10,000

KATHERINE SORRELL

TIPS

HOW TO DO ALMOST EVERYTHING

Quercus

CONTENTS

1 HOME & GARDEN 6

2 FRIENDS & FAMILY 64

3 BEAUTY & WELLBEING 116

4 HEALTH & FITNESS 158

5 WORK & EDUCATION 198

6 HOLIDAYS & TRAVEL 232

7 FOOD & DRINK 274

8 YOU & YOUR MONEY 334

9 FUN & GAMES 356

10 FOUR WHEELS & TWO 382

INDEX 408

INTRODUCTION

I, for one, wish I'd had a copy of *10,000 Tips* when I got married, when I was decorating my house and when I was having a baby. Not to mention when my kids started school and that time when someone backed into my car. Because what this book contains is a compendium of helpful tips that apply to all areas of our lives, from (quite literally) the cradle to the grave. Many of the tips are useful on a daily basis, others every once in a while and some only in the event of an emergency – in which case, you will be even more pleased that you've got this book to hand.

10,000 Tips is divided into ten straightforward chapters: Home & Garden, Friends & Family, Beauty & Wellbeing, Health & Fitness, Work & Education, Holidays & Travel, Food & Drink, You & Your Money, Fun & Games and Four Wheels & Two. So there is something here for everyone, whatever your stage of life, your hobbies and interests, or your responsibilities. Within each chapter we have given a whole host of expert tips, from the absolutely vital to the incredibly useful, via the amusing, the remarkable and the quite unexpected. In all, we have covered 1,000 different topics that will help you save money and spend your cash wisely, learn new skills and polish up existing talents, keep safe, get healthy and go green – among many other things. From walking in high heels to getting a flight upgrade, dealing with a bike puncture to making a fancy dress outfit, it is all here, right at your fingertips. In short, this book is a one-stop, go-to reference book that no home should be without. But be warned: it could become highly addictive!

KATHERINE SORRELL

HOME & GARDEN

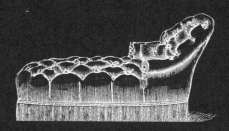

Moved into a new house or in the midst of renovating an old one? Want to pep up your patio or plant out a vegetable plot? From choosing colours for your living room to redesigning your garden, you'll find all sorts of tips to help with home life here.

PLAN A ROOM

1 Plan your room with its end purpose in mind. Whether you're designing from scratch or doing a quick overhaul, think about absolutely everything according to how you are going to be using the room – from the big picture to the smallest detail. If you get a plug socket in the wrong place, trailing wires could cause you irritation for the next ten years.

2 A case for professional help? Architects and interior designers seem expensive, but if your project is large-scale they will almost certainly be cost-effective in terms of managing budget and builders. They may even save you money. What's more, they're worth their weight in gold when it comes to ingenious ideas that you might not have thought of.

3 Budget, budget and budget again. Get it right and everyone will be happy; get it wrong and it's a recipe for disaster. There is no point in being too optimistic. If you can decide on every tiny detail in advance, there's less chance that things will need changing halfway through. This is a major cause of over-spending. The other is unforeseen problems. They can only be catered for by allowing at least an additional ten per cent.

4 Limited budget? Don't despair. Always spend money where it really matters and save on less important areas. You could always make do with minimal furnishings for a while, or scour second-hand shops for vintage finds.

5 What are the major considerations? First, measure the room and, as accurately as you can, draw a plan of it (graph paper makes this easier), marking in existing windows, doors, built-in cupboards, radiators, plug sockets, light fittings and so on. Do you need to move a wall or radiator, enlarge a window, hang the door the other way around or add some extra plug sockets? In bathrooms and kitchens, work out where the existing pipework is and whether that needs to be altered.

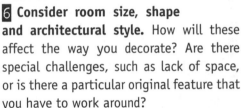

6 Consider room size, shape and architectural style. How will these affect the way you decorate? Are there special challenges, such as lack of space, or is there a particular original feature that you have to work around?

7 Decide where your furniture will go. Sketch the approximate shapes of your furniture onto a separate sheet of paper (the same scale as before), as if you were looking at them from above. Cut them out.

8 Place the furniture cut-outs on your master plan and assess how well they fit in to the available space. Move them around as necessary. Allow adequate room for movement between and around them. Eventually, everything will fall into place and – bingo! – you've got the basics of a functional and comfortable room.

9 Investigate local planning regulations. Ensure that work you're contemplating won't contravene local planning or building laws/regulations. Check with the relevant authority if you are in any doubt.

10 Use your DIY skills. If you have the proper tools, equipment and know-how you can save money by doing all the work yourself. It's both satisfying and economical. However, it's important to know your own limits and always keep safety in mind. Leave specialist work to the professionals.

MAKE A MARVELLOUS MOOD BOARD

1 **Ask retailers for samples** of your favourite fabrics, wallpapers, carpet and tiles.

2 **Cut out pictures** of flooring, furniture, light fittings and accessories from magazines and brochures.

3 **Choose paint colours** by clipping from magazines, using colour chips from paint manufacturers or by mixing your own.

4 **Use a large piece of stiff cardboard** for the mood board – a neutral colour works best – and some glue. Now for some fun!

5 **Arrange all your elements** on the mood board, but don't stick them down yet.

6 **Keep samples roughly in proportion** to their real-life size, so that a curtain-fabric swatch is much larger than a cushion. Reduce or enlarge images on a photocopier.

7 **Place swatches and images** according to their position in the real room – flooring at the bottom, curtain fabrics near the top, furnishings in the middle.

8 **Assess the overall look** and rearrange the elements as necessary. If things look crowded or empty, remove or add elements.

9 **Think about combinations.** Do you have a nice mix of colours and patterns? Is there a variety of textures? What about the scale of furnishings? Do they sit well together?

10 **Stick down everything** once you're happy with the overall effect. Repeat the process for every room you're planning.

GET CLEVER WITH COLOUR

**TOOL KIT
ESSENTIALS**
1 Screwdriver
2 Spanner
3 Pliers
4 Hammer
5 Scraper
6 Chisel
7 Saw
8 Knife
9 Tape measure
10 Spirit level

1 **Think about which colours you are naturally drawn to** and which will go with your existing furnishings.

2 **Select colours that set a style.** Historic colours are lovely in an older house, while 'retro' colours work well with vintage finds. Bolder, contemporary shades look great with modern furnishings.

3 **You can't go wrong with neutrals –** they're the 'little black dresses' of interior design – good-looking for all occasions.

4 **Search for interesting colour combinations.** Be inspired by colours in your garden, in books or magazines, or in paint manufacturers' brochures.

5 **Paint a room entirely white** to make it seem bigger and brighter.

6 **Think about 'warm' and 'cool' colours.** Blues/greens are 'cool', ideal for 'enlarging' small rooms. Reds/yellows are 'warm' – great for making large rooms cosy.

7 **If you want to use a bold colour,** beware of it being too overpowering. Try painting just one wall.

8 **Establish a visual link from room to room.** Use a gentle range of colours: start with a very pale colour in a narrow hallway, with slightly darker hues in a living room and a warm tone in a dining room.

9 **Think about 'practical' colours.** A darkish colour is best for a busy room that gets a lot of wear and tear; reserve paler colours for less-used upstairs rooms.

10 **Colour can affect the way you feel.** In a bedroom avoid bright, lively colours in favour of soft, 'restful' shades.

USE PATTERN PERFECTLY

1 **Choose a single-patterned fabric** or wallpaper and team it with plain colours.

2 **Combine a busy pattern** with simple stripes, checks or spots for a jazzy look.

3 **Mix and match a variety of patterns.** Tricky, but it can be very effective, too, provided the colours tone in.

4 **Same colour, different pattern?** Get a unified look by matching the same colours in different patterns precisely.

5 **Think about scale.** Don't put a large-scale pattern next to a small-scale one.

6 **Look at pattern size.** Big patterns work in large rooms; small in small spaces.

7 **Steer clear of pattern/style clashes.** Georgian floral doesn't go with a sixties abstract, even if the colours do coordinate.

8 **Use pattern in small areas to add interest:** a feature wall or a set of cushions.

9 **Steal ideas!** Manufacturers' wallpaper/ fabric books show how to mix and match.

10 **Use small swatches to experiment with different ideas.** Your patterns will eventually fall into perfect place!

DECIDE ON A DECORATING STYLE

1 **Think about your own style!** Sassy modern minx or a die-hard traditionalist?

2 **List your decorative likes and dislikes.** What do you really love and really loathe?

3 **Find inspiration anywhere and every-where:** in friends' homes, restaurants, hotels, shops, on TV and in films.

4 **Put together a scrapbook** of images clipped from magazines.

5 **What's your home's architectural style?** You can emphasize or disguise it in your decorating.

6 **Use a historic or generic 'look'** – such as Art Deco, English country house or mid-century modern.

7 **Use a key object to develop a style:** a rug, a painting, a chair or a vase.

8 **Make sketches or a mood board** to work out how your style will pull together.

9 **Concentrate on atmosphere.** Don't get hung up on recreating a style down to the very last detail.

10 **Be individual.** Don't feel you have to follow fashion or other people's taste.

PICK THE PERFECT PAINT

1 **Confused by huge colour charts?** They usually vary in colour from left to right, but in shade from top to bottom.

2 **Avoid nasty colour clashes** by choosing shades from the same colour 'family'.

3 **Buy tester pots** so you can experiment with the colours at home.

4 **Choose colour tones according to what you are decorating.** Pick darker tones for woodwork; lighter ones for walls.

5 **Test the result on white cards.** Paint two coats. The bigger the area of paint, the more intense the colour. Stick the painted cards up on each wall.

6 **Live with your colour cards first.** You may love or hate a particular colour immediately. Or you may have to live with it for a while before you can decide.

7 **Observe your colour cards at different times of day**, with lights on and off.

8 **Paint finishes are an important consideration.** High gloss, soft sheen or ultra matt? Choose paint texture with as much care as you choose colours.

9 **The shinier the finish, the paler the colour** will appear – you may need to compensate by choosing a darker shade.

10 **Get paint specifically mixed** if you're in love with a particular colour (say of your favourite dress) and want to copy it.

WONDERFUL WINDOW TREATMENTS

BRING LIGHT INTO YOUR LIFE

1 Masses of mirrors
2 Extra light fixtures
3 Bright lightbulbs
4 Transparent furniture
5 Glass doors
6 Large windows
7 Skylights
8 Glass walls
9 Bright white paint
10 A glass floor!

1 **To let maximum light into your room,** hang curtains, blinds or shutters so that, when open, they don't obscure the window.

2 **Full, thick curtains and long blinds need more stack-back space** than thinner, shorter ones.

3 **To make a fabulous feature of your window,** select an eye-catching colour or pattern for your curtain/blind and go to town on the style of arrangement.

4 **Choose short curtains** to go over radiators or windowseats, on stairways or at kitchen-sink windows; otherwise, floor-length is more fashionable.

5 **Pick a curtain-hanging style to suit your room.** Pencil, goblet and box pleats are all worth considering.

6 **Show off a curtain pole –** plain wood or curly wrought iron, sleek steel or traditional brass with ornate finials. Or go for a minimalist track or tensioned wire.

7 **Consider unusual fabrics** such as blanket, tweed, fleece, mohair, canvas, a sari, vintage embroidery or a chintz quilt.

8 **Need an inexpensive solution?** Roller blinds are cheapest, but can look severe. Roman blinds pull up into lovely soft folds for a chic effect.

9 **Want to block out sound and light, insulate and add extra security?** Install wooden shutters: Shaker-style or American with tilting louvres are great choices.

10 **Apply stick-on window film for cheap privacy.** Choose plain or patterned.

LIGHTING SCHEMES WITH VA VA VOOM

1 **Design your desired lighting scheme** when you are planning room use and furniture position.

2 **Think about lighting effects.** Decide where you want the light to be, how much you need at different times of day and what lighting atmosphere (dark and moody or efficient and bright) you want.

3 **Better lighting on a budget?** Plug in extra table or floor lamps in dark corners.

4 Plan for light to come from a variety of sources and directions. Designers talk about 'layering' for function and interest.

5 You'll need a combination of four types of light: good overall light for general activities, bright 'task' lights for reading, accent lights to illuminate features and atmospheric lighting to set a mood.

6 Think about different fittings. Browse retailers for downlights, spotlights, track lights, uplighters, wall-washers, floor or table lamps and shelf or display lighting.

7 Install two or more lighting circuits in one room. Then you can have one or more sets of lights on at any particular time.

8 Change all light switches to dimmer switches. Check bulbs are dimmable for quick and easy lighting improvement.

9 Change your bulbs. Brighter, softer or coloured bulbs will make a big difference and are a cheap way of upgrading.

10 Don't forget about the most beautiful, elemental forms of additional light: candlelight and firelight.

DECLUTTER WITHOUT TEARS

1 Give yourself a deadline to declutter your chosen areas by – and stick to it.

2 Set aside time for sorting through stuff: ten minutes a day or one room a week.

3 Make decluttering fun by blasting out your favourite music while you work – and promise yourself a reward when it's over (a bar of chocolate or a trip to the movies?).

4 Mark up six bags/boxes: rubbish, recycling, giving away, mending, to do and moving elsewhere.

5 Assign a 'not sure' container. Don't be tempted to put too much into it, though.

6 Sort your stuff into the marked-up boxes or pop it back into its rightful place.

7 Deal with the boxes before you get used to having them around and they turn into yet more clutter.

8 Create storage that really works for you and your belongings – and use it!

9 Designate a specific place or corner where 'pending' clutter can be kept out of the way and sort it out at regular intervals.

10 If you tidy up as you go along you won't be stuck with lots of decluttering – encourage your family to do the same.

CREATE SUPER STORAGE

1 A good storage target is about ten to 20 per cent of each room.

2 Don't store heavy items higher than shoulder height or lower than knee height.

3 If you're short of space choose bespoke built-in cupboards that happily fit into an awkward corner or go up to the ceiling.

4 Stacking boxes look great and save space – but don't put things you often need in the bottom-most boxes.

5 Ready-made storage gives greater flexibility. Whether it's an antique apothecary's chest or a woven-willow log basket, there's a free-standing storage option to suit you.

6 Wash and re-use jam jars, plastic tubs and pots for storing small toys.

7 Store rarely used possessions in attics, basements, sheds or on cupboard tops.

8 Don't store too much on open shelves unless you can keep them clean and tidy.

9 Look for multi-functional furnishings doubling as storage: tables or beds with drawers, lidded bench seats, basins and baths with built-in drawers or cupboards.

10 Office, catering, retail and industrial fixtures and fittings are sturdy and capacious. If they don't suit your decorative theme, they may be ideal for a home office.

DESIGN DELIGHTFUL DISPLAYS

1 Plan displays at the same time as planning colours, fabrics, furnishings and lighting in the rest of the room – so that they coordinate.

2 When grouping objects together, stand back in order to get an overview of the effect. Rearrange as necessary.

3 In a formal room, a symmetrical display of traditional objects may work best.

4 In an informal room, choose randomly arranged natural objects.

5 Match object size to the display area – a tiny vase is best suited to a small ledge rather than a large shelf, for example.

6 Large objects need space around them to 'breathe' or they look cramped.

7 Mass a small group of similar objects together for instant effect.

8 Easy mantelpiece display? Pop a pair of identical objects at either end (candlesticks, vases or antique 'fire dogs').

9 Range three or more objects in order, perhaps the smallest to the tallest, palest to darkest, smoothest to roughest and so on. Or why not opt for a group, putting the smallest pieces in front, largest at the back?

10 Improve your display with lighting. Try spotlights, uplights and downlights and specialist lit shelf/cabinet fittings.

MAKE OPEN-PLAN WORK

1 Introduce hints of colour, pattern or texture onto one wall to add a little bit of character, interest and drama.

2 Choose the same paint colour all the way through for an unbroken look and to emphasize space. Or create 'zoned' areas by varying their colour.

3 Use lighting to delineate different areas and illuminate distinct sections.

4 When it comes to flooring, run the same material throughout the space for a flowing look or choose a variety of flooring types to differentiate between areas.

5 Include flexible division for truly flexible living. Folding doors, moveable screens or ceiling-mounted panels work well.

6 To blend the kitchen and living areas seamlessly, continue kitchen unit styles into adjacent areas for storage, choosing a design that will suit, for example, both a TV stand and a cutlery drawer.

7 Install a decent extractor fan to avoid drifting smells percolating different areas.

8 With fewer walls there's less wall space for storage. Use some tall, open shelving to double as a room-divider. Mount a flat-screen TV on a media wall with storage for DVDs concealed behind.

9 Look for larger-than-average furnishings and light fittings and bear in mind that they must look good from all angles, not just from the front.

10 Create cosy sitting areas with two sofas facing and tables and lamps behind.

MAKE ROOM FOR GUESTS

1 Sort your spare room. Put clutter in a shed, under the stairs or under your bed.

2 Add a bedside table and space to hang or fold away a few clothes to make a spare room comfy for your guests.

3 If you don't have a spare bedroom, buy a sofabed, folding bed or inflatable mattress. You could put up a screen to provide a little privacy in a shared space.

4 Double up by providing bunk beds for children. Or acquire a truckle bed, which wheels out from under the main bed.

5 Temporary clothes storage? You can buy special hooks and racks that simply hang over the back of a door.

6 To accommodate extra diners, an extending table with leaves is ideal.

7 Extra lightweight folding chairs can be stored out of the way when not in use.

8 If you're holding a party, clear the room of clutter first. Push large furnishings against the walls to maximize floor space.

9 Make room in your fridge and kitchen cupboards for extra food and drink.

10 Clear space in your hallway for extra coats and shoes.

COPE WITH TINY SPACES

1 On a tight budget? A small room means less furniture but more available budget for each piece: a higher-quality look.

2 Look for clever space-saving features – furniture on wheels, foldaway pieces and special compact furnishings.

3 When floor space is precious, don't overcrowd – minimize furnishings.

4 Don't overwhelm the space – avoid tall, bulky or busy-looking furnishings.

5 Pale colours enhance a feeling of space.

6 Choose furniture raised on legs to increase the visible floor area. This will make the room seem larger.

7 Choose dual-purpose items such as a sofabed or storage seat.

8 Search for see-through or reflective furniture to help increase visible space.

9 Choose small-scale patterns on a pale, open background.

10 Maximize light by minimizing window treatments and adding table and floor lamps.

DEAL WITH AWKWARD SPACES

1 Sloping ceilings? Don't even think about using the areas in the lowest points as living space. Instead, build in useful storage cupboards.

2 Odd corners or alcoves that can't be used are ideal for wall-to-wall shelving.

3 In low-ceilinged rooms, choose correspondingly low furnishings.

4 If your room is strangely shaped it may be hard to find conventional furniture to fit it. Your best bet? Go tailor-made so that you can use all the space.

5 Curtains on poles may not be ideal if your windows are oddly shaped. Try ceiling-mounted tracks to bend around corners, bespoke blinds or swing-arm rods.

6 Carpeting oddly shaped rooms may be pricey due to wastage during cutting. Save money by sanding and painting floorboards and piling on soft rugs.

7 Very large rooms can be problematic. Purchase large-scale furnishings and big patterns that won't be dwarfed by their environment. Group in cosy seating areas.

8 An unused landing space can be kitted out with a small desk plus shelf above and used as an informal office.

9 In a hallway, a slender console table and a shelf with hooks are ideal for storing coats, hats and keys. A bench with a hinged lid is great for keeping clutter out of sight and makes a useful seat, too.

10 Landings are ideal places for slim bookshelves, fitted or free-standing.

PLAN THE ULTIMATE KITCHEN

1 Consider your kitchen requirements. Who will use it? When and how?

2 Count how many plug sockets you need and decide where to put them – you probably require more than you think, especially if you like to use a lot of gadgets.

3 How much storage do you want? What type? Do you prefer solid or glass cupboard doors, or maybe open shelves?

4 Think about unfitted elements, such as a dresser or butcher's block. Would you prefer built-in or free-standing appliances?

5 Choosing wooden work surfaces or flooring? Think hard first! Wood needs tender loving care to prevent marking and warping. Select from stainless steel, composite, stone or laminate worktops and rubber, cork, vinyl or lino for flooring.

6 Likely to drop your crocks? Ceramic or stone flooring will be unkind to dropped breakables as well as being cold underfoot.

7 What about ergonomics? Design a kitchen layout that makes it easy to get from fridge to sink, from cooker to worktops and from dishwasher to cupboards.

8 An island unit is great for maximizing space, but it must be carefully positioned. It should be within one step of other worktops and not so deep that you are unable to reach across it.

9 Provide an area for dumping shopping bags before unpacking and ensure that the rubbish bin is close to the chopping board.

10 Avoid fashion fads and invest in a quality kitchen that will be comfortable and functional, standing the test of time.

DESIGN A BRILLIANT BATHROOM

1 Consider your bathing requirements. Who will use the bathroom and how frequently? What fixtures would you like? How much space do you have available?

2 Plan the bathroom to scale on graph paper, noting the positions of pipework, radiators, windows and doors. Leave elbow room around the basin and towelling room beside the bath/shower.

3 For a small room a shower-bath may be better than separate bath/walk-in shower.

4 Avoid moving existing pipework, if you can, to keep costs down.

5 Invest in moving parts such as shower doors and taps, and save a bit of cash by selecting some economical options such as simple white ceramics.

6 If you're buying fittings from more than one source be wary – the whites may not match up exactly.

7 Underfloor heating gives an efficient, overall heat while freeing up space against the walls – perhaps for a towel-warmer.

8 Lighting is crucial for creating the right atmosphere: bright and efficient for a wake-up morning shower or subdued but relaxing for a leisurely evening bath.

9 Don't overlook your bathroom storage options. Hide all your fiddly bits and bobs in built-in vanity units, wall and floor cupboards, baskets and trolleys.

10 Limit expensive tiles to small areas such as splashbacks, or combine with one-colour tiles to create borders or insets.

SUPER-COOL KIDS' ROOMS

1 For colour schemes that will suit fast-growing kids, keep walls, floors and furniture neutral; just change colourful accessories, such as rugs and blinds.

2 Children need plenty of play-space. Arrange furniture at the edges of the room and consider buying raised sleeper beds.

3 To pep up the walls attach a large magnetic board or paint a single wall with blackboard paint for easy scribbling.

4 For added ceiling interest put up bunting, maps or delightful fairy lights.

5 Make use of wooden floorboards by painting on paw prints, a race track or a giant game of snakes and ladders.

6 Don't go for carpets. Soft surfaces may spell disaster should spillages occur. Floors should be hard-wearing, non-slip, easy to clean and not too hard. Wooden or laminate boards plus a soft rug (plus anti-slip mat), vinyl, lino, cork or rubber are ideal.

7 Storage is crucial. Most toys can be kept in plastic buckets or in colourful drawstring bags. Make sure shelves are low enough for small kids to reach easily.

8 Storing small toys and felt-tip pens is easy in recycled ice-cream tubs or old, sturdy shoe boxes. Cover them in pretty wallpaper offcuts to create a fun look.

9 Floor cushions and bean bags are fun, comfortable, practical and cheap for reading, quiet play and lounging about.

10 Teenagers' rooms should be a cosy dens, with chill-out zones and study areas, where hobbies, socializing and sleep-overs can all take place comfortably.

FRONT-DOOR POT PLANTS

1. Japanese maple
2. Dwarf rhododendron
3. Box
4. Dwarf conifer
5. Olive
6. Miniature rose
7. Bay
8. Lavender
9. Rosemary
10. Camellia

CREATE A SUPERIOR EXTERIOR

1. **Clear away windswept leaves**, mow the lawn and prune back straggly plants.
2. **Clean surface grime off brick walls** and repoint mortar. Repair any render that's bulging, cracked or blemished.
3. **Replant your windowboxes and pots** so that they're fresh-looking and inviting.
4. **Consider replacing door furniture.** New ironmongery gives real wow-factor.
5. **Polish your windows** until they gleam.
6. **Ensure gutters and pipes are properly attached,** clip back any flapping cables and align satellite dishes.
7. **Wash and press your curtains.**
8. **Make your paintwork pristine** – pay attention to any gates and railings, walls, fences and front and garage doors.
9. **Give your bins a really good scrub.**
10. **Polish your knobs, handles and latches** for a full frontal with pizazz.

EXTEND YOUR HOME

1. **Space at the back of your house?** You could add a useful rear extension and create a multi-functional family room.
2. **Check out your local regulations** before you think of building an extension.
3. **Add a second storey to your extension** to create a new bathroom and bedroom.
4. **Convert your loft space** to add a bedroom with bathroom, office or den.
5. **Dig down deep** and convert your unused cellar/basement into a useful utility area, home office or self-contained annexe.
6. **Add a conservatory or garden room** to create extra living (and plant) space. This is one of the cheapest extension options.
7. **What about a handy shed?** If you can't extend your home but have plenty of space outside, build a home office, games room or chill-out area in the garden.
8. **Turn under-stairs space into a small extra room.** It'll be perfect for a ground-floor WC, extra shower or a handy study.
9. **Transform your garage into additional living space.** The foundations may need strengthening, but it could make a great bedroom, living area or home office
10. **Make sure your new-built extension is well insulated and well lit,** has good head height and that the style chimes in with your existing home.

REGULAR HOME MAINTENANCE

1. **Check your roof** for any broken or dislodged tiles or accumulating moss.
2. **Make sure your gutters and drains** are clear and that all the pipework is sound.
3. **Examine all pointing on brickwork** – if it's damaged, rake it out and re-do it.
4. **Trim back ivy and all climbing plants:** they could damage your walls.

5 **Have your chimneys swept annually.**
6 **Protect all pipes that might freeze** by wrapping them securely in foam tubing.
7 **Check that smoke/carbon monoxide alarms** are in good working order.
8 **Sand and re-paint windows** as soon as you detect faults in the paintwork.
9 **Have your heating and hot water system serviced** once a year.
10 **Keep an eye on all electrics** and replace any cords or plugs at the first signs of damage.

DIY SAFETY

1 **When lifting heavy weights,** keep your back straight and use your knees.
2 **Use the right tool for the right job.** Not only will it be safer, but the work will be easier and the results better.
3 **If you're using unfamiliar, hired tools,** ask for a proper demonstration and follow all operating instructions precisely.
4 **Cordless power tools are safest,** but if your tool has a cord, check that it's not worn and always use a circuit-breaker.
5 **Maintain your tools carefully.**
6 **Be especially careful with ladders** – they're a major cause of accidents.
7 **Supervise young children and pets** around DIY equipment and make sure it's stored out of their way when not in use.
8 **Wear protective goggles, a mask and gloves** when necessary. Tie back long hair.
9 **Never attempt any electrical work you don't feel competent to handle,** and treat every job with caution.
10 **Keep a first-aid kit handy.** You never know when you might need it.

USE A LADDER

1 **Choose the right ladder for the job:** stepladder, short ladder, double or triple extending? It should be kept within easy reach and be light enough to move around.
2 **Check that your ladder is in good condition,** especially if you haven't used it for a while or if it's hired.
3 **Carry a ladder upright,** leaning against your shoulder – one hand supporting it at shoulder height and the other lower down.
4 **A ladder should rest against a wall at an angle of about 70 degrees.** Don't lean it against gutters, pipes or glass.
5 **If you're working on uneven ground,** use a stabilizer. If the ground is soft, place a wide board under the feet and screw a batten across it to hold the ladder in place.
6 **When you extend your ladder,** overlap sections by a quarter of their length. Make sure they're locked in position.
7 **Never climb to four rungs or less from the top** – you'll run out of handholds and won't be able to balance properly.
8 **Always keep both feet and one hand on the ladder.** Never lean out to one side.
9 **Add hooks and trays for holding things** – don't hold things in your hands!
10 **Put the ladder away afterwards.**

GET DRILLING!

1 **Choose a good-quality drill** with a powerful motor, variable speeds and a hammer action for drilling into masonry.

2 **Never lift a corded drill by its flex,** and use a purpose-made extension lead.

3 **To work at a remote site or at the top of a ladder** use a cordless drill with rechargeable battery.

4 **Unplug a drill before fitting bits or attachments,** and remove the chuck key before you switch on.

5 **Select the correct bit size for the job,** suitable for the material you're drilling.

6 **Mark the point you wish to drill,** place the drill bit on the mark, gently squeeze the trigger and give it a gentle push.

7 **For drilling right through a piece of wood,** cover the exit point with a piece of masking tape to prevent splintering.

8 **If you are only drilling to a certain depth,** mark the measurement on your bit by wrapping tape around it.

9 **To remove the bit, once drilled in**, slowly pull it out while spinning it gently.

10 **When drilling in screws,** don't force them too far in.

UNBLOCK BASINS & WCS

1 **Don't ignore early blockage warnings!** If water drains slowly, use chemical cleaner.

2 **For a blocked basin,** try using a plunger.

3 **Try a hand-operated pump,** forcing a jet of water along the pipe. Block the overflow with a wet cloth first.

4 **If a plunger or pump isn't enough, undo the trap.** Pop a bucket underneath, unscrew the trap and clear out the gunk.

5 **Check nearby pipework.** Unscrew access plugs, then dig with a bent hook.

6 **If more than one fitting is affected,** the problem is in outside pipework.

7 **Clear leaves, moss and debris from outside drainage systems.** From a ladder poke a cane downwards and from below use a piece of bent wire.

8 **Blocked yard gully?** Bail out as much water as possible with a disposable container. Scoop out muck by hand (gloved).

9 **Does the water in your WC rise when you flush it?** Use a plunger or auger.

10 **Blocked soil pipe?** Use a drain auger and do it yourself if it's a plastic stack with access points. Or give yourself a break and hire a professional.

PERFECT PAINTWORK

1 **Use the right brush for the job:** a natural bristle is best for oil-based paints, synthetic for water-based paints.

2 **'Cut' into corners and edges** of ceilings and walls first, using a medium brush and a roller/extension. Paint in strips.

3 Paint a large area all in one go, otherwise you'll be able to see the joins.

4 Painting a whole room? Start with the ceiling, then tackle walls and woodwork.

5 For even paint coverage on walls, make strokes going in different directions.

6 If you don't like the orange-peel effect of a normal roller, use a short pile, micro-fibre sleeve for a smoother finish.

7 Matt finishes are best for uneven walls.

8 Before you paint woodwork, remove built-up paint, fill cracks and sand.

9 For a smooth, even finish with gloss paint, use a brush or mini roller.

10 Ideal order for painting a panelled door: mouldings around panels; the panels; central vertical section; cross rails. Finish with the outer verticals and the edge.

PUT UP A SHELF

1 To fix shelves in an alcove, use wooden supports on side walls. For a wide alcove add support along the back.

2 Cut alcove shelves individually for a perfect fit – walls are rarely straight.

3 Fit panels across the fronts of alcove shelves to hide supports or conceal lights.

4 To run leads from electrical equipment to a socket, cut a small hole in a back corner of each shelf.

5 If your wall's plasterboard, you may need to attach the shelf to the wall studs.

6 To put up shelf brackets, mark two vertical guidelines. Hold one bracket against a guideline at the right height. Use a spirit level and mark holes. Drill and screw the bracket in place.

7 More than one shelf? Measure the heights of objects destined for the shelves.

8 When fitting a shelving system on long upright supports, check that your wall doesn't lean. To help correct the tilt, place packing behind the uprights.

9 For the sturdiest shelving, choose solid timber or blockboard. Veneered chipboard is cheap, but is the most likely to sag.

10 Sagging shelves? Add a bracket, move them closer together or use a thicker shelf.

HANG UP A PICTURE

1 Use an awl/drill to make holes in the frame back, about one-third from the top.

2 Stretch cord or twine between the screw eyes or D-rings, doubling and knotting.

3 Use mirror plates for heavy frames.

4 Get someone else to hold the picture against the wall to see where it should go.

5 To position the hook, measure the distance between the tops of the wire and the frame. Mark the wall with a pencil.

6 For a plasterboard wall, use a picture hook, nail or a plastic multi-pin hook.

7 For large frames use double hooks.

8 For brick, cement-and-plaster or concrete walls drill a hole and use a wall plug.

9 Use a spirit level to straighten.

10 If the picture is too high/low, tighten or loosen the wire on the back.

UNUSUAL PAPERS FOR EYE-CATCHING INTERIORS

1 Old maps
2 Wrapping paper
3 Sheet music
4 Handmade paper
5 Faux-effect wallpapers
6 Posters
7 Vintage wallpaper
8 Brown paper
9 Crêpe paper
10 Cellophane

WALLPAPERING FOR ALL

1 **Before you start wallpapering** paint the ceiling and woodwork.

2 **Use the right tools –** a long pasting table, a large brush for applying paste, a paper-hanging brush or sponge to smooth the paper once on the wall, long scissors/ trimming knife and a seam roller.

3 **Remove old wallpaper first** and fill in any holes or cracks.

4 **Put up lining paper** for a smooth base on bumpy walls. Hang it horizontally.

5 **When cutting each length of paper,** allow a 5cm (2in) overlap at both ends.

6 **Use a plumb-bob and a pencil** to mark the vertical lines.

7 **The easiest way to start** is by papering the longest uninterrupted wall first.

8 **When hanging patterned paper,** centre your first piece over a fireplace for symmetry and then work outwards.

9 **If you get an air bubble in the paper,** cut a cross in it using a sharp knife and paste the flaps down.

10 **Hide joins** in a corner of the room.

TOP-CLASS TILING

1 **Check that the tiling surface is even.**

2 **To level out defects in the wall,** first apply a thin coat of tile adhesive.

3 **'Setting out' is important:** mark a row of tiles (including spaces) on a straight batten and use it to gauge tile positions, working from the centre vertical outwards.

4 **Always use a spirit level –** don't trust floor and walls to be level.

5 **Only apply enough adhesive** to cover about 1sq m (1sq yd) at a time. Any more and it may dry too soon.

6 **To make each tile stick,** use a little twist while pushing against the adhesive.

7 **Don't push the tile down too hard –** adhesive will come up between tiles.

8 **If you're only tiling part-way up a wall,** finish with a whole tile at the top.

9 **Check your tiling progress regularly** to ensure it's completely straight.

10 **Make a level tiled surface.** Place a batten over the tiles and push protruding ones in by tapping it with a rubber mallet. If a tile is too low, add more adhesive.

ERECT A GARDEN FENCE

1 **To make sure your fence lasts years,** choose good-quality posts and set them solidly in the ground.

2 **Mark where your fence posts will go** by stretching string between two pegs in the ground. Avoid any obstructions such as tree roots.

3 **To be a good neighbour,** erect your fence with the posts and rails facing your property, rather than theirs.

4 For a firm foundation, bury a quarter of each post, packing with hardcore.

5 Use a spirit level to check each post is vertical before top-filling with concrete.

6 Get help if putting up a pre-fabricated panel fence. Put one post into its hole, then ask your helper to push a panel, supported on two piles of bricks, against the post, while you nail it in place.

7 To stop a fence panel rotting, either raise it completely off the ground or fit specially treated boards along the bottom edge. Or set posts in metal post supports.

8 On a slope, set posts vertically. Step the fence panels and fill the gap with treated boards or retaining walls.

9 Post-tops rot if cut horizontally. Bevel them so that rainwater runs off, or finish them with a protective cap.

10 Panelled picket fences are easy to put up. Use metal brackets to attach a pair of panels to each post.

LAY FLOORBOARDS

1 If you are re-laying existing boards, number them as you take them up.

2 Buy new boards in advance and leave them to acclimatize for at least a week in the room where they'll be laid.

3 When cutting boards to fit, allow for an expansion gap of 10mm (3/8in) around the edges of the room.

4 Balancing on the joists isn't a good idea! Work on a steady platform made by resting loose boards across the joists.

5 Fix the first board, then lay four to six boards before clamping and nailing down.

6 Make the job of laying floorboards easier by hiring a floorboard cramp and nail punch.

7 Drive the nails just below the surface or use 'secret' nailing.

8 When butting two short boards end to end, make sure that the joint is positioned over a joist for support.

9 Avoid creating an ugly row of butt joints by arranging several boards in one go time and staggering the joints.

10 Use a jigsaw to scribe the last board to fit against the wall.

CHOOSE A BRILLIANT BUILDER

1 Ask neighbours friends/family
2 Use trade associations
3 Use the internet
4 Ask owners of local renovated properties
5 Check references
6 Check insurance
7 Get three quotes
8 Never pay upfront
9 Agree work in advance
10 Agree a start/finish date

PLASTER LIKE A PRO

1 When repairing old plasterwork, first cut away any that's damaged until you reach sound material. Brush away debris.

2 The key to successful plastering is a well-prepared surface. Treat dry or absorbent surfaces with a PVA bonding agent.

3 Mixing plaster is messy – protect floors with a dust sheet and wear old clothing. Afterwards, wash everything before the plaster sets.

4 Only mix as much as you can work with at a time, and throw away plaster that's started to set – adding more water won't help.

5 Apply the plaster with an upward stroke of the trowel, pressing it into the wall so it sticks. Angle the trowel closer to the wall, but don't put it flat on to it – you'll pull the plaster off again.

6 **Work from right to left** if you're right-handed; vice versa if you're left-handed.

7 **Level the new surface** by holding a batten against the wall. Run it gently from side to side, working up from the bottom of the wall, removing excess plaster.

8 **To check that your surface is flat,** shine a torch at an angle across it.

9 **Smooth the final surface** of plaster by lightly spraying with water and trowelling it to a matt finish. Don't overwork it.

10 **Never try to dry plaster quickly** by heating it. It might crack.

WHERE TO INSULATE
1 Roofs
2 Cavity walls
3 Solid walls
4 Around windows
5 Around doors
6 Under floors
7 Ducts
8 Basements
9 Above an unheated garage
10 Crawl spaces

EASY-AS-PIE DRAUGHTPROOFING

1 **Find the worst draughts** by dampening the flat of your hand and holding it against the suspected area.

2 **Stop cold air coming up between gappy floorboards** by filling in the gaps. For small gaps use flexible filler; for large gaps cut strips of matching floorboard.

3 **Check your skirting boards don't have gaps below them** and seal if necessary. Cover with wooden moulding.

4 **For a draughty letterbox/front door,** fit a clever hinged flap plus bristly draught excluders. Hang a thick curtain in front of a draughty front door.

5 **Pop an inflatable chimney balloon** up an unused chimney to cut draughts.

6 **Make sure all doors and windows fit properly** and seal gaps with a draught-excluding strip. Self-adhesive foam strips are cheap and easy, but metal or plastic strips with brushes/wipers last longer.

7 **Make a sausage-dog draught excluder.** Stitch together old socks and add stuffing.

8 **Add curtain linings.** Buy a special thermal lining or use extra-heavy fabric.

9 **Fit external keyholes with coverplates.**

10 **Cover pipework openings** leading outside with a hinged flap.

INSTALL SOUNDPROOFING

1 **Find out where the sound is coming from** by turning everything off and listening. Do it at different times of day.

2 **Soak up sound** by maximizing soft materials, such as carpets and upholstery.

3 **Thick curtains help a lot** if the noise is coming in through windows.

4 **Draughtproof around doors and windows to help reduce outside noise** as well as draughts. Seal any obvious gaps.

5 **Add proper airtight secondary glazing or wooden shutters.**

6 **Install double or triple glazing** for a big improvement.

7 **Make sure doors are well-fitting** and replace lightweight doors with solid ones.

8 **Add extra plasterboard,** plus insulation to partition walls. The thicker the better.

9 **It's easier to insulate a floor than a ceiling.** Cork tiles or carpet plus underlay

are a good start, but you can also buy specialist insulating materials.

10 **If all else fails,** get advice from a soundproofing professional, who can give you more detailed information about wall linings and false ceilings.

SAND YOUR FLOORBOARDS

1 **Is your wooden floor worth sanding?** Too many nails, woodworm or poor-quality wood might mean it's better to replace it.

2 **Before sanding, mend or replace** any damaged boards with second-hand ones.

3 **If the floor is very gappy,** lift the boards and re-lay them tightly butted, filling in the last gap with an extra board. Alternatively, fill gaps with timber slips.

4 **Hammer in protruding nail heads** below the board surface before you start.

5 **To deal with sanding dust,** clear the room, open windows and seal built-in cupboards with tape. Wear mask/goggles.

6 **Start with coarse sanding sheets** and work your way down to fine ones.

7 **Sanding machines are very powerful.** Keep them moving for an even finish.

8 **Use an edge sander for the edges** of the room and get into corners by hand.

9 **Sand *with* the wood grain,** not across.

10 **Collect clean sawdust from your sander's dust bags** and mix with PVA glue to make a matching wood filler to fill gaps.

DEAL WITH DAMP

1 **Find out what's causing the damp.** If you can't work out where it's coming from, consult a qualified professional.

2 **Do you have rising damp?** Decaying skirting boards or floors, stained plaster or peeling paint and wallpaper may indicate rising damp. Get professional help.

3 **Stains on walls or ceilings?** These are likely to be caused by water from outside. Usual causes are faulty gutters, pipes, overflows, roofs, windowframes, pointing or rendering.

4 **To deal with condensation** dripping down walls/windows, wipe wet windows and sills every morning and open them to let damp air out or install a good extractor.

5 **Avoid creating moisture** by putting lids on cooking pans, closing kitchen and bathroom doors and drying clothes outside. Improve insulation and heating

6 **Repair damaged roof flashings** or rotting window frames.

7 **Check roofs regularly** and re-fix dislodged slates or tiles straight away.

8 **Keep gutters clear of leaves, moss and other debris.** Also check for gaps, cracks or damage to all rainwater goods.

9 **Check bathroom and kitchen fittings** for overflows, leaks and poor pipe joints.

10 **Cracked pointing or render will allow moisture in.** Rake out old pointing and re-point. Fill cracks in render.

HOUSEHOLD RECYCLING

1 **Sort out a good-sized storage place** to put your items for recycling. Make sure it's handy but out of the way. Equip it with a range of stacking boxes.

2 **Buy a smaller kitchen bin** – it will remind you to recycle every day.

3 **Make sure your recyclables are clean.** Wash out bottles and tins and squash tins and plastic bottles to take up less space.

4 **Re-use old envelopes** by sticking on a new address label.

5 **Give your old magazines to friends** or surgeries'/dentists' waiting rooms.

6 **Use lidded glass jars** for putting your home-made preserves in.

7 **Donate recyclables to schools** for craft work/learning resources (fabric scraps, wrapping paper, ribbons, cardboard, tubs).

8 **Don't discard takeaway containers or ice-cream cartons** – use them for small items (toys, nuts, bolts, clothes pegs).

9 **Ask local charities if they'd like old furniture,** kitchen kit and bedding (in good condition). They may even collect.

10 **Clothes are ideal for recycling.** Give to a charity shop or swap with a friend.

REDUCE YOUR CARBON FOOTPRINT

1 **Insulate your loft and draughtproof doors and windows.** Closing curtains at dusk stops heat escaping.

2 **Buy energy-efficient appliances.**

3 **Switch off electronic items at the plug** when they are not in use.

4 **Change to energy-efficient light bulbs** and remember to turn off all the lights whenever you leave a room.

5 **Install double-glazing.**

6 **Turn down your thermostat** just a little – it will make a big difference.

7 **An indoor ceiling fan** uses less energy than air conditioning.

8 **Buy an electricity monitor** – it's a great way to focus the mind on energy use.

9 **Switch to a smaller fridge.**

10 **Upgrade your heating/air conditioning system** and service it regularly to maximize its efficiency.

GO FOR ALTERNATIVE ENERGY

1 **Installing renewable technology** can be simple and could save you money. It may also reduce your carbon footprint and add value to your home.

2 **Cut down your energy usage.** Ensure your home is energy-efficient by insulating, draughtproofing, double glazing, saving water and making sure your heating/hot-water systems are super-efficient.

3 **Consider solar power.** It can be used to make electricity or to heat water.

4 **Enough space for boilers and pumps?**

Ask a registered installer to advise.

5 **A stream or river running past your home?** Use it to generate electricity. It must have a strong flow, with a difference in height over a reasonably short distance.

6 **Consider having a wind turbine.**

7 **Put in a new biomass boiler/heat pump:** they are more cost-effective.

8 **Seek insider advice from local people** who have acquired similar technologies.

9 **Check whether you need permission** for any installation and whether your home insurance policy would need adjusting.

10 **Make money by being green.** Find out about grants. You may be able to earn money by selling back surplus electricity.

BE WATER-WISE

1 **Don't let the cold tap run** while you are cleaning your teeth or washing your hands.

2 **When running the hot tap,** save the cooler water for watering your houseplants.

3 **Take showers**, though power showers do use more water. Install a water-saving shower head. Fill baths half-full or share.

4 **Collect rainwater in a water butt** and use it to water your garden.

5 **Redirect rainwater from your roof** for using in your washing machine or WC.

6 **Use all water-using appliances fully loaded.** Choose eco programmes.

7 **Check for hidden water leaks.** If you have a meter, read it, then don't use any water for an hour. Check again for the same reading. If it's different, you have a leak.

8 **Fix a dripping tap** straight away.

9 **Fit a water-saving device** in your loo cistern to use less water at every flush.

10 **Jet washers are water-wasters.** Clean your car with a bucket and sponge.

ENERGY-CONSCIOUS CLOTHES CLEANING

1 **Reduce the number of washes you do.** Wear clothes more than once and refresh them by hanging them outside.

2 **Select low temperatures –** cooler washes are fine for many once-worn items.

3 **Wait until you have a full load** before running a wash. Small loads waste energy.

4 **Choose a high final-spin speed –** it will remove more water from your clothes.

5 **Put up simple clothes-lines outside.** Stack lines above each other and hoist them out of the way. Or use a fold-up whirligig dryer.

6 **If you don't have a garden** make use of breezeways and airy indoor areas.

7 **A dedicated laundry room** is perfect for drying clothes indoors. Buy an extractor.

8 **Ceiling- and wall-mounted airers** are great for keeping drying clothes out of the way. Don't drape clothes over radiators; it prevents the heating working efficiently and encourages condensation.

9 **Make sure your dryer filters are fluff-free** so that it runs ultra-efficiently.

10 **Don't run your dryer for longer than you really have to.**

GORGEOUS GREEN DECORATING

1 Use eco paints. They are breathable, non-toxic and come ready mixed.

2 Use traditional lime wash as a wall covering. It has a chalky finish, is anti-bacterial and insecticidal and can be coloured with natural pigments.

3 Environmentally friendly wallpapers are great, but don't use them in humid areas such as kitchens and bathrooms.

4 Re-use old furniture and avoid buying new. Seek antique, vintage or second-hand items and update unwanted furnishings.

5 Linoleum flooring is made from natural, renewable materials, is hard-wearing and easy to clean.

6 When searching for fabrics, look for organic wool, cotton, linen and felt.

7 Recycled textiles are great for making into a beautiful patchwork quilt.

8 Choose light fittings that are suitable for low-energy lightbulbs.

9 Use recycled glassware – it's green, good-looking and durable.

10 Opt for towels made from bamboo: they're soft, fluffy, ultra-absorbent, naturally anti-bacterial and sustainable.

TURN WOODEN CHAIRS INTO TREASURES

1 Repair
2 Re-cane seat
3 New solid seat
4 Fabric seat cover
5 Strip and wax
6 Paint
7 Découpage
8 Frilly seat cover
9 Tie-on seat cushion
10 Slip cover

UPCYCLE YOUR FURNITURE

1 Brush up on DIY skills to make the most of broken, old or just plain boring furnishings. Ask a friend/relative for tips, borrow library books, research on the internet or even go on a course.

2 Only tackle furnishings that are inexpensive and not too old. If a piece is valuable or antique seek expert help.

3 Save the life of a wobbly chair by evening up its legs with a saw. Or shorten the legs of an unwanted dining table and turn it into a useful low-level coffee table.

4 Ugly or out-of-proportion knobs and handles can ruin furniture. It's easy to transform it by unscrewing them and attaching good-looking replacements.

5 Use patterned, sticky-backed plastic to line for old chests or wardrobes, creating a smooth finish for storing delicate clothes.

6 Liven up the flat panels of wooden furniture by pasting on wallpaper, wrapping paper, maps, music or posters.

7 Upright wooden dining chairs often have removable seats. Staple a gorgeous new fabric cover over the top of the existing one. Choose interesting fabric remnants that coordinate with the room colours.

8 Give a new lease of life to a worn-out piece of wooden furniture with a bright new coat of paint. Unexpected colours can look brilliant on vintage or modern, lacklustre pieces – imagine a 1950s sideboard repainted with lime-green gloss.

9 Before you paint furniture, carry out all the necessary repairs. Remove the drawers, handles, knobs and sand everything thoroughly. For a really professional finish, rub down between each coat with wet-and-dry sand-paper. Finish with a top coat.

10 Newly painted pieces blend in best if painted the same colour as the walls.

CHEAP, CHIC IDEAS FOR WINDOWS

1 **Recycle an old curtain** into a simple roller or softer roman blind.

2 **Look for funky, vintage-print second-hand curtains** in charity shops, garage sales and at auctions.

3 **Use a flat sheet to make a curtain** – but line it to give it the necessary body.

4 **Vintage tablecloths** can make beautiful curtains, especially if they are embroidered.

5 **Get warm and toasty with a curtain** fashioned from a thick, cosy blanket.

6 **A length of sari fabric** will add a real splash of exotic colour and style.

7 **Inject new life into a dull old curtain** by adding on a patterned border made from a cleverly coordinating fabric.

8 **Fleece is cheap,** it comes in lovely colours and it sews oh-so easily.

9 **Choose sheer muslin** for a floaty feel.

10 **Interesting trims add class** to inexpensive curtains and blinds – ricrac, ribbons, bobbles and bows.

NEW CUSHIONS FROM OLD FABRIC

1 **Consider using a mix of fabrics,** not just project leftovers but also old curtains, bed linens or clothes.

2 **Use curtain-fabric remnants** to really coordinate your room expertly.

3 **Have fun with interesting textures** such as silk, felt or corduroy, but avoid very thick or sheer fabrics.

4 **If you only have tiny scaps of fabric,** cut out squares and stitch them together to make a pretty patchwork cushion.

5 **Think about other cushion shapes.** How about rectangles, circles, ovals, triangles or even sausage-shaped bolsters?

6 **To make an appliquéd cushion front,** cut clever motifs from a patterned fabric and stitch them onto a plain background, using striking contrasting thread.

7 **Cushion fronts and backs don't have to match,** but it's good if they coordinate.

8 **Fantastic ideas for fastenings** include buttons, poppers, zips, ties or a simple envelope-style overlap.

9 **Large-patterned motifs** look better if they are centred on the cushion front.

10 **Use interesting trimmings** (buttons, ribbons, ricrac, sequins, ruffles, feathers, fur) to make your cushions truly original.

IMPROVISE A HEADBOARD FOR A BED

1 **To revive a painted wooden headboard,** sand and repaint it for fresh appeal.

2 **Make a headboard from a wooden panel.** Add decorative trims or mouldings.

3 **Cover your headboard with fab fabric.** Cut your fabric to the shape and size of your headboard, allowing 10cm (4in) all the way around. Spray-glue the board, before stretching the fabric over and stapling it smoothly to the back.

4 **Add a luxurious touch.** Lusciously soft and tactile fabrics are a wonderful choice – think velvet, moleskin or lambswool.

5 **For leaning against your headboard in comfort** add a layer of extra-deep wadding.

6 **Throw a lovely old eiderdown or soft blanket** over the existing bed head.

7 **Make a rectangle of quilted fabric** with ties positioned at each corner so that it can be attached to a metal bed framework.

8 **For divan beds,** a rectangular headboard can be attached to the wall or bed frame.

9 **For a temporary solution prop a fabric-covered/wooden screen** behind the bed.

10 **Give the illusion of a headboard** with a rectangle of fabric hung behind the bed.

IRRESISTIBLE TRIMMINGS TO LIVEN UP YOUR STYLE

1 Ribbon
2 Lace
3 Ricrac
4 Bobbles
5 Buttons
6 Beads
7 Pom-poms
8 Braid
9 Diamanté
10 Tassels

REVIVE A WORN-OUT SOFA

1 **Wash loose covers or use upholstery cleaner** to get rid of dirt and grime.

2 **Neatly stitch repairs** to any worn areas of the sofa arms or back. Or make pretty patches/appliqué from contrasting fabrics.

3 **If just one arm is worn,** simply throw a nice folded blanket, shawl or quilt over it.

4 **Cover a worn-all-over sofa** with a huge throw and tuck in. Pile high with cushions.

5 **To stop throws constantly rucking up** use two – one for the seat and another over the back. They'll stay in place better.

6 **Make a brand-new loose cover.** Choose fabric to complement the room.

7 **To save money on a loose cover,** use cheaper fabric on areas you can't see, such as the seat beneath the base cushions.

8 **Make a fashionable, patchwork cover** using lengths of different fabric.

9 **Piping adds a professional touch,** but you need to be good at sewing.

10 **If you can't deal with sewing zips** in your new loose cover, use simpler tie fastenings, or hook-and-loop tape.

REVAMP A LAMP

1 **Repaint a wooden lamp base** for an instant refreshed new look.

2 **On a metal lamp,** use a coat of primer before you start painting.

3 **Think patterned as well as plain** – stripes, spots or an animal print would all look interesting on a repainted lamp base.

4 **Wrap raffia, string or ribbon** around the base to transform its looks.

5 **Use stickers or découpage** to decorate the base after a fresh lick of paint.

6 **Re-cover a fabric shade** with a small amount of new or vintage fabric.

7 **Embellish the shade edge** with glued-on binding, ribbon, braid or buttons.

8 **To make a ruffle** to add to the shade's lower edge, gather up a strip of fabric.

9 **Paint or stencil designs** onto a fabric or card shade using watered-down paint.

10 **Punch holes in a card shade** using an ordinary needle – the light will cast the pretty shadows of your design.

SORT A SQUEAKY FLOOR

1 Stand beneath the squeaky floor and get a friend to walk above you – to locate the problem area precisely.

2 Look at the joists from below – if there's a gap between them and the sub-floor, fill by forcing in a tapered shingle.

3 Install a screw, angled, through a joist and into the sub-floor to attach them firmly. Ask your friend to stand on the floor above to help press the two layers together.

4 Your surface flooring may not be properly attached to the sub-floor. From below, drive a screw through the sub-floor into the underside of the surface flooring. Make sure the screw is the right length to reach into the flooring, but not pop out through the top of it.

5 Check that a nail isn't sticking out and rubbing against a joist. If so, cut it off with diagonal cutters.

6 Squeaks from between floor joists may mean extra bridging is needed beneath the sub-floor. Screw and glue a small rectangle of 1.5cm (¾in) thick plywood under the squeaky seam.

7 If access is a problem, you'll have to work from above. Try hitting the area with a hammer. It may force any loose nails back in.

8 Try lubricating the squeaky area by working a little powdered graphite or talcum powder in between the floorboards. Vacuum up the excess.

9 Drive spiral flooring nails, at a slight angle, through the board and down into the sub-floor. Press down as you're drilling.

10 Always pre-drill nail holes in floorboards so that the wood doesn't split. But don't pre-drill the sub-floor or the nail won't hold.

TYPES OF FLOORING
1 Wood
2 Cork
3 Carpet
4 Ceramic tiles
5 Leather
6 Vinyl
7 Lino
8 Rubber
9 Stone
10 Natural fibre

DEAL WITH A DRIPPING TAP

1 Before you start, put the plug in the basin so you don't lose any small tap or tool parts that may fall in.

2 Disconnect and drain the water supply to the tap.

3 Identify the problem: a dripping spout usually means a faulty washer or worn seal; a drip from the head of the tap when in use indicates a faulty O-ring or gland packing.

4 Lever off the hot/cold disc with a knife and undo the small retaining screw below. Or look for a screw on the side and undo it.

5 Pull off the head of the tap. It may pull or screw upwards or else rock it from side to side as you go. Or you may need to tap it gently from below with a hammer.

6 Unscrew the headgear nut, just above main body of the tap and lift out the assembly.

7 Replace the worn washer, O-ring or gland packing, or tighten the gland nut, and reconnect all the parts again in the right order.

8 If the tap continues to drip then its metal seat may need regrinding. Either buy a specialist tool or ask a plumber to do it for you.

9 If you have a dripping ceramic-disc tap, it may simply be caused by debris stuck inside. Remove the cartridge and wash it in warm, soapy water, checking for damage – in the cartridge and to the rubber seal below it – at the same time.

10 **Remember that ceramic-disc cartridges are 'handed'** so, if you do have to replace one, make sure you buy one that turns on and off in the right direction.

EASE A STICKING DOOR

1 **Loose screws in the hinges** can make a door drop. Tighten as necessary.

2 **Pull the hinge (and the door) in** by replacing the middle screw of the hinge where it's attached to the jamb, using a 10cm (3in) screw and a drill.

3 **If the top of the door is sticking,** adjust the top hinge; the bottom hinge if the bottom of the door is sticking.

4 **If the door is straining on its hinges,** insert thin pieces of cardboard under the hinge flaps to pack them out.

5 **If the hinges are old and worn,** either fit new hinges or swap the old ones over (the wear on the pins will be reversed).

6 **Excess humidity can make doors stick** because the timber has swollen. Open kitchen and bathroom windows and avoid drying clothes on radiators.

7 **Bump in the floor?** Try resetting the door hinges so that the lower one sticks out slightly more than the higher one. As you open the door, the misaligned pins should force it up a little.

8 **If the door sticks on newly laid carpet,** replace the hinges with rising butt hinges. Remember that they are made for either right- or left-handed openings.

9 **If paint on the door's edge is causing the problem,** sand it a little at a time.

10 **If all else fails,** take the door off its hinges and shave off a thin layer of wood.

REPAIR A BROKEN WINDOW

1 **For a short-term repair,** stick waterproof tape over the crack. If glass is missing, tape a plastic sheet over the whole window.

2 **First floor or higher?** It's probably best to remove the whole window, if possible, and work on it at ground level.

3 **If you're handling a large piece of glass,** ask someone to help. Never work with glass outdoors in windy weather. Always wear gloves and protective goggles.

4 **Grip each shattered piece of glass** separately and work loose to remove. It's safest to work from the top of the window to the bottom.

5 **Remove all old putty** and pull out the sprigs (small nails holding the glass) with pincers. Seal any bare wood with primer.

6 **Measure your window to the insides of the rebates and have new glass cut.** It should be 3mm ($1/8$in) smaller than your measurements all around.

7 **Linseed-oil putty can be tricky** to work with. To absorb excess oil, wrap in newspaper. If stiff add more linseed oil.

8 **When puttying-in the glass,** wet the knife with water to stop it dragging.

9 **Don't paint the putty** for three weeks.

10 **Clean any excess putty** from the glass with methylated spirits. Paint slightly over it and onto the glass to form a seal.

RESUSCITATE DAMAGED FURNITURE

1 **Got a shallow dent in wood?** Try sitting a few drops of water in the hollow, so that the compressed timber swells up again.

2 **Lightly sand away a cigarette burn,** then cover the area with a furniture-patching wax stick in the correct colour.

3 **White spots or rings** formed by water or hot dishes may disappear just by firmly buffing with liquid furniture polish. Or use a soft cloth dampened with a mix of one part turpentine and one part linseed oil.

4 **If a table top has a dark water stain,** you'll probably have to remove the finish, bleach the stain and refinish the surface.

5 **To stop drawers sticking,** look for obstructions/loose parts. Try rubbing hard wax on drawer sides and bottom or lightly sand the bottom edges. If your drawers have sticky plastic runners, wipe them and spray the rollers with silicone lubricant.

6 **To cover a small scratch in wood,** crack open a Brazil nut or a walnut and rub the oil along the scratch to darken it. Or use a permanent felt-tip marker

7 **Test solvents/stains** in an inconspicuous place before you actually use them.

8 **Don't try to repair veneered furniture.** Leave the task to a professional.

9 **Fixing a wobbly chair** depends on how it's made. Screw the leg in more tightly, re-glue the dowel, or tighten/replace the screw, bolt or corner plate.

10 **Remove leather upholstery stains** by rubbing with an art gum eraser.

ZZZZZZZZ – SELECT A NEW BED

1 **Spend at least ten minutes trying out a new bed** in the shop. Lie down on it and practise rolling over. If the bed is for two, it's important to try it out together.

2 **Too hard or too soft?** Lie on your back and put your hand under the small of your back. If you can pull it out easily the mattress is too hard; if you can't move it at all, the mattress is too soft. The term 'orthopaedic' may not necessarily mean it's good for your back – it's just extra firm.

3 **What about length?** A bed should be at least 15cm (6in) longer than the tallest person who will sleep in it. Buy as wide a bed as possible for comfort.

4 **If you need extra bedroom storage,** choose a divan bed with drawers.

5 **Remember that antique beds** are much smaller than modern ones – we've grown!

6 **When buying a mattress separately,** check that it will fit your bed properly.

7 **How far apart should wooden slats be?** No more than 6cm (2½in) wide for good ventilation and no more than 4cm

(1½in) apart to prevent the mattress sagging through them.

8 **If you're allergic to house dust mites,** a foam or latex mattress is a good option.

9 **A memory foam mattress is great** for relieving pressure on painful joints.

10 **Make sure the new bed is the right height.** Can you get in and out of it easily?

PURCHASE TOP-NOTCH BED LINEN

1 **It's worth investing in quality linen.** It feels a lot more luxurious, will wash well and last you for years.

2 **Basic, plain bed linens,** in white or a solid colour, are inexpensive and easy to coordinate with your bedroom.

3 **Look for interesting design details,** from pintucks, cording and scalloped edging to hemstitch, embroidery and lace.

4 **Linen sheets are breathable,** cool, crisp and they soften as time goes by.

5 **Silk bed linen** keeps you warm in winter and cool in summer; it's even said to reduce wrinkles and keep your hair glossy. It can go in the washing machine, too.

6 **Pure Egyptian cotton** is the most popular bed linen and is a brilliant all-rounder.

7 **Look for a thread count** of more than 200 and up to 600 for real luxury linen.

8 **If you want easy-care linen,** go for a 50:50 or 60:40 mix of cotton and polyester.

9 **Choose from different weaves of cotton bed linen:** percale, sateen, waffle, jacquard, flannel, seersucker and twill.

10 **Wash new linen** before use to get rid of finishing agents and allow for shrinkage.

BARGAIN OPTIONS FOR FURNISHINGS

1 Sales
2 Special promotions
3 Ends of lines
4 Factory shops
5 Clearance outlets
6 Online shopping clubs
7 Online comparison sites
8 Store-card discounts
9 Discount vouchers/codes
10 Second-hand shops

CHOOSE YOUR IDEAL DUVET/PILLOW

1 **If you suffer from allergies,** avoid feather or down duvets and pillows. Alternatives are synthetic fibres or silk.

2 **Looking for a natural filling?** Goose down is the most luxurious as it's warm and light and duck down is a good alternative. Both are often mixed with feathers to add greater resilience.

3 **Choose a duvet according to warmth.** Look for the tog rating, which goes from about 4 (summer weight) to a toasty 15 (for freezing winters).

4 **Choose a duvet one size larger than your bed** if you don't want to have a nightly fight with your partner over it.

5 **Children need a lower tog** value because they have naturally higher body temperatures than adults.

6 **Side-sleepers need a high pillow,** or a firm bottom pillow and softer top one, to keep the spine straight.

7 **Back-sleepers are better off with** a softish, medium-height pillow.

8 **Stomach-sleepers need a low pillow** to reduce pressure on the neck.

9 **Get extra support** for your neck by using a shaped foam pillow.

10 **Use pillow and mattress protectors** for extra comfort and to prolong the life of your bed linen, pillows and mattress.

SPLASH OUT ON A SUPER NEW SOFA

1 **Test the strength of the sofa frame** by lifting one front leg about 15cm (6in) off the floor. If the other leg hasn't lifted a little, too, the frame has too much 'give'.

2 **Never buy a sofa that is just held together with nails, glue or staples.**

3 **If possible, feel the springs through the upholstery;** they should be close together and nicely firm.

4 **Know your stuffing –** goose down and feather is luxurious and expensive and will need frequent plumping. Foam may harden or flatten quickly. Look for high-resilience foam for durability and comfort.

5 **Choose heavy, smooth, closely woven fabric,** which will last. Seams should be straight, strongly stitched, not puckered.

6 **Size matters –** choose a sofa that seats as many as you need, but it's important that it will neither crowd a room nor get lost in a large space.

7 **Your sofa's dimensions should suit your body** and provide enough support for comfortable sitting. You should be able to put your feet on the floor while sitting, and stand up easily.

8 **Cushions should be neither floppy nor overstuffed** and the covers not too tight.

9 **Be a style diva** and go for a look that suits you and your room. Skirts or bare legs (the sofa, not you!), number of seat cushions, style of arm – they all make a difference.

10 **Ensure that your sofa will go through your front door or window when it is delivered.** If you have problem access, then perhaps choose a model that has removable feet, arms or back – or even a modular version.

ACQUIRE ANTIQUES

1 **Research antiques before you buy:** look at and handle as many items as possible and get an idea of prices.

2 **Think carefully about how an antique piece will fit into your home.** Dark wood furniture can be bulky and heavy-looking.

3 **If a price seems too good to be true** – it probably is.

4 **It can be difficult buying with investment in mind.** The best advice is to buy because you love something. Then if it goes up in value it's an added bonus.

5 **Don't get a rush of blood to the head when you are buying at auction.** Set yourself a top price and don't go over it.

6 **Look at a piece underneath,** check for signs of intervention and ask lots of questions. A reputable dealer won't be afraid to answer them.

7 **Understand what descriptions are all about:** Louis XV 'style' doesn't necessarily mean it's really Louis XV.

8 **Condition is paramount** for collectors. Choose the best quality you can afford.

9 **Watch out when you buy old radiators** (or other plumbing pieces) or electrical items. If they haven't already been restored, add on the cost of getting it done.

10 **Ask dealers (politely!) whether a discount is possible.** 'What's your best price on this?' is a good line of approach. It's almost expected.

GIVE YOUR KITCHEN A MAKE-OVER

1 **Stain or repaint cupboard doors and drawer fronts.** Replace knobs and handles.

2 **Buy replacement doors or drawer fronts** for an instant, dramatic change. Check sizes carefully and ensure that hinge holes are in the right places.

3 **Opt for free-standing furnishings** such as a dresser, sideboard, butcher's block or chest of drawers. Ensure they're the same depth as existing fitted items.

4 **Create your own dresser** with a minimum of expense by hanging a couple of shelves above a chest of drawers and painting them all the same colour.

5 **Replace worktops.** Laminate is cheapest and timber is not too expensive (but don't locate timber adjacent to a sink).

6 **A new splashback looks stylish.** To be ultra-smart, have it in the same material as the worktop. Cheap alternatives include ceramic tiles, painted tongue-and-groove timber, mirror tiles or a sheet of toughened glass or acrylic.

7 **Swap a boring ceiling-mounted track** for a good-looking new light fitting.

8 **Fit dimmer switches** to add atmosphere at different times of the day.

9 **Maximize storage space** with hooks, racks and rails

10 **Coordinate all your kitchen kit:** why not hide any ugly pieces and display matching, interesting, crockery and glassware. You'll get far more enjoyment out of your kitchen.

A NEW-LOOK BUDGET BATHROOM

1 **Change the taps.**

2 **Replace an old shower curtain** with a glamorous glass screen.

3 **Replace the shower handset.**

4 **Add a decorative mirror.**

5 **Use eye-catching mosaic tiles** to jazz up small areas – try using broken crockery.

6 **Put up a new window blind.**

7 **Coordinate towels** – one colour is good!

8 **Re-grout tiles** and replace old sealant.

9 **Sort out your storage** with pretty baskets, hanging tidy-aways and pots or tubs to hold all your bathroom bits.

10 **Buy a colourful new seat for your WC.**

SUCK IT UP! CHOOSE A VACUUM CLEANER

1 **Are you the upright type?** Upright cleaners give better control and are ideal for large areas of carpet.

2 **Cylinder machines are compact** and easy to use on stairs, around furniture and on upholstery. They're good for hard floors.

3 **Would you like a bag with that?** Bagged cleaners are usually cheaper – but you will have to keep buying new bags. How easy are they to fit?

4 **Before you decide to buy a bagless version,** check how easy it is to empty.

5 **Have you got allergies?** Choose a cleaner with a sophisticated filter system.

6 **If you have pets,** consider a cleaner with a charcoal filter – it can get rid of unwanted odours.

7 **If you want to clean upholstery, rugs or curtains, variable power is a boon.**

8 **What about power?** On a cylinder machine, the higher the wattage the more powerful the machine. On an upright cleaner, the brush makes all the difference.

9 **Try before you buy** – is the machine easy to manoeuvre? Can you pick it up easily? Is handle height adjustable?

10 **A longer cable is handy in a big house.** It also means less moving of plugs.

LOOK FOR A NEW WASHING MACHINE

1 **Think about what clothes you wash and how often.** Do you need a quick-wash facility, gentle wash or variable temperature control? Or perhaps all of the above.

2 **If you don't often wash many clothes at a time,** a half-load facility is useful.

3 **If you want to switch on your washing when you're not at home,** choose a machine with a timer-delay function

4 **How about extra capacity?** Useful if yours is a large household – sometimes big machines will even wash duvets.

5 **Front or top loader?** A front loader fits under a worktop, but you won't have to bend down to use a top loader.

6 **Choose an integrated machine** (hidden behind a door that matches your kitchen) to make it blend in seamlessly.

7 **A machine with a high spin speed** will remove more water from your clothes.

8 **Ask about energy efficiency.** An ultra-efficient machine could save you money.

9 **A combined washer/dryer** is good if space is tight, but you'll only be able to dry half a wash load at a time.

10 **Make sure you install** the machine on a level, solid base, that the hoses are not kinked and that the plumbing is easily accessible so you can turn it off quickly in an emergency.

FLAT OUT: BUY AN IRON

1 **If you rarely iron, buy a basic model.** No point in paying for extra features you'll never actually use.

2 **If you need your iron to generate lots of heat,** look for a higher wattage.

3 **For ironing curtains or hanging garments,** choose a 'vertical steam' facility.

4 **Steam generator irons can cut ironing** time in half – but they are more bulky, so check your space.

5 **If you have young children,** choose an iron with cord storage or a safety cut-out.

6 **For the easiest glide on an iron,** a sole plate should be highly polished stainless steel or have a non-stock coating. A dimpled pattern helps, too.

7 What watt? For most people, 1600W is quite enough.

8 Heavy irons press well but can be tiring to use. Lighter ones mean more pushing back and forwards. Aim for a compromise that's comfortable for you.

9 A bigger water tank means less refilling and waiting for the steam. A transparent tank is handy.

10 If you happen to live in a hard-water area, look for a model that combats the build-up of scale.

WHERE TO BUY SECOND-HAND

1 Markets
2 Car boot/yard sales
3 Auctions
4 Private dealers
5 Salvage yards
6 Jumble/garage sales
7 Antiques fairs
8 Junk shops
9 Small ads
10 The internet

HOW ABOUT SECOND-HAND FURNITURE?

1 Watch out for woodworm – remove drawers and look underneath for telltale signs (tiny holes and dust).

2 Get old electrical fittings checked by a professional before use.

3 Don't be too rigid in your expectations. The surprises found in a second-hand outlet are all part of the fun.

4 Even if it's cheap, don't buy something broken, poorly made or unattractive – unless you're sure you can renovate it.

5 Never leave home without a tape measure and a list of relevant dimensions.

6 Salvage yards can be mucky places. So you can explore them fully, wear work clothing and sturdy shoes.

7 Consider asking (politely) if the seller will offer a discount. They will often be prepared to do a deal.

8 Worried about buying at auction? Go to one or two first and watch.

9 When buying online, don't forget to factor in the cost of delivery.

10 Being patient is a golden rule of buying second-hand. Eventually you *will* come across your ideal piece.

FURNISH FOR FREE

1 Go 'dumpster-diving' or 'skip-dipping' for unwanted items from people's skips.

2 If you spot something in a skip you like, never trespass and always ask the owner's permission before taking it.

3 Sign up to an internet-based network which connects people who have unwanted items with those who want them. If you get something free through such a site, offer something in return.

4 Sometimes you'll spot unwanted furniture left on the street with a note: 'please take'. Grab it while you can.

5 Scan the small ads – sometimes people advertise furnishings as 'free to collector'.

6 Swap things you don't want with things you do want from a friend/family member. Or repay them by bartering a service.

7 A local charity may be able to help. Perhaps volunteer some time in return.

8 Make your furniture yourself.

9 Buy lots from one dealer. They may feel able to throw in an item for nothing.

10 If all else fails, perhaps a distant member of your family will leave you some gorgeous antiques in their will!

RENOVATE FOR LESS

1 **Try to buy fittings from trade suppliers** rather than high-street retailers.

2 **Hire or borrow expensive tools.**

3 **Do as much as you can yourself** and ask friends/family to help. Leave specialist tasks to the professionals.

4 **Look for good-condition second-hand fixtures/fittings.** Check auction sites, ads in local papers and reclamation yards.

5 **Wait for seasonal sales,** or search factory outlets and discount warehouses.

6 **Buy wallpaper and fabric from ends-of-line** and discount suppliers.

7 **Use materials in standard sizes only.** Unusual dimensions take up more material.

8 **If you can't afford carpets,** sand back and stain, varnish or paint floorboards and add rugs for a contemporary look.

9 **Instead of bespoke curtains,** roller blinds can be cut to fit most windows.

10 **Use online comparison websites** to ensure you always get the best deal.

REMOVE LAUNDRY STAINS

1 **Deal with stains before they dry** and become harder to remove. No time to treat a stain straight away? Soak in cold water.

2 **Blot away excess,** then push the stain out from the back, working from the outside inwards to avoid spreading.

3 **Cold water is better than hot for stains** – heat can set them permanently.

4 **Different types of stain need different approaches.** For protein stains soak in cold water with salt or a biological pre-soak.

5 **Non-soluble stains** such as nail varnish, paint or glue should be removed with a solvent and then washed.

6 **Test a specialist stain-remover** on an inconspicuous part of the fabric first.

7 **For stubborn underarm stains,** mix half a cup of bicarbonate of soda with half a cup of salt and a few drops of cold water to make a paste. Cover the stain and leave for half an hour. Rinse with cold water.

8 **For grass stains,** soak in white vinegar.

9 **Greasy stains** can often be removed by rubbing in baking powder and leaving for half an hour. Rinse off, then wash.

10 **To clean grimy collars,** use washing-up liquid, then pour on bicarbonate of soda and use an old toothbrush to scrub. Wash.

BANISH WASHDAY BLUES

1 **Sort dirty laundry as you go** to save time. Keep whites and colours separately.

2 **Make the most of your laundry room space** by fitting shelves above your washing machine to store all your kit.

3 **A drying rack on a pulley** holds masses and can be hoisted out of the way. Mount above a radiator if possible.

4 Add hooks to the back of the door to hold peg bags and other paraphernalia.

5 Paint a laundry room brilliant white for a feeling of serene cleanliness all round.

6 If you haven't got cupboard space for concealing laundry essentials, hang a gorgeous curtain in front of shelves/alcove. Or choose matching storage.

7 Make your laundry room welcoming.

Keep a radio, TV or sound system there to help keep you amused.

8 Decant washing powder into an attractive jar (label as necessary).

9 Good lighting is essential, so you can see what you're doing.

10 Keep laundry products well stocked so you don't run out unexpectely. They're cheaper to buy in bulk.

USE WHITE VINEGAR IN YOUR LAUNDRY TO...

1 Whiten fabrics
2 Brighten colours
3 Prevent static cling
4 Get rid of smoky smells
5 Neutralize body odour
6 Remove soap residue
7 Get rid of musty smells
8 Soften fabrics
9 Remove perspiration stains
10 Clean your machine

KEEP YOUR WHITES WHITE

1 To lightly bleach whites in your washing machine, add half a cup of lemon juice to the rinse cycle.

2 Hard water can make whites grey. Add half a cup of vinegar to your rinse water.

3 Whites made of natural fibres will benefit from being line-dried in the sun.

4 Add half a cup of borax or washing soda to your wash to brighten up whites.

5 To prevent colour transfer, wash whites separately from coloured clothes or linens.

6 Don't overload the washing machine. It needs space to agitate whites properly and for the detergent to cleanse effectively.

7 Launder white garments after you've worn them, even if they look clean – body oils can turn a garment yellow.

8 To brighten white fabric, use a commercial colour remover.

9 Use bleach carefully – an oxygen-based bleach is usually safer.

10 Try a nappy or net-curtain cleaner.

MAXIMIZE YOUR WASHING MACHINE

1 Clean your machine regularly: unclog the filter monthly and wipe out the detergent drawer before it clogs up.

2 To prevent lime scale and mildew, run the machine empty regularly. Choose a hot wash and add vinegar or soda crystals.

3 Check garment pockets and remove tissues, sweets, coins and so on as such objects will cause machine damage.

4 Do up zips, hooks and poppers, and turn anything that might fade inside out.

5 Turn down that temperature dial: most

clothes can be washed at 30°C (85°F).

6 Never be tempted to overload the machine – the clothes won't wash properly and the machine could be damaged.

7 Wash delicates in a special mesh bag, or use an old pillowcase.

8 Repair any tears or holes before you wash them, and pre-wash heavily soiled items separately.

9 Take damp washing out of the machine straight after the programme has finished.

10 Don't spin-dry stretch fabrics.

EFFICIENT TUMBLE DRYING

1 **Add a clean, dry towel to wet laundry.** It can cut drying time by 25 per cent.

2 **Dry towels and other heavier items separately** from lighter garments.

3 **Clean the dryer lint filter every time.**

4 **Use the correct heat setting** for the fabric you're drying.

5 **Turn fadeable clothes inside out.**

6 **Don't overload the dryer –** everything will end up wrinkled if you do.

7 **Check the dryer vent regularly** to ensure it's not blocked.

8 **Don't over-dry your clothes.** Use the moisture sensor, if your machine has one. If everything ends up too dry, add a damp towel for a minute or two.

9 **If your clothes get static cling,** add a ball of aluminium foil to the dryer.

10 **Cut a dryer sheet in half –** it'll be quite enough to do the job.

BRILLIANT IRONING

1 **When you take clothes out of your washing machine or dryer,** shake them briskly and hang up – they'll need less ironing. Line-drying often eliminates it.

2 **Always choose the correct temperature for the fabric you're ironing.** Test first on an inconspicuous area of the garment.

3 **Most fabrics are best ironed inside out,** to avoid shiny patches.

4 **Dampen the fabric as you iron,** using the built-in sprayer or a spray bottle.

5 **Irons heat up faster than cool down,** so avoid waiting and start with garments that require a cool setting.

6 **To iron a shirt,** start with the collar, then the sleeves/cuffs. Finish with the front and back. Use spray starch if you like.

7 **Iron delicates or embroidered fabrics** on the reverse side, using a pressing cloth.

8 **Put freshly ironed items on a hanger** or clothes-horse to air before putting away.

9 **Banish lime scale from your iron** by filling it with a mix of water and vinegar for a couple of hours. Then rinse.

10 **Polish the iron's soleplate** when it's cold, using a soft cloth. Get rid of sticky marks by using a damp cloth and heating the iron up.

STORE CLOTHES SAFELY

1 **Don't let moths get your woollens –** wash items, then store in moth-proof bags. Use mothballs/natural cedar blocks.

2 **Vacuum storage spaces** regularly to keep pests away.

3 **Use all the hanging loops** on clothes so they stay in shape.

4 **Create enough space in your wardrobe** for everything you need to hang. Crushed clothes will only need ironing again.

5 Ditch wire hangers – they can wear holes in clothes. Choose kinder wooden ones or, for delicates, padded ones.

6 Knitwear and anything heavy and stretchy is better folded than hung.

7 Stack folded clothes with the heaviest items at the bottom.

8 Very delicate or beaded items might snag on other garments. Keep them folded in separate, tissue-lined boxes.

9 After dry-cleaning remove the plastic and allow clothes to air before storing.

10 Store dirty washing in canvas laundry baskets to allow air to circulate.

CHORE-NO-MORE REGULAR CLEANING

1 A slightly dampened duster is more effective than a dry one. Use an anti-static duster on electronic equipment.

2 Dust small, detailed items with a soft paintbrush or toothbrush.

3 Books attract a lot of dust – wipe with a soft cloth or use your vacuum cleaner's upholstery attachment.

4 Keep carpets and rugs in good condition by regular vacuuming. Spot-clean and shampoo once or twice a year.

5 Vacuum wooden floors along the grain.

6 Always sweep or vacuum before you mop, to get rid of dust. Use a mop in a sweeping motion, not circular.

7 Keep your kitchen germ-free by dealing with scraps, spills and splashes immediately. Clean up every time you cook by wiping down oven/hob and worktops.

8 Get into a cleaning routine that suits you, whether it's all day every Saturday or a midweek morning. If you don't have time, prioritize the most important tasks.

9 Store all cleaning products within easy reach (but well out of the reach of children) and replenish them before they run out.

10 Spend a little time each week tidying, dusting and vacuuming. You'll only need to do an occasional thorough clean every now and then.

SPARKLING SPRING CLEANING

1 Make a list of tasks in a logical order. You may not feel like tackling the whole house all at once. Do one room at a time.

2 Have a major sort-out and a really good tidy before you start.

3 Always clean from top to bottom of the house and do wet jobs first, then dry.

4 Wash down painted walls with a sugar-soap solution. Protect furniture first.

5 Hire a carpet cleaner.

6 Clean underneath all furniture, including concealed areas.

7 Turn your mattresses and have any bedding that you can't wash cleaned.

8 Wash curtains and clean slatted blinds.

9 Remove light fittings and clean them. For cobwebs use a long-handled duster.

10 Do your cleaning on a bright and breezy day, throw open the windows. Crank up the music. Enjoy!

MAKE YOUR WINDOWS SHINE

1 Start by cleaning the frames, using a wet, soapy cloth. Rinse with fresh water.

2 A mix of half water, half vinegar is a great cleaning solution for windows.

3 Use lint-free cloths or you'll end up spreading tiny fibres all over your windows.

4 Wash a couple of panes at a time, then sweep away the liquid with a squeegee.

5 If dirt has built up in window-frame corners, tackle the spot with a cotton pad.

6 Clean top to bottom to catch drips.

7 Use a soft, dry cloth to polish smears.

8 For a tried-and-trusted method of polishing windows use crumpled-up newspapers. It really works!

9 Wait for a cloudy day to wash your windows – the heat from the sun makes them dry too quickly, causing streaks.

10 Ask a professional window cleaner to do the outsides of upstairs windows.

CLEANING KIT ESSENTIALS
1 Cloths
2 Dusters
3 Dustpan and brush
4 Broom
5 Vacuum cleaner
6 Bucket
7 Mop
8 Old toothbrushes
9 Scouring pad
10 Squeegee

CLEAN YOUR KITCHEN KIT

1 To get burnt-on food off stainless-steel pans, fill with a solution of 15ml (5fl oz) biological washing powder for every 1 litre (2pt) water and boil for ten minutes. Repeat then wash.

2 Cast-iron pans can rust when soaked. Get rid of grease by sprinkling with salt, then washing and drying.

3 For oven-proof glassware with cooked-on food, try filling with water, add a few effervescent antacid tablets and soak.

4 Refresh your dishwasher by running it empty with a cup of white vinegar or lemon juice on the top rack.

5 For washing lots of greasy pans, use 2tbsp baking soda with washing-up liquid.

6 For stains on enamelware, fill with warm water and a tablet denture cleaner.

7 Remove burnt milk by wetting the pan and sprinkling salt over it. After ten minutes a quick scrub should do the trick.

8 Clean copper pans with ketchup.

9 Cooked-on food in your microwave? Microwave on high for a few minutes with a bowl of lemon juice/water. Clean.

10 Descale your kettle by filling with half water, half vinegar and leaving overnight. Empty, refill and boil twice before using.

GIVE YOUR FRIDGE A MAKEOVER

1 Wipe spills as soon as they happen with a clean, damp cloth.

2 Have some cool bags ready before you start a thorough clean-out. Turn the fridge off, throw anything away past its best, and bag up the rest of your food.

3 Remove all the shelves and drawers; wash in hot, soapy water and leave to dry.

4 Wash down the inside of the fridge with a soft cloth and soapy water, or a mix of 1 litre (2pt) hot water and 2 litres (4pt) bicarbonate of soda.

5 **Clean the rubber seals** with a solution of white vinegar.

6 **Use an old toothbrush to clean out all the nooks and crannies.**

7 **Can you get at the coils behind the fridge?** Vacuum them gently if you can.

8 **Wipe down the front of the fridge door** and the handle every day.

9 **Get rid of any mould** by wiping with a mix of bleach and water. Rinse off and dry.

10 **Defrost the freezer every few months.** Empty, turn off and put bowls of boiling water inside to speed up defrosting. Wipe away melting ice and clean.

CLEAN YOUR COOKER INSIDE & OUT

1 **Clean your oven regularly to prevent grime building up.** Do it once a week, if you cook every day.

2 **Soak any removable parts** (knobs, drip trays, pan supports) in hot, soapy water while cleaning the rest of the cooker.

3 **For an oven with stay-clean linings,** don't use ordinary detergents. Follow the manufacturer's instructions.

4 **For ovens lined with untreated enamel,** mix a thick paste with a few drops of water and bicarbonate of soda. Paste over the inside, leave overnight, scrub off.

5 **Stainless-steel oven panels need a proprietary cleaner.** Rub away finger marks with a soft cloth and baby oil.

6 **Make an oven easier to clean** by putting a bowl of water inside for about 20 minutes at a high temperature. The steam should loosen the grime.

7 **For the glass in oven doors,** use a multi-surface kitchen cleaner.

8 **To clean a hob,** wait until it is cool before you tackle it. Mop up light spills with kitchen paper or a damp cloth.

9 **Problems getting at hob crevices?** Use a small scouring pad or an old toothbrush.

10 **Keep your cooker hood clean.** Wash the inside regularly with warm, soapy water and remove grease with a blunt knife. Wash metal filters; replace paper and charcoal ones as recommended.

BACK TO NATURE WITH ALTERNATIVE CLEANERS

1 Vinegar
2 Bicarbonate of soda
3 Lemon juice
4 Salt
5 Non-gel toothpaste
6 Baking soda
7 Oxygen bleach
8 Soap nuts
9 Natural detergents
10 Washing balls

BRIGHTEN UP YOUR BATHROOM

1 **To shift WC stains,** put soda crystals in overnight and flush in the morning.

2 **Before you start cleaning the bathroom,** pop some cleaner down the WC, so it can get to work while you do the rest.

3 **Really dirty baths** will benefit from an overnight soak with warm water plus two scoops of biological washing powder.

4 **Use separate cleaning cloths and wear rubber gloves when cleaning the WC.** Soak the cloths in a solution of bleach after you have finished.

5 **Work from the least germy to the most** – basin and bath, then WC.

6 **In hard-water areas,** clean the WC with a combined cleaner and lime scale remover.

7 **Pour boiling water down plugholes** every now and then to prevent blockages – especially if you use bath oils regularly.

8 **Drop a mesh strainer in the plugholes** to catch hair before it blocks your drains.

9 **Don't leave products on too long –** it's quite likely that they'll cause discoloration, especially if there are worn areas or tiny cracks in the glaze.

10 **Avoid abrasive cleaning products;** nylon-bristled brushes and elbow grease are much, much better.

A SQUEAKY-CLEAN SHOWER

1 **Descale a plastic shower head** by removing it and soaking overnight in vinegar. Scrub, rinse and reattach.

2 **For a metal shower head,** use a liquid descaler and follow the manufacturer's instructions carefully.

3 **To get rid of mould on sealant and grout** use a bleach solution and an old, soft toothbrush.

4 **Dry the shower cubicle with a clean towel following every use.** Use a plastic squeegee, too. This will help keep mildew under control.

5 **To prevent a shower curtain mildewing,** cut off excess length before hanging and spread it out to dry following every use.

6 **Remove mildew from a shower curtain** by washing it in soapy water or a bleach solution and drying it in sunlight.

7 **To restore life to your tiles,** add a few drops of washing-up liquid to warm water and rub with a soft cloth. Rinse with fresh water and dry.

8 **Glass tiles need a special cleaner.** Don't use anything abrasive or acidic or you'll damage the surface.

9 **Test new products somewhere inconspicuous before you use them.** Tiles and shower cubicles can be made from all sorts of different materials.

10 **If grout or sealant are too mouldy to rescue,** scrape them out and re-do them.

CARE FOR WOODEN FURNITURE

1 **Avoid over-using spray polishes –** they may form an unpleasant coating.

2 **Rub in beeswax a few times a year.**

3 **Apply spray-polish to the cloth,** not the furniture. Buff well to remove.

4 **Get rid of sticky marks with a soapy cloth,** wrung out well to get rid of excess water. Rinse with a damp cloth, then dry.

5 **Bright sunlight and direct heat can damage furniture.**

6 **Restore old, dry wood** by rubbing in a little petroleum jelly.

7 **Never use abrasive cleaners or cloths.**

8 **Wooden antiques can be high-maintenance.** Research care techniques before you decide to buy.

9 **To clean varnished wood,** use cooled, black tea.

10 **Dust wooden furniture regularly** to keep the shine spot on.

KEEP YOUR BBQ BRILLIANTLY CLEAN

1 **To stop the food from burning/sticking and to make cleaning easier,** coat the rack with oil before you start cooking.

2 **Use a wire brush** for cleaning the racks – do it when they're still warm.

3 **Burn off cooked-on food.** After cooking, close the lid and turn up the heat.

4 **For normally dirty racks,** you can't beat a good soak in hot, soapy water.

5 **For stubborn rack dirt,** remove them, spray with an oven cleaner and pop into a plastic sack overnight. Rinse with water.

6 **Clean a charcoal grill regularly** by brushing out the ashes and scraping away the gunk that's accumulated at the bottom.

7 **For a gas BBQ,** check the burners regularly to ensure they're not clogged.

8 **Lava rocks/ceramic briquettes?** Replace when they are encrusted with food.

9 **To re-paint a grill,** use a wire brush then sandpaper to get down to the metal. Finish with several thin coats of BBQ paint.

10 **Use an old toothbrush** to clean the controls, burners and other fiddly bits.

SHINE UP YOUR SILVER

1 **Rub white toothpaste** onto the tarnish and polish with a soft cloth.

2 **Make a paste of baking soda and water.** Rub on with a clean, damp sponge, rinse with warm water and polish.

3 **Silver-polishing gloves are handy.**

4 **Wear plastic/cotton gloves, not rubber,** if you're using a commercial cleaner.

5 **Prevent tarnish forming** by storing silver in a cool, dry place, rolled in a soft cloth and then sealed in a plastic bag.

6 **For cracks and crevices,** in small pieces, line a dish with aluminium foil, pour in hot water plus a little baking soda to cover the silver. Rinse, dry and polish with a soft, clean cloth.

7 **Avoid using abrasives/chemicals –** they can scratch and wear the surface.

8 **If you are using silver plate or cutlery,** don't let it stand with food on it.

9 **Spray on a clear lacquer to achieve long-term protection.**

10 **Use silver frequently –** it's really the best way to stop tarnishing.

DEAL WITH HOUSEHOLD PESTS

1 **To deter pests in the first place,** clean all surfaces and cupboards regularly.

2 **Cover food and don't leave piles of dirty crockery** around for too long.

3 **Empty and clean bins regularly.**

4 **Seal any small gaps** through which pests and rodents might squeeze.

5 **Track where ants are coming from** to locate the nest, then pour ant powder or boiling water down into it.

6 Hate commercial fly spray? Try burning strongly scented essential oils.

7 Eradicate carpet beetles by treating areas with insecticide. Put small items in a sealed bag in a freezer for two weeks. Wash clothes, fabrics, rugs in hot water.

8 Discourage mice by storing food in sealed containers. Leave bait or use traps.

9 If you find a bees' nest, search for a beekeeper who can safely remove it.

10 To eliminate cockroaches and wasps, get professional help.

BANISH BAD SMELLS

1 Sprinkle a stinky carpet with bicarbonate of soda, leave for 15 minutes and then vacuum thoroughly.

2 Spray stale curtains with a solution of two parts' water/one part vinegar.

3 Cooking fish can leave a terrible pong. Boil a pan of water and add the juice and rinds of two/three lemons. Continue boiling for 20 minutes or so.

4 To absorb general cooking smells, leave a bowl of vinegar next to the stove.

5 If your fridge smells, spread a layer of baking soda or fresh coffee grounds on a tray and leave in the fridge overnight.

6 Use a fan to help circulate air as well well as opening doors and windows.

7 For smoky smells, wash the tar off surfaces with hot, soapy water and shampoo carpets thoroughly.

8 To freshen the air, light a candle.

9 For drain odours from garbage disposal, grind a couple of chopped lemons.

10 For a smell of fresh laundry, tape fabric dryer sheets over air vents.

CHOOSE A HOME COMPUTER

1 Laptop, desktop, notebook or tablet? Think hard about the trade-off between portability and function.

2 Plan ahead. How will you use your computer both now and in the future?

3 Is screen size important? Will you want to watch films, play games, design graphics or just write emails?

4 Will you want to plug external devices (printer, TV, monitor, scanner or camcorder) into the computer? If so, check that it has enough appropriate ports.

5 Think about space on the hard drive. It's surprising how quickly it can fill up, especially if you store pictures or music. But there's no point in paying for more memory than you'll need. At least 320 GB is a good starting point for most people.

6 Mac or PC? Each has its ardent fans.

7 Get enough RAM (random access memory) so that your computer will run efficiently. Aim for at least 2 GB.

8 Check what disc drive is included. Do you need one at all? As a basic you'll probably want a CD-ROM drive that reads CDs and plays music. You may also want to play Blu-ray films, record music or write to blank disks.

9 **For word-processing, spreadsheets and internet research** you won't need as much memory, disk space and processing speed as if you're planning to use the computer for gaming and graphic design.

10 **The more you spend,** the more likely you are to get the latest software. It might last longer than a cheaper model, too.

THE PERFECT HOME PRINTER

1 **Inkjet or laser?** Inkjets tend to produce higher-quality photo prints; laser printers are better for text.

2 **Only printing photographs?** Consider a mini photo printer – they can connect straight to your camera.

3 **An all-in-one printer is ideal** if you want to print, scan, photocopy and fax but need to save space in your room.

4 **Want to print wirelessly?** Look for a wireless-enabled printer.

5 **Need high-quality printing?** Choose a printer with a high resolution.

6 **Got large documents to print?** Then go for a printer that can cope with large sizes of paper as well as standard.

7 **Tortoise or hare?** Check out your prospective printer's speed before you buy.

8 **Borderless printing is great** when you want photos to fill the entire page.

9 **A printer that can print double-sided** will save energy and money.

10 **The cost of replacement ink cartridges can really mount up.** You need to factor this in when you are budgeting for a new printer.

CREATE YOUR OWN WEBSITE

1 **What's going to be on your website?** Plan your words and pictures carefully.

2 **Look at other sites** to work out what to emulate and what to avoid.

3 **Choose and register a domain name –** it could be your business name or something that people will find easily.

4 **Choose a web host** and sign up for an account with them.

5 **Start to design your pages** (or hire a professional web designer). You'll need a web editor: some are free, some not.

6 **Test your pages as you design them,** to make sure they work properly with all the main browsers. Test all links, too.

7 **Make sure your site is easy to navigate.** Minimize clicking around. There should be a link to the home page and a menu on every page.

8 **Each page should hold a reasonable amount of information –** but not too much. Readers don't want to have to scroll through loads of words.

9 **Movies, sound and animation can slow your site down** and annoy visitors. Unless they're vital to your site, avoid them.

10 **Think about what the user will want to see on your site.** Go for clarity, simplicity and useful information – you can always add the bells and whistles later.

WRITE A BLOG

1 Decide on your message. What are you going to write about?

2 Want to try to make money? Work out whether there's a potential income stream related to your topic. For example, is there related merchandise?

3 Choose a blog platform that suits your needs. Generally, the 'hosted' ones are free or cheap and easy to set up, but aren't as flexible as the stand-alone type.

4 Use your own tone of voice to convey your personal enthusiasms.

5 Make your writing interesting/useful.

6 How much should you write? Bear in mind that most people don't spend much time reading content online.

7 Visual content (photos) adds interest.

8 Make your blog interactive. Not just comments, but perhaps polls, videos or tutorials. It will keep your readers involved.

9 Use categories for each post, tagging elements. Visitors will find info easily.

10 Blogs often fall by the wayside. Set aside time to update yours regularly.

WHAT TO LOOK FOR IN A MOBILE

1 Does size matter? Some people prefer tiny phones; others prefer to use easy-to-use buttons or large screens.

2 What about shape? Choose between bar-shaped phones, sliders and clamshells/flip phones – it's a personal thing.

3 Touch-screen phones have the keypad on the screen. They may be cool, but may take getting used to.

4 Check out battery life; the longer they last the better.

5 Do you require internet access? If so, you'll need a web-enabled phone.

6 Lots of contacts? Find a phone that can store plenty of names and numbers.

7 Instant messaging/email important to you? Ensure the phone supports them.

8 Get snap-happy with a camera – some are better than others. Look for high megapixel resolution and built-in flash.

9 Consider Bluetooth technology. If the phone has it, you can connect with a headset and sync data with other devices.

10 Conventional or smart phone? Smart phones can access a vast array of apps, ranging from games to business tools.

TEXT MESSAGING FAUX PAS TO AVOID

1 Rambling
2 Rudeness
3 Bad news
4 Sad news
5 Dumping a partner
6 Spelling mistakes
7 Drunkenness
8 Middle of the night
9 Wrong number
10 Confidential info

CHOOSE A PHONE PROVIDER

1 Work out exactly how much you'll use your phone, for calls, texts and surfing the internet. You can do a rough calculation from your last six months of bills.

2 Choose a provider that offers the cheapest tariff for your needs – it's expensive to go over your allowance. Build a little leeway into the monthly fee.

3 **If you use your phone most at off-peak times,** find a provider that has a tariff to match.

4 **If you regularly call one person or a small group of people,** look for discounts.

5 **Need coverage in rural areas or abroad?** Check coverage maps to see what's available to you.

6 **Already got a handset?** Then you'll get a better deal if you just buy a sim card with the tariff.

7 **If you want to buy a specific handset,** do online comparisons for the best deals.

8 **Pay-as-you-go contracts are good for lighter users,** and they don't tie you down.

9 **Research reliability.** Some providers come higher than others in surveys.

10 **Check the contract** and question whatever you're unclear about. Don't sign up for a long one unless you're sure you want it. A short contract lets you shop around again sooner.

TVS FOR TECHNOPHOBES

1 **What screen size suits you best?** Think about your home space and how far away you'll be sitting from the screen.

2 **Which screen type?** Plasma is great for colour accuracy and smooth action scenes, LCD is cheaper and good in bright rooms, while LED is energy-efficient and displays blacks well.

3 **Love films and sport?** A high-definition TV offers the best picture quality.

4 **Want to get online via your TV?** You'll need a Smart TV or a network media player connected to your TV, wireless router and broadband.

5 **Can't get enough of 3D?** Then choose a 3D TV – but remember that you'll have to sit there wearing the glasses.

6 **Stereo or surround-sound?** Sound quality is as important as the pictures.

7 **Save space by buying a TV with a built-in DVD player.**

8 **Save space by wall-mounting your TV.** Choose from fixed, tilting or articulated.

9 **TVs dominate a room –** so think carefully about colour and style.

10 **It can be tricky to set up a new TV.** Why not get a professional on the job if you're unsure what to do?

AWESOME MUSIC SYSTEMS

1 **All-in-one systems are convenient,** but for optimum sound quality, go for separate components.

2 **Invest in your amplifier –** it's the key to a good system. Make sure it has plenty of inputs so that you can add new components when necessary.

3 **Want to listen to radio, too?** Then choose an amp with a built-in tuner.

4 **What will you connect to your system** – CD player, turntable, iPod dock, laptop or network music player (for listening to streamed music from the internet)?

5 **The right speakers are vital.** Biggest

isn't always best – how much space do you have? What styles do you prefer? How loudly will you crank up your sounds?

6 For music in more than one room, either buy an amp with two sets of outputs or invest in a wi-fi system.

7 Buy a good-quality DAC. It converts digital to analogue signals to give richly detailed, clean sound.

8 Optimize your system's performance with quality cables and keep cable runs as short as possible.

9 Place speakers at ear level on stands and make sure they're level and rigid.

10 Optimize speaker positions for the best sound. They need to be about 2.1m (7ft) apart and 2.7m (9ft) away from you to create the ideal listening triangle.

SET UP A HOME CINEMA

1 Don't be put off by home cinema system acronyms. The basics are similar to setting up a music system.

2 A typical home cinema system includes a receiver, DVD player/recorder, subwoofer and mini speakers.

3 In a small room you might not have space for loads of separates, especially five speakers. Opt for an all-in-one unit.

4 Cables clogging up your room? Buy a little extra length and run them under the skirting boards for tidiness.

5 It's all about positioning. Put front speakers about 1.5m (5ft) away from the TV on either side. The centre channel goes above/below the TV, centrally, at the same height as the front speakers. Place the rear speakers behind your sofa on either side and try out spots for the subwoofer until everything sounds great.

6 Buy the best cables you can afford – especially the ones carrying video signals.

7 Connect your games console to the system to get more fun from gaming.

8 Add a media streamer/network media player to your system so you can watch movies from your hard drive/internet.

9 Store your digital music/films on an external device, to avoid using computer space. It can be accessed at all times.

10 Make life easier with a universal remote that controls all your kit.

PREVENT IDENTITY THEFT

1 Shred old bank statements, bills, ATM receipts or anything else printed with your personal information.

2 When buying online, check that the website has good security – usually indicated by a small padlock at the bottom right of the screen, or an 's' after the http.

3 Take care at the ATM. When entering your PIN number, make sure no one's looking over your shoulder.

4 Check your bank/credit card statements regularly and diligently.

5 Review your credit report at least once a year, so you can spot any anomalies.

6 **Choose secure passwords** (a mixture of upper and lower case letters and numbers) for online security. Change them often.

7 **Before you dump a dead computer,** make sure the drive data is destroyed. You might need technical help to buy a product.

8 **To make it easier to cancel cards** if there's a problem, stick them all on a photocopier once in a while and keep the single sheet of paper in a secure place.

9 **Don't give out personal information** unless it's absolutely necessary. Never, ever give it to cold-callers.

10 **Don't keep personal documents in your wallet** and only carry the credit/debit cards you need on the day.

ESSENTIAL GARDENING TOOLS

1 Spade
2 Fork
3 Rake
4 Hoe
5 Watering can
6 Secateurs
7 Trowel
8 Bucket
9 Wheelbarrow
10 Kneeler

GARDEN BASICS FOR BEGINNERS

1 **Who will use the garden and what for?** Whether you're updating an existing garden, rescuing a jungle or starting from scratch, think about design. If your garden is a space for family fun, it needs to be planned differently from a formal garden, or one in which you want to grow vegetables, sunbathe or keep chickens.

2 **What's your style? It will influence your garden design.** Cottage garden abundance or modern minimalism? Do you like colourful flowers, tall trees, neat containers, water features or decking? How much space do you need? How much time do you want to spend caring for it?

3 **Put fundamentals in place before luxuries.** You may love fountains, ponds or sculptures, but a shed, washing line and water butt may be more practical.

4 **Work out which way your garden faces and how much sun it gets, and when.** Some plants thrive in full sun and dry soil; others prefer dark, damp places. Where do walls, fences or trees create shade?

5 **Work out which areas are prone to receiving frost, wind or sun.** Choose the right plants for the right places.

6 **Know about your soil type.** Choosing plants to suit it could make the difference between success and failure. Have you got a decent depth of topsoil? If not, import some. Is it mostly clay or sand? Sticky clay soils retain water while gritty, sandy soils are good for drainage. Buy a PH testing kit to find out whether your soil is acid or alkaline. There are plants for each type.

7 **If you're taking over a badly neglected garden,** clear weedy areas with chemicals or by strimming and covering with old carpet for several weeks. But don't rush to cut everything down. There could be gems among the horrors once you've tidied up and given them space and light.

8 **Get to know plant classifications.** Annuals live and die in a year, biennials in two years, while perennials regrow yearly. Shrubs have woody stems and are usually bush-like. If you are time-poor, choose low-maintenance herbaceous perennials and grasses/shrubs, avoiding delicate plants.

9 **When drawing up your planting plan,** mark choices with a circle indicating final spread. Put the tallest plants at the backs of borders and include 'star' and 'supporting' plants in complementary colours and shapes for year-round interest.

10 **Gardening isn't a quick fix** – it's a long-term thing. It takes time and trial and error to find out which plants thrive and which ones fail in your garden.

LAY A NEW LAWN

1 Preparation is key. Mark out the position of the new lawn and clear the area of plants or weeds. Remove large stones and use a garden fork to break up the soil surface. Add a thin layer of topsoil and even some granular fertilizer if your existing soil isn't too good.

2 The lawn area must be level. Once you've raked it and allowed it to settle, tread it firmly to compact it. Don't do this when the ground is too wet. Water lightly.

3 The easy method of laying a new lawn is to unroll turfs. Get them delivered the day you need them and lay them straight away. For neatness, overlap the edges of the area by about 5cm (2in) and trim later.

4 Butt edges, but stagger the joints between rolls, so you don't get a long line. Work a layer of sand/fine soil into gaps.

5 Use wooden boards as pathways, so that you don't tread on your new turf while you are laying it.

6 Get rid of any air pockets by tamping down newly laid turf with the back of a garden rake.

7 Grass seed is cheaper than turf, and not too difficult to use. Choose the correct seed for your garden – shady, drought-tolerant, fine or family-friendly.

8 Sow grass seed either in spring or at the end of summer on a calm day. Use the correct amount to cover your area, sow evenly, then lightly rake the surface.

9 Don't walk on the new lawn, or mow it, for at least a couple of weeks.

10 Water the new lawn every day for a fortnight, then regularly until it's well established.

MOW LIKE A PRO

1 Mow the lawn once a week from early spring to late autumn, unless the weather is very dry. Regular mowing, when done little and often, encourages a vigorous growth and deters weeds.

2 Pick up any sticks, stones or debris before you start.

3 Mow when the grass is dry, to reduce clumping, improve mulching and avoid spreading disease over the lawn.

4 Trim any hard-to-get-at areas first, then mow the lawn in straight lines and finish with a 'clean-up' lap that goes around the edges.

5 Only cut off one-third of the leaf blade, to help the grass thrive.

6 Mow in many different directions to prevent wear patterns, encourage upright growth and give a smart, stripy effect.

7 Don't leave cut grass to clog up your lawn. Instead, put the clippings onto your compost pile.

8 Grass clippings make a good top-dressing for the lawn at the beginning and end of the season.

9 If your grass gets very long, don't chop it all in one go. It's less of a shock to the plant if you cut it back over two or three mowing sessions.

10 Keep sharp! Blunt mower blades won't work properly and can spread disease.

DEAL WITH SLUGS

1 Place commercial traps or recycled margarine tubs on top of the soil. At dusk fill them with cheap, fresh beer. Next morning, they should be filled with dead drunken slugs. Repeat every evening.

2 Caffeine is effective at dispatching slugs. Surround plants under attack with a mulch of used coffee grounds to deter the critters and feed the plants.

3 Leave citrus rinds out overnight near slug-prone plants, then collect and throw away (covered with slugs) next morning.

4 Iron phosphate in a commercial, slug-attracting bait is very effective. Scatter pellets around plants in peril.

5 Use a spray bottle of white vinegar for slugs that aren't actually on the plants.

6 Go for a toad. Avoid pesticides, provide water low to the ground and a damp shady spot for them to hide. These wonderful nocturnal predators will eat lots of slugs.

7 Lay old planks between beds. The slugs will crawl underneath. Come morning, lift the planks, scraping all slugs into a bucket.

8 Buy copper plant guards or adorn raised bed frames with copper flashing.

9 Crushed eggshells and sharp grit will deter slugs from attacking tender plants.

10 Get a duck! These feathered friends are among nature's finest slug-eaters.

MAKE YOUR OWN COMPOST

1 Buy or make a suitable compost bin. Alternatively just create a heap, preferably topped with a piece of hessian-backed carpet to keep the heat in.

2 Choose a good site for your bin. It'll be best in sun or partial shade and directly on soil. If you have to put it on concrete, tarmac or patio slabs, layer soil and twigs on the bottom to persuade worms and other creatures to move in.

3 Start your compost bin in spring, and for best results combine 'greens' (soft, green, nitrogen-rich material), and 'browns' (dry, brown, carbon-rich material), in even quantities.

4 Place woody material at the bottom to help air circulation.

5 Don't put loads of grass clippings in together. Combine with some woody, brown material to create a better mix.

6 Chop stems and leaves up with a spade. Hire a shredder if you have lots of woody material.

7 Leave out weeds that have seeds or strong roots, diseased plants or any that are contaminated with weed killer. Avoid cooked food, meat, fish and dairy products, which can attract rats, and never put in cat or dog waste.

8 Turn your compost with a fork to help it rot down more speedily. You could also add a nitrogen-rich 'activator'.

9 After nine to 12 months your compost should be ready to use. If some of it isn't fully broken down, pick it out and add it to your next batch. It will rot eventually.

10 If your compost bin smells, it's probably too wet. Simply turn it and add more dry materials. Seal in the smell by topping with spent potting compost.

MAKE & USE MULCHES

1 Mulching – what's that? A layer of material is spread over the soil to regulate temperature, suppress weeds and retain moisture. It's best done mid to late spring.

2 Clear weeds before mulching.

3 Cover whole beds rather than just surrounding the plant bases.

4 Choose organic mulch to improve your soil. It gradually breaks down and releases nutrients into it.

5 Make organic mulches from garden compost, manure, composted bark/straw, wood chips or mushroom compost.

6 Leaf mould makes an excellent mulch. Gather fallen leaves in open-topped plastic sacks and let them stand for a year or two.

7 Spread organic mulches 10cm (4in) deep, but not too close to plant bases.

8 Inorganic mulches are great for better surface drainage. They discourage moss.

9 For decorative effect, choose gravel, grit, stone chips or pebbles and lay it about 2.5–5cm (1–2in) deep.

10 For really efficient weed suppression, use a woven fabric/plastic sheeting, cut to fit, disguised with another mulch on top.

GARDEN SHED ESSENTIALS
1 Mower
2 Leaf blower
3 String trimmer
4 Edge cutters
5 Hedge clippers
6 Plant pots
7 Seed trays
8 Potting soil
9 Fertilizer
10 Radio

ALL ABOUT ORGANIC GARDENING

1 Avoid chemical fertilizers. Use compost, leaf mould, manure or seaweed.

2 Green manure is good for veg patches. Plant mustard, rape or phacelia in vacant ground and dig in before they set seed.

3 Use organic mulches to improve your soil, retain water and keep weeds at bay.

4 Trap or gently pick off pests rather than killing them with chemicals.

5 Shun poisonous weed-killers. Weed by hand with a hoe or fork, or cover the area with plastic or old carpet.

6 Employ contract killers. Introduce roundworms to tackle slugs, for example.

7 Look out for plant-derived alternatives to synthetic pesticides, such as derris, pyrethrum and soap solutions.

8 Save rainwater and install a butt, connected to a shed or greenhouse roof.

9 Use 'grey' water to water garden plants – but not crops, lawns or seedlings.

10 Healthy plants can defend themselves better from pests. Buy quality seeds or plants and take care of your soil.

WILD & WONDERFUL WILDLIFE GARDENING

1 Build a pond in a sunny place, away from trees and attract everything from dragonflies to newts and frogs. Don't add fish, though!

2 Set a slope up on one side of your pond so amphibians can crawl out, and plant the pond with non-invasive oxygenators. Clean it regularly.

3 Provide a nesting box and feeding station (with food!) to attract birds.

4 To tempt butterflies and bees, you need plants that have plenty of pollen and nectar, as well as open blooms.

5 Chuck a couple of logs in an undisturbed corner and wait for helpful creatures to move in.

6 Buy or make a bee box and give that solitary bee a home.

7 Choose plants with seeds and berries for birds in winter. Don't cut seed heads back too early.

8 Avoid using chemicals in the garden – it's a sure-fire way to banish wildlife.

9 Leave a patch of lawn uncut to provide seeds and nectar for insects and birds.

10 Your compost bin is the ideal breeding ground for insects, worms, mites and other animals.

PLANT A HANGING BASKET

1 Use peat-free, multi-purpose compost mixed with a handful of controlled-release fertilizer granules and water-retaining gel.

2 Before planting, keep your basket steady by standing it in a pot.

3 Line the basket with coconut fibre or suitable liner material.

4 To retain water, lay a plastic bag on top of the fibre and cut around the edges.

5 Put a 2.5cm (1in) layer of compost in the base. At soil level, make three slits through the liner and fibre at the sides.

6 To prevent damage to roots and stems, wrap the plants for the sides of the basket in tubes of paper. Push the tubes through the holes, from the inside, until the plants' root balls lie snugly against the liner. Unwrap the paper and firm the soil around the root balls.

7 Fill two-thirds of the basket with soil, then add another layer of plants. Fill with compost, leaving a 3cm (¾in) gap at the basket lip and finish by planting the top. Water really well.

8 Only hang your basket outside once all risk of frost has passed. Water daily.

9 Encourage more flowers by removing spent blooms two to three times a week.

10 For brilliant blooms, boost plants with a weekly liquid feed.

BRILLIANT HANGING BASKET PLANTS

1 Begonia
2 Diascia
3 Fuchsia
4 Helicrysum
5 Impatiens
6 Lobelia
7 Nepeta
8 Pelargonium
9 Petunia
10 Viola

GROW A HEDGE

1 Be considerate to neighbours. Hedges take up more space than fences, create shade and need care on both sides.

2 Formal or informal? Choose an informal hedge that's a mix of different shrubs and hardly needs pruning or a formal hedge, all of one type, clipped into an even shape.

3 Good choices for a formal, evergreen hedge include yew, Lawson cypress, box, privet and shrubby honeysuckle. Deciduous hedges, such as hawthorn and hornbeam, are better for windy gardens.

4 For a successful hedge, it all starts with soil preparation. Six weeks before you plan to plant, clear away perennial weeds and dig over a trench the length of the hedge and about 90–120cm (3–4ft) wide, adding plenty of garden compost or well-rotted farmyard manure.

5 **Buy a few more plants than you'll need** in case some die. Keep them in containers until you're sure the hedge is a success.

6 **To mark the line of your hedge** use a couple of pegs and a length of string. Check that the planting intervals are correct, depending on the species, and dig holes for the plants.

7 **Once you've planted** – at the original planting depth – firm the plants in by pressing down with your feet around them, then water really well and cover the area with a mulch.

8 **Water a young hedge** in dry spells and fertilize it every spring.

9 **If you want a formal hedge,** clip it as it grows to create a wedge shape.

10 **While your young hedge is growing,** put up a temporary boundary with wire netting or bamboo. The hedge will eventually grow around them.

BEST IN SHOW: GROW VEGETABLES

1 **Great home-grown vegetables need four key ingredients** – good soil, shelter, sunshine and water. So choose the position of your vegetable patch wisely, or your produce will not flourish.

2 **Aim for decent topsoil depth.** At least 20cm (8in) is good, but 30–45cm (12–18in) is better. Add organic matter, such as manure or mushroom compost.

3 **Truly terrible soil?** Make raised beds and fill them with imported topsoil.

4 **If you have marauding wildlife nearby** – such as rabbits or deer – fence them out or they'll go crazy for your crops.

5 **Aim to 'rotate' your crops** – in other words, plant different things in the beds each year. This will help to maintain the quality of the soil and avoid a build-up of pests and diseases.

6 **Never tread on your growing beds –** so about 1.2m (4ft) is a good maximum width, meaning you can reach to the middle from either side. It's useful to lay paths between them that are wide enough to take a handy wheelbarrow.

7 **Dig in plenty of organic manure and fertilizer every year.**

8 **Most vegetables are grown from seed.** An easy way to do this is to sow direct into the ground. Start as soon as you see seedlings appear in your garden. The soil should be fine and you'll need to thin out the seeds once they have a pair of leaves.

9 **Protect tomatoes, cucumbers, early crops and some squash** by sowing them in containers and keeping them under cover (in a greenhouse, cold frame, polytunnel or on a sunny porch).

10 **If you haven't got room to grow vegetables in your garden,** use containers instead. Choose good-sized ones with holes in the bottom for drainage and use multi-purpose compost. Water and fertilize them regularly.

TASTY TOMATOES

1 Think about sun and shade. Small tomatoes are fine planted outside against a sunny wall, but larger varieties prefer a greenhouse in which to ripen properly.

2 Tomatoes hate wind and frost. Grow them in a sheltered position and, if they're at risk from cold, protect with fleece.

3 For fabulous fruiting, just before planting your tomato seedlings, add organic potash to the soil. Good sources are fresh wood ash and chopped comfrey.

4 When planting tomato seedlings, pop them in deep to encourage root growth.

5 Keep roots moist but not waterlogged. Regular watering prevents the fruit splitting. To get water to the lower root system, sink a pierced plastic bottle into the soil next to each plant and add a litre (2pt) of water a day in hot weather.

6 If you're growing tomatoes in pots or bags, feed them every week.

7 Use supports. Tie your tomatoes loosely to a cane or string so they don't go floppy.

8 'Pinching out' is a regular job for tomato growers. It means snapping off the small sideshoots, which would otherwise use up valuable water and nutrients. Don't do it on bush varieties, though.

9 Don't water just before you pick your tomatoes – the plant absorbs water so quickly it will reduce flavour intensity.

10 Save your seeds! Scoop some out of the tomato, leave it to dry and store in a labeled envelope, in a cool, dry place.

A ROSE BY ANY OTHER NAME

1 There's a world of roses out there. Make sure you choose a type that suits the spot in which you want to plant it – large, mini, rambling – the choice is yours.

2 Rambling roses are fine near trees, but other types don't like too much competition from large roots.

3 Soak up the sun. Roses like a position where they'll get a few hours' sun each day.

4 Add manure before planting. Put well-rotted manure/compost into the hole.

5 Plant your rose at the correct height. The base of the stem should be about 2.5cm (1in) below the soil level.

6 Feed your rose with fertilizer at the start of the growing season. If it's a repeat-flowering variety, feed again two or three months later.

7 Roses prefer cool, moist roots. Cover the surrounding area with deep mulch and give them the occasional lavish watering.

8 Pruning roses is an art. Do it every year just before spring growth starts. On all roses, cut away weak, dead, diseased, crossed, straggly or woody stems.

9 Cut repeat-flowering shrub roses back by one-third to two-thirds, but cut back bush roses by a half to three-quarters. Leave non-repeating shrubs and ramblers alone, or prune lightly to shape. With climbers, remove older stems and cut back last year's flowering shoots to 15cm (6in).

10 If you want hips, don't deadhead your flowers. All roses produce hips, which make great food for birds and a variety of other wildlife.

FABULOUS FRUIT

1 For a really good harvest, plant two different varieties of the same fruit tree. If you only have room for one variety, choose one that's self-pollinating.

2 The essentials for growing any fruit are good, well-drained soil and plenty of sunlight. Fruit also needs lots of water.

3 Plants/trees need water most when they're flowering and developing fruit.

4 Classic orchard trees require space. Plant at least 2.4m (8ft) apart. If you're short of space, consider growing dwarf trees or berry bushes.

5 A great way to grow fruit without taking up masses of space is to train the tree flat against a wall or fence.

6 It takes several years for trees to produce fruit.

7 Most fruit will grow in a sunny garden, but if yours is shady, choose alpine strawberries, acid cherries, red or white currants or gooseberries.

8 A late frost can be fatal for fruit. Avoid planting in frost pockets and, if sub-zero temperatures are forecast, move containers indoors or protect temporarily with fleece, polythene or a glass cloche.

9 Use netting and fences to protect fruit from birds and small mammals.

10 Keep diseases at bay by removing fallen leaves and fruit, cut off parts that appear infected and prune on a dry day.

SUCCESS WITH SEEDS

1 Remember the things a seed needs to grow: warmth, air, light and water.

2 Collect seeds from plants in your own garden. Choose your healthiest plants and pop the whole seed head in a paper bag, cut off, label and date the bag. Store in a cool, dry, dark and well-ventilated place.

3 Don't throw away commercial seed packets – they give useful information.

4 Most seeds can be planted as they are, but some require special treatment to help them germinate. Information on the packet will tell you whether you have to soak them overnight, nick with a knife, rub with sandpaper or chill in the fridge.

5 Some seeds can be sown straight outdoors, but many must be started inside. Sow at the recommended depth – the larger the seed, the deeper.

6 When sowing into a pot, use your index finger and thumb to sprinkle seeds sparingly onto the compost. Cover with a fine layer of vermiculite or sieved compost. Water and keep warm and dark.

7 Bring the seedlings into the light as soon as you see little shoots. Keep them moist but not waterlogged.

8 When seedlings are large enough to handle, prick out to avoid overcrowding. Use a dibber to help pull them out by their leaves and re-plant in individual pots. Put the weakest ones in your compost.

9 A few weeks before you want to plant them out, get your sensitive seedlings used to the cold by gradually moving them into colder spots during the day.

10 Once they're hardened-off and the weather is OK, plant in your garden.

BEAUTIFUL BULBS
1 Iris
2 Daffodil
3 Tulip
4 Crocus
5 Anemone
6 Dahlia
7 Lily
8 Begonia
9 Cyclamen
10 Snowdrop

DIVIDE TO MAKE NEW PLANTS

1 **If you have a large herbaceous potted perennial,** divide it before planting it out in your garden.

2 **Just choose from the healthiest plants** – others aren't worth the trouble.

3 **Divide from early spring to late summer.** The ideal time depends on each plant – research carefully before you start.

4 **Water your chosen plant** a few hours before you dig it up.

5 **Cut down stems** to see your progress.

6 **Carefully dig up the whole crown and shake off excess soil.** Remove any weeds.

7 **The best parts of the plant for dividing** are usually around the edges.

8 **Pull the crown or mass of roots apart** with your fingers or a garden fork. You might need to cut it with a knife/secateurs.

9 **Each smaller segment you create** should have healthy roots and strong buds.

10 **Re-plant your segments straight away,** at the same depth as before.

WHAT TO GROW WITH KIDS

1 Sunflowers
2 Runner beans
3 Cress
4 Sweet peas
5 Chives
6 Strawberries
7 Pansies
8 Lamb's ears
9 Marigolds
10 Lettuces

TAKE CUTTINGS

1 **Always choose a healthy plant** to take cuttings from.

2 **To avoid spreading diseases,** always use fresh compost and a clean container.

3 **Buy special, free-draining cuttings compost,** or make your own by mixing sieved leaf mould with horticultural sand.

4 **Space out your cuttings once planted** – their leaves should not touch each other.

5 **Cover trays of cuttings** with a lid, or pop a plastic bag around a pot.

6 **Choose healthy, young, non-flowering stems** of softwood cuttings in spring and early summer.

7 **Take root cuttings in winter.** Only remove a few roots from each plant.

8 **Remove hardwood cuttings** from deciduous trees, shrubs, roses and climbers after the leaves have fallen. Take a long, straight stem that has plenty of buds.

9 **Take semi-ripe cuttings** from broad-leaved evergreens, climbers, conifers and tender perennials between mid-summer and mid-autumn.

10 **Only transplant cuttings once you have a good root system** as well as leaves. Softwood cuttings root in a couple of months; for others it could take six months.

PERFECT DEADHEADING/PRUNING

1 **Why deadhead?** It stops plants from setting seed and persuades them to keep producing flowers for longer. Snap off whole dead stalks if they're long or just nip off the dead bloom. For bulbs, snap off the dead head and leave the stalk.

2 **Deadhead any time** from when the bloom is past its best.

3 **Prune any branches that are dead,** diseased, broken, crossed or too crowded.
4 **When pruning lots of tall, slender stems** (grasses) tie the tops together.
5 **To make a plant more bushy,** pinch out the tip of the main growing stem when it's about 5–7cm (2–3in) tall.
6 **When to prune?** Usually before spring growth begins or after flowering.
7 **When pruning a shrub,** cut each branch off just above a young sideshoot.
8 **Make every cut clean and at an angle** to prevent disease taking hold.
9 **Make pruning easier by selecting the right tool for the job,** depending on the thickness of the stem or branch to be cut.
10 **Care for your pruning tools.** You'll do a better job if you keep secateurs, loppers, pruners, knives and saws sharp. Wipe any sap off after use and oil lightly.

BRRRR: PREVENT FROST DAMAGE

1 **Choose plants that can survive your local climate.** If in doubt, observe what does well in neighbouring gardens.
2 **You may get pockets of frost.** Choose hardy plants for these areas of the garden.
3 **If frost is forecast,** move plants in containers to a sheltered spot or put them against a south-facing wall. Tender plants need to be brought indoors.
4 **A glass cloche** makes a pretty protector.
5 **Wrap some horticultural fleece around plants that need protecting,** keeping it well fastened or pegged down. You can also use straw, newspaper, sacking or a very light blanket.
6 **Pots can suffer in frost, too.** Wrap them in fleece and raise them on feet.
7 **Don't walk on frosty grass** – it will cause damage.
8 **Shrubs can be lifted out of the ground by frost.** Firm them back in.
9 **Add a thick layer of mulch** to the soil to stop it freezing.
10 **Lag outside tap pipework.**

COOL TOOL STORAGE

1 **Clean all the soil off your tools** before you put them away.
2 **Never put your tools away wet.**
3 **Wipe metal blades with a little oil** every time you use them.
4 **Neatly coil away cables and hoses,** checking for kinks as you go.
5 **Clean pots** and stack them by size and shape – they'll take up less space.
6 **Hooks are ideal to hang tools** out of the way but close at hand.
7 **Rub linseed oil into the wooden shafts of garden tools** to preserve them.
8 **Sharpen blades before putting away** – secateurs tend to blunt the quickest.
9 **Tie canes in a bundle,** in length order, and stack them.
10 **Always store weed-killer and other potentially dangerous chemicals** out of the reach of animals and children.

GARDENS FOR OUTDOOR LIVING

1 Use screens, changes of level or plantings to create different areas.

2 Cheap and easy garden pep-ups include painting an unattractive fence or lopping back overhanging branches.

3 Allocate a space near the house as a dining area. Whether decked, paved, tiled or bricked, it should be stable and level.

4 Add a generously sized table and comfy chairs. Store all cushions inside.

5 Create a play area for children – visible for younger ones, more private for teens.

6 Provide lighting to allow you to enjoy your garden after the sun has set.

7 You'll need shade, especially over a dining table/play area. Permanent shading could be a gazebo, arbour or fabric awning fixed to hooks in walls or trees. A garden umbrella is an inexpensive option.

8 Create a private corner for quiet relaxation: anything from a hammock to a sun lounger, a bean bag to a steamer chair.

9 Children love dens and treehouses. Or make a tepee by knotting bamboos together and throwing a blanket over it.

10 Storage is important outside. A small shed is vital for BBQ accessories, folded furniture, cushions, toys and lanterns.

PLANTS FOR A SCENTED GARDEN

1 Butterfly bush
2 Escallonia
3 Verbena
4 Rose
5 Jasmine
6 Katsura tree
7 Sweet bay
8 Honeysuckle
9 Tobacco plant
10 Night-scented stock

DESIGN HARD LANDSCAPING

1 Try to invest in high-quality materials where you can, reserving cheaper ones for unseen areas, such as behind garden sheds.

2 Choose solid materials near entrances/ seating – gravel gets too scattered.

3 Keep paving sizes in proportion to the overall size of your garden.

4 Avoid shallow steps between different levels – they're all too easy to trip on.

5 Economize by using standard sizes/ designs to minimize cutting/wastage.

6 Consider how material types will work with the style of your house and garden.

7 Stick to two landscaping materials (plus lawn) to avoid an overly fussy look.

8 Ask for samples from yards/merchants and try them out in your garden first.

9 Check that stones, tiles and bricks are frost-proof before you buy.

10 Bring new life to dull or cheap paving by painting with outdoor floor paint or topping with fresh gravel/pebbles.

WONDERFUL WATER FEATURES

1 Classical fountain or modern minimal spout? Ensure that the feature you've got your eye on suits your garden style/ size.

2 Off-the-peg garden features may be too small for most normal garden spaces.

3 Location is key. Do you want to sit and look at the feature, discover it in a hidden corner or hear it wherever you are?

4 Listen before buying. A water feature can create a relaxing backdrop or a racket that you can't wait to switch off!

5 How will the feature look when it is switched off? It won't be on constantly.

6 Maintenance is vital. Work out how much you'll have to do before you decide which one to buy.

7 In a patio garden or a courtyard, choose a container water feature such as a stone trough, wooden barrel, old sink or large pot which has all its drainage holes blocked up.

8 Add a long, shallow ramp to attract wildlife to your water feature.

9 Prevent algae growing by shading the feature. Adding a little beneficial bacteria should help – or get scrubbing!

10 It's 'safety first' wherever children and water are in proximity. A bubble fountain or shallow birdbath is safest. If in doubt, fence off your feature.

LIGHT UP YOUR GARDEN IN STYLE

1 Pop tea lights into jars and set along pathways for a magical night-time effect.

2 Solar lights are easy to put in, but they tend to fade and aren't terribly bright.

3 Plunge torchères into the ground for dramatic, temporary lighting.

4 Some plug-in fairy lights can be used outside – check you buy the correct type.

5 Permanent lighting should always be installed by a qualified electrician.

6 Illuminate trees, shrubs or sculptures by angling the lights upwards.

7 Use rope lighting to create a defined border for a path, patio or gazebo.

8 LED lights are a great option – bright, easy to fit and energy-efficient.

9 Bright, white lights create sculptural, effects – these are especially good for water/architectural features. For foliage, a softer light enhances colours and shapes.

10 Don't overwhelm your garden with too much lighting.

CHOOSE GARDEN FURNITURE

1 Good-quality second-hand furniture looks great if you're on a tight budget.

2 Colour-wise, mid-toned shades are best. White or silver furniture can be glary, while black can get very hot in bright sun.

3 If you want to move your furniture around, choose lightweight aluminium.

4 What furniture styles suit your garden?

5 Teak is the most durable wooden outdoor furniture. But check certification.

6 A hammock is great if you have two sturdy trees a suitable distance apart.

7 If you want a dining set, measure the space available and work out size options.

8 Before you buy, try out chairs and make sure they're really comfortable.

9 Keep wooden furniture covered/stored in a weather-proof shed in winter.

10 Pressure-wash/repaint old furniture to give it a new lease of life.

BZZZZ: GET STARTED IN BEEKEEPING

1 Get support from a local beekeeping association. Read a book or take a course.

2 New equipment is best. That way diseases won't be passed on.

3 Order bees, hives and equipment in autumn or winter, because the best time to start beekeeping is spring.

4 Ideal hive location? South-facing on a hill, with a deciduous tree to provide shade in summer and a windbreak behind.

5 Bees need water. Fill a shallow pan and put rocks in it for the bees to rest on.

6 Wear the correct protective clothing – bees can sting through jeans.

7 Don't keep all the honey for yourself. The bees need some to last the winter.

8 Spend half an hour per hive per week mid-April to August.

9 Most beekeepers get stung a few times at first – you'll build up immunity.

10 Smoke calms bees, facilitating hive inspection. Burn compressed sawdust/cotton fibres or use pine needles/cones, cardboard, sawdust or wood chippings.

FEED BIRDS IN YOUR GARDEN

1 Garden birds will benefit from feeding all year round, not just in winter.

2 Site a bird table in a quiet, sheltered spot, with a good all-round view, away from fences from which a cat could pounce.

3 Entice ground-feeding birds by placing food on wire mesh just above the ground, away from bushes that could conceal a cat.

4 Clean bird tables regularly. Move them around to avoid mess build-up underneath.

5 Leave the seed heads on plants to encourage bird-feeding.

6 Provide your own bird food. Some birds enjoy apples, raisins or grated cheese.

7 Make your own fat block by melting suet/lard into a mould (a coconut shell) or over seeds, nuts, dried fruit or oatmeal.

8 Remove nylon mesh from commercial food; it can trap and injure birds.

9 Provide water for drinking and bathing, too. Break ice in cold weather.

10 If squirrels and/or other birds are a problem, consider installing a feeder with a guard.

CLUCK! HOW TO KEEP CHICKENS

1 Who will care for the chickens when you go away? They can't be left.

2 A coop should have nest boxes, ventilation and perches.

3 Your coop will be highly visible, so make sure it looks good in your garden.

4 Allow coop floor space – minimum 30cm sq (12in sq) per bird, plus perch space of 30–40cm (12–16in) long each.

5 Cover the floor with straw or bits of

chopped cardboard. Compost after use.

6 **A big outdoor run** will keep chickens healthy. Bury chicken wire 20cm (8in) to stop predators and cover the roof, too.

7 **Choose ready-mixed feed** over kitchen scraps as it contains the correct nutrients.

8 **Buy your birds from the same breeder** in one go. They'll settle in more easily.

9 **Hens love to be free-range –** but they'll scratch away your garden, eat plants and leave droppings. Give them their own run.

10 **Supply flint grit** and oyster-shell grit. If you can't buy the latter, bake eggshells for ten minutes, then crush.

GROW IN A GREENHOUSE

1 **Site a greenhouse away from buildings, fences or trees** that would create shade. Choose a level area, away from gusting winds. Avoid the bottom of a slope – it could be a frost pocket.

2 **Don't let your greenhouse get too hot** in summer. Louvres and windows that open are vital – an automatic opener is handy.

3 **Add shading if heat is a problem.** Blinds are pricy but good-looking, while paints are cheap and functional.

4 **Don't let delicate plants get chilly in winter.** Insulate your greenhouse.

5 **For a warm-as-toast winter greenhouse** add a stand-alone heater or have one powered by electricity from your house.

6 **Include plenty of staging and shelving** to make the most of the space.

7 **To create a humid atmosphere** in hot-weather spells, spray the greenhouse's path and gravel with water.

8 **Clean the glass/structure** to let in light and discourage pests/diseases.

9 **Add a gutter and purchase a water butt** to facilitate watering.

10 **Install an automatic, capillary or irrigation watering system** for peace-of-mind watering.

HERBS FOR A WINDOW SILL
1 Mint
2 Rosemary
3 Basil
4 Thyme
5 Marjoram
6 Oregano
7 Parsley
8 Chives
9 Lavender
10 Tarragon

HAPPY HOUSEPLANTS

1 **A warm room with an even temperature** all year round is best for houseplants.

2 **As light levels fall in winter,** move plants nearer to windows.

3 **Avoid placing houseplants too near to sources of heat/cold,** such as open fires, radiators, draughty doors or windowsills.

4 **Create a humid atmosphere for your tropical plants** by misting them or grouping them on a tray of damp gravel.

5 **Don't over-water in cold weather.**

6 **Never let a houseplant sit in water.**

7 **Feed houseplants only when they're growing;** reduce or stop feeding in winter.

8 **Choose a controlled-release fertilizer** for long-lasting effect.

9 **You'll need to repot houseplants every year or so.** The best time is spring and don't forget to water before repotting.

10 **Keep plants looking smart.** Remove diseased/dead leaves and faded flowers regularly and softly dust large leaves.

FRIENDS & FAMILY

People! There are plenty of do's and don'ts for making sure things go with a swing. Pick up some wonderful tips for helping life with your significant others run just a little bit more smoothly – everything from wooing your beloved, tying the knot, bringing home a precious first babe to doting on your darling grandchildren.

CREATE YOUR INTERNET DATING PROFILE

1 A well-written online dating profile is crucial to success. It's how you make your first impression. Start by thinking very carefully about what to include. Put yourself in the shoes of the person reading it. What's unique about you? What would attract someone to you? A good look through other profiles will show you what sort of information people include – as well as what kind of info is over-used.

2 Don't be too brief – include enough to make yourself sound interesting. Take each point and elaborate on it in an engaging way. But don't go on for too long, either. There's no need to include your entire life history!

3 Be positive – an upbeat, cheerful tone is best. There's no need to dwell on past bad dating/relationship experiences. Potential dates are bound to be put off by self-pity or a negative attitude.

4 Be careful how you use humour. Demonstrating that you have a good sense of humour is great, but jokes can sometimes backfire if the reader can't discern your tone of voice. Sarcasm and black humour are almost never a good idea before you've actually met. If in doubt, tone it down. You can showcase your fantastic wit when you meet.

5 Check your grammar and spelling. While some people won't notice mistakes, others will pick up on them and count them against you. Also, avoid teenage-type texting abbreviations – they'll just make you look silly.

6 Think about the sort of person you want to meet, and describe your priorities clearly, but without sounding fussy. Don't be overly particular, though – it's worth keeping an open mind at this stage.

7 Be honest. There's no point in creating a profile of a person who is not actually you – you'll only get caught out when you start meeting your dates in real life. This doesn't mean you shouldn't angle your profile in a positive way, but downright fibbing is unfair to people and bound to backfire on you eventually.

8 Strike a balance between boasting and being overly modest. No one likes a bragger, but underselling yourself is pointless. Think about how your best friend would describe you to someone who doesn't know you. In fact, why not ask your best friend to help write your profile? He or she will be able to be both positive and objective.

9 Avoid clichés and be original. Everyone says they love 'romantic walks on the beach' or 'cuddling up on the sofa with a glass of wine', but these are a tad obvious. Why not come up with a few original ideas? Explain them in your own, individual way and it will attract the right sort of reader to your profile and give them a great first impression, as well as a few talking points to help your first date go with a swing.

10 Add a picture. It will boost the number of people who contact you – as long as it's a good one. Smile, look at the camera and make sure there are no other people (or distracting objects) in the background. The image should be fairly accurate but flattering, too. Never use an out-of-date photo and never use software to 'enhance' your photograph – most people can tell it's been altered and, once you meet, your date will be able to see the real you anyway.

WHERE TO FIND A PARTNER

1 Parties
2 'Lonely hearts' ads
3 Festivals
4 Singles events
5 Dating agencies
6 At work
7 Clubs/classes
8 Bars/pubs
9 Art gallery
10 Supermarket

A GREAT FIRST IMPRESSION

GOOD FIRST-DATE VENUES

1 Coffee shop
2 Sports event
3 Art gallery
4 Wine bar/pub
5 Flea market
6 Mini golf
7 Museum
8 Zoo
9 Wine-tasting event
10 Dance lesson

1 **Smile! It really helps.** And try to relax.

2 **Be chatty, but don't talk too much,** especially about yourself. Find some common ground that suits you both.

3 **Ask questions – it's not being nosy.** Show you're genuinely interested in your date and give them your full attention. Look them in the eye, listen carefully and respond appropriately.

4 **Be really positive about dating.** Avoid discussing past disasters and ex-partners.

5 **Turn your phone off,** or at least put it on 'silent'.

6 **Be yourself.** If you try to create a false impression it's bound to backfire and will be stressful to keep up long term.

7 **Look well turned out.** Clean teeth, hair and shoes, a nice fresh perfume/aftershave, pressed clothes – they're all important.

8 **Offer to pay half,** but make sure you have the wherewithall to do so!

9 **Stand tall.** Good posture is much more attractive than slouching and makes you look and feel confident and appealing, too.

10 **Enjoy yourself.** If you feel relaxed and happy, your date will, too.

STAY SAFE ON YOUR FIRST DATE

1 **Tell a friend where you are going** and approximately what time you intend to be back. If you decide to stay out later, you can always phone or text them.

2 **Go to a public place** where there will be other people who could help in the event of a problem. Don't go back to your date's home until you've got to know them well.

3 **Don't get drunk.** You might find your judgement is impaired or you find it harder to get out of a tricky situation. Arrange a daytime date and avoid alcohol altogether?

4 **Carry a personal attack alarm.**

5 **Choose clothes carefully.** Low-cut tops or very short skirts could be misinterpreted.

6 **Ask a friend to call you at a particular time –** if things are going badly use it as an excuse to leave straight away.

7 **Research your date in advance.** Find out some background infomation. If anything puts you off, cancel.

8 **Don't leave food/drink unattended.**

9 **Keep cash/cab number handy.** Don't accept a lift from your date the first time.

10 **If you get bad vibes** or feel unsafe, for whatever reason, leave immediately.

BE IRRESISTIBLE TO THE OPPOSITE SEX

1 **Be friendly, approachable and smile.**

2 **Be comfortable in your own skin.** If you're not happy with who you are, how can anyone else be? Modest confidence is an attractive trait.

3 **Be genuinely interested in your date.**

We are all well disposed to someone who wants to know more about us.

4 Display your sense of humour, but don't laugh at everything (no sleazy jokes!)

5 Your passions truly enhance you. Discuss the things you really love.

6 Dress to bring out your best bits. Women! Men do love skirts and dresses. Men! Women absolutely adore smart suits.

7 A little flattery goes a long way.

8 Smell great! Go for a combination of clean hair, teeth and clothes with a touch of nice perfume or aftershave.

9 Get healthy. Eat well and try to exercise regularly. You'll improve your figure, feel on top of the world and be more attractive.

10 Be kind and caring. Not just to your date but to others, too. It's appealing.

JUST GOOD FRIENDS

1 Be honest about the kind of friendship you want. Would you really prefer your relationship to be romantic? Don't start a friendship with a different aim in mind.

2 One-sidedness isn't an option. Make sure you both understand that the relationship is purely platonic.

3 Openness and communication is vital. Talk to your own partner and your friend's and explain there is no reason for jealousy.

4 Involve your own partner in your social life with your friend.

5 Have other friends, too. Concentrating solely on your friend could feel confusingly similar to a romance.

6 Don't flirt or get too touchy-feely. It's open to misinterpretation.

7 If you take your opposite-sex date to an event where everyone is in a couple, people may assume that you're one, too. If that's a problem, avoid such situations.

8 Don't discuss dating and romance. Tempted to ask for advice from the other sex's point of view? It could get tiresome.

9 If your friend starts up a new relationship, they may not have so much time for you – be happy for them.

10 Be as loyal to your opposite-sex friend as you would to any other. Don't treat them differently.

LONG-DISTANCE LOVE

1 Agree a realistic time-frame for the long-distance part of your relationship. It's easier to make it work if you have a date for being together again.

2 Schedule regular visits to each other – as often as you can manage.

3 Communicate as much as possible. Agree a schedule so that you know what

messages and calls to expect and when.

4 Set up a cheap deal on long-distance communication. You might also want to video chat. And don't forget texts, instant messaging, email and good old snail mail.

5 Get away to other destinations, too. Just because you're living apart it doesn't mean you can't take holidays together.

6 Don't get jealous. Your partner'll be more independent than if you were together all the time. Socializing with others isn't a problem if you can accept it.

7 Create intimacy in as many ways as you can – special trips you can reminisce about, love letters or unexpected gifts.

8 Make your time together fun. It's easy to be negative, but a shame to be grumpy when you don't see each other too often.

9 Be good to your own friends. If your partner's not around, you'll need your friends to be there for you sometimes, too.

10 Look after yourself well. Build some enjoyable activities into your spare time so that you don't feel lonely and miss your partner too much. Create your own life and live it to the full!

MOVE IN TOGETHER

1 Talk about your expectations. Is this the start of the rest of your lives together or just a practical way of sharing the bills? Make sure you're both on the same page.

2 Don't let money be a problem. Agree how to divide up household bills. You might want to set up a joint bank account.

3 Expect niggles, but don't let them get to you. They are worth putting up with for the sake of a committed relationship.

4 Compromise. Then again. And then a bit more. Find that middle ground.

5 Don't bottle up your feelings. When you first move in together you're bound to have issues to resolve. Talk to your partner calmly about what's bothering you before you let anger build up explosively.

6 Reserve a space/room in your new home where you can be alone.

7 Divide up the chores fairly so that you contribute equally and are both happy.

8 Accommodate some of your partner's belongings, even if you don't like their style. He/she will appreciate your effort.

9 Check on sleeping habits. If one of you is a night owl, the other an early bird, decide how to avoid disturbing each other.

10 Create quality time. You're seeing a lot more of each other, but you still need to do special things together.

A PERFECT PROPOSAL

1 Are your feelings reciprocated? Get a pretty good idea of the likely answer before you actually pop the question.

2 Why not ask for her parents' blessing? It might be old-fashioned, but if you know they support you it can only help.

3 Consider your partner's personality. Shy or extrovert? Outrageous or romantic? Your gesture will be most appreciated if it's something that suits her style.

4 Does the proposal style suit you, too? Love the idea of a public demonstration or prefer a private moment?

5 Is your chosen location suitable? Visit it at the same time of day/night as you're planning to propose.

7 Plan everything down to the last detail. It's not unromantic – in fact, it will ensure that things run so smoothly it will be the most romantic thing ever.

3 What kind of ring? Look at what type of jewellery she usually wears to help you choose. Classic styles won't date.

4 Get the ring size by borrowing one she normally wears on her ring finger and either hold it against a chart or take it into a jeweller's. If it's wrong it can be adjusted.

9 Choose the right date. An anniversary, a birthday, Christmas or Valentine's Day are all traditional, or it could be another date that's meaningful for both of you.

10 Include some heartfelt words in your proposal: a poem, song or a few simple phrases about why you want to marry her.

ENDING A RELATIONSHIP WELL

1 Be quite sure you want to end the relationship. Discuss everything with trusted friends. Maybe even get counselling.

2 Don't split up in anger. If you've just had an argument, wait until you've calmed down, then think things through calmly.

3 Choose a suitable venue, where you'll both have privacy (not a restaurant).

4 Get the timing right. Just before an exam is not advisable.

5 Stick to your guns, however much your partner protests – don't change your mind.

6 Be kind. There's no need to be brutally honest about every tiny flaw. He/she will be feeling bad enough already.

7 Don't be surprised if anger is in the air. Arrange to talk things through again once you have both calmed down.

8 Spend time alone. A clean break is a good idea. You can always be friends with your ex at some point in the future.

9 Use the break-up as an opportunity to learn from what went wrong.

10 Don't split up via phone/email/text.

BE A GOOD FRIEND

1 Love your friend for who they are: don't be judgemental.

2 Be kind and respectful and try never to hurt your friend's feelings.

3 Loyalty is important. Don't dump your friend because something or someone 'better' has come along.

4 Keep up with what's going on in your friend's life. You don't have to meet up in person all the time – phone/email/text are great for touching base.

5 Laugh together; cry together.

6 Be truthful and honest, so your friend knows you're always trustworthy.

7 Don't be jealous – accept that your friend has other friends as well as you.

8 Be supportive to your friend in all their decisions – even if you disagree.

9 If things get rough, hang in there. If your friend has big problems, they will need you more than ever.

10 Never broadcast your friend's secrets.

BE A GOOD NEIGHBOUR

1 Get to know your neighbours. Smile and say hello every time you see them. Ask how they are. Good communication is vital.

2 Keep noise down and work out where it might be annoying to others – via shared walls or floors and through open windows.

3 Keep your garden tidy. Discuss issues such as hedges/trees/fences which affect both of you. Be prepared to compromise.

4 Dog-owner? Don't let your dog bark or run around on your neighbours' property.

5 Park considerately. Try not to park outside neighbours' houses or block access.

6 When planning a party, invite the neighbours, if it is appropriate. Otherwise, warn them and don't crank the music up too loud. Ask guests to leave quietly.

7 Obey rubbish/recycling rules. Put it in the right place at the right time

8 Be considerate about BBQs/bonfires. Will wind blow smoke towards a neighbour's washing line? What about food smells?

9 Keep a close and watchful eye on your neighbours' property if they are away.

10 Look after elderly/infirm neighbours. Can you shop for them or clear their paths?

WEDDING THEME IDEAS

1 Beach
2 Vintage
3 Fairytale
4 Christmas
5 Valentine
6 Rock 'n' roll
7 Favourite colour
8 Medieval
9 Natural
10 Hollywood

PLAN YOUR OWN WEDDING

1 Religious or civil? Decide on the type of ceremony you want and that will lead to a decision on the most appropriate venue.

2 Set a suitable date. Ask your family to inform you of dates they can't make and work around the availability of your venue.

3 Reserve your chosen venue early as popular locations may be booked up several years in advance for summer Saturdays.

4 Agree on a budget. Will your families want to contribute anything?

5 How many guests? Ask your parents. Their views may differ from yours.

6 Check legal requirements and documentation needed for your ceremony.

7 Book the honeymoon as early as possible to ensure that you get what you want at the best price.

8 Start to research invitations, catering, entertainment, photography, transport and flowers. Look at magazines for ideas.

9 Choose your best man, groomsmen, matron of honour and bridesmaids early, and start looking at dresses/suits.

10 Consider wedding insurance in case you're let down by suppliers or venues.

A WONDERFUL WEDDING-PARTY VENUE

1 Decide on your preferred venue style – somewhere formal or quirky, traditional or contemporary, a marquee or a castle?

2 Think about transport. If ceremony and reception are in different places, how will guests get from one to the other?

3 Make a shortlist of venues within your budget. Visit and ask lots of questions.

4 Check that your chosen venue is free on your preferred wedding date. Sounds a little obvious? Mistakes have been made!

5 Will other functions be taking place before/after yours? Will this affect you?

6 What's included in the hire price?

7 Who will decorate the venue? Costs?

8 Does the venue provide catering/staff, or can you arrange your own?

9 Is there accommodation on site, or are there places to stay nearby?

10 Check any restrictions. Are confetti/candles banned? What time must music finish by?

YOUR ULTIMATE WEDDING DRESS

1 Your dress should be appropriate for your venue – whether it's a tropical beach, a summer marquee or gothic-style castle.

2 What time of year? Light fabrics are ideal in summer, but for winter you may want a heavier fabric and long sleeves.

3 Not a stick-thin model? Join the club! But there's something gorgeous out there just for you, whatever your size or shape. Consider what's most flattering for you.

4 Get clued up on colour. White is traditional; colours may suit you better.

5 Start searching for your dress early. Even if it isn't going to be made from scratch, your dress may need to be altered specially. Or it may have to be ordered several months in advance.

6 Try on different styles – even ones you don't think will be right. You may be surprised at what looks good on you.

7 Take a trusted friend or relative with you when you're trying on dresses. A second opinion really helps.

8 Don't blow your budget. If you can't afford something fancy, don't despair. Consider vintage, home-made or a sales bargain. Or buy second-hand online – but factor in time and the cost of alterations.

9 Comfort counts. If the dress doesn't feel right, don't buy it. You've got to wear it all day and feel great in it, after all.

10 Don't choose a dress that's too small. Beware of going on a drastic pre-wedding diet. What if it doesn't work?

WHICH WEDDING SUIT?

1 A full-on formal morning suit looks fabulous in photos, but will you really feel comfortable all day?

2 Hiring is often the best option for a full morning suit, if you think you're unlikely to wear it again.

3 If you want a more casual approach, go for a three- or two-piece suit (with or without a separate waistcoat).

4 Do you think you're a fashion-forward type? Choose a slim cut in an interesting fabric or colour.

5 Buying a bespoke suit will be costly, but you can choose fabric and cut. Ask for a suit lining to reflect your personality.

6 If you hire a suit, check the small print. What about damage? Perhaps you could take out insurance cover.

7 Try on a range of suit styles and keep an open mind about what you like and what looks good. You never know – you may be surprised.

8 It's important to feel comfortable. You don't want to spend the day dying to change into something more relaxed.

9 If you've chosen a three-piece lounge suit, coordinate the waistcoat to the wedding colour theme.

10 Ties can be chosen to match the bridesmaids' dresses.

WOW-FACTOR WEDDING HATS

1 Don't go crazy! A hat should complement your outfit, not become a talking-point.

2 Try on hats with your wedding outfit, including your shoes and bag.

3 Consider hiring a hat for the big day if you want designer style on a budget.

4 Take a friend or relative with you – impartial advice can be really helpful.

5 Suit your hat to the season – suede, wool or velvet for winter and chiffon, lace, linen, taffeta, organza or straw for summer.

6 Look at a range of different hats, especially if you don't often wear one.

7 If your outfit is richly decorated, your hat should be fairly plain, and vice versa.

8 For a really smart look, match your hat to your handbag and shoes.

9 Buy a plain hat and decorate it with feathers, flowers or trimmings yourself.

10 To avoid hat-hair, style your hair with extra volume and use stronger hairstyling products than normal.

SAVE MONEY ON A WEDDING

1 Second-hand dress
2 Fewer guests
3 Weekday ceremony
4 Make your own invitations
5 Buffet reception
6 Do your own flowers
7 House wine
8 Photographer friend
9 Avoid May–September
10 Advance booking

THE ALL-IMPORTANT WEDDING CAKE

1 Size is your first consideration. How many guests? Will you need extra to send to those who couldn't make it?

2 Start thinking about your cake a few months in advance. Planning takes time.

3 Need some clever cake ideas? Look through wedding magazines for cake ideas. Visit confectioners and bakers to see what suggestions they offer. They may have their own original ideas, too.

4 Consider some unusual wedding-cake options. What about sponge cake, cheesecake, a stack of yummy profiteroles, a giant pavlova or a display of mini cupcakes?

5 Accessorize your cake with flowers, ribbons, candles or trimmings that match your overall wedding colour scheme.

6 Don't overlook the taste in favour of how it looks. Can your cake-maker provide a sample for you to try?

7 Make the cake yourself if you want to economize (or ask a relative or friend), but have it professionally decorated.

8 Create your own sugared-icing adornments – from flowers to figures, or doves to hearts.

9 Think outside the box! What shape will your cake be? Anything is possible, but you'll get more servings from a conventional circular shape.

10 To get the 'big-wedding-cake' wow-factor, choose a normal tiered cake. If you don't really need the whole thing, include dummy cakes decorated to match.

SORT OUT YOUR WEDDING CATERER

1 Must you really call in the pros? If the guest list is less than 20 do the food yourself – hire staff to serve.

2 Some venues insist you use their own caterers. If this is a stumbling block, you may have to choose a different venue.

3 Meet with several caterers – it's OK to shop around. Discuss dates and times, guest numbers and costs.

4 Sample the caterer's wedding menus.

5 Find out whether the caterer can serve special diets. What about kids' prices?

6 Costs are usually quoted per head. Check what's included corkage, deliveries, travel expenses and insurance?

7 Establish the latest date for finalizing numbers. You don't want to pay for extra meals if guests drop out last minute.

8 What facilities does the caterer need? This is especially important if they haven't worked in your chosen venue before.

9 Discuss the table layouts and seating plans with your caterer and ask how many staff they provide and what uniforms.

10 Check who is going to provide china, glasses, utensils, the cake stand/knife.

ENTICING WEDDING INVITES

1 If the bride's parents are hosting, a traditional invitation is sent out in their name, requesting the 'honour of your presence at the marriage of their daughter'.

2 If the couple are paying, and the wedding is informal, you might opt for something like 'John and Sara would be delighted if you would attend our wedding'.

3 Include the essentials: date, time and location. Use a full postal or zip code for guests who use sat nav.

4 Tell your guests what event to expect. If you're not serving a full meal, say 'and afterwards for cake and champagne'.

5 Include a reply deadline if you want to get more replies, more quickly, and include a stamped, addressed reply card. Maps and local accommodation are useful.

6 Give guests an idea of attire: black tie, semi-formal, smart casual and so on.

7 If you don't want little ones there 'adult reception' sounds nicer than 'no children'! You'll just put parents' backs up.

8 Hand-write invitations using a calligraphy pen for a personal feel.

9 Writing invites and envelopes neatly can become a bit of a chore. Allow yourselves plenty of time and don't rush it.

10 Invitations are traditionally posted six weeks beforehand, but earlier is fine.

YOUR WEDDING GIFT LIST

1 Choose a gift-list service that suits your style as a couple. A department store is great if you need toasters, kettles and household items, or why not place your list in a more unusual shop?

2 Some companies let you create gift lists from a range of stores. And there are also lists for vouchers, travel and even donations to charity.

3 Ask gift-list services what facilities they offer. Can guests order by phone and online? Are there any perks, such as discounts? Personal shopper facility?

4 If you feel a bit uncomfortable about including your gift list with your wedding invitations, spread the word in person or even create a wedding website with a link to the list.

5 Create as long a list as possible and choose gifts at a wide range of prices. A range of smaller gifts means guests can buy more than one thing, or they can club together for a pricier item.

6 The bride's mother usually looks after the gift list, but if you'd rather do it yourself, that's fine.

7 Take dimensions and pop a handy tape measure in your bag to make sure you select the right-sized houseware.

8 Include a range of types of gifts, so that older relatives may choose more traditional items, while young friends can opt for something more quirky.

9 Start thinking about your gift list at least three months before the wedding. Select your gift list about eight weeks before, so that guests can start buying from about six weeks before.

10 Write thank-you notes as soon as possible after the wedding.

SAVE ON WEDDING STATIONERY

1 Call or email the guests with your invitation if you're on a tight budget.

2 Make your own invitations. Use your computer or supplies from a craft store.

3 Avoid thick or heavy embellishments that will make the invitation heavy and push up the cost of postage.

4 If you are using a professional printer, get several quotes and don't be tempted to go over your budget.

5 Don't send a stamped RSVP card with the invitation – just include your email address or phone number.

6 Keeping your invitation simple will save money and no one will mind. Fancy engraving, embossing and metallic printing all bump up costs.

7 Limit professional printing to your most important stationery (probably the invitations) and do all the rest (place names etc) yourself.

8 The orders of service need not be professionally printed – do them yourself on a home printer, using quality paper.

9 Write out the seating plan yourself. If you're good with a computer or fancy yourself as a calligrapher have a go.

10 Buy thank-you cards in bulk from stationer's/online. Or write them out by hand for the personal touch.

THE BRIDE'S BIG DAY

1 **Eat breakfast!** It's vital to eat something – it'll settle your nerves.

2 **Dress first – before you tackle hair/ make-up.** Don't get make-up on the dress!

3 **If you do put on your dress afterwards,** loosely cover your made-up face with a scarf first to stop any transfer.

4 **Make sure your helpers have clean hands** (or white gloves) and no shoes on.

5 **Allow at least half an hour** to put on your dress, shoes, veil and jewellery.

6 **Raise a glass with your bridesmaids and helpers –** but don't get tipsy!

7 **Allow enough time to arrive at the church** five minutes before the ceremony is due to start. This will give you a chance to get out of the car, smooth your dress, check your hair and arrange your veil.

8 **Try to speak to as many people as possible once you arrive at the reception,** especially those who are alone, have travelled a long way or who don't know many other guests.

9 **Gracefully accept invitations to dance.**

10 **Before throwing your bouquet, take out a few stems first** to dry as a keepsake.

GREAT WEDDING ENTERTAINMENT
1 Band
2 DJ
3 String quartet
4 Ceilidh band
5 Magician
6 Comedian
7 Karaoke
8 Casino
9 Fireworks
10 Caricaturist

A GREENER WEDDING

1 **Hold your ceremony and reception at the same venue** to cut down on transport and reduce the number of decorations.

2 **Buy a lovely vintage dress,** or, if you're handy with a needle, sew your own.

3 **Choose organic and natural materials** for all the wedding outfits and accessories.

4 **Use environmentally friendly** papers and inks for the wedding stationery.

5 **Source ethical metals and gems** for rings or re-use family heirlooms.

6 **Ask your florist for locally grown** flowers, herbs/foliage or grow your own.

7 **Choose seasonal, local and organic ingredients** for your wedding breakfast.

8 **Ensure your confetti** is biodegradable.

9 **Don't give single-use cameras to every guest.** Ask them to take their own photos and send them to you afterwards.

10 **Give home-made wedding favours.**

FABULOUS WEDDING FLOWERS

1 **Select a style for your bridal bouquet that is all about you –** hand-tied posy, tear-drop-shaped cascade, arm-held long stems or something more unconventional.

2 **Flowers in season are cheaper.** Don't choose anything delicate or short-lived.

3 **Remember scent, as well as colour and shape, is important –** especially for a bouquet that needs to last the whole day.

4 **For bridesmaid's flowers, echo the bridal bouquet,** but have them smaller, using colours that go with their dresses.

5 **Give very young bridesmaids** a basket filled with petals to scatter down the aisle before the bride's entrance.

6 **Men's buttonholes** can complement the bridal bouquet or the colour of the groom's outfit. For something a little different, what about thistles or herbs?

7 **When designing corsages** for the female members of the wedding party, coordinate colours with their outfits. But if you're in any doubt, white is good.

8 **Check what flower arrangements** you are allowed to have at the ceremony venue, where you can put them and how garlands will be attached.

9 **Decorate small trees (bay or olive),** to place outside the venue entrance, then transfer them to the reception.

10 **Silk flowers are great** if you suffer from hay fever, want to take them on honeymoon or simply want to keep them as a permanent reminder of your big day.

A FABULOUS WEDDING FEAST TABLE

1 **Add colour to white/ivory table cloths** with runners, napkins, flowers and glasses.

2 **Don't use too many patterns and colours.** The effect will be overly busy rather than cool and elegant.

3 **Hire vintage crockery** for a unique, memorable look that's so very 'now'.

4 **Centrepieces should be low enough to see over or tall and thin** so that they don't impede conversation across tables.

5 **Consider different ideas for centrepieces –** candles, bonbons or balloons.

6 **Put in a touch of sparkle to the table** with metallic confetti or sequins.

7 **If you want a country look** sprinkle flower/paper petals on the tablecloth.

8 **Little decorative touches,** such as colour-coordinated ribbons, raffia or ricrac tied around the napkins/menu cards, work well.

9 **Scatter small gifts** such as sweets, chocolates or a mini bottle of bubbly.

10 **Create a jolly party atmosphere** by putting out sparklers, balloons, poppers, games and disposable cameras.

SUPER SEATING PLANS

1 **What combinations of tables are possible?** Is there any flexibility about position? Find out from your venue.

2 **Start by sketching a plan of the room,** and cut out pieces of paper to represent each table.

3 **Write guests' names on sticky notes,** so that you can move them around.

4 **Spread all the ushers out** around the tables and try to alternate the sexes.

5 **It's best to seat people of similar ages all together.** But instead of tables composed entirely of friends, why not intersperse them with a few new people?

6 **Worried about distant relatives?** Ask your parents' advice about who they know or who they might like to meet.

7 **Display your seating plan prominently.**

If yours is a large wedding, you may need to display two in different locations.

8 **Allow around 30 minutes** for guests to find their places and sit down.

9 **Highlight guests with special diets** on the seating plan and make sure that your caterers have their own copy.

10 **Keep a few blank name places handy** just in case there are last-minute changes to the guest list.

WRITE YOUR OWN VOWS

1 **Check that whoever is officiating at your wedding ceremony** is in agreement with you writing personalized vows.

2 **Talk to your partner at length** about what kind of vows you'd like.

3 **Do you want one vow for both of you,** or individual vows?

4 **Before you write your vows, think carefully.** What first attracted you to your partner? Why do you want to marry them? What does marriage mean to you?

5 **Research poetry and passages from literature** that you might incorporate.

6 **Write a first draft.** Read it out loud several times to make sure it sounds right.

7 **Keep your vows short and sweet.** Long and rambling might be over the top.

8 **Read your vows** to a trusted friend or member of your family and get their opinion. If the vows seem insincere or you're tempted to laugh, change them.

9 **Practise reading your final vows** until you know them almost by heart.

10 **Even if you've memorized your vows**, write them out on a card to keep close by, just in case of memory lapses.

BEST-EVER BEST MAN'S SPEECH

1 **Starting the speech is easy:** introduce yourself, read out messages from friends/relatives who couldn't attend the wedding.

2 **Short, entertaining and heartfelt** (no more than ten minutes) is much better than long and overly detailed.

3 **Don't try too hard for humour** if it doesn't come naturally to you.

4 **Include a little background info** on how long you have known the groom, his personality, how the couple met and a light-hearted insight into their relationship.

5 **Don't forget to talk about the bride,** but be sure to pay her lavish compliments!

6 **Include a funny story,** if possible. The aim is to make your audience think you have embarrassed the groom – but try not to make him feel too bad!

7 **Avoid smutty or shocking content**. You need to appeal to all generations: old, young and all those in between.

8 **Finish off with a charming summary** of how you see the couple's future together.

9 **Practise by reading your speech out loud** until you feel completely confident.

10 **Your last bit is easy, too** – a toast to 'Mr and Mrs (married name)' or just their first names if this is too formal.

MAKE A GRAND WEDDING EXIT

1 **Timing is crucial –** you don't want to miss the best party ever; nor do you want to be the last ones lingering at the end.

2 **Schedule your going-away time into your running order for the day,** but allow for last-minute adjustments.

3 **Do you want to change your outfits?** If so, where will you do it? Arrange for going-away clothes to be stored at the venue in advance and for someone to collect the clothes you've left behind later.

4 **Make sure your wedding clothes can be cleaned** and, if necessary, returned to the hirers while you're on honeymoon.

5 **Arrange for someone to announce your departure –** the MC, DJ or best man.

6 **Make the announcement** just a few minutes before you plan to leave.

7 **It's traditional for the bride to throw her bouquet.** Turn your back to the crowd and throw gently over your head – surreptitiously aimed at someone you think would like to catch it!

8 **Ask the best man to check that your going-away transport has arrived** and that any documentation is safely inside.

9 **The best man and ushers might want to 'decorate' the vehicle** with tin cans and spray-on messages – though what they can get away with depends on whether or not it's hired.

10 **Putting on a firework display is a great send-off.** Or how about giving guests a sparkler each?

ORGANIZE A SPECIAL HONEYMOON

1 **Decide what type of honeymoon –** adventurous, exotic, active or relaxing? Set a budget before ideas get out of hand.

2 **Don't be swayed by the idea of a traditional romantic honeymoon if that's not what you want.** This is a great chance to have the holiday of a lifetime – just the two of you – whatever that may be.

3 **Simple or luxurious?** If you want to organize a simple honeymoon, use an agency, or for more flexibility why not put together your own independent itinerary. If you can splash the cash, you might opt for a specialist luxury travel agent.

4 **Choose your dream destination first** and then look at accommodation options – bed and breakfast, gîte, hotel, hostel, self-catering, camper van, tent...

5 **Be sure to shop around for a good deal.** Just because it's a honeymoon, it doesn't mean you can't economize.

6 **Book early.** Not only might you get a better deal, but you'll have more time left to concentrate on the wedding itself.

7 **Mention that you're booking a honeymoon** and you may receive discounts, upgrades or free flowers or chocolates!

8 **Extras may make the honeymoon extra-special –** don't forget to book day trips, spa packages or breakfast in bed.

9 **Buy a travel insurance package** for complete peace of mind.

10 **Leave yourselves some downtime at the start of your honeymoon.** Allow for the fact that you'll probably feel quite tired for the first few days. Relax!

THE PERFECT PARTY HOST

1 The secret's in the planning. Invite a good mix of guests and choose menus, drinks, music and décor well in advance so that you're relaxed on the night.

2 Invite your guests in good time, and ensure they know where to come, at what time. Give them your telephone number in case they get lost.

3 If you want a dress code and/or a finishing time, explain in advance.

4 Ask whether any guests have food allergies or special dietary requirements.

5 Ensure your guests have plenty to eat and drink. Watch out for empty glasses, but don't be too pushy with drinks.

6 Make introductions and make sure that everyone has someone to talk to.

7 Clear spills/breakages without fuss.

8 Scan the room regularly to check for wallflowers and those who look ill at ease.

9 Accept offers of help graciously.

10 Stay awake and reasonably sober until the end. It's very rude to retire early from your own party.

PARTY THEMES FOR ADULTS

1 James Bond
2 Cocktails
3 Hoedown
4 Casino
5 Rock 'n' roll
6 Luau
7 Masked ball
8 Wine- and beer-tasting
9 Fortune-telling
10 Vintage

WHAT MAKES A PERFECT PARTY GUEST?

1 Respond to invitations promptly and, if you say you'll attend, do so.

2 If you're unavoidably delayed, call to let your hosts know. Never arrive early.

3 Bring a small gift appropriate to your hosts and to the occasion.

4 Offer to help – such as pouring drinks, handing round food or taking coats.

5 Don't hog the buffet or chase the canapés around the room. The same goes for the drinks tray.

6 Never look over someone's shoulder when you're talking to them to see who else is around. If you're bored, think up a polite excuse to get out of the conversation.

7 Chat to as many other guests as you can and make the effort to circulate.

8 Be careful not to drink too much.

9 Don't outstay your welcome. If the party's winding down, leave.

10 Thank your host before you go and follow up with a phone call/note next day.

EXCELLENT PARTY ENTERTAINMENT

1 Personal recommendation is always best and, if possible, attend an event where the entertainer is performing.

2 Check references and ask whether your entertainer has all the necessary licenses and/or insurance.

3 Approaching an individual yourself is cheaper than going to an agency, though they will represent a range of entertainers.

4 If you book a solo performer, ask what would happen if they're unwell or can't get to your event at the last minute.

PARTY ESSENTIALS

1. Lively guests
2. Good food
3. Well-chosen drinks
4. Cool music
5. Atmospheric lighting
6. Floor space
7. Comfy seating
8. Great decorations
9. Fun and games
10. Someone else to clear up

5 Choose a party act that suits the occasion and your guests. Older guests might appreciate a big band, for example, while teenagers might prefer karaoke.

6 Remember that children are often scared of clowns. A magician or balloon artist might be a better choice.

7 Sort out where the act will perform. Do you need a stage or to clear a space?

8 Check how long the act/performance will last. Will there be a break?

9 How about a performer who visits tables doing up-close magic or drawing caricatures?

10 Agree a payment schedule in advance and get a signed contract.

THROW A DIVINE DINNER PARTY

1 Choose a good mix of guests who you think will get on well with each other.

2 Send invitations out in good time – four to six weeks is about right, unless it's a casual get-together.

3 Choose a menu that suits your guests – taking into account allergies or dislikes.

4 Make sure you can cook your planned meal competently and prepare as much as possible in advance.

5 Choose atmospheric music and decorate the table – candles, flowers, napkins.

6 Greet your guests warmly and put their coats and bags somewhere safe.

7 Offer drinks and nibbles as soon as your guests have settled in.

8 Place seating cards to avoid confusion. Or at least have a seating plan in your head and direct people to their places.

9 Clear away dirty dishes between courses. Don't leave them lying around.

10 Keep conversation flowing and avoid controversial subjects (politics and religion are probably best avoided).

A TERRIFIC TEA PARTY

1 Make delicates finger sandwiches – preferably cucumber – with the crusts off.

2 Keep sandwiches in top condition by covering with a clean, slightly damp, tea towel, in a cool place – until you serve.

3 Go for a retro vibe with meringues, scones, éclairs, brandy snaps, cream horns, tarts or cupcakes.

4 A matching set of chintz cups and saucers is divine, darling – or collect odd flowery pieces of china from second-hand sources for an eclectic look.

5 The cake stand is crucial. Two or three tiers, in pressed glass or floral china.

6 Use the proper kit: teapot, vintage cake forks and linen napkins.

7 There are lots of teas to choose from, but always make tea with freshly drawn and boiled water. Milk goes in first.

8 Pretty posies of flowers will decorate the table nicely.

9 Play dance-hall music for atmosphere.

10 Dress to impress in a gorgeous retro tea dress, with hair and make-up to match.

UNDERSTAND DRESS CODES

1 'White tie' means very formal. Men should wear a black, single-breasted tail coat, black trousers, white shirt, waistcoat and bow tie, plus black patent lace-up shoes. Women should wear a long gown

2 For men 'black tie', dinner jackets or tuxedos means a single-breasted black jacket with black trousers, a white evening shirt and black bow tie.

3 For women, 'black tie' means a smart dress, long or short (not mini) in any colour.

4 Formal men's socks are black silk, long enough to cover bare legs when seated.

5 Only hand-tied bow ties will do for a smart event. Avoid novelty designs.

6 Morning dress, or formal day dress, is traditional wedding garb. For men, this is a black/grey tail coat, with grey (plain, striped/hounds' tooth) trousers, plain shirt and waistcoat and tie/cravat.

7 Attend to your waistcoat buttons. If it's double-breasted, fasten them all; if single, leave the bottom one undone.

8 'Lounge suits' means business suit, with shirt/tie. For women, this means a skirt- or trouser-suit, cocktail dress/ball gown. Ask your host for clarification.

9 'Smart casual' means no trainers, sportswear/jeans. Men can choose a shirt/tie or open collar. For women, it's trousers/skirt, blouse/sweater and jacket.

10 It's rarely compulsory to wear a formal hat. Top hats at weddings should not be worn indoors or in the photographs.

ALL ABOUT INTRODUCTIONS

1 The traditional order of introductions is men to women, young people to older people and individuals to groups first.

2 Surnames aren't necessary unless it's a formal occasion.

3 Smile, maintain eye contact and repeat names as clearly as possible.

4 Break the ice by adding a bit of information about the person.

5 Bad memory? Check names in advance.

6 In a large party, introduce your guest to those nearest/those you're talking to.

7 Forgotten a name? Apologize and ask.

8 It's polite to stand up when you're being introduced to someone.

9 No introduction? Introduce yourself.

10 If you're asked, 'How are you?', a short and positive response is best.

WRITING A THANK-YOU LETTER

1 Prompt
2 Brief
3 Sincere
4 Personal
5 Refer to event
6 Accurate spelling
7 Snail mail not email
8 Nice paper/card
9 Neat writing
10 Clearly addressed

YOUR ENGAGEMENT PARTY

1 Hold the party within a couple of months of announcing your engagement.

2 You might want to have two parties: one for family and another, less formal one, for friends your own age.

3 Check dates with your most important

guests before deciding when to hold it.

4 **Only invite people you're definitely going to want at the wedding.**

5 **Champagne a go go!** Or sparkling wine if you're on a tight budget.

6 **Add some nibbles –** from bowls of crisps to a full-blown buffet.

7 **Choose romantic decorations:** balloons, bunting, fairylights and candles.

8 **Introduce strangers –** they'll be pleased to meet up again at the wedding.

9 **Speech! Speech!** A quick speech from the father of the bride is a nice touch.

10 **Write thank-you letters** for any gifts.

BAR/BAT MITZVAH CELEBRATIONS

1 **Discuss with your child** whether to hold a formal event or a themed party.

2 **Decide on a mix of guests –** mostly your child's friends, family, or both?

3 **Start planning a couple of years in advance –** synagogues and venues have busy schedules.

4 **Send invites about six months beforehand.** If relatives are coming from far and wide, give even more notice.

5 **Save money by inviting guests for a meal at the synagogue** after the Saturday afternoon service rather than booking a separate party location.

6 **Remember that many guests will be teenagers or younger –** make sure they'll enjoy the food and music.

7 **It's tempting to keep adding extras –** set your budget and try hard to stick to it.

8 **It's best for gifts to be given at the reception** rather than at the service.

9 **Pen the poem** for the candle-lighting ceremony well in advance and practise it with your child.

10 **Plan the ceremony in detail –** how many candles, who will light them and in what order. Enjoy it but don't let it go on for too long.

GET YOUR EASTER EGGS CRACKED!

1 **If you intend to eat the eggs later,** hard-boil them first.

2 **For a permanent (if fragile) display, blow out your eggs.** Pierce the shell with a knife tip at both ends, making one hole slightly larger. Push a paper clip into the yolk to disperse it, then hold the egg over a bowl and blow the contents out of the larger hole.

3 **To make a dye,** mix food colouring with hot water and a little vinegar. Then dip the eggs in one by one, holding them carefully with tongs.

4 **Draw or write on the egg with a wax crayon first –** the dye won't stick to these areas, so your design will show through.

5 **Attach small stickers to the eggs** before dyeing to create a masked design. Experiment with leaves and flowers, too.

6 **Let the eggs dry;** you could re-dip parts of them in a different dye to create a multi-coloured effect.

7 **To achieve a marbled effect,** add a little olive oil to the second dye.

8 **A simple solution for hard-boiled eggs?** You could simply paint or draw straight onto them with felt-tip pens, or use colourful stickers to create a design.

9 **For Easter eggs with bling,** cover them with glue and then roll them in glitter.

10 **Fill a small basket** with your decorated eggs for a charming Easter display.

BOO! TRICK-OR-TREAT ON HALLOWE'EN

1 **Cheap and spooky costumes –** an old sheet for a ghost or a mummy wrapped in toilet tissue.

2 **To whiten hair effectively and temporarily** use talcum powder. It will add a really creepy finishing touch.

3 **Thinking about masks?** They can get hot, sweaty and uncomfortable. Creative face paint might be a better option.

4 **Only let children go trick-or-treating to houses** they know and accompany younger ones. Older kids should take a phone and have agreed a return time.

5 **Take along a torch,** wear a reflective costume or carry a glow stick.

6 **Look for houses that look as if they'll welcome trick-or-treaters –** usually with visible Hallowe'en decorations.

7 **Don't choose a flimsy or paper container for treats,** but make sure it's easy for little ones to hold and not too heavy.

8 **Smile and say 'trick or treat' nicely.**

9 **Go in small groups –** large ones can be too intimidating, especially for the elderly.

10 **Adapt the Hallowe'en outfit to the weather.** Wear wellies if it's raining.

CARVE A SCARY PUMPKIN

1 **It's going to get messy!** Cover your work area with newspaper or plastic.

2 **Draw a circle** about 15cm (6in) diameter on the top of the pumpkin and cut it out carefully. This will be your lid.

3 **When cutting out the lid,** hold the knife at 45 degrees so that you create a 'shelf' for the lid to sit on.

4 **Spoon out the inside of your pumpkin,** then scrape it so that it's really clean.

5 **To make carving the eyes and mouth easier,** scrape away a bit more of the inside area where you're planning to cut.

6 **Download a design from the internet** or draw freehand – but practise on a piece of paper first.

7 **Use non-permanent pens** to draw the features on your pumpkin first.

8 **To make precise cuts,** start by making shallow cuts, then go deeper.

9 **Test the design every now and then** by closing the curtains and using a torch.

10 **Coat the edges of the finished carved pumpkin** with petroleum jelly to stop it drying out. Keeping it in a cool place helps, too.

THANKSGIVING DECORATIONS

1 Dried corn
2 Gourds
3 Willow wreath
4 Wheat sheaf
5 Nuts
6 Pine cones
7 Dried leaves
8 Mini pumpkins
9 Flowers
10 Candles

GREAT CHILDREN'S
STOCKING FILLERS
1 Bouncy ball
2 Colouring pens
3 Hairclips
4 Toy car
5 Tiny teddy
6 Bubble mix
7 Keyring
8 Chocolate coins
9 Bath bubbles
10 Diary

AN INCREDIBLE CHRISTMAS TREE

1 **The fresher your Christmas tree is when you buy it,** the longer it will last.

2 **Choose a tree that's bright green** and sheds very few needles when you shake it lightly. Ideally, it should be displayed in water and out of direct sun and wind.

3 **Cut an extra 12mm (½in) off the bottom of the tree** as soon as you get it home. This will help it absorb more water.

4 **Put the tree in water immediately,** out of direct sunlight and heat sources.

5 **Don't let the tree dry out.** Use a stand that holds water and replace it often.

6 **Trim away any low-down and interior branches** that you don't need.

7 **If your tree starts to look a bit dry,** try refilling the stand with hot water as it's absorbed more quickly.

8 **Add a couple of cups of corn syrup** as extra food in the water.

9 **Use LED lights on the tree –** they don't give off heat so won't dry it out as much.

10 **Why not have a live tree in a pot?** You can plant it in your garden afterwards.

CONSTRUCT A CHRISTMAS WREATH

1 **To make your own wreath base,** use wire coat hangers bent into circles and bound, or bundles of willow/vine tied into a circle with string, raffia or florist's wire.

2 **Cut sprigs from the garden –** conifer, holly, laurel and ivy all work well. Strip excess foliage from the sprigs' lower ends.

3 **Wind florists wire around the lower part of a sprig or bunch of sprigs** and attach to the base. Don't cut the wire.

4 **Overlap one sprig after the other,** going in the same direction, winding the wire around again. Keep going until the base is covered.

5 **To finish the last one,** lift up the base of the first sprig you attached and slip your last sprig under it.

6 **Trim any untidy bits** with scissors or pruning shears.

7 **Decorate your wreath** by wiring on fresh, dried or artificial flowers, ribbons, raffia, moss, cones, seed heads or baubles.

8 **A red ribbon bow** finishes the whole thing off nicely. Wire-edge ribbon is best.

9 **Spray on fake snow or glitter.**

10 **To hang up the wreath** attach a strong loop of wire or string, or simply prop it on a shelf or mantelpiece.

HOME-MADE CHRISTMAS DECCIES

1 **The easiest Christmas stockings can be made from felt.** Just trace the shape, cut out and sew edges together. Add a cuff for a professional look and make sure the whole thing is big enough to hold presents!

2 **Hang ginger biscuits on the tree.**

Before baking, pierce a hole near the top of each one. When cooled, thread with a ribbon and hang (out of reach of pets!).

3 Pine cones *au naturel* or sprayed with metallic paint look great arranged in a large bowl on a coffee table.

4 Dried oranges threaded with ribbon look seasonal. Slice them thinly and dry out in the oven on a low temperature.

5 Collect sprigs from the garden with vibrant red berries and arrange in a vase.

6 Cover mini-pegs in glitter and use them for hanging up Christmas cards.

7 Make a shimmering centrepiece by arranging foliage, berries and cones around a gorgeous oversized candle.

8 Cut some long, skinny rectangles from coloured or foil paper and hang twirling from the ceiling.

9 For an advent calendar that will last forever, use mini-pots numbered with elegant calligraphy. Just add the gifts!

10 Top the tree with a peg-doll angel. Wrap and glue a fabric remnant for her dress, stick on wool for hair, add cut-out wings and then draw on her features.

FIREWORKS: SAFE AS HOUSES

1 Only use fireworks outdoors.

2 Obey any local regu(lations. Don't use fireworks if they're illegal in your area.

3 Keep a hose/bucket of water close by.

4 Never try to tamper with fireworks, or combine more than one.

5 Read the instructions carefully.

6 Never relight a firework that fails to go off first time. Leave it for 20 minutes before dunking it into a bucket of water.

7 Stand well back when you're watching.

8 Wear safety glasses if you're the one setting fireworks off. Spectators need to be careful of sparks and smut, too.

9 Don't drink alcohol before setting off fireworks.

10 Hold sparklers at arm's length – they're very hot even after they've finished.

MAKE MOTHER'S DAY A TREAT

1 Breakfast arranged on a tray in bed is the perfect mother's day treat.

2 Write a personal poem to your mum and enclose it in a card or frame it.

3 Make your mum a book of special promises – to 'tidy up', 'give you a back rub' or 'make you a cup of tea'.

4 Take her to her favourite restaurant.

5 A hand-made card is a real treat.

6 Compose your own message about what your mum means to you and how much you really appreciate her.

7 Organize a trip to the movies – see a film she's been dying to see for ages.

8 Have a family picture framed as a gift, or use a website to make a collection of photos into a printed album.

9 Take her to a day spa for some relaxation and luxurious pampering.

10 If all else fails, chocolates never do.

A DREAMY VALENTINE'S DAY

1 Fry a scrumptious egg inside a heart-shaped cookie cutter for a really romantic breakfast. Or make heart-shaped pancakes.

2 Write sweet messages and pop them inside your loved-one's pockets, to be found accidentally later in the day.

3 A home-made card is more heartfelt than a bought one .

4 Give him/her a 'love voucher' promising a romantic night in.

5 It's the surprise that counts! Book a babysitter and go out on a 'date' somewhere totally unexpected.

6 Dig out your old photos and go all gooey over them together.

7 Turn off your phone and computer and make sure your time together is wholly dedicated to your loved one.

8 Skip the overpriced restaurant and cook up a storm at home. Add candles and music for a really romantic atmosphere.

9 Make up a mystery box holding charms, notes, pictures and sentimental items – just for your loved one.

10 Don't leave it too late! The best Valentine's Day treats get booked up.

FLAGS FOR THE FOURTH OF JULY

1 Only have the flag on display from sunrise to sunset – unless you plan to light it up at night.

2 Don't let the flag touch the ground.

3 The union (stars) should be at the peak of the flagstaff.

4 The stars should be visible on the upper left-hand side.

5 Don't display the flag in bad weather.

6 Hoist the flag briskly.

7 The flag should always be flown above any flags of states, cities or localities.

8 When flying the flag of the USA with a flag of another country, they should be on two separate flagstaffs, at the same height and roughly the same size.

9 Don't display a worn or damaged flag.

10 After you have finished displaying the flag, lower it ceremoniously and carefully fold into a triangle.

KIDS' PARTY THEMES

1 Pirates
2 Wild West
3 Knights/ princesses
4 Rainbow
5 Ballet/fairy
6 Dinosaur
7 Football
8 Super-heroes
9 Under the sea
10 Cartoons

YIPPEE! KIDS' PARTY GAMES

1 Make games age-appropriate so that younger ones don't get frustrated or older ones bored.

2 Set everything up well in advance and have plenty of games planned – kids can get through them surprisingly quickly!

3 Don't start the games too soon. Quieter kids need to find confidence, while bouncy ones need to let off steam first.

4 Mix noisy games with quiet ones.

5 Plan the party according to the kids. If they seem boisterous, give them loads of physical games and vice versa.

6 If you've planned outdoor games, have back-ups ready in case of rain.

7 Ensure games don't drag on too long if they're not being enjoyed.

8 If competitive games don't go down well, avoid disappointment by giving small consolation prizes to the losers, too.

9 Set up a space with quiet activities so that kids who don't want to join in, or who've been eliminated from a game, have something to do.

10 Ask other parents/older kids to help supervise the games.

A FABULOUS FAMILY GET-TOGETHER

1 If you find it difficult to spend a long time with your family, don't! Stay the minimum time possible to be polite, offer a believable excuse and leave again.

2 Book a hotel rather than staying in a relative's house if that's too tricky.

3 Avoid controversial subjects such as politics, religion or money.

4 Keep some harmless topics up your sleeve – books, films, the weather.

5 Your family usually means well, even if they do seem very annoying.

6 Don't get riled by personal questions that you don't want to answer. Change the subject politely.

7 Bring a friend along for moral support.

8 If it all gets too much, take time out. Go for a stroll or spend time with the kids.

9 Don't take sides or get dragged into other people's rows.

10 Keep calm – make an effort to enjoy it. It mightn't be as bad as you think.

A BABY SHOWER FOR A FRIEND

1 Pre- or post-birth shower? It's traditional to hold the shower in the last two months of pregnancy, but some couples like their new baby to be a guest of honour.

2 Why not invite men (and maybe kids) to enjoy the occasion, too?

3 Choose a suitable location. You could hold the shower in your home, or you might prefer to book a café or restaurant.

4 Send out the invites at least three weeks beforehand.

5 Decide whether to theme the shower. Choose a main colour or a theme such as animals or the alphabet.

6 Thinking about the menu? Tasty but easy-to-eat finger foods are ideal. They need to be pregnancy-friendly, too.

7 Alcohol or not? Bubbly's ideal, but check with the mother-to-be first.

8 You'll be asked for advice on gifts – get the lowdown from the parents-to-be so you know what to say.

9 If you want to include some games, plan them beforehand and assemble equipment and prizes.

10 Decorate! Put up balloons, streamers and a few flowers, or perhaps something to match your theme. And have fun!

IDEAS FOR BABY PRESENTS

1 Silver spoon
2 Photo frame/album
3 Silver bracelet
4 Case of wine
5 Savings bond
6 Money box
7 Baby china
8 Cashmere blanket
9 Silver rattle
10 Collectable teddy

CHRISTENING/NAMING PARTIES

1 Dress the baby in his/her cutest outfit at the last possible minute. You'll avoid messing it up before the big event.

2 Take a change of clothes for baby, lots of wipes and all your usual kit for a day out. Pop them in a pretty bag.

3 Practise holding your baby in a way that's both comfortable for you and looks good in the photographs.

4 If you haven't got a family heirloom gown for your baby to wear, a sailor suit or normal white party outfit will do just fine. Is it comfortable and appropriate for the weather?

5 Check if it's OK to have photography during the ceremony.

6 Choose a venue for your party that's fairly close to the church/naming venue.

7 Economize by holding the party at home and doing the food yourself.

8 If you arrange a morning party you won't be expected to offer alcohol.

9 Organize activities to keep young children on the go. Colouring-in equipment, push-along cars/tractors, or even just balloons to bat around.

10 A short toast by a godparent will provide a memorable moment.

WRAP PREZZIES WITH PANACHE

IDEAS FOR ALTERNATIVE WRAPPING
1 Brown paper
2 Music score
3 Tissue paper
4 Calendar
5 Fabric
6 Comics
7 Japanese newspaper
8 Wallpaper
9 Map
10 Child's drawing

1 Pop awkwardly shaped presents into a box before you embark on wrapping them.

2 Assemble everything you need before you start wrapping: a clear space on a clean table top, sticky tape, long-bladed, sharp scissors and a range of ribbons.

3 Thick wrapping paper is less likely to tear. Avoid frustration!

4 Use stickers and decorative stamps to embellish your wrapping paper.

5 Add some pretty embellishments: a bow, tassel, button, charm or flower sprig.

6 Add a band of contrasting-coloured, patterned paper for a snazzy effect.

7 Use two sheets of different-coloured tissue paper and fold back one layer.

8 A fancy ribbon can make plain paper look really upmarket.

9 Good alternatives to ordinary ribbon: raffia, ricrac and twine.

10 Make your own gift tags: cut down old greetings cards with pinking shears.

A WARM WELCOME FOR HOUSE GUESTS

1 A comfy bed and clean sheets/towels are a must. Clear out plenty of space for their things in drawers, too.

2 For an extra special touch, add a bottle of mineral water and a posy of flowers on the bedside table.

3 Can guests connect to the internet? Give them the details, if so.

4 **Let guests know of any 'house rules'** in advance.

5 **Provide guests with a rough timetable,** especially mealtimes, so that they know what to expect and when .

6 **You don't have to entertain guests** all the time. They'll appreciate downtime.

7 **Establish how much guests will contribute** to the running of the house – if you could use a little help, ask politely.

8 **Tell guests what they can help themselves to,** so they don't have to ask for everything.

9 **Show guests where things go,** so they can tidy up after themselves.

10 **Don't try to do all your usual chores!** Your guests will want to spend time with you, not wait around while you work.

TRACE YOUR FAMILY TREE

1 **Start by finding out as much as you can by speaking to your relatives.** Write it all down, checking first, last and maiden names, locations and occupations, and making sure dates are as accurate as possible. Keep your notes well organized – you're going to have a fair few of them! It may pay to set up a small filing system, too, in which you can keep photographs, documents, print-outs and so on.

2 **Note down some information about the youngest members of your family.** Then move on to your parents, grandparents and great grandparents. You'll probably want to narrow down your search to just one branch of the family tree at first and trace the others later.

3 **Get help from societies.** Is there a local family history society? Their records may hold relevant information or be able to offer practical advice. Think about joining an online genealogical society, which could help to cover a lot of ground. Your local library may hold useful records.

4 **Go up in the attic or down into the basement!** Drag out those old boxes of memorabilia. You might find lots of interesting letters, postcards, photographs, work records, newspaper clippings, accounts, coins, souvenirs or medals. Clues of any sort will help you in your detective work.

5 **Look on the backs of photographs.** Pull them carefully out of old albums and you'll often find family names and dates written on the reverse. These could help with a missing part of your puzzle.

6 **Once you've gone as far as possible with immediate family members,** start working backwards, using key records. What you use will vary as you go along, but might include birth, marriage and death certificates, census returns, electoral rolls, military records, church records, wills and trade directories.

7 **There are many websites that can help you trace your family tree,** using millions of names in online databases. They're easy to use and can provide quick results, but you'll have to pay to subscribe to them. It's therefore worth doing as much research of your own as possible first, and really making sure that you're focused on a particular area of research.

8 **Start with five key questions: Who? Where? When? What? Why?** Who were your ancestors? What were their names and perhaps nicknames? When did they live? Where did they live? What did they do for a living? And why are they interesting? What did they do in their spare time? What made them unique and noteworthy? Don't forget that old family stories may be fascinating, but they may not necessarily be founded on fact – sometimes the truth gets embroidered.

9 Don't be shocked by what you find. They say that whenever anyone traces their family tree, there is a likelihood that they'll uncover a criminal or lunatic in their past. But you never know, you may also be connected to royalty, too!

10 Don't give up. Tracing your family tree can often be frustrating, overwhelming and difficult. But if you don't have luck with one route, try another. Ask advice, too. You'll get there in the end. It will be incredibly rewarding – and a wonderful gift to pass on to future generations.

THE RIGHT NAME FOR YOUR BABY

1 Don't leave choosing a name until the last minute – unless you really want to feel under pressure!

2 Is there a family tradition that you wish to follow? Ask your parents for input.

3 Read name books and discount all the ones you hate; highlight ones you like.

4 Make lists of any names that have special meaning for you or your family.

5 Will your chosen name be shortened? You might like Charlotte, but hate Lottie, for example.

6 Unusual names may be hard to spell, or not typically gender-associated. Will that make life hard for your child?

7 How does the name (and any middle names) work with your last name? Are the initials OK or do they spell something?

8 Say your chosen name out loud. A lot. Does it sound good?

9 Make sure you and your partner are equally happy with your chosen name.

10 Accept advice graciously, but it's your decision in the end.

FIRST DAYS WITH YOUR NEWBORN

1 Sleep! As much as you can. Whenever you can. Switch off the phone and draw the curtains if it helps.

2 Shut the door. If you're too tired/busy to entertain visitors, don't.

3 Share as much care as possible with your partner. You're in this together! Take time to chat and cuddle, too.

4 Involve the older siblings. They'll be anxious and in need of extra attention.

5 Hang the housework. If you let your usual standards slip for a while, does it really matter?

6 Eat and drink healthily and regularly. You need to look after yourself so you can look after your baby properly.

7 Talk to someone. Once the initial euphoria has subsided, you may feel a little lonely and down. A fellow new mum is ideal for sharing worries, or you could invite a friend or relative round for a chat.

8 **Accept any offers of help.**

9 **Do things your way.** Plenty of people will offer advice, but you don't have to follow what they say if it doesn't suit you. After all, 'mother knows best'!

10 **Enjoy this precious time with your baby.** It will vanish all too quickly.

TERRIBLE TODDLER TANTRUMS

1 **Compromise.** It's better to avoid tantrums, so if you don't mind giving in a little it will save you both a lot of stress.

2 **Organize things so that they are less frustrating for your little one.** If he/she doesn't get upset there's no need to throw a tantrum.

3 **Can you make the difficult thing any easier for your toddler to cope with?** With kindness and lateral thinking you might be able to steer clear of tantrums.

4 **Stay calm.** Anger exacerbates things.

5 **In the throes of a tantrum,** hold your toddler gently so that no damage is done. If they can't bear this, at least keep them clear of anything breakable.

6 **Don't try to reason with your toddler** in the middle of a tantrum. They won't be capable of responding.

7 **Make sure the tantrums don't lead to rewards or punishments.** If your toddler learns that having a tantrum changes nothing, he/she is less likely to learn that such actions get results.

8 **Don't be embarrassed by tantrums.** If you need to take your toddler to the shops, then go to the shops.

9 **Sympathize.** Toddlers are torn by their emotions and don't usually do it on purpose. They feel as bad as you do and need a good cuddle afterwards.

10 **This stage will pass.** If your toddler's negative emotions are wearing you down, try to focus on their many happy times.

SENSIBLE TOILET TRAINING

1 **Wait until your child is physically ready.** He/she will start to recognize the signs of needing the toilet soon enough.

2 **A good potty is vital:** stable, comfortable, easy to clean. A 'throne' may appeal. Or your child may want to start straight away with a special toilet seat.

3 **Let your toddler get to know their potty.** Explain what it's for and let your little one play with it and sit on it with a nappy on.

4 **Never force your toddler** onto a potty against their will.

5 **Don't make the process of toilet training about being 'good' or 'naughty'.** It's a skill to master, not a moral issue.

6 **Imitation helps.** Let your child see you using the toilet.

7 **Bare all.** Try letting your child just have a bare bottom, or else use trainer pants with a plastic lining.

8 **Avoid piling on the pressure.** Praise

success and be sympathetic with accidents.

9 Provide prompt help. Fetch the potty, assist with clothes, wiping and disposing.

10 Carry a potty and clean pants with you whenever you go out and find out where all the public toilets are.

BED-WETTING? SORTED!

1 Wet nappies every morning? Don't take them off at night yet. Just no point.

2 Don't make a big deal of a wet bed. Anxiety will only make things worse.

3 Plastic sheets are essential. But do find ones that are comfortable not crinkly.

4 Don't stop evening drinks, but go easy on fizzy and caffeine-containing drinks.

5 Be patient. Your child can only be dry at night once their body has started making a hormone that slows down urine production. No one can control that.

6 If your child has been dry for a while, and then starts wetting again, it could be caused by an infection. See your doctor.

7 Insecurities can cause bed-wetting. If there are problems at home it may be time to go back into night-time nappies again – just for a while. Just give lots of support.

8 Genes count. Bed-wetting can run in families, so if you or your partner were late being dry you'll need to be extra patient.

9 Encourage your child to use the toilet just before bed. Opinions vary as to whether you should 'lift' them in the night to take to the loo, but if it suits you, do it.

10 Keep spare bedding/nightwear handy for quick and easy night-time changes.

HELP A LEFT-HANDED CHILD

1 Don't make assumptions about which hand your child will use until about the age of four. Handedness can change.

2 Allow your child to use whichever hand suits them. Sometimes hand usage may be different for different activities.

3 When they start cutting-out, buy a pair of left-handed scissors. The blades are set differently, making cutting easier.

4 Position paper correctly for writing: place the paper to the left of your child and rotate the top to the right, at an angle.

5 Teach your child to hold their pencil correctly. He/she should grip the pencil between thumb, index and middle fingers.

6 Moulded, triangular pen/pencil grips may be a good idea; consider buying a specially designed left-handed pen.

7 Some left-handed children try to write from right to left. Draw a tiny cross in the top-left corner of the paper so he/she knows where to start.

8 Place drinking cups to the child's left side, as well as a spoon/knife.

9 Tie shoes standing opposite to your child or in front of a mirror, so that they can practise their way round.

10 When your child starts using a computer, a special left-handed mouse may be a good idea.

SEE TO SIBLING RIVALRY

1 **If you have a jealous toddler,** spend as much time as you can with him/her.

2 **Listen to your children** and take what they're saying seriously. Talk about how they feel and how they might resolve their problems for themselves.

3 **Remind your kids that they don't need to compete** for your love or attention.

4 **Hold back a little.** Your kids need to learn how to resolve problems themselves.

5 **Don't let fights get out of hand.** Listen to what's happening and step in if things start to get violent.

6 **Have a change of scene.** A trip to the park or a run around the garden may provide a welcome diversion.

7 **Don't get into the blame game.** Taking sides will get you nowhere. Unless it's really obvious who's at fault. You must be as impartial as you can.

8 **Give your children individual attention** as often as you can.

9 **Separate your kids** if the fighting gets too much.

10 **Set rules for things** like name-calling and physical fighting. Stick to them.

BOOST YOUR CHILD'S CONFIDENCE

1 **Give your child lots of praise.**

2 **Let your child know** that it's quite OK to make mistakes sometimes.

3 **Listen carefully to your kids** and make sure you've understood their problems. Respond, but let them keep talking.

4 **Help your child to express his/her feelings** and acknowledge them.

5 **Don't let your child think that you're criticizing them** as a person, just their bad behaviour.

6 **Take an interest in your child's life,** in their schoolwork and friends.

7 **Encourage your child to try out plenty of new things.** Succeeding at something will give them a massive confidence boost.

8 **Never ever laugh at your child.**

9 **Focus on your child's successes** rather than on any perceived failures.

10 **Don't put yourself down.** If they think you have poor self-esteem they may start to feel the same way about themselves.

TRIPS OUT WITH YOUR TOT

1 Ride the bus
2 Train journey
3 Zoo
4 Park
5 Gardens
6 Shops
7 Swimming pool
8 Museum/gallery
9 Play group
10 Library

TODDLER MEALTIMES WITHOUT TANTRUMS

1 **Conflict over food is always counterproductive.** Try not to get frustrated or angry with your fussy eater.

2 **Gentle, calm encouragement is best.** Try not to sound too desperate!

3 **Routine helps:** eat at the same times.

4 **If family mealtimes are hectic,** feed your toddler separately.

5 Variety is good, but it's not always essential – eating similar things most days is fine, as long as the food's nutritious.

6 Cook inexpensive foods and simple recipes – you're less likely to take it personally if you're child doesn't eat them.

7 Don't worry too much about eating foods in the 'wrong' order – if pudding is eaten before the main, it's fine, as long as what he/she eats is nutritionally balanced.

8 Don't make your toddler sit for hours over a half-eaten plate.

9 Let your child eat with his/her hands if necessary.

10 Never, ever physically force your child to eat.

TEACH YOUR TOT TO TALK

1 Talk and sing to your little one as much as you possibly can.

2 Listen to what your tot says and respond in an appropriate way.

3 Use lots of meaningful, individual words and repeat them all the time.

4 If your toddler says a 'wrong' word, don't criticize; simply use the correct one yourself when you repeat the phrase.

5 Offer praise when your tot repeats your words and sounds.

6 Read to your child every day and discuss what's in the story and pictures.

7 Involve your tot in all your activities so that all the new words become familiar.

8 Avoid just talking 'baby talk'. This might well hold up language development.

9 In a large family, try to find some one-to-one talking or reading time.

10 Remember that children develop at different rates. Einstein was three before he started to talk.

DISCIPLINE FOR LITTLE ONES

1 Encourage toddlers to express feelings. If children know they can, they are more likely to do what you ask them to do.

2 Only make hard-and-fast rules about really the important things – you can be flexible about the rest.

3 Don't punish your child for behaving like one. Children are high-spirited.

4 Talk to your partner and agree on a consistent disciplinary approach.

5 Praise the good behaviour and either ignore the bad or else explain calmly what was wrong.

6 Don't make empty threats. Your child will soon learn to ignore them.

7 Don't keep telling a child he/she is naughty or nasty – they will end up living up to the description.

8 When things go wrong, tell your child that you love him/her, but not the bad behaviour.

9 No point in dishing out punishment later. It should be immediate or not at all.

10 Never hit. If you're pushed to the point where you're about to lose it, step out of the room until you've calmed down.

BEST BEDTIMES

1 **Make your child's bedroom** into a comfortable, cosy place to be.

2 **Attractive bedding and nightwear** will make bedtime more appealing.

3 **Place a pretty light near the bed** that your child can control.

4 **Have favourite toys around the bed** to encourage solo play.

5 **Don't use bedtime as punishment.**

6 **Warn your child about upcoming bedtime,** so that activities can be finished.

7 **Establish a routine** in which there's something to look forward to at bedtime, whether it's a story, song or telling jokes.

8 **Leave the door ajar** so your child feels safely close to you.

9 **Say that you'll be back to check on your child in a while –** he/she will feel more secure and will have a deadline for going to sleep.

10 **If your child gets out of bed,** return him/her there straight away, without fuss.

HELP YOUR CHILD GET TO SLEEP

1 Routine
2 Milky drink
3 Warm bath
4 Calm
5 Story
6 Music/song
7 Nightlight
8 Cuddle
9 Soft toy
10 Leave decisively

HELP YOUR CHILD MAKE FRIENDS

1 **Talk to your child's teacher.** They might suggest a reason why he/she isn't making friends. You may need to help with shyness.

2 **Be a role model.** Your child will learn by watching you interacting with your own friends, neighbours and relatives.

3 **Making friends is all about developing social skills.** For a younger child, act out playing with friends using toys.

4 **To help older children socialize, talk through different scenarios** such as how to join in a game or how to take turns.

5 **Invite a potential friend to play.** Plan an activity in advance that the children will enjoy together and supervise carefully.

6 **Praise your child** when he/she gets on well with friends.

7 **Can you see an argument brewing?** Don't let it get out of hand and put your child off making friends. Step in kindly and help them sort it out.

8 **Arrange activities with other people** – clubs, outings and so on.

9 **Don't get anxious** if your child has few friends. It changes through childhood.

10 **Not all children need lots of friends** – some are happy with just one close friend or spending time alone.

TEACH YOUR CHILD TO SWIM

1 **Start by teaching safety around water** and then building confidence with lots of games in the bathtub and swimming pool.

2 **Toddlers often think they can swim** when in fact they can't. Don't leave them alone for a second.

3 **First of all, encourage floating** on the back while he/she kicks.

4 Blowing bubbles under water is a good way to teach your child how to get the face wet without swallowing water.

5 At four/five years your child may be ready for formal teaching. But don't force it. And remember that a child may love swimming one day and hate it the next. Be patient and they'll get there in the end.

6 Teach your child to relax and lie flat in the water, using a life vest, lying in your arms or holding onto the side of the pool at first.

7 Get your child to push off from the side towards you, so that he/she is moving while floating.

8 Get your child to start kicking independently – he/she shouldn't bend the knees too much.

9 Put in strong, slow arm movements.

10 When your child feels confident, demonstrate how to breathe by putting your face to the side, alternating with your arms. Your child will need lots of practice, but the basics are in place.

HAIR-WASHING WITHOUT TEARS

1 Make the whole of bathtime fun so that it's not an event to be dreaded.

2 Let your child see you washing your own hair so that it becomes a normal, painless thing to do.

3 Try a 'ring' that pulls over the head and sits below the hairline to stop water going into the eyes.

4 Get your child to hold a clean, soft flannel over the face to stop drips.

5 Encourage your child to help squeeze out the shampoo and lather.

6 Use a gentle, child-friendly shampoo.

7 Some children enjoy pouring water over themselves. If so, encourage it.

8 Bath toys may provide a distraction.

9 Be as quick as possible so the hair-washing is over without too much fuss.

10 Finish with a gentle conditioner to make combing through easier.

WHICH MUSICAL INSTRUMENT?

1 Let your child listen to a variety of instruments. He/she may immediately have a strong preference for one sound.

2 Play with toy instruments. Does your child show an interest in one in particular?

3 Visit a music store and try instruments from each separate group: woodwind, brass, strings, piano/ percussion.

4 Does the instrument physically fit your child? Some are too big or heavy for a small child, and it's worth him/her holding and playing an instrument a few times before committing to it.

5 If an instrument is too big, try an alternative – a flute instead of a clarinet or a cornet instead of the trumpet.

6 Is your child coordinated? Keyboards and strings are generally better suited for younger children than brass and woodwind.

7 Consider what tuition is available in

your area, and how much it will cost.

8 Group lessons are usually more fun, and cheaper, so choose an instrument your child can play with friends.

9 If you don't want to commit to buying an instrument just yet, rent one to begin with. Some schools loan them when you book lessons.

10 When you do decide to buy, get the best quality you can afford.

SAFETY FROM STRANGER DANGER

1 Don't dwell on unlikely, horrific possibilities. Concentrate on routine safety and make sure your child understands the rules.

2 Make sure your child knows never to accept gifts or sweets from strangers.

3 Tell your child never to go anywhere with anyone – even a friend – without asking you first.

4 Instruct your child to shout 'no' loudly if approached by someone they don't know and run to a safe place.

5 Don't advise: 'Don't talk to strangers'. Your child may need to ask for help from someone they don't know.

6 Tell your child what to do if you get separated when you're out and about.

7 Teach your child who to approach: uniformed policeman, security guards or shop-keepers if they need help.

8 Help your child to memorize his/her name, address and home phone number.

9 Encourage your child not to necessarily believe stories someone might tell them, such as mummy needing help or going to see some kittens.

10 Make sure your child knows he/she should tell you straight away if someone does approach them.

HORRID HEADLICE

1 Check your child's head for headlice at least once a week.

2 Use a pale-coloured comb. You'll see the dark lice more easily.

3 Check everyone who's been in contact with your child. They all need treatment.

4 Wet-combing is traditional, using a very fine-toothed comb on wet hair. Leave in some conditioner to ease combing.

5 Shorter hair is easier to comb.

6 Re-comb the hair on days five, nine and 13 to catch lice as they hatch, but before they lay eggs.

7 A medicated lotion or spray may be effective: ask your pharmacist for advice, and use it according to the instructions.

8 No need to wash/fumigate clothing or bedding. Headlice can only survive on humans and die after one/two days away from a scalp.

9 Even if you remove all headlice, your child can be re-infested if they come into contact with someone with headlice.

10 Getting headlice doesn't mean your child is dirty. Anyone with hair can be affected. And they love clean hair.

EASE CHILDHOOD AILMENTS

POSSIBLE SIGNS OF A SERIOUS ILLNESS

1 Stiff neck
2 A fit
3 Breathlessness
4 Severe abdominal pain
5 Unusually drowsy
6 Very pale
7 Spotty, purple-red rash
8 Repeated vomiting
9 Unresponsiveness
10 Turning blue

1 **Relieve the itching of chickenpox spots** by dabbing them with calamine lotion or essential oil of lavender.

2 **Ease the nasty congestion of a cold** by sitting your child in a 'tent' made from a towel over a bowl of steaming water. Add a few drops of essential oil of cinnamon to the water.

3 **To help a persistent cough,** avoid dairy products, offer plenty of fluids and encourage your child to sleep on his or her side rather than back.

4 **For croup,** sit in the bathroom with the door shut and hot taps running until the room fills up with steam. If the attack is severe, see a doctor immediately.

5 **For diarrhoea,** don't give your child solid foods but offer plenty of fluids (but not fruit juice or squash). See a doctor if the complaint lasts more than 48 hours, if there is blood in the diarrhoea, if your child is vomiting at the same time or if he/she has severe stomach ache.

6 **For mild ear ache,** crush some fresh garlic and mix with olive oil, then strain and soak a cotton ball in the mixture. Gently push the ball into the outer part of your child's ear to draw out the infection.

7 **For a mild tummy ache,** try a warm-water bottle on the stomach and give your child plenty of water.

8 **Lower a temperature** by taking off your child's clothes and sponging him/her with tepid water. Give paracetamol and cool drinks and see a doctor if the temperature is very high, lasts more than 24 hours or your child shows other symptoms.

9 **If your child is vomiting,** give very small sips of water, semi-skimmed milk or diluted fruit juice or squash. See a doctor if the problem persists or if you are worried in any way.

10 **Help prickly heat** by putting your child in loose, cotton clothing and giving him/her a cool bath or shower. Avoid heat and humidity: a fan will help, too.

ALL ABOUT POCKET MONEY

1 **Start giving pocket money** once your child understands that different things have different values.

2 **What does your child need/want to spend their money on?** If you think their requests are valid, you can work out an appropriate amount together.

3 **Rather than giving your child cash** you could open a bank account and deposit in it money regularly.

4 **Stick to the amount you have agreed** unless there are exceptional circumstances.

5 **It's quite reasonable to ask your child to do age-appropriate household chores** in return for pocket money.

6 **Set a day on which the chores must be done** and give pocket money straight after.

7 **Give small bonuses for extra chores,** or deduct money for bad behaviour.

8 **Raise pocket money** as time goes by.

9 **Encourage your child to save** a little of their pocket money each week.

10 **Keep a close eye** on how the pocket money is being spent.

OUCH! A CHILD WHO BITES

1 **Keep your reaction low-key.** Biting shouldn't be a means of getting attention.

2 **Say 'no'** and, if your child is old enough to understand, explain that biting is definitely not OK.

3 **Try to get your child to say sorry and then move on.**

4 **Never, ever bite back.** You'll be letting your child know that it's OK for you to bite.

5 **If your child looks as though he/she's about to bite,** try a diversionary technique to distract him/her.

6 **Stay close and watch** for signs of anger building up.

7 **Biting may be a sign** of tiredness, hunger or frustration. Deal with those issues and the biting should stop.

8 **Substitute a teething toy.** Sometimes a teething child will bite.

9 **If biting persists,** try a negative consequence such as not playing with your child for five minutes.

10 **Reward your child** for good (non-biting!) behaviour.

KEEP YOUR CHILD SAFE ON THE INTERNET

1 **Your child should never give out personal information** such as full names, addresses, name of school/work or phone numbers for themselves or family members.

2 **Your child should treat people they 'meet' on the internet** as if they were a stranger on the street.

3 **They should never post pictures** of themselves without consulting you first.

4 **Advise your child not to choose a provocative username.**

5 **People can pretend** to be anyone they want to be on the internet. Ensure your child understands that.

6 **Your child should never ever agree to meeting anyone** they've encountered on the internet without your permission.

7 **If your child does meet someone** from the internet in real life, a parent or trusted adult must go with them.

8 **Tell your child to never respond to rude/threatening messages.** Ask them to tell a parent or teacher instead.

9 **Don't let your child open emails** from someone you don't know.

10 **Consider using a filter** that only allows your child access to a pre-approved list of websites.

ADORABLE TWEENAGERS

1 **Reinforce a sense of security and self-esteem** by telling your child you love them and are proud of them, no matter what.

2 **Understand your pre-teen better** by getting to know their friends and asking what they do in and out of school. Talk about peer pressure and avoiding risky situations.

3 **Keep communicating with your child:** talk to them, listen and respond.

4 **Assign household chores –** it will give your pre-teen a sense of responsibility and self-esteem.

5 **Set clear rules about study hours,** curfews and behaviour, with fair, consistent consequences if they are not obeyed. If thing go wrong, discuss how your child should have behaved.

6 **Monitor friends, behaviour and his/ her whereabouts,** without snooping.

7 **Decide on a fair limit for time spent** on computers and other entertainment media. Encourage a wide variety of other hobbies and interests.

8 **Modify your rules and expectations** as your pre-teen matures. There's a heap of difference between an eight-year-old and a 12-year-old.

9 **Don't be offended** if it feels as though your child is pushing you away. He/she still needs you, but is starting to establish independence now.

10 **Establish trust** by giving your child a (safe) taste of independence.

SURVIVE SEX EDUCATION

1 **Make sure you know what you're talking about.** Do research if necessary.

2 **Have appropriate books, videos and articles available** to back you up.

3 **Map out what you plan to say.** Practise by talking to your partner first.

4 **Don't wait for your child to bring up the subject;** better to start the conversation yourself.

5 **Avoid making a big lecture.** Let your child ask questions and check how he/she is responding.

6 **Keep the conversations ongoing.** It's not a one-off, but a long-term topic.

7 **Make the atmosphere seem more casual** by having 'the chat' while you're both doing something else, like washing the dishes or walking the dog.

8 **You could start a conversation in response** to watching a love scene on TV.

9 **If you feel embarrassed, say so.** It could ease the tension.

10 **Don't be critical of your child's responses.** Listen calmly and make sure they know you're happy to talk further whenever they want.

MISTAKES TO AVOID MAKING WITH TEENAGERS

1 Lecturing
2 Not listening
3 Inconsistency
4 Unreasonable goals
5 Negativity
6 Ignoring problems
7 Not talking
8 Avoiding family time
9 Standing back
10 Giving up

CO-EXIST WITH A TEENAGER

1 **Expect some conflict** as your child becomes more independent. Just don't let it get out of hand.

2 **It's all about communication.** Listen, stay calm and decide what you want to

stand firm on and where you could make a few compromises.

3 **Teenagers need clear boundaries,** just like younger children.

4 **Respect your teenager's views,** even if

they are different to your own. But you can ask them to respect yours.

5 Take an interest in their friends, hobbies and schoolwork. Be supportive without piling on the pressure.

6 Ensure your teens tell you where they are going, who with, and what time they will be back. Do the same in return.

7 Clear a little time in your schedule so you can do ordinary things together.

8 Give teenagers their own space and respect their privacy.

9 Cultivate reserves of patience.

10 Encourage and praise teenagers and let them know that you love them and will always be there for them.

TELL-TALE SIGNS OF A DRUG PROBLEM

1 Change in appearance
2 New friends
3 Different interests
4 Loss of appetite
5 Disrupted sleep
6 Moodiness
7 Lack of communication
8 Lack of motivation
9 Poor school work
10 Out late

MAKE SURE TEENS STAY SAFE

1 Teenagers should keep valuables out of sight when they're out. Tell them not to fight back if someone tries to mug them.

2 Teens should be alert to what's around them. They should stick to well-lit roads. and consider carrying a personal alarm.

3 Educate yourself about drugs and talk frankly to your teenager about them.

4 Don't talk to your teen about drugs when you suspect they might be high. Keep calm and try not to overreact. If necessary, get help from a professional.

5 Warn your teen not to carry a weapon for self-defence. It is against the law and could be used against them.

6 Help your teenager develop a healthy attitude towards alcohol. Explain the risks and ensure that, if they drink, it is under parental supervision and limited.

7 Make sure your teen can get home safely at night.

8 Talk to your teen about sexually transmitted diseases, and discuss how they can stay safe.

9 Discuss the consequences of risky behaviour with your teen and suggest ways of dealing with peer pressure.

10 Place the computer in a family room so you can keep an eye on what your teenager is doing on it. Think carefully about the consequences of your teen having a computer in their own room.

JUGGLE WORK & CHILDREN

1 Stick to a consistent routine that is easy for everyone concerned to follow.

2 Prioritize the most important tasks, and don't worry about the non-essentials.

3 Make it easier to remember things by creating a to-do list, a calendar, diary or personal organizer, or set up reminders on your phone or computer.

4 Delegate as many tasks as possible. Children can tidy their own rooms and dads can do the cooking, for example.

5 Relieve any stress with some gentle exercise – go for a workout or a walk in the fresh air during your lunch break.

6 Find a school near to work – you'll be able to fit drop-offs, pick-ups and teacher meetings into your schedule more easily.

7 Make the most of family time together by eating as a family and setting aside time to relax together.

8 Have a back-up plan for when your child falls sick on one of your working days.

9 Try not to feel guilty. Everyone has to make compromises – do the best you can.

10 Take time for yourself occasionally. You deserve it.

BE A SUPER SINGLE PARENT

1 Develop a support network – family, friends, maybe even a local single-parent group. You'll need reliable childcare and people to turn to in an emergency.

2 Spend as much quality time with your children as you can.

3 Be respectful towards your ex-partner and never say anything negative about him or her in front of your children.

4 Never force your kids to take sides.

5 Give yourself time to relax and stay healthy. Eat as sensibly as you can and get plenty of exercise, too.

6 Boost your children's self-esteem with plenty of love and praise.

7 Accept help whenever it's offered.

8 Try not to over-indulge your children in an effort to compensate.

9 Don't involve your children in your problems, frustrations, anxieties or anger.

10 Don't dwell on your own problems more than you have to. Talk to someone else, if necessary, and learn from any mistakes you might have made.

BE A BRILLIANT DAD

1 Be an example. Your kids will learn everything from the way you behave rather than what you actually say.

2 Get involved with all aspects of child-care. Don't leave it to your partner.

3 Spend time alone with your kids doing special 'dad' things.

4 Cultivate patience and tolerance. You're going to need lots of both.

5 Think laterally. Not all parenting problems have an obvious solution.

6 Be flexible. Rules are good – but there are times when compromise is better.

7 Sharpen up your sense of humour. There aren't many tricky situations that can't be laughed away.

8 Listen properly to your children and respond appropriately.

9 Try to maintain your calm. Shouting and aggressive behaviour won't help anything. Quite the reverse

10 Support your child's schoolwork and hobbies – attend parent-teacher meetings and go to watch sports matches.

BE A MIRACLE MUM

1 **Aim high** – but don't expect perfection, of yourself or others.

2 **Be a mother first, not a friend.** Set boundaries and stick to them.

3 **Trust your instincts.**

4 **Give lavish praise and lots of love** – but avoid spoiling your kids with too many material things.

5 **Eat together,** at least some of the time.

6 **Don't hot-house your children** into over-achieving.

7 **Involve your partner** in all aspects of family life.

8 **Learn to let go.** Allow your children to be independent.

9 **Always be ready to listen or help.**

10 **Don't be a martyr to motherhood.** Make time for yourself, too.

FABULOUS GRANDPARENTHOOD

1 **Consider how involved you want to be.** Establish some ground rules with your son/daughter so that everyone knows how often you're happy to babysit, for example.

2 **Child-proof your home** so that there's nothing dangerous or breakable around.

3 **Kids need consistency** so be clear on your expectations of your grandchildren's behaviour. Ensure they chime with your son/daughter's own disciplinary system.

4 **It's not your job to raise your grand-children.** Don't over-step your role.

5 **Check with your son/daughter first.** Are they happy for you to give your grand-children sweets or other gifts?

6 **Don't indulge misbehaviour.**

7 **Spend quality time** doing activities with your grandchildren. Choose things they wouldn't get a chance to do normally.

8 **Share your hobbies or interests** with your grandchildren – these give them a different perspective on life.

9 **Create a sense of family history** for your grandchildren: tell them about what life was like when you were young and what your children were like as youngsters.

10 **Long-distance grandparents need to make a special effort** to keep in touch. Use the phone, letters, email and video calls so you stay involved with each other.

KEEP YOUR MARRIAGE ALIVE

1 **Create time to be alone together at home.** Put the children to bed a little earlier, if necessary.

2 **Keep in touch during the working day** with an email, phone call or text message

telling your partner that you care.

3 **Make time to go out together** – but not to the movies. Go where you can chat.

4 **Do something surprising and nice** for your partner every now and then.

5 Keep talking – your partner can't read your mind and grumpy silences won't help.

6 Have a break from your usual routine. Have a night out, a weekend away or perhaps try out a new activity together.

7 Listen to your partner, pay attention to their needs and be happy to support their interests.

8 Have time apart to do things you each love, and talk about them afterwards.

9 Have healthy arguments. Resolve your differences without getting upset and emotional and clear the air so that you can move on.

10 Have sex! Take turns to initiate and, if necessary, schedule in a 'date night'.

COPE WITH YOUR PARTNER LEAVING

1 Accept that the relationship is over – don't try to coerce or guilt-trip your ex back into it.

2 Don't dwell on damaging feelings of guilt or failure.

3 Avoid over-indulging in alcohol or other substances – it won't help.

4 Try to relax and find time to look after yourself.

5 If you're finding it hard to sleep, try herbal remedies or see your doctor.

6 Stick to your normal working routine.

It will help to give you focus.

7 Make an effort to see your friends, even if you don't feel very sociable.

8 Think about why the relationship is ending, so you can learn from any mistakes – but don't obsess or try to second-guess your ex's reasons.

9 Avoid seeing your ex for a while – it will only be harder to let go again.

10 Don't start thinking about a new relationship until you're sure that you've definitely moved on.

DEAL WITH DIVORCE

1 Try not to argue with your ex, even if he or she provokes you.

2 Never use the children as weapons. Their welfare should be top priority for both of you.

3 Create a support network of people who care for you.

4 Stay busy. Go to work, and keep your social life on track.

5 Prepare for your new life. Take up a new hobby or activity, make new friends and be positive about being single again.

6 Don't pry into your ex's personal life. It's no longer your business.

7 Cope with stress by keeping healthy, relaxing and talking to friends or seeing a professional.

8 Remain civil with your spouse, and set up systems for communicating, whether it's about children, finances or your home.

9 If you're feeling overwhelmed, take some time out. Rest and re-evaluate.

10 Give yourself time to get over it. It's OK to feel bad; the hurt will ease eventually.

HELP KIDS GET OVER DIVORCE

1 Expect your kids to be stressed, sad and confused at first. Listen to them, be patient and offer reassurance.

2 Provide routines so kids feel secure.

3 Tell the truth (broad brushstrokes not unsuitable details) about what's happened, in a simple, non-scary way.

4 Reassure them that you both love them and will always be there for them.

5 Be diplomatic. Criticizing your ex to your children will make them unhappy and could cause long-term damage.

6 Explain the practicalities clearly, so that your children know where they'll be at what times and with whom.

7 Listen to your children and acknowledge their feelings. Make sure they know that the divorce isn't their fault.

8 Never argue with your ex in front of the children; don't ask them to take sides.

9 Set aside your feelings about your ex and work with your kids' welfare in mind.

10 Both of you should remain involved in your children's lives.

SECOND MARRIAGE SUCCESS

1 Work out what went wrong in your first marriage and make sure you're not in danger of repeating the same mistakes.

2 Set aside embarrassment and talk to your new partner about all your deepest thoughts and beliefs about marriage. Ensure you know what you're getting into.

3 Let down your barriers. It can be hard after a divorce, but your new partner needs to know the real you.

4 Move house. A new marriage won't thrive if it's haunted by the old one.

5 Don't recreate the habits/routines of the old marriage – new partner, new life.

6 Be prepared to change and make compromises. If you're stuck in a rut the new marriage might end up in it, too.

7 Leave behind negative feelings from your first marriage. This is a fresh start.

8 Deal with financial issues head-on. There may be alimony or child support in the picture, and you need to know that everything has been resolved fairly.

9 Sort out the practicalities of dealing with children and stepchildren.

10 Try pre-marriage counselling to make sure you're establishing a strong foundation for your new lives together.

STEPCHILDREN – WHAT TO EXPECT

1 Don't expect stepchildren to be thrilled that you've married their mum/dad. Let them accept you on their terms.

2 Acknowledge stepchildren's feelings of loss, insecurity or resentment and show that you understand.

3 **Make sure that your stepchildren know that they are still loved** by everyone and just as important to both their parents as they were before.

4 **Look at your overall parenting styles.** Are they similar to your partner's?

5 **Spend time together as a family** on group activities. Have fun.

6 **Expect that genuine love or affection will take time to develop.**

7 **Routines help kids feel secure** as life in a stepfamily can be complex.

8 **Ask everyone in the new family to treat each other respectfully.**

9 **Build your own broad shoulders.** Don't take a negative attitude or lack of enthusiasm from stepchildren personally.

10 **Try holding family meetings** so that everyone can feel as though they're having a genuine say in what's happening. Be polite and never ignore others, no matter how young. Don't feel hurt or withdraw.

MAKE YOUR WILL

1 **Make a list of all your dependants,** and anyone else to whom you'd like to give something. They are your 'beneficiaries'.

2 **How much money would your dependants need** in the event of your death? Write a list of all your assets and liabilities and work out how much you should give and to whom.

3 **Be clear about individual items you want to give** – in some cases it will be necessary to describe them.

4 **Include full names and addresses of all your beneficiaries** so that they can be properly identified.

5 **Choose a guardian for your children** (if they are under 18) and get their agreement to do it. You may want to have a second choice in case your first choice cannot take on the responsibility. Decide at what age you want your children to receive their inheritance.

6 **Choose trusted executors** who are not only capable of the job, but are unlikely to die before you do.

7 **Be wary of DIY wills.** If you do go for one, get it checked by a legal professional who has the relevant experience.

8 **Include your wishes** for funeral and burial arrangements.

9 **Update your will** if personal or financial circumstances change.

10 **Keep the will somewhere safe** – usually either with your solicitor or in a bank vault.

CARING FOR AN ELDERLY RELATIVE

1 **Consult your relative,** if possible, over all important decisions and what they really want.

2 **Check if plans have already been made** for dealing with certain situations, such as health care or finances.

3 **Organize your important documents,** especially anything relating to finances.

3 List all of the medication that your relative is taking and check with your relative's doctor that the medicines are not interacting.

4 In a period of transition, establish a routine to structure each day. This will help organization and reassure the relative.

5 If you don't know your relative well, find out about their likes and dislikes, and try to establish a genuine bond with them.

6 Give yourself regular planned breaks, so you can recharge your batteries.

7 Consult with your siblings or other relatives on long-term care issues.

8 Try to avoid a situation where one person feels they are doing all the work. If this does happen, make sure that person receives plenty of moral support.

9 Be patient and try to understand issues from your elderly relative's point of view. How would you want to be helped if you were in their shoes?

10 Make the most of any local services for the elderly.

CHOOSING CARE

1 Consult your relative, who may have strong opinions about being/not being moved into a home. Discuss the options.

2 Check the services and care offered by any prospective care home. Assess your relative's needs. Do they simply require help at mealtimes or have they got medical issues that require 24-hour supervision?

3 Visit prospective care homes at different times of day. Drop in unannounced. Ask questions.

4 Is the home clean, tidy and homely?

5 Are the staff warm and welcoming, caring and patient?

6 Location is important. Do you want your relative to be near by? If they go out by themselves, is the new home near shops, clubs, friends and transport?

7 Research the costs of different homes. The most expensive home may not necessarily be the best.

8 Money is an issue. Is there insurance? If not, who will pay? How much money is available? For how long? What state-run facilities are available?

9 If you and they prefer for them to stay in their own home, is this possible? Would their home have to be modified? Who would come to look after them? How often? Who would finance this?

10 Consider asking your relative to move in with you. How would you and your family cope? Is it really what your relative wants?

COPING WITH BEREAVEMENT

1 Go easy on yourself for a while. Expect that you'll feel more disorganized than usual and perhaps make mistakes.

2 Get proper sleep and eat healthily.

3 Take some exercise – you'll feel better for it.

4 **Limit alcohol intake.** It may make you feel better initially, but you could end up drinking too much or relying on alcohol to get you through this difficult time.

5 **Treat yourself.** A sweet-smelling bunch of flowers or a coffee with a friend will give you a boost.

6 **Talk to a good friend** – it's best if they're not too closely involved. Air your feelings and it will help to ease the pain.

7 **Consider joining a local bereavement support group.**

8 **Remembering the good times** is a healthy part of the healing process.

9 **Don't rush into making big changes to your life.** Take things slowly and wait until you have properly adjusted to your loss.

10 **Don't expect to 'get over it' by a certain time.** We all heal differently, but the pain will lessen eventually.

A CARING CONDOLENCE LETTER

1 **Write and send the letter promptly,** preferably within a fortnight of the death.

2 **Hand-write the letter** – it will seem more personal.

3 **Don't get fancy.** A poem is fine if it comes naturally to you, but otherwise keep it simple and just write how you feel.

4 **Write down a little about the special qualities** of the deceased.

5 **Add any meaningful memories** or a favourite anecdote.

6 **You might want to offer help of some sort.** A specific offer may be better than a general 'call if you need anything' – you could help with shopping, the children, housework or cooking.

7 **If you were very close to the deceased person or their family,** you may want to write a fairly long letter. But if they were a passing acquaintance or someone you didn't know well, a short note is enough.

8 **Draft the letter first,** to avoid making mistakes. Read it through carefully.

9 **Choose appropriate stationery** or an illustrated card.

10 **End the letter with a sympathetic word or phrase,** such as 'you are in our thoughts' or 'my love is with you always'.

ARRANGING A FUNERAL

1 **Don't rush to make decisions.** It's fine to take whatever time you need.

2 **Check the deceased person's papers** – their will, for example, may state how they wish to be buried.

3 **If no funeral decisions have been made,** decide on burial or cremation, a traditional or modern service, religious or otherwise and any special touches

4 **Who will pay for the funeral?** There may be a provision in the will. Check whether the deceased had an insurance plan or pension scheme that covers it.

5 **Funeral expenses can mount up.** There's no harm in shopping around. Check the details to see exactly what's included.

6 **Put an announcement** in the newspaper and/or relevant publications.

7 **Compile a list of people to invite –** you may need to consult other members of your family.

8 **Would you like people to send flowers?** Some people prefer to ask for donations to charity instead.

9 **Include as many personal elements** in the service as possible, from music and poems to flowers and photographs, to help with the healing process.

10 **Will you need caterers for after the funeral?** Decide whether you will do this yourself, book a professional or go to a restaurant, pub or other public venue.

THE IDEAL PET FOR YOU

1 **Think about why you want a pet.** Is it for companionship, to get you out on walks, for the children? Do you want a cuddly pet, one that can learn tricks, or one that doesn't require much attention?

2 **Consider how much time you can spend looking after a pet.** Reptiles, for example, require great care in setting up and maintaining, while mice or rats, which are relatively easy to look after, require regular cleaning out. Dogs need walking and some require frequent grooming.

3 **What about costs?** Pedigree animals can be expensive and all pets cost money to keep. Budget for food, insurance, training, spaying/neutering, enclosures, vet visits, holiday care, grooming and toys. Least expensive pets include small birds, hamsters and goldfish, while the most expensive are rare breeds or exotic pets.

4 **Look at your available space.** You're better off having some outdoor space if you decide on a dog or cat, while small mammals, reptiles, birds and fish live happily indoors.

5 **Do you have any animal-related dislikes, fears or allergies?** Lots of people wouldn't like a pet snake or spider, while some are allergic to cats, dogs or horses. Try handling your prospective pet before

you commit to buying it.

6 **Are you out a lot?** If you are at work all day or at night, a dog won't be right. Cats can be left alone all day, but like to be fussed once you're home.

7 **Are you allowed to keep a pet where you live?** In some properties, you might be allowed a fish tank but not a dog. If you are planning to get an exotic animal, check whether there is legislation that might require you to register it.

8 **Do you have a baby or young children?** If so, whatever pet you choose must be safe for them. Small mammals such as gerbils may bite, or be too quick for kids to handle easily, and even the cutest kitten has scratchy claws. Dogs can be ultra-gentle, snappy or risky, while fish may not be the most exciting family pet .

9 **How will you handle problems and emergencies?** Pets do get sick or injured and you'll need to get them treated as quickly as possible. Are you properly set up for this?

10 **Who will look after your pet when you're away on holiday?** Most areas have kennels and catteries, or pet-sitters, or you may have a friend or neighbour who is willing to help.

CHOOSE THE RIGHT DOG

1 Pedigree or crossbreed?
2 Rescued dog?
3 Lively or couch potato?
4 Does size matter?
5 Gentle or guard dog?
6 Good with other pets?
7 Good with kids?
8 Affectionate or aloof?
9 Non-moulting?
10 Puppy or adult?

HEEL! PUPPY-TRAINING

1 Allow plenty of time and be patient. Your puppy wants to please you, but it may take a while to get everything right.

2 Several short sessions a day are better than one long session. Like children, puppies have a short attention span.

3 Puppy class is great for teaching your dog to socialize with others and for you both to learn some basic skills.

4 Be committed and consistent.

5 Be firm but kind. Dogs work best when they are rewarded for good behaviour, not punished when they go wrong.

6 Learn what motivates your puppy – food, a toy or simply a word of praise.

7 Repeat, repeat, repeat. Your puppy learns by doing the same thing over and over again.

8 Take your puppy around with you (in a carrier if he hasn't had all his shots) to meet different people and experience as many different situations as possible

9 Consider 'clicker' training, which is a simple and effective way to 'shape' your puppy's behaviour.

10 Don't stop training just because you've finished the course or your puppy has grown up. Continue all your dog's life.

PAMPERED POOCH POWER

1 Buy 'complete' or 'balanced' food and remember that a dog's nutritional needs can change over the course of its life.

2 Ceramic food dishes are the ideal choice as they are heavy enough not to tip over, can go in the microwave and dishwasher and last for years.

3 A dog can't tell the difference between an old shoe that you don't mind him chewing and a new one. Give him toys that don't resemble precious items that you'd prefer him to leave alone.

4 Old soft toys make a good dog toy, but if your dog likes to chew them up, remove button eyes, wires or other potential choking hazards first.

5 Keep a plastic water bottle and a bowl in the boot of the car so your dog has something to drink straight after an energetic walk.

6 Tinned or dry food? Tinned food is appetizing but can't be left out for long; dry food is good for your dog's teeth and is often better for dogs that are prone to gaining weight.

7 Clip your dog's nails if they touch the floor when he is standing. Wait till he's sleepy or relaxed, use special trimmers and clip where the nail curves, just above the pink quick.

8 Brush your dog regularly – it stimulates blood flow and distributes natural skin oils. If your dog's fur is matted, work some baby oil through the area first.

9 Check your dog's paws regularly for cuts, cracks or punctures. Small cuts should be cleaned and covered with anti-biotic ointment. For dry foot pads, apply a light coat of petroleum jelly.

10 Clean your dog's teeth with a doggy toothpaste and either a soft brush or some gauze wrapped around your finger.

CUTE KITTENS! ALL YOU NEED TO KNOW

1 **Kittens need extra protein,** so give them special kitten food, not cat food.

2 **After weaning or because of stress kittens can suffer from diarrhoea.** This can cause dehydration, which may be fatal if not treated quickly by a vet.

3 **Eye problems in kittens are common;** take yours to the vet if you are worried.

4 **Use a litter tray from when they are four weeks old.** Pop the kittens in after every meal. Gently rub their paws in the litter as if they were scratching, to give them the right idea.

5 **Expose your kitten to as many different experiences as possible,** so he/she can get used to all aspects of life, from being around the vacuum cleaner to going in the car.

6 **Stop your kitten from clawing the furniture** by getting a scratching post and using repellant spray or stick-on strips anywhere you don't want destroyed.

7 **Don't let little children pick up kittens unsupervised –** they squeeze and the kitten bites or scratches. It's best if the child sits down with an adult and lets the kitten approach them.

8 **Don't let a kitten go outside** until all the vaccinations are complete.

9 **Introducing a new kitten to other pets?** Do it slowly and give him/her space to approach them or run away. Fuss over the others, so they don't get jealous.

10 **Ignore a kitten's bad behaviour and reinforce the good** with cuddles and rewards of food or toys.

FELINE FACTS: CARE FOR YOUR CAT

1 **Cats need a hiding place or they can become stressed.** Make sure your cat can always get to one. High-up places are a good option, if there's a choice.

2 **Place your cat's litter tray in a quiet place,** well away from where she eats or sleeps. Clean it regularly.

3 **If you have two or more cats,** make sure they have room to get away from each other if they want to.

4 **Cats can't be vegetarian.** They need several small, meat-based meals a day and plenty of water. A good-quality, complete dry food is best.

5 **Give your cat plenty of opportunities for exercise and play –** toys, scratching posts, feathers and small balls to chase (a scrunched-up piece of foil is perfect).

6 **Don't shout at or punish your cat –** he/she won't understand what's going on, and if they behave badly it is usually a sign of stress or illness.

7 **Don't give your cat cow's milk.** Water is best, or for an occasional treat give special cat milk.

8 **A cardboard box lined with a towel makes a great cat bed.**

9 **Don't use a cardboard box as a cat-carrier –** they're too easy to claw through. A proper plastic one or a basket is best.

10 **After you have moved house,** keep your cat indoors for at least a week. Don't let her out until you're sure he/she is properly settled in.

LOOKING AFTER A RABBIT

1 You need a lot of space if you want to keep rabbits. Provide room for hopping, running, jumping, digging, stretching out when lying down and standing on back legs without the ears touching the roof of the hutch.

2 Rabbits need somewhere safe to hide (a cardboard box or a pipe) if they feel afraid. They should have separate areas for food, rest and going to the toilet.

3 Let rabbits make friends – they are sociable animals and like to be kept with at least one other friendly rabbit.

4 Give your rabbit a chance to exercise every day. They're most active in the early morning, late afternoon and at night.

5 Give your rabbits toys to play with and interact with.

6 Encourage foraging by giving your rabbit hay in a rack, tube or box and then scatter food in it.

7 Rabbits should always have access to good-quality hay, for their dental and digestive health.

8 Give your rabbits their own sandbox for digging in.

9 Rabbits may nibble electrical wire, house plants and soft toys. Make sure your home is bunny-proof before you set your pet loose inside.

10 Cut the carrots. Rabbits should mainly eat hay or grass. Give the occasional root vegetable as a treat only.

HOW TO KEEP GUINEA PIGS

1 Not too hot and not too cold: guinea pigs are sensitive to temperature changes, and should be kept in an environment that is 15–26°C (60–78°F).

2 Keep guinea pigs calm. These are creatures of habit and they don't like too much noise and activity.

3 Bust guinea pig boredom. Guinea pigs are intelligent and like to explore, play and gnaw. Give them toys and an interesting environment and play with them.

4 Provide a safe space. Guinea pigs need a place to hide, where they feel secure.

5 A great guinea pig home is dry, draught-free, well ventilated, spacious, with a shelter and some horizontal pipes for them to get some exercise in.

6 Dogs and cats are guinea pigs' natural predators. Keep them well away.

7 Avoid giving guinea pigs oranges and other citrus fruit. Give hay, fresh grass, leafy greens and pellets. Small amounts of root veg/fruit make a good treat.

8 Be gentle. A guinea pig won't understand shouting or punishment and it will only scare them. Bad behaviour indicates stress or a medical problem.

9 Most guinea pigs prefer to live with another friendly guinea pig.

10 Handle your guinea pig gently from a young age – it will see you as a friend and companion.

SOOTHING TROPICAL FISH

1 Choose your fish before setting up your aquarium, as different fish have varying requirements.

2 It's easiest to start with freshwater fish, as looking after a marine aquarium is a far more complex prospect. Choose a hardy species and remember that some fish are only ever happy if they are a member of a shoal of a certain size.

3 The bigger the tank the better – more water means it's better quality and there's less chance of compatibility problems between fish.

4 A good lid on top of the tank is important – some fish like to jump and you don't want them to jump out!

5 Consider fishy water requirements. For fully grown fish, allow a minimum of 45 litres (10g) of water, with 4.5 litres (1g) of water for every 2.5cm (1in) of fish.

6 Add water plants to provide oxygen and somewhere for the fish to hide.

7 Add a filter, a light and a heater. Choose a straightforward system that will be easy to look after.

8 Don't put your aquarium in direct sunlight such as on a windowsill. It will affect the water temperature and may cause green algae to grow.

9 Don't put fish straight into a new tank. Allow three weeks or so to establish a healthy microbial colony first.

10 Change the water regularly as stale water can be very harmful to fish.

TWEET! A BIRD FOR A PET

1 Choose as large a cage as possible. Your bird should be able to spread both its wings out and turn around without touching the sides of the cage.

2 Larger birds like to climb, so they need a high cage, while smaller birds like to be able to fly within the cage, so require a longer enclosure.

3 Provide perches with different diameters to prevent foot problems. Clean, natural branches are good for this.

4 Ensure the door has a bird-proof latch and that your bird can't get any parts of its body wedged between the bars.

5 Supplement dry seed with fresh green seeds, fruit, vegetables and perhaps vitamins and minerals.

6 Check your bird regularly: it should have bright eyes, clean, shiny feathers, a good appetite and be energetic and active.

7 Don't let your bird fly free inside the house unless you're certain you've shut all the doors and windows. Turn off ceiling and floor fans, close the toilet lid, cover air ducts and either pull blinds/close curtains or put a sticker on the window to warn your bird it's there. Supervise your bird whenever it's out of the cage.

8 Parrots can be very destructive. Encase electric wiring in plastic tubing and keep an eye on them when they're loose.

9 Be careful with cleaners and sprays – birds are very sensitive to airborne toxins.

10 Dogs and cats are natural predators – ensure the cage is safe and shut other pets away when the bird is flying free.

ELIMINATE ANIMAL SMELLS

1 **If your pet has peed,** soak up as much as possible by blotting the spot with paper towels. Clean it thoroughly with warm, soapy water and allow to dry.

2 **For stale urine smells,** sprinkle baking soda over the area, leave for 20 minutes or so, then vacuum up.

3 **White vinegar neutralizes odours.**

4 **Try a commercial cleaner,** but avoid anything containing ammonia, as the smell can actually encourage cats to pee again in the same place.

5 **Spot-test any cleaners in advance** in case they stain your flooring.

6 **Don't use a steam-cleaner or blow-dryer on pet stains:** the warmth can set the stain and odour more firmly.

7 **For persistent smells,** lift the flooring to check whether pee has gone through. If it's necessary, clean the underside of your carpet or vinyl, as well as the sub-floor.

8 **To keep your carpets smelling fresh,** sprinkle baking soda or commercial powder freshener on the carpet once a week before vacuuming.

9 **Have carpets professionally cleaned** once or twice a year.

10 **Groom and wash your pet regularly.**

CHOOSE A PET-SITTER

1 **Ask the pet-sitter to come to your home** and meet your pet. Do they get on?

2 **Ask about training and experience.**

3 **What services does the pet-sitter offer?** As well as checking your pets are OK, feeding them and keeping their toilet area clean, sitters may also exercise pets, play with them and groom them.

4 **Have they got insurance?**

5 **If your pet needs medication,** is the sitter happy to give it?

6 **Get references from other clients.**

7 **When would the sitter check on your pet?** For how long and how often?

8 **What happens if your pet becomes ill?** Is the sitter associated with a vet or will they use yours? What about payment?

9 **If the sitter become ill or is unable to look after your pets,** do they have a back-up arrangement?

10 **Write a written contract** that details all terms and conditions, services and fees.

PET-PROOF YOUR HOME

1 **Be careful about plants in your house and garden.** Many common species are poisonous to animals.

2 **Make sure your pet can't get at** your cleaning products, rat poison, ant-killer, insecticides or medication.

3 **Make your fences and gates secure,** and check them regularly.

4 **Keep chocolate out of reach of your dog** – it's a danger to pooches.

5 **Find any small holes** that your pet could squeeze into and screen them off.

6 **Keep the lid on your rubbish bin.** Don't let your cats/dogs rummage through potentially hazardous stuff.

7 **Hide or cover up electrical wires.** Dogs, cats, rabbits and other pets may be tempted to gnaw through them.

8 **Take care when using bleach, anti-freeze** and other products. If you spill them, flush the area well with water in case your pet tries to lick them up.

9 **Get a good book** that lists common pet poisons, symptoms of poisoning, and what to do in case of emergency.

10 **Keep your vet's and emergency vet's** telephone numbers handy.

GIVE MEDICINE TO YOUR CAT/DOG

1 **Check if the medicine should be given** with food or on an empty stomach.

2 **Wrap a pill in a piece of meat,** a cube of cheese or some peanut butter.

3 **A capsule can be broken and mixed** into tasty wet food to disguise it.

4 **Check before you crush pills and mix them into wet food** – some types need to be taken whole.

5 **Dip a pill into a small amount of butter** to help it slide down a cat's throat.

6 **If you have to hold your cat to give it medicine,** it may help to gently wrap a towel around it to stop it clawing you. This can work with a bird, too.

7 **Buy a plunger** to help get a pill or liquid to the back or side of a cat's mouth.

8 **Once you've popped a pill into a cat's mouth,** hold the mouth closed and stroke the cat's neck or blow on its nose to help it to swallow.

9 **Don't mix medication with a whole meal.** If your pet doesn't finish the meal, he won't have received the proper dose.

10 **Be calm, talk in a happy voice.** End the session with praise or a treat.

STOP YOUR PET GETTING LOST

1 **Pet-proof outdoor areas** with fencing or chicken wire so pets can't get out.

2 **Keep garden gates shut.** Put up a sign to tell visitors to shut them, too.

3 **Transport cats in a secure carrier only.**

4 **Keep your dog on a lead** in an unfamiliar area, and anywhere else if you are not certain it will come when called.

5 **Don't let your pets roam free.**

6 **Put a collar on your cat or dog,** with your current phone number on it.

7 **Have your pet microchipped.** If its collar comes off it can still be identified.

8 **Train pets to come to a call or whistle.**

9 **Take good-quality photos** so that you can put up posters if your pet goes missing.

10 **Spay or neuter your pets** – they'll be less likely to wander.

FIND A LOST PET

1 Search the house
2 Walk the neighbourhood
3 Ask around
4 Call your pet
5 Listen out
6 Advertise
7 Ask at vets
8 Put up posters
9 Check animal rescue
10 Offer a reward

BEAUTY
& WELLBEING

Wondering how to max your clothes appeal or pep up your crowning glory? Look no further. Here you'll find all the tips you need to help you look your very best – everything from selecting a perfect little black dress, looking stunning in a swimsuit to maxing your memory.

LOOK GOOD AS THE YEARS GO BY

1 Invest in a good haircut that suits your age and stage. Find a good stylist who will be objective. There's no point opting for the latest style if it's too young – but you don't have to look 'old' either. Don't cling to your past – move forward with grace and imagination. Long hair looks wrong past a certain age so go for a chic short cut. If you are greying, shorter hair is more suitable. Gentle colours are best for dyes – dark colours can look too harsh.

2 Sleeves are the way forward – at a certain age, it's best to cover up. Sleeves are so much more, well, stylish. Look for styles that maximize arm coverage – for added elegance. Then you won't need to worry about bagginess you can't control.

3 When it comes to wearing make-up as you age, less is more. Don't leave home without a touch of make-up, but don't overdo it, either. A little lipstick is all you need – there's no need to go for the full slap. Don't choose dark shades of lipstick – go for a shade nearest your natural colour. Try eye pencils instead of liquid liners, which are too harsh on older eyes. Choose eyeshadows carefully to make your eyes stand out, but softly. Defining your eyes can make you look younger, so a touch of mascara and curling your lashes creates a youthful look.

4 A glowing skin can take years off you so devote time to good skincare. Don't just cleanse and moisturize, exfoliate weekly and consider taking antioxidants and vitamin-A products.

5 It's a fine line between looking dowdy and dressing age-appropriately. Don't wear clothes that really are too young – nor too old either. Be honest about what looks good and use a three-way mirror when trying things on. Dressing younger won't make you look younger, but you don't have look dull either – go for elegance instead. There are many ways to show off your best points without trying to look like your daughter – or granddaughter. Have confidence in your personal style.

6 Dress for your best feature. Accentuate the positives. Whether you have lovely eyes, gorgeous hair, nice legs, good hands – play up the good bits; downplay the rest. Nice hands deserve to be shown of with pretty rings, for example.

7 Update your wardrobe with seasonal accessories not the latest fashionable clothes. Small items such as scarves and necklaces can be great value; they are on trend for a short time, but can make you look really up to the minute.

8 Invest in classic clothing styles. Go for simple, enduring looks. It's worth spending out on good-quality items that you can wear year on year. Care and repair will make them last. Buy basic well-cut trousers, jackets, skirts and mix and match with colourful blouses and sweaters.

9 Learn what colours look best on you and build your wardrobe around them. Solid colours are more sophisticated than patterns and offer more opportunities to accessorize with the latest trends. Save time by just choosing from your personal colour palette and ignoring all the rest. Don't be afraid to go for strong shades. Red can be a flattering accent colour, so don't shy away from it!

10 Always stand up straight! Posture becomes more important as time goes by and slouching can really pile on the years. Don't forget – there's nothing wrong with getting older. We all have to do it!

CREATE A CAPSULE WARDROBE

1 Jeans
2 Long-sleeved shirts
3 T-shirts
4 Cardigan
5 Sweater
6 Trousers
7 Jacket
8 Skirt
9 Dress
10 Coat

DRESS SLIM

WARDROBE CLASSICS

1 Tailored dress
2 Ballet pumps
3 Cinch belt
4 A-line skirt
5 Camisole top
6 Perfect bra
7 Tailored shorts
8 Chiffon blouse
9 Trench coat
10 Petticoat

1 **Dress all in one plain colour** (dark colours are more slimming) – it will create a held-together look that is smarter and sleeker than lighter shades and patterns.

2 **Black is still the most slimming colour** – until someone invents another one!

3 **Loose, shapeless clothes don't hide the flab.** In fact, they'll often have the opposite effect, making you look bigger.

4 **Colour-blocking is a great concept for slimmers!** Carefully juxtaposed strong shades distract from unappealing parts.

5 **Shoulder pads can make you look slimmer.** Back to the eighties!

6 **Wear vertical not horizontal stripes.** Slimming and nice and fresh in summer

7 **Tapered trouser legs can help give you a slimmer look.**

8 **Don't wear your clothes too tight!** Body-con is for young, thin things – it's a mistake to think that constraining, stretchy clothes are slimming. Go for tailored items that flow over your shape gracefully. As for undies – straps that dig in and shapers that bite only enhance the very things you want to conceal.

9 **Heels are good –** the higher the heel, the slimmer you will look.

10 **Longer cuts are best.** Short jackets are less flattering, but if you do wear one, keep it unbuttoned to display additional vertical lines.

ALL ABOUT EXCELLENT UNDERPANTS

1 **Comfort is everything.**

2 **Boyshorts are great for ladies with boyish figures,** but not if your waist is small and your thighs wide.

3 **Cotton lets you breathe.**

4 **If you choose satin and lace they may itch or rub.**

5 **A visible pantie-line must be avoided.** So choose carefully when you are teaming underwear with clothes.

6 **Figure-shaping underwear can feel hot** and restrictive.

7 **Thongs and g-strings must fit well.** If they are too loose or too tight they can be dreadfully uncomfortable.

8 **When buying for your partner,** don't guess – get their size first.

9 **There are 'green' pantie options.** Look for eco cottons online.

10 **Change your panties every day.**

ACQUIRE A WELL-FITTING BRA

1 **Measure yourself accurately** or use a personal bra-fitting service. Most good stores do this for free.

2 **Make sure that the band across your back** lies horizontally.

3 **You shouldn't be able to pull the band**

away from your back more than 5cm (2in).

4 **The shoulder straps should not dig** into your shoulders.

5 **The cups should contain your breasts,** the nipples should be in the fullest parts.

6 **Move up a cup size** if your breasts bulge over the bra.

7 **Move down a cup size** if you notice wrinkles in the bra fabric.

8 **The wire should sit behind the breasts.**

9 **The bra fabric between your breasts** should lie flat on your breastbone.

10 **Try on lots of brands and styles** to find out what suits you best as they vary.

STUNNING IN A SWIMSUIT

1 **Preparation is key before you go shopping for a swimsuit.** Before you strip off, update hair removal, get a pedicure and have a quick spray tan.

2 **If you like swimming, diving, surfing or sailing, go all-in-one.** It's more likely to remain on your person.

3 **A tankini suits those who want a two-piece effect** without flashing the flesh.

4 **If you're small on top,** go for a cozzie with ruffles/fringes for an enlarging effect.

5 **If you have a bigger bust,** go for an underwired top-half rather than fly-by-night stringy things.

6 **Put bright colours and bold prints on or around your best bits.** Stick to dark colours on parts you wish to downplay.

7 **Don't forget the accessories.** You can get away with wearing that old black favourite if you dress it up with a wonderful floaty caftan. A wide-brimmed sunhat and pair of sexy shades pile on the glamour.

8 **Good quality's worth the extra.** Bust support, linings and stomach control panels are worth their weight in gold.

9 **Minimizer swimsuits can be great** for a slimming effect. They smooth out bulges, but be careful about creating extra ones.

10 **Embellishments such as beads and embroidery** can look good, but can easily get caught on all manner of things, such as seaweed, sunbeds and other swimmers.

DRESS UP FOR A BIG NIGHT OUT

1 **Keep your attire simple when you're going clubbing,** but add a bit of sparkle and bling, clever accessories, heels suitable for dancing and a small shoulder bag.

2 **Choose between showing cleavage and legs – never both at the same time.** Pair a top with a plunging neckline with skinnies or trousers and if you're wearing a short dress, keep the neckline high.

2 **Hair can go 'big' and your make-up loud.** Now's the time to be brave and bold.

3 **Smart jeans are fine** when you're spending the night in pubs and wine bars. They're good teamed up with a glitzy blouse or sparkly sweater. Add eye-catching accessories to pull your look together.

4 **Dinner parties are up for grabs,** though smart with a hint of glamour is ideal.

5 For a meal in a restaurant, smart casual is the order of the day. This could mean a skirt and top with heels – it all depends on how upmarket the venue is.

6 Pay attention to shapes. Always put a skinny top with a full skirt; a floaty top with narrow jeans.

7 If your outing has a theme – go for it, but if you're on public transport, think practical. Otherwise smart casual.

8 Your little black dress will come into its own at a Christmas party. Dress it up or down, depending on your mood or the venue and company.

9 Wear something glamorous for the office bash – different from what you usually wear for work. Be warned, though, plunging necklines and extra-short minis may attract the wrong type of attention.

10 Long gowns suit a formal dinner dance – perhaps halter-neck or strapless. You'll need a clever little clutch bag, too.

TEETER IN HEELS

1 Start small. Start with a two-inch heel and work your way upwards.

2 Don't break in a new pair of heels on your first date with someone. Wear your shoes a few times first to wear them in.

3 Take small steps. Wearing heels makes your stride shorter, so don't expect to walk as fast as you normally do.

4 Sit down every ten minutes or so. You'll last longer in them that way.

5 Customize your heels and cushion them. Once you've worn your shoes in and have detected areas that rub, put in gel cushions and rub-relief strips to make things really comfy.

6 Walk heel to toe, not toe to heel. Your stride will look natural and you'll be more balanced. Watch how models do it.

7 To stop you slipping in your heels, put a traction pad on the bottom of the shoe. Or, for a quick fix, roughen up the bottoms of your soles with coarse sandpaper.

8 Try wearing heels with eyes closed first – before you start walking. This will help you focus on your core muscles to assist your balance.

9 Step as if walking on a straight line. This'll give you the 'model sway'.

10 Don't wear high heels all day, every day. Alternate them with flats. Perhaps take trainers in your bag to change into for the journey home.

ULTIMATE ACCESSORIZING

1 Going for a large, ornate hat means you have to keep the rest of your outfit streamlined and simple. A compact hat might go better with a more ornate outfit.

2 Don't over-accessorize. Choose one piece as your focal point. Try chandelier earrings and a cocktail ring rather than big earrings and an ornate necklace.

3 The size of the accessories should mimic the size of the person.

4 **Necklaces are great** if you want to fill in a scooped, V-shaped or low neckline. Long chains or strings of beads add style and sparkle and can be extremely flattering.

5 **Don't use day accessories for an evening event** and vice versa.

6 **Bags and shoes don't always need to be the same colour.** Choose one in a colour or pattern and the other neutral.

7 **Make sure you put on stockings and tights straight,** to avoid patterns or seams twisting in an unsightly fashion. Black tights look good with short skirts and boots, while flesh-coloured ones are great with strappy shoes and floaty dresses.

8 **Scarves add a splash of colour** near the face and give you a fresher look. They also fill that awkward gap.

9 **A good bag is every girl's must-have accessory,** but it should be practical. A lovely, well-chosen bag, organized with pockets and places to keep all the things you need to hand is a sheer delight.

10 **Brooches are versatile –** why not wear one on your hat, on a headband or on your hair?

WHAT YOU NEED IN A PERFECT WOMAN'S SHIRT

1 Crisp cotton
2 Bust darts
3 Shapely sleeve
4 French cuffs
5 Long body
6 Well-shaped collar
7 Curved bottom
8 Close fit
9 Hidden buttons
10 Generous sleeve heads

BRILLIANT BLING

1 **Use jewellery boxes that contain partitions** and soft, padded interiors to avoid damaging your jewellery.

2 **Use a non-abrasive jewellery cleaner** or a solution of mild soap and water for gold, platinum and gemstones. Rinse well and buff dry with a soft, lint-free cloth.

3 **For silver, use a non-abrasive silver polish** applied with a soft cloth and gently work it into tarnished areas. Polish and buff to a bright shine afterwards using a soft, lint-free cloth.

4 **Wearing silver jewellery frequently** can prevent it becoming tarnished.

5 **Avoid exposing jewellery to perfume, cosmetics or perspiration** as it will stain.

6 **Remove gold jewellery before you take a shower.** Soap can aid the formation of a film that will make it look dull.

7 **Restring bead and pearl necklaces every two years or so,** depending on how often you wear them. This will prevent accidents happening.

8 **Platinum needs treating with care as it scratches easily.** Store pieces separately from each other.

9 **Beware of chlorine in hot tubs and swimming pools.** It can damage stones and metal and even solid gold.

10 **Keep chains fastened when you're not wearing them,** so that they don't get tangled up.

ALL-IMPORTANT HANDBAG ADVICE

1 **Think about your handbag needs:** day-to-day, smart occasion, evening, holiday, work, shopping and outings.

2 **Carry a bag that's right for your body size.** Larger gals look silly with tiny, delicate bags. If you're petite, go for a

smaller size – a large bag will swamp you.

3 Remember the matching shoes and bag thing? Well, if you can't manage this go for a black bag.

4 Bags get you organized. You'll need a bag with separate places for your personal items such as keys, phone and sunglasses.

5 Some bags are easier to snatch. The safest kind is an over-the-body version.

6 Change your handbag with the seasons and give your winter model a rest come summer – change it for one that's light and summery. Or use a capacious basket.

7 If you like a designer bag, it's safer to buy direct from a proper shop or designer outlet – there are a lot of fakes out there.

8 Don't overfill bags – it'll be hard to find things and the bag will become misshapen. Polish and clean it once in a while.

9 Segregate stain-causing pens and make-up – these can do a lot of damage.

10 An adjustable strap allows you to fit your bag comfortably to your individual height and shape.

TEND YOUR SHOES & BOOTS

1 If your shoes or boots get drenched, stuff them with newspaper to absorb all the moisture overnight.

2 Smelly footwear? If your shoes are on the whiffy side, sprinkle a little salt in them and leave them overnight. The salt helps controls moisture, which contributes to odours. Bicarbonate of soda also works.

3 To get rid of watermarks on leather shoes, add one tablespoon of vinegar to 240ml (8fl oz) water and apply with a soft cloth. Wipe and polish in the normal way.

4 Don't wear the same pair every day as the moisture needs time to evaporate.

5 Don't polish patent leather or suede. A soft cloth dipped in vinegar is fine for patent; a suede brush is best for suede.

6 If your shoelaces get frayed and you can't thread the laces through the eyelets, try dipping the ends in clear nail polish.

7 You can wash some trainers in the washing machine. Remove the laces and inserts first, though.

8 Tackle shoe scuffs by rubbing a little non-gel toothpaste into the affected spot. Then wipe the paste away with a soft cloth and polish briskly. Test a small area first.

9 Using shoe trees in your dress shoes will increase their lifespan; they prevent shrinkage and unwelcome creases.

10 Tall boots need careful care. Roll up a magazine tightly and insert it into the boot. The magazine will gradually unfurl to create a firm insert.

CONSIDERATE CLOTHES CARE

1 You can wash almost everything by hand in cool water – even the items that are labelled 'Dry clean'.

2 If your item is labelled 'Dry clean only', you can still probably wash it by hand, but approach with caution and do it very carefully, possibly in cold water – unless it's really dirty, in which case take it to the dry-cleaners.

3 Store all your out-of-season clothes in a vacuum-pack on top of the wardrobe, under the bed or in the attic. This will enable you to look through your remaining seasonal clothes, get things repaired or donate them to your favourite charity. This will free up plenty of wardrobe space if you need to make any new purchases.

4 Buttons always falling off? When you buy something new, dab the centre of each button with a tiny amount of clear nail polish to seal the threads.

5 Use tissue paper to wrap delicate, silky items or anything that is embroidered with beads. Hanging will cause wear and tear and damaging snagging.

6 Are moths a problem in your home? Moth-proofing products should be placed high up in the wardrobe since fumes filter down, not up. Clean all clothes before storing them to remove moth eggs.

7 If you spot any nasty stains on your clothes, it's best to tackle them straight away. If you've already washed the item, ensure that the stain is quite gone before you put it in the dryer, otherwise it could be there for ever. The heat has a tendency to 'set' the stain.

8 Need to eradicate fluff and lint from smart clothes? Wind a piece of sticky tape around your index finger, sticky side out, and gently brush your garment with the nap to remove all bits and pieces.

9 If your zips have a habit of getting stuck, try rubbing the teeth with the stub of a candle.

10 De-wrinkle your favourite blouse or dress in a hurry by hanging it up in the bathroom while you are running a lovely hot bath or having a shower. The steam will smooth out crushed fabrics in a trice.

LOOK GREAT IN SNAPS

1 Messiness always shows up in photographs so take care over your hair and make-up. Apply make-up a little heavier than normal because the camera bleaches out cosmetic colour – especially with flash photography. If you want your teeth to look whiter, apply lipstick a shade brighter than normal.

2 Think about what you are wearing. In general, simple necklines and clean, unfussy lines photograph better. One colour or similar shades head to toe will streamline your appearance. Wear classic styles as trendier items will date more quickly. Don't clutter things with too much jewellery, scarves and accessories.

3 If you want your hips to look slimmer, angle your shoulders towards the camera and your hips three-quarters on.

4 To look thinner, keep your arms and elbows slightly away from your body.

5 To avoid a mug-shot photo, put one foot behind the other, have your shoulders and head at different angles and always put your weight on your back foot.

6 **If you have a large nose or a double chin,** try turning your head straight to camera and raise your chin slightly.

7 **Avoid having your picture taken in direct sunlight,** especially at midday. Overcast skies provide a flattering even look; morning and sunset are the times for the most flattering lighting.

8 **Camera angles can seriously affect your appearance.** Have the picture taken from a high angle to look thinner and more glamorous. Tilt your head down and look just over the camera. A low camera angle will shorten a long nose.

9 **If your smile feels a little faked,** your best plan is to think about something that's genuinely funny. If that doesn't work, try breathing in and smiling as you breathe out. It relaxes your face, making your smile look more natural.

10 **If you are sitting down in the photo,** extend your neck and tilt your head down slightly to get rid of a double chin.

YOUR COLOURS & YOU

1 **Choose the right colour clothing for your skin, eye and hair colouring.** The wrong choices can make you appear older and heavier.

2 **Seasonal colour analysis** is a system that divides colours into winter, summer, autumn, spring and helps you decide which shades are best for you. This depends on skin tones and hair and eye colouring.

3 **If your colours are 'winter',** choose subtle blue undertones – emerald green, holly-berry red, royal blue and magenta.

4 **If your colours are 'summer',** choose shades that are muted with blue undertones – baby blue, slate blue and powder pink.

5 **If your colours are 'autumn',** choose rich burnt oranges and reds, golden yellows and sludgy greens. Examples are pumpkin, mustard yellow, burnt orange, brown, camel and avocado.

6 **If your colours are 'spring',** choose shades tinged with yellow undertones: red, orange, coral and yellow.

7 **Not everyone fits neatly into a particular season.** Flow-colour analysis goes deeper, dividing the colour palette into 12 categories instead of four.

8 **Not into the seasonal colour system?** Get all your clothes out of the wardrobe and sort them into piles according to colour. For each separate category drape the garment under your chin and look in the mirror. See what the colour does to your hair, eyes and skin. Does it make you look grey, yellow, orange or blue? Does it throw shadows onto your face and make youir skin look sallow? Does it make your eyes and teeth look dingy or dull? Or does it make your skin or hair look somewhat lifeless? If it helps light up your face, makes your eyes sparkle, generating a healthy look, then this is the right colour for you.

9 **No need to throw out clothes** that aren't in your best colours. Make them work better for you by minimizing the amount of the wrong colour reflected onto your face. This only applies to colours above the waist, so you can add a jacket, cardigan or scarf in the right colour.

10 **To get an accurate colour analysis** use professional colour analysis service.

TIE A DICKIE BOW

1 Place the bow tie around your neck, situating it so that the left-hand side is about 5cm (2in) longer than the right.

2 Cross the left end over the right.

3 Bring the left up and under the loop.

4 Double end the right over itself to form the front base loop of the bow tie.

5 Loop the left piece over the centre of the loop you have just formed.

6 Holding everything in place, double the left piece back on itself and poke it through the loop behind the bow tie.

7 Adjust the bow tie by tugging gently at the ends of it and strengthening the centre knot.

8 Straighten the tie, although some people like a bit of a tilt.

9 The finished size of the bow should never be broader than the widest part of your neck or extend beyond the tips of your shirt collar.

10 To untie, pull the single ends.

THE IDEAL TIE

1 The front point of the tie should be long enough to touch your trouser waist.

2 The knot of the tie should be proportional to the collar size – it should fit neatly within the collar space.

3 The texture of your tie should go with your other clothes – a shiny silk goes with a silk shirt.

4 Avoid wearing clip-on ties, unless you are six years old.

5 A bow tie tends to lend an 'arty' air if it is coloured and dressy for weddings and formal events.

6 The proper width for a tie is around 8–9cm (3¾in) and the standard tie length is 130–150cm (51–59in) and anywhere within that range would be fine.

7 The quality of a tie is reflected in the cut across the fabric that allows the tie to fall straight forward after knotting.

8 The main colour of a patterned tie should complement your suit. A secondary colour should pick up your shirt.

9 The colour of the tie should not clash with your outfit, but it should not be so similar that it 'disappears' into the shirt.

10 Tie your tie in front of a mirror – make sure your shirt is buttoned up and your collar up first. Keep the knot of the tie tight throughout.

WHAT YOU NEED IN A PERFECT MAN'S SHIRT

1 Crisp cotton
2 Button-fly front
3 Pocket
4 French cuffs
5 Business collar
6 Tailored fit
7 Double-stitch seams
8 Bright white or a dashing colour
9 Traditional-shaped hem
10 Wrinkle-resistant

CUTE IN A SUIT

1 Choose the right jacket style for you. If you are on the skinny side, you can go straight for a double-breasted number. Single-breasted, with two buttons, is the style that will probably never go away – and it suits most shapes.

2 To button or not to button? Now, that's a question! Double-breasted suits should always be buttoned so that they hang properly.

3 Which material suits which season? Cotton and linen are by far the best fabrics for hot weather, while wool worsted is the best choice for the rest of the year. It's wise to give polyester a wide berth, whatever the weather.

4 Does your suit pass the wrinkle test? Try crunching the fabric between finger and thumb.

5 Trouser style, sir? For a dressy look select pleats and turn-ups. Flat-fronted troos take off the pounds while the no-turn-up look will add inches to height.

6 And now for the trouser fit. The waist is where a trouser should sit, not hips, and the hems should slightly overlap the shoe.

7 Check that you're not wearing ankle-swingers – oh, and your socks shouldn't be on display when you're on the move.

8 The jacket should fit right, too. Those inspecting your back view should only be able to glimpse 6mm (¼in) of shirt collar. Your shoulders need to be padded lightly, to give you that 'real man' appeal (there's something about a man in a suit, isn't there?). And so to the sleeves. They should fall 13cm (5in) above the tip of your thumb – but who's counting?

9 Off-the-peg suits give you a far more limited suit choice. Mixing and matching might be the way to go if you happen to have an unorthodox shape.

10 When you're buying off the peg, make your choice according to the jacket rather than the trousers. Why? Because people will check out the jacket first, not the trousers.

YOUR IDEAL LITTLE BLACK DRESS

1 Think what aspects you want to show off. Your back, cleavage, legs? Choose an LBD that flatters your favourite bits.

2 Make sure you select a comfortable style of dress. Consider whether you'll be walking, sitting or dancing – or all three.

3 Go for a dress with a lining.

4 Buy a dress made from good-quality fabric such as silk – it'll last much longer.

5 Accessorize your LBD. Choose a floaty scarf or accent jewellery. You can wear your LBD at virtually any occasion – add or remove accessories for different looks.

6 An unusual feature will set your LBD apart from the crowd: a slashed neckline, plunging back or criss-cross straps.

7 Dress your LBD up or down by adding a jacket or a chunky sweater.

8 An A-line LBD looks great on any shape, both small and not so small.

9 Don't ruin the elegant effect of your LBD by wearing it too short. Just above the knee is short enough.

10 If your LBD is strapless, ensure your skin tone looks good and your upper arms are firm.

VINTAGE CLOTHES — SO HIP!

1 **Search ordinary markets for vintage.** Surprising finds may surface. It's worth your patience to have a bit of a rummage.

2 **Local garage and church sales will offer up a wealth of riches.** But get there early to bag your bargains.

3 **Inspect garments carefully before making a purchase.** Nasty sweat stains can perish old fabrics all too easily.

4 **Vintage accessories are well worth searching for too:** bags, shoes, hats and scarves — as well as jewellery.

5 **Sizes have changed since the olden days.** Try things on as you may find that people are bigger nowadays.

6 **Visit the smarter areas of town** to find good-quality vintage designer buys. Out-of-town second-hand stores can yield great finds — better than city locations.

7 **'Vintage' ever changes.** Keep your eyes peeled for the next big thing.

8 **Look for great vintage fabrics.** They'll really make you stand out and are the true test of 'vintage'. If the garment is past its best, decide whether you might use the fabric to repurpose it into something totally different.

9 **Way back when, dress-making skills were more expert** and more fabric was used to make a garment. If something is a tad on tight side, see if there's enough seam allowance to let it out.

10 **Trawl through your grandma's attic.** You may be able to track down dreamy long-forgotten gowns that are badly in need of a home.

ETHICAL FASHION

1 **Buy second-hand** so that you are not constantly buying new items. Search in thrift stores and garage sales for bargains.

2 **Reuse/revamp your existing clothes.**

3 **Source items made from sustainably grown fibres.** Some brands specialize in them. Industrialized ways of growing cotton make it quick and cheap to produce, but this may mean it uses unsustainable amounts of water and insecticides.

4 **Has the item clocked up thousands of air miles to reach the stores?** That extra plane mileage might be costing the earth.

5 **Has child or slave labour been used in the manufacture of your garment?** You may have purchased it very cheaply, but perhaps at the expense of someone who has been paid a pittance to make it.

6 **Is the item really too cheap to be true?** Ethical shopping may mean spending more to acquire items that have been manufactured locally for realistic costs.

7 **Don't buy cheap clothing only to discard it after a couple of wearings.** Think whether it might be better to spend more on garments that last longer.

8 **Synthetic fur can be very much like the real thing.**

9 **If you are vegetarian,** consider buying shoes made from synthetics.

10 **Don't be a slave to fashion.** There's no need to keep changing fashions with each season and it's expensive, too. Buy classics that have a longer lifespan.

TEN THINGS TO BIN

1. Flouncy skirts
2. Single socks
3. Hotpants
4. Slogan T-shirts
5. Shrunken items
6. Combat pants
7. Holed items
8. Warrior belts
9. Dated patterns
10. Shapeless knitwear

DO A WARDROBE DETOX

1 Go through your wardrobe on a regular basis. Every six months or so take everything out of your wardrobe/drawers. Divide items into three piles: things you wear often, things you sometimes wear and things you only wear occasionally. Take the 'occasional' pile and put it in a storage bag. If you don't want to wear any of them after six months, donate them.

2 Alter anything that you want to get further wear out of. Could you shorten a long dress? Make cut-offs from an old pair of jeans?

3 Get your wardrobe organized! Getting up and at 'em in the mornings must be a streamlined operation. So create order in your wardrobe. Put rarely used items at the back and hang your clothes according to colour and frequency of wear. Get rid of items that could be defined as 'clutter'.

4 Before you put away off-season clothes, make sure that everything is clean first. It will deter moth attack.

5 Dump all duplicates. Some people buy the same thing over and over again – such as black jumpers or jeans. Does this sound like you?

6 Do your detoxing in chunks if you find it an overwhelming task. Give yourself clearly defined goals (such as sorting your shoes) and complete the task in one go – don't break off halfway through.

7 Recruit others to do your sorting for you. It's expensive, but it might be worth it if you really can't stand it. You can also hire stylists to teach you what suits you.

8 Look through your accessories: belts, scarves, hats, jewellery and handbags that you use all the time. Get rid of the rest. Don't keep things that are only there 'just in case'. You won't miss them.

9 After your detox, assess what is left. Are there are any gaping gaps in your wardrobe? This could be time for a little thoughtful retail therapy.

10 How about selling your surplus gear online, doing a clothes swap with friends, or holding a garage sale?

HOST CLOTHES-SWAPPING PARTIES

1 Get some friends together with their cast-offs and get swapping to refresh your wardrobe cheaply.

2 Make sure everyone is paired with at least one other person the same size.

3 Everything must be squeaky clean. So remind your friends to make sure their offerings are daisy-fresh beforehand.

4 One woman's cast-off is another's dream find. Don't fuss about what to bring – someone else might love it.

5 Space for rummaging and trying on? Ensure your venue has room for everyone to sample their finds and go home with great additions to their wardrobe.

6 Everyone must be able to see themselves properly to try things on – provide two full-length mirrors.

7 Short of friends, time or just too disorganized? Go online. Internet sites hold public swapping events.

8 If two people want the same item toss

a coin or try a mini catwalk strut to see who gets most applause.

9 If your party is at home, support your favourite charity and charge an entry fee.

10 Don't forget about shoes, accessories and jewellery. These can be swapped, too.

BARGAIN CLOTHES-SHOPPING

1 Just because something is discounted, it doesn't mean it's right for you. It's been reduced for a reason – probably because it's not very nice! However, regular stock clearances may mean you can find something special that's a bargain, too.

2 Stay focussed. If you're watching the sales with one item in mind, don't be sidetracked by last-year's must-haves just because they're cheap. They're over!

3 Try the last day of the sales, rather than the first. Some items may be reduced even further if they don't sell quickly.

4 Some stores restock sales rails daily – so keep looking for fresh supplies.

5 Get a store card, even if you don't often use it. It may inform you of special sale previews for card-holding customers.

6 Go online! You'll get regular updates about upcoming designer sales.

7 Only buy timeless fashion in the sales. Classic clothes will earn their keep by lasting for years. Trendy clothes date fast: you'll look like last season's news.

8 Evening-wear bargains are best found in January – when shops want to free up their rails.

9 If a gorgeous gown in the sales is still outside your budget – why not share the dress with a same-sized friend?

10 Is it a proper sale? The sign might lure you in, with only a few items on sale.

CUSTOMIZE OLD GEAR

1 If you've got a pair of jeans that fit, but with ragged, worn hems, cut off the legs and fray the edges for a real summer-holiday look. Yes, cut-offs are still in!

2 Create a corsage for an old jacket by cutting flower petals from colourful felt.

3 Try a little embroidery. It's easier than it looks. No need to stick to particular stitches; invent your own. Choose bright silks and decorate a plain skirt. A simple running stitch can enliven a hem.

4 Home-dyeing is a cinch. Hot-dye in the machine or buy cold-water dyes.

5 Buttons can make a big difference and you can change the look of an old cardigan radically by snipping off the old ones and sewing on new.

6 If your old heels needs pepping up, stick sparkly sequins all over the heels for an eye-catching backview.

7 Attach a pretty white lace collar for a smart revamp to a plain old sweater that could do with a facelift.

8 Use colourful trimmings on skirt hems to give your old favourite an exotic gypsy or peasant look.

9 Unravel your old sweater and knit something new.

10 Cut the fingers off old woollen gloves and keep them warm but active.

SEW YOUR OWN CLOTHES

1 **Home dress-making can be really great if you know what suits you –** both the design and the fabric. But be warned. You must like sewing, as dress-making can be labour-intensive and results need to look professional. Making your own won't necessarily save you money either, because patterns are pricey and fabrics can be, too.

2 **If you are new to the art of dress-making, choose the simplest patterns** you can find first of all and graduate to more complex styles as confidence grows. A simple blouse or tunic top in cotton might be the simplest design you can find.

3 **Measure yourself,** checking your size corresponds to measurements on the pattern. Don't guess your measurements and size. Later you may want to acquire a personalized dummy to fit your clothes on to. Buy the right-sized pattern.

4 **Check that the fabric you've chosen is suitable** for what you want to make. You'll find suitable fabric suggestions on the pattern envelope.

5 **Study the instructions before you start,** so you know what to expect. Spend time getting acquainted with the pattern.

6 **Try your pattern on first** by pinning all the pieces together, pinning the darts and then either slipping it on to your dummy or on yourself. You will then know if the fit is correct or needs altering.

7 **Lay out the pattern pieces on the fabric,** making sure you have folded it according to the instructions. Mark all the notches and dots clearly. Pin the pieces on to the fabric, making sure you are following the straight grain of the fabric and cut out. Most of the pieces will need to be double.

8 **Follow the steps** according to the pattern instructions, pinning the pieces before tacking them together.

9 **If the pattern advises that you use interfacing,** use it for collars, cuffs and facings. It will help the garment look more professionally finished.

10 **Always press seams and darts as you go along.** The garment will look well made.

MAKE–UP BUYING MADE EASY

1 **A product with fancier packaging will cost you more,** regardless of what's inside.

2 **Make-up has a limited life span** and you shouldn't hang on to it for years on end. Chuck it out!

3 **It's worth spending more** to get the

best brands of foundation you can afford. Foundation looks different in different lights and on different skins, so select the right one for you. Test it on the back of your hand and seek advice from beauty consultants.

4 Buy the right shade of concealer. The wrong shade can over-emphasize the spots that are covered up, making them even more prominent.

5 Go for either water-soluble or water-resistant mascara. The first can be taken off easily without remover while waterproof is great for summer and monsoons.

6 Pencil and felt tip eyeliners are easier to control than liquid eyeliners. Use them like pens to sketch the desired look.

7 Older woman alert! Pastel shades look much classier.

8 An eyelash curler is essential.

9 Where brushes are concerned choose one for blusher, one for powder, one for foundation and a couple for eyeshadow.

10 You can get away with buying cheaper mascaras, cleansers and moisturizers, but not blush, bronzers and powders.

MAKE-UP ESSENTIALS

1 Blusher
2 Eye shadow
3 Eyebrow color
4 Eyeliner
5 Face powder,
6 Foundation
7 Concealer
8 Lip-liner
9 Lipstick
10 Mascara

PUT ON MAKE-UP

1 Cleanse and moisturize your face before you start putting on make-up. Use the correct types for your skin.

2 Apply concealer that is one shade lighter than your foundation.

3 Always use a foundation that matches your skin tone exactly – apply it in dots over the central part of your face and blend it out with a make-up sponge or your fingertips – until it covers your face.

4 Put on eyeshadow before you apply your mascara or eye-liner. There are many variations in eyeshadow types. It can look subtle for day wear and darker and more sultry for evening.

5 Use powdered eyebrow shadow on your brows instead of a pencil, which can look too harsh, dark and false.

6 To keep your foundation on for longer, use a looser, pressed powder on top. This is useful for touching up your make-up when you are out and about.

7 Eye pencils are usually easy to manipulate and get a subtle result. With liquid eye-liner it can be hard to get an even effect on both eyes. Put on eye-liner after you put on eyeshadow and before mascara.

8 If you are fair, choose brown mascara and brown-black or black if you are dark. Mascara makes a world of difference as it defines your eyes.

9 Locate the apples of your cheeks by smiling. Apply blusher above or below.

10 Apply a lip-liner after putting on your lipstick if you want to emphasize your lips even more.

GENTLE MAKE-UP REMOVAL

1 Do not use baby wipes. They are too astringent for such delicate skin.

2 Start by removing eye make-up. Use either a proprietory eye make-up remover or vaseline. Apply to a cotton pad and gently press down on your eyelids and lashes. Then wipe off to the sides.

3 To stop towels getting mucky, use a

clean pad until the eyes are make-up free.

4 Use eye make-up remover on your lips to remove long-lasting lip colour.

5 Choose a skin cleanser that can also remove make-up.

6 Don't use cleanser for eye make-up – it's way too harsh for the delicate eye area.

7 Use lukewarm water for eye make-up removal.

8 If your facial skin is super-dry, use a cleansing oil on a cotton pad. Massage in the oil to loosen dirt and make-up. Wash with a foam or gel cleanser. Apply moisturizer while your skin is still damp.

9 If your pores are clogged, steam them before cleansing to open them up and dislodge the make-up more easily.

10 To close pores splash with cold water.

PUCKER UP FOR PERFECT LIPPY

1 Choose darker colours for night time and lighter ones for day wear.

2 Select your lipstick according to the natural colour of your lips and skin.

3 Test out different shades and inspect them under natural daylight before you buy – on your fingertips.

4 Choose a lip-liner one shade darker than the main colour, but in the same colour family.

5 Put the liner on after you've applied the main colour, not before.

6 Texture is important. Matte thins lips; glossy makes them look fuller.

7 Think about lipstick colour with eye make-up. Bold lipstick shades go with light eye make-up and natural with heavy.

8 Liquid versus solid? Solid is the most usual, but liquids give you better control.

9 Fed up with constantly reapplying lipstick? Try lip stains, which come in liquid and gel form.

10 If you just need a touch of colour, try out coloured lip glosses.

HAPPY HAIR REMOVAL

1 Plucking
2 Bleaching
3 Sanding
4 Epilating
5 Shaving
6 Waxing
7 Sugaring
8 Electrolysis
9 Laser
10 Threading

WHAT THE PLUCK! PERFECT EYEBROWS

1 First off, wash your face with cleanser and warm water and blot-dry with a washcloth. Now put a little lotion onto your eyebrows to soften them. This will make it easier to pluck them.

2 Make sure you pluck your eyebrows in good light. Either sit by a window or under a bright light with a good mirror, preferably magnified.

3 Look at which way your eyebrow hair grows – this is generally outwards from your nose towards your hairline.

4 Choose a good pair of tweezers with a slanted edge and a good grip.

5 Hold the tweezers in your hand as though they were a pencil, with the open end upwards.

6 A good eyebrow shape is slightly arched. Start with one eyebrow and decide what shape you are going for. Pluck above and below the brow, so that edges are smooth both top and bottom.

7 You can hold your skin taught as you pluck – don't take too many hairs at once.
8 Carefully pluck out the hairs in the direction of growth. Position the tip of the tweezers as close to the root of the hair as you can and pull, keeping them angled as near to the skin as possible.
9 Continue plucking until you have achieved a neat and tidy result. Repeat for the other eyebrow.
10 Threading is an effective way to get a great shape.

MIX UP CLEANSERS & SCRUBS

1 Try a milk cleanser for oily skin. Mix one teaspoon of powdered milk with one of water. Massage in for two minutes.
2 A yogurt cleanser loves sensitive skin. Mix one teaspoon of baking soda with one of plain yogurt. Leave on for two minutes and then gently massage into the skin.
3 An oatmeal cleanser is worth trying on a sensitive skin. Mix half a cup of oatmeal with plain yogurt to form a paste.
4 A yogurt almond scrub is good for blemished skin. Mix three tablespoons of ground almonds with half a cup of yogurt.
5 An almond mayonnaise scrub is perfect if your skin is dry. Grind quarter of a cup of almonds until they form a paste. Add one-eighth teaspoon mayonnaise. Rinse with vinegar before rubbing in the scrub. Leave on for ten minutes, rinse off with vinegar.
6 If your complexion is normal, add an abrasive ingredient, such as sugar, milk, orange or lemon juice, pineapple juice, vinegar and yogurt. Mix to a paste. Scrub.
7 Using a washcloth will exfoliate further.
8 If you suffer from acne, try a pineapple juice cleanser. Mix three tablespoons pineapple juice with one to two tablespoons sugar/baking soda. Scrub into your face.
9 Fruity cleansers are good because they make exfoliating easier and allow moisturizers to penetrate the skin.
10 Reduce irritation by rinsing well and patting your skin rather than rubbing it.

GREAT FACE MASK COMBOS
1 Honey & lemon
2 Oatmeal & banana
3 Avocado & yogurt
4 Olive oil & avocado
5 Peaches & cream
6 Cucumber & egg
7 Tomato & mint
8 Orange juice & yogurt
9 Apple & honey
10 Coconut & pineapple

FACIAL CLEANSING

1 Remove all your mascara with a cotton pad dipped in eye-cleansing lotion. It helps if you tie your hair back.
2 Use eye-cleansing lotion to remove your eyeshadow. Wipe your eyelids gently with clean cotton wool dipped in it.
3 Clean your face with a good-quality facial cleansing cream. Put a blob of it into the palm of one hand. Dab it over your nose, chin, forehead and cheeks.
4 Massage the cleansing cream into the skin. Start below your throat and work up.
5 Carry on massaging right up to your forehead using your fingertips.
6 Massage from your eyes to your nose.
7 Work the cream back over your chin using the tip of your index finger.
8 Remove the cream with cotton wool,

starting under your chin, working over your cheeks and up to your forehead.

9 Apply a little toner to your forehead and cheeks, nose and chin creases using cotton wool pads.

10 Finish by moisturizing.

ZAPPING SPOTS

A CLOSE (MEN'S) SHAVE

1 Wet or dry?
2 Sharp blade
3 Warm water
4 Hot flannel
5 Shaving cream
6 Smooth movement
7 Pat dry
8 Styptic pencil
9 Cold rinse
10 Aftershave

1 Don't squeeze. You'll get scarring and infections. But if you really must, wash your hands and lightly squeeze the top with a tissue/cotton pad. Clean the area.

2 Get a good skincare routine going! Wash your skin twice a day, but don't scrub as this stimulates the sebaceous glands.

3 Use an oil-free anti-bacterial concealer to help your blemishes blend in.

4 Try a mud mask. This will have a drying effect, which will help to shrink spots.

5 Oily skin is more likely to get spots. Shower or bathe in tepid water as hot can strip your skin of the moisture it badly needs. Avoid using cleansers that over-dry the skin as it will create even more oil.

6 Diet is important for healthy, clear skin. Eat fresh fruit and vegetables and drink lots of water. Eat foods rich in zinc, which is an anti-bacterial agent and carrots, which are high in vitamin A, to strengthen the skin's protective tissue.

7 Keep your hair off your face – wear it short or tie it back. Avoid fringes. The hair contains oil, contributing to break-outs.

8 Wash pillowcases frequently. They absorb oils and reapply it to your face.

9 Avoid wearing make-up. It contributes to clogging your pores, causing more pimples and blackheads to develop.

10 If make-up is a must, choose a water-based brand.

SOOTHE YOUR DRY SKIN

1 Wash or shower in luke-warm water. Hot water robs the skin of moisture – this applies to your hands, face and body.

2 Keep your showers short. Shower once a day only to reduce drying-out effect.

3 Skip taking hot baths, but if you really can't, avoid using bubbles and opt for bath oils instead.

4 Moisturizer is far more effective on a properly exfoliated skin. Exfoliate on a weekly or twice-weekly basis.

5 Soaps can have a highly drying effect, so stick with a creamy, moisturizing cleanser that contains glycerine or petrolatum.

6 If you have dry hands and feet, put on your moisturizer and your gloves before you go outside.

7 If you have a very sensitive skin, avoid rinsing your face with tap water and use a cold cream to cleanse your face. Or use bottled water.

8 If your feet are particularly dry, lather them up in thick moisturizer and encase them in cotton socks for maximum effect.

9 Don't forget about getting dry lips; they contain less moisture than the rest of your skin. Use a lip balm all the time.

10 **Have you got really super-dry skin?** Then it might be worth thinking about investing in a proper humidifier. You'll be surprised at the results – it really does make all the difference.

CHILL – IN YOUR OWN HOME SPA

1 **Clear the bathroom of clutter and distractions.** Create a private, calming environment just for you.

2 **Find a couple of soft towels** – the fluffier the better. You'll need a large one for your body; a smaller one for your head.

3 **Arrange scented candles around the bath.** Lavender is a great perfume to choose for relaxation.

4 **Put some home spa treatments out,** where you can reach them easily from the bath (hair conditioner, scrubs, gorgeous soaps and shampoo).

5 **Run the bath and add lavender oil** to the water for deep relaxation. Try a rich mud mask to moisturize your face.

6 **Turn off all the lights and illuminate the candles.** Sink into your bath. Put on your facial mask.

7 **Apply exfoliating scrub** and then relax completely in your bath.

8 **Wrap up** in your lovely soft towels. The fluffier the better.

9 **Sip delicious jasmine tea.**

10 **Give yourself a home manicure** on both your hands and feet.

QUICK HOME-BEAUTY FIXES

1 Face mask
2 Massage
3 Bubble bath
4 Steam inhalation
5 Meditation
6 Creams & oils
7 Compresses
8 Foot spa
9 Manicure
10 Good night's sleep

PERFECT YOUR OWN PERFUME

1 **Try a vegetable-based oil for the base,** but use the perfume quickly as it will become rancid. Try almond/grape seed oil.

2 **Use artificially created fragrance oils rather than essential oils** unless you're prepared to spend out. But compare prices as orange, citrus and some herb essential oils may be cheaper.

3 **Collect old bottles with tight-fitting stoppers.** Dark-coloured bottles are the preferred choice as light damages the oils.

4 **Fill each bottle about two-thirds full** with base oil. Use a funnel to avoid spills.

5 **Add fragrances drop by drop** and use a different dropper for each scent. If you want to mix aromas, mix a few drops of oil

until you get a mixture you're happy with. Try grouping notes: floral, woody, green/fresh, fruity and spicy and create a balance.

6 **Test the aroma by smelling the jar** (don't stick your nose right into it) to see whether it's right for you.

7 **Place the new perfume in a cool, dark place** for two weeks to infuse.

8 **Use your scent for different purposes.** Try it in a candle or a home-made soap.

9 **If you want an eau de toilette,** dilute it with perfumer's alcohol. Use ten per cent perfume oils and 90 per cent alcohol.

10 **Write down your perfume recipes,** so that if you get a real success you can re-create the same one at a later date.

A FINE FRAGRANCE

1 Decide which perfume group you like best: floral, woody, spicy or fresh.

2 Think about when you'll be wearing the perfume: lighter scents will suit daytime, whereas more pungent ones are better for evening wear.

3 Perfumes react differently to various types of skin and in different conditions, such as body temperature, diet and weather. So if you like a specific perfume on some-one else, beware – it may not smell the same on you.

4 When sampling perfumes, don't try out more than three at a time. Your sense of smell will become desensitized and you won't be able to tell one from another.

5 To take a 'smell break' when trying out scents, take a sniff of coffee beans or just take a deep breath through the nose and smell your sleeve or cuff.

6 Decide how much you want to spend. There is a wide range of prices attached to perfumes.

7 Spray a trial amount of perfume onto your skin – don't just sniff the bottle. The perfume will change on your skin.

8 Apply perfume to pulse points behind the ears, on the wrists and lower neck. Or wherever you would like to be kissed!

9 Don't keep bottles of perfume for years. Once opened, shelf life is a year and if the bottle is not stored in a dark, cool place deterioraton is even quicker.

10 Spicier fragrances are said to arouse sexual feelings, while fruit and floral scents are calming and sensual.

DO THE FILING: PERFECT MANICURE

1 Remove old nail polish. Douse each fingernail in nail-polish remover and using cotton balls, rub until the nails have returned to their natural colour.

2 Emery boards are kinder than nail files. Use them to make all your nails into a uniform shape, smoothing rough edges.

3 If you want to reshape or shorten your nails use nail clippers. You should do this about once a month, though it depends on how fast they grow. Be careful not to trim them right down to the quick.

4 Remove your cuticle altogether or push it down. You can use a cuticle stick.

5 If you wear nail polish most of the time, give your nails a two-day nail polish break, every now and then.

6 Choose a varnish to go with your skin colouring or whatever you are wearing. Use the integral applicator and a steady hand for applying the colour. Or why not ask a friend to be your manicurist?

7 Use evenly loaded, regular brushstrokes, making sure you do not apply too much varnish at once. Brush from the base of the nail to the tip.

8 If you make a mistake, immerse cotton wool in nail-polish remover. Take the varnish off, then recoat.

9 Add a second coat of polish after the first has dried. Do this after about ten minutes.

10 Quick-drying varnishes are a real boon if you are going out shortly.

SUCCESS WITH A FAKE TAN

1 **Do a patch test on a small area of skin** 24 hours before applying the fake tan – if you have a sensitive skin.

2 **Exfoliate thoroughly two to three days** before self-tanning to give a smoother surface for the tan to be applied to. It will also stop it being uneven.

3 **Moisturize your skin daily,** avoiding oil-based moisturizers which can prevent the absorption of self-tanning products, creating a patchy effect.

4 **Remove any unwanted hair** at least 24 hours before applying the tan.

5 **Get rid of all make-up** before you start with a non oil-based remover.

6 **Take off all jewellery** and don't wear perfume or an oil-based body lotion.

7 **Wear gloves** to protect your hands.

8 **Apply fake tan to your face using your fingertips –** in the same way as putting on foundation. Use only a minimum amount around the eyebrows and hairline, the ears and behind the ears.

9 **Allow the tan to dry thoroughly,** without coming into contact with water. Do not shower for at least six to eight hours. So ideally apply the tan before bed and then shower in the morning.

10 **After the tan has developed** avoid using harsh exfoliating products, facial scrubs, body brushes, soaps, loofahs and mitts. Gently pat the skin dry after showering. Refrain from going swimming – it will shorten the life of the tan.

SCALPEL-FREE FACE LIFTS

1 **If your skin is thinning and dry** use warming and moisturizing ayurvedic beauty treatments. Treatments work on energy junctions around the body. Pressure stimulation clears energy blockages and helps the flow of prana.

2 **Acupuncture reduces fine wrinkles and folds in the face,** lifts sagging eyelids and improves muscle tone and collagen production.

3 **Try reiki healing,** which restores natural chi energy flow to the facial muscles/skin.

4 **An aromatherapy facial massage** using essentials oils de-stresses facial muscles and smooths out fine lines, leaving your face feeling soft and supple.

5 **Do a facial massage** using almond oil for all skins, olive oil for dry and jojoba oil for sensitive and oily skins. Massage stimulates and tones the tiny muscles of your face, acting as a natural face lift.

6 **Do plenty of facial exercises –** the muscles become toned and the overlying skin becomes taut and lifted.

7 **Try a facial wrap,** which is like a body wrap. It uses minerals and herbs that are applied to your face to help your skin to release toxins, toning and firming the skin.

8 **Make a home-made anti-ageing facial mask** from bananas mixed with cream and organic honey.

9 **Smile as much as you can.** This will improve your facial muscle tone and tighten up any slackness in your face.

10 **Anti-ageing skincare products,** such as toners, may help.

WATCH OUT FOR SUN DAMAGE

1 Stay out of the sun as much as you can, particularly during the hottest part of the day. Even if it's cloudy, UV rays still cause 'secondary exposure', penetrating and burning. The sun starts damaging your skin after just ten minutes.

2 Cover up when you are out in the sun. Wear a wide-brimmed sun hat, a long-sleeved shirt, long skirt or trousers made from firmly woven cotton. Wear sunglasses.

3 Use a sunshade when you're on the beach – but you may still suffer skin damage, especially around midday.

4 Use high-factor sun protectant and reapply it every two hours. Experts recommend an SPF of 15 or higher for those with fair skin.

5 Apply sun protectant to all exposed skin, especially the face, ears and neck. If you are bald or have thinning hair, apply it to your scalp as well.

6 Outdoor activities such as gardening and walking expose you to more sun, so cover up and use sun protection.

7 Sun beds are just as damaging.

8 Sun creams lose their potency over time. Check expiry dates and throw out any that are past their time. Don't leave sun cream in the sun or in a hot place.

9 Sweating, swimming and showering will mean you need to reapply sun cream. You'll also need to apply it around 15 or 30 minutes before you go out.

10 Go for a spray tan.

KEEP WRINKLES AT BAY

CHOOSING AGE-DEFYING FOODS

1 Berries
2 Artichokes
3 Cinnamon
4 Wholegrains
5 Salmon
6 Leafy greens
7 Red/kidney beans
8 Prunes
9 Apples
10 Pecan nuts

1 Sun protection is a must as loss of elasticity is caused by UV light. Keep yourself out of the sun – it's the worst cause of skin wrinkles.

2 Start moisturizing at the earliest possible age and keep doing it. Moisturize daily with deep moisturizing cream and then try anti-wrinkle creams plus other anti-ageing products.

3 If you have been out in the sun, use products containing aloe vera.

4 Use a skin lotion during the day with SPF 15 or higher and reapply regularly to prevent wrinkles from forming. Use a higher-strength sunblock for long periods outside, even if the weather is cloudy.

5 Exfoliation is vital to skin-cell turnover – use a facial scrub regularly. The new cells give your skin a younger look.

6 Moisturizers work a lot better on an exfoliated skin.

7 Look for a moisturizer containing anti-ageing aloe, beeswax, alphalipoic acid, lanolin and selenium.

8 Use different moisturizers for day and night. Your day moisturizer defends against the sun and pollution, while the night one is for repair and nourishment.

9 Don't smoke – it ages the skin and causes wrinkles to appear.

10 Eat a diet rich in vitamins/nutrients especially vitamins A, C, E and K.

BEAT CELLULITE INTO SUBMISSION

1 **A powerful massage** increases blood flow and breaks down cellulite.

2 **Renounce sweets and fatty foods.**

3 **Include plenty of fresh fruits and vegetables** in your daily diet.

4 **Drink plenty of water.** It will help repair the connective tissue in your body, making it harder for cellulite to accumulate.

5 **Salon treatments include painless radio frequency** to break down fat pockets.

6 **Dry body-brushing can be effective.** It works because it stimulates the lymphatic system. Use a firm body brush on dry skin before your shower. Brush in long strokes, working towards the heart.

7 **Cellulite tights and control pants** make curves look smoother.

8 **A fake tan doesn't actually get rid of cellulite,** but it makes it look much nicer.

9 **Cardiovascular and aerobic exercises** are very important. They reduce cellulite accumulation and can greatly strengthen the connective tissue in the body.

10 **Anti-cellulite creams** can improve the way your skin looks. They temporarily plump the skin with moisture.

BANISH BODY ODOUR

1 **Wash, shower or bathe daily –** morning or evening.

2 **Use soap all over.** Choose anti-bacterial versions, but not those with high levels of perfume or alcohol. Do not use those that have a moisturizing effect.

3 **Use a deodorant with anti-bacterial and anti-perspirant together.** Do not choose deodorants that have high perfume or alcohol content.

4 **Change your clothes every day.**

5 **Don't borrow other people's clothes.**

6 **Wash your clothes as soon as you can** – especially if they are sweaty.

7 **Watch what you eat.** Fatty and oily foods and meats are to be avoided.

8 **Eat green, leafy vegetables and fruit.**

9 **Drink plenty of water** throughout the day to prevent dehydration.

10 **Store your clothes in an airy environment** rather than a confined wardrobe and use scented lining paper in your drawers. Hanging garments up after wearing may be more effective than folding them away.

HAIRBRUSH HARMONY

1 **Paddle brushes create** smooth styles for longer hair.

2 **Use a cushion hairbrush for medium-length hair –** it's great for sleek styles.

3 **A brush with close-set bristles** allows you to control your hair more easily.

4 **A vent brush** is good for ventilating the hair during blow-drying.

5 **Bobbles on bristles are good –** they protect your scalp from scratching.

6 **Bristles are worth thinking about.** Metal ones can damage hair, while boar bristles cause less friction and distribute sebum. Synthetic materials massage the scalp, stimulate oil release and are easy to clean and cheaper than natural bristles.

7 **Ceramic hairbrushes help** to speed up drying and add volume. The metal centre is heated up by the heat in your dryer.

8 **Styling brushes are suitable for all hair types** and are great for shaping, styling and creating volume.

8 **Choose a round-bristled brush** for curly or wavy hair that you blow-dry.

10 **Maintain the condition of your brush** by washing it regularly in a mild shampoo.

HUNT FOR A HAIRDRYER

1 **It may not be worth paying for a more expensive dryer –** especially if it's a 'professional'. If you've got an easy-to-maintain cut, a cheaper hairdryer will do fine. Simple combined heat and speed settings will be adequate for daily needs.

2 **Heat causes damage to hair.** Look for a dryer with heat-control and a 'cool' button.

3 **If your hair is more high-maintenance** and you need to consider shape and volume, go for a pricier dryer with style-setting attachments.

4 **Make comfort one of your considerations.** How much noise does the dryer make and how heavy is it?

5 **Pay attention to wattage** as this determines the dryer's effectiveness. 1600 is enough to style and blow-dry it quickly.

6 **Ceramic technology features** straightening, heat retention and even distribution of heat, helping to prevent frizz.

7 **Bonnet dryers are top-of-the-range.** They blow very hot air and are usually best left to the professionals.

8 **If your dryer has a plastic or metal heating element,** it works by blowing hot air over wet hair to evaporate the water. Eventually your hair will start to break. The best hair dryers use ceramic heating elements, which dry your hair through radiant heat. This process is much gentler .

9 **Use the lowest heat and speed setting possible** to reduce hair damage. Just use high temperatures when you are in a hurry.

10 **Higher-speed hair dryers are great for styling;** they're OK for short periods.

DIY HAIRCUTS

1 **Wet hair is easier to cut.**

2 **A cut with the hair the same length all over is easiest.** Cut a little at a time. Comb a small section out and hold it taut. Measure to the length you want and snip off excess. Continue, one section at a time.

3 **To maintain a professional cut,** trim the same amount from all over monthly.

4 **If you have long hair the same length all over,** first comb it all forward. Smooth sections through your fingers and cut all in one line, straight across. Work in sections.

5 Check the cut by tugging your hair towards your eyes, nose, chin and jaw.

6 To cut curly hair, cut your hair longer than you want it to end up when dry.

7 Hold small sections if your hair is thick or coarse. If you try to cut too much at once, the hair will bend between the scissor blades and your cut will be uneven.

8 Men: try hair clippers. These allow you to set the blades to your desired length.

9 Recruit a friend to help get your hair even in hard-to-reach areas.

10 To cut a fringe, part your hair in the centre. Take an equal amount of hair from each side and comb it forward. Smooth the hair and cut across in a straight line.

SETTLE ON A HAIRSTYLE

1 Have a long, hard look at the shape of your face in the mirror and assess the shape. If you have an oval-shaped face, you'll find almost any style suits you.

2 Get ideas from hair magazines. They show fashionable styles for all lengths.

3 Consider the texture of your hair. If your hair is fine, avoid long tresses – a shorter cut will contribute body. If your hair is thick, layers might be right.

4 If your face is long-shaped, long hair can make it look even more so. Consider putting in layers, above-shoulder length or a fringe with a side parting.

5 To elongate a round face, grow your hair to just below your chin.

6 If you have a square-shaped face, think about soft, curly styles.

7 A heart-shaped face will benefit from a style that is fuller at the bottom.

8 Move with the times. Your style ten years ago may look old-hat now.

9 Beware of having super-long hair if you are very short or past your teens.

10 Get to know your hairdresser. He/she will be honest about what suits you.

LONG-HAIR CARE

1 Avoid sleeping with your hair plaited or in a ponytail or keeping it like this for too long. The tightness can break hair.

2 Use hairbands or scrunchies that are intended for hair. Ordinary rubber bands are damaging because they pull and tear.

3 To eradicate split ends, trim your hair once every three months, even if you want to keep growing it.

4 To keep long hair the same length, trim the ends every six to eight weeks.

5 De-tangle long hair before washing, using your fingers or a wide-toothed comb. Don't use a brush – it stretches the hair and may cause it to break off. Be gentle and work from the tips to the roots.

6 Don't rub long hair dry with a towel. This will cause it to tangle. Blot the water out instead with a thick towel.

7 Brushing is important when caring for

long hair, because it spreads the oils along the length of each strand. Use long strokes starting from the roots.

8 **To remove static from long hair after brushing,** stroke down its length.

9 **Use a satin or silk pillowcase.** This allows your hair to slide across the pillow without getting caught or broken.

10 **Wear a satin or silk scarf** over your hair at night to prevent it breaking.

COPE WITH CURLS

1 **Don't shampoo curly hair more than twice a week.** It will strip the hair of its natural oils.

2 **Use a conditioner on curly hair** every time you shampoo – it is likely to be more brittle, dry and prone to frizziness than straight hair.

3 **Use wide-toothed combs** in preference to narrow to avoid curly hair breaking.

4 **Let curly hair dry naturally** to reduce frizziness and don't brush or towel-dry.

5 **Deep-condition your curly hair** once a month to re-moisturize the hair and scalp.

6 **Use a small amount of a moisturizing product** to add moisture and keep your hair from frizzing. Add the product when your hair is still moist and style it with your fingers.

7 **Avoid touching or fiddling** with curly hair as the friction will cause it to tangle or frizz.

8 **It's best to get tangles out in the shower,** using your fingers and then a wide-toothed comb, working from the ends up to the roots. If you do this when the hair is dry, you risk adding frizziness.

9 **Look out for curly-hair shampoos.**

10 **Warm up a couple of drops of style serum** in your hands and palm it over your head to calm down dry, frizzy curls.

HOW TO ACHIEVE GLOSSY, VOLUMINOUS HAIR

1 Conditioner
2 Cold rinse
3 Serum
4 Layered cut
5 Finger-drying
6 Olive oil on hair
7 Natural hair colour
8 Head massage
9 Taking fish oils
10 Shine spray

WASH-NIGHT FOR YOUR HAIR

1 **Wash your hair every two to three days –** even if you are tempted to do it more often. If you have 'bed hair', wet and dry it normally. Daily shampooing will strip it of its natural oils. If your hair is greasy, wash it every day or every other day.

2 **To start the wash,** give your hair a good soaking in medium-hot water.

3 **For effective shampooing,** put a small amount into the palm of your hand and rub it gently into your scalp.

4 **Massage your shampooed hair with** your fingertips. Avoid mounding longer hair and massaging as it will tangle.

5 **Rinse until the water runs clear.**

6 **Use a flat comb or just your fingers** to smooth your hair before you condition.

7 **Leave the conditioner on** your hair for just a couple of minutes.

8 **Rinse all the conditioner out** until the water runs completely clear.

9 **Finish rinsing with icy water.** This will add a wonderful shine to your hair.

10 **Drying your hair is a must** if you are

going out straight away. If you are towel-drying, pat and leave the hair to dry naturally. Hairdryers can have a damaging, drying effect.

A TOUCH OF HAIR COLOUR

1 **Salon-dyeing will cost you a lot more than doing it yourself at home.** However, a salon is the best choice for intricate procedures such as streaking.

2 **Choose the right colour for you.** Look for natural shades, even if you are tempted by bright colours.

3 **If this is your first attempt at dyeing,** why not go for a temporary dye? This washes out after a few weeks, allowing you to experiment with different shades.

4 **Test products on a few strands first.** Try putting it on hair that is underneath the rest and doesn't show – before putting it on your whole head.

5 **Condition before you dye your hair.** Your crowning glory needs to be in the best possible condition before you start.

6 **When your original-coloured roots start showing through,** just touch up the regrowth areas, otherwise your hair colour will get progressively concentrated.

7 **To prolong the life** of your dyed hair colour use a special colour shampoo.

8 **If you are dyeing your hair yourself for a special occasion –** do it a few days beforehand to avoid disappointing results.

9 **If you are pregnant, consult your doctor.** Chemicals in dye could be absorbed into your system. Wait until the second trimester of pregnancy before dyeing.

10 **Vegetable dyes may be an option if you are pregnant.** Check ingredients first; chemicals are sometimes included.

HEAVENLY HAIR-STRAIGHTENING

1 **Make sure your hair is clean and conditioned** before straightening.

2 **Use a heat-protective spray** whether you are using commercial hair-straighteners or an ordinary hairdryer.

3 **Get as much moisture out of your hair** as you can after washing.

4 **Use a wide-toothed comb** to part and comb before and during blow-drying.

5 **Choose the best brush for your hair length –** a round, bristle brush for short hair and a paddle brush for long.

6 **Use a blow-dryer extension** so that you can position the dryer as close to your scalp as possible.

7 **Point the dryer downwards** while you are drying. An upward angle can create a frizzy effect.

8 **Blow-dry your hair in sections –** this will have a straightening effect. Start from the bottom half of your hair.

9 **For longer-lasting straightening** consider a permanent keratin-based method to relax the hair.

10 **If your hair is still frizzy, try anti-frizz serum.** Apply all over your hair.

THE DREADED DANDRUFF

1 **To prevent dandruff appearing** in the first place, when shampooing massage the scalp and don't scratch it. Rinse thoroughly.

2 **Use specialist anti-dandruff shampoo.**

3 **Brush your hair daily** to improve circulation and remove flakiness. Brush forwards from the nape of the neck.

4 **Massage your scalp** using your fingertips before or after brushing to stimulate circulation, dislodge dirt and dandruff and to encourage hair growth.

5 **Use a teaspoon of fresh lemon in your final wash rinse.** This removes stickiness, preventing dandruff.

6 **Clean hair helps minimize dandruff** as it stops dead skin cells accumulating.

7 **How is your diet?** A well-balanced diet is important for scalp health. Too much sugar, salt and spice may worsen dandruff.

8 **A preventative diet** needs to contain vitamins E, B6 and B12, selenium and zinc. Flax seed oil is also said to help.

9 **For stubborn dandruff,** use a scalp preparation containing selenium, zinc, coal tar and coconut oil or salicylic acid.

10 **Try anti-fungal shampoos containing ketoconazole,** but be patient as they can take up to six weeks to work.

GET AROUND HAIR LOSS

1 **Before you attempt to conceal your hair loss,** consult your doctor about its cause. There may be a medical solution that you can explore first.

2 **Wear a hat or a scarf –** these are both on trend. Shaving might be acceptable.

3 **Have a hairpiece made to fit in** with your remaining hair.

4 **Try a different hairstyle** that can effectively cover thinning or bald areas.

5 **Consider hair weaves or extensions.**

6 **Try a regrowth product –** either over-the-counter or on prescription.

7 **Wigs are a good option** and some very stylish ones are available.

8 **Think about having a hair transplant** if you really are worried.

9 **There are forms of surgery,** such as scalp reduction, available.

10 **Blow-drying your hair can fluff it out,** giving the appearance of a fuller head of hair.

FLASH A BRILLIANT SMILE

1 **White teeth are the order of the day** and you'll more feel like smiling if you've got them. There's really no need for them to be whiter-than-white *à la* Hollywood, but yellow fangs are to be avoided.

2 **Brush/floss regularly** to reduce stains.

3 **Try whitening toothpastes,** though no one seems clear about their efficacy.

4 **Regular dental cleaning is a must** for keeping your teeth tip-top.

5 **If your teeth really are discoloured think about getting veneers,** though it is the most pricey form of treatment available.

6 **Bleaching can be effective,** but you may have to repeat it after a while. It can cause tooth sensitivity.

7 **Smile from within.** If your smile is genuine, you will seem to glow.

8 **Smile with your eyes, too.** This will make your smile come alive. If necessary, practise in front of the mirror.

9 **If your teeth are crooked** and making you self-conscious, think seriously about having orthodontestry.

10 **What do you consume?** Red wine, tea, blueberries all stain. Quit smoking.

SPORTING DENTURES

1 **When you get your new dentures,** it may take a while to speak in the way that you used to. You may occasionally bite your tongue or cheek. Practise by yourself, by speaking aloud in front of a mirror.

2 **To get used to chewing with dentures,** start off with a soft/liquid diet.

3 **Your gum tissue will take a while to become firm again,** so get your dentures adjusted. But don't try to do it yourself.

4 **Bring balance to your bite.** Position equal amounts of food on both sides.

5 **Avoid eating sticky/hard foods** to begin with.

6 **Try sucking sugar-free mints** or boiled sweets the first few times you wear your dentures. You may salivate more because your body thinks your dentures are food.

7 **Clean your dentures twice a day** with a denture brush and a non-abrasive cleanser.

8 **Experiment with the amount** of denture adhesive you use.

9 **Don't wear your dentures at night;** your mouth and gums need to rest.

10 **Soak the dentures in warm water** and denture cleaner overnight.

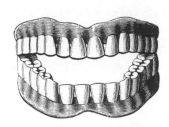

TERRIFIC TOOTHBRUSHES

1 **Replace your toothbrush as soon as it begins to show wear,** or every three months. If you've had a cold, change the brush anyway.

2 **A soft-bristled brush is the best for removing plaque.** It will be more gentle on your teeth and gums.

3 **Choose a small-headed brush.** It will be better able to reach all areas, including your hard-to-reach back teeth.

4 **Bristles with rounded teeth a**re better at protecting your teeth when you brush.

5 Select whatever handle is most comfortable for you. You'll find a non-slip grip or flexible neck on offer.

6 Bristles should not fall out of your brush if you are using it normally. If they do, replace the brush.

7 A powered toothbrush can do a far better job of cleaning your teeth and suits those with brushing problems.

8 Consider a floss-action brush head for accessing crevices between the teeth.

9 When choosing between manual and powered, powered costs more but if it helps to keep your teeth cleaner, you may make up for the cost of extra dental care.

10 If you can find a brush that you actually like to use, you'll feel more like brushing for two minutes.

SELECT FLATTERING SPECS

1 Assess your face shape with your hair off your face.

2 Oval faces can take any style of frame because they are balanced top and bottom.

3 A long, thin face can take larger frames, either round or rectangular, to suggest width. Or you can experiment with a wide, rectangular shape with some colour or decorations at the sides. This will also have a widening effect.

4 Square faces need softening. Try round frames made out of thin metal.

5 Heart-shaped faces are shown off to their best advantage in frames that are wider at the bottom than at the top.

6 Avoid round frames on a round face.

Rectangular ones are better. Choose light frames – darker ones are heavy.

7 Small faces need small frames – and it's important that frames don't protrude past the widest part of your face. Large heads need large frames.

8 Make sure that your eyebrows line up with the topmost part of the frame.

9 If you're in the upper age range, go for an up-to-date style and don't shy away from unusual colours and designs. A well-chosen on-trend pair will make you look fashion-conscious and they will be one of the first things someone notices.

10 If you sport a beard, choose smaller frames to avoid facial swamping.

GET ON WITH CONTACT LENSES

1 Choose contact lenses according to your lifestyle. They come as soft, gas-permeable, daily, extended wear.

2 How can you tell if your lens is inside out? Place the lens on your fingertip so that a cup is formed. If it makes a U-shape it's the correct way out.

3 Always make sure you wash your hands thoroughly before you put your contacts in, but avoid scented or oily soaps.

4 Always apply the first contact lens to the same eye so that you avoid the mixing up the lenses for right and left eyes.

5 If you wear eye make-up with your

lenses, buy new make-up regularly, at least every three months. Over time bacteria will get into the make-up and then into your eyes. Never share make-up.

6 **Carry hypoallergenic artificial tears** with you at all times, but make sure they're safe for contact-lens wearers.

7 **Take disposable contact lenses out when you get home.** It is important to allow your eyes time to breathe.

8 **Don't sleep with contact lenses in,** unless approved by your optician or you use extended-wear contact lenses.

9 **If your contact lens shifts off your eye** or to the side, gently close your eye and blink until the lens shifts into place.

10 **Care for your contact lenses every time you take them out** and leave them in the case for an extended period of time. You'll need to use a proper solution.

PERFECT YOUR POSTURE

1 **If you're conscious of the alignment of your back and neck,** you'll notice that your posture will improve.

2 **Make sure that your weight is evenly distributed on both feet.** This may feel as though you are slightly leaning forwards, but in fact you are not.

3 **Using a mirror, get your ears, shoulders and hips in alignment,** whether sitting or standing. Don't push your head forwards. Proper alignment will place your shoulders above your hips.

4 **Do exercises and stretches** to strengthen your upper back and shoulders. Be sure to repeat several times a day.

5 **Take ballet classes –** it's an excellent dance form for good posture.

6 **Do yoga.** The combination of breathing and posture alignment really helps

7 **Pilates will help strengthen your core muscles –** excellent for improving and building muscles leading to good posture..

8 **Use a high-quality chair with proper lumbar support.** The back rest should have a natural curve fitting the hollow of your back. Keep the soles of your feet flat on the floor. If you are sitting for most of the day, get up and walk around frequently.

9 **Avoid wearing high heels for prolonged periods** or every day. Heels alter the body's centre of gravity and throw the body out of alignment.

10 **Keep your spine straight as much as you can,** even when you are bending over to pick up something – don't be tempted to fold at the waist.

BE KIND TO YOUR FEET

1 **Wash your feet every day,** especially when you've taken brisk exercise.

2 **If you take showers in the morning rather than at night,** you need to wash your feet thoroughly at night.

3 **Wear shoes for comfort and fit.** Avoid designs that rub, pinch, are too big/small.

4 **Don't restrict blood flow to your feet**

by wearing tight shoes or socks or by sitting for too long with legs crossed.

5 **Re-energize your feet with some foot exercises** such as circling your ankles or tapping your toes, gripping and letting go.

6 **Do foot-stretching exercises,** which are beneficial for the lower leg.

7 **Have a home pedicure** every two weeks by soaking and exfoliating.

8 **Cut your toenails straight across to prevent ingrown toenails.** If you want to achieve a rounded effect, use an emery board after cutting to smooth the edges.

9 **Moisturize your feet daily.** Rub lotion into your feet at night and wear socks.

10 **Reflexology massages** are the ultimate relaxation. Use wooden foot rollers to give your feet a real treat.

A PERFECT FIT FOR SHOES

1 **Get your feet professionally measured.**

2 **The best time to have them measured is late in the day,** when they are largest.

3 **Don't choose shoes according to the size marked,** but according to their fit.

4 **Fit a new pair of shoes to your larger foot** – most people have one foot slightly larger than the other.

5 **Choose a shoe that is shaped** in a complementary way to your foot.

6 **During fitting, make sure that there is enough space for your longest toe** at the end of the shoe when you are standing up with your feet flat on the floor.

7 **Make sure the ball of your foot fits** the widest part of your shoe in comfort.

8 **Do not buy shoes that feel too tight in the shop** in the expectation that they will stretch to fit – they may not and they may rub your foot instead.

9 **Your shoes should not ride up and down on your heel** when you walk.

10 **Leather shoes reduce the possibility of skin irritation.**

AVOID VARICOSE VEINS

1 **Don't stand for long periods of time.** Move your legs, lifting and flexing your ankles to get your blood circulating.

2 **If you are sitting for extended periods of time,** say on a plane, get up and move around every 35–40 minutes.

3 **Take regular walks** to increase blood flow and to help exercise leg muscles.

4 **Avoid clothes that may restrict blood flow to the legs,** such as tight trousers.

5 **Try to keep your weight down** so that you reduce pressure on your legs.

6 **Raise your legs whenever you can,** especially when you are sitting down.

7 **Reduce your salt intake** to help prevent leg and ankle swelling.

8 **Apply witch hazel to the legs.**

9 **Try supplements** such as gingko biloba, gotu kola and capsicum.

10 **Take vitamin C with bioflavonoids,** to reduce blood-clotting tendencies, promote healing and strengthen the blood vessels.

WHAT? CHOOSE A HEARING AID

1 **How severe is your hearing loss?** Go for a hearing test before you choose a hearing aid – some types are more suited to mild hearing loss while others to severe loss. Seek professional advice before you make a final decision.

2 **The smaller the hearing aid is, the less powerful it will be,** the shorter its battery life and the more it will cost.

3 **The most-used type is the behind-the-ear hearing aid.** This type minimizes feedback, meaning it's less likely to whistle. It can also amplify more than other styles and is appropriate for all kinds of hearing loss and all ages.

4 **If you do a lot of sport, don't choose the behind-the-ear style.** The microphone remains outside the ear, so the wearer loses the natural resonance of the ear. This type also tends to pick up all wind noise and other noises besides and it can be knocked out of position all too easily.

5 **The best choice of hearing aid for children** is the behind-the-ear style – as the child grows and changes the aid can easily be adjusted.

6 **In-the-ear hearing aids are less visible,** but they require a lot more care and maintenance. Those who are physically active find them useful.

7 **Completely in-the-ear hearing aids** are for mild to moderate hearing loss in adults.

8 **Open-fit hearing aids are especially effective** for people suffering from high-frequency hearing loss.

9 **Digital hearing aids are more finely tuned to your hearing loss** and use a computer chip which converts the incoming sound into code.

10 **Half-shell and full-shell types** are made to measure, but are highly visible.

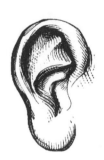

AVERT INCONTINENCE

1 **Do pelvic floor exercises.** They improve muscle tone over a lifetime. Tighten up muscles around back/front passages and imagine you are lifting them inside you.

2 **If you are overweight, try to slim down** and tone the abdomimal muscles.

3 **Watch your fluid intake.** Avoid drinking large amounts in one session. Rather, drink water steadily throughout the day.

4 **When you are working out, take little sips of water all the time.** Drinking too much too quickly can strain your bladder.

5 **Drink alcohol and caffeine just in moderation** as they stimulate your urine production. Overuse of either can weaken the muscles that control the bladder.

6 **Urinate whenever you feel the urge,** as holding on for too long can weaken the bladder and lead to urine leakage.

7 **Eat plenty of fibre-rich foods** as constipation can worsen incontinence.

8 **Stop smoking** – smokers are more likely to develop urinary incontinence.

9 **Reduce your stress levels.** Stress can lead to incontinence. For example, practise controlled breathing techniques.

10 **Visit your doctor if your urination** becomes more frequent or more painful.

TRY A LITTLE HAPPINESS!

1 Keep physically active – your body will respond to the extra endorphins, which will lighten your mood. Go for a run, wash the kitchen floor or dance a little jig.

2 Aim to have a good life-work balance. Don't take work worries home with you.

3 Take time to do the things you really enjoy outside working hours.

4 Listen to nature. You will get a quiet contentment from hearing natural sounds.

5 Singing lifts the spirits. Take singing lessons or join a choir. Or sing in the bath.

6 Try out new things.

7 Let go of all those grievances you can do nothing about. This will allow you to move forward in your life more positively.

8 Get plenty of sleep – it's crucial to your health and wellbeing.

9 Why not go on a pilgrimage? This can bring peace, connection and healing.

10 Try volunteering. Doing good works can raise your happiness levels.

HOW TO MEDITATE

1 Find a comfortable place to sit – cross-legged or on a straight-backed chair.

2 Check your posture and consciously relax your body, starting with your toes and working up to the top of your head.

3 Close your eyes. Focus attention on your breathing. Count four beats, inhaling, hold your breath for four beats, exhale for four beats and hold for four beats. Repeat this six times.

4 On the following exhale, breathe out the word 'om'. Focus your mind on the sound. Repeat 'om' with every exhale. You may find that this sounds quite loud. Just let the sound flow out. The syllables should resonate through your body. Do six 'oms' and then try six cycles of breathing silently.

5 Check your posture and physical tension. Relax tense muscles.

6 Repeat the cycle again.

7 Don't rush from one 'om' to the next and keep on inhaling through your nose.

8 Come back to full consciousness.

9 Now shake out your limbs or rub your hands together.

10 Feel energized and calm.

HELP WITH DE-STRESSING

1 Aromatherapy
2 Chi gung
3 Colour healing
4 Crystal healing
5 Reiki
6 Massage
7 Yoga
8 Neuro-linguistic programming
9 Pilates
10 Reflexology

GET A SENSE OF CALM

1 If you are constantly plagued by worry and don't know how to stop it, use 'thought-stopping'. Take time every day to close your eyes and say to yourself 'Stop'.

2 Make yourself a dream pillow. Blend lavender, mugwort, hops, rosemary and rose petals and stitch into a cotton pillow.

3 Try doing chi gung. This ancient Chinese discipline harnesses energy to combat illness and promote longevity.

4 B-complex vitamins combat symptoms and causes of stress and keep you calm.

5 Take a stress-relief bath. Add essential oils to your normal bath oil or bath milk: 24 drops of neroli, 12 drops of clary sage, 12 drops of lavender and 6 drops of cedar wood. Light candles, put on soft music and allow your tension to flow out of you.

6 Have a head massage. Massage in a little almond oil.

7 Cut out caffeine. Don't drink more than two or three coffees a day.

8 Pilates is calming.

9 The candle-gazing technique can have a wonderfully calming effect. Sit with a lit candle a short distance away in your line of sight. Gaze at the flame and after a few minutes close your eyes. You should be able to see a calming residual image.

10 Boost your blood-sugar levels. Eat regularly so that you maintain energy levels. This will keep moods more even.

ESSENTIAL AROMATHERAPY OILS

1 Clove
2 Eucalyptus
3 Grapefruit
4 Lavender
5 Lemon
6 Peppermint
7 Patchouli
8 Pine
9 Rosemary
10 Tea tree

OVERCOME A PHOBIA

1 It's important not to avoid the feared situation or object. Write down a hierarchy for your feared situation/object. If you hate snakes the range would run from reading about snakes to picking one up.

2 Confront the least-frightening item in the range and try to regulate your anxiety. Remain in the situation until anxiety decreases. Move to the next item.

3 If you entertain frightening thoughts relating to your phobia, write them down and find good arguments against them.

4 Take small steps. If you try to rush you may feel overwhelmed and discouraged. But if you don't take any steps at all, you may never be able to get over your phobia!

5 Learn relaxation techniques to help you manage your anxiety and fear.

6 Try positive thinking. Stay optimistic when facing your fears. Remind yourself that you do have the power to overcome your phobia; there is no real danger.

7 Empower yourself in other areas of your life. Take up a hobby, join a club or take a course. This may help you feel more confident and able to conquer your fears.

8 Find out as much as you can about your condition.

9 Promote a positive frame of mind in yourself. You have all the tools you require to overcome your phobia – you just need to believe in yourself.

10 There are therapies available: psychotherapy, counselling, hypnotherapy.

FEAR OF FLYING

1 Lack of familiarity may be causing your fears. Find out what to expect.

2 Research statistics that will reassure you about flying safety.

3 Lack of air may make you nervous. Use the cool-air valve above your seat.

4 Sitting in the centre of the plane, may help to reassure you.

5 Pretend you are really on a bus.

6 Stretch your muscles throughout the flight to help relax you.

7 Try smiling! Putting on a smile will make you feel positive and you'll have a positive effect on other people, too.

8 Repeat positive affirmations to yourself. For example, 'I am calm'.

9 Listen to music. Background music will help lighten your mood. Choose blues, jazz or mood music. Don't choose sounds that energize you, though.

10 If you've tried absolutely everything, why not visit your GP for a sedative?

INSTANTLY IMPROVE YOUR SENSE OF WELLBEING

1 Get physical
2 Eat well
3 Sleep
4 Laugh
5 Socialize
6 Fulfilling work
7 Engrossing hobbies
8 Spoil yourself
9 Massage
10 Be kind to others

RAISE YOUR SELF-ESTEEM

1 Build on your personal successes. Think of something you can do easily. Every time you complete a task well, move on to complete a new task and do that well, too. Start with small things.

2 Imagine yourself the way you want to be. Create an image of yourself in your mind's eye. Practise seeing yourself in this way for ten minutes every morning.

3 Improve your life socially. Contact a friend you haven't seen for a while. Think of other friends you haven't seen recently.

4 Think of what you fear doing most and do it. Then do it again! It will seem a lot less threatening afterwards.

5 Think about the things you are really good at. Do them more and more.

6 Write down your personal goals. This will make them a reality and you will be less likely to put off achieving them.

7 Think about the parts of your life that need your attention. List the main areas of your life and then rate yourself out of ten for each one. Work on the areas you scored lowest on first – once you start getting results, you'll have the confidence to work on all areas.

8 Be with people who build you up. Avoid those who put you down.

9 Give yourself encouragement. Count all the things you do well in and congratulate yourself on them.

10 Stop comparing yourself to others. Just do the best you can for you and yours.

ARTFUL ANGER MANAGEMENT

1 Anger can be healthy. Think about whether your style of anger is healthy or unhealthy.

2 Calming yourself down is important. Divert your mind by thinking about something completely different.

3 If someone has angered you, ask them for time to think. If you really cannot control yourself, leave the room.

4 Calm down your angry mind by playing music and listening to it closely.

5 Take some form of exercise: go for an energetic walk, a swim or a run.

6 Tense and relax muscles alternately – hold for a few seconds and then release.

7 Give yourself a massage, especially

your stomach and chest area.

8 Imagine a relaxing scene. Think of laughing at yourself and the situation you are in after the angry scene is all over.

9 Think about where the anger comes from. If it comes from inability to assert yourself, consider assertion training.

10 Avoid stimulants.

FOIL YOUR FOOD CRAVINGS

1 Chocolate is the number-one craving! Try just having chocolate when you're already full. Your cravings may weaken.

2 Sugar and sweets are big, too. You get an instant 'lift' to your energy levels, but this falls again rapidly, causing you to crave them again. Never skip meals and try a protein snack to break your habit.

3 If you crave chips and savoury snacks, choose lower-fat versions. Make your own low-fat chips or munch on baked bread slices instead – it has the 'crunch' effect.

4 Bread and pasta are favourite comfort foods. Carbs stimulate serotonin release, which could be part of their appeal. Control portions and restrict butter/creamy sauces.

5 When you feel a food craving coming on, try changing your location. Your surroundings may be sending signals that trigger you to desire a certain food.

6 Change what you are doing. This will focus your mind on a different activity for a while. You'll forget about your desires.

7 Distract your taste buds. If you want something salty, eat a spicy food item, although lower in calories. If you want something sweet, eat a sour food.

8 Give yourself a reward for avoiding your cravings! But not chocolate!

9 Don't starve yourself. You'll be lowering blood-sugar levels and weakening your will – you'll binge on the very foods you want.

10 Eat calcium-rich foods. Sometimes food cravings can be traced to calcium deficiency, so your body starts fancying certain foods to make up for it.

IMPROVE YOUR CONCENTRATION

1 Perhaps your physical environment is distracting you. Move to a more controlled place. It may be easier to concentrate in a library rather than working at home.

2 Focus on one thing at a time. Put aside time for your task and then focus just on it. If your mind wanders, make it return to what you are doing.

3 If unrelated thoughts come into your mind, ignore them and switch them off.

4 If random thoughts are persistent, detach from them.

5 If your work is difficult, realize that concentration on it will be harder, too. Simplify your work down to basic concepts.

6 Meditation works! Empty your mind. Every time it tries to latch on to a thought, dismiss it and return to emptiness.

7 Give yourself goals to improve concentration over several weeks. Reduce the time your concentration is poor. Then reduce that further. Then further.

8 Practise concentration games. Look at a number of objects hard, then remove them and list everything you can remember.

9 Try saying 'Be here, now' when you notice thoughts wandering. When they do the same again, say it again and again.

10 Reserve a daily slot for thinking about the things that distract you. Plough through these things. When your mind starts going into 'distraction mode', remind yourself that you have already thought about it in your daily slot.

MAX YOUR MEMORY

SUPPLEMENTS TO BOOST WELLBEING

1 Rescue remedy
2 St John's wort
3 Marjoram
4 Echinacea
5 Glucosamine sulphate
6 Manuka honey
7 B-vitamins
8 Ginseng
9 Fish oils
10 Evening primrose oil

1 Nurture your brain by giving it a good diet and top nutrition. Your ability to use your memory will improve. Bulk up on omega-3-rich fish. Limit saturated fat.

2 Exercise well! This will increase oxygen to the brain, reducing the risk of disorders leading to memory loss such as diabetes and cardiovascular disease.

3 Get plenty of sleep. If you're sleep-deprived, your brain won't be able to operate at its full capacity.

4 Use mnemonic devices to make your memory work. Visual images work well.

5 Pay attention so that the information hits your memory and stays there.

6 Use your senses and relate information to colours, textures, smells and tastes.

7 Relate information to what you already know so that new data is connected to what you already remember.

8 If you find that a concept is too complex to remember, focus on the basic ideas and remember those.

9 Review what you already remember so that it sticks in your memory.

10 Use mental images to label or 'hook' information in your brain. To remember a particular item, you recall the label.

BRILLIANT BRAIN EXERCISES

1 Try singing – it exercises the right side of your brain, which helps you to become a more effective problem-solver.

2 Do puzzles, such as crosswords, to help to keep your brain agile.

3 Try something different every day, such as taking a different route to work or talking to a different colleague.

4 Try to build up your memory and concentration skills.

5 Combine two brain activities, such as driving and doing maths in your head. This forces your brain to do more in the same amount of time.

7 Develop your language skills. Try expanding your vocabulary by reading about topics that do not attract you.

8 Learn a new skill every day.

9 Physical exercise is important for the brain because it influences the rate of creation of new neurons.

10 Swapping hands to do everyday tasks strengthens pathways and connections on the opposite sides of your brain.

USE AROMATHERAPY STRESS RELIEF FOR:

1 Nervous tension
2 Anxiety
3 Apprehension
4 Low self-esteem
5 Anger
6 Insomnia
7 Depression
8 Interpersonal relations
9 Nervous exhaustion
10 Lack of concentration

RELAXING RELAXATION

1 Yoga is an exercise system ideally suited to help stress and anxiety.

2 Reiki is a relaxing healing practice. Energy is transferred to the practitioner's hands and then to the receiver.

3 Essential oils are very relaxing.

4 Aerobic exercises are great for alleviating stress and anxiety.

5 Reflexology is renowned for stress-relief. It uses pressure points.

6 Many crystals are useful for relieving stress and calming the mind, including tourmaline, aquamarine and green calcite.

7 Sandalwood incense can have a calming and cooling effect when you are driving. Leave the incense unlit.

8 Chi gung stimulates blood flow around the body. Balancing the flow of energy can help you let go of tensions.

9 Guided imagery for relaxation is a variation on tradional meditation that requires you to employ not only your visual sense but your other senses, too.

10 'Being in the moment' can be used for de-stressing, bringing your nervous system back into balance.

PERK UP YOUR TIME–MANAGEMENT

1 Don't jump from one activity to another, leaving a trail of incomplete tasks in your wake. Complete one task before you move on to the next.

2 Set aside blocks of time to accommodate the competing demands in your life: work, home and leisure. Identify areas when you waste time.

3 Be realistic when assessing what can and cannot be achieved.

4 Learn to say 'no' if your experience tells you the task cannot be completed in the allotted time.

5 Learn to let go and delegate work to others if at all possible.

6 Prioritize everything that needs doing. Make a list of jobs to be done.

7 Review your list during the day, update and re-prioritize as necessary.

8 Don't procrastinate. The task will prey on your mind. Get it out of the way.

9 Set realistic and achievable goals. Reward yourself when you have achieved some or all of your goals.

10 Break tasks into components so you accomplish them one step at a time.

GET OVER SHYNESS

1 **Why are you shy?** It will help if you can work out the root causes of your condition.

2 **Practise 'as if'!** When you are on your own, behave as if you are supremely confident. You will see results the next time you go anywhere.

3 **Make eye contact and smile.** This will make a real difference to the way people react to you and add to your confidence.

4 **Talk to strangers.** It's a great way to practise conversation skills.

5 **Observe the shy-free.** See how they behave and how they react to others.

6 **Look your best.** This will boost your confidence and help reduce shyness.

7 **What's the worst that could happen?**

8 **How do you handle rejection?** Imagine scenarios in which you are told 'No' and test out your reactions in private.

9 **We are all afraid of the same things** (embarrassment, insecurity, lack of self-worth); some cope better than others.

10 **Learn to read body language.** It will help you develop your social skills.

BEEF UP YOUR ENERGY

1 **Eat smaller, more frequent meals** to help you maintain a steady energy.

2 **Drink lots of water.** About eight glasses a day will stop you feeling sluggish.

3 **Take control of your body clock** by waking up and going to bed at the same time every day, even weekends. You'll remain alert all day.

4 **Take more exercise.** If going to the gym regularly is a step too far, go for power walks round the block.

5 **Losing weight will boost your energy.**

6 **Take power naps.**

7 **Wear bright colours** to boost your mood and make you feel more energetic.

8 **Light, energy-packed meals** will give you the boost you need to go out on the town. They should be high in protein, low in fat, with a complex carbohydrate.

9 **Some foods sap energy.** These include: saturated animal fats, butter, alcohol, caffeine, processed food and additives.

10 **Regular meditation** helps recharge your batteries.

BE SAFE ON FOOT

1 **Be conscious of your surroundings** when you are out and about – particularly if you are on your own.

2 **Have your keys ready** as you approach your vehicle or your front door.

3 **Project yourself as a confident person.** If you come across as weak and frightened you are more likely to be victimized and possibly attacked.

4 **Don't have valuables,** such as jewellery,

a phone, watch or camera on display.

5 **When you are in a threatening situation** remember that material things can be replaced.

6 **If you wear a backpack,** transfer it to your front so that it can't be pickpocketed.

7 **Wear a shoulder bag across your front.**

8 **At night, stick to well-lit streets** and try to avoid known dangerous areas.

9 **Wear comfortable shoes** that you are happy to run in – or take a pair with you.

10 **Take self-defence classes.**

SAFETY FIRST IN CROWDS

1 **Look for the emergency exit signs** as you enter a large venue.

2 **Check to see where the first aid and security offices are.**

3 **In the rare event of a crowd stampede,** move sideways to the crowd until you get to a wall. Press yourself against it until the crowd disperses or you find an exit.

4 **Wear clothes with zipped pockets for carrying valuables.** Bags are not advisable in crowds as they tempt pickpockets and easily get lost or stolen.

5 **Set up times to connect with friends or family,** even if it's just by phone.

6 **Establish a meeting place** in the event that you become separated.

7 **Think about leaving before the end of the event** – get away before the rush.

8 **Look at the weather forecast.** Changing weather conditions can cause conditions to deteriorate. Wear sturdy shoes.

9 **Keep kids in sight at all times** and go with them to the bathroom. Dress them in bright clothes and hats. Discuss what they should do if they get separated.

10 **Write a label with your child's full name, address, phone number** and attach it to their clothing in a hidden spot.

BEEP BEEP! ROAD SAFETY

1 **Always check that you have enough petrol, oil and water** before you set out.

2 **Research alternative routes** in case your chosen one becomes impassable or a traffic jam develops.

3 **Keep a travel blanket and a spade** in the boot of the car.

4 **Take a special survival bag** on road trips. It should contain water, snacks, first aid kit, a blanket, a torch, some comfortable shoes and extra clothes.

5 **Take a map with you,** even if you use sat nav. Know where you are.

6 **Don't use your phone while you are driving,** unless it is hands-free.

7 **Keep valuables, such as bags, out of sight** when you're driving. Don't leave valuables in the car between trips.

8 **Before you get into your car,** check that there's no one hiding in the back.

9 **If you are worried about car-jacking,** wearing a seat belt and locking your doors may help keep trouble away.

10 **Don't give lifts to strangers.**

HEALTH & FITNESS

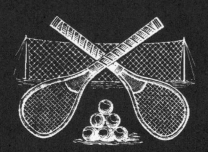

Good health is vital for a happy, healthy and productive life – and there are a whole lot of things we can do to improve and keep good health. It really pays to take good care of yourself and maintain your fitness – that way you'll be able to enjoy everything in life, both now and in the years to come.

STICK TO AN EXERCISE PLAN

1 Take a realistic view of exercise. Start with simple, achievable goals – such as going to the gym twice a week. It's easy to get frustrated and give up if you're too ambitious and think you'll go every day – you just won't be able to stick to it. Feelings of failure will follow. A realistic goal that really works for you is your best bet and it will achieve slow, steady results.

2 Put your plan down on paper and record your progress. This will help you to stay motivated. You could ask a personal trainer to help you work out your plan. He/she can assess you and will know what is best for your age and stage.

3 Get into the exercise habit, but if you experience a lapse, try not to worry too much. Everyone has off-days or is ill for a short time. It happens. When you've had to miss a few sessions, just ease yourself back into your regime gradually – your original schedule will return soon enough. Choose sports and physical activities that you really enjoy. If you're not actually relishing working out, then try tackling something different, but don't stop activity completely. Perhaps think about starting a class in something you haven't tried before.

4 Try to take a flexible approach to your exercise regime. If you're too busy or tired to work out, take a day or two off and start again when you can. If you miss a workout – don't be too hard on yourself. You'll need to take breaks for holidays, too.

5 Incorporate physical activity into your daily routine – you'll be far more likely to stick at it. A brisk walk to the bus is a good start. Try taking the stairs instead of the lift. Use your lunch break for a quick game of squash, a visit to the gym or to squeeze in a yoga class. You can do simple stretches while you are still sitting at your desk. It also helps motivate you if you don't need to buy special clothes and equipment, get changed or take showers.

6 Don't beat yourself up. If you decide to skip a class, don't waste time feeling too terrible. Don't try and punish yourself by over-exercising the next day. If you really can't put the guilt aside, set yourself a time limit for blaming yourself and then move on. Let it go!

7 Join forces with friends or colleagues. Invite other people to join you when you exercise and don't be tempted to break arrangements you've made with them. You can all join a class to help with technique and motivation and you'll make new friends there, too.

8 Play sport with children. You'll benefit just as much as they will. You'll be getting some exercise and they'll be getting the fitness habit for life – and even maybe learning some new ball skills at the same time. Make a habit of taking them to the park, no matter what the weather is.

9 Reward yourself. Short- and long-term successes merit a little pat on the back. Treat yourself however you like, but perhaps not with a bar of chocolate! If you need to give yourself some encouragement, treat yourself to some new music or buy a new gym outfit. This will really help to motivate you.

10 Think of someone who inspires you. Whenever your fitness enthusiasm seems to be flagging, bring to mind someone you can use as a role model. This might be an older person who swims regularly or a young kid you know who never misses his football practice. If they can do it then, surely, so can you!

GREAT OUTDOOR SPORTS

1 Cricket
2 American football
3 Rugby
4 Golf
5 Sailing
6 Football
7 Softball/baseball
8 Fishing
9 Hockey
10 Netball

THE PERFECT GYM FOR YOU

GREAT INDOOR SPORTS

1 Badminton
2 Squash/racquet ball
3 Basketball
4 Swimming
5 Volleyball
6 Tennis
7 Bowling
8 Snooker
9 Table tennis
10 Gymnastics

1 **Convenience is key.** If the gym takes too long to get to, you'll be less likely to go. Find one that's on your route to work – you'll have a hard time avoiding it.

2 **Is the gym clean and tidy?** Inspect the changing room and see whether it is spick and span.

3 **Is the gym safe?** Are lockable lockers provided to leave valuables in? Do you feel safe? Might you prefer a same-sex facility?

4 **Look at the equipment.** Is it up to date and in good repair? Is it the type of equipment that you want to use?

5 **Beware of 'weekend warriors'.** Find out how well used the gym is. Some gyms are overcrowded at certain times.

6 **Talk to the instructors and trainers.** Are they available, friendly and helpful?

7 **Sit in on a class.** Is it well attended? Does the teacher seem good?

8 **TVs and music may be on tap.** Is this what you want?

9 **Consider what facilities you need?** Does the gym have a pool, sauna, yoga and dance studios? What about weights?

10 **Is the gym good value or are there hidden extras?** Will you have to pay on top for towels, lockers and classes?

GET THE MOST FROM YOUR GYM

1 **If your gym offers personal training, evaluations or classes,** avail yourself and make sure you get regular assessments and updates from your trainer.

2 **Use all the machines on offer.** Ask a trainer to teach you how to use machinery you've never tried before and set up a workout plan for you.

3 **Try out a range of classes.**

4 **Get the gym habit!** Get into a regular routine of going to the gym a certain number of times per week.

5 **Don't leave long gaps between visits to the gym.** The longer you leave it, the harder it will be to return.

6 **Invest in a brand-new workout kit.**

7 **Listen to motivating music** while you are working out – it will keep you focused.

8 **Don't get distracted by your phone.** Leave it in your locker.

9 **A workout buddy** can help you stay focused and it's more fun.

10 **Bring water, drinks and snacks** with you to keep your energy levels up.

FINDING A PERSONAL TRAINER

1 **Decide how much you want to spend.** Normally trainers charge by the hour and prices depend on location, experience and how much they are in demand.

2 **Search a professional directory for trainers in your area.** Or ask at your gym.

3 **Contact at least three trainers** and call them to discuss what you are looking for. If you don't like anything about any of them, then discount them immediately.

4 **Meet your selected trainer in a public place** – preferably at your gym.

5 **Check the trainer's credentials.** There should be no problem accessing them. How long have they been working in this job?

6 **Follow up references** and ask them what they really think.

7 **Ask questions and get clarification** about anything you are unclear about.

8 **It's vital to feel comfortable with your selected trainer.** Are they pleasant and interested in your wellbeing? Do they listen and ask relevant questions in return?

9 **Your trainer must be able to tell you how your training will be planned** and what they have in mind for you.

10 **Ask the trainer about his/her achievements** and success stories.

DON'T GIVE YOURSELF SPORTS INJURIES

1 **Get into shape before you embark on the sport** – especially if you haven't played for some time.

2 **You need to train for each specific sport you take up.**

3 **Know and abide by the rules of the sport** – they are designed to keep everyone safe and the sport running smoothly.

4 **Courtesy is good!** Look out for other team members. If someone's shoe has come undone, tell them.

5 **Get properly warmed up** before you start. Do plenty of stretches.

6 **Wear the correct clothes and use the proper equipment.** Make sure everything is the right size and that it fits you.

7 **Rest is a critical component of your training.** It makes you stronger and prevents injuries caused by over-training, poor judgement and fatigue.

8 **Don't play if you are very tired or in pain.** Pain indicates a problem, so pay attention to warning signs.

9 **Always listen to and obey the coach or referee.**

10 **Be aware of old injuries.** If you have been injured before, you are much more likely to be hurt again.

YOUR FIRST GOLF CLUBS

1 **Do not buy the best golf clubs,** since investing in high-quality, high-priced clubs as a beginner could be counter- productive and a waste of money. Decide on a reasonable budget to spend and stick to it. If you are going to play often, it is worth spending a bit more.

2 **New or used?** All-new is good but could be more than you want to spend. A used set could be a bargain, but be cautious. Before purchasing, double-check all clubs. If there are missing head covers or worn grips – do not buy it!

3 **Ask for recommendations.** A pro shop

or golfing friends will be able to advise you. It's a great way to get ideas.

4 To save money look for complete sets as this is where bargains are to be had.

5 The larger the club face on the driver, **the bigger the sweet spot** and the more it will decrease the chance of making a miss-hit.

6 Buy a driver with more loft, not less. Additional loft of at least 12–15 degrees will help increase the height of your shots.

7 Opt for a mallet putter with an offset. The lines on the putter head aid you in lining up your putts. The offset shaft is designed to get your eye over the ball, as

it allows you to line up your shots more easily than a straight shaft.

8 Choose irons that are perimeter-weighted and cavity-backed. These are geared to higher-handicappers.

9 Steel or graphite shaft? Graphite is lighter and can help generate swing speed; steel is more durable and cheaper. Women and seniors will most likely benefit from graphite shafts with a softer flex. Younger, stronger men might go with regular or stiff shafts, but most teaching pros say many golfers use shafts that are too stiff.

10 All golfers should use standard-length clubs unless he/she is short or tall.

FORE! IMPROVE YOUR GOLF SWING

1 Make sure that you grip the club correctly. Place your left hand on first; your right goes over the top.

2 Adopt the correct stance. Your feet need to be in the right positions for the type of shot you are going to take.

3 Align yourself with the flag. Find a small leaf or stone that is in a direct line between the flag and your ball and use it to position yourself.

4 Never take your eye off the ball.

5 Keep your head down and keep it still. A common mistake is to lift the head during the swing.

6 Don't rush your swing or you will lose your balance and miss-hit the shot.

7 Practise the rotation movement of your swing by holding your club across either the front or back of your shoulders. Rotate your whole body either to the right or to the left, as in the swing. This keeps your back at the correct angle.

8 Remember! You're not hitting the ball – you're swinging through it.

9 Always follow your shot through the ball and into a full swing.

10 Make your practice swing your real swing – stance, correct grip and all.

THE TENNIS RACQUET FOR YOU!

1 For more power as a less-experienced player, choose a larger racquet head size. It has a bigger sweet spot

2 Choose a light-headed racquet if you are a more experienced player. Its weight is more evenly distributed throughout, allowing you to have more control.

3 **Think about the grip.** Hold a racquet in your normal forehand grip – you should be able to squeeze a finger in between your palm and fingers.

4 **The thicker the shank** the more powerful the racquet.

5 **Between sizes?** If you are a junior and still growing, it is best to go for a slightly larger grip.

6 **Pre-strung racquets** are geared towards recreational players and are very versatile for beginners.

7 **Unstrung racquets** are for intermediate to advanced players, allowing you to choose a racquet type and size and then tailor the string to your game.

8 **All racquet frames come with manufacturer's recommendations** on string tension. Stay within those limits.

9 **Only buy natural-gut strings** if you are more advanced. They need to be changed frequently and aren't as durable.

10 **What shaped head?** The tear-drop shape allows almost the entire face to become the sweet spot. The oval-shaped racquet has its sweet spot in the bottom half only.

ANYONE FOR TENNIS?

1 **Tennis is a game of the mind,** so it's vital to concentrate or you'll make errors.

2 **Keep moving during play.** Exercise your knees and bend them whenever you can. This helps to prevent injury.

3 **Keep your eye on the ball** to help you concentrate and coordinate your shots.

4 **Check your grip** and keep it relaxed.

5 **Maximize time practising your strokes** by always using the correct technique – even when the ball is not in play (for example during the warm-up).

6 **Don't play too horizontally on groundstrokes.** Play from low to high, to lift the ball over the net.

7 **Toss the ball high when serving**, to help you generate more power and speed.

8 **Don't drop your tossing arm too early when serving.**

9 **When volleying, step out with your outside foot first and then cross over.** Make sure that you are closer to the net than when you started.

10 **Keep the ball in play.**

RUN FOR YOUR LIFE!

1 **Wear good-quality running shoes.**

2 **Women should wear a good supportive sports bra** and anti-chafing clothes.

3 **Learn the correct upper-body form and stride.**

4 **Breathe in through your nose and mouth** to make sure that you're getting enough oxygen while running. Take some deep belly breaths to prevent developing side stitches.

5 Stay hydrated before/during your run.

6 Eat some protein and a good amount of carbohydrates beforehand. During the run, eat to replace the sugar, electrolytes and salt you are losing through sweating.

7 Always warm up and cool down every time you run.

8 Don't do too much too soon – it can lead to injury. Take walk-breaks during your training runs. By alternating running and walking you will find you can cover greater distances.

9 Alternate faster and longer run days with shorter and slower run days. This allows your body to recover and progress.

10 To get the most out of your running workout, do a hill-train once per week. Or try power-walking up the hill.

GREAT AEROBIC EXERCISES

1 Step aerobics
2 Cycling
3 Skipping
4 Running
5 Jazz aerobics
6 Water aerobics
7 Yoga
8 Swimming
9 Cross-country skiing
10 Inline skating

YOGALICIOUS WORKOUTS

1 Use a proper sticky yoga mat to help improve your grip.

2 Keep your feet bare throughout the programme.

3 Wear loose or stretchy clothing.

4 Do yoga on an empty stomach or about one to two hours after a meal. Drink water and eat an energy bar/piece of fruit about an hour before class.

5 Practising first thing in the morning is a great way to revitalize mind, body and spirit before your day starts.

6 Relaxation between exercises is important – it gives the body a chance to assimilate the energy that is now circulating. The body rejuvenates, heals and recharges.

7 Enhance relaxation periods by turning your eyes upwards while closed and 'look out' through the centre of your forehead to help to activate the third eye – the seat of intuition and awakening. This centre is a key aspect of progress in yoga.

8 Mentally chant a mantra to enhance relaxation further – you'll get more out of your session and you'll develop your concentration and spiritual energy.

9 Get a good yoga instructor. You can learn from a book, however they are usually best used as reminders of your class.

10 Choose the right kind of yoga for your age and stage. There are several different types, from very active and fast to quiet and contemplative.

SWOOSH! BEGINNER'S SKIING

1 Before you learn to ski, make sure your body is physically fit and that you have sufficient physical endurance – it's a demanding sport!

2 Rent or borrow clothes and equipment until you are sure you want to ski seriously. It's expensive to buy and it's all readily available for hire.

3 Stop your feet getting cold by wearing correctly fitting ski boots. You should be able to wiggle your toes. If your boots fit properly they will be warm and you won't need to wear very thick socks or more than one pair – you'll lose circulation and your feet will get cold.

4 **Make sure your ski pants, jacket and gloves are all waterproof.** You'll be falling down a lot to begin with.

5 **Padded ski pants are preferable** as they protect your body from bruising and keep you warm on the ski lift.

6 **You can't just set off without instruction.** Take lessons or enlist a good friend to teach you.

7 **Have reasonable expectations as a beginner.** You will fall down a lot, it will be hard to get up and six-year-olds will be skiing expertly all around you.

8 **When falling, try to fall uphill –** on your backside.

9 **Choose a suitable ski resort with good beginners' slopes –** you want wide rather than steep slopes.

10 **Check ahead for snow conditions.** If it's icy, forget it. Ice is way too dangerous for beginners.

LET'S GO SNOWBOARDING!

1 **Determine your snowboard stance.** Is your left or right foot forward? To find out, if you push someone backwards on the chest, whichever foot they step back onto is their back foot.

2 **Adopt a solid stance** that spans slightly wider than your shoulders.

3 **Strap on the front snowboard binding first.** You may want to sit down to do this.

4 **Take lessons** from a proper instructor.

5 **Practise the basic positions and movements on the flat.** Find a spot on a carpet and use a doorframe for balance.

6 **Build up your muscle strength** by doing squats, lunges and leg-presses.

7 **Falling uphill,** if possible, will reduce the impact. If you do fall downhill, relax and roll with the fall rather than resisting it with your arms and legs.

8 **When you fall backwards,** make your hands into a fist, punch the snow and sit on your backside.

9 **Skate on your board when you're moving across flat areas.** Attach the front foot only and leave your back foot free. Make a skating motion.

10 **Do not drop your board on a slope.** Carry it like a book under one arm.

BE A SURFING DUDE

1 **Ensure that your board lies flat in the water –** the nose/tail shouldn't dip.

2 **Make a mark on the board** where your chin should be.

3 **Always paddle using a crawl stroke.** This provides constant speed.

4 **The key to sitting well** on your board is to be calm and still.

5 **Practise standing on your board** in the sand or on a large bed as a lot of control is required – having someone to watch and critique your performance is a good idea.

6 **Wear a leg rope tied to the board** so that you don't lose it.

7 **Consider wearing a vest, rash guard or T-shirt** to avoid your stomach and chest getting a rubbed rash.

8 **Never attempt to position your board** between yourself and the oncoming waves.

9 **To avoid collision** with others keep a safe distance.

10 **When you fall off your board,** cover the back of your head with your hands, wrists over your ears and elbows together.

START SWIMMING

1 **If you're afraid of the water,** start by staying in the shallow end of the pool and practise gradually going deeper under the water, holding your breath at the same time. Relax and do it slowly – until your head is fully immersed.

2 **Try not to wear any floating devices.** You need to learn to float on your own.

3 **To learn about breathing,** take a breath and go under water. Exhale by blowing out bubbles rather than holding your breath. This keeps you relaxed.

4 **Always practise** in a safe environment.

5 **Practise arm motions independently** from leg motions.

6 **Try swimming goggles** – you'll be more relaxed as you'll be able to keep your eyes open without getting water in them.

7 **Use dry-land training** at home to perfect your technique.

8 **Get a waterproof digital camera** and ask a friend to film you swimming. This is a great way to observe your own mistakes and then improve on them.

9 **Wear a nose clip** when swimming free-style – you'll be able to concentrate on your mouth and breathing correctly.

10 **Wear silicone ear plugs** if you swim in cold water. This helps prevent irritation and infection.

GET A SIX-PACK

1 **Become as lean as possible** in the stomach area. Eat a diet that is low in fat and high in protein.

2 **Reduce your body fat to around ten per cent** in order to get a visible six-pack. Running, cycling and swimming are all good exercises for this.

3 **Aerobic exercises** help to burn fat.

4 **To build your entire mid-section** do rotation exercises such as ab-twists.

5 **Use standing moves** to burn more fat.

6 **Aim to train** at least three to four times per week.

7 **Focus on other muscles** as well as your abs, to keep your physique balanced.

8 **Do as many different ab exercises** as you can. You'll keep the muscles stimulated and developing constantly.

9 **Work your abs** by doing sit-ups.

10 **Make your exercise gradually harder.** Aim to increase the intensity of your workout by ten per cent every four weeks.

WHICH SPORTS KIT?

1 If you work up a real sweat think about the material used for your kit. Look for fabrics that wick-away moisture and keep you cool.

2 Use specialist sports shops to buy better-quality goods. Mass-market stores sometimes sell fashion-item goods that aren't up to the job.

3 Layering clothing works better for outdoor pursuits such as hiking and mountaineering. You can peel off or add on according to the demands of the weather or your activity levels.

4 Put comfort, fit, suitability for use and practicality before fashion. Try on before you buy and try out the movements you will need to make in your sport.

5 Don't cut costs when it comes to safety and protective equipment such as helmets, pads and hand protection.

6 Look out for core vents on jackets or thigh vents on trousers if you perspire from a high-energy activity.

7 To keep out snow and cold, wear a jacket-to-trouser connect system while skiing and snowboarding.

8 Remember your eyes – wear sunglasses or goggles with UV protection when skiing and sailing.

9 Wear specific footwear for the sport you are pursuing. You will perform better.

10 Lightweight, light-coloured clothing is best in hot weather. Ventilated shorts and T-shirts let heat dissipate.

BUYING A PAIR OF TRAINERS
1 Comfort
2 Protection
3 Durability
4 Purpose
5 Price
6 Shock absorbency
7 Add sports socks
8 Measure feet
9 Do research
10 Shop around

WONDERFUL WETSUITS!

1 Rent a wetsuit before buying and dive in it so that you can work out whether it's the correct fit for you.

2 Fabric thickness is the most important factor. Choose thickness on the basis of the type of water and use. The thicker the wetsuit, the warmer you will be.

3 Wear a shortie in warm waters. It has short arms and legs to just above the knee.

4 A hood is for cold-water diving.

5 Quality of construction is important. Check the seams before buying. The glued seam stitch will deteriorate fastest. The basic overlocked stitch has a ridge, which can be uncomfortable. The blind stitch is the strongest. Flat-lock stitching is found in many warm-water wetsuits.

6 Sizing can be tricky. The suit should feel snug. If it is too loose, water will flow freely through it and you will get cold. The wrists, ankles and neck should fit snugly.

7 Take proper care of your wetsuit and it will last longer. Most shrink eventually, though. Rinse your suit in fresh water and hang it up to dry on a plastic hanger before storing. Store it flat and not in direct sunlight. Never put it in a dryer.

8 Shampoo your suit using a special wetsuit shampoo or baby shampoo every once in a while to prolong its life.

9 Inspect your wetsuit for any tears and rips – they're easier to fix while still small.

10 Do not use aerosol spray near your wetsuit as it can degrade the neoprene. The same goes for car exhaust, so your garage is not the best place for storage.

LOSE WEIGHT EFFECTIVELY

1 Eat more soup. Preferably not cream-based. You will feel fuller for longer and soups tend not to be calorific.

2 Eat fewer calories by upping your intake of healthy fruits, vegetables and wholegrains.

3 Stop having little snacks in between meals. Conventional snacks, such as crisps, tend to contain high amounts of fat and salt. If you really must snack, choose fruit.

4 Drink skimmed or semi-skimmed milk rather than whole milk. Eat natural low-fat yogurt rather than full-fat varieties.

5 Stop putting sugar on cereal – scatter raisins or chopped fruit on it instead.

6 Exercise more and try to lead a more active life. Adults should get at least 150 minutes of exercise per week. If you find it hard to fit in to your lifestyle, try getting off the bus a stop earlier or park further away from your destination.

7 Don't go on crash diets. Steady weight loss works best and there's less chance you'll put it all back on again.

8 Join a slimming club if you feel you need the encouragement of others and people to compare notes with.

9 A very low-calorie diet (VLCD) of less than 1,000 calories per day could be the answer, but should only be undertaken intermittently or for 12 consecutive weeks. It is not recommended for pregnant or breastfeeding women or for children.

10 Surgery should be the last resort. If you've tried, and failed, to lose weight, this could be the answer, but shouldn't be undertaken lightly. Consult your doctor first. The best-known type is gastric banding.

SLIM THE SAFE WAY

1 Take photos of yourself as the weeks go by so that you can see how well you're doing – it will help to motivate you.

2 Weigh yourself monthly not weekly. Otherwise if you have a one-off bad week and gain weight you'll get disheartened.

3 Walk up and down stairs as much as possible. When you're out, take the stairs rather than the escalator or the lift.

4 Do a meditation in which you visualize the new, slimmer you. Imagine yourself wearing a skinny pair of jeans or a nice new dress.

5 Reduce the size of your portions and tell anyone who cooks for you to give you smaller platefuls, too.

6 Set small targets that you know you can achieve rather than one big one.

7 Fad diets can be good for losing weight quickly, but not so good for keeping the pounds off permanently. And they can be unbalanced nutritionally, too.

8 Eat off smaller plates – you'll be eating less without really realizing it. Your plate will look full.

9 Check food labels carefully for added sugar and ingredients that could pile on the pounds, such as fats.

10 Take note of food packaging if calorie-counting is your weight-loss tactic. It tells you exactly how many calories a food item contains. Keep a daily tally.

HOW TO PILE ON THE POUNDS

1 **Consume more calories** every day than you burn in activity. Eat larger amounts of food, more often, containing more calories.

2 **Choose foods that are nutrient-dense.** These include fruit, vegetables and whole grains. Foods that are nutrient- and energy-dense include legumes, nuts, seeds, olives and avocadoes.

3 **Increase your intake of full-fat dairy foods, meats, seafood and poultry.**

4 **Limit your physical activity** so that you don't burn up calories that your body requires for putting on weight.

5 **Eat more meals.** Have three full meals a day: a good breakfast plus proper lunch and an evening meal. Add energy-dense snacks in between meals. If eating large meals is difficult, eat several small meals throughout the day.

6 **Increase your portion sizes.** Do this gradually, adding a little more to your plate every day. Have second helpings.

7 **Use larger plates and fill them up.** Dinner plates come pretty large these days be sure to load them up.

8 **Add some extra servings of additional nutrients** to your balanced diet of protein, carbs and fat, such as potatotes, sweet corn, rice or pasta.

9 **Add toppings** such as extra butter, rich sauces, olive-oil and extra cheese. This is a great way to add calories without noticing.

10 **Add calories to creamed soups** by adding a spoonful of dry milk powder.

SNIFF SNIFF! COLD RELIEF

1 **Spot early symptoms:** the earlier you catch a cold, the earlier you can help your body to recover.

2 **Get plenty of rest and sleep more than usual.** Use extra pillows to prop up your head to relieve congestion. You may not actually need to take to your bed for long, but early nights will help.

3 **Lie on the couch** if you can't actually go to bed. Take in some daytime TV.

4 **Keep up your fluid intake.** Colds can drain your body of fluids, so drink plenty of water/juice all day. Hot drinks, such as herbal teas and soups, help rehydrate, too.

5 **Eat regularly and healthily.** It's vital that you eat as normally as you can so that your body regains its strength. Spicy foods and hot soups can calm sore, tickly throats.

6 **Don't go for antibiotics** – they will have no effect. Colds are caused by viruses. If you're achy take pain relief and use a nasal spray to keep your nose unblocked.

7 **Vitamin C and echinacea** have been proven to help prevention and relief of cold symptoms.

8 **Inhaling steam from very hot water** can help loosen a blocked nose.

9 **If work stress levels are high,** your immune system may be challenged, making colds more likely to come along. Take a few days off work and remove the factors that are causing you stress.

10 **Give up smoking.** Smokers suffer from cold symptoms for longer than non-smokers as the smoke irritates the nasal membranes and worsens symptoms.

BEAT A SORE THROAT

1 Honey in warm water
2 Lemon tea
3 Salt-water gargle
4 Cold drinks
5 Ice lollies
6 Throat lozenges
7 Cool-mist vaporizer
8 Humidifier
9 Over-the-counter pain relief
10 Dissolvable aspirin gargle

EXAMINING YOUR BREASTS

BOOSTING IMMUNITY

1. Sufficient sleep
2. Wash hands often
3. Don't smoke
4. Don't drink
5. Steam inhalation
6. Exercise
7. Chicken soup
8. Vitamin D
9. Massage
10. Good nutrition

1 **Examine your breasts once a month.** This way, you can get to know how your breasts normally look and feel.

2 **If you feel a lump, don't panic!** Some women are lumpier than others.

3 **The upper, outer area of your breast** tends to be lumpier than the rest in the normal course of events.

4 **The lower half of your breast** may feel like little pebbles.

5 **The area beneath the nipples** may normally feel like large grains.

6 **Does one area of your breast seem different from the rest?**

7 **Has anything changed** since the last time you checked?

8 **If you notice a change** that doesn't go away/or gets worse after a full month's cycle, go to your doctor.

9 **Write a diary** to record what you find in your regular self-examinations.

10 **Draw little 'maps'** of your breasts and include notes to help you remember where everything is and what you find.

TAKING YOUR TEMPERATURE

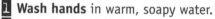

1 **Wash hands** in warm, soapy water.

2 **Wash the thermometer** in cold water.

3 **Check the position of the mercury.** It should be down near the bulb.

4 **To get the mercury down near the bulb,** hold the thermometer at the end furthest from the mercury and shake it with a downward wrist flick.

5 **Insert the thermometer** well under your tongue. Close your mouth.

6 **Leave the thermometer in your mouth** for one minute.

7 **To read the thermometer,** hold it near to the light and rotate it until you see the silver column of mercury.

8 **Your temperature is** the number on the thermometer positioned at the very top of the mercury column.

9 **Rinse the thermometer** in cold water.

10 **Before storing,** wash it in alcohol.

HEAVE HO! LIFT SAFELY

1 **Test every load** before you try and lift it. Push it gently with your hands or feet to see whether it moves.

2 **A small size** doesn't necessarily mean a light load.

3 **Is the load well balanced and packed correctly?** Loose items can be dangerous.

4 **Get a tight grip** on the load before you try and lift it.

5 **Add handles** to help you lift the load safely – if you can.

6 **Avoid back strain** by using slow, smooth movements.

7 **Don't be tempted to twist.** Face the

item square-on and keep facing it while you are lifting.

8 **Keep the load as close to your body as you can.** Reaching out to lift and carry may hurt your back.

9 **Lift with your legs** if you can straddle the load. Bend your knees, not your back, pick up the load, keeping your back as straight as possible.

10 **Carry the load** in the area between your shoulders and your waist. You'll be less likely to strain your back muscles.

BEAT MINOR BACKACHE

1 **Sit at your desk correctly,** if you work in an office. Check your posture if you spend a lot of time sitting down.

2 **Eat a good diet and drink plenty of plain water** to keep the intervertebral discs properly hydrated.

3 **Get up from your desk** and walk around at regular intervals.

4 **If you are overweight – lose it.** Surplus pounds can put a strain on your back.

5 **Try over-the-counter painkillers** and then perhaps anti-inflammatories to help with minor back pain.

6 **Do plenty of exercise** and keep moving. Swimming, yoga and Pilates are great ways to exercise if you have a bad back – they help to build core strength.

7 **Use a hot-water bottle/cold pack** if you do get minor back pain. Stop what you're doing, get comfortable and keep warm for a little while.

8 **Consider having manipulation** from a qualified osteopath or chiropractor.

9 **Physiotherapy** may help.

10 **Keep moving** and take plenty of exercise – it will strengthen your back.

CORRECT DESK POSTURE

1 **Your lower back needs to be properly supported** at all times.

2 **Adjust your chair –** consider its height, back position and tilt.

3 **Can you use your keyboard with your wrists/forearms straight?** They should be level with the floor.

4 **Your arms need to form an L-shape at the elbow.**

5 **Place your feet flat on the floor.** Use a footrest if you need to.

6 **Have your screen at eye level.** Get a stand to raise it if necessary.

7 **Your keyboard should be in front of you,** with a gap of 100–150mm (4–6in) for resting your wrists.

8 **Your mouse should be close.** You may need a wrist pad to help you keep your wrist straight.

9 **Keep everything within reach.** Avoid stretching and twisting to reach frequently used things such as your phone, your mug of tea or your calculator.

10 **Don't cradle your phone** between your ear and shoulder. It can put a strain on your back muscles.

BEAT THE BLUES

1 **Identify some attainable personal goals –** this will give you an upbeat focus in your daily life.

2 **Try a few simple things to help improve your mood,** even if you are low in energy. Go for a walk or see a friend.

3 **Take one day at a time** and one step at a time. Give yourself little rewards when you feel you have achieved something new or different from usual.

4 **St John's wort** has been found to be a natural mood-booster and is helpful for SAD (seasonal affective disorder).

5 **Reach out to friends and family –** it will help lift your mood and keep the blues away. Learn to trust your supporters.

6 **Keep up social activities.** It's hard, because you don't feel like it, but being with others will help lift your spirits. Mix with people who are positive and upbeat.

7 **Join a support group.** You may find that sharing with others in the same boat can help relieve your sense of aloneness.

8 **Pets can help.** They make you feel less isolated and take you out of yourself.

9 **Challenge your own negative thinking.** Keep a diary to record negative thoughts. If you are always hard on yourself, try to be more forgiving.

10 **Try not to generalize from a negative perspective** or indulge in 'all or nothing' thinking, such as 'I'm no good at....'

FOODS TO AVOID FOR EXCESS WIND

1 Baked beans
2 Broccoli
3 Brussels sprouts
4 Cabbage
5 Carbonated drinks
6 Chewing gum
7 Apples/pears
8 Peaches
9 Boiled sweets
10 Lettuce

TAKE THE HEAT OUT OF HEARTBURN

1 **Elevate your head in bed.** Fluff up your pillows so that your sleep posture helps heartburn that comes at night.

2 **Do not drink acidic drinks,** especially at night (grapefruit, orange, tomato).

3 **Avoid spicy, processed, greasy foods.**

4 **Watch what you drink.** Do not have caffeine-containing and carbonated drinks.

5 **Don't wear belts or clothes that are tight-fitting** around the waist.

6 **Lose any extra pounds.**

7 **Try increasing Vitamin A and carotene:** these have useful anti-inflammatory qualities (mangos, apricots, carrots, spinach, chard, beet greens and watercress).

8 **Don't eat within two to three hours of going to bed.**

9 **Bananas may help –** they may protect the stomach from acids.

10 **Eat smaller, more frequent meals.**

SIDE-STEP INDIGESTION

1 **Don't chew with your mouth open** and don't talk while you chew.

2 **Smaller meals may help –** your stomach

won't have to work overtime to digest large amounts.

3 **Don't eat large meals late at night** and

avoid making late-night trips to the fridge.

4 Don't bolt your food. You'll be taking in large amounts of air at the same time, which can cause indigestion. Chew each mouthful thoroughly and make mealtimes a leisure activity.

5 If they give you indigestion, avoid eating spicy foods – and any other foods that you think may be causing the problem. Likely suspects are foods that are more acidic such as tomatoes and citrus fruits.

6 Stress in your life may be contributing.

Do what you can to make life less stressful. Learn how to manage stressful situations.

7 Alcoholic beverages and smoking may be irritating the stomach lining – cut back or stop drinking.

8 Relax after meals, but don't lie down. Sleep with your head higher than your feet to allow the digestive juices to flow to the intestines and get to work.

9 Keep track of the foods you eat that cause indigestion. Avoid them in future.

10 Drink after the meal, not during it.

CONQUER CONSTIPATION

1 Eat plenty of fibre. Insoluble fibre passes through the body unchanged, bulks out stools and softens them. Foods high in insoluble fibre include: wholegrains, fruits and vegetables.

2 Make sure you drink enough. This will make bowel movements easier to pass.

3 Limit your consumption of alcohol- and caffeine-containing drinks. They can be dehydrating.

4 Biofeedback therapy may help with constipation resulting from pelvic floor dysfunction.

5 Acupressure is a simple home remedy that may work. It involves finger pressure to specific acupuncture points. A point that is often recommended for constipation is

Large Intestine 4. Do not use this acupressure point if you are pregnant.

6 A deficiency of the mineral magnesium may contribute to constipation. Magnesium is found naturally in fresh green leafy vegetables, nuts, seeds and wholegrains and in supplements.

7 Engage in regular physical activity. A deficit can lead to constipation.

8 Don't put off what needs to be done. The longer you delay, the more fluid is absorbed from the stool and the harder it becomes to pass a movement.

9 Probiotic supplements may help deal with constipation.

10 Laxatives may be the answer. Herbal laxatives include: rhubarb, aloe and senna.

DIARRHOEA CAN BE CAUSED BY:
1 Underlying infection
2 Food poisoning
3 Antibiotics
4 Gastroenteritis
5 Stress
6 Anxiety
7 Too much alcohol
8 Tropical disease
9 Eating unsuitable foods
10 Intestinal disorder

COPE WITH IBS

1 Take steps to avoid stress in your life. This is a common trigger for IBS. Take vigorous exercise, do deep breathing,

meditation and try positive thinking.

2 Make small changes to your diet. Break meals up into four or more smaller meals throughout the day. Large meals, especially late in the evening, can trigger IBS. Try to eat your meals more slowly.

3 **Cut down your caffeine consumption,** alcohol and eating fatty foods.

4 **Avoid drinking diet colas** and similar.

5 **Take a gentle walk after your meals** to help speed up your digestion.

6 **Keep a diary to record symptoms,** triggers and coping techniques so you can plan your activities around episodes.

7 **Educate your friends and relatives** about the unpleasant symptoms you have to deal with. They'll be more understanding and helpful.

8 **Increase your daily intake** of fibre.

9 **Join a support group** that offers classes on symptom management, stress management and moral support.

10 **Stop smoking –** it's a must.

HOME HELP FOR CONJUNCTIVITIS

1 **Make an eye wash** from honey and warm milk. Use equal parts, mix them together until it is smooth. Use an eye dropper to drop a few drops in your eye several times a day.

2 **Try placing sliced potatoes on the eye.** Peel/slice a potato (natural astringent) and apply it to the affected area.

3 **Try applying cooled teabags to the affected eye.** The tannin in the tea reduces and soothes inflammation.

4 **Consume more vitamin A** (whole milk, yogurt, butter, carrots, pumpkin, green veggies, tomatoes, mangoes).

5 **Consume more vitamin B2** (green leafy veggies, almonds, citrus fruits, bananas and tomatoes).

6 **A warm-water compress** will relieve itchiness and provide some pain relief.

7 **Carrot juice with spinach added** can provide relief.

8 **To remove crusts on the eyelashes –** dip a sterile cotton ball in warm water and press against the eye.

9 **To help itchiness in the eye,** make a poultice of yogurt and apply it to the eye.

10 **Use separate towels** until the problem has completely cleared up.

TAKE THE PAIN OUT OF A SPRAIN

1 **Raise the affected area.** It helps speed the healing process and pain relief.

2 **Protect the injured part –** usually by providing support.

3 **Rest helps healing** take place as quickly as possible. Allow about two days.

4 **Keep the sprained limb straight.**

5 **When you are lying in bed,** keep the limb in the same position – as straight as you can.

6 **Use a stack of pillows** to support the sprained limb.

7 **Make a cold pack.** Wrap ice cubes in a soft towel and apply to the affected limb. Cool the skin for 15 minutes, then stop for 15 minutes, cool again and so on.

8 **Put some ice cubes in a plastic bag** and place over the sprained area – cooling helps to limit the internal bleeding.

9 **You can purchase custom-made cooling packs,** which contain a special gel – keep them in your freezer.

10 **Bandage the damaged area in order to limit movement as much as possible.** Apply a pressure bandage at first and then tape the limb when all the swelling has gone down. Watch the areas surrounding the bandages.

SOOTHING MILD SUNBURN

1 **Avoid direct sunlight** by covering the affected areas and staying indoors or at least in the shade until the sunburn has completely healed.

2 **Sponge the skin** with lukewarm water or take a cold shower/bath.

3 **Put on a cold compress,** such as a cold flannel, to the affected area.

4 **Drink fluids** to help cool down and replace those lost through sweating.

5 **Try not to drink alcohol** as it will de-hydrate you further.

6 **Apply a cooling moisturizing lotion** or aftersun cream several times a day to hydrate the skin and help moisturize it.

7 **Use creams containing aloe vera** to help soothe.

8 **Dab on some calamine lotion to** relieve itching and soreness.

9 **Use over-the-counter painkillers** to relieve pain and reduce inflammation.

10 **Wear loose-fitting cotton clothes** so that they do not rub against the burnt skin. If you are at home, wear as little as possible to allow the air free contact with the sunburned area.

STOCKING A FIRST-AID KIT

1 Adhesive bandages/tape
2 Tweezers/scissors
3 Disposable gloves
4 Sterile gauze pads
5 Antiseptic ointment
6 Bandages
7 Antiseptic wipes
8 Thermometer
9 Antibiotic ointment
10 Hydrocortisone cream

DEALING WITH A MINOR BURN

1 **Flood the injured area** with cold water for ten minutes to stop the burning and relieve pain.

2 **Remove any jewellery, watches, belts or constricting clothes.** If you have them, put on fresh disposable gloves.

3 **A cool bath, or shower,** will help to soothe the burn.

4 **Cover the area with a sterile dressing** or clean, smooth pad and bandage loosely.

5 **Do not use ice, iced water, creams or greasy substances** to soothe the burn.

6 **Use a clean plastic bag** or a piece of kitchen film instead to cover the area if you do not have access to bandages.

7 **If the burn is painful,** take a mild over-the-counter painkiller.

8 **Don't be tempted to interfere with the burn, or break any blisters.** If the burn is very painful, or seems to be getting worse, visit your doctor for advice.

9 **Do not attempt to remove anything that is stuck to the burnt skin** because this could cause more damage.

10 **Make sure that the person keeps warm,** using a blanket or layers of clothing.

TACKLE BITES & STINGS

1 **Stings are usually painful not dangerous** unless you suffer from an allergy, in which case seek emergency help.

2 **If you can see the sting, brush or scrape it off** with a blunt knife or edge of a credit card. Don't use tweezers.

3 **Raise the affected part,** if you can.

4 **Apply an ice pack or cold compress.** Hold in place for at least ten minutes.

5 **Avoid scratching the area** because it may become infected

6 **Take over-the-counter painkillers.**

7 **To prevent itching,** use a spray/cream containing local anaesthetic, antihistamine or mild hydrocortisone (one per cent) – available at pharmacies – on the area.

8 **Take an antihistamine tablet** to help reduce swelling.

9 **If you have been stung and the wasp or hornet is still buzzing about,** walk away calmly to avoid being stung again.

10 **If pain persists,** see your doctor.

STOP A NOSEBLEED

1 **Nose bleeds usually stop on their own,** but help speeds up recovery.

2 **Pinch your nose firmly** just below the bridge with your thumb and finger.

3 **Lean your head forwards** and breathe through your mouth.

4 **Keep up the pressure** for ten minutes.

5 **If the bleeding does not stop,** carry on

applying pressure for a further ten minutes.

6 **Don't tip your head back –** you'll just swallow blood.

7 **Bleeding should stop** in 30 minutes.

8 **Avoid bending down.**

9 **Do not blow your nose** for the next twelve hours.

10 **If bleeding continues,** see your doctor.

ALL ABOUT FAINTING

1 **If you see someone fainting,** try to break their fall.

2 **Call for emergency help** to request an ambulance. Make the person as comfortable as possible while you are waiting.

3 **If someone faints and doesn't regain consciousness** within one or two minutes, put them into the recovery position: place them on their side, supported by one leg and one arm; open their airway by

tilting the head back and lifting the chin. Monitor breathing/ pulse.

4 **Remain with the person** until official help arrives.

5 **If someone seems about to faint,** help them to lie down, preferably with their head down and legs raised.

6 **If lying down is impossible,** sit the person with head between knees. Gently push their head down while they try to push their head up. This encourages blood flow to the brain and will assist recovery.

7 **To make sure you don't faint,** be sure that you don't become dehydrated. Drink plenty of water.

8 **Check out the symptoms properly.** Before fainting they are: light-headedness, dizziness, nausea and sweatiness, ears ringing and general weakness.

9 **Don't assume the person is right as rain** after they've recovered. They might feel woozy or nauseous for a while.

10 **Don't let the person try to get up** too quickly afterwards.

AVOIDING FOOD POISONING

1 **Store and prepare all raw and cooked foods apart from each other** to prevent cross-contamination.

2 **Put raw meats in the bottom of the fridge** to stop juices contacting other foods and contamination them.

3 **Clean all of your work surfaces,** chopping boards and utensils every time you change over to preparing a different food.

4 **Cook all types of meat right through** – especially poultry and pork.

5 **Wash your hands thoroughly** with soap before you start preparing food.

6 **Eat food by the use-by date.**

7 **Don't eat raw eggs** or uncooked foods made from them, such as mayonnaise.

8 **Elderly, sick, babies/pregnant women shouldn't eat soft-boiled eggs.**

9 **Don't let chilled or frozen foods warm up in the boot of the car** after purchase. Take insulated bags on supermarket shopping trips.

10 **Cook all foods thoroughly** and heat leftovers right through until piping hot.

TREAT FOOD POISONING

1 Don't get dehydrated
2 Oral rehydration salts
3 Easily digested foods
4 Small, frequent meals
5 Avoid alcohol
6 Don't smoke
7 No caffeine
8 No spicy foods
9 No fatty foods
10 Rest

ANTI-ADDICTION TIPS

1 **What are your high-risk states?** Make a list of them. Are you hungry, angry, lonely or tired at the end of the day, making you more vulnerable?

2 **Avoid going to the places and seeing the people who might tempt you to slide back.** If you're a drinker, pubs and old drinking friends are best steered clear of.

3 **Avoid high-risk situations.** Being aware of them will help you prevent a tiny craving turn into a major urge.

4 **Try calming meditation to learn to relax.** People use addictive substances to escape, relax and reward themselves – to relieve tension. Relaxation techniques can help you cope and recover.

5 **Look after yourself better.** For example, eat well during the day so that hunger at night doesn't put you at risk.

6 **Join a twelve-step group** to avoid feeling isolated and to learn the skills that will help you cope better.

7 **Learn relaxation techniques** so that you can let go of anger and resentment.

8 **Develop good sleep habits** so that you're less tired and vulnerable.

9 **Keep motivated** by staying abreast of current findings and taking an interest in your general health.

10 **Be totally honest** – with friends and family, your supporters, your doctor – and, most importantly, with yourself.

STOP! SMOKING

1 **Write down a list** of reasons why you want to quit smoking. Read them whenever you feel like lighting up.

2 **Decide on a date** for stopping smoking and then stop.

3 **Tell everyone you know that you are giving up.** Friends and family will be only too happy to support you.

4 **Organize a team effort.** Find other friends/family who want to stop, too, and do it together.

5 **Mark off the days on a calendar.** Look at it whenever you feel the urge to smoke.

6 **Get rid of all smoking paraphernalia:** cigarettes, lighters and ashtrays.

7 **Be ready to suffer nicotine-withdrawal symptoms.** They peak after one or two days and fade over two to four weeks.

8 **Tell people you don't know that you don't smoke.**

9 **Be prepared for wanting to eat more,** but fight the urge.

10 **Attend a 'stopping smoking' clinic** to get support and help in stopping.

LESSEN STRESS IN YOUR LIFE

1 **Identify the causes of stress in your life.** Work? Family? Money problems?

2 **Be the one who takes control over your life** – and keeps it.

3 **Learn to say 'no' to people's demands.** Know what your limits are and make sure you stick to them.

4 **If someone causes you stress,** stop spending so much time with them or terminate the relationship completely.

5 **Is your environment stressful?** If you can, make changes to it. If bad news on the radio makes you tense, turn it off.

6 **Prioritize your commitments.** Make a list of the things you must do now and the things that can wait. Cross off the things that can wait completely.

7 **Avoid dwelling on the people and events** that upset you.

8 **Get it off your chest!** Don't bottle up something that is on your mind.

9 **Find the middle ground.** Be prepared to compromise in an argument and expect the other person to as well.

10 **Think things through** so that you are not always running late. Allow enough time to get to your appointments without rushing. You'll feel more relaxed.

LOWER YOUR BLOOD PRESSURE

1 **Eat less salt** – it raises your blood pressure. Watch out for the salt content in ready-made snack foods such as crisps, but also in less-obvious things such as breakfast cereals.

2 **Don't add salt** to your cooking or to your plate when you are eating.

3 **Increase your fruit and vegetables.** Make sure you get your five-a-day. They will help lower your blood pressure.

4 **Dried, frozen and tinned fruit/veg are fine** if you don't like/can't get fresh.

5 **Drink less alcohol.** Too much will raise blood pressure. Count units (one unit is half a pint of beer, a small glass of wine, a measure of spirits). The limits are 21 for men and 14 for women per week.

6 **If you are overweight, lose it.** This will help lower your blood pressure and reduce risk of health problems. Eat low-fat, low-calorie foods and move around more.

7 **Make small changes to your diet and exercise regime.** Give yourself some goals, but make sure you can stick to them.

8 **Become more active.** Take 30 minutes' exercise five times per week to keep your heart healthy. This may lower your blood pressure.

9 **Stop smoking.** Smoking injures blood vessel walls and speeds up hardening of the arteries.

10 **There are medicines** available to help control your high blood pressure. Consult your doctor.

GET A HEALTHY HEART

1 **Don't smoke.** Chemicals in tobacco can cause damage to the heart and blood vessels, leading to a dangerous narrowing of the arteries. Nicotine in cigarette smoke makes your heart work harder by narrowing down the blood vessels and increasing heart rate and blood pressure.

2 **Exercise for 30 minutes a day** (on most days). If this is problematic, break your exercise slots up into smaller chunks and fit them into your busy day. Choose a mixture of different exercise types to prevent boredom from setting in.

3 **Walking is a good exercise to choose** as you can fit it in to your everyday life. Use a pedometer to monitor how many steps you take in a normal day.

4 **Have your cholesterol levels measured.**

5 **Be sure to eat two portions of oily fish a week** (for example mackerel, salmon, sardines and herring).

6 **Eat a diet that helps keep your heart healthy.** Choose foods that are low in fat, cholesterol and salt and rich in fruit, vegetables, wholegrains and low-fat dairy.

7 **Keep to a healthy weight.** Calculate your body mass index (BMI) to determine whether you are carrying too much fat for your height and age.

8 **Be sure to get your blood pressure tested regularly.**

9 **Get yourself screened for diabetes,** which is a risk factor for heart disease.

10 **Check out your genetic history** – your family tree may mean that you're more at risk of heart disease.

HUFF PUFF! IMPROVE YOUR BREATHING

1 Install a carbon monoxide detector in your home if you have any type of natural gas heating or appliances.

2 Put a humidifier in your bedroom, or place a large, open container of water by your bed.

3 Use anti-allergy pillow cases designed to repel tiny dust mites and bed bugs – they may be causing the problems.

4 Arrange lots of clean-air plants around your home. Philodendron are recommended by NASA.

5 It's way better to breathe through your nose as nose hairs filter air before it enters the body. If you breathe through your mouth this filtration takes place in the lungs.

6 Get the vacuum cleaner out every day. Vacuuming on a daily basis will help eliminate dust mites and get rid of pet dandruff and fur. Some vacuum cleaners have anti-allergy filters or attachments.

7 Wear a facial mask while using strong household cleaning products. These may cause breathing problems.

8 Use anti-bacterial wipes for cleaning computer keyboards and door knobs, especially if a member of your family has a cold. Colds and flu can often lead to serious breathing problems.

9 Spray perfume below the face and neck area, keeping it as far away from your face as you can.

10 Focus on your breathing and breathe deeply. This will help you to concentrate and stay alert.

STOPPING MOTION SICKNESS

1 Keep your eye on the horizon or a fixed point. Take deep breaths and stare into the distance.

2 Choose a seat where you experience the least motion. The middle of the plane, over the wing. The lower-level cabins near the centre experience less motion. Sit in the front seat of a car.

3 Don't sit facing backwards from your direction of travel.

4 Don't read while you are moving.

5 Over-the-counter medicines can be very effective for short trips and mild cases.

6 Get some fresh air. On a ship, go above deck in the centre, if you can. On a plane open the air vent above your seat and in a car open the window.

7 Sit away from other people who are suffering – hearing people talking about it and becoming ill might set you off, too.

8 Eat ginger. Try this about 12 to 24 hours prior to setting out on your trip. Find it in ginger biscuits, powdered ginger on toast or in muesli and in crystallized chunks. Suck on ginger sweets.

9 Avoid strong food smells. This may prevent feelings of nausea.

10 You can buy anti-motion wrist bands.

DON'T TEMPT A MIGRAINE

1 Identify your migraine triggers (such as chocolate, cheese, monosodium glutamate, citrus fruit, aspartame, caffeine or alcohol, especially red wine) by keeping a diary. Write in all the circumstances that surround your migraine including sleep patterns and meals eaten.

2 Reduce stress and anxiety in your life as these are thought to make migraines worse. Yoga, meditation and controlled breathing exercises are all excellent for relaxation and stress reduction.

3 Wear sunglasses as bright light and glare can bring on a migraine.

4 Don't change your routines. A change in sleep patterns at the weekend or going without breakfast or lunch can bring on a migraine. A change in your blood sugar is the cause. If taking regular meals becomes a problem, be sure to carry snacks such as oatcakes, fruit or a muesli bars.

5 Take more exercise. Keeping active may stop you getting migraines.

6 Keep hydrated. Dehydration is a major cause of migraine.

7 Try either a hot or cold compress on your forehead to ease your migraine. Discover which type works best for you. For a cold compress try an ice pack wrapped in a towel or for a hot compress, use a hot-water bottle.

8 Apply pressure to the pulse points on the side of your forehead or neck.

9 Try acupuncture to help relieve migraine symptoms.

10 See your doctor if you get frequent, severe migraines as there is treatment available for severe cases.

EASING A TENSION HEADACHE

1 Over-the-counter pain relief
2 Relaxation/yoga techniques
3 Hot compress
4 Cold compress
5 Good posture
6 Acupuncture
7 Massage
8 Deep breathing
9 Biofeedback therapy
10 Hot bath

HAVE A HEALTHY DETOX

1 Eliminate all the possible toxins: alcohol, coffee, cigarettes, refined sugars and saturated fats.

2 Drink 2 litres (4pt) of water daily.

3 Eat plenty of fibre, including brown rice and organically grown fresh fruits and vegetables. Beets, radishes, artichokes, cabbage, broccoli, spirulina, chlorella, and seaweed are excellent detoxifying foods.

4 Cleanse and protect your liver by including herbs such as dandelion root, burdock and milk thistle in your diet, and drinking green tea.

5 Take vitamin C, which helps the body produce glutathione, a liver compound that drives away toxins.

6 Breathe as deeply as you can to allow oxygen to circulate more completely through your system.

7 Practise hydrotherapy by taking a very hot shower for five minutes. Follow this with a cold-water shower for 30 seconds. Do this three times and then get into bed for 30 minutes.

8 Sweat in a sauna so your body can eliminate wastes through perspiration.

9 One hour's exercise a day is the most important way to detoxify. In particular, try yoga or chi gung for their detoxifying or cleansing powers.

10 Remove toxins through your pores by dry-brushing.

SAFE ALCOHOL IMBIBING

1 Restrict your alcoholic intake to 21 units per week (for men) and 14 units per week (for women).

2 Eat before and at the same time as drinking alcohol. Your body will be better able to absorb the alcohol. Choose food that takes longer to digest (bread, cheese, pasta), so that your stomach is lined. Milk has the same effect.

3 Drink plenty of water at the same time as drinking alcohol. Your body won't dehydrate so much and you won't be so likely to develop a headache.

4 Minimize your drinking time by intentionally arriving about half an hour later than everyone else.

5 Start the drinking session off with a soft drink or a large glass of water to quench your thirst first.

6 Pace yourself. Go slow – your body can only process one unit of alcohol per hour.

7 Don't mix drinks. Stick to one type of alcohol the whole night.

8 Know thyself! Be aware of what your limits are and when enough is enough. You know it makes sense!

9 Have alcohol-free spells every now and then. One day per week or per month will give your body a rest.

10 The hair of the dog? It may seem as though it helps, but really it's just putting off the hangover for even longer.

CURING A HANGOVER

1 Sleep
2 Fruit juice/water
3 Avoid caffeine
4 Orange juice
5 Sports drinks
6 Mineral-rich foods
7 Shower
8 Exercise
9 Aspirin
10 Hair of the dog

PREVENT ENVIRONMENTAL ALLERGIES

1 Keep all windows closed during the pollen season.

2 Air-conditioning or an air-filtration system can actually remove mould-friendly moisture and filter out some allergens.

3 Wash your shower curtain monthly.

4 Identify cleaning products containing substances you may be allergic to.

5 Buy an ionizer.

6 Let the extractor fan run or open the window after your shower/bath. This will dry out the room and stop mould growing.

7 Use a carbon monoxide monitor.

8 Clean out your gutters! Clogged gutters may cause water to seep into your house, leading to the growth of mould, which can exacerbate allergies.

9 Ask smokers to always smoke outside.

10 Use envionmentally friendly paint when decorating.

HAY FEVER HAPPINESS

1 Watch the pollen count. These often come with weather reports.

2 Stay indoors, if you possilby can, when the pollen count rises to high levels.

3 Try a little vaseline just inside your nose – it should reduce symptoms.

4 Wrap-around sunglasses will help prevent pollen getting into your eyes.

5 When you're driving, try to keep the windows closed and in high-pollen season use the air-conditioning system to stop pollen coming into the car.

6 Keep bedroom doors and windows closed mid-morning and early evening – this is when pollen levels are at their peak.

7 Don't go to parks or fields – especially during early evening.

8 If you have a lawn that needs mowing – get someone else to do it for you.

9 Don't lie around on freshly cut grass. Tempting – but a no-no!

10 When you come home change into clean clothes – wash everything you were wearing outside.

BEAT BAD BREATH

1 Find natural breath enhancers in your kitchen. You'll find plenty of useful herbs and spices. Carry around a little baggie of breath-refreshing cloves, fennel or anise seeds to chew on after a meal out.

2 Brush your tongue. While you are doing so, sweep the upper surface of your tongue to disperse food and bacteria.

3 Gargle with extracts of sage, calendula and myrrh gum four times a day.

4 If you can't brush your teeth after a meal, rinse instead. Sip water, swish around to wash the food odour away.

5 Parsley's good for bad breath. Chew a little sprig after meals. Or make a parsley juice to sip anytime.

6 Cheeses aren't too great for breath – especially the strong ones.

7 Avoid coffee, beer, wine and whiskey. These all leave residues that attach to plaque and then get into your digestive system. The result? Bad breath.

8 Carry a spare toothbrush around with you and brush straight after meals.

9 Try a minty mouthwash – though the effect is temporary: only twenty minutes.

10 Mint and gum are great as cover-ups, but the effect only lasts a little while.

ALLEVIATE ECZEMA

1 People may be triggering your eczema. Avoid all those who may be contributing to your stress.

2 Try stress-relievers such as yoga and meditation.

3 Document what you eat as diet is important for keeping eczema under control. Citrus fruits can cause flare-ups, so avoid eating and handling them.

4 Regular, thorough moisturizing is vital as it prevents dry skin forming that leads to the intense itching. Take moisturizer with you wherever you go.

5 Take extreme care over cleansing your skin. Wash the day's dust off so that the skin can breathe. Showering is preferable.

6 Wear loose, breathable cotton clothes that don't fit too tightly.

7 **Moisturize after washing, but before you dry yourself –** to help lock the moisturizer into the skin.

8 **A Gortex-covered mattress** may help cut down the incidence of dust mites, an allergy to which may cause eczema.

9 **Keep an eczema diary.** Record times when your eczema seems better and when it is worse.

10 **Consider going to holiday spots that are temperate.** This climate will suit your skin condition better than hot ones.

HIC, HIC HICCUPS

1 **Take a deep breath and hold it** for 30 seconds before releasing it.

2 **Breathe into a paper bag** five times.

3 **Swallow a teaspoon of dry white granulated sugar.** This overloads the tongue's nerve endings with sweetness, which can stop hiccups.

4 **Dip your whole face into ice-cold water** and hold it there for 30 seconds.

5 **Put your fingers in your ears.**

6 **Take ten sips slowly** from a glass of water without taking a breath.

7 **Gargling,** so that your breathing is disturbed, may be effective.

8 **Drink water while your head is inverted.** Fill a large cup and bend at the waist with your head between your legs. Try not to breathe as you drink.

9 **Try taking an antacid.**

10 **Chew gum** or suck a peppermint.

PUTTING UP WITH PERIOD PAINS

1 **Some gentle exercise can be effective.** Though this seems counterintuitive, rest may actually make things worse.

2 **Try taking the first dose of over-the-counter pain relief as soon as your pain begins,** or as soon as the bleeding starts, whichever comes first. Some doctors advise starting the tablets the day before your period is due.

3 **Take some over-the-counter pain relief** throughout the day, not just when the pain is too difficult to cope with.

4 **Hot-water bottles or warm towels** on the abdomen have a calming effect.

5 **Treat any stress** you may be experiencing: it can make the pain worse.

6 **A warm bath** may bring relief.

7 **Take the combined oral contraceptive pill.** As well as offering contraception it can lessen painful or heavy periods.

8 **Try the intra-uterine system (IUS)** if you need long-term contraception as it also reduces the amount of pain and bleeding during periods.

9 **Transcutaneous electronic nerve stimulation (TENS)** is widely used for period pains. Small electrodes are placed on the abdomen to stimulate the nerve in the pelvic area, reducing pain.

10 **If you have severe pains,** go to your doctor, who may arrange for you to take further tests.

HELPING FEMALE MENOPAUSE

1 **Supplement your basic healthy diet with calcium** for weakened bones (take it in milk, yogurt, cheese) and soy, which is effective in combating hot flushes and helps control osteoporosis.

2 **Keep a postive outlook** on the changes taking place in your life and take time out for yourself.

3 **Commit yourself to regular exercise** to help keep you agile and healthy. You will improve muscle tone and flexibility.

4 **Learn how to deal with stress.** Review your approach to stress: get extra physical exercise and try yoga and meditation.

5 **Regular intercourse** keeps the vagina lubricated, preventing vaginal dryness. Use vaginal lubricants or moisturizers specifically for vaginal dryness.

6 **Cut down alcohol and caffeine.**

7 **Take St John's wort** – it may improve your mood swings.

8 **Try hormone replacement therapy.**

9 **Phyto-oestrogens may help.** They are found in soybeans, chickpeas, red clover and other legumes. Oilseeds such as flaxseed (present in cereals, vegetables, legumes and fruits) may help, too.

10 **Stop smoking.**

FOOD FOR HEALTHY BONES
1 Milk
2 Yogurt
3 Cheese
4 Fortified orange juice
5 Fortified cereals
6 Broccoli
7 Spinach
8 Salmon
9 Tuna fish
10 Sardines

STOP SNORING

1 **Raise your head at night** by using a thick, firm pillow or two thin ones.

2 **Don't drink alcohol before bed** – your muscles will relax and limit breathing.

3 **Don't go mad on dairy products before bed** – they can cause a mucus build-up.

4 **Lose weight.** Shifting the pounds can help reduce snoring by increasing the space in your air passage.

5 **Sleep on your side not your back** – it causes snoring. Sew a tennis ball into your nightwear to make you turn over.

6 **Don't eat a heavy meal just before bedtime.** A full stomach pushes up on your diaphragm, limiting your airway.

7 **Stop smoking** – or at least don't smoke before bedtime. It inflames the throat and will cause snoring.

8 **Get into a solid, regular sleep routine.**

9 **Nasal strips may be able to help.** They open the nostrils to allow more air to enter, reducing snoring.

10 **Take up singing.** It increases muscle control in the throat.

FIGHT INSOMNIA

1 **Don't try too hard to fall asleep.**

2 **Put your clock out of sight** so that you don't keep checking what time it is.

3 **Don't toss and turn.** This keeps you more alert than you should be for going to sleep. Just try to keep still.

4 If going to the bathroom in the middle of the night wakes you up for hours limit what you drink in the evening and avoid caffeine-containing drinks.

5 Reduce the stress in your life. Worries will keep you awake before you go to sleep and then wake you later. And then you'll worry about not being able to sleep.

6 Listen to light, soothing music as you drop off. Some people swear by having the radio on and listening to chat.

7 If you really can't sleep, get up and do something for a while.

8 A hot bath before bed with calming aromatherapy oils or soaps (lavender or marjoram) may help.

9 Try using a herbal sleep remedy such as valerian, chamomile, lavender or passion flower – either in tea or capsule form.

10 If you fancy a midnight snack, choose tryptophan-high foods to help you relax (turkey, bananas, figs, dates, milk, tuna).

GET A GOOD NIGHT'S SLEEP

1 Get a good strategy going! Develop good sleep-helping habits for good-quality sleep night after night.

2 Go to bed at the same time every night. Select a time when you feel naturally tired. Don't break this routine.

3 If you want to change your bedtime for a holiday, change it slightly every day.

4 Wake up at the same time every day. If you are getting enough sleep, you should be able to wake up naturally at the same time without an alarm.

5 If you suffer from insomnia, napping might not be such a good move. If you must, have 30 minutes in early afternoon.

6 A short daytime nap is better than sleeping in in the mornings.

7 If you feel drowsy after dinner, do something to wake yourself up for a while. Otherwise you'll wake in the night.

8 Don't use your TV or computer to wind down in front of. The light suppresses melatonin production and stimulates your mood rather than relaxing it.

9 Keep your bedroom dark. The darker it is, the better you'll sleep. Use heavy blackout curtains or use an eye mask.

10 If you get up in the night, use a torch rather than switching on lights. It'll be easier to get back to sleep.

HOW TO GET PREGNANT

1 If you're a tad overweight, you might consider trying to lose a few pounds. If your BMI (body mass index) is over 30, your fertility might be affected. And if your partner is overweight, this could be affecting sperm production.

2 If you're on the skinny side (if your BMI is under 20), your fertility might be affected (oestrogen levels are affected). Take steps to gain weight.

3 Try superfoods to help your libido. They include pomegranates, avocados, figs, bananas, dates, asparagus, almonds, garlic and oysters.

4 Give up smoking and drinking. Both of these can diminish fertility in both sexes.

5 Is your life a bit stressful? Stress may decrease libido in both sexes. It can also disrupt the menstrual cycle.

6 Are you taking painkillers (such as aspirin)? Excessive use can affect your ability to become pregnant.

7 Calculate your fertile periods. It makes sense to know when the best times are likely to be – then aim for them.

8 Does your man like his trousers snug? It could be that heat caused by prolonged wearing of tight trousers are causing sperm production problems. Semen motility can be affected by drug use, heavy alcohol use, smoking and free radicals in the diet.

9 Have your man take zinc and vitamin C to improve sperm (number and quality).

10 Lastly, are you getting enough?

HELP WITH MORNING SICKNESS

1 Eat little and often so that you don't get hunger pangs. Frequent healthy snacks are the order of the day.

2 Eating something before you actually get out of bed (low blood sugar levels are thought to be at least partly responsible.

3 Avoid fatty or spicy foods – so put the Friday-night curry habit on hold (sob!).

4 Eat 'bland', easy-to-digest foods such as dry, plain biscuits, rice cakes and proper porridge made from oats.

5 Peppermint tea is good for combating nasty nauseous tastes in the mouth.

6 Ginger is great for nauseous feelings. Try ginger biscuits, ginger tea, ginger capsules or crystallized ginger.

7 If your sickness is worse in the mornings, eat a dry biscuit when you wake.

8 Acupuncture has been shown to help with pregnancy sickness. If you don't want to go the whole hog with needles, you can purchase wrist bands to wear on your acupressure points.

9 Anti-emetic drugs can be prescribed by your doctor and are known to help severe cases of pregnancy sickness, but they should be used as a last resort.

10 Drink plenty of fluids all day long so that you don't get dehydrated as a result of repeated vomiting.

FOODS TO AVOID IN PREGNANCY

1 Unpasteurized/ blue cheese
2 Patés/cooked meats
3 Raw fish/shellfish
4 Raw/undercooked eggs
5 Chilled foods
6 Ready-washed, bagged salads
7 Raw/undercooked meat
8 Unwashed fruit/ vegetables
9 Liver
10 Large predatory fish

PURCHASING MATERNITY CLOTHES

1 Don't go mad on maternity clothes, save your pennies for the baby. Wear leggings and loose tops that won't break the bank. Try charity shops/second-hand shops if you don't mind other people's cast-offs.

2 Maternity briefs provide vital support for your bump.

3 Support tights are a must in the later weeks of pregnancy, to stop varicose veins developing, feet and legs swelling and fluid retention. If you have to be on your feet a lot, they will be helpful. Socks should be cotton, not synthetic, and avoid knee-highs as they are too constricting.

4 **Try wearing a belly band –** mums swear by them as they help to support the growing babe comfortably. It can also fill the gap between your top and your waistband as your bump grows – great if you want to carry on wearing your favourite tops as the months go by.

5 **A trouser expander is useful.** It is an elasticized belt that can help you carry on wearing your normal trousers while your belly expands. You can also hold trouser openings together by looping a hair band across the opening – through the buttonhole and back.

6 **Layer with loose knits in cold weather.** It's easier and a whole lot cheaper than splashing out on a new maternity coat that will only be worn for one season.

7 **Borrow clothes from your partner or friends –** especially if they are slightly larger than you. Do swaps, too. Maternity clothes tend to be hardly worn and almost as good as new.

8 **Use large shawls, shrugs and wraps to wear with your normal coat.** It'll fill the gap nicely when your bump is too big to close your coat.

9 **Choose safe shoes** to avoid tripping or falling if your balance goes awry during pregnancy. Wear flat, comfortable shoes rather than heels. Velcro fastenings are great later in pregnancy when tying laces and fastening buckles are one step too far.

10 **A good supporting bra is essential** during pregnancy. Just buy a couple at a time – you will get bigger as the months go by.

PACKING FOR HOSPITAL

1 Birth plan
2 Dressing gown
3 Slippers
4 Nightdress
5 Disposable underwear
6 Sanitary towels
7 Nursing bra
8 Breast pads
9 Toiletries
10 Drinks/snacks

PREGNANCY CONCERNS

1 **Treat haemorrhoids** by drinking plenty of water and increasing dietary fibre. Upping your exercise will help, too.

2 **Simple, non-perfumed oils and creams** can be very effective for itchy skin. There's no need to buy expensive versions. Wearing cotton clothes will keep skin cool.

3 **Flex a cramped leg or foot** in the opposite direction in order to ease painful night-time cramps.

4 **See your doctor if you get a lot of headaches.** Severe headaches could mean high blood pressure.

5 **Try wearing an orthopaedic/maternity belt** if you get a lot of back pain. But see your doctor anyway.

6 **Eat iron-rich foods along with vitamin C-enriched food or drink** for anaemia.

7 **Add a few drops of vinegar to your bath** to ease common vaginal infections or try live yogurt. Reduce your intake of sugar and yeast and wear cotton underwear. Avoid tights and close-fitting trousers.

8 **Rest with your feet up,** but not for too long, if you suffer from swollen feet and ankles, which are a common feature of late pregnancy. Make sure you intersperse the rest with times of normal activity. Wearing maternity stockings/tights will also help.

9 **Wear a properly fitted bra** and a soft sleep bra at night if you experience breast tenderness.

10 **Avoid large meals,** especially at night if you suffer from indigestion. Try sleeping in a propped-up position, with your head higher than your feet.

EXERCISE IN PREGNANCY

1 **Pelvic-floor exercises are a must** for pregnancy and beyond. They'll avert stress incontinence in later life. Do them whenever you think of it.

2 **Avoid high-impact sports from the second trimester onwards.** These include jogging, skiing, horse-riding and tennis.

3 **The best exercises** for pregnancy are cycling, walking and swimming.

4 **Inform your fitness instructor that you are pregnant** – if you are gym bunny.

5 **Always carry out the correct warm-up stretches** before undertaking any exercise in pregnancy and build up your stamina and fitness gradually.

6 **Avoid exercising in very hot conditions** as this may be harmful to the baby.

7 **You can do yoga and Pilates** throughout pregnancy, but under expert supervision only. Tell the teacher you are pregnant. In yoga, relaxation and breathing are helpful in preparation for the birth. In Pilates the hands and knees position is ideal, taking stress off the back and pelvis.

8 **Swimming is excellent** exercise throughout pregnancy, but wonderful in the later months because of the weightlessness.

9 **Don't exercise near traffic** as you may be affected by pollutants.

10 **Stop exercising immediately** if you experience dizziness, shortness of breath or pain in your back/pelvis. If you are overheating or feel too exhausted, stop straight away.

PEN A BIRTH PREFERENCE PLAN

1 **Think about your birth plan.** It includes details about what kind of birth you would like to have and is a general guideline of preferences, not something that has to be, or will be, adhered to.

2 **Be specific** (birthing pool, upright position, home birth), who your birth partner is, pain relief, how you feel about your waters being broken, induction, episiotomy, breastfeeding and whether you want your partner to cut the cord.

3 **Discuss your plan with your birth partner and midwife.** It is useful if your partner has to advocate on your behalf.

4 **For dads** – don't impose your views if your partner feels strongly about something. Respect her feelings, but make sure you are aware of pros and cons.

5 **A good time to think about the birth plan** is during the second trimester.

6 **Include personal considerations** such as whether you are on a special diet, your religious faith if you have one.

7 **Make sure that your personal birth plan is straightforward and accessible.** Give copies to everyone involved.

8 **It's important to be realistic.** Your plan will help you to think about the overall picture. There are many different ways of experiencing labour.

9 **Plans are great, but be prepared for any eventuality.** The main objective is to give birth safely. Don't be disappointed if you have to abandon your plan after all.

10 **Keep your baby's best interests in mind** at all times.

BRINGING ON LABOUR

1 Making love
2 Nipple stimulation
3 Walking/exercise
4 Raspberry leaf tea
5 Acupuncture
6 Castor oil
7 Curry/spicy food
8 Pineapple
9 Homeopathic remedies
10 Herbal remedies

NURSERY BASICS

NURSERY EXTRAS

1. Nightlight
2. Playmat
3. Music
4. Mobile
5. Comfortable chair
6. Room thermometer
7. Blackout blind
8. Nursery frieze
9. Toys
10. Baby gym

1. **Reusable nappies are cheaper in the long run,** though the outlay is greater. You can choose Velcro-closing versions.

2. **Disposable nappies are convenient** and fewer changes are necessary because they are super-absorbent and wick urine away from the skin. They cause less nappy rash.

3. **Choose a Moses basket or cradle for your newborn.** They sleep much better in confined spaces. But these cradles are quickly outgrown.

4. **Go for a drop-sided cot for ease of access.** An adjustable-height version may mean that your baby can use it right up to moving into a 'proper' bed. You also need mattress protector, fitted sheets, cotton sheets or sleeping bag and light cellular blankets. And don't forget a mobile.

5. **Take care over the baby's mattress.** If you buy a second-hand cot, it's important to buy a new mattress made with an all-cotton filling and wool casings. Avoid mattresses that include chemicals used in fire retardants.

6. **Make sure the changing table has a lip all round** to stop the baby falling off. You might want to select one with shelves and cupboards underneath so that you can store changing things within easy reach.

7. **Go for an easy-to-wash changing mat.** The plastic versions can be used on the floor as well as on the changing table. They are easy to wipe down after use and you can line them with a soft towel for baby's comfort.

8. **Muslin cloths are a must.** Use them for protecting your clothes as well as your baby's during feeding and winding.

9. **Use a baby monitor** to keep an ear out for your baby when you have to be in a different room. When your child moves into his/her own bedroom a monitor will help you to listen out for cries in the night.

10. **A bouncer seat is handy.** You can move it from room to room and they are suitable for very young babies (with inserts added). Your baby can see what's going on and be safe and secure at the same time.

GETTING TOGETHER A BABY LAYETTE

1. Cotton vests
2. Hat
3. All-in-one suits
4. Nappies
5. Jacket
6. Mittens
7. Shawl/cellular blanket
8. Muslin squares
9. Bootees or cotton socks
10. Sleeping bag

ADJUSTING AFTER THE BIRTH

1. **Maximize your rest.** Ask help from your family and friends and accept all offers. They can help keep your home tidy, cook meals, go shopping and watch over the baby while you catch forty winks.

2. **Deflect sibling jealousy** by involving any other kids in caring for their new brother or sister.

3. **Don't become isolated** – try to get out – even if it's just for a short walk.

4. **Seek out other new mums** and make new friends by joining a local support network such as a baby-sitting circle.

5. **Get as much help in the house as you feel you need.** Pay for it if necessary – it'll be worth the extra expense.

6. **Make sure that you eat regularly and sensibly.** Pay attention to having a good balanced diet. If you're breastfeeding you'll need to take extra calories to keep your milk flow going well.

7. **Give yourself a treat** from time to time.

Accept offers of babysitting help so that you can go out between feeds.

8 **If you think you might have baby blues,** but can't seem to shake them don't suffer in silence. See your doctor as soon as possible. Talk to your partner and/or family to see if they can help.

9 **Don't feel a failure if your baby cries a lot –** some cry more than others!

10 **Let your baby lead the way** and don't worry if things seem a bit chaotic in the first few weeks. A routine will emerge after a while and you'll start to feel on top of things again soon.

BONDING WITH YOUR NEW BABY

1 **If your baby has to spend time away from you** (say in special care), don't worry. Bonding can still take place. Touch, caress, talk to, sing to and perhaps feed him/her.

2 **Help bonding** by spending waking time with your baby, who will sleep a lot.

3 **Don't worry if bonding doesn't come easily.** You need time to adjust.

4 **Dads! Be prepared to bond with your baby** in a different way to the mother.

5 **Make eye contact with your baby** as much as you can. Even newborns can interpret shapes and outlines.

6 **Go for physical contact.** Try to keep your baby in contact with you as much as possible – your presence is reassuring. You

could try carrying him/her in a sling.

7 **Let the baby hear your heartbeat –** it will be reassuring.

8 **Use your voice.** Your baby recognizes your voice – so sing and talk to him/her as much as you can.

9 **There's no difference in bonding** between breast- and bottle-fed babies.

10 **Give and take.** Give as much love to your newborn as you can – it will be returned to you magnified in the years to come.

ALL CHANGE!

1 **Keep clean.** Wash and dry your hands – both before and after changing a nappy.

2 **Don't get a roll-over.** Make sure your baby cannot roll off the changing table. If you are unsure, it's safer to change a baby on the floor (on a soft surface). Watch the baby at all times.

3 **Gather everything you need together** before you start so that you don't have to

leave the baby alone to fetch something.

4 **Hang a pretty black and white mobile** above the changing station to keep your baby happy. Newborns don't see colour straight away.

5 **Lay a soft muslin square on your baby's tummy** to soothe him/her during nappy-changing. Some babies hate being changed and cry a lot.

6 **Practice makes perfect!** But don't worry, you'll get plenty of that. A newborn baby will need between eight and 10 nappy changes a day during the first few weeks.

7 **If you are a bit worried about being showered by your baby boy mid-change,** try changing him as quickly as possible or place a clean muslin cloth over him just while you clean him up.

8 **If you are out and about,** use two plastic bags to put a used nappy in – the smell can be overpowering!

9 **If you feel that using disposables is not helping climate change,** try switching to cloth nappies. You could use them sometimes or just while you're at home.

10 **Sticky tabs and water or cream don't go!** Beware of getting water or cream on new nappy tabs – they just won't stick and you'll have to start again.

SUCCESSFUL BREAST-FEEDING

1 **If the milk comes down too fast,** slow the flow by expressing a little first.

2 **Use both breasts every time you feed,** to keep the flow going on both sides.

3 **If your nipple is soft and small and your baby can't latch on,** put a cold damp cloth on it just before you feed to firm up the nipple.

4 **Start feeding** from the heavier breast first of all.

5 **The first five minutes are important.** because your baby's sucking reflex is much stronger then.

6 **To remove the baby from your breast,** slip your finger between the areola and your baby's cheek and place your little finger into the corner of the baby's mouth. This will break the suction.

7 **Be sure to support your arms and back** with cushions or pillows. Use a pillow to raise your baby's head, too.

8 **If you're tired or if you don't want your baby lying on you,** try adopting a side-lying position and put baby beside you.

9 **Keep a glass of water or milk by you** while you are feeding to keep hydrated.

10 **Breastfed babies may need more frequent feeding** than those who are bottle-fed because they digest their feeds more quickly.

STRAIGHTFORWARD BOTTLE-FEEDING

1 **Always wash your hands thoroughly** before sterilizing, preparing and giving bottle-feeds.

2 **Sterilize everything to do with making up bottles,** including teats, bottles, the work surface and spoons.

3 **Don't make up feeds in advance –** give them to your baby when they are ready.

4 **Don't keep leftover milk** for the next feed. Discard any that is left over.

5 **Stroke your baby's cheek** to get the sucking reflex going.

6 **Talk to your baby as you feed** and hold him/her close to you.

7 **Don't feed your baby while he/she is lying flat.** This could bring on gagging.

8 **Never leave your baby to feed from a bottle that is propped up on a pillow.** Your baby could choke and/or become very uncomfortable through swallowing air.

9 **Don't make your baby finish the whole bottle** if he/she doesn't want it.

10 **Bottle-fed babies feed much less frequently** than breast-fed ones because formula takes longer to digest and contains a little more protein.

BATHING A NEW BABE

1 **Use a portable bath in the bedroom** while your baby is still tiny. It's likely to be warmer and it's easier, too.

2 **Warm the bathroom first** so the baby doesn't get cold. Make sure the room isn't too draughty.

3 **Gather everything you need together first,** so that you don't have to put the baby down to fetch something.

4 **Wear a waterproof apron** with a large soft towel across your lap.

5 **Bath water should be warm rather than hot.** Test the temperature by dipping your elbow in first.

6 **Before you put your baby in the bath,** hold your babe under one arm, with a towel wrapped around him/her and gently wash the hair. Use mild shampoo and rinse gently with warm water.

7 **Support the baby's shoulders** with one hand, holding the upper arm firmly. Use your free hand to wash him/her with a soft washcloth or sponge.

8 **Wrap your baby up quickly in a warm, fluffy towel** when you take him/her out of the bath. Pat your baby dry all over. Hooded towels are convenient.

9 **Baby towels with hoods are useful.** They allow the baby to feel secure, comfortable and warm.

10 **No need to use talcum powder** – it could cause irritation.

BABY BATHTIME ESSENTIALS

1 Baby bath
2 Bath support
3 Flannel
4 Hooded towel
5 Bath towel
6 Nappy
7 Sleepsuit/ sleeping bag
8 Baby bath oil
9 Shampoo
10 Sponge

GETTING YOUR BABY TO SLEEP

1 **Get into a bedtime routine** (bath, song, bed) even when your baby is tiny. This will become enjoyable for parents/baby that will last through childhood.

2 **Wrap your young baby firmly.** This will help him/her feel more secure.

3 **In very cold weather, put a hot-water bottle in the cot** before bedtime and then be sure to remove it just before you pop your baby in.

4 **Keep the baby's bedroom dark at night.** Older babies and young children often like a nightlight.

5 **Is the baby's room warm enough?** 16–20°C (60–68°F) is about right.

6 **When your baby wakes up to be fed,** don't be tempted to play with him/her.

7 **Check that your baby is warm enough** by touching the back of the neck. It should feel the same temperature as your skin.

8 **Baby's extremities are often cooler** – ensure that they are warm enough and then keep them warm.

9 **Lay your baby on his/her back** with the feet touching the foot of the cot. That way there is less risk of him/her wriggling under the covers.

10 **Some babies are far more wakeful** than others – so you will need to work around your baby's routine.

BABY SAFETY GEAR FOR THE HOME

1 Stair gates
2 Playpen
3 Baby monitor
4 Corner/edge protectors
5 Socket covers
6 Fridge lock
7 Cupboard locks
8 Non-slip mats
9 Cordless blinds/ curtains
10 Glass stickers

CHOOSING & USING A BABY MONITOR

1 **Decide what level of reassurance you want.** Monitors come with different sensitivities – from knowing whether your baby is crying or not to whether he/she is breathing or not.

2 **Consider a moving-lights sound display** so that you can still check on your baby if the volume is turned down or off.

3 **How about dual channels?** A choice of channels reduces the interference your monitor picks up and improves reception.

4 **A talk-back facility** is sometimes useful. You can talk to your baby, maybe to soothe him/her by talking into the parents' unit.

5 **What about a temperature sensor?** If you're worried about your baby getting too hot or too cold, some monitors can keep you informed about the temperature of the baby's room.

6 **Get optional mains/battery operation.** This allows you to plug the monitor into the mains or use the battery – whichever is most convenient.

7 **If you are really worried about your baby, a sensor pad might be the answer.** This fits right under the mattress and rings an alarm should the baby stop moving around/breathing.

8 **Go for lower power and/or out-of-range warning options.** This lets you know whether the monitors are within a suitable distance of each other.

9 **Buy a smartphone app** which allows you to use your phone as a baby monitor.

10 **Some monitors come with a handy nightlight** on the baby unit. This adds a comforting glow to the room as the baby drifts off to sleep.

TACKLING NAPPY RASH

1 **Don't leave a wet nappy on for too long.** It's best to change it as soon as it becomes wet. Moisture makes skin more likely to chafe and over time urine irritates the skin.

2 **The same applies to a soiled nappy.** Digestive agents in the stool attack the skin, making it more prone to a rash.

3 **After a bowel movement,** cleanse with a soft cloth and water.

4 **Expose the baby's bottom to the air** whenever you can. You could try doing this for a while each day.

5 **When you're out use wet wipes.**

6 **Wash the baby's bottom with water.** Soap can cause irritation.

7 **Make sure the skin is completely dry** before you put on a clean nappy. Pat thoroughly with a towel by patting rather than rubbing.

8 **Use a good-quality barrier cream** to protect the skin from moisture – rub on a thin layer before putting the nappy on.

9 **There's no need to use talcum powder during a rash –** it may irritate the skin even more.

10 **Don't use tight-fitting plastic pants** over the top of the nappy – they tend to hold in moisture and and make the rash even worse.

TAKING THE PAIN OUT OF TEETHING

1 **Use a cold cloth.** Take a wet, clean cloth and place in the freezer for a couple of minutes. Let the baby suck on it – the coldness will alleviate the pain. Keep an eye on the baby at all times in case he/she tries to eat the cloth.

2 **A gum massage may help.** Wash your hands thoroughly and rub the gums, exerting a little pressure.

3 **Try out cold food on your baby.** Freeze a banana or carrot and offer it for the baby to chew on. But stay close by in case he/she chokes.

4 **Experiment with a hard teething ring.** Many are specially designed to make it easy for the baby to hold.

5 **Let your baby chew on soft, chewy teething toy.** Some have water inside – so pop them in the freezer first. This relieve pressure on the gums and ease pain.

6 **Use a little clove oil.** Apply one drop diluted in one tbsp of olive oil to the affected gums. Do not use in excess – it can cause gum blistering.

7 **Try a numbing teething gel.** Though be careful as some contain small amounts of sugar. And never use more than the recommended dose.

8 **Hard rusks for the baby to chew** on may help calm things down.

9 **Your baby may love chewing on hard toys.** However, you need to watch carefully to make sure anything put into the mouth is completely safe.

10 **Be extra patient** and give your baby lots of cuddles.

COPING WITH COLIC

1 **Rub a little lavender in a carrier oil on your neck** before you hold your colicky baby. This will help calm him/her down and send him/her off to sleep.

2 **Add a couple of drops of either lavender, chamomile or geranium to a bowl of warm water.** Soak a flannel in it, wring it out and place it on the baby's stomach.

3 **Diffuse a little lavender or chamomile** in the baby's room.

4 **A baby massage may help to eliminate wind.** Warm your hands and using gentle fingertips, stroke from the right hip up around the tummy and down on the left side. Massaging above the navel and in the webbing between thumb/finger helps too.

5 Cranial osteopathy may be worth a try. Ensure that you use a properly qualified cranial osteopath.

6 If your baby is breastfed, think about what you have been eating that may be causing colic. Spicy food, fruit and orange juice can affect the baby's stomach.

7 If your baby is bottle-fed, perhaps change to another type of milk powder.

8 Walking your baby around may help. The motion may provide distraction.

9 A white noise CD will distract the babe.

10 Holding the baby in an upright position when you are feeding may help.

WORRY-FREE WEANING

1 The time to start weaning is usually around halfway through the first year. You'll be able to tell when the time is right – your baby will fill up with milk but still seem hungry.

2 A good moment to introduce your baby to the first tastes of solids is halfway through a normal feed, when he/she is not too hungry or tired.

3 Scoop a little taste of purée onto a soft-edged spoon and place it gently between his/her lips.

4 Make your own purées from fresh fruit such as apple or banana. Remove seeds first and cut up into small pieces before pureeing. Add a little milk.

5 Don't add salt, sugar or flavouring. Your baby doesn't need them.

6 Ready-prepared foods are easy and convenient – especially if you're out. Choose good-quality brands which don't include seasoning or preservatives.

7 Introduce your baby to drinking from a cup at around six months.

8 When your baby is taking solids in any quantity he/she will need water to drink, too. Feed him/her from a cup – either open or with a spout.

9 Finger foods are a great way to get your baby involved in feeding him/herself. Choose fruit and vegetables such as apple, carrot or broccoli cut into chunks that can be easily held.

10 Try not to get tense at mealtimes! Your baby will sense the atmosphere and possibly rebel.

HIGHCHAIR HIGH JINKS

1 Put your older baby in a highchair to sit up at the table. This will help him/her get used to family mealtimes. They are at the same eye level as other family members and will soon start 'chatting'.

2 When your baby is old enough, remove the high-chair tray to pull the chair right up at the table.

3 Put the highchair on a large sheet of plastic so that dropped food and drink doesn't get onto the floor or carpet and spillages can be dealt with.

4 **Put finger foods on the highchair tray** for your child to pick up – this encourages self-feeding.

5 **Always use the harness** when your baby is sitting in a high chair.

6 **Use an additional bumper** as extra padding in the high chair when your baby is small.

7 **Draw circles or shapes on the high-chair tray** to show where the bowl, mug or spoon should go.

8 **Think about what space you have available** in your home for a highchair. Do you need a chair that folds up easily and quickly or are you able to leave it out all the time?

9 **You can get multi-function high chairs** that can be converted into a separate low chair and table, which your child can use when they are older.

10 **Safety tip:** never ever leave your child alone while he/she is eating or drinking.

BEST BUGGIES

1 **A forward-facing pushchair** with lie-back facility is great for newborns. With four wheels, it's convenient, light and easy to manoeuvre.

2 **A two-in-one** can be used upright as a buggy or flat like a pram. Some face the parent while others are outward-facing.

3 **A three-in-one** is just like the two-in-one except that it has a detachable carry-cot, which is great for newborns.

4 **A three-wheeler** is really for fitness-freak parents. You can steer it one-handed and it's robust enough for a variety of surfaces. However, it's quite bulky should you need to stow it in the car.

5 **Go for broke and get a 'travel system'.** This has all the bells and whistles. It's a normal pram/pushchair, with a carrycot as well, and also a clip-on car seat. It's a great choice if your life involves a lot of car travel.

6 **The stroller or buggy is a lightweight item,** though not usually suitable for newborns. They're really for older babies and going out and about on public transport. Some of them can be folded with one hand.

7 **Considering an old-fashioned pram?** Great for sleeping in, but not so good for stowing in the front hall. It's a high-cost item which really only has limited use these days.

8 **Think about your lifestyle before you buy.** Do you live in an upstairs flat? Do you use public transport or a car? Will you be carrying heavy shopping while you wheel? Foldability and weight are the key considerations.

9 **Check safety standards** carefully if you are buying a second-hand buggy.

10 **Consider some useful extras** to make life easier: rainhood, matching changing bag, sunshade, cositoes, hooks and racks for carrying bags safely. And don't forget, the more expensive the pushchair, the more expensive the accessories.

WORK & EDUCATION

How to earn a living and become educated are issues that require a lot of careful thought. Whether you're looking for a career for yourself or a new school for your child, want to gen up on how to find a babysitter or help your teen settle into college, this chapter will help you to focus on all the most important things.

A CAREER FOR LIFE

1 To work out what your future career might be, sit down with a piece of paper and pencil and make a list of all your talents, interests and personality traits. Think about what your real passions are. Don't hold back and don't stop until you've run through everything you can think of. Flag up items that must form part of your perfect career, as opposed to things that might be nice but aren't essential.

2 For the moment, leave money out of the equation and consider what jobs would really make you happy and lead to fulfillment. This is serious as you may well need to work for forty years – so you might as well enjoy it. Remember – as long as you are fairly paid, money will find you. Top-dollar jobs may sound good at the outset, but can sometimes suck you in to long hours and stress – perhaps in a field that doesn't truly interest you.

3 Know thyself! Self-knowledge is vital. Look for insights on 'you' by asking fond friends what they think you are really like; what they consider your strengths and weakness to be and what makes you tick. Use this information to guide you in your search, in writing your CV and in interviews. Then use it to pitch for the perfect job.

4 Do some serious careers research. Read blogs by people involved in your chosen career to get first-hand insight into what it's all about. Read all about available positions, job descriptions and statistics. Find out what qualifications you need.

5 Brainstorm with your friends about their careers. You probably know people in a wide range of fields. Ask them to tell you honestly whether they are happy in their work, what they get out of it, whether it uses their skills and training.

6 Job-shadow or do an internship. Find out about a specific career by getting in on the act. Even though you may not be paid at first, ask to take on real assignments and try not to be fobbed off with tasks such as making coffee. Your proactivity will show that you really are keen. If you are in a full-time job already, take time out to volunteer. You'll build skills to help you follow your dreams and find out whether you really want to make the career jump.

7 Think about your qualifications. Have you got the correct bits of paper for your career? If you don't, think about doing some courses to get you started. If you already possess the correct qualifications, consider whether they need updating.

8 Contacts are important. Are yours good? If they aren't, join professional networks and get connected to people in your chosen field. You may be able to make contacts online and even attend face-to-face events to do some networking. Go to public lectures and free events and stick around afterwards to chat to people. Don't be nervous about introducing yourself to people you haven't met before. You never know where a new contact might lead.

9 Think long-term. What you want from a job will probably change during your life. It's very unlikely you will have the same career aspirations in a couple of decades' time that you do now. Many careers start as junior positions, in which you carry out a range of basic administration skills and then progress into management.

10 Think about your work/life balance. If you think you may want to divide your time between work and other things, look at finding a career that is flexible enough to accommodate your desires.

WHAT TO LOOK FOR IN A JOB

1 Creativity
2 Autonomy
3 Company reputation
4 Opportunities
5 Learning
6 Skills
7 Interest
8 Flexible hours
9 Remuneration
10 Part-time/full-time

JOB-RELATED SKILLS
1 Buying & selling
2 Helping others
3 Teaching
4 Writing
5 Designing
6 Presenting
7 Planning
8 Administering
9 Handling money
10 Making money

TRACK DOWN THE PERFECT JOB

1 Go to potential employers you would really like to work for rather than waiting for job vacancies to come up – they may never happen or you may miss them.

2 Market yourself as the person an employer is searching for. Approach companies who want what you can offer: personality, skills, experience and aptitude.

3 Make your CV stand out, though focused on the job you are searching for. For example, if you are a graphic designer, showcase your typographic and design skills and your creative abilities in your CV.

4 Create an impressive web presence. Online CVs with colleague recommendations are quick and easy for prospective employers to access – get yours ready.

5 Business cards are the real deal. Choose a great design that highlights your skills and qualifications. Cards are good to take to interviews and business encounters as they underline you to new contacts.

6 Seek and get attention by being unique and doing something that shows off your talents. For example, start an online campaign using social media.

7 Go in for contests and competitions. These are important and definitely worth the time, effort and expense. Take time to enter competitions that will demonstrate your skills. Prizes and awards on your CV will impress others and make yours shine.

8 Do what you love. Could you turn a beloved hobby into a career? Could leisure activities be turned into work/a business?

9 Think about a 'portfolio' career, with a range of related skills that can be used in different settings – this gives you far more scope in the jobs market.

10 Keep your skills finely tuned and up to date and be prepared to go on training courses to keep them tip top.

WHERE TO LOOK FOR A JOB

1 Tell everyone that you are looking for a job. A friend or family member may notice an advert you haven't seen.

2 Network! Attend professional meetings in your chosen career. Be sure to note people's names and contact them directly after meetings. Make use of association directories to find further names.

3 Contact your local employment office.

4 Make an appointment with your university or school careers adviser. Pick their brains and use their resources.

5 Search trade journals and relevant newspaper job listings.

6 Go online. Use internet job boards, online newspapers and search engines to find business website addresses and classified ads. Also many business websites have job listings pages.

7 Go on foot. Smarten yourself up and visit businesses to inquire about openings in person. Take printouts of your CV with you to hand them out to those you meet.

8 Phone businesses direct. It helps if you have a relevant name to ask for.

9 Register with a recruitment agency.

10 Attend job fairs and talk to anyone who is prepared to talk to you.

PEN A BRILLIANT CV

1 **Include all your contact information.** List your full name, address, home phone number, mobile number and email address. You do not have to include information about your age, race, religion or sexual orientation, though perhaps age may be relevant. Many people attach a photograph. You don't have to do this, though it may help quick identification at interview.

2 **Tailor your CV specifically on the job you are applying for** and include the same keywords that appear in the job description. That way, you will increase your chances of it matching available positions – and of you being selected for an interview.

3 **Format your CV so that it's easy to read.** Limit yourself to one or two fonts and avoid adding clip art or fancy flourishes – too many gimmicks can be irritating to those who only have limited time.

4 **Prioritize the CV content** so that your most important and relevant experience comes first, with key accomplishments at the top of each position.

5 **Keep your CV concise.** Two pages is a good length to aim for; anything shorter will possibly skimp on detail about your work history, accomplishments and education.

Anything longer is cumbersome and could discourage a recruiter from reading it.

6 **Your CV must be perfect –** do not make any mistakes. Proofread it and the covering letter and ask someone else to check it over, too. If you are applying for posts where spelling, grammar and writing matters this is even more important.

7 **Explain absences from the workplace** such as unemployment, maternity leave or periods of travel. Be honest and open, otherwise it will look as though you're trying to conceal something.

8 **Write a personalized covering letter** rather than a generic one. Tailor it to the job you are applying for and your own experience and use it to tell the employer why you are interested in the position.

9 **Don't be tempted to manipulate the truth.** Positive emphasis and strong presentation is good, but falsehoods will count against you once someone has noticed it. For example, don't claim to have qualifications you do not.

10 **If you have good references,** make sure your prospective employer knows about them and that they are available to talk to them. But ask your referees first.

GO DOWN WELL AT INTERVIEWS

1 **Do some in-depth research** about the company. Learn as much as you can before the interview. Come up with good questions about the job and the company itself.

2 **Arrive a little early –** to collect your thoughts and appear relaxed. If you are late it won't make a good impression.

3 **Prepare some answers** for the type of questions you may be asked. You must know why you want the job, what your strengths are, how you'd tackle challenges and what your achievements are so far.

4 **Bring along some props –** copies of printed reports you have written, for example, – physical proof will impress and give you an advantage over those who just talk about what they've done.

5 Decide what to wear and get your clothes ready the day before. Aim for a neat, clean and tidy appearance.

6 Take three CVs with you – one for the interviewer, one for you and a spare. This will look efficient and act as a prompt.

7 Engage the person(s) interviewing you. Look them in the eye. Be sure to learn their name(s).

8 Be polite and friendly. Give a firm, dry handshake, appear confident, sit up straight and be sure to smile.

9 Think how you will deal positively with questions about negative issues such as illness or redundancy. Tell the truth. Don't gloss over things that could put you in a negative light.

10 Follow up the interview with a letter or email (and then a phone call) so that they know you are keen. Do this as soon as you can after the interview.

A GIRL'S SMART WORKING WARDROBE

1 Notice what your boss wears and then mirror his/her style.

2 Colour is very important in creating a professional image. Traditional career colours include red, navy, grey and black and they work well in teaming trousers with jackets, skirts and shoes. Mix them with softer, feminine colours such as ice blue, lilac, soft pink and ivory.

3 Simple jewels, please! Stud earrings and single bracelets are best. Jangling and dangling is distracting and unprofessional.

4 Choose a structured handbag that makes you look organized. Slouchy, soft styles can look too informal. A briefcase or laptop bag adds a professional touch.

5 Inspect your nails. Your hands will be on show, so your nails should be clean and neat and not talon-like or decorated. Avoid wearing brightly coloured varnish.

6 If you go for tailored work clothes, pay attention to fit. Trousers should be fitted and skirts, especially straight styles, should be loose enough to sit down in and not ride up. A jacket should be buttoned.

7 Your blouse shouldn't gape between the buttonholes – oh, and cleavage is a real no-no.

8 Designer labels are great, but heavily logo-ed clothes and accessories are out.

9 Shoes need to be well polished and scuff-free. Keep them in good repair.

10 Your hair should look neat and your make-up should be subtle.

GET THAT PROMOTION

1 Got a mentor? If your company has a mentoring scheme, use it, but if it doesn't, try to build relationships with people who are higher up in the company. Do this informally and naturally. Such individuals can help you make career decisions.

2 Keep a record of everything you do for the company. These are the things that promote the company and they show your loyalty and commitment to it.

3 Promote yourself. You don't need to be a show-off, but if no one knows about your good points, they can't make use of them.

4 Looking for promotion? Let people know – someone may recommend you.

5 Use the appraisal system to discuss your promotion aims plus recent achievements. If there are stumbling blocks to promotion this is a good place to discuss them. Make sure your boss knows you are committed to the company.

6 Take up training opportunities. Aim to take on fresh skills to benefit the company.

7 Be sociable and be sure to make friends at work. If people know you, know what you can do and how good you are, the more likely your name will come up when opportunities arise.

8 Ask for some extra responsibilities. This shows you want to help your company succeed. It will spotlight your value.

9 Be a real pro. Be dependable, professional and cooperative. Dress the part, ask questions when you aren't sure how to do something and be a bit different so that you stand out. Be positive, don't complain, don't always blame others, don't be a clock-watcher and always be a problem-solver. Don't go running to your boss every time there's a problem. If a difficulty crops up, be the one to suggest a solution.

10 Teams are the thing. Share successes and avoid blaming others for failures. You'll increase your value to the company.

NEGOTIATE A PAY RISE

1 Do the research. Find out what the typical salary rates in your field are.

2 Be objective about your market worth. Look at similar jobs outside your industry and compare them to your own job.

3 Ask for a face-to-face meeting with your boss. This is better than writing a letter as it is a two-way communication allowing you to build mutual understanding of the situation.

4 Think about when you will arrange the meeting. First thing Monday or last thing Friday may not be the best moment. Choose a time when your boss will not be rushed and can give you full attention.

5 Don't be afraid to negotiate. Ask for a little more than you actually want, to make room for some negotiation. Know your arguments and present your case clearly. Always be polite and reasonable.

6 Wait for a moment when your boss is more likely to say 'Yes'. If the company's going through a difficult financial situation, this is not a good time to ask.

7 If your request for a rise is turned down, ask for extra work and responsibilities and link this to a future pay rise.

8 Ask for a performance-related bonus or a pay increase subject to you achieving more, based on an increased output.

9 What about taking perks rather than an actual pay rise? This could be in the form of extra holiday, a higher car allowance or increased training and development.

10 As a last resort, resign. Your employer may offer you more money to stay. Some companies have a policy of not taking action until they have to. But it's risky.

KEEPING FIT AT WORK

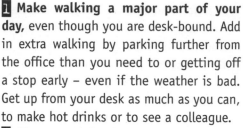

1 **Make walking a major part of your day,** even though you are desk-bound. Add in extra walking by parking further from the office than you need to or getting off a stop early – even if the weather is bad. Get up from your desk as much as you can, to make hot drinks or to see a colleague.

2 **Sit up straight,** keeping your vertebrae aligned. Adjust your monitor screen so that you look straight at it.

3 **Check whether your office chair is correctly positioned** for your desk height and monitor position.

4 **Do sitting or standing exercises at your desk.** Keep small weights by your desk. Why not squeeze a stress ball to relieve tension in your hands and wrists?

5 **Do some neck exercises** by relaxing your shoulders and letting your head roll forwards. Rotate your head without straining your neck and repeat five times.

6 **Pay attention to your shoulders** as they tend to absorb and retain a lot of stress. Shrug your shoulders, holding them up for 15 seconds. Then release and repeat.

7 **Rearrange the things on your desk regularly** so that you are not repeating the same stretching and reaching movements over and over again.

8 **Drink plenty of fluids,** especially water, throughout the day.

9 **Eat healthily at work.** Avoid sugary snacks and comfort food – even if you are under pressure. Eat a nutritious light lunch, away from your desk if you can.

10 **Do something different in your lunch hour,** as well as eating, so that your brain takes a break as well as your body.

DESK ERGONOMICS

1 Monitor height
2 Monitor distance
3 Monitor glare
4 Monitor angle
5 Bifocals needed?
6 Keyboard angle
7 Chair height
8 Minimize your head-turning
9 Light mouse-hold
10 Feet flat on floor

OFFICE ETIQUETTE

1 **When you are away from your desk,** divert or activate your voicemail – your ringing phone will annoy others.

2 **When you go on holiday activate your 'out of office'** facility so that others know where you are and when you are due back. If possible, leave the contact details of an assistant who can act in your place.

3 **Be punctual.** Be on time for work – always! And never be late for meetings.

4 **Turn down your speaking volume** so that other people aren't disturbed. This is important in open-plan offices.

5 **Stay at home if you get the sniffles** – it doesn't do to spread your germs around. Perhaps work from home if you can.

6 **Ask before borrowing** colleagues' pens, staplers and scissors. If you use someone else's desk while they're away, leave it exactly as you found it.

7 **Leave the office kitchen tidy** after you have used it. Do your washing up and don't leave unwanted food in the fridge.

8 **Respect the need for peace and quiet.** If a colleague is having lunch at her desk, don't start on a work-related conversation until she's finished.

9 **Be sensitive about whiffs** – strong-smelling flowers, pungent perfumes and the dreaded BO can upset people.

10 **Keep all your sounds to yourself.** If you're using headphones, turn them low.

WATERCOOLER DON'TS

1 Don't be tempted to gossip. It can be very damaging if negative chat spreads abroad – with your name attached to it.

2 Don't be bitchy. Be positive about everyone – talk about their good points.

3 Don't be a flirt – you might send out the wrong messages and office romances aren't known for running smoothly.

4 Don't get personal – it makes you seem very unprofessional.

5 If you're leaving the company or switching to a different department, don't discuss it with colleagues as it might get back to your boss before you've told them.

6 Don't talk about what you are earning unless you want everyone else to know.

7 If you don't want something to be broadcast around the company, don't talk about it around the water cooler..

8 Don't whinge – negativity spreads like forest fire.

9 Don't air personal problems.

10 Don't be inconsiderate. When the water has all gone – refill the cooler.

COPING WHEN YOUR JOB'S UNDER THREAT

1 Increase your cash reserve. Save at least three to six months' living expenses.

2 Update your CV so that you are ready to start looking for a new job.

3 Avoid performance anxiety at work – you'll only make things worse.

4 Keep your whole life in perspective and don't let your threatened job ruin the satisfaction you get from other areas of your life – family, hobbies, holidays.

5 Take a close, hard look at your sector and be realistic about what might happen to your job. Who is up and who is down? Who is hiring and who is firing?

6 Make sure you appear committed, enthusiastic and contributing.

7 Update your skills – especially if you haven't done so recently.

8 Put yourself forward to do something that no one else wants to take on.

9 Forewarned is forearmed. Talk to your boss, your union representative if you have one, human resources contact or legal expert.

10 Remember: there's no such thing as a job for life. Perhaps now could be the time for you to move on.

DEALING WITH REDUNDANCY

1 If it's an option, leave straight away. No need to upset yourself with questions from colleagues. Or if you are serving out a notice period, work just as you normally do, so that your reputation stays intact. You may need to ask your old boss for references for your next job.

2 Be sure to get a reference from your

boss which, in addition to recommending you, explain the reasons for the redundancy.

3 Discuss and receive the correct redundancy package. But be sure to finalize all the arrangements before you actually leave. It's hard to backtrack later.

4 Tell your family and friends.

5 Sort out your financial situation. How long can you survive without a job?

6 Find out about any benefits you and your family may be eligible for.

7 Consider short-term therapy.

8 Make use of any help your company may offer to redundant staff – anything from career assessment to free use of the photocopier to help you find a new job.

9 Start job-hunting immediately. This will give you something positive to do when you are used to working all day.

10 Search online for the latest jobs and volunteering opportunities – so you can learn new skills while looking.

START UP YOUR OWN BUSINESS

1 Your new venture needs to be something you really care about.

2 Start your business while you are still employed. The money you are still earning will keep you afloat while setting up.

3 Have a support system in place, such as family, friends or mentors.

4 It's more fun to work with a colleague or two. You'll need sympathetic listeners to bounce ideas off at first.

5 Draw up a realistic business plan.

6 Do as much research as you can about your product or service. Know everything you can about the field you're getting into. You need to know what the competition is,

understand what you are providing and its intended market place.

7 Professional help is a must. You will need a book-keeper and an accountant.

8 Where is the money going to come from? You need to know how you will be putting your finances in place.

9 Sort out your legal and tax issues and get them right at the outset. It will save a lot of fuss down the line.

10 Just pitch in! It's best just to get going, rather than waiting until everything is perfect before you start. Don't be afraid of hiccups or even of failing. Don't let money get in the way of a good vision.

BLISSFUL WORKING FROM HOME

1 Be disciplined – when you are at work, be at work one hundred percent. If the day seems tough and you feel like stopping – keep going anyway. You'll feel a sense of achievement just by persevering.

2 It helps to set up your office in a

particular room, so that you can be single-minded and purposeful about what you are doing. It indicates boundaries to others.

3 When you are working, close the door to your room so that others realize you are working and won't disturb you.

4 Try to stick to office hours, at least to begin with. Work a full day, even if it's not normal working hours. Some people work better in the mornings or evenings.

5 Get a routine going and you'll feel more business-like – get dressed and don't hang around in your dressing gown.

6 Stay connected with old work colleagues and make new contacts.

7 Go to professional meetings to keep up to date and in circulation.

8 Be sure to meet, and exceed, all your client's expectations.

9 Take a lunch break, eat well and take some exercise. You'll feel better able to tackle the afternoon workload.

10 Know when to stop at the end of the day. Don't let work take over your life.

A SUCCESSFUL HOME OFFICE

1 A room of one's own
2 Wi-fi connection
3 Ergonomic desk
4 Proper office chair
5 Telephone
6 Printer
7 Good lighting
8 Filing cabinet
9 Copier
10 Kettle

A HAPPY CAREER MOVE

1 Think about your current job – why do you dislike it?

2 Look back over jobs you liked in the past and think about what they gave you that you don't get now.

3 Discuss your skills and talents with people who know you well and who might be willing to advise you.

4 Pick out areas for career research. Read up as much as you can on each area.

5 Test out your interests by volunteering your services, interning or work-shadowing. This will help to give you some first-hand experience.

6 Have you got all the skills and qualifications you'll need for your new career? Look at educational opportunities to get fully skilled-up in your new field. Short courses might be available.

7 Your existing job might provide some day courses and training schemes in your new field.

8 Move sideways. Think of moving to a different job within the same company.

9 Restructure your CV to suit your new career choice. You'll probably find that there are a lot of items that can be left in, but just need tweaking for a new audience.

10 You may have to accept a slightly lower salary, new location or lower job status. But this may be well worth it in the longterm.

PERFECT PART-TIME WORKING

1 Take your job as seriously as if it were full-time – be a real pro, then others will think of you that way, too.

2 Bring all your energy, efficiency and enthusiasm to your part-time position. You are working less, so you should be less tired and jaded.

3 Don't feel that you've got to achieve more in less time – don't work longer hours than you are contracted for.

4 Make sure your pay is the same pro rata as it would have been full time.

5 Work to the very highest standards: be better than the full-time crowd.

6 Negotiate which days, or half-days, of the week suit your own arrangements and those of your workplace. You need to be able to balance a mixture of demands and there must be give and take.

7 Are all your life backup systems in place? You must be a reliable worker. If other people pick up your children or help keep your household going – make sure arrangements are watertight.

8 When you're at work, 'be' fully at work. Don't wish you were elsewhere.

9 Make sure that you're getting the same training as full-time staffers.

10 Insist on having proper job appraisals – just the same as full-time colleagues.

DO A JOB-SHARE

IDEAS FOR VOLUNTARY WORK

1 Charity/thrift store
2 Hospital
3 Hospice
4 School
5 Schemes abroad
6 Mentoring
7 Sports coaching
8 Senior citizens
9 Fundraising
10 Religious groups

1 Make sure you know and like the person you're sharing a job with – though you may not have a choice.

2 Set up a forum for getting to know your job-sharer.

3 Get a good idea about how your job-sharer works before you start.

4 Agree some ground rules.

5 Share out tasks fairly so that resentments don't build up.

6 Communicate freely and readily with your job-share partner – even if this eats into your free time.

7 Schedule a handover time during the week when you can update one another on what has happened. Or make arrangements to email to do the same.

8 Be clear about how you store information you'll both need so that you can both access it – this could be electronic or in a filing cabinet.

9 Know what your manager expects. Make sure that they are not expecting double just because there are two of you.

10 Can you both get access to training if it applies to both of you?

RETURNING AFTER A CAREER BREAK

1 Don't feel guilty if you are a parent returning to work. You and your family will both benefit from it.

2 Mug up on any new skills you may now need to add to or update.

3 Perhaps go part time and build up the hours gradually.

4 If you are returning after a maternity break, consider switching to a career that's more flexible and fits in with your family commitments.

5 If you feel your confidence has taken a knock – perhaps seek help in assertiveness training.

6 Give yourself time to adjust to the changes of being back at work.

7 Don't forget – you will have acquired many life skills to add to your professional talents. For example, parenting teaches you time management and negotiation. It's all goes into the pot.

8 Sort out your wardrobe. If you have

been at home for a while in your jeans, it could be time to go shopping for a smart working wardrobe.

9 Get yourself ready for returning to work a few months ahead of time. It's such a significant change that it requires intensive planning.

10 Recall an occasion at work when you were at your peak and try to relive it. Take this feeling to your workplace.

LEARN TO TOUCH-TYPE

1 Learn the correct finger placement from the start. Rest your fingers on the home keys and move back and forth from there – you won't get lost.

2 Just learn the home keys first and type as fast as you can with them – perhaps even faster than feels comfortable. Add the other letters gradually.

3 Do a little practice every day.

4 If you need structure, enrol for a class. There are online tutorials, too.

5 Don't be tempted to look at the keyboard or your hands. Touch-typing will come more easily if you train yourself not to from day one. It may help to 'hide' the keyboard and your hands under a cloth.

6 If you find some of the less-used keys hard to learn at first, peep when you need to.

7 Don't worry too much about making mistakes. Correct them and move on. Speed and confidence in moving around the keyboard are more important.

8 Only move the finger you need. Leave all the others on their home keys.

9 Be aware of your posture. Your feet should be flat on the floor and you should be sitting as straight as you can.

10 Don't sit too near to the keyboard.

LEARN SHORTHAND

1 Use a ring-bound reporter's notepad. The width is perfect for quick note-taking.

2 Keep the left-hand margin for noting key words so you can identify them later.

3 Write as small as you can so that you can go faster.

4 To get in some practice, write out articles and features you have read in shorthand and read them back to see how well you've noted them down.

5 Choose an easy-gliding pen and press lightly. Blue or black biros are good. Keep a spare one handy. Pressing hard will make you feel tense and slow you down.

6 Keep as calm and relaxed as you can. Take deep breaths if necessary.

7 Flex your fingers every now and again to keep them supple and relaxed.

8 If you miss out a word, leave a space. Go back and write in the whole word.

9 Transcribe someone else's shorthand to practise recognizing other people's outlines and words.

10 If you are noting down speech, leave a line of space between each sentence to make it clearer to read your notes back.

EFFECTIVE PUBLIC SPEAKING

1 **Do your homework** and make sure you know the subject inside out. The more you know, the more confident you will be.

2 **Watch the masters.** Study what makes a speech good and check out different styles and delivery techniques. Emulate them.

3 **Practise what you're going to say.** Write it down or make notes you can refer to easily. Practise in front of friends and family and take their feedback on board.

4 **Pay attention to your appearance.** All eyes will be on you, so make an effort to look smart. You'll feel more professional.

5 **Eye contact is good** as it makes the audience feel involved. Make eye contact with different people, but not for too long.

6 **Give the audience something to look at** – apart from you, of course! Use power-point presentation, slides and visual aids.

7 **Handouts can be a plus** – if there is information that the audience might like to take home. But keep it simple – a summary of points made might be best.

8 **If you are a tad nervous about public speaking,** build up your self-confidence by concentrating on making your presentation as good as it can be rather than wondering how you are going to survive it.

9 **Visit the venue first** and adjust your presentation to what is there. Will you need a microphone to make yourself heard? Will you need a lectern? Test everything you are going to use out beforehand.

10 **If you ask for questions** from the floor at the end, make sure you know enough to be able to answer them.

DEAL WITH YOUR INBOX

1 **Delete the emails** you do not need to keep – straight away.

2 **If you feel pressurized to keep looking** in your inbox and dealing with it, close your 'email notification' so that you can't see new messages coming in.

3 **Only look in your inbox at specific times of the day** and deal with everything then. That way, you'll be less distracted from your routine work. Some people say it's better not to start your day by dealing with your inbox.

4 **Consider whether it's really necessary to receive and read emails** you've been copied in on. Also think about who you send emails to. Does everyone really need to be copied in?

5 **Send links rather than attachments.** The latter take up a great deal of space on your computer.

6 **Act on a message when you get it** rather than opening and closing the message several times.

7 **File your emails** when you've dealt with them. Don't keep them all in your inbox – only the ones you haven't finished dealing with yet.

8 **Delete items in your 'sent' folder** regularly to save storage space.

9 **Empty out your 'deleted' items folder** at regular intervals.

10 **Create subfolders for archiving** your messages. Filing is essential for general organization and creating paper trails.

MANAGE A PROJECT

1 **Agree on the project scope,** specification or terms of reference. This should give an accurate description of what the project aims to achieve and how.

2 **Plan the project in detail.** Build in timing and costs, who is going to be involved and how. Plan the reporting-back process and find out about contingencies.

3 **Assemble the team** and let everyone know what the plan is. This elicits their support and gets them on side.

4 **Delegate actions.** This involves describing all the tasks and activities and assigning them to people.

5 **Identify the key steps** or stages of the project and work out how it will progress.

6 **Motivation is key** when the project is under way. Encourage everyone, to get the best out of them. Consider how people work together and be prepared to pass on information and handle conflicts.

7 **Check and review progress** as the project goes along. Document everything.

8 **Be prepared to adjust** your original plan and keep everyone informed.

9 **'Praise loudly, but blame softly'** is a good approach. When the project is completed, review it and thank the team. Reflect on anything that could have gone better and point out mistakes objectively.

10 **Follow-up and learn from mistakes.** Give extra training where helpful.

SOLVE ALL YOUR PROBLEMS

1 **Accept that the problem exists** rather than fretting about it, which might be making the issue bigger in your mind than it really is. Acceptance will help you start to solve your problem.

2 **Try talking.** Get together with the relevant people and see if there was a misunderstanding. It may be possible to calm things before people start to panic.

3 **What's the worst that can happen?** This idea will help put the problem into perspective and make you feel you can tackle and solve it.

4 **Find out as much as you can about your problem.** Educating yourself may help to calm you down. The issue might not be as serious as you first thought.

5 **Ask other people** how they tackled similar/the same problem(s).

6 **Ask for help.** This is not an admission of defeat. Two heads are usually better than one and people are often willing to hand on their expertise.

7 **Keep an open mind.** The solution you first thought of may not be the right one. You may be overlooking or ignoring an important solution through having a closed mind.

8 **See if you can break the problem into chunks.** This will stop it overwhelming you and seeming too big.

9 **Is there an opportunity within your problem?** See if you can find the positive behind the difficulty. This will reduce the negativity and its emotional impact and help you learn from the situation.

10 **Think first.** Problems often crop up because we don't think things through.

BRILLIANT BRAINSTORMING

1 **Think about why you are brainstorming** (normally it's to produce a wide range of ideas, not whether they are good or bad) and use the process to extend the ideas, not just to collect them.

2 **Understand the best ways to facilitate brainstorming.** All contributions are equal (including your own).

3 **Write all the ideas down,** as they come up. In a group a flipchart is good.

4 **Don't allow too much general discussion –** wait until after you've collected all the ideas together.

5 **Don't let the participants criticize** one another's suggestions.

6 **Allow one idea to lead on to another** and include everything.

7 **If you are brainstorming on your own** you may feel you're running out of ideas – just see if you can keep going for a further five minutes so see what comes up.

8 **Set a definite time limit.** Half an hour is probably quite long enough for most brainstorming sessions.

9 **When you have finished,** look through the ideas and start discussing them with a view to narrowing down the list.

10 **Write up the session,** listing all the ideas and the discussion and conclusions arrived at. Note actions decided on.

DEVELOP YOUR SALES SKILLS

1 **Work out who your product is aimed at** and don't approach people who won't be genuinely interested. Draw up a list of criteria for prospective clients.

2 **Find clients who want to buy** what you have to offer – from you.

3 **Build up good rapport with your clients –** be a people person. Move outside your comfort zone and go for those you don't immediately click with.

4 **Use voicemail.** If you can't get to the person you need to deal with, try personalized voicemails. Focus on who you are speaking to and make your message individual to them. Your message will almost certainly be returned.

5 **Devote some time and energy to presentations.** Make yours different from everyone else's. Get your audience involved by making your descriptions and stories as

rich as possible. They are bound to want what you are selling.

6 **What can your product do for your client?** How can it improve their life? Go for broad brushstrokes and don't explain fiddly details.

7 **Do your homework on the person you are trying to sell to.** The more you know about them, the more accurately you can pitch your product to them.

8 **Always follow up a promising lead.** If you make a successful first cold call, follow this up with another and perhaps make an appointment to see them.

9 **Enjoy selling!** Think about your goal (closing a deal) and work towards that. Everything else is the responsibility of your client. Don't absorb his/her stress.

10 **Go for sales skills training** if you get the opportunity.

NETWORK FOR BUSINESS

1 **Work on mutually helpful connections.**

2 **Look at your goals** and decide whether networking is really useful to you.

3 **Visit a variety of networking groups.** Which ones might be helpful to you?

4 **Volunteer** to help run networking organizations. This will raise your visibility and let you contribute to those who may have helped you in the past.

5 **Ask open-ended questions** when you are networking. This will open up discussions and create two-way interest.

6 **Set yourself up as a valuable resource.** If people feel they can turn to you, this will reinforce you in their minds.

7 **Be sure about what you do and why.** What makes your service unique? This will help you network effectively.

8 **Know what you are looking for in others** and how they can help you.

9 **Follow up all referrals** quickly and efficiently. This will inspire confidence and reinforce the respect of others.

10 **Chase up contacts** with a call/email.

RESOLVE CONFLICT

1 **Stay cool, not confrontational.** You'll be in a stronger position if you are still and silent. If the other person is angry, they will want to provoke you into becoming angry yourself.

2 **Let the other person talk** – just listen. Sometimes people just want to be heard.

3 **Think about the other person's point of view.** Is there validity in what they're saying? Put yourself in their place.

4 **Look for the areas in which you both agree** and build on those.

5 **Don't tell the other person they're 'wrong'.** Go for positive validation of what

they are saying, even if you don't agree.

6 **If an argument does flare up,** suggest a postponement of the discussion.

7 **If you think you might be wrong after all, admit it** and move on.

8 **Suggest that you 'might' be wrong,** even if you still believe you are right. Then look at the facts again. This may bring the other person on to your side.

9 **Use visualization techniques** to imagine a tyrannical person as sweet and loving.

10 **Use experiences of dealing with past conflicts** – learn from mistakes and use things that worked to your advantage.

MANAGE OTHER PEOPLE

1 **Think of yourself as being responsible for other people's work** rather than just contributing your own work.

2 **Establish your immediate goals** by setting up a checklist of team targets, regular meetings and productivity reviews.

Be prepared to change it over time and regard it as a changing document.

3 Get to know your team. Be aware of everyone's strengths and weaknesses and what makes everyone tick.

4 Match people with the tasks they are strongest in. It's usually best for people to work to their strengths at first. Put people together with complementary skills.

5 Meet team members regularly. This is to get to know them better and give feedback on their performance, provide goals, learn more about staff issues, ask for ideas and to motivate everyone.

6 Don't hide away. It's important not to be isolated from the team, otherwise you will seem remote and uninvolved.

7 Keep written records of your team's recent performance.

8 How you deal with problems will be what your role is all about.

9 If things go well, make sure your team knows that you are happy. Think about how to recognize achievement.

10 Coaching your team is important. Be prepared to be a teacher, to impart all the correct procedures, and this will lead to you getting the results you want.

HANDLE BUSINESS MEETINGS

1 Make sure the meeting has a specific overall goal and that it sticks to it. If you need to tackle separate issues, put aside time under an 'Any other business' heading.

2 Set an agenda beforehand and circulate it to everyone concerned.

3 Circulate the minutes of the previous meeting and take time to review it at the beginning of the meeting.

4 Ask someone to take minutes and circulate them afterwards.

5 Don't always rely on the same styles of presentation. Use audio-visual aids, break people up into small groups or pass around items to look at.

6 Start the meeting with an ice-breaker. This might be a single question to get the ball rolling with informal chat.

7 Invite guest speakers. A new person in the room will stimulate fresh ideas.

8 Ask people to write their questions down. This lets everyone think about what they want to know and why more carefully. Allow time for questions.

9 Repeat a question, to make sure everyone has heard and understood it. The person who asked the question can check that their question is correctly worded.

10 Start and end on time and make sure drinks/snacks are on hand.

MANAGE YOUR TIME

1 Make deadlines work for you. Create mini deadlines and meet them. The main 'big' deadline will become more achievable.

2 Use your time well. Be disciplined about distractions. For example, set times for making phone calls and going through your inbox so that you can carry out uninterrupted spells of work and feel you have achieved something.

3 **Get organized.** Set up filing systems, both physical and electronic, so that it is easier to find things quickly. This will cut down time you waste searching for things.

4 **In-trays can be useful.** You then know how much you really have to deal with.

5 **If you maintain an open-door policy,** accept that people will disturb you – otherwise have a closed-door policy.

6 **Do you really need to attend routine meetings?**

7 **When you are setting deadlines for others, give them a date** a couple of days beforehand, to allow for lateness.

8 **Do you really need to read everything you are sent?** Some people send emails just to prove they are doing their job.

9 **Don't supervise unnecessarily.** Decide how much you really need to supervise your staff. Why not trust them to do what they said they would do?

10 **Don't postpone jobs that you don't like doing.** Do the things you don't like first, followed by the things you do like and perhaps give yourself a small reward.

GO TEAM GO!

1 **All team members must understand the goals of the team.** They also need to be committed to achieving them.

2 **Team members must trust each other** so that they feel happy to take reasonable risks and be able to disagree with each other if they have to.

3 **Members must communicate easily** and feel they can be open and honest.

4 **Does everyone feel they belong to the team?** Belonging is important, so that members get behind actions and decisions.

5 **Team members need to feel they are individuals** with their own personalities and opinions. They will then feel they have something unique to contribute.

6 **Positive feedback** should be part of the team culture. Negative comments should have a constructive message.

7 **The team should be able to analyse how it is working,** so that it can improve ways of working and team interaction.

8 **Ways of solving problems** should be agreed by the team, so that clashes can be looked at and dealt with quickly.

9 **There needs to be a team leader** who is supported by all members.

10 **There should be an understanding** that the team can produce high-quality work and support each other in this.

BODY-LANGUAGE CUES

1 Body position
2 Closeness to others
3 Facial expressions
4 Eye movements
5 Touching ourselves
6 Touching others
7 Connection with objects
8 Clothes
9 Breathing
10 Perspiration

WRITING A REPORT

1 **What are your main aims in writing the report?** If you are not sure, talk to the person who briefed you before you start.

2 **Always think about who is going to read your report,** taking into account their background, education, age and assumed knowledge of the subject.

3 Where will your information come from? Check your resources.

4 Think about the presentation of your report. What will the layout be like? How long will the report be?

5 Look at your writing style and its suitability for your reader. Will it be appropriate? If you need to, adjust it.

6 Map out the sections of your report. The main components might include: title, summary, contents, introduction, the main report, conclusion, recommendation, appendices, bibliography, glossary and index.

7 Make notes of the report outline.

8 Pull the information together from all your selected resources.

9 Write your report, drawing your own conclusions and recommendations. Check facts, spelling, punctuation and grammar.

10 Read your report through carefully one last time before presenting it.

ACHIEVE YOUR GOALS

1 Be fully committed to achieving your goal before you start on the task. If you can't do it, go back and see whether your goal is, in fact, the correct one.

2 Monitor how you are getting on. Create a chart to see your progress taking place. This will help you feel you are achieving something.

3 If you find your goal is overwhelming, consider chopping it up into smaller goals.

4 Ask someone for support. Even if you can't take on practical help, just getting someone to take an interest and offer advice may encourage you.

5 Be prepared to tweak your goal. If your initial aims now seem unrealistic, revise them.

6 Think about the end result. Contemplating success will spur you on.

7 Use your own systems to assess your progress. When you are thinking about your progress, track how you are getting on. This will encourage you.

8 Accommodate further changes. As time goes by you may need to change your goals even more to keep them current.

9 Thinking positively can really help you to achieve your goals. Being negative can wreck your plans.

10 Give yourself a pat on the back when you are eventually successful – make sure that you celebrate and congratulate yourself in a way that really means something to you.

WRITING A REFERENCE

1 If you have nothing positive to say and don't want to write the reference, politely decline to do so. The person can then move on to asking another referee.

2 If you are not sure what to say, ask the person for their CV and any other relevant information about the post. Is there anything they would like you to focus on?

3 **State your own post** and qualifications.

4 **Start by saying how long you've known the person** and in what capacity. Include relevant dates.

5 **Describe the person's skills,** performance, competency and what makes them suitable for the post. Include some outstanding attributes.

6 **Don't dwell** on their weaknesses.

7 **Provide your own contact details** in case there needs to be any follow-up.

8 **Include a strong summary** but don't overdo it with overblown praise.

9 **Be succinct;** don't go over one page.

10 **Check over your reference** for spelling and grammatical mistakes.

DEAL WITH A DIFFICULT BOSS

1 **Learn how to manage your boss.** Find out how they want things done. Work 'with' rather than against them.

2 **Look carefully at your own performance.** Consider your own actions and see whether they are perfect – or not. Ask others what they think of your work.

3 **Talk things over with your boss,** but develop a plan B (such as another job offer) in case this gets you nowhere. This gives you confidence and clout.

4 **Don't react emotionally to your boss** if they are harsh and critical. Remain neutral so that they have no power over you and can't undermine you.

5 **Go into discussion mode.** Remain objective and avoid confrontation – talk instead. If your boss is critical, use the

main points being made for interesting discussion and ask for advice.

6 **You can't change the boss' personality.** Change how you think about them. It's 'the boss' not 'the idiot boss'.

7 **Always remain professional –** it's not necessary or desirable for your boss to be your friend. Your job is to follow your boss' instructions.

8 **See what your colleagues think.** They probably find your boss difficult, too. You'll feel better if others share your concerns.

9 **Don't go higher up unless all else fails.** It could make things worse.

10 **If things continue to go badly, write everything down.** If you decide to stay and battle it out, you'll need documentary evidence about your complaints.

CHOOSE A NURSERY

1 Friendly, professional staff

2 Staff-to-child ratio

3 Clean & tidy

4 Colourful

5 Well organized

6 Good atmosphere

7 Parent participation

8 Affordable

9 Convenient hours

10 Healthy meals & snacks

THE RIGHT CHILDCARE FOR YOU

1 **What kind of childcare do you and your family need?** Do you want full-time childcare? Are your kids at school but need care until you get home and during school holidays? Do you need someone to live with you and provide before-school care

and holiday care, too? Are you looking for someone to care for a small baby? The main options are: full or part-time daycare, live-in help, live-out help, employing a childcare professional in their own home, au pair, mother's help, informal babysitting.

2 Think about arrangements in good time before you return to work. Some childcare centres run long waiting lists. Don't miss out through late planning. Be aware that some times of year are less busy than others – in summer a lot of people are on holiday as well as you.

3 Consider what you can afford. If you have to pay for full-time childcare out of your salary, this will be a big expense, but you may consider it worth it.

4 Think about travel to and from the childcare. Adding this on to your daily commute might mean extra driving and early starts/late finishes. Live-in help may suit you better.

5 What style of care would best suit your child? Some kids love lots of company and benefit from childcare, but others prefer one-to-one and love being at home. This also depends on their age.

6 Think through your contingency plans. You need to have watertight back-up plans in case of sickness (yours or your child's), school holidays and other eventualities.

7 Prepare your child and family for this change in their lives. Your normal routine will be affected and it will take time to adjust to the new regime. You can help the transition by bringing bedtimes forward and sticking to regular mealtimes.

8 Do you need 'wrap-around care' for older kids? This involves term-time care before and after school and you may also need someone to drop, pick up, cook meals and supervise homework.

9 Do your kids have a wide age range that you have to arrange suitable care for? This will bring other issues into the frame.

10 Do you have friends and relatives who might be prepared to help – even if only in the short term?

SURVIVE SCHOOL HOLIDAYS
1 Garden camping
2 River swimming
3 Park picnics
4 Art/craft projects
5 Zoo outings
6 Museum visits
7 Play dates
8 Games/puzzles
9 Scavenger hunts
10 Odd jobs for pocket money

HOW TO FIND A BABYSITTER

1 Look around your local community. You may find a suitable person in your church, local schools, place of work, community centres, youth groups and local shops. Look on notice boards.

2 Take references seriously. If you don't know sitters personally, look for those who are happy to supply them. Be rigorous about following them up. When you get in touch with referees, ask if there have ever been any problems, how many children the sitter looked after at once and information about their personality and reliability.

3 Ask the sitter about their previous experience. If they have already looked after a lot of kids or have younger siblings, this is all to the good. But those new to

looking after kids shouldn't be discounted.

4 Arrange interviews in your home and make sure the kids are present. Notice how the sitter relates to them. Are they open and friendly? Do they like children?

5 Do you trust the babysitter? You may need to use your instincts. Do you feel happy about leaving this person in charge of your kids? Do you feel relaxed about leaving the sitter in charge of your home?

6 Discuss money at the outset, after you have researched the going rate and asked your sitter what he/she is used to earning. Come up with solutions for late evenings and transport home.

7 When you have signed up a sitter – ask them to come to the first appointment early so that you can show them around.

8 **Talk through house rules** and ask the sitter to stick to them. You need to tell her/him about the kids bedtimes, what their routine is, whether they are allowed to watch TV and whether they need to do homework. If you anticipate problems, tell the sitter how to deal with them.

9 **When you are out call home** to see if everything is going OK.

10 **Leave numbers** for your babysitter to contact you and emergency services.

SETTLE YOUR CHILD INTO NURSERY

1 **Prepare your child** by talking about nursery positively some weeks beforehand.

2 **Read stories to your child** about going to nursery.

3 **Practise leaving your child** with a friend or relative in the weeks beforehand to get them used to being without you.

4 **Arrange taster visits** to the nursery for your child. Stay with your child.

5 **Meet your child's key person,** who will guide you through the settling-in process and be your main point of contact.

6 **Take your child's favourite toy** or comfort blanket to nursery, too.

7 **Set up a two-way relationship with the nursery** by giving the key person the information they need to care for your child, including allergies, their likes and dislikes, going to the toilet, meals, dressing and putting on their shoes.

8 **Stay with your child** for a little while on the first day.

9 **Try not to seem anxious** about leaving your child in nursery for the first time – they will become anxious, too.

10 **If your child cries, try not to worry.** Experienced nursery staff are trained to have strategies for helping your child.

STARTING PRIMARY SCHOOL

1 **Take your child into the school** every day and be there to pick them up at the end of the day. If another carer is collecting your child, make sure your child knows them well and is expecting them.

2 **Limit weekday TV** and computer use.

3 **Make sure your child goes to bed** in good time and gets plenty of good-quality sleep on school nights.

4 **Stick to a 'school night' routine.**

5 **Invite school friends round** at weekends to support new friendships.

6 **Make sure that your child eats** a good breakfast (include some protein).

7 **If there is any homework to be done,** create a quiet space/time for doing it. Be available to give help. Encourage the child to do it before they turn to other activities.

8 **Talk to the teacher occasionally** to see how your child is settling in.

9 **Limit their after-school social life** and activities to avoid over-tiredness.

10 **Prepare the night before** – clothes, reading book, lunchbox and games kit.

SCHOOL UNIFORM PLUSES

1 Comfortable fit
2 Room to grow
3 Long-lasting
4 Hard-wearing
5 Washes well
6 Easy to put on/ take off
7 Suits school policy
8 Value for money
9 Good for layering
10 Looks nice

HELP YOUR CHILD LEARN TO READ

1 **Read to your child from an early age** so that they become interested in stories.

2 **If your child's school asks parents to help them** read school reading books do this regularly – make a time before bed.

3 **Find out what the school's preferred reading method is** and use it.

4 **Ask your child questions about the story,** so that they become involved. Ask them what they think about the characters.

5 **As your child starts to read,** gradually let them start reading to you instead.

6 **If your child doesn't know a word's meaning,** help look it up in a dictionary.

7 **If you encounter an interesting new word,** spell it out in fridge magnets.

8 **Join a library with a good children's section.** Make regular visits and help your child choose new titles to read at home.

9 **Follow your child's interests** and reinforce these by suggesting extra books on the subject.

10 **Let your child browse** your book collection and introduce suitable titles.

HELP WITH WRITING/SPELLING

1 **Start taking an interest** when your child is first learning as it's hard to put right bad habits later on.

2 **Encourage them to hold the pencil correctly.** Check with your child's teacher if you aren't sure.

3 **Observe whether your child is left- or right-handed** and don't attempt to change this once it's established.

4 **Help your child to view writing and spelling as fun activities.**

5 **Write out words and sentences** for your young child to copy.

6 **Help your child to draw** and be proud of the results as this is closely connected to writing. Put your child's drawings and paintings up on display at home.

7 **Inspire your child** by showing examples of good handwriting.

8 **Get your child to handwrite** thankyou letters for presents.

9 **Encourage your child to keep a diary,** especially on holiday. Give them a special diary as a present.

10 **Get your child to write stories in a special book.** Suggest inspiring and imaginative themes and encourage him/her to add illustrations.

NUMBERS, NUMBERS, NUMBERS

1 **Show your child numbers in everyday life:** house numbers, bus numbers, clocks and calendars.

2 **Count out things** with your child in daily life: household things, food items, and during everyday activities.

3 Collect things when you are out and count them: shells, conkers and pebbles.

4 Play lots of counting games and sing along to counting songs.

5 Talk 'big numbers' in your general family chat. Compare and contrast thousands, millions and more – your child will soon catch on to their meaning.

6 Teach your child the times tables – up to twelve is quite sufficient. Chant with them to make it fun – they'll stick for ever.

7 If your child has been taught to use a calculator at school, make sure they understand the theory behind the method.

8 Ask your child to assist you with shopping – get them to find two packets of cereal, four bananas or three oranges.

9 Let your child go on shopping errands for you so that they get used to handling money and counting it out for real.

10 Encourage your child to love numbers and they'll be happy to try maths later on.

ASSIST YOUR CHILD WITH HOMEWORK

1 Create a comfortable, quiet desk space for your child to get on with home-work – somewhere near to you.

2 Be on hand to give help if you are asked. Always reinforce the teacher's goals – check with them if you're in doubt.

3 Choose a good time for doing homework – when they are in the right frame of mind and not too tired.

4 Be enthusiastic and light-hearted. Use humour if it helps.

5 Offer praise and encouragement, but not too much – or too little.

6 Provide extra materials if this helps your child.

7 Find connections between what your child already knows and what they are already learning.

8 Don't do the work for your child.

9 Help your child to think independently.

10 Don't push your child too hard. Take plenty of breaks.

FIND THE SCHOOL OF YOUR CHOICE

1 Admissions criteria
2 Sibling already there
3 Catchment area
4 Waiting list
5 Faith school
6 Disability
7 Application deadlines
8 Visits
9 League tables
10 Atmosphere

FIRST DAYS AT SECONDARY SCHOOL

1 Pin up a school timetable so that you and your child know what is going to happen every day and are prepared for it.

2 Encourage your child to pack what is needed for the next day themselves.

3 Limit TV time on school nights.

4 Create a quiet space/time for study and make sure homework is done at a reasonable time. Check it over to make sure it has been done properly.

5 Ensure your child gets enough sleep.

6 Give your child a nutritious breakfast containing some protein every day.

7 Talk to your child about school and create an atmosphere in which anything can be discussed openly and supportively.

8 Get to know your child's main teacher.

9 Attend parent-teacher meetings.

10 Support new friendships by inviting friends round at weekends.

GET THROUGH THAT COURSEWORK

1 Take an active interest in your child's coursework. Encourage and praise.

2 Get your child to take coursework seriously – it's not a 'soft' option but an important part of their work. Don't let it be left until the last minute and then rushed.

3 Provide a good comfortable study space with desk, suitable chair and light. It should be reasonably quiet.

4 Help your child prioritize homework and coursework – create a calendar with deadlines on it.

5 Suggest resources. Help your child use the local library and search for online sources. They should learn to distinguish between reliable and unreliable sources.

6 Stop your child copying resources. Show them how to write things in their own words and use information for their own work in an acceptable way.

7 Help your child be self-disciplined about internet use. Limit use of social sites, games and instant messaging when coursework is being done.

8 Check over what coursework your child has produced and offer useful feedback about structure, content, writing style, spelling and punctuation.

9 If your child really is floundering with coursework, contact the teachers for advice on how to proceed.

10 Try not to nag your child about coursework. This will be counterproductive and create a bad atmosphere.

TIME FOR SCHOOL EXAMS

1 Make sure that your child does some revision every night so that they get used to doing it by the time the exam period comes along.

2 Don't allow the TV to be kept on while your child is studying for exams and restrict access to the computer. Background music can be soothing, but it shouldn't be too loud and stop the child working.

3 Encourage your child to review their schoolwork every night so that it starts to stick in their mind. It's a great study habit to get into – it'll last a lifetime.

4 Create a revision timetable together, well before exam time, and stick it up over your child's desk so that they know they must do some every night. You can put stars on it for encouragement.

5 Show your child how to revise – or discuss different ways of tackling it. Find out about any advice they have been given at school and complement this approach. Don't go against teachers' advice.

6 Ask your child if they would like you to test them. Make this aspect as relaxed as you can – no stress!

7 Encourage your child to take regular breaks and provide good-quality snacks and plenty of water to drink.

8 Give your child nutritious meals and make sure they get plenty of good-quality sleep and exercise.

9 Little rewards can be a good idea when your child has tried hard.

10 A lucky mascot may bring comfort in the exam itself.

POOR EXAM RESULTS

1 Be disappointed 'for' your child's results, not 'by' them. This will show that you are empathetic rather than blaming.

2 Think about possible reasons for the poor results – was there a one-off reason, such as illness, or do they reflect reality?

3 Look forward. Focus on solutions to bad results and suggest a plan of action.

4 Don't be put off if your child seems depressed for a few days – it's natural.

5 Think about re-sits, if this is helpful.

6 Talk to teachers about why your child did badly – they may make suggestions.

7 Don't say 'I told you so' – negativity won't help. Ultimately your child needs to experience what the lows are like in order to change their own behaviour.

8 Consider extra coaching and support.

9 Bad results may be a wake-up call to your child to work differently next time. Children who do well every time often have an inflated view of their own abilities.

10 Go over the exam questions to see whether your child has a knowledge gap. Perhaps they were away from school when that subject was being taught.

DEAL WITH BULLYING

1 Can your child tell a trusted adult? Talk to the teachers yourself.

2 Ask your child to avoid being alone with the bully. Be part of a group.

3 Can your child possibly ignore the bully? Bullies thrive on the reaction they get, so ignoring their behaviour might work.

4 Advise your child not to get angry as bullies thrive on creating anger. Being cool and calm is a good way to deflect bullying behaviour.

5 Ask your child not to be tempted to take a swipe. Getting physical will show the bully how angry they are and will only give them exactly what they want.

6 Help your child get confident! If they can feel good, this will deter bullies.

7 Make sure that your child takes lots of exercise and toughens up physically. Feeling fit and strong will help confidence and it will lift low moods, too.

8 Encourage your child to confide in friends – it helps to share.

9 Find out whether your child is eligible for counselling sessions.

10 Be on your child's side.

SUPPORT A GIFTED CHILD

1 Give your child plenty of quality time. Spend time alone with them to listen to their ideas and share their interests.

2 Read to your child every day – even if they already know how to read. This gives you both a forum for sharing ideas.

IS YOUR CHILD GIFTED?

1 Alertness as a baby

2 Sleeps less

3 High activity levels

4 Reactive to stimuli

5 Reaches milestones quickly

6 Outstanding memory

7 Quick to learn

8 Loves reading

9 Curious to learn

10 Logical thinking

3 **Stimulate your child's interests** with trips to the library, museums, cinema visits, walks and outings.

4 **Praise your child's effort** rather than the results. Amazingly, underachievement is an issue for gifted children and sometimes they only try when they know they will achieve high rates of success.

5 **Talk to your child's teachers.**

6 **Contact other families** with similar children. Your child needs to be with others who are like him/herself.

7 **Find a support group** in your area.

8 **See whether your child is eligible for special help** at school.

9 **Talk to other parents** and share ideas and experiences.

10 **Accept a gifted child for who they are** and don't make excuses, be negative or feel guilty when talking to other parents.

DYSLEXIC CHILD?

1 **Help your child to learn things by rote** while you're on car trips. This can be short poems, spellings or times tables.

2 **Mark your child's shoes** or encourage wearing shoes with different-coloured laces to help distinguish between right and left.

3 **Get your child a mobile phone.** Texting, though at first it may be inaccurate, will help with your child's writing fluency and confidence.

4 **Give your child a dry-erase board** for learning spellings. If mistakes occur there will be less frustration – wrong letters can be rubbed out and quickly corrected. Coloured pens are fun to use, too.

5 **Let your child use audio books.** He/ she can follow the words in the printed book and read books that are pitched at a higher/more suitable reading age.

6 **If your child has trouble telling left from right** and following directions, let her wear a bracelet on her left hand (this can be called her 'leftie').

7 **Fridge magnets** are a great way to practise spellings at home.

8 **Moulding letters out of clay** or writing them in sand or rice may help with spelling difficulties.

9 **Mnemonics may help with spelling,** especially if they are visual.

10 **Tinted glasses** can make a big difference to reading ability.

HOME-SCHOOLING IDEAS

1 **Check what the law requires** of you before you start home-schooling. It varies.

2 **Are your basic literary and number skills good enough** to be able to follow the curriculum and teach your child? Enrol in adult classes to get yourself up to speed.

3 **You must want to learn yourself.** If you are not familiar with certain subjects, you will need to mug up on them.

4 **Do you get on well with your child?** It's important to have good rapport and patience with your child – you are going to be spending a lot of time together. You need to be able to communicate well, too.

5 Are you sensitive towards your child? Their progress is in your hands, so you need to be aware of how they are doing.

6 Get your sense of humour going! You're going to need it – every day! If your child gets stuck and frustrated, will you be able to defuse the situation and carry on?

7 Are you organized? Each day needs to be well thought out, structured and made productive. You will need to have the right teaching aids and equipment and have your teaching and learning area arranged for maximum efficiency. You should devise daily lesson plans and schedule in the rest of your family life, too.

8 Home-schooling is about finding and benefiting from learning opportunities together. Get involved in hobbies, languages, reading and common interests.

9 Be prepared to receive some negative criticism! Home-schooling has a lot of critics and there are people who won't hesitate to tell you what they think.

10 If your kids would really rather go to school, re-examine your own motives for home-schooling.

EXTRA TUTORING

1 Is extra tutoring necessary? Talk to your child's teacher first to see whether help could come from the school or from you – in the first instance.

2 One-to-one help may make all the difference. Your child may be distracted by other children in the class and a generally noisy atmosphere.

3 The earlier you catch the problem, the better. It's best to nip it in the bud. Small problems can turn into bigger ones.

4 Is your child lacking in confidence? Tutoring may help build it up.

5 Find a tutor your child likes. This is key to successful tutoring.

6 Why not ask friends and family? A teenage neighbour may be willing to help talk your child through a minor maths problem. One of the child's friends may be able to fill in on missed lessons.

7 Tell your child's tutor which areas you want them to focus on.

8 Keep an eye on your child's progress and be prepared to suggest changes to your child's tutor if necessary.

9 Make sure that your child does the tutor's homework rigorously and attends all the sessions.

10 The tutor should complement the child's schooling not undermine it.

HOW TO TELL IF YOUR CHILD NEEDS EXTRA HELP

1 Falling grades
2 Negative behavioural changes
3 Lack of motivation
4 Teacher suggests tutoring
5 Poor confidence
6 Badly done homework
7 Lack of attention span
8 Stomach upsets
9 Headaches
10 Nail-biting

CHOOSE A DEGREE

1 What do you really love? It's important to select a subject that you are truly interested in rather than one which seems to be a 'good' reliable career prospect.

2 What are you already good at? Think about the skills you've nurtured from

GET ONTO THE COURSE YOU WANT

1 Exam results
2 Skills & qualifications
3 Research
4 Personal statement
5 Filling out forms
6 Application date
7 Open days
8 Interviews
9 Entrance exams
10 Acceptance & rejection

childhood – this may give you ideas.

3 **What job are you aiming for?** Where do you see yourself in five years' time? And after that?

4 **Don't live out the dreams of others.** Don't be swayed by what your parents want you to study. It's your life.

5 **Think about location.** Some universities are better than others for certain subjects.

6 **Why not travel abroad to study?** It may suit you to broaden your horizons for a few years.

7 **Narrow your choice down** to five or six establishments that you would be completely happy with.

8 **Choose a course** that suits your preferred study style.

9 **Are your existing qualifications** up to scratch and are they the right ones?

10 **Need more time to think?** Consider taking a gap year before you apply. Your time off from study could be just what you need to have a hard think about your future life.

PREPARE FOR UNIVERSITY

1 **Read the information pack!** It's worth the time and effort. There may be forms that you need to fill out and return plus other useful tips on settling in.

2 **Consider what to take.** Before you load up with everything (including the kitchen sink), check what you really do need and what is already provided.

3 **Check where everything is on campus.** Find your accommodation via a map before you turn up with all your stuff.

4 **Find out where and when** you need to register for your course.

5 **Get the paperwork done early.** You'll need pass cards, passwords and membership cards for gaining access to sites, libraries and essential information.

6 **Sort out your money now** (grants, scholarships, loans and bank of mum and dad) and how to access your funds.

7 **Find out who your tutor is.**

8 **Register with a doctor.**

9 **Don't sign up** for too many extra-curricular activities at the outset – you may find it hard to fit them all in.

10 **Need extra help or advice?** Student counselling services are available in all colleges and universities.

FIND STUDENT DIGS

1 **Don't leave it too late.** There will be plenty of other students hunting for a place to live, too.

2 **Check out the area.** Your accommodation needs to be convenient for getting to lectures, shops and for leisure pursuits.

3 **What is the transport like?**

4 **You have the same legal rights** as any ordinary tenant.

5 **Visit the student housing officer.** Most universities keep lists of available and recommended accommodation.

6 Sharing with friends? Choose people who you know you'll be able to get on with – more or less. Living alone has its advantages – why not try it?

7 Be prepared to sign a tenancy agreement and pay a deposit. One person may be called upon to be the main contact and you may have to find someone else to act as a guarantor.

8 Is the area safe? There may be a downside to cheap accommodation.

9 If you cause damage to the property you will be asked to forfeit your deposit. Tidy up at the end of your tenancy.

10 Don't forget to budget for utilities – you can set up a kitty system for paying for joint expenses such as gas and electricity and internet connections.

CHOOSE A UNIVERSITY OR COLLEGE

1 Best teaching
2 Big city
3 Rural setting
4 Campus
5 Social facilities
6 Sports facilities
7 Halls of residence
8 Living at home
9 Costs
10 Distance learning

SHARE YOUR LIVING SPACE

1 Think about a bit of give and take. Sharing is all about compromise – so choose your housemates carefully.

2 Establish clear house rules before you move in. Have monthly house meetings for people to air grievances.

3 Consider the number of people you will be sharing with. Does the accommodation have enough bathrooms and living space for everyone?

4 Get everyone's permission first before you invite guests to stay.

5 Make a rota for taking out the garbage and cleaning communal areas.

6 If the bedrooms are of different sizes, might you adjust the rent accordingly or share larger rooms?

7 Are things going to get noisy? Agree beforehand about late-night revelries. Some people like to sleep.

8 Decide about food. Are you going to share shopping and cooking or just fend for yourselves?

9 Fridge etiquette is important. If you aren't sharing the food, allocate shelves to different people – no picking!

10 Delegate one person to act as the contact with the landlord.

RETURN TO STUDY AFTER A BREAK

1 Develop your network of like-minded spirits. You are bound to come across other returnees just like you.

2 Plan your time carefully. Create a timetable. This will help if you are juggling study and family commitments.

3 How do you learn best? Are you an early bird or a night owl?

4 Prioritize your activities. You may not be able to cover everything you need to do – just do the most important things.

5 Are you up to speed with current technology? If not, do some extra courses.

6 Be sure to have realistic expectations of yourself. You'll be wanting to get high marks as a mature student – don't be too hard on yourself. Failure can be very demotivating.

7 Stay focused. Look at the bigger picture of your course as a whole. Go over your reasons for deciding to study.

8 Give yourself rewards when you have completed a difficult task and share your successes with your significant others.

9 Keep in contact with your tutors. If you experience home difficulties that prevent you completing work, tell them.

10 Know where to get help.

SURVIVE THE FIRST TERM

STUDENT ESSENTIALS

1 Bedding
2 Computer
3 Sound system
4 TV
5 Cooking equipment
6 Crockery
7 Pans
8 Sports equipment
9 Study materials
10 Teddy bear

1 Be open and friendly with everyone. Don't make snap judgements about people. If they seem stand-offish it could be that they're shy and nervous.

2 Join societies and sporting activities – this will help you meet new people with common interests.

3 Keep your work organized. Put lecture notes in a file and look over them.

4 Get to know your tutor and see them as your advocate. They are there to help you succeed.

5 Go easy on the alcohol. Eat before you drink and alternate drinking a glass of water with alcoholic drinks.

6 Remember that you are there to study – for at least some of the time.

7 Keep up with assignments – there may be serious penalties for late work or for not doing it at all.

8 Attend all lectures and tutorials.

9 Avoid getting into debt – if at all possible – you'll only regret it later.

10 Don't forget to eat and sleep.

STUDY EFFECTIVELY

1 Plan your meals around your study. Eating a big meal before study may make you feel drowsy. It's best to have small, frequent meals and snacks in between, if necessary. Drink plenty of water.

2 Go easy on caffeine and sugar. You may get an energy surge initially, but this could be followed by a crash.

3 Like to study at night or during the day? Think about when you are most alert.

4 If your desk is loaded up with distractions, clear it before you start.

5 Take plenty of regular breaks. Every hour is sensible, but think what works best for you. It may be best to take infrequent long breaks rather than frequent short ones.

6 For a quick refresher, take a few deep breaths to get more oxygen to your brain and get up to walk around often. Do a few stretches to improve your circulation.

7 Use the same time, same place theory. This helps you associate time and place with studying and concentration.

8 Choose a quiet study place. You'll find concentration a whole lot easier. Don't have the TV or music on at the same time.

9 Avoid doing an all-nighter before an exam. You'll perform less effectively.

10 Understand the material rather than trying to memorize it.

RESEARCH ONLINE

1 State your research problem. Sometimes phrasing it as a question will direct your line of enquiry more precisely.

2 Use multiple search engines so that you get a range of information.

3 Select key words with care to eliminate irrelevant sites.

4 Think hard about where the information comes from. Is it reliable?

5 Use online encyclopedias.

6 Post a request for information on internet news groups in your subject.

7 Visit chatrooms that are related to your subject matter.

8 Look for online library catalogues.

9 Visit sites on internet research. They may make useful suggestions and perhaps even do some of the research for you.

10 Produce more focused search results by altering your key words slightly.

HOW TO WRITE AN ESSAY
1 Research
2 Analysis
3 Brainstorming
4 Thesis
5 Outline
6 Introduction
7 Paragraphs
8 Conclusion
9 Formatting
10 Notes/ bibliography

BENEFIT FROM THE LIBRARY

1 Check computer databases to see what's available in your research subject.

2 Check the card catalogue and practise using it – it may contain useful details that aren't on the computer database.

3 Need help? Ask the librarian.

4 If you need extra research material, browse the surrounding stacks.

5 Someone else taken out your book? Ask about inter-library loans.

6 Check for non-book resources for the information you need: microfilm, audio resources or DVDs.

7 Use the library for your studying. Most libraries supply desks, power points, good lighting, scanners and even wi-fi.

8 No need to take out the whole book if you only need part of it. Use the photocopier for copying individual pages. When photocopying, note down all the book's details to add to your bibliography.

9 Go to the library off-peak – it'll be easier to find a quiet spot to work and resources won't already be in use.

10 Specialist libraries such as historical societies and archives may exist in your area, though you may need to get special permission to use them.

PREPARE A PRESENTATION

1 Prepare stories to illustrate your points. These will engage the audience better than mere facts.

2 Create a strong beginning, a middle and an end.

3 Get to the presentation location early to check the facilities.

4 Keep your notes as prompts on cards and try not to look at them all the time.

5 Prepare more material than you can

actually use, but also be prepared to use less if necessary.

6 **Try to time your presentation** so that you don't run under or over time. Run through it in advance so that you can tighten up the timing if necessary.

7 **Use pictures** to put your ideas across.

8 **Keep visual imagery simple** – avoid complex charts and graphs.

9 **Limit the text on powerpoint slides** and make sure the type is big enough to be read by the audience.

10 **Less is more.** Don't create an unnecessarily complicated structure.

PART-TIME STUDENT JOBS

1 Bar work
2 Restaurants
3 Cafés
4 Shops
5 Office temping
6 Babysitting
7 Cleaning
8 Call centres
9 Supermarkets
10 College administration

GIVE A PRESENTATION

1 **Know your audience** and decide how you want to pitch your presentation before making a start.

2 **Tell the audience what you are going to say** at the beginning. Tell them what the timeframe is.

3 **Either tell people that they can interrupt with questions** or take all questions at the end.

4 **Give a quick introduction** and summary and then go straight into the main presentation. Finish with a powerful finale.

5 **Remind your audience** of what you said at the end of your speech.

6 **When you are planning a powerpoint** presentation, make sure that the slides just pick up the salient points and do not replicate your script exactly.

7 **Don't read from your slides** – use your own notes and let the slides pick up the salient points.

8 **Go nice and slowly and don't rush.** Pause to take breaths and to let strong ideas sink in.

9 **If you make a mistake, don't say you're sorry** – it will just draw attention to it. If you mess up, move on.

10 **Use humour – but not too much.** It's good to smile and crack the odd joke or two. But don't be tempted to overdo it.

STUDY FOR COLLEGE EXAMS

1 **Create an achievable revision plan** and stick to it.

2 **Don't be tempted to cram,** but pace your learning over a long revision period.

3 **Read through your class notes** at regular intervals.

4 **Discuss topic issues** with friends.

5 **Highlight major topics and sub-topics** in your notes in different colours.

6 **Use background music** if it helps you.

7 **Refresh your memory by rewriting your notes** – this will help you to lodge the information in your mind.

8 **Ask yourself questions** that relate to the material.

9 **Repeat the questions out loud** – this reinforces the main points.

10 **Lecture to yourself using your hands** – this will help you to recall information when you need it.

EXAM CALM

1. **Get** a good night's sleep.
2. **Eat** a good breakfast.
3. **Arrive early** at the exam room.
4. **What** can you take in with you?
5. **Read** the instructions.
6. **Read through** the paper.
7. **Answer** what you can first.
8. **Save** the difficult questions for last.
9. **Keep an eye** on the time.
10. **Check** through your answers.

COPE WITH STUDENT SOCIAL LIFE

1. **You'll be tempted to join a lot of societies early on –** limit yourself to what is realistic so that you don't take on too much and have problems fitting everything in along with your studies.
2. **Avoid emotional entanglements** to begin with – if at all possible.
3. **Get enough sleep.** It'll be tempting to stay up all night, but you really need as much sleep as you can get.
4. **Stay within your budget.**
5. **Limit your party time.** It's great to party, but all too easy to let social life take over from study.
6. **Get enough exercise –** perhaps join a gym or a running club.
7. **Eat sensibly.**
8. **Make a good friend,** someone you can share your problems and concerns with.
9. **Don't feel that you have to follow the crowd.** If you don't want to go out, don't.
10. **Call home.** It's good to be in touch.

BETTER STUDENT BUDGET IDEAS

1. **Make a budget.** Write down your income and expenses. You will be able to work out exactly how much you can spend each day after your monthly bills are paid.
2. **Avoid making cash withdrawals** more than once a week and don't carry your cashpoint card with you at other times.
3. **Get a part-time job.** Try a supermarket or café. You may get discounted food.
4. **Look for good discounts,** student and otherwise. Supermarket deals, money-off vouchers and student discounts in shops, cinemas and restaurants.
5. **Check with your welfare office** to see if there are college hardship funds.
6. **Get free student banking** and go for bank accounts with extra freebies.
7. **Learn to cook.** Even making sandwiches will cut down on your daily expenses.
8. **Sell off all your unwanted possessions,** especially used textbooks, fiction, CDs, DVDs, clothes and sports equipment.
9. **Don't smoke.** It is expensive and bad for you, too.
10. **Don't buy new.** Shop in charity/thrift stores – it's cheaper and greener.

CHEAP STUDENT EATS

1. Pasta
2. Vegetable curry
3. Beans on toast
4. Risotto
5. Casseroles
6. Omelettes
7. Soup
8. Chilli con carne
9. Pancakes
10. Stir-fries

HOLIDAYS & TRAVEL

It's great to get away! Holidays are an important part of everyone's year these days and it's vital to find a break that suits you, your family, your interests – and your purse. Peruse these handy tips and put together your perfect vacation package. You'll return refreshed and revivified – with plenty of stories to tell everyone.

TRAVELLING WITH CHILDREN

1 Travel at night – especially if you're embarking on an extended car journey. Put the kids into their jammies first if it makes things easier – as the excitement will be explosive! Another idea is to leave very, very early so that they can get a few hours' extra kip in before you make a breakfast stop. Long plane journeys go far more easily for kids if you can take a night flight – hopefully they'll just sleep for most of the time.

2 Are we nearly there yet? Car games help the journey go by. Try the ones that involve the kids looking out of the window as this can help prevent car sickness as well as keep them happy. They can each 'collect' a different thing that they see, such as men wearing hats or red cars. The person with the most wins.

3 If you are driving alone with children, consider attaching an extra rear-view mirror so that you can spot what they're up to without having to turn around in your seat. If a real rumpus breaks out – pull into a service area and stop before trying to sort out the problem.

4 Attach a bag for each child on the back of the seat in front – so that they can help themselves to their own amusements (books, snacks, drinks, mags, music and games) when-ever they like. This will help keep track of everything, too. For babies, bring toys that you can attach to the car seat – otherwise someone will have to keep retrieving toys from the car floor.

5 Take plenty of drinks and healthy finger foods – a long journey can be de-hydrating plus snacks are a welcome distraction for kids. Put everything into an insulated cool bag. Don't forget to include a few special treats such as cookies and sweets – now might be the moment to relax your junk-food rules a little.

6 Stop at regular intervals to let everyone run around. It's bad for kids to stay still for long periods and frequent loo breaks can't be put off. If you have a baby on board it's even more important to have plenty of stop-offs for feeding and changing. Babies hate remaining in cramped car seats for too long.

7 Audio and music will give everyone something to take their mind off the boredom of a long trip. Sing-along tunes can be fun for the whole family – as can engrossing talking books.

8 Bring along your kids' favourite toys and perhaps add in something new that your child hasn't seen before. This will help calm things down when everyone's feeling a bit fed up. Cuddly toys and comfort blankets will be indispensible, too, when it comes to dozing off – so make sure they're not left behind.

9 When travelling by air, investigate using private departure lounges. Even if you're travelling economy, you can often buy day passes to lounges and it might be worth the extra expense. They often supply toys and entertainment for children plus food, drinks and snacks, movies and music. It's a major plus if you have a long wait with fidgety little ones.

10 Will you be able to take everything you need for your baby in your hand lugg-age onto the plane? Check when you arrive at the airport. There are restrictions on taking fluids on board. You may be able to get away with milk and drinks as long as they are in baby bottles, rather than the original carton.

DOCUMENT CHECKLIST

1 Passport plus photocopy
2 Credit cards
3 Debit cards
4 Membership cards
5 Business cards
6 Phone card
7 Health/travel insurance
8 Driving licence
9 Vaccination documents
10 Visas

HOW TO PACK PERFECTLY

1 **Travel light** – don't take more than five or six days' clothes with you, no matter how long you're going for. Wash as you go.

2 **Check with the airline** what your weight restriction is – some airlines make you pay for extra weight.

3 **Toiletries should be the smallest kind** you can get hold of and packed in sealable plastic bags – no spills that way!

4 **Place all your heavier things** at the bottom of your case first.

5 **Roll your clothes up.** Partly fold your garments and then roll them up tightly to get a neat sausage shape. Slot them in.

6 **Pack an extra flattened holdall** – you're bound to bring back extra goodies.

7 **Plan your wardrobe around one main colour** so that you can mix and match.

8 **Wear your heaviest items** on the plane. You'll save loads of space in your case.

9 **Stuff your shoes** with small, rolled items such as socks or underwear and put them in separate plastic bags around the perimeter of the case.

10 **Avoid trying to squeeze too much in.** Take out half after you've packed it.

NO MORE WRINKLES!

1 **Pack your things nicely!** To avoid wrinkling, use all the flat pockets (inside and out) and the extra spaces in your case.

2 **Roll up linens, woollens and denims** to avoid creating hard fold lines.

3 **Choose linen** if you favour that safari look. It tends to appear slightly crumpled even if you've just ironed it.

4 **Opt for fabrics that blend** a synthetic with a natural fibres. Fewer creases!

5 **Wool and silk contain some elasticity,** which stops them creasing so much.

6 **Buy wrinkle-resistant clothes** from specialized travel shops – it's worth it if you travel a lot and/or are unable to hang your things up on overnight stops.

7 **Knitwear is far less likely to wrinkle** than woven fabrics – fact!

8 **Unpack and hang up your clothes** as soon as you arrive – to minimize the amount of time your togs stay folded.

9 **Hang clothes in a steamy bathroom.** Creases will just fall out – amazing!

10 **Spritz your garments lightly** with water and hang in the bathroom overnight. The creases will have vanished by morning.

CAPSULE BEACH HOLIDAY WARDROBE

1 Swimsuit
2 Beach towel
3 Sunglasses
4 Sarong
5 Sandals/flipflops
6 Sunhat
7 Shorts
8 Linen trousers
9 T-shirt
10 Floaty dress

PHEW! WHAT A SCORCHER!

1 **Take a fold-up, wide-brimmed sunhat.** It protects your tender head and face from the sun and your peepers from bight light.

2 **Consider the local sensibilities.** Just because it's hot it doesn't mean you can strip off. Women may be expected to cover up – shoulders, knees and heads. Take a scarf or hat just in case.

3 Investigate quick-dry fabrics for trousers. Denim takes a long time to dry.

4 Take rubber flipflops to wear in the shower/bathroom – some floors are best avoided. A pretty pair doubles up for the beach and going out in the evening.

5 Sarongs are such useful multi-purpose items. Use one as a cover-up on the beach, to shelter from the sun, cover your head in a temple or to rub down after a swim.

6 Take a hi-tech water filter (which can remove/kill viruses) and a collapsible water carrier – drink all the time.

7 Insect repellants and antihistamines are vital if there are mozzies around.

8 A cardigan or shawl will be needed in case it gets cool in the evenings or if you spend time in air-conditioned buildings.

9 Take one smart item – even if you are backpacking. You never know when you might want to dine out in style or get invited to the opera.

10 Lighter colours reflect the sunlight and keep you cooler.

WRAP UP FOR COLD WEATHER

1 Think layers. Don't take different coats for different conditions – just bring a variety of useful garments that can be worn on top of each another.

2 Longjohns under trousers make all the difference!

3 Wool will keep you very warm and a woolly hat is a must. Choose wool trousers instead of denim – they're far cosier.

4 Silk is a good fabric for keeping you warm. It's cosy, packs tightly and dries fast. You can buy silk thermals, if you like, to keep you really snug.

5 Insulated leather boots and gloves will keep your extremities really toasty.

6 Just take one heavy knit and wear it on the plane.

7 Removable quilted or fleece linings are a good idea in a waterproof coat.

8 Pack up your woolly sweater in a zip-lock bag with all the air removed – it will compress right down and take up far less space than normal.

9 Beware of having chilly gaps between one garment and another. Take a woolly scarf to keep your neck warm.

10 Don't forget – hand- and foot-warmers are useful to take along as are lip balm, moisturizer, sunscreen and sunglasses – whatever the weather.

CAPSULE SKI HOLIDAY WARDROBE

1 Jeans
2 Sweaters
3 Ski jacket
4 Ski trousers
5 Warm socks
6 Hat/helmet
7 Gloves
8 Scarf
9 Goggles/sunglasses
10 Thermal underwear

TRAVEL SMART

1 Always carry loo paper with you – it's not always on offer.

2 Take a comfortable pair of shoes – you need to feel happy about wearing them the whole day and walking long distances.

3 Carry your valuables in a money belt concealed underneath your clothes – pickpockets are commonplace in many parts.

WHAT TO ORGANIZE BEFORE YOU GO

1 Pay bills
2 Inform bank
3 Redirect post
4 Medical supplies
5 Inform others of itinerary
6 Valid visa/ passport
7 Currency
8 Travel insurance
9 House-sitter
10 Animal-sitter

You can also get waistcoats with inside pockets to seal against theft.

4 **Buy your own multi-size bath plug –** sometimes they're not supplied or are missing from hotel bathrooms.

5 **Find out all about local customs** and culture and respect them.

6 **Support the local economy.** Even if your trip is all-inclusive, make an effort to buy at local shops and eat in the local restaurants – you'll have a more authentic experience.

7 **Carry the right adaptors** for your phone recharger and other plug-ins.

8 **Bring gifts from home** as a gesture for local hospitality.

9 **Take a sleeping sack and pillowcase** in case your linen isn't changed regularly.

10 **Earplugs or headphones are a good idea –** some places are very noisy.

GOING SOLO

1 **Leave all your travel details,** itinerary, passport copy, flight and ticket information with someone at home.

2 **Don't wear jewellery –** even cheap things can cause temptation and you'll attract attention to yourself, too.

3 **Be confident:** always look as though you know where you're going.

4 **Find out where you are going** or ask someone for directions. Hotel concierges are probably the best people to ask. If you are out and about, ask family groups.

5 **Use the hotel safe if it has one –** so that you are not carrying valuables around with you all the time.

6 **Be sure to find out where** the unsafe areas are, especially at night.

7 **Choose a hotel in a busy street** with convenient transport nearby.

8 **Use your peephole** before opening your hotel room door.

9 **Check that your room is secure,** with functioning door and window locks.

10 **Choose to dress conservatively** and inconspicuously when you are travelling – especially if you are a woman.

TAKE FIDO ALONG

1 **Update your pet's vaccinations** and take the paperwork with you.

2 **Equip your pet with a collar** showing your home address and phone number. It may be suitable to include other useful information, too.

3 **Use a restraint for your pet.** A carrier is ideal, but you may need special harnesses or safety belts.

4 **Carry your pet's food with you** plus any other bedding, brushes and dishes.

5 **Take clean-up bags.** A little nervousness may make your pet want to go more often.

6 **Motion sickness applies to pets** as well as their owners. Give your pet a light meal a few hours before leaving and don't give them any food during the journey. Offer frequent drinks.

7 **Don't let your dog ride in the car** with their head out of the window.

8 **Notice the temperature –** your pet can't tell you if they're too hot or too cold. Always have the window open in hot weather. Consider shades on the windows.

9 **Take breaks,** if you can stop.

10 **If you are making a long trip** and your pet has not travelled before, try them out on a weekend trip first.

MAKE IT EASY FOR SENIORS

1 **Allow extra time** so that you can go more slowly. Everything takes longer with an elderly person.

2 **Take medical records with you** plus a summary of their medication.

3 **Sensitivity to change –** whether in climate or environment – will affect the elderly traveller. It's good to be prepared for this if possible.

4 **If the person has a hearing aid –** make sure he/she takes extra batteries along.

5 **It may be difficult to get hold of denture adhesives** in some places.

6 **Check the weather before you pack –** be prepared with all the correct clothes, shoes, an umbrella and a raincoat.

7 **Pack light – if possible.** Your elderly friend will need to pack a lot of things, but will be less likely to get flustered if there are fewer items to look after in transit.

8 **If you are travelling by plane or train,** see whether you can get special assistance – it makes a difference as you can avoid crowds, walking long distances and waiting in queues at customs.

9 **Remember that the elderly** are more vulnerable to pickpocketing. Make use of money belts and inside pockets.

10 **Think about tours and cruises.** They are more likely to be elderly-friendly.

ARRANGING SELF-CATERING

1 **Speak with the owner/agency –** ask lots of questions about the accommodation and the location and write them down.

2 **Make sure you get a booking form** and the owner/agency's terms and conditions – read and understand them thoroughly.

3 **Read accommodation reviews.**

4 **Check the location thoroughly before you book.** Find out what the local area provides – restaurants, transport links, shops and sights.

5 **Pay with a method of payment** which is traceable – so that the money can be tracked should anything go wrong.

6 **Breakages.** Notify the owner/agency of any breakages when you arrive. Otherwise you could be made to pay for them.

7 **Keep a copy** of all email communication.

8 **If anything is amiss** or not as described be sure to take photographic evidence.

9 **Baby equipment may be provided –** check whether you need to take it.

10 **Any complaints?** Any reputable rental company will have a complaints procedure.

HOTEL HINTS

1 **Prioritize!** Price or location?

2 **What amenities** are you looking for?

3 **Are you taking your family along?** If so, is the hotel family-friendly?

4 **In the market for a spot of luxury?** A nice hotel might be just the thing to mark a special anniversary.

5 **Want ambience and local flavour?** You decide.

6 **Do your own booking** – find places off the beaten track as well as regular chains.

7 **Want something a little unusual?** How about an igloo or a castle?

8 **If you book directly with the hotel** you may be able to get a discount.

9 **Is eco-friendliness important to you?**

10 **Join a hotel loyalty scheme** if you travel a lot.

SAVE ON ACCOMMODATION

1 **Try couch-surfing.** There are websites that connect travellers with free accommodation hosted by people in different cities. It's a fabulous way to explore local culture and meet new people. Be aware that the site should be bona fide – look out for authentic recommendations.

2 **Hostels are a great option for budget travelling.** Simple dorm-style rooms give you basic but adequate facilities.

3 **Home exchanges are great value.** Swap homes with a similar household in another country and explore their neighbourhood.

4 **House-sitting is an option.** Look after someone's home while they are away and get to see their locality. You may have to take care of their pets or water their plants.

5 **Short-term rentals** such as furnished apartments are cheaper than hotels.

6 **Time-share rentals** can be good value. They are great for older travellers.

7 **Home-stays,** whereby you rent a room from a family and are treated like their guest, is a great way to get to know a different culture and its people close up.

8 **Bed and breakfasts may be cheaper** than hotels and home-cooking is often a feature. They may also be more atmospheric than hotels.

9 **Try booking directly** with the hotel or hostel for a cheaper or last-minute deal.

10 **Keep your eye on local or national newspapers.** They sometimes offer special coupon deals for cheap accommodation.

TRY A HOUSE-SWAP

1 **Trust is important.** You are allowing a complete stranger into your home and they are letting you use theirs. It usually works!

2 **The hassle is well worth it.** The plus is going on a holiday and staying in a real home in a different part of the world.

3 Flexibility is vital. If you're open to different locations and timings, you may well find yourself visiting a wonderful place that you'd never formerly considered.

4 Don't oversell your own home and community in your written description. Honesty is the best policy.

5 Communicate with the other family as much as you can beforehand. It's the only way to build up trust and get a sense of what to expect when you get there.

6 Get tidied up! Your house needs to be lickety-split before you hand it over. And leave their house as you found it!

7 Ease yourself into house-swapping. If you're not sure about it, try out a weekend swap first to see if you like it.

8 If you don't want certain things to be used, make sure the guest family knows.

9 Write a complete report about your house and area – do it as well as you can because you only have to do it once. The other family needs to be fully informed on every aspect of your life and environment. Leave behind local guide books, maps and tourist information for their perusal.

10 Check all insurances are up to date and will cover the intended uses.

PACKAGE HOLIDAY – YES OR NO?

1 Find out what the potential cost of your holiday is going to be so that you can budget fairly precisely. For example, find out if the package includes meals.

2 After a bargain? Package operators can get good discounts due to high volume, so your package deal is likely to work out significantly cheaper.

3 You may feel that you are missing out on seeing other places if you have an all-in holiday – this could be a bad thing.

4 Optional side-trips? It could be cheaper to book with the seller direct.

5 Don't just jump into the nearest taxi at the airport. Find out whether transport to and from the airport is included.

6 A good package operator will make sure you get home in the event of a natural catastrophe or political unrest.

7 Look at part packages. Some operators offer some of the deal – you organize the rest. This may suit you better.

8 Do you need to feel secure? The package tour operator has an obligation to look after you, so if anything goes wrong they will help you sort it out.

9 Package holidays are a great option for families. They often offer good facilities, such as bars and pools, so that you can find everything in one location.

10 Claim compensation if the package is not what you were led to believe.

ACTIVITY HOLIDAYS

1 Dancing
2 Singing
3 Yoga
4 Painting
5 Writing
6 Photography
7 Walking
8 Ceramics
9 Cooking
10 Cycling

ALL-INCLUSIVE HOLIDAYS

1 Find out just how all-inclusive your holiday is before you book. Are tips to waiters/bartenders/tour guides included?

2 No need to worry about where your next meal is coming from – it will be waiting for you. The downside is that after a few days the food might seem samey.

3 Don't like to be hassled? You'll be able to miss out on local life such as street sellers and beggars.

4 Take your family on a special family package. You will be offered children's facilities such as kids' clubs and the children will have plenty of company.

5 Get a break from your children. Some venues offer a babysitting service or alarms, nannies and kids' entertainment.

6 Check out which perks are included.

These may be snorkelling, sailing and diving, games and activities, outings and barbecues.

7 Find out whether holiday insurance is included in the price.

8 If you want to get out and about day tours may be available, but be aware that there may be extra cost.

9 Avoid long queues for the ski lift on an all-inclusive ski holiday.

10 Fancy some local flavour? You are under no obligation to stay put so get out and explore the local sights if you want to.

PICK THE RIGHT TOUR GROUP

ADVENTURE HOLIDAY EXPERIENCES

1 Shark-cage diving
2 Safaris
3 Scuba-diving
4 Mountain climbing
5 White-water rafting
6 Rail journeys
7 Ballooning
8 Boat journeys
9 Trekking
10 Polar voyages

1 Tours can be wonderful for first-time travellers or if you want to travel alone but with others' company (if you want it).

2 Check the reputations of the tour companies you are considering.

3 Are you getting the best value for money? Ask where the money goes and how it is spent.

4 Find out whether there are any extras to pay for at specific sites such as tour guide tips and entrance fees.

5 Some tours don't include the costs of all the meals. It's good to know.

6 Explore the tour company's target market. Older people, younger people,

families? You want to find one that has the sort of people you will get on with.

7 Make sure that the company uses knowledgeable local guides who are experts in their fields.

8 Are the proper safety requirements being followed by the company?

9 Look at the itinerary. Is it balanced with activities you want? Is there free time? Excursions? Some tours organize plenty of activity and some not enough.

10 If there are long distances to be travelled by road, check how long journeys are and how early you will need to start in the mornings.

LAST-MINUTE TRIPS

1 Look at local websites – they tend to contain more up-to-date information than the global ones.

2 Shop around. Check more than one site for what is available.

3 Visit or phone your local travel agent; they may have more recent information.

4 Sign up to low-cost airline newsletters. They may offer newly available discounts.

5 Approach the hotels directly. Why not

ring them to see what they can do for you?

6 **Local tourist offices** may be able to help you.

7 **'Last-minute' doesn't always mean 'discounted'.** If you can, find out what the original price is to make sure that it really is a discount.

8 **Prices may have changed** since last season. Don't rely on last year's catalogues Information is updated all the time.

9 **Be prepared to be flexible** in order to get the discount you want. You may have to travel at unsocial times.

10 **You may have to take your trip in a place you hadn't thought of –** but it's an opportunity to go somewhere new.

MAXIMIZE MINI-BREAKS

1 **Plan your break in advance,** then you can just get stuck in when you get there. Research what's available, using a guide-book/map. Create a logical itinerary.

2 **Read up on the history of the place** so that you are well informed before your arrival. Having some prior knowledge will make your hols more enjoyable.

3 **Book some evening activities.** If you want to go to a concert or a play, you may want to book ahead to secure good seats.

4 **Hire bicycles.** Going by bike lets you see the place close up and personal. You get a better feel for the atmosphere.

5 **Talk to people.** Try out your language skills on the locals and take a dictionary to help you out. Be brave!

6 **Go on foot** so that you see places slowly and take it all in. Take comfy shoes.

7 **Hang out in cafés and bars –** they're relaxing and atmospheric.

8 **Try out the local cuisine.**

9 **Get off the beaten track.** Once you've checked out the touristy areas, wander away from the crowds and explore the less well-known spots.

10 **Time your arrival** to get there early in the morning and leave late in the evening – this gives you more daytime in your chosen location.

HOW TO TRAVEL GREEN

1 **Choose a small tour group,** which will have less environmental impact.

2 **Use a tour company that uses local services,** guides and hotels owned by local people rather than chains.

3 **Don't buy souvenirs made from endangered animals** such as ivory, seashells and tortoiseshell.

4 **Use rechargeable batteries** so that you don't have to throw away and buy new ones. Look for quick-charge features.

5 **Treat your own water** by taking a water-purifier and reusable bottle with you. Buying bottled water means that you are leaving a trail of plastic and the water may not even be purified anyway.

6 **Avoid using plastic bags.** Take a re-usable fabric shopping bag instead.

7 Stay on the main trail when hiking. If you start a new trail, others may follow you and do environmental damage.

8 Use biodegradable soap that can be used for different purposes: body and laundry. It's gentle on local water systems.

9 Try to buy only locally made products. Mass-produced souvenirs may be shipped in from abroad and be contributing to global warming.

10 Use local transport and your own two feet rather than hiring a car.

EXCHANGING CURRENCY

1 If you exchange money at home – just change enough to cover travel and transport until you are settled. It will be cheaper to exchange money once there.

2 Beware of high transaction charges in hotels and airports.

3 Credit cards may offer the most favourable exchange rates.

4 Although they are fading in popularity, travellers' cheques still offer excellent benefits – they can be replaced if they are lost or stolen.

5 Local banks offer far more convenience and are a relatively low-cost option for changing your money when you need it.

6 ATMs are usually easy to find and usually offer reasonable exchange rates.

7 Check that your debit or credit card fees will be OK for foreign use.

8 Alert your bank that you are travelling beforehand – your account may be frozen if you try to take money out abroad.

9 No-fee currency exchange booths are usually the most expensive way of changing money. Their exchange rates tend to be higher than banks that charge a fee.

10 Use credit cards for large purchase: it's usually safer and cheaper.

SHOP TILL YOU DROP ON YOUR HOLS

1 Shop around. Compare goods and prices before you make your final decisions.

2 Don't be afraid to haggle if it's the done thing in that country.

3 Be firm with shopkeepers. In some countries they may seem overly keen to get your custom.

4 Look for high standards.

5 Seek out the unusual – it's fun to find things you never see at home.

6 Learn the basics of the local lingo. It will help your confidence when you are shopping and give you an advantage.

7 Get to grips with the local currency so that you know exactly what you are spending. Carry a ready reckoner.

8 Go for good value. Exchange rates may mean that there are great bargains to be had if you search for them.

9 Buy locally made goods to support the local economy.

10 Will it travel? Some things look really odd when you get them home and you will wonder why you bought them.

HAGGLING IS A HOOT!

1 You can haggle in tourist shops, in markets and with beach vendors. In some places you also haggle for taxis.

2 Don't show you're interested in the item you want to buy. Just be neutral about it and act cool.

3 Look at lots of items, including the one you want and ask about prices.

4 Notice flaws and point them out – this should bring about a reduction.

5 Propose your price – about two-thirds lower than the original one.

6 Say you'll think about it and move to leave. You may find that the price magically drops just as you are walking away.

7 You could tell the seller that a good price means you'll bring all your friends.

8 Keep your sense of humour intact. You'll have a lot more fun that way.

9 Be prepared to leave the shop without buying the thing you want.

10 There are some places where you don't usually haggle – in restaurants with menus, shops and for pre-paid taxis.

PAY LESS WHEN YOU EAT OUT

1 Prices may be higher at weekends, when there is more eating out going on and restaurants are more in demand.

2 Take your kids for free. Some restaurants have 'kids eat free' nights – especially during the week.

3 Perhaps eat out during the day – evening meals tend to be pricier.

4 Try eating early in the evening. Some restaurants have 'early bird' specials before the venue gets busy.

5 Choose all-inclusive set menus – the choice is more limited, but prices will be cheaper. Choose from two or three courses.

6 Happy-hour deals may mean you can economize on the drinks at least.

7 Order 'specials of the day' – these are usually cheaper and are guaranteed to be freshly cooked.

8 Look for kids' and senior meals, for those whose appetites are smaller. Prices will be lower.

9 Some restaurants may offer 'theatre suppers', before or after the shows. They are usually more economical.

10 Root around for discount coupons on websites or the city's entertainment information publications.

AVOID TRAVELLER'S TUMMY

1 Don't drink the water or eat ice cubes.

2 Don't eat salads – they may be washed in dirty water or not washed at all.

3 Eat peelable fruit and peel it yourself.

4 Foods and water that have been boiled thoroughly are fine.

5 Beware of buffets. Don't eat food that's been sitting around for long periods.

6 Don't eat undercooked meat.

7 Eat pizza – the high cooking temperature of the oven tends to kill harmful bacteria.

8 Don't go any where near dairy foods in hot climates – tempting though it is.

9 Don't eat ice cream.

10 Purify all your water with purifying tablets – even tooth-brushing water.

HIRE A CAR

1 Safety standards vary from one country or company to the next. Choose a reputable car-hire company so that you're confident about their safety standards.

2 The cheapest deal may not be best.

3 Get some personal recommendations as prices vary. Smaller car-high places may be able to give you a better deal and larger ones may give discounts for early booking.

4 Do your homework and read the small print before you choose a hire company.

5 Make sure your hire contract is trans-lated into your language.

6 Use a credit card for payment as this may provide you with some cover.

7 Don't hand over your passport if the hire company asks for it as a guarantee.

8 If you have a second driver, do your homework – this can sometimes cost more.

9 Check out your insurance – it's often limited to the legal minimum of the country/state you hire the car in and you can be held personally responsible for any claim over this limit.

10 Make sure any existing damage to the car is recorded before you set off.

WHAT TO HAVE IN YOUR CAR WHEN DRIVING ABROAD

1 Spare lightbulbs
2 Warning triangle
3 Snacks/water
4 Torch
5 Blanket
6 First-aid kit
7 Shovel
8 Ice-scraper
9 Mobile phone
10 Jump leads

DRIVING ABROAD

1 Find out what the legal requirements are. Is your licence valid?

2 If you're in your own car – remember to take your car registration papers with you as proof of ownership. Carry your photo ID with you at all times.

3 Check your insurance for breakdown and comprehensive cover before you depart. Costs can skyrocket abroad.

4 Do you have the right car kit for where you are going? Check country identifier signs, headlight adjustors, spare lightbulbs.

5 Take spares: car keys, driving glasses and basic tools.

6 Take a phrase book with a good section of motoring terms.

7 Load your sat nav with the right area and take a good paper map as well.

8 Read up on local driving laws – they vary from country to country. For example, in some countries you are expected to keep your lights on throughout the day.

9 In the event of an accident, call the police and take photos of the damage. If in doubt, contact your consulate.

10 If you are used to driving on the other side – watch out! The worst time for making a mistake is the following day.

DECIPHER A ROADMAP

1 Make sure that you are using an up-to-date map. Buy a new one every five years. Roads change, or are up- or downgraded. Junctions are added/altered.

2 Whenever you read a map, keep a mental image of the four main directions.

3 Look at road colours and legends to see what type of road you are on.

4 To visualize right/left turns, you may need to turn the map on its side or upside down. But this can add to the confusion.

5 When planning exits and entries to/from main roads, make sure that you really will be able to drive on/off. The road you want may pass under or over you.

6 Take the scenic route. Look at the map and plan out a route on smaller roads. You'll take longer to get there, but it will be more interesting and you'll be able to make stops along the way.

7 If you want to arrive at your destination fast – the quickest option may be to take the biggest roads – even if the distance is greater.

8 Maps in books are convenient but the place you want may be lost in the binding. Get a better idea of your route by looking at a smaller-scale map first.

9 Look out for arrows at the map-page margins to see which page to turn to next.

10 Use sat nav by all means, but have a map in the car, too, in case of malfunction or the need to check your position. Technology can go wrong.

BUY CHEAP BUS & TRAIN TICKETS

1 Book early for cheap journey prices.

2 Travel off-peak for cheaper seats.

3 Buy two single tickets instead of a return ticket – it sounds mad, but it works.

4 Use young person and senior railcards and concessions.

5 Get a railcard to get reductions.

6 Buy group tickets if you are travelling with others – six is about the right number.

7 Take advantage of special offers such as family travel concessions.

8 If you're booking at the last minute check whether advanced tickets are still available – they may well be.

9 If you're a commuter, use your ordinary season ticket.

10 Travel overnight – you'll be saving on accommodation.

SURVIVE A LONG BUS JOURNEY

1 Choose your seat with care. Front seats have good leg room and you won't be sitting over a wheel. But if you don't like witnessing the quality of the driving, move further back.

2 Take your own pillow to make sleeping

KIDS' ACTIVITIES ON A BUS/TRAIN

1. I-Spy
2. Hangman
3. Tic tac toe
4. Visual scavenger hunt
5. Sticker books
6. Word searches
7. Draughts/ checkers
8. Chess
9. Colouring-in
10. Card games

a little more comfortable. And your own blanket might be worth the effort, too. Otherwise snuggle up under your coat.

3. **Take your earplugs and headphones** to block out noise.

4. **Travel at night.** There'll be far fewer stops and things will be much quieter – most people sleep.

5. **Use a reputable bus company** that runs the most direct services. The buses are likely to be more comfortable.

6. **Take plenty of entertainment:** a very good book and your favourite music.

7. **Bring your own food and drink.** There's no knowing what the restaurant stops will be like or how often they'll come up. Have plenty of water with you.

8. **Comfortable clothing, perhaps in layers, is a must** – shoes that come off easily and loose sweats are good.

9. **Time your pit stops** – drink plenty of water but not so much that you need to go all the time – this may cause discomfort if the bus only stops occasionally. The restroom on board, if there is one, may not be up to scratch. Take toilet paper.

10. **Take what you need in your hand luggage.** Keep your valuables with you whenever you get off and don't pack them in your main luggage.

GET A CHEAP FLIGHT

1. **Sometimes it can be a lot cheaper** to buy two single flights from two different airlines. Though this is a bit of a hassle.

2. **Make use of comparison websites.** The best search engines are those that aren't affiliated with any airline and will list the cheapest deals across the board.

3. **Search for deals early** and book as soon as you can. Cheap flight companies release a limited number of seats more cheaply on a first come, first served basis.

4. **Go no-frills.** Fly to secondary airports using cheaper carriers.

5. **Be flexible with your travel dates.** It's always cheaper to fly midweek than at a weekend and after major holidays rather than before.

6. **Take the long way round** and try alternative routes – it may save you.

7. **Direct flights** are always more expensive than connecting flights.

8. **Sign up for a frequent-flyer programme** – you'll get points to put towards companion tickets, free upgrades and discounted fares.

9. **Join mailing lists** to be kept informed of last-minute, cut-price deals.

10. **Take advantage of student discounts.**

GET A FLIGHT UPGRADE

1. **Family or friend work for the airline?** Try asking.

2. **Look for special promotions** when you book. Ask, as it may only take a nominal fee to upgrade you.

3. **Get on to a frequent-flyer programme,**

which may entitle you to certain upgrades. Perhaps you'll be able to use points to upgrade seats, if there is spare capacity.

4 **Get to the airport early and ask early.** Your chances of an upgrade will be better.

5 **Dress smartly.** Your efforts will get you nowhere if you look too scruffy to be allowed out of economy.

6 **Travel alone.** Kids will almost certainly disqualify you from upgrading.

7 **Be willing to move when asked** – it might be to the seat of your dreams.

8 **Be nice!** Politeness and kindness will go a long way – if you treat airline staff well, they might be more prepared to do something for you. But be subtle – an outright demand for an upgrade will probably get you nowhere.

9 **Just married?** Then let everyone know about it! Staff may feel inclined to make a fuss of you – including giving you an upgrade.

10 **Buy an upgrade.** You may even be able to find them in the classifieds.

BEAT JET LAG

1 **Start resetting your body clock** in advance of your flight. Move your bedtime an hour or two in the right direction several nights before you leave.

2 **Find sleeping tricky on a plane?** If you only ever snooze on flights, plan yours to arrive late afternoon so that you'll be tired when bedtime comes around.

3 **If you can sleep on planes,** take a night flight and arrive fresh and bouncy.

4 **When you first get on board,** reset your watch to the time of your destination. This will help you get your head round the time difference. Your body will then follow.

5 **Drink water!** Lots of it. Take plenty – both before, during and after your flight.

6 **Eat lightly.** A little and often is easier

on your body than large meals – both before, during and after the flight.

7 **Avoid drinking alcohol** – it may assist your relaxation on the flight, but it won't help your jetlag later.

8 **Move around the cabin** – exercise will lessen the dreaded effects of jet lag.

9 **Don't go to bed the very moment you arrive.** Stay up – even if you can hardly keep your eyes open. Then go to bed at the same time as everyone else. You'll adjust to the time difference more easily.

10 **Get outside** into the fresh air when you get there. It will help you reset your body clock more quickly – your head will start adjusting and your body will catch up more rapidly.

DEALING WITH A FLIGHT DELAY

1 **If you enjoy people watching** – this is a great chance. People of all sorts will be passing before you – so now's the time to

inspect humanity's variety and richness.

2 **Play!** Airports offer all sorts these days: kids' play areas, cinemas, video games and music pods – make the most of your time.

3 **If you have hours on your hands –** why not leave the airport and explore the city? Some airports offer quick city tours for those between flights.

4 **Window shopping is fun** when you've got some spare time. Take your pick from trying out perfumes, browsing the latest bestsellers and inspecting designer wear that you don't necessarily want to buy.

5 **If you need some quiet time** for de-stressing – most airports offer quiet rooms and prayer rooms.

6 **Try a spa treatment or massage –** but don't get too relaxed; you don't want to miss your flight.

7 **Hit the gym!** Serious delays may give you a chance to keep up your fitness pro-gramme. If not, take a brisk walk around the terminal. But don't run!

8 **De luxe lounges** may not be off-limits for a small fee. You can access time-consuming goodies such as showers, free movies, snacks, newspapers and wi-fi.

9 **Sample the local cuisine.** Many of the bigger airports make a feature of the local food. If you don't fancy airline food on the plane, eat your fill now and you won't be hungry later!

10 **Get back to de-stressing nature.** Some airports have green areas, rain forests and gardens for quiet contemplation.

WHAT TO PUT IN YOUR CARRY-ON
1 Travel documents
2 Money
3 Jewellery
4 Medication
5 Keys
6 Change of clothes
7 Mini toiletries
8 Books & mags
9 Music
10 Snacks & sweets

COPE WITH A LONG-HAUL FLIGHT

1 **Minimal transfers make long plane trips more bearable.** If you can afford it, book direct flights or at least change planes as few times as possible.

2 **Wear loose, comfortable clothing.** If you can't be seen in your old joggers, buy clothes with a loose fit made from soft fabrics. They won't get scrunched up. Jeans are too restricting. Layers are good idea as temperatures zoom up and down.

3 **Book a window seat early.** You won't be disturbed by people climbing over you to get to the toilets. If you're a legroom fanatic, book early seats next to the exits and in front of the bulkheads.

4 **Get comfy –** use a neck rest/cushion. Take your own pillow if you've got space. If not, just get yourself into sleep mode with flight pillows, blankets and folded-up clothes. Eye shields and earplugs are also a boon and will help get you settled.

5 **Grab any empty seats early on** in the flight. If the flight isn't fully booked, you may notice clusters of empty ones in other parts of the cabin.

6 **Take lots of good, hard exercise** before you get on the plane. You'll feel a lot less stressed out and more likely to relax – and possibly even sleep.

7 **Entertainment will help to pass the time.** Take a guaranteed page-turner.

8 **Drink as much water as you can lay your hands on –** to stay hydrated. The air in the cabin is moisture-free.

9 **Alcohol is best avoided** as it has a dehydrating effect and will be a lot stronger than it is when you drink it on the ground.

10 **Keep moving.** Walk up and down the aisles at regular intervals and do some simple moving and stretching. Take ad-vantage of stopovers to walk around. If you are stuck in your seat, try simple stretches to promote good circulation, especially in your legs.

FLYING WITH A BABY/TODDLER

1 Book a fold-down bassinette. These usually suit babies up to around a year old and are useful for putting the child into for spells even if they don't sleep a whole lot. (You probably won't have a seat for the baby.) If bassinettes aren't available, you may need to book an extra seat and perhaps take a car seat from home.

2 Everything takes longer with babies – so allow plenty of time for check-in and going through security and customs. You may have to deal with emergency nappy-changes just when you don't need it.

3 Deal with ascents and descents by giving your baby a bottle, breastfeed – to make them swallow and alleviate discomfort. Give children sweets.

4 Take extras of everything. You'll get through more than you think: clothes, nappies, wipes, baby food and bottles. Take spare clothes for yourself – in case your baby is sick over you or your small child spills their drink on you.

5 Can another adult come with you? Another pair of hands will be invaluable.

6 Take a lightweight stroller as hand luggage. This will help no end if you have to walk distances in airports and will be somewhere for the baby/small child to sit. For small kids a sling/baby carriers will help transport them around airports.

7 Check in advance how much baby food and drink you can take on board. This varies with the airline and regulations change. Ask for children's meals when you book and ask the attendants to warm up bottles well before the baby needs them.

8 Take a night flight – if you have any choice in the matter. If you're covering distances your baby/child will sleep more.

9 Take some toys along, too – though you'll probably find that an empty cup and spoon will help keep a baby amused. Don't forget the all-important soothing cuddly blanket/soft toy. If your child is older, why not take along a small toy they've never seen before? They will love packing their own mini backpack.

10 Walk around the plane with the baby/small child. New faces and a change of scenery help keep them amused. You'll get the chance to stretch your legs, too.

TAKE A BREAK IN THE UK

1 Manners are important and you'll hear people saying 'Sorry' a lot. If you brush into someone on the street it's expected, whether you're in the wrong or not. If you're out walking in the countryside, say 'Hello' to everyone and anyone.

2 No need to tip when you're buying a drink in a pub or bar. You just walk up to the bar and buy your drinks – then find a seat, sit down and take the first sip. Ah!

3 Beer is bitter and it's served at room temperature. There are many different local brews, so it's worth experimenting.

4 It doesn't rain all the time – but you may well experience three seasons in one day. Take waterproof clothing and an umbrella, but be prepared for a heatwave or a snowstorm.

BEST CITIES FOR A WEEKEND BREAK

1 Paris
2 Barcelona
3 New York
4 Amsterdam
5 Berlin
6 Istanbul
7 Prague
8 London
9 Hong Kong
10 Bangkok

5 There are outdoor music festivals in the summer all over the country, from June to September – hundreds of them, covering all genres of music. Go for one day or even a whole week. The big three are Glastonbury, Leeds and Reading.

6 Get around on trains and coaches. Book online early for the best deals.

7 Black cabs are expensive. You could try one for the experience, but they run on meters. Calling a private taxi company will be cheaper.

8 Local dialects can be a challenge, with different accents and word usages. Be patient and listen carefully.

9 Leave London – it's great, but you need to take in the rest of the country, too.

10 Don't stay in chain hotels. Try bed and breakfasts to get a flavour of being in someone's home, with all the quirks.

LIVELY LONDON

1 Book a ticket to visit the Houses of Parliament. You can watch members of parliament waving their order papers at each other during sessions.

2 Buckingham Palace is a must for the famous wedding-kiss balcony. It's the famed London home of the British Royal Family. You can only go inside during the summer months, though.

3 Soar above the city on the London Eye – it's a great view, but over all too quickly.

4 The National Gallery is tops for historical art and you can take a stroll beneath Nelson's famous column, too.

5 Watch Tower Bridge open up to let ships pass up, or down, the Thames.

6 Inspect all the Queen's bling at the Tower of London and see where traitors were incarcerated in times gone by.

7 Yummy mummy? The British Museum has a vast collection of Egyptian artefacts.

8 Enjoy a top-notch lunch at the Victoria and Albert Museum café in the sumptious William Morris rooms.

9 Walk across the 'wobbly' bridge to get to Tate Modern and visit magnificent St Paul's Cathedral afterwards.

10 St Paul's has a great big dome to climb up for a wonderful view of the river and the city.

MUST-SEE SIGHTS IN PARIS

1 Eiffel Tower
2 Musée du Louvre
3 Notre-Dame de Paris
4 Musée d'Orsay
5 Montmartre
6 Château de Versailles
7 Centre Pompidou
8 Sacré Coeur
9 Cimetière du Père-Lachaise
10 Arc de Triomphe

FABULOUS FRANCE

1 When in France, take the train – it's the quickest and cheapest transport.

2 Don't get caught out by France's limited opening hours. Shops, supermarkets, boulangeries and cafés all open and close at unpredictable times.

3 Skip hotel breakfasts in favour of a croissant and coffee in a café or boulangerie – cheaper and far more delicious.

4 Slow down and go at the French pace.

5 At least try to speak French. It's the trying that matters. People will then be more friendly.

6 Always say 'Bonjour' to the shop owner

when you enter a shop and say 'Au revoir, merci' when you leave – even if you don't actually make a purchase.

7 **Start every interaction with** 'S'il vous plaît, Madam/Monsieur'.

8 **The French go on holiday in August.**

Prices go up correspondingly. Also, many shops will be closed during that month.

9 **Meals can go on for longer than you'd expect.** Relax and enjoy!

10 **If you want to look French,** wear black and tie a scarf about your person.

SENSATIONAL SPAIN

1 **They eat late.** Don't expect to have company if you have your evening meal before 10.00pm. If you don't want to wait that long, go to one of the many tapas bars for delicious snacks, which can be quite filling if you eat a few of them.

2 **Bartering happens** on market stalls, but not in shops.

3 **The Prado Museum in Madrid** is now open on Mondays as well as the rest of the week, and in the evenings it's free. No excuses for giving this splendid galley a miss now!

4 **Take high-speed trains (AVE).** They are sometimes quicker than taking planes.

5 **Don't forget your loo paper** when you go to bars, restaurants and petrol stations.

6 **Siesta time!** Plan on having lunch between 2.00 and 5.00pm, because that's when the shops are shut.

7 **Life happens outdoors in Spain,** so things can be noisy and it goes on all night. Take some effective earplugs.

8 **Be assertive!** When ordering at a tapas bar, waiting patiently won't get you anywhere – it's expected that you will shout out your order – unless there is obviously someone ahead of you.

9 **Pedestrians have right of way** on every cross-walk without traffic lights. Cars won't always stop, however, so it's best to look as though you are going to cross and then wait for the car to slow down.

10 **Try the menu of the day** for great value and be sure to go to traditional restaurants rather than chains.

BEAUTIFUL BARCELONA

1 Sagrada Família
2 Park Güell
3 Casa Milà
4 Casa Batlló
5 Barcelona Cathedral
6 La Rambla
7 Picasso Museum
8 Montjuïc
9 Gran Teatre de Liceu
10 Palau Música Catalana

BELLA ITALY!

1 **Check when Italian bank holidays are** and steer well clear of them – hotels and restaurants will be more crowded.

2 **Buses are often cheaper** than the train, but for the visitor with little Italian, the trains are easier to use.

3 **Plan to visit** either in April–May or September–November. The weather is still warm, prices are lower and queues shorter.

4 **For the best food** go straight to the place of origin. For example, to Parma for prosciutto and Liguria for pesto Genovese.

5 **If you don't want to stick out** like a sore thumb, refrain from having a cappuchino after 10am.

6 **Cover up in churches** and don't wear

AMBLE THROUGH AMSTERDAM

1. Canal tour
2. Rembrandt Museum
3. Rijksmuseum
4. Van Gogh Museum
5. Anne Frank House
6. De Wallen area
7. Bike tour
8. Stedelijk Museum
9. Jewish Historical Museum
10. Bloemenmarkt

shorts. Bring a scarf to cover the shoulders.

7 Driving in Italian cities is not for the faint-hearted.

8 Florence is the best city in Italy for buying great-quality gold souvenirs.

9 Tuscany is still the place for villas – long or short stays. You'll need to rent a car to explore the whole area.

10 Be prepared to feel a bit tatty – Italians are still the world's most stylish.

REMARKABLE ROME

1 Visiting the Pantheon is like stepping back in time. See it in different lighting conditions – awe-inspiring.

2 The Colosseum lets you 'live' history and is a marvel to behold. It was originally a sports complex where gladiators fought. Dress-up gladiators out front demand money in return for happy snaps, but if you're on a budget pass them by.

3 St Peter's is the largest and most important church in Christendom. Try climbing the dome or visiting the Vatican when the Pope is giving an audience.

4 Take a good guide book to make sense of what you are seeing at the Roman Forum and Palantine Hill as they are ruins now. Be sure to take an umbrella as there is very little shade and a lot of sun.

6 Piazza Navona showcases some dramatic fountains by Bernini. Have a snack or a drink and do some people-watching at the same time. It's a good, central place to stay, too, and probably offers the best ice-cream in the world.

5 San Clemente – descend through history and discover the layers below the present building. It's not well known, so you can get away from the crowds.

7 Trevi Fountain is a wonderful baroque creation – if you throw a coin into it, you will be sure to return to the city. The world-famous Spanish Steps are near by.

8 Capitoline Museums are the oldest public museums in the world. They are full of Greek and Roman sculptures, art and frescoes. It's a good idea to visit these at the same time as the Forum.

9 St John Lateran is the official cathedral of Rome – but you need to be keen on looking at relics.

10 The Vatican Museums and the Sistine Chapel are a must-see and are free on the last Sunday of every month – but be prepared to brave the long queues.

VIVACIOUS VENICE

1 Get lost in Venice. Wander aimlessly through its tangled streets and alleyways. You'll come across some charming deserted squares way off the usual tourist track.

2 Buy a vaporetto ticket and spend half a day going round Venice the long way. It's a relaxing way to spend time on the water.

3 Go to St Mark's Square when it is empty – early morning/late evening. Otherwise you'll be exercising crowd-control skills.

4 St Mark's Basilica is free if you just want to go into the main part. Booking an entry time online is free, too – enabling you to avoid the queues.

5 Walk around Murano, the island where they make all kinds of glass objects. Find a glass-blowing studio so that you can see exactly how it's done.

6 The Rialto market is a great way to see how Venetians restock their larders. Point at the produce you want and the vendor will select it and wrap it up for you. Whatever you do, don't touch.

7 You may want to give gondola rides a miss. They are very pricey and possibly not all they're cracked up to be. Shame!

8 Stay on the main island and be right in the thick of it.

9 Don't plan everything too precisely. You'll get lost in the maze of passageways and extra time is required for finding your way around. Be late!

10 Don't pay too much attention to addresses – they often only refer to the district and the number rather than to a street. Buy a good, detailed map.

MUST-SEE SIGHTS IN PRAGUE

1. Prague Castle
2. Charles Bridge
3. Old Town Square
4. Astronomical Clock
5. St Vitus Cathedral
6. Jewish quarter
7. Vyšehrad Castle
8. Petrin Tower
9. Wenceslas Square
10. Prague Zoo & Botanical Gardens

LOVELY LAPLAND

1 Autumn is the perfect time for a visit – low season means it's a lot cheaper and the bonus is that there are fewer insects.

2 Forget about driving – trains are super-fast and extremely efficient.

3 Don't try out your English on the locals! Finns are quite bilingual but would love it if you could learn a few words of their language. Oh – and they seldom make the first move conversationally.

4 Father Christmas is big! These tours are expensive, though they can provide an unforgetable experience for kids that's, well, Christmassy!

5 Saunas are ubiquitous – why not try one? They are great social centres, but there are things you should know. Everyone is in their birthday suits, for starters. Go with the flow – you'll be fine.

6 Eat dill pickles to replace lost salts after your sauna.

7 Like to stay up? Then go to Finland's northern-most region where they get ten weeks of unbroken sunlight in summer – it's called the White Nights.

8 Wrap up warm! It can be cold all year.

9 The Sami people have 300 words for snow – that should tell you something!

10 The best time to see the Northern Lights is between September and March, though weather conditions need to be clear and calm to get the full effect.

NEW YORK, NEW YORK!

1 To hail a yellow cab in New York – step off the kerb and hold up your arm. If the light is lit the cab is available. It's harder to get one when it's raining and pre-arranged pick-ups are unheard of.

2 Don't be afraid to wander – New York

MUST-SEE SIGHTS IN NEW YORK

1 Times Square
2 Central Park
3 The Statue of Liberty
4 Rockefeller Center
5 Empire State Building
6 Grand Central Terminal
7 Greenwich Village
8 Staten Island Ferry
9 The Metropolitan Museum of Art
10 Brooklyn Bridge

is one of the safest large cities in the US. The grid system makes it easier.

3 Long queues outside a pizza place are a good sign. Sample by buying a slice – if you can't eat the whole thing.

4 Eat dinner early or late. Make reservations a week in advance for the most popular restaurants. If this isn't possible, try before 7.00pm or after 10.30pm.

5 Venture into the Lower East Side to find small clothes shops full of exciting new local designers.

6 Don't just eat in the tourist spots but explore to eat well. Travel to the city's ethnic enclaves to sample their fare.

7 Buy tickets for Broadway shows at a discount booth at the South Street Seaport location, which is usually a lot less busy than the one in Times Square.

8 You can enjoy free concerts in the summer in Central Park.

9 Don't hit the big department stores at peak times – choose weekday evenings.

10 Respect New Yorkers' sidewalk etiquette. Walk on the right and don't stop to peer at maps in busy spots.

COOL SAN FRANCISCO

1 Watch out – the weather in the city is variable. Take an extra sweater and prepare for changes in temperature and fog coming in off the ocean.

2 Look for parking lots if you are driving in the city. Parking on the street can be problematic – you need stamina to find parking metres.

3 Watch out for seagulls – they'll swoop down and grab your picnic lunch if you are anywhere near the water.

4 You cannot smoke – anywhere. This applies to public places, inside and out.

5 Don't pick up the cable car on the waterfront. Walk a few blocks further up the route. You'll find it easier to get a ride.

6 Consider the night tour to Alcatraz for extra creepiness.

7 Resist the urge to call it 'San Fran' or 'Frisco' – the locals hate it. It's 'The City'.

8 Get a good view, climb up Tank Hill – a secret spot for panoramic views of the Golden Gate Bridge, downtown and the Bay Area. It's gasp-worthy!

9 Be an old hippy and explore the delights of Haight-Ashbury.

10 Go for a street-car ride in a lovingly restored vehicle from other world cities. It's an economical way to tour the City and you get a lesson in mass-transit history.

FEEL-GOOD FLORIDA

1 South Florida is a great place for a winter holiday, but beware the high season (December to April) – rooms will be harder to find and the rates higher.

2 North Florida is best during the summer months – for the legendary sunshine.

3 Ride through the Everglades in an airboat – you may see alligators. But take earplugs – the engine noise is deafening.

4 Plan for the theme parks. There are special deals galore and it pays to do some research to know when and where to go. Work the park from the exit rather than joining the crowds at the first attraction.

5 Don't waste your money on souvenirs in the theme parks. You can buy the same thing cheaper in souvenir stands and flea markets in the surrounding cities.

6 If you want to go hunting or fishing you will need to buy a licence and these are readily available at bait shops and sporting goods stores.

7 Driving around Florida? Always carry your current driver's licence and proof of liability insurance on your person.

8 Rest areas will offer you coupon booklets and travel discount brochures free for the taking. They contain maps, directions and money-off discounts.

9 US Highway 1 down the 1,700 islands of the Florida Keys is a two-lane only – so expect traffic delays. Renting a boat might be a better option.

10 Be bilingual when in Miami. Even a smattering of Spanish will help – especially in the Little Havana area.

WE'RE GOING TO BARBADOS!

1 It's best to go December to April.

2 Check out the coastal differences. The west coast is ideal for snorkelling and water-skiing, the east coast for surfing, while the south coast is known as one of the world's best for windsurfing.

3 Get off the beaten track. Rent a car and explore – you'll have a richer experience away from the plush hotels/holiday areas.

4 Like music? The Crop Over summer festival is Barbados' most popular and colourful festival. Its origins can be traced back to the 1780s, when Barbados was the world's largest producer of sugar.

5 Buy from the local stall-holders and shop-keepers rather than sticking to the hotel shops. You'll get greater variety and help the local economy, too.

6 All Barbados's beaches are public – although some hotels like to make it difficult to get to them.

7 Look out for the green flash at sunset.

8 Eat flying fish – it's an island speciality.

9 The fabulous Oistins Fish Fry is the second highest-rated attraction in Barbados and can't be missed.

10 Study architecture. Visit the grand old plantation houses, rich with centuries of history and look at the chattel houses, sometimes sporting ornate trims.

WINTER SUN HOLIDAY SPOTS
1 Florida
2 Hawaii
3 The Canaries
4 Mexico
5 Trinidad & Tobago
6 Red Sea
7 Caribbean
8 Gambia
9 Goa
10 North Africa

PUFF PUFF! PERU

1 High altitude may affect you with nausea and headaches, but hotels have oxygen and medication available.

2 Never exchange money on the street. Go to 'casa de cambios' instead.

3 If you're travelling to Cusco by train

don't forget to take your camera. The journey is spectacular.

4 Don't hail taxis on the street in Lima. Ask your hotel to call a taxi for you or use a hotel car. It's more expensive, but it's far less risky than taking a street taxi.

5 Lima is only a few hours' flight away from Easter Island. Flights only operate a few days a week, so book well in advance if you plan to go in the high season.

6 The best time to visit Peru is in the dry season, from May to September. The rains from mid-November to March can make walks and jungle trips challenging.

7 Keep lots of small change for taxis, tips and trinkets.

8 Trek the Inca Trail to Machu Picchu. Good health is required as it is a demanding trek with several nights' camping en route. Book in advance as permits are limited.

9 If trekking isn't an option, you could stay in Aguas Calientes and catch the early-morning bus to Machu Picchu. The earlier the better, in order to avoid the hoards. You can walk to the site from the town.

10 Remember that the sun sets early (6.30pm), even at summer solstice, since Peru is close to the equator.

AWESOME AUSTRALIA

1 When planning your trip, remember that Australia is vast. It's best to fly between the major cities.

2 The best months to visit Australia are September and October.

3 Drive with a good supply of drinking water with you and stay with your car if you break down.

4 Don't touch any sea creatures – they might bite or sting you, sometimes with fatal consequences.

5 Wombats, kangaroos and other animals are capable of wrecking your car – be careful. Kangaroos hang out on grass verges at dusk (nibbling the nice green grass) and are prone to jumping out at unsuspecting cars – with dire consequences.

6 Are you a wine buff? South Australia is the place to go wine-tasting.

7 Mug up on the regulations about importing animal and plant products.

8 Give road-trains a wide berth. You'll be buffeted by displaced air when you pass in the other direction.

9 Thick-soled shoes are a must when walking on reefs – for combating stone fish and other poisonous creatures.

10 Check approaching storm fronts for signs of hail storms – which can give you a severe battering.

PLACES TO SEE IN AUSTRALIA

1 Uluru (Ayers Rock)
2 The Great Barrier Reef
3 The Sydney Opera House
4 Tasmania
5 The Gold Coast
6 The Great Ocean Road
7 Kakadu National Park
8 Wine country
9 Whitsunday Islands
10 Kimberley

MUST–SEE SIGHTS IN TOKYO

1 The Imperial Palace is the residence of the Japanese Royal Family. Closed to the public normally, you can wander around the inner grounds and see members of the royal family for the New Year's Greeting and the Emperor's birthday every year.

2 **Look for the famous gate lantern** at the Sensji Temple, Asakusa. It's part of what is supposed to be the first temple ever built in the Tokyo area.

3 **Shinjuku Gyoen Park provides** breath-taking views of blossoms every April. Don't just go to see the glorious displays, take a peep at artists painting them, too.

4 **Enjoy a little peace and quiet** close to nature in Ueno Park. It's near to Tokyo's top museums and you can see beautiful displays of lotus flowers in season.

5 **The Tokyo Tower sports a fabulous display** of colourful paper fish at its entrance. The view from the top is not for the faint-hearted, though.

6 **Go to Ginza for all your gadgets.** It's Tokyo's best-known shopping area – jam-packed with all you could possibly want.

7 **The Tsukiji Fish Market is the world's largest fish and seafood market.** Go and admire the vast arrays and displays – the giant blue fin tuna attracts attention at auction – sometimes tourists have to be banned as they get in the way!

8 **If you like ferris wheels –** you just have to go on the one at Odaiba as it's the biggest in the world.

9 **Hang around the Yoyogi Park entrance at Harajuku on Sundays** to see crowds of young people all dressed up as anime characters, lolitas and goths – it's a blast!

10 **No trip to Tokyo is complete** without a trip to admire the famed Mount Fuji.

UNMISSABLE INDIA

1 **Avoid the attentions of shop-keepers** trying to get you into their shops by putting on your earphones and pre-tending that you can't hear them. Just cruise past – unless you do want to go in, that is.

2 **Don't ask for directions.** Even if the person doesn't know the way, it's impolite for them not to respond – you might find yourself misdirected. Find out what the nearest landmark is and jump into a taxi.

3 **You will get ill in India –** it's almost a certainty. Be prepared so that it won't ruin your holiday. Don't drink the water without purifying it or buy bottled water that has not been properly sealed. Also smell it. Check for filtered water in restaurants. Drink canned, soft drinks.

4 **Eat locally made yogurt** during your first few days to let your stomach adapt.

5 **If you are in a group,** leave one person in charge of watching the luggage.

6 **Take official taxis from taxi booths,** where you can get a receipt. Don't be tempted to use informal drivers.

7 **Ask the hotel receptionist** to write down your destination on a piece of paper. You can show this to drivers and be sure they will take you to the right place.

8 **Beggars are a fact of life in India** and it can all get a bit too much. If you really feel hassled, don't engage and move along. If you do want to give, do it when you're on the point of leaving – otherwise you will be mobbed. Carry sweets or small foreign coins to give to children.

9 **Avoid making public displays of affection –** even at the beach.

10 **Dress appropriately – especially if you are female.** Keep covered up and remember that shoulders, arms, cleavage and legs, in particular, should be loosely covered. Tight-fitting clothes aren't on.

PLACES TO SEE IN INDIA

1 Taj Mahal
2 Golden Temple, Amritsar
3 Varanasi
4 Forts/palaces of Rajasthan
5 Goan beaches
6 Khajuraho temples
7 Rishikesh
8 Bandhavgarh National Park
9 Ajanta and Ellora Caves
10 Kerala backwaters

EVOCATIVE EGYPT

MUST–SEE SIGHTS IN EGYPT

1 The Pyramids at Giza & Sphinx

2 Khan El-Khalili, Cairo

3 Abu Simbel

4 Temples of Karnak

5 Valley of the Kings

6 Siwa Oasis

7 Luxor Temple

8 Egyptian Museum, Cairo

9 Al-Azhar Gardens

10 River Nile

1 **Consider your dress.** Avoid wearing shorts and short-sleeved shirts. Women should take a scarf for temple visits.

2 **Take a box of cheap ballpoint pens.** Children (and many adults) are happy to receive them.

3 **Toilet paper is often at a premium at historical sites** so take a roll along. Loos at many sites are not 'western' so arrange toilet trips in hotels and restaurants.

4 **Take plenty of water** and make sure it's sealed. Don't eat salads or ice.

5 **Ask hotel reception to get you taxis.** They have certain taxis that they know well and deal with daily.

6 **Women should wear trousers inside the pyramids.** You may have to go up and down ladders and crawl through narrow passages. Men should avoid wearing shorts.

7 **Take along small notes for tipping.**

8 **Take a small torch when visiting the sites.** Many tombs and temples only use natural light. A small mirror can be used to highlight a relief. Halogen torches will not be acceptable – they cause damage.

9 **Prices are marked up for tourists** so offer at most one-third to half of the asking price and work up. Or just keep saying 'no' and let them lower the price.

10 **Baksheesh is a tip in Egypt for just about anything –** from carrying bags at the airport to offering to have a picture with you or showing you around a tomb. Pay with the smallest notes possible.

UNFORGETTABLE SAFARIS

1 **Want to take the kids?** Do your research – some companies have age limits and don't allow small children along.

2 **Let your guide know what sort of wildlife you are hoping to see.** They can tailor your trip to your interests.

3 **Be safety-aware around animals.** Don't stand up in an open vehicle or stick anything through a car window. Always follow the guide's advice.

4 **Tip your guide, driver and porter.** It's a common courtesy. Find out from your hotel what might be expected.

5 **Carry cameras in dust-proof bags on safari.** You'll need a powerful telephoto lens to be able to photograph wildlife.

6 **Take advantage of special dawn rides** to see the animals feeding and watering.

7 **Take a pair of binoculars** so that you can view wildlife close up. The more powerful it is the better.

8 **Ask permission before you photograph local people.** Otherwise you may cause serious offence. Some people will need to be paid before you photograph them.

9 **Think about the clothes you take.** Camouflage colours are best. Don't wear white, which gets very dirty. Black is too hot and attracts flies. A safari jacket is useful to keep you warm in early mornings and evenings.

10 **Hats must be worn –** the wider the brim the better – to protect you from the sun and glare. They'll help you get a better view of the animals, too. Sunglasses are a must as well.

A TERRIFIC CRUISE

1 Plan ahead – start a year in advance. Read reviews so you know what to expect.

2 Book through an agent rather than directly with the cruise company. Agents are able to get some great deals.

3 Check what's included in the package.

4 Choose a balanced holiday to avoid having to be on board for days at a time and perhaps more sea-sickness, too. A good idea is to choose a trip that has a day or two of being at sea for every week away.

5 Book cabins that are higher up in the ship. This will afford you better views. Also, the lower ones are nearer to the engine and likely to be noisier and stuffier.

6 Research ports of call – you'll enjoy the trip more if you know something about the culture and history of each place.

7 Be flexible – you are at sea, so plans and itinerary because of bad weather and other factors may change along the way.

8 Illness can spread quickly on a ship. Be vigilant and wash hands before and after handling food and after loo breaks.

9 If you want a quiet holiday, don't choose a cruise that caters for families.

10 Thinking of taking your family? Select cruises offering kids' activities – some have kids' clubs and babysitting services as well as more spacious cabins.

MOST POPULAR HOLIDAY SPOTS
1 Spain
2 France
3 Great Britain
4 Greece
5 Italy
6 USA
7 Turkey
8 Egypt
9 Croatia
10 Thailand

A ROMANTIC ANNIVERSARY GET-AWAY

1 Ladies need serious pampering. Have a facial, a manicure and a pedicure. Get your hair done. Make-up must be flawless.

2 Book a chauffeur – either to or from the airport – just for a treat. It will make the occasion even more special.

3 Pack romantic items: CDs, scented candles and aromatherapy massage oils.

4 Arrange to have duplicates of your wedding flowers decorating your hotel suite when you arrive.

5 Ask the chef to recreate your wedding meal for your first dinner after arrival.

6 Go for a massage together.

7 Take a walk to a romantic viewpoint.

8 Try something completely new: white-water rafting, bungee-jumping, take a balloon ride or try sky-diving.

9 Have a candle-lit dinner in your room – or on the balcony. Try wishing on a star.

10 Don't talk about the kids, money or the broken-down washing machine.

FANTASTIC FAMILY TRIPS

1 Book a Bedouin desert adventure. Try Oman, with its expansive beaches, child-friendly resorts and enticing desert dunes.

2 Fiji is good for parents who want a rest. Some hotels have dedicated nannies, letting you recharge parental batteries.

3 Camp in a tipi, a yurt or stay in a treehouse. The kids will just adore it.

4 Do Christmas in Lapland with sleigh rides, Santa's home and ice hotels.

5 Rajasthan is a great introduction to India for family travellers. Its ancient desert cities are living fairy tales.

6 Climb aboard a camel in Cairo. A visit offers a citywide cacophany, guaranteed to stun the most reticent teenage traveller.

7 Road-tripping in the land of Oz. Have a campervan hol in the back of beyond.

8 Bright lights, big city, Tokyo. Children will go wild for a holiday in the home of all things high tech and high kitsch.

9 Take a camper van coast to coast in the USA. The thrill of the open road awaits all family adventurers.

10 Go monster-hunting in Loch Ness, Scotland. Tacky but fun.

IDEAS FOR A BRILLIANT WEEKEND

1 Wine-tasting
2 Cookery course
3 Camping
4 City break
5 Hiking & hill-walking
6 Outdoor music festival
7 Old school reunion
8 Sailing & windsurfing
9 Diving
10 Cycling

THEME PARK THRILLS

1 Book tickets online in advance. It will be cheaper and you won't have to queue.

2 Wear comfortable footwear – you will need to walk distances. Make sure shoes are fastened securely so you don't lose them on some of the more intense rides.

3 Go for the 'big' rides early in the day – before the queues build up. Arrive at the park 30 minutes before it opens.

4 Avoid doing the 'wet' rides at the end of the day – you might not be able to dry out before the trip home. Or take a change of clothes.

5 To avoid the biggest crowds, visit during term time and/or weekdays.

6 If you want to save on food – take a picnic. Theme park food can be expensive. Or you could share meals.

7 Regular visitor? If you want to visit the park more than once per year, look at buying an annual pass.

8 The best time to get on popular rides is at mealtimes or during a parade or other main event show.

9 Take a digital picture or your group at the start of the day! If you lose someone, it might be useful for tracking them down.

10 Get dizzy on big rides or roller coasters? Don't close your eyes – it will make things worse.

GO ON A RETREAT

1 Try a monastery with all mod cons to sample the spiritual life in comfort.

2 Get away from it, but all close to home. Choose an hotel in quiet countryside.

3 A silent retreat will give you a break from a noisy lifestyle and a welcome relief if you need a break from talking.

4 A meditation retreat might be just what you need. Come prepared with loose clothing, a meditation cushion and perhaps a shawl, too.

5 Build a little exercise into your retreat schedule – especially if you are sitting still for much of the time.

6 Think in small chunks of time – just sitting and walking (if that is what your retreat offers) may seem daunting, but it gets easier once you get used to it.

7 Don't be too hard on yourself if the benefits of the retreat aren't immediately clear to you. It may take a few days to get used to a different regime. Practise relaxed awareness.

8 Trust in the process and don't start wondering why you came. The format is tried and tested and proven to work.

9 What works best on a writing retreat? A specific task or two. For example, perhaps you need to make a big effort to finish a piece of writing – now's your chance!

10 A yoga retreat in a luxury spa may sound like a great idea, but the standard of yoga instruction might not be as high as you expect or are used to.

WHY GO ON A PILGRIMAGE?

1 New spiritual path
2 Inspiration
3 New perspectives
4 Learning meditation
5 Purification
6 Penance
7 Harmony of natural world
8 Spiritual adventure
9 Concentration
10 Peace

PRE-WEDDING BREAK IDEAS

1 Indulge in the hedonistic paradise that is Las Vegas, just made for the bride or groom's last nights of freedom!

2 New York, the city that never sleeps. You'll have a fantastic time in this energy-packed town.

3 Have a dancing weekend. It could be salsa, ballroom, cha-cha-cha or even Bollywood. Take lessons from a pro and dance the weekend away.

4 Organize a golf weekend in a luxurious country-house hotel with a sweeping course and practise that swing.

5 Pamper yourselves. Have a spa and beauty treatment weekend.

6 Paintballing! Get down and dirty.

7 Sun, sea and shopping? Barcelona has it all. Relax by the pool on the beach or indulge in some serious water sports.

8 Rent a cottage in the country and relax in front of the fire after exploring the surrounding countryside.

9 Have a yachty weekend. Learn to sail or just enjoy the ride.

10 Don your wetsuits and learn to surf – exhausting but great fun.

THE WONDERS OF A SKIING HOLIDAY

1 Rent skis rather than buying them, but do buy your own boots. You'll be advised to break them in before you go – walk around the house in them.

2 Practise on artificial ski slopes – start a few weeks before you depart.

3 Work on your muscles – it'll pay off. Running and hill-walking are good preparation exercises.

4 Research your ski resort beforehand for facilities. Some have spas, which are great for après ski relaxation and recovery.

5 Take lots of layers – high activity in a chilly climate means you need to be able to control how much you have on.

6 Don't forget sunscreen to prevent skin damage. It'll also protect your skin from the wind.

7 Keep an eye on your hydration. Even though the climate will be cold, your body still needs plenty of water.

8 Research top spots – conditions vary from place to place and country to country.

9 Learn ski lingo – skiing has a whole language of its own. You'll be in the know if you can get to grips with some of it.

10 Experience après ski. Some resorts are noisy and energetic – go for it!

SAFETY ON THE SKI SLOPES

1 Get fit before you go. You'll be less likely to injure yourself. Go on a ski exercise programme at least a few weeks before you depart.

2 Wear the correct ski gear to avoid hypothermia and frostbite. The weather can worsen all too rapidly.

3 Use the right equipment and make sure it is in good repair – to avoid cold feet and blistering, for example.

4 Wrap-around or goggle sunglasses are a must for preventing sun-blindness.

5 Don't ignore signs and flags where avalanche danger is present. Don't ski on closed runs – they are unsafe.

6 Wear a helmet if you are going to ski fast – they are increasingly the norm and could be a life-saver. Kids should always wear them.

7 Be aware of mountain rules – they vary from one area to the next. Familiarize yourself before you go.

8 Take care of children – they won't know their limits and are more susceptible to hypothermia and frostbite. They may not be able to understand all of the dangers involved in skiing.

9 Alcohol can slow your reactions at high altitude – so drink very carefully, especially at lunchtime if you are returning to the slopes afterwards.

10 Know your own ability – and no showing off! Have respect for others and don't ski too near them and obstacles.

HOW TO SURVIVE SUN & HEAT

1 Don't forget vaccinations. A last-minute break to a tropical country may mean inadequate time to get protection from tropical diseases – be safe!

2 Re-apply sun lotion after prolonged periods in the water, there is no sun cream that is guaranteed fully waterproof!

3 Wear a T-shirt. If you are pasty white after a few months of autumn or winter you will need lots of sun protection. A T-shirt is the equivalent of sun-factor 25.

4 Don't fall asleep in the sun!

5 If you do get sunburned apply cold vinegar over the sore areas. It will soothe and prevent peeling.

6 Avoid large, protein-rich meals that increase metabolic heat and warm the body.

7 Sun without jetlag? Choose a hot destination that is in the same time zone.

8 For gentle sun, go to the islands – the

Canaries, Malta, Cyprus, the Algarve, Madeira or the Azores.

9 Prone to heat rash? Don't put on lots of layers of tanning product. Your pores will clog and irritation will set in.

10 Never drink an iced drink in the blazing sun – it may make you feel ill. Have a body-temperature drink while in the sun and wait until you cool down in the shade before having a very cold drink.

THE RIGHT SHADES FOR YOU

1 Always buy UV-protected glasses. Read the label carefully before you buy, as full protection is not necessarily a given and isn't pegged to price. The vulnerable eyes need protection from UV rays in all climates. Standard protection is at least 60 per cent but 100 per cent is desirable.

2 Polarization is great if you are doing water or snow sports. The glasses reduce light off reflective surfaces.

3 Don't be sucked in by style. Mirrored sunglasses are highly reflective and will filter some light, but they are more of a style statement than useful.

4 Durability is vital when you're out and about. Scratch-resistant lenses help.

5 High-contrast lenses offer added filtering, aiding in-depth perception. However, they can distort colour and may not be suitable for driving.

6 Presciption sunglasses let you enjoy the great outdoors while maintaining good vision. Look for versions which adapt to varying light levels to avoid having to take two pairs of specs.

7 Consider what lenses are made of. Glass lenses are heavy but offer best clarity. Plastic are lightweight but may scratch more easily. Polycarbonate lenses are strongest and resistant to shattering.

8 Colour is important – different shades offer varying protection and enhancements.

9 Think about frames. Metal frames are strong but rigid so they can break or bend permanently. Nylon and plastic frames are often used in sports sunglasses and are lightweight, strong and flexible.

10 Rubber coating on the bridge and earpieces allows specs to stay on your face – important if you're being very active.

KIDS! STAY SAFE IN POOLS

1 Don't allow kids to swim without adult supervision – even if they know how to swim. Accidents can happen.

2 Enclose your pool with a high childproof fence that can be locked. If latches are self-closing, make sure they are out of reach of tiny hands.

3 Keep a life-saving flotation device by the pool at all times.

4 Learn life-saving skills.

5 Keep children away from spas and hot tubs – kids are susceptible to overheating.

6 Don't let kids run around the pool perimeter – they will slip on wet tiles.

7 **If the pool has a cover,** make sure that it is covered completely when not in use and that children don't walk over it.

8 **For little kids and toddlers,** there should always be an adult within grabbing distance just in case.

9 **Avoid giving kids inflatable swimming aids** – they give little ones a false sense of security and slow them down when learning to swim.

10 **Children are not ready for swimming lessons** until after their fourth birthday.

SEASIDE SAFETY DO'S & DON'TS

1 **Look for safety flags** and know what they mean. Ask one of the lifeguards if you are in any doubt about whether to swim.

2 **Only swim on beaches** that have a lifeguard patrol on duty.

3 **Don't swim after drinking alcohol.**

4 **Don't swim alone** – always take a swimming buddy with you.

5 **Don't swim straight after a meal.**

6 **Don't dive off breakwaters.**

7 **Don't use inflatable lilos or toys in the sea** – someone could be swept out.

8 **Don't misuse safety equipment.**

9 **Supervise children** at all times.

10 **If you get into trouble in the sea,** wave your hand in the air and shout for help. If you see someone else in trouble call the lifeguard straight away.

TYPES OF TENT
1 Ridge
2 Dome
3 Steel-frame
4 Geodesic dome
5 Touring
6 Hoop/tunnel
7 A-frame
8 Pop-up
9 Bell
10 Yurt

BUYING A TENT: WHAT TO LOOK FOR

1 **Think about how many people you need to accommodate** and how much kit you will take. You might want to allow for more people in order to increase the space.

2 **Don't get blown away.** Look for a tent that is sturdily constructed.

3 **Don't give yourself a struggle.** Find a tent that's easy to put up and down.

4 **Who's coming too?** Will you be taking kids along? They'll need their own sleeping space and maybe extra area to hang out in during bad weather.

5 **Will you be carrying your tent** from place to place or just popping it on the top of a car?

6 **Are you using the tent for short trips or longer stays?** For weekend breaks and festivals or lengthy touring trips?

7 **Will want to stand up in the tent?** If the weather is going to be mixed, you might want to think about the size of the living area – you'll be spending more time in it if the weather turns nasty.

8 **Dome tents are better than A-frame and walled tents** because they're more spacious and offer good stability. They're also easy to clean and dry.

9 **Tents need to have good ventilation.** They should have openings on all sides and mesh screens to admit the air without letting in insects.

10 **Think about the time of year.** There are three-season and four-season tents. It all depends.

POP UP A POP-UP TENT

1 **Choose a flat, non-sloping pitch** – if possible higher than the surrounding area so that when it rains, water drains away.

2 **Don't pitch underneath a tree** unless you need the shade. Falling branches can be dangerous.

3 **Choose a pitch that's a polite distance from other campers** – unless you have no choice. You can hear everything through tent walls and you'll need plenty of space for guy ropes. A 6-m (20-ft) gap between yourself and the next tent is advisable.

4 **Look around the area** and pick up any objects such as stones – otherwise they'll poke through your groundsheet and give you a sleepless night.

5 **First off, take your tent out** of its carrying case and tip out the tent pegs.

6 **Remove the band** that stops the tent popping up when you don't want it to – and let the tent pop up – magic!

7 **Decide which direction you want the tent to face** – think about which way the wind blows, which way the sun rises and sets and any other important factors. If you're near a path you may not want your tent entrance to face passers-by. If you're pitching on a slope, direct the entrance uphill so that rain water doesn't flow in.

8 **Push or hammer the pegs** into the ground at a 45-degree angle. Use all the available loops so that your tent is secured.

9 **Peg out all the guy ropes** and adjust their tautness.

10 **Check the guy ropes and pegging** at regular intervals – they can come loose.

CAMPING ESSENTIALS

1 Tent & pegs
2 Tarps
3 Sleeping bag
4 Camp stove
5 First-aid kit
6 Cooking essentials
7 Water carrier
8 Torch
9 Matches
10 Mallet

TENDING YOUR TENT

1 **Seal all the seams with sealant** – if your tent is nylon or synthetic. Otherwise find a tent that has taped seams.

2 **Cotton tents need to be weathered.** This means getting them naturally wet and letting them dry out by themselves. You can do this with a garden hose at home.

3 **Dry out your tent after use** and remove all the mud – before you stash it away.

4 **Don't use detergents on your tent** – they affect the waterproof coating. Just brush or gently wash with mild soap.

5 **If you can store tents opened out** this is the best plan – in a warm, dry place. If you can't do this – make sure the tent is completely dry before packing it up.

6 **Store pegs and poles separately.** It's a good idea to keep everything in separate bags – less likelihood of tearing the fabrics.

7 **Lubricate zips** to make sure they keep running freely.

8 **Take off your boots** before you go into the tent – this reduces wear and tear.

9 **Check your tent before and after use** for rips and tears – before they worsen.

10 **Reproof your flysheet** at intervals.

KIDS GO CAMPING!

1 Experiment with camping in the garden before you go so that the kids learn how to pitch a tent, use all the equipment and get used to sleeping under canvas.

2 Take extra clothes and shoes – way more than you think you'll need. Everyone will get dirtier and wetter than they usually do – but then it probably won't matter.

3 Take their favourite stuff, too – soft toys and cuddly blankets. It may help if there's a little overexcitement and difficulty getting to sleep.

4 Plan to arrive just after lunch so that you can sort out the camp before it gets dark and everyone gets cold, cross, tired and hungry after the long journey. Hopefully you won't need to dig a pit latrine as well!

5 Glo-sticks are fun and may help allay night-time fears, if there are any.

6 Give all the kids their own camp chores – they'll love collecting water, doing washing up at the campsite block, collecting firewood (if it's allowed), tidying up the tents, airing the sleeping bags, fetching the milk – there's a lot to do!

7 Drop the routine and reconnect with the kids – just relax! If you let things go a bit, everyone will have a lot of fun.

8 Is the site safe for kids? While it's a good time to let the kids go wild, there are limits. Check out any potential hazards, such as cliff tops and deep lakes, first.

9 Pack a play tent. This can become a base for stashing their toys, for playing in during bad weather or making into a den. It'll stop the main tent getting mucky, too.

10 Take extra blankets to put under the kids' sleeping bags – they'll keep warmer at night that way.

THINGS TO DO WHILE CAMPING

1 Midnight walks
2 Star-gazing
3 Bird-watching
4 Fishing
5 Swimming
6 Hiking
7 Songs around the campfire
8 Writing a camp diary
9 Collecting flotsam & jetsam
10 Story-telling

CAMPSITE GAMES & ACTIVITIES

1 Have a scavenger hunt – see how much of the following you can collect: shells, driftwood, pine cones and pebbles.

2 Go on an alphabet hike – find or spot items that each begins with a different letter of the alphabet.

3 Hold a cloud-watching contest. See who can find shapes in the clouds.

4 Have a tug of war – you need a whole crowd for this one, plus some strong rope.

5 Go sketching in a group. Equip every-one with pencils and paper and get them to look at scenery, plants and animals while they draw.

6 Make a camping scrapbook. Help kids collect, identify and stick in flowers, leaves, bus tickets, entrance stubs – anything to help them remember and identify things they saw on their hols. It'll make a wonderful keepsake.

7 Make leaf rubbings. Use charcoal or pastels and lining paper.

8 What am I? In a group of kids, relate your questions to the camp surroundings: animals, plants, trees, mountains or lakes.

9 Campfire story games are fun. One person starts by giving the first sentence of a story and each person adds to it, one by one, around the fire.

10 Try playing 'poison balls' (it needs a

large group with lots of tents) – three coloured balls (one ball per three tents) are planted in different tents. Every time someone finds a ball in their tent they have to plant it in someone else's without being caught (using all their cloak-and-dagger skills). Devise your own reward system if you like.

CAMPFIRE CUISINE

1 Take a jar or two of curry paste. You can make a yummy curry out of almost anything and it only takes one pan. Think laterally – potatoes, veggies or beans.

2 Forgotten your chopping board? Use a handy Frisbee instead. It's lightweight and the rim stops everything sliding off.

3 Go foraging – you might be able to find wild food for your supper: wild strawberries, blackberries, mushrooms (but identify them properly before you eat them), wild garlic, plums, dandelions and nettles.

4 Tin foil is vital if you're going to cook over a campfire – for baked potatoes, corn on the cob and fresh fish.

5 Think one-pot basic dishes such as risotto, casseroles and stir-fries.

6 Caught some fish? After gutting, cut slits in the skin and rub in a mix of olive oil and salt. Use a skewer to hold it all together while it's being cooked.

7 Get your fire going before everyone gets hungry. It takes longer to settle down than you think and there's nothing worse than starving campers!

8 Non-pan cooking is the way to go if water's in short supply. Use a peeled stick to make kebabs from meat and veggies.

9 For a quick nutritious pudding make banana boats. Scoop out the banana to look like a canoe and mix it with marshmallow/banana, nuts and raisins, replace the mixture, wrap in foil and bury it in hot coals for ten minutes. Delicious!

10 Use a tin-can stove if you only need a little water – say, for hot drinks.

CAMP KITCHEN NECESSITIES
1 Olive oil
2 Curry powder
3 Dried herbs
4 Stock cubes
5 Tomato purée
6 Garlic purée
7 Cornflour
8 Flour
9 Chilli powder
10 Soy sauce

GLAMPING? IT'S GLAMOROUS CAMPING

1 Glamping costs quite a bit more than ordinary camping, but if you like your mod cons and even, sometimes, breakfast in bed, this may be the answer for you.

2 Try a traditional tipi or a bell tent – great fun for the kids. These traditional tents can accommodate crowds and are often supplied with mattresses and woodburning stoves.

3 Yurts are comfortable, cosy and already put up for you – some even boast en suite facilities. Everything you need is there and they're really big – with real carpets, beds and kitchens. You won't need to take anything at all with you.

4 Treehouses sound a bit Swiss Family Robinson, but they can be very atmospheric and comfy, once you're up there. Some even hoist your breakfast up to you in a basket in the mornings.

5 **Covered wagons or gypsy caravans (vardos)** are yours to move around in and you get your own horse, too.

6 **De luxe tents can run to** proper beds, duvets, lovely rugs, soft cushions – even chandeliers and hot tubs.

7 **Want to be eco whilst glamping?** Many sites use solar power and pride themselves on minimum impact on the environment. Some offer delicious organic meals.

8 **Consider a caravan –** you can enjoy the great outdoors but still have all the your own shower and fridge on hand. Airstreams are the old-fashioned kind of caravan and they're really cool, too.

9 **Some glamping sites are open all year** – so if you fancy a cosy winter break, this may be the answer.

10 **For something a little more low key** – just take a silk sleeping bag liner and an air mattress. They will make all the difference between luxury and roughing it.

CHOOSING A CAMPSITE

1 Group size
2 Pets
3 Kids
4 Forest
5 Beach
6 Mountains
7 Lake
8 Campfires
9 Glamping
10 Views

LOW-IMPACT CAMPING

1 **If you want to have less impact** on the environment just go in a small group – they do less damage and are quieter, too.

2 **Reduce your rubbish.** Leave as much packaging as you can at home. Put your food into reusable containers and avoid tin, aluminium and glass. You won't have to throw anything away.

3 **Stay on the trail** – regardless of how muddy it is. Passing to one side or the other will simply widen the path. Wear as light a boot as possible for the conditions.

4 **Don't camp in fragile areas** – it will take them a long time to heal after you have left. Choose durable surfaces instead.

5 **Wear camp shoes** while you are moving around the camp – sandals, moccasins, sneakers – they will minimize impact on the camp ground.

6 **Don't use soap and shampoo –** or if you do, use it 60m (200ft) away from water sources and use as little as possible.

7 **Don't pick up too many things to take away,** such as flowers, stones, feathers – otherwise others won't be able to enjoy them. Photograph them instead.

8 **Minimize fire impact –** it scars the environment and uses valuable resources. Use a backpacking stove instead. If you really must, contain your fire in a fire pan.

9 **Don't feed animals –** otherwise they'll get a taste for human food.

10 **Leave no trace.** Take all your rubbish home and collect that dropped by others.

SURVIVE BAD-WEATHER CAMPING

1 **Keep a 'wet stuff' area** near the tent entrance and take your footwear/jackets off every time.

2 **If torrents are coming in,** you might be able to divert it by digging a small drainage channel (check with the site owner first).

3 If your tent leaks use dirty clothes and towels to mop up pools of water.

4 If you haven't got a built-in groundsheet, make sure your belongings are raised off the ground.

5 Pack some waterproof overclothes and boots to avoid the onset of trench foot – it's no joke!

6 Use windbreaks to buffer the wind – move them around according to changing wind directions. Make use of your car for the same purpose.

7 Pack extra pegs and spare guy ropes so that you can knock in extra pegs in high winds and storms – such fun!

8 Pitch your tent facing downhill in cold weather. Cold air enters the tent when the entrance faces uphill.

9 A four-season tent and sleeping bag might be a good idea if you're planning a lot of poor-weather camping.

10 Know what to expect. Do your research before you set off. Is the weather likely to be bad? Have you got the right equipment? Is the site exposed to wind and rain? If conditions become bad, don't let bravado get the better of you – know when to quit.

AVERT CAMPING CRISES

1 Don't place cooking, heating or lighting kit near the sides of the tent – it could easily catch alight.

2 Keep tent exits clear at all times – in case you need to get out quickly.

3 Put a torch in a handy place by the exit – for loo trips in the night.

4 Condensation is not the same as leakage – make sure the tent is well ventilated at all times.

5 Carry spare poles and tent repair kit.

6 Put fluorescent tags on your guy ropes so that people don't go flying in the dark.

7 Don't eat in your tent or store food in it as food smells attract animals. It's probably best to keep it in the car.

8 Lighting campfires is only allowed on certain sites and then only in special locations on the site. Find out in advance what is allowed and what is not.

9 Select a flat site that is at least 6m (20ft) away from the next tent.

10 Don't camp under trees – they drip long after the rain has stopped, drop sap, bird droppings and are a lightning risk. In very hot climates they can provide shade.

TOP LITTLE THINGS FOR FESTIVALS

1 Loo paper
2 Wet wipes
3 Hand sanitizer
4 Suntan lotion
5 Wet-weather gear
6 Battery lantern
7 Food & drink (lots)
8 First-aid kit
9 Insect repellant
10 Hat

CAMPSITE HEALTH HAZARDS

1 Don't leave a campfire unattended and put it out completely before you leave it. Keep a bucket of water and shovel near your campfire.

2 Build or use a campfire pit away from overhanging tree branches.

3 Check for potential hazards before you set up camp – such as poison ivy, bees, ants, sharp objects, nettles and snakes.

4 **Teach your kids to recognize landmarks** and not to get lost.

5 **If kids do get lost,** teach them to remain where they are and blow whistles.

6 **Don't drink water from streams and rivers –** you don't know whether there's a dead sheep lying in it upstream.

7 **Tell kids not to go near wild animals** and never feed them.

8 **Take a fully stocked first-aid kit.**

9 **Don't cook inside your tent –** there's a danger of fire and carbon monoxide poisoning.

10 **Don't use naked flames inside a tent** – candles and lighters. And don't smoke in your tent.

CONSIDER A <u>VOLUNTEERING</u> BREAK

1 **Think about your motivation –** ask yourself why you want to volunteer and if you can't answer, reconsider.

2 **How much time can you give?**

3 **Think about what skills and experience** you have to offer.

4 **Research reputable companies –** speak to them in person if you can and ask as many searching questions as you can think of.

5 **If you're not quite sure what you want** – don't fall victim to companies who want you to give them a deposit fast.

6 **Speak to former volunteers before you depart.** Good recommendations from people you trust are all you need.

7 **Learning the local language** will help you get the most out of your experience.

8 **Be realistic** about what you can achieve in the time you have available.

9 **Find out whatever you can about your host country –** local culture and history will help you fit in and be useful.

10 **Where does your money actually go?** Make sure that everything seems legit.

DREAM GAP-YEAR JOBS

1 Yacht steward
2 English teacher
3 Ski instructor
4 Game research worker
5 Travel writer
6 Wind-surfing instructor
7 Bartender
8 Tour driver
9 Movie extra
10 Swimming instructor

GREAT GAP-YEAR TRAVEL TIPS

1 **Buy a good guidebook and read it** cover to cover before you go. It will give you a real head start in terms of settling in and you'll be less likely to cause offence or break local laws.

2 **Do you need any vaccinations?** Go to your doctor or travel clinic at least six weeks beforehand.

3 **Is your passport up to date?** It must be valid for six months after your return and not be too battered and bruised.

4 **Check whether you need any visas.**

5 **Take enough money** and/or make sure you will be able to access money.

6 **Create a realistic budget –** and stick to it (barring disasters, of course).

7 **Set up a secure email account** and make an effort to keep in touch with those left behind. They may be a little anxious about your travels. Put their minds at rest.

8 **Don't go mad on your mobile phone** – some places carry heavy charges.

9 **Give your friends and family all your contact details** plus your itinerary and flight information.

10 **Book a flexible air ticket** – this will give you scope to leave and arrive when you choose.

SAFE GAP-YEAR TRAVEL

1 **Read up on the customs** and cultural norms of the places you are visiting. Misunderstandings wil be less likely.

2 **Look after your important documents.** Make copies and keep them separate from the originals. Leave a copy at home.

3 **Split up your money** and don't carry more than you need to at once.

4 **Use the buddy system** and don't travel alone – especially at night.

5 **Be alert and be on your guard,** but without being unfriendly.

6 **Don't drink too much** – you become more vulnerable to ne'er-do-wells.

7 **Keep your eye on your belongings** at all times – even if it means taking large bags into toilets.

8 **Use lockers** for your valuables.

9 **Leave your valuables at the hostel front desk** to keep in the safe (don't forget to get a receipt).

10 **Be careful** who you trust and exercise caution before leaving your valuables in someone else's charge.

CHOOSE A BACKPACK

1 **Buy a backpack** that's proportional to your body and which can hold about 9kg (20lb) weight.

2 **The fabric should be semi-waterproof** – add a tarp in a downpour. If it gets wet, dry it out so that it doesn't get musty.

3 **Front-panel loading is a boon.** It allows you to rummage without having to take everything out. Repacking is much quicker. This is especially important if you have a large pack.

4 **Make sure each compartment** has two zippers so that you can lock them together.

5 **Multiple compartments are a must.**

6 **The backpack should have an internal frame** – the rods won't get caught up and the bag will be slimmer and lighter.

7 **You'll need a padded hip belt** to support the weight of the backpack – one that you can tighten or loosen.

8 **Padded shoulder straps** will take the pressure off your lower back.

9 **A chest strap** distributes the weight evenly across your upper body and takes the pressure off your shoulders.

10 **A contoured padded back** spreads the weight of the pack more evenly and makes everything more comfortable.

PACK A BACKPACK

1 **Pack all those things** you will only need occasionally right at the bottom.

2 **Put your sleeping bag in next** or tie it underneath the pack.

3 **Place all the heaviest items** on top of the sleeping bag – but make sure that they don't stick into your back.

4 **Keep your water bottle separate** – most backpacks have a separate place for this – for easy access.

5 **Clear plastic bags are a good idea** – separate different types of clothes this way. It helps you keep track of everything. Ziplock plastic bags are good for toiletries so that they don't leak onto your clothes.

6 **Distribute the weight evenly** from side to side of the pack.

7 **Fill the pack up** with the rest of your clothes – with the heaviest things near the top, next to your back, going lighter towards the outer edges.

8 **Take full advantage of the space** by packing smaller items inside other things. Put socks and underwear inside shoes.

9 **Use all the pockets** and put everything back in the same place each time – that way you'll know where everything is.

10 **Don't take 'just in case' items** – you probably won't need them and they just take up valuable space. Think streamlined!

BEST PLACES FOR BACKPACKERS

1 **Take a trekking trip to Patagonia** to see the jaw-dropping glaciers.

2 **Kazbegi, Georgia, is off the beaten track.** It's cheap, the people are wonderful, and it has glaciers, gorges and mountain villages – accessible yet unspoiled.

3 **In Ho Chi Minh City, Vietnam,** a city of nine million souls, the culture and the people will keep you fully occupied – no need to visit special attractions.

4 **Guatemala offers all the amenities a backpacker could want.** Trek up a volcano, take in breathtaking cultural sites or just relax with a beer.

5 **Honduras is a stunning destination.** Idyllic beaches and the hidden wonder of La Mosquitia, a huge expanse of jungle. Travel is only possible in Cayucos on the rivers, and just to arrive requires a biplane landing on a grass strip.

6 **New Zealand is a dream.** It combines stunning scenery with adrenaline-pumping activities, which will keep the pickiest of backpackers happy. It also has a good selection of big cities, providing you with some respite from all the bungees and skydives – if they get too much.

7 **India is a rich stomping ground for backpackers.** Wonders of the world, exotic beaches and desert landscapes are just the start. You'll be hard pushed to find a country which provides so much to see and do. And that's not counting the food!

8 **Turkey has an incredible history** and a never-ending list of things to fascinate the discerning backpacker. Fly high in a hot-air balloon over Cappadocia, visit the stunning ruins of Ephesus or explore the wonders of Istanbul. Throw in some beautiful beach getaways and the barren mountains of

Anatolia and you've got yourself a great backpacking destination.

9 Morocco is a stunning country with a rich culture. Flowing deserts, snow-capped mountains or beaches and great surf; it's got everything a backpacker could possibly want. Start off by trekking in the High Atlas mountains, visit the quiet beach town of Taghazoute and go on a long trip into the Sahara and Erg Chebbi.

10 Take a backpacking break on Koh Lipe, Thailand, for a glorious beach experience. The island is only accessible by boat, so you can avoid the crowds.

ALL ABOUT INTERRAILING

1 Look at train schedules and timetables on the internet – you can plan your trips all over the world from your armchair.

2 Use night trains so that you don't have to spend extra on accommodation.

3 Don't take unnecessary clothes – wash them. You'll have to carry everything.

4 Make your reservations a day or two in advance to travel in popular countries. When you arrive in the city, make your departure arrangements straight away.

5 Choose travel companions carefully – you'll be spending a lot of time with them.

6 Book your accommodation in advance.

That way you won't arrive without anywhere to lay your head.

7 Use a money belt for all your valuables and wear it under your clothes. Don't wave wads of notes around.

8 Take a small sleeping bag – you can use it as a pillow on trains.

9 Wet wipes are a boon – you'll find showers in short supply on trains. Be sure to carry a bottle of hand sanitiser, too.

10 Save a travel day by going at night – on the first day leave after 7pm and arrive after 4am – then only the day of arrival will count on your travel pass.

TOP TEN INTERRAIL DESTINATIONS
1 Rome
2 London
3 Paris
4 Geiranger (fjord)
5 Istanbul
6 Lake Bled
7 Santorini
8 Venice
9 Lisbon
10 Budapest

EARN WHILE YOU TRAVEL

1 Write for online travel magazines.

2 Start a travel blog – even though you may not make money straight away. Once you build up some traffic you can get advertisers to place ads with you.

3 Take travel photographs and sell them to publications or put them on stock photography websites.

4 Bars and restaurants are often looking for temporary help.

5 Cruise ships need staff of all kinds.

6 Follow the ski season and get to clean and cook in ski chalets.

7 Teach English as a second language all around the world.

8 Fruit-picking is seasonal and fun – you meet lots of people, too.

9 Woofing is a great volunteer scheme whereby you can go and work on organic farms in return for keep.

10 Hostel work may provide a live-in job to tide you over.

FOOD & DRINK

For some, food and drink is simply fuel; for others it's artistic fantasy. But for all of us it is a source of health and happiness. After all, we are what we eat. Here you'll find ideas on foods from asparagus to zucchini, with tips on round-the-world cuisines, feeding the family, entertaining with style or simply perfecting your pancakes.

BE A REALLY GOOD COOK

1 Be prepared – it's the basis of everything you cook. Not even the most expert of chefs can create something out of nothing, so make sure your store cupboard is always well stocked with basic ingredients such as pasta, beans, flour, sugar and all the staples. Keep a running list of what you need and, if you're going to cook a special recipe, check what's in your larder before heading for the shops.

2 Know your hygiene. Washing hands properly is a number-one priority, but it's also important to keep appliances and surfaces squeaky clean, and to know how to store things so they don't develop bacteria and go off, or worse, make you ill.

3 The building blocks of cooking are not difficult to learn. If you can read you can cook – certainly to an adequate level. They say the first time you cook a dish is always the best – because you have really paid close attention to the recipe, measured ingredients carefully and followed the exact method. Don't start experimenting until you've got a little experience.

4 Great cooks learn all the time. Recipe books have so much information in them – you can read them like novels and they'll teach you a lot.

5 Experiment if you're feeling confident. If you have a good repertoire of dishes but want some extra excitement, adapt them, add new ingredients or alter the method. Try new recipes – maybe set yourself a chall-enge of cooking one new dish each week. Invite friends round to enjoy the occasion. You could even take some cookery lessons to develop your skills.

6 Make the most of every morsel. Don't throw away leftovers, but store them carefully and use them as the basis for another meal. If you have a glut of fruit, make jam. If someone gives you a load of onions, make chutney. Wasting food is a terrible shame. Develop your cooking skills – you'll never waste food again.

7 Plan ahead. A shopping list, a menu-planner, maybe a computerized reminder – whatever suits you best. But planning is a cook's best friend and, although it takes a little time in the short term, it will save you plenty long term.

8 Buy the very best ingredients you can afford. They always taste much better. And although they will cost more they may be better value. When the flavour is stronger, for example, you may find that you can use a smaller quantity. If you can't always afford premium foods, learn techniques to get the most out of them, such as marinating.

9 Eat food in season. It's nutritionally better and, if you avoid eating food that's been flown thousands of miles, it's good for the planet, too. Support your local farmers' market and buy great, seasonal produce – you'll be able to find out exactly where it's come from. Organic food is highly recommended, too.

10 Try to make as many meals as you can from scratch. That can be a bit of a mission, but if you perfect a few simple recipes that your family enjoys you'll all feel better for it. There's nothing like the satisfaction gained from sitting around the table and eating something you've made yourself – cooking is creative!

ESSENTIAL KITCHEN KIT

1 Sharp knives
2 Whisk
3 Good pans
4 Mixing bowl/ spoon
5 Rubber spatula
6 Chopping board
7 Measuring jug
8 Scales
9 Peeler
10 Colander/sieve

KEEP IT SAFE!

1 Wash your hands thoroughly before preparing food. Appoximately half of food-related illnesses are the result of not washing your hands properly.

2 Don't leave food uncovered.

3 Store raw and cooked foods separately. Some raw foods may contain bacteria that can make you ill.

4 Read through all the cooking instructions carefully. Food must be cooked for the right length of time, at the right temperature, to kill germs.

5 Always store food at the appropriate temperature.

6 Be sure to wash fruit, vegetables and salad leaves thoroughly.

7 Check that cooked food that has been stored is still fresh. If in doubt, throw it out. Don't keep rice for more than a day or two in the fridge.

8 Use different chopping boards for raw and cooked foods, or wash them thoroughly between uses.

9 Use clean water for cooking food.

10 Check the labels on fruit and veg. Unless it is labelled 'ready to eat', wash thoroughly by submerging in a bowl of water and scrubbing, or peel.

MAKE THE MOST OF YOUR FRIDGE

1 Keep it full. Your fridge will have to work less hard with lots of cold stuff inside. If you don't keep much in it, add full bottles of water (or perhaps white wine!).

2 Minimize time with the door open.

3 Defrost food in the fridge. It keeps it colder and reduces energy consumption.

4 Buy a new fridge! Older models use four times as much energy as newer ones.

5 Vacuum the hard-to-get-to coils behind the fridge – if you can get at them. Too much dust on them reduces efficiency.

6 Keep all dairy on one shelf, and all condiments together, with labels showing.

7 Your salads should go in the bottom drawers to keep them crisper.

8 Store all drinks, milk and juice in the door, as they're the most frequently used.

9 Most hard cheeses are best kept on the top shelf of the door. Wrapping it in film can make it go mouldy.

10 Don't try to refrigerate tomatoes/ avocadoes/bananas. Tomatoes and avocadoes won't ripen and bananas go black.

FOOLPROOF FREEZING

1 Begin with good-quality food. Freezing can retain quality, but not improve it.

2 Freeze food as fast as you can. Use the fast-freeze facility if you have one.

3 Many vegetables need to be blanched (plunged in boiling water and then put in iced water), to prevent enzymes reacting with the freezing process – this causes them to lose colour and flavour.

4 **Don't freeze large quantities of food all at once –** it will slow down the freezing process and lose quality.

5 **Prevent air getting in and moisture escaping** by sealing food in plastic containers or film.

6 **Undercook the food slightly before you freeze it** to avoid over-cooking when it is reheated.

7 **Label food so you know what it is,** and date it so you know when you have to take it out of the freezer.

8 **Freeze fruit and veg at their freshest possible.** Clean them well first and cut into bite-sized portions.

9 **Cut fruit into bite-sized portions** and cover with a mixture of ascorbic acid and sugar syrup to prevent browning.

10 **Remove food from the freezer before it has been in there too long.** Follow recommendations on the packaging.

COOL FOOD STORAGE

1 **Turn it down.** Check that your fridge is below five degrees centigrade

2 **Keep your food cool.** When preparing ingredients, take them out of the fridge at the last possible minute. Don't leave them sitting around.

3 **Cool leftovers rapidly –** don't leave them standing for more than 90 minutes.

4 **Make sure food is cool before putting it in the fridge,** or you'll raise the temperature inside.

4 **Never put open cans in the fridge.** The metal may transfer to the contents.

5 **Clean your fridge regularly.**

6 **Always cover food or wrap it in film.**

7 **Store raw meat or poultry** in clean, sealed containers on the bottom shelf of the fridge so they can't drip onto, or touch, other foods.

8 **Keep cooked meat away from raw.**

9 **Don't eat food that's gone past its 'use-by' date.**

10 **Food past its 'best-before' date is safe to eat,** but may not taste as good.

GADGETS FOR THE
EXPERIMENTAL COOK
1 Sous vide
2 Blow torch
3 Smoke cooker
4 Whipper
5 Antigriddle
6 Evaporator
7 Smart scales
8 Spherification kit
9 Gastrovac
10 Molecular gastronomy kit

PICKING PERFECT POTS & PANS

1 **First, what type of cooker have you got?** If yours is a halogen hob or a solid-fuel cooker, use pans with thick bases to withstand high temperatures. Avoid pans with shiny bases if yours is a halogen hob.

2 **If you have an induction hob,** it won't work with pans made of aluminium or copper. Go for cast iron or stainless steel.

3 **What will you be cooking?** Pasta for a large family or tins of soup for one? Match the sizes of your pans to your ambitions.

4 **Cooking long and slow?** Cast-iron pans retain heat well so are good for stews, for example. But they're heavy; even heavier once full of food. Make sure you can pick them up without too much difficulty.

5 **Copper pans are preferred by the pros** because they heat up and cool down so quickly. But they're pricey, and you have to take care cleaning them. If you prefer a more leisurely cooking style, choose stainless steel instead.

6 **If you don't want to spend hours** over the washing up, check that your pans will be dishwasher-friendly.

7 **For stainless steel,** quality is 18/10 (18% chromium, 10% nickel).

8 **How do your pans feel?** Are the handles comfortable? If they're riveted on they'll be extra strong. Check they'll remain cool even if the pan is hot.

9 **Do you want pans that can go in the oven** as well as on the hob? Check for size and whether the materials are suitable.

10 **Lids should fit snugly** but be easy to take on and off. Glass lids are a convenient choice, enabling you to see what's going on inside without taking it off.

GADGETS FOR THE KEEN COOK

1 Food processor
2 Pasta-maker
3 Ice-cream maker
4 Spice-grinder
5 Deep-fryer
6 Bain-marie
7 Bread-maker
8 Wok
9 Steamer
10 Griddle

COOKWARE CARE

1 **Never put an empty pan** on a hot burner or in a hot oven.

2 **Don't pour cold water into a heated pan.** Leave it to cool before washing.

3 **Don't scour away at stuck-on foods** – leave the pan to soak in soapy water before you wash it.

4 **Is your pan a non-stick version?** Then avoid metal utensils, scouring pads and any abrasive cleaners.

5 **Make sure that your pan is at least the same size as the heating area.** If it's smaller the handle could get burned.

6 **Cooking with high heats can damage** non-stick surfaces.

7 **Pans should be completely dry** before being put away.

8 **Stack pans carefully** so you don't dent them by accident.

9 **Never turn the gas up so high that it laps up the sides of your pan.** It may cause damage to the outside of the pan.

10 **Once you've washed and dried a non-stick pan,** condition it by wiping a little cooking oil over it with kitchen paper. It helps prolong the life of the coating.

AS SHARP AS A KNIFE

1 **Avoid cheap, one-piece stainless steel knives** that may not sharpen properly. For better quality, look for tempered stainless steel with a high carbon content.

2 **Carbon steel knives are cheaper than stainless** and sharpen really well, though acid foods may corrode/stain them. To prevent this happening, use a thin coating of vegetable oil applied to the blade.

3 **Always try to buy a knife** with a tang that extends to the end of the handle and is securely fixed with rivets.

4 **A knife's weight should be evenly distributed** along the blade and handle.

5 **Some top-of-the-range knives have a hollow handle** that's integral to the blade.

They're made from stainless steel with molybdenum and vanadium added for extra strength and corrosion resistance.

6 Keep blades sharp by sharpening them a little and often. Choose a steel that suits your knives.

7 Be sure to always chop on a wooden or polyethylene board. Never cut plastic with a knife unless you want to blunt it.

8 Don't put knives in the dishwasher – it blunts them.

9 A hand-held steel is ideal for sharpening. Beware cheap sharpeners that can wear down the blade quickly.

10 Store all your knives in a block, magnetic wall rack or even a canvas knife holder. Don't let them knock around in a drawer with every-thing else.

CUT CLEVERLY

1 For vegetables, use an all-purpose cook's knife with a deep, curved blade tapering to a tip and a handle that curves at the end to prevent it slipping out of your hand.

2 Use a cleaver for tough jobs such as chopping through bones or when you are preparing meat, fish, herbs and vegetables for Oriental dishes. Treat with caution.

3 For peeling and scraping, choose a light knife with a comfortable handle and short blade – an extension of your hand.

4 The best thing for sliced bread is a straight, firm knife with a long, serrated edge that will cut easily through a crust.

5 A knife with a long, thin blade is best for cold meats.

6 For oranges and lemons (and tomatoes and cucumbers, too), a small, serrated, stainless-steel blade is ideal.

7 A mezzaluna has a crescent-shaped blade. Rock it over herbs, strips of meat, garlic and vegetables to mince them finely.

8 A pizza cutter is more effective for cutting pizza cleanly than any knife is – it's a wheel with a sharp edge.

9 Looking for kitchen scissors? They might be used for anything, so choose serrated blades that cut evenly right down to their tips and a lower handle that has room for three fingers, giving extra power.

10 If you eat a lot of grapefruit, oysters or hard Italian cheese, consider investing in special knives to prepare/eat them.

GET JUICY WITH A JUICER

1 What do you want to juice? There are lots of different types of juicers, and not all of them juice every type of fruit or veg, so check what it's capable of.

2 You really do get what you pay for. The juicers that can cope with anything are the most expensive. But if you only want to juice a couple of oranges every morning, save money by just buying a manual citrus juicer.

3 How noisy is the juicer? All juicers are noisy, but some are worse than others.

4 The motor power is important for quick and effective juicing. Try for one that has at least a 250-watt motor .

5 Is it easy to use and clean? Some are complicated to take apart and will put you off the whole idea of juicing.

6 If you choose a less well-known brand it may be difficult to get hold of accessories or spare parts.

7 Is the juicer durable? Look for a good warranty – it says that the manufacturers have confidence in their product.

8 Is it nice enough to keep out on the counter? It may be a nuisance to put your juicer away, so get a good-looking model.

9 Decide between a basic model that will cost you less, or one that has lots of extra features, from variable pulp control to a place in which to store the plug cord.

10 If you choose a model with a small feed tube, you'll have to cut up your fruit and veg before you can fit them in.

INVEST IN A NEW DISHWASHER

1 How much crockery will you need to wash at one time? Check the dishwasher's capacity (the number of place settings it can wash).

2 How many programmes will you use? Quick-wash, economy, half load, delicates?

3 A countdown function is convenient.

4 Find out how noisy the dishwasher is. This can be an issue in an open-plan kitchen.

5 Flexible shelving inside the machine may suit you better than fixed. Look for top racks that fold up or are height-adjustable.

6 Energy-efficient machines often cost more to buy, but should be cheaper to run.

7 Check how much water the dishwasher uses. Modern ones can clean thoroughly on just a few litres.

8 If a full-sized dishwasher won't fit into your kitchen, look out for a slimline or compact model.

9 Where will the machine go? To make plumbing-in easier, put it near the kitchen sink. It also helps if it's close to the cupboards/drawers where you'll be putting away the glasses, cutlery and crockery.

10 Choose an integrated model to blend into your kitchen – concealed behind a door that matches your kitchen units.

SHOP FOR A NEW COOKER

1 How do you like to cook? How often do you cook and for how many people on a regular basis? Serious home chefs will want to combine controllability (gas or induction hob) with oven capacity and versatility.

2 Consider an eye-level oven if bending down is a problem for you.

3 What size is your kitchen? Suit your oven's dimensions to those of the room.

4 If easy cleaning is important, ceramic and induction hobs are best, and pyrolytic ovens are the most efficient.

5 In a compact kitchen, a built-in cooker is an ideal solution for space problems.

6 **If you choose an induction hob** you may need new pans, as they only work with stainless/enamelled steel or cast iron.

7 **If you want to keep your bills down,** choose an energy-efficient model.

8 **Don't pay extra** for fancy oven features you may possibly never use (including rotisseries, pizza stones and auto timers).

9 **Are you concerned about safety?** Look for triple- or quadruple-glazed doors, anti-tip shelves, closed-door grilling, automatic cut-out and a child lock.

10 **Buy a nifty cooker hood** to get rid of cooking smells and moisture.

COOL IT! BUY A NEW FRIDGE

1 **Think about what you need.** Do you need a larder fridge, one with freezer compartment, or a fridge freezer? What sizes would be most useful?

2 **How much space do you have?** In a small kitchen, an under-counter fridge is ideal. If you have a large kitchen then a huge, side-by-side American-style fridge-freezer would be great.

3 **If you'd like your fridge to blend in** with the rest of your kitchen, then choose an 'integrated' model with a front panel that matches your units.

4 **Measure access areas –** will it go into your house? This is especially important if you're considering a very large fridge.

5 **Consider whether you want to pay extra** for special features, such as auto defrost, dynamic cooling system or anti-bacterial surface coatings.

6 **Check the energy efficiency** of your chosen fridge. Buy one that uses less electricity and you'll save money.

7 **Do you want to site your fridge in an out-house?** Check it can cope with the outdoor temperatures.

8 **Fridges need room to breathe!** If you plan to put it under a counter, allow a gap of at least 2.5cm (1in) at the top, back and sides for air to circulate.

9 **Fridge doors are reversible.** It's usually a fairly easy job to swap a door over so you can open it from the other side.

10 **After your fridge has been delivered,** keep it upright and switched off for at least six hours. The gases need to settle.

SUPER COOL: WHAT'S IN A FREEZER?

1 **How much capacity do you need?** Chest freezers are ideal for large households, while upright ones are less spacious but can coordinate with kitchen units. Mini freezers are an option for tight spaces.

2 **Where will it go?** It might be convenient to keep it in a garage or utility room (but check manufacturer's recommendations), or it may be better in the kitchen.

3 **Chest freezers are great for holding lots of stuff,** but you need to be organized about how you store things in them, otherwise you'll spend hours rummaging around to find what you're looking for.

4 To conceal a freezer in your kitchen, consider the integrated option, behind a door that coordinates with your units.

5 Energy efficiency varies – check with the retailer, as an 'eco' fridge will save you money as well as the planet, but the best ones usually cost more to buy.

6 In an upright freezer, bin-style drawers (as opposed to wire ones) help retain the cold inside when you open the door, making them a little more efficient.

7 Go frost-free and you won't have to defrost your freezer. It also means that ice crystals don't form inside your food – tastier and nutritionally better.

8 A thermometer placed on the outside is handy, but not absolutely essential.

9 Your new freezer should be kept up-right and left for six hours (for the gases to settle) before you switch it on.

10 Don't put food into your new freezer until it has reached its optimum temperature. Usually, leaving it overnight is best before you put your food in.

BUY A BLENDER/FOOD PROCESSOR

FOOD PROCESSING FOR PROS

1 Grate cheese
2 Chop herbs
3 Slice vegetables
4 Make bread dough
5 Make cake mix
6 Crush ice
7 Purée veg for soup
8 Make stock
9 Crumb bread
10 Grind coffee beans

1 What do you want to do? Simple, hand-held machines are ideal for quick and easy jobs, while all-in-one food processors suit those with more ambitious ideas.

2 Look at the type of motor: the cheaper the machine, the more basic the motor.

3 Higher wattage is particularly useful if you need your gadget to multi-task.

4 If you're cooking for a family or for parties, you'll need a bigger bowl.

5 If you haven't got much space on your worktop look for pint-sized gadgets.

6 Retro or no? There are lots of gorgeous-looking vintage-style appliances on the market, often in appealing colours. But you may prefer to have a sleek, modern look or something understated that simply blends in with everything else.

7 Hand-mixers are handy to have around. Look for a range of attachments if you desire versatility.

8 If you use a 'stick' blender all the time, why not upgrade to a model that has an automatic sensor that can tell what speed is needed for the job? Gee whizz!

9 If you're buying a gadget with lots of accessories, think about how and where you'll store them. Will they simply languish in the back of a drawer?

10 Buy the basic model first, but choose one that has a choice of accessories so that you can add them later.

HOW ABOUT A HOB?

1 A hob doesn't have to go above an oven. If that's not the best place, put it somewhere else.

2 How wide? If you do a lot of cooking, the bigger the better; if your kitchen's bijoux, opt for a smaller model.

3 The best configuration of hob burners/ zones is to have one large, two medium and then a single one for simmering.

4 **Look at special burners** for fish kettles, deep fryers, woks and more.

5 **If using a gas hob,** automatic ignition makes things easy, while flame-failure cut-out means the gas will turn off if the flame goes out.

6 **Induction hobs are pricier,** but cheaper to run. They heat faster and are easier to control than gas/electric hobs.

7 **If you yearn for versatility,** 'domino' hobs could be just the thing. Small and rectangular, they offer different types of cooking so you can build them up into a cooking 'hub' that suits you.

8 **If you have a regular hob but it's not enough,** add a single domino unit and extend your cooking choices.

9 **Do you love Japanese food?** Consider a teppanyaki hob. You buy a plate to fit over your existing hob, or even have a special teppanyaki hob fitted separately.

10 **With a glass or ceramic hob,** choose light cookware, to avoid scratches.

MARVELLOUS MICROWAVING

1 **What do you want it for?** Basic models will defrost, reheat and cook food, but some are combined with a grill, and even a convection oven for more flexibility.

2 **If you do a lot of freezing,** then make sure your chosen model is really good at defrosting. If you love re-heating, then look for a turbo reheat function.

3 **Want an easy life?** Choose one with automatic timing, sensor cooking, pre-set programmes and self-cleaning liners.

4 **Have you got enough space on your worktop?** If not, consider a built-in micro-wave. But you'll still need a worktop near by for plates and utensils.

5 **If speed is of the essence,** go for a microwave which has the highest wattage available – it will cook your food faster.

6 **Looks aren't everything** – but they are important. Colours and finishes vary: choose a model you'll enjoy having around.

7 **How big is the turntable?** Some dinner plates are too big to fit on a small micro-wave's turntable – watch out!

8 **Capacity counts:** it really varies. So be sure to check out the different sizes.

9 **Height is also important.** Measure the dishes you'd want to put in it and check they'll fit comfortably.

10 **Microwaves need to be installed** with enough space for air to circulate. Take this into account when measuring.

BEST WAYS TO USE A MICROWAVE

1 **Defrosting meat in the micro?** It's all too easy to partially cook it at the same time, so cook it thoroughly straight away on the stove or in the oven.

2 **Is your dish suitable for the micro-wave?** Place a cup full of water and the dish you want to test in the microwave at full power for one minute. The water should get hot while the dish remains cool.

3 Cook veg quickly, with no added fat, by chopping, placing in a safe container and cooking on high for one to two minutes.

4 Cut meat and veg into uniform sizes to ensure they cook evenly.

5 Stir vegetables, stews and casseroles during microwaving, and turn dishes, to avoid cool and hot spots.

6 Remove large bones from meat before microwaving. They can prevent the area around them from cooking at the same time as the rest.

7 Get more juice from a lemon or other citrus fruit by popping in the microwave on full power for 30 seconds.

8 Put a paper towel around sandwiches, sausage rolls, bread and baked goods. It will absorb moisture that would otherwise make them horribly soggy.

9 Put chips on a paper towel and heat briefly to retain more crunch.

10 Make peeling tomatoes, peaches or other fruits easier. Heat for 30 seconds on high and stand for two minutes. The peel will just slip off.

GET ALL STEAMED UP OVER STEAMING

1 Steaming is great if you're on a diet. It will give you the most nutritious, low-fat meals in existence.

2 Seafood is ideal steamed with herbs. But don't put too many in. Mussels are great steamed in a pot with a little wine.

3 If you don't have a specialist steamer you can use a pan with a tightly fitting lid. Even better, cover the pan with a tea towel and then put the lid on top.

4 Vegetables that are ideal for steaming: broccoli, cauliflower and asparagus.

5 Try wrapping vegetables such as courgettes and asparagus with herbs, then steam.

6 Steam en papillote (in parchment) by wrapping tasty parcels of fish plus veg, herbs and spices with a small amount of liquid in a parchment paper parcel. Light, healthy and full of flavour.

7 Use a multi-tiered plastic or bamboo steamer to cook more than one ingredient at the same time.

8 Use a pressure cooker when you want maximum flavour from a variety of ingredients in minimum time. This is especially useful for making stocks.

9 Don't let the water run out in your steamer. Top it up with boiling water.

10 Arrange food with space between so the steam can circulate. Don't steam meat or fish from frozen because cooking times are impossible to gauge.

SLOW DOWN WITH A SLOW COOKER

1 Reduce the amount of liquid in a conventional recipe by up to half when using a slow cooker. It retains the moisture more effectively than normal cooking does.

2 Make sure that you buy roasts or other large cuts of meat to fit in your cooker

or you will have to trim them down a bit.

3 **Root veg (carrots, potatoes and onions) should be placed underneath the meat.** The bottom of the cooker cooks more quickly and the vegetables tend to take a bit longer.

4 **To thicken a sauce,** turn the heat up just before the end of the cooking time.

5 **Colours may fade in slow-cooked food** so garnishes, such as chopped eggs, tomatoes, chives, peppers, cheese, sour cream or yogurt can liven them up.

6 **Don't lift the lid.** It will add at least 20 minutes' cooking time.

7 **When buying a slow cooker,** look for one with a removable liner. They are much easier to clean.

8 **Bring the temperature to 60°C (140°F)** as quickly as possible. Keep it there for the first hour, then turn down to low to ensure the meat is cooked safely.

9 **Only fill the cooker one half to two-thirds full.** The food will not cook properly if it's filled to the brim. However, if it is less than half full it will cook too quickly.

10 **Use cheaper cuts of meat in a slow cooker.** Any tough cuts will be gorgeously tender if they are slow-cooked.

WHAT A CARVE-UP!

1 **A sharp knife is crucial** to cut thinly and safely. You'll also need a large carving fork to hold the joint steady.

2 **Avoid prong holes in your carved meat** – turn the carving fork over and hold the meat with the fork's safety guard rather than the tines.

3 **To create uniform slices,** cut across the grain of the meat.

4 **Want to make carving easier?** Ask your butcher to remove your chicken's wishbone.

5 **Don't use a giant knife** if you're only carving a small joint or chicken.

6 **Carving a ham?** It's a good idea to cut both from the cushion (round) end and the side (perpendicular to the bone), giving you two different cuts of meat: one leaner, the other fatter.

7 **Let the knife do all the work for you.** If it's sharp enough, you won't need to use a hacking action.

8 **Keep a close eye on the point of your knife.** It should be in line with the handle, for even slices.

9 **Watch out if you are carving a joint** on stainless steel or china. These materials may blunt your knife.

10 **Give yourself plenty of elbow room** if you are carving at the table. Make sure all the diners give you a wide berth.

CHOP-CHOP VEGGIES

1 **Always use a sharp knife,** especially on tough root veg. A blunt knife needs more pressure and can slip out of control.

2 **To chop vegetables like a pro,** rest one hand on the back of the blade, at the tip, keeping it in contact with the board, while the other hand rocks the handle up and down, moving the knife across the veg.

3 For rough chopping, raise and lower the whole blade.

4 Cut round vegetables in half lengthwise, then put the flat side down before further cutting, to keep stable.

5 To dice a vegetable into small cubes, first cut it lengthwise into even slices. Bundle them together and cut into sticks. Then cut crosswise into cubes.

6 To slice an onion, use a knife twice as long as the onion. Cut it in half, laying halves cut side down. Cut 15cm (½in) off the root and stem ends. Then peel off the skin. Cut three/four times in each direction.

7 To chop an onion, cut in half, leaving the root on. Peel off the outer skin. Gently slice into the onion, towards the root tip but without cutting through it, four or five times. Repeat in the opposite direction, holding together. Turn and slice across your cuts.

8 To julienne a carrot, slice four sides to create a rectangle. Cut lengthwise into 2.5cm (1in) slices. Stack and again, cut lengthwise into 2.5cm (1in) strips. Voilà.

9 Broccoli can be chopped with a small kitchen knife or even scissors.

10 To get the most flavour from a clove of garlic, simply crush it with the flat side of a knife. Add a little sea salt and, with a rocking motion, slice in one direction, then the opposite, until it is finely minced.

ONIONS WITHOUT TEARS

1 Partially freeze the onion before you start (not too much, though, or it will be impossible to cut).

2 Hold a metal spoon upside down in your mouth.

3 Pop a chunk of white bread into your mouth – then eat it!

4 Chop the onion with the root still on. It prevents it from bleeding.

5 Cut as rapidly as you can.

6 Cut onions under cold, running water (warning: don't cut yourself!).

7 Use a really sharp knife – less juice will be released as you chop.

8 Light a candle to draw the gas from the onion to the flame.

9 Chew gum (in fact, generally breathing through your mouth rather than your nose should help).

10 Wear swimming goggles!

STORING & USING EGGS

1 Store eggs on their side in a container in the coldest part of the fridge – not in the door. The vibration of opening and closing the door thins the white and consequently decreases nutritional value.

2 Put eggs in a sealed container. They're porous and can take on fridge smells.

3 Is the egg fresh? Crack and smell. If it smells bad throw it away. If it doesn't, it's fine. It's as easy as that.

4 **Want to test an egg's freshness without cracking it?** Pop it in a glass of water. If it floats it's too old to use.

5 **Use three- or four-day-old egg whites** to make a better meringue or mousse.

6 **Never buy commercial mayonnaise.** Simply whisk eggs, wine vinegar, lemon and mustard, adding a continuous drizzle of olive oil until the mixture gains the right consistency.

7 **If you separate eggs** you can store yolks and whites in the freezer. Defrost in the fridge before using.

8 **For pancakes, make sure the batter isn't too thin** (think double cream rather than single) and stand for at least 15 minutes before using.

9 **Use a whisked egg** to seal the edges of pastry or glaze all over to make it shiny and crisp.

10 **Don't bin egg shells.** They'll add vitamin C to your compost.

EGG-CELLENT EGGS

1 **Use the freshest possible eggs.**

2 **Before you boil an egg,** carefully puncture one end with a fine, sharp needle. This will stop it from cracking.

3 **To boil an egg** – simmer in a small pan to prevent them moving around too much and cracking.

4 **When frying an egg sunny side up,** spoon the hot oil over the yolk and white to cook the top as evenly as the bottom.

5 **Hard-boiling an egg takes about ten minutes** – but take it out of the pan and immerse it in cold water so that it stops cooking. Otherwise you'll get a dark ring around the yolk.

6 **It's hard to peel a hot hard-boiled fresh egg.** Run under a cold tap first.

7 **The most efficient way to soft-boil an egg** is to simmer for a minute (use a timer), then remove the pan from the heat, cover, and leave for six more minutes.

8 **For a poached egg,** lower a fresh egg carefully into gently simmering water. A vigorous boil will break the egg apart.

9 **When scrambling eggs,** remove the pan from the heat a minute or two before they are ready – they will continue cooking.

10 **The yummiest scrambled eggs** are cooked in lots of butter. The diet will just have to start tomorrow.

PERFECT OMELETTES EVERY TIME

1 **If you don't have an omelette pan,** use a heavy, non-stick frying pan.

2 **Don't use too big a pan** – your omelette will spread too thin.

3 **Cook omelettes in oil or, for the best results, clarified butter.** Ordinary butter will burn at the high temperature needed to brown an omelette but leave the inside slightly runny.

4 **Cook quickly** – slow-cooked omelettes are flat and tough. It's vital to make sure that the oil or butter in your pan is really

hot before you add your beaten eggs.

5 If you like a very light, soufflé-like omelette, whisk the egg whites separately, then fold the yolks into them before you start cooking.

6 To add milk or cream, or not? There are no hard-and-fast rules – it really depends on your taste.

7 A 'naked' omelette is delicious, but how about adding cheese, ham, smoked salmon, chorizo or veggies?

8 Pre-cook any additional ingredients. They won't cook quickly enough in the short time it takes to assemble and cook your omelette.

9 If you are making omelettes for more than one person, it's generally better to cook one at a time rather than making a big one and cutting it up.

10 When you've used your pan, don't wash it, but just wipe clean using kitchen paper instead.

MAKE YOUR OWN PIZZA TOPPINGS

1 Tomatoes
2 Parmesan/ cheddar/ mozzarella/blue cheese
3 Prosciutto/ chorizo/hams or sausage meats
4 Rocket/basil
5 Poached or fried egg
6 Chicken/duck
7 Meatballs
8 Squid
9 Aubergine/ mushrooms/ peppers/onions
10 Almonds/ pistachios

PERFECT PIZZA

1 Home-made dough is much nicer than anything you can buy in the shops. Use ultra-fresh flour and yeast.

2 Sift the flour to get plenty of air into it – to create a lighter, more airy, crust.

3 Add a couple of tablespoons of mashed potato to the dough to increase the pizza dough's elasticity.

4 Knead until the dough is silky and smooth. If you don't knead long enough, your pizza will be flat. Leave to rest and rise for at least half an hour.

5 Use a pizza stone, preheated in the oven, to get a crisp crust.

6 Or start the pizza off on a griddle and transfer to the oven once slightly cooked. This will crisp the underside.

7 Bake at a very high temperature – but remember it will only take a few minutes to cook, especially if it's very thin.

8 Make several batches of dough at once. Store in the fridge for up to a week or the freezer for up to a month.

9 Don't make your toppings too thick, or they won't cook through.

10 Cool the baked pizza on a wire rack for a couple of minutes before you cut it – the crust will stay crisper.

RUSTLE UP ROAST SPUDS

1 Use floury potatoes for preference.

2 Peel thinly and cut the potatoes into equal-sized chunks.

3 Par-boil the potatoes in unsalted water for about eight minutes – they mustn't cook right through. You can tell when the potatoes are ready by scratching the surface with a skewer – if it stays smooth, cook for a little longer.

4 Cool completely. Scratch the surfaces with a fork and season with salt.

5 Try draining the water, leaving the potatoes to dry out for a few minutes, then shake them up and down in the pan (hold the lid on!) to roughen up the edges.

6 **Some people swear by a thin coating of flour or semolina** to crisp the potatoes on the outside.

7 **Pour 0.5cm (¼in) sunflower/groundnut oil into a roasting tin** and heat (oven) until sizzling hot. Use goose fat/duck fat/dripping for fuller flavour.

8 **Place the potatoes** gently in the pan and turn or baste them straight away so they're completely covered in oil.

9 **Roast for 45 minutes,** or until brown and crisp. Turn at least once.

10 **Serve straight away,** sprinkled with a little salt. They'll go soggy if you leave them waiting.

CHEAP AS CHIPS!

1 **Choose the right type of potato.** Maris Piper or King Edwards are ideal.

2 **Use a good-quality potato cutter** or a mandolin. You can choose different widths, from matchsticks to farmhouse.

3 **For the crispiest chips** use groundnut or peanut oil. For flavour, use lard.

4 **A thermometer is crucial –** your oil must be heated to the right temperature. Or use an electric deep-fat fryer.

5 **Simmer the raw chips** in a large pan of salted water for ten minutes. Cool on a cake rack then chill in the fridge.

6 **Never put too many chips** in the oil at one time – it will lower the temperature of the oil and they'll go soggy.

7 **The secret of success is to cook the potatoes twice.** First, for ten minutes at 130°C (266°F), then chill in the fridge.

8 **Do the second fry** for 4–5 minutes at 190°C (375°F) or until crisp and golden – it depends how thick your chips are.

9 **Always drain your chips** on kitchen paper to remove excess oil.

10 **Serve your chips** with plenty of salt and malt vinegar.

OTHER SPUDDY IDEAS

1 **Don't be tempted to eat green potatoes** – they're toxic. But if you find little sprouts on your spuds, cut them off and carry on.

2 **Choose potatoes** according to how you plan to cook them. New or first early varieties (waxy) are good for boiling or salads; winter main-crop potatoes (floury) are better for mashing and roasting.

3 **New potatoes should be used as fresh as possible** for optimum flavour.

4 **Cook potatoes in their skins** for more flavour. Plus, most of the goodness is just under to the skin. If you do decide to peel, take off the minimum amount possible.

5 **To make a nice lightly mashed potato,** whisk egg whites till fairly stiff then fold in. For richness, add whisked egg yolks.

6 **For a quick and tasty baked potato,** first microwave to cook, then crisp in the oven with a little oil and sea salt on the skin. No need to wrap in foil.

7 **When boiling potatoes,** start them off

in cold water and bring to the boil. Don't pour boiling water over them to start with.

8 You can peel potatoes before you need to cook them – keep them covered, in cold water, for up to two hours.

9 Avoid freezing cooked potato dishes.

They get very watery when reheated.

10 Make home-made crisps by slicing raw potatoes very thinly and soaking in cold water to remove starch. Drain and dry, then deep-fry in olive oil till golden. Dry on kitchen paper and serve with salt.

COOK PEAS, BEANS & LENTILS

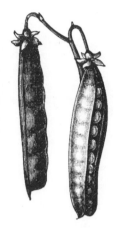

1 Always pick through dried beans and separate out any grit or beans that appear shriveled or discoloured.

2 Cooking dried beans? Soak for at least four hours – or preferably overnight. Or you can boil them for two or three minutes and then just soak for an hour.

3 Once you've soaked, rinse several times and discard the water.

4 Check out the packaging – some beans come pre-soaked.

5 Never cook tinned beans in the liquid from the tin. Rinse the beans several times and then drain them.

6 There is no need to pre-soak dried

black-eyed peas, peas, split peas or lentils.

7 When cooking your pulses, don't add salt until your dried beans, peas or lentils are tender – it will prevent them absorbing water and going soft.

8 Don't add any acidic ingredients, such as wine, vinegar, juice or tomatoes, until the dried peas, beans or lentils are thoroughly cooked.

9 You know they're done when they can easily be mashed with a fork.

10 Cooked dried beans, peas and lentils freeze really well. You need to immerse them in cold water first, then drain them well. Ziplock bags are good for storing.

STORE-CUPBOARD ESSENTIALS

1 Rice
2 Tinned tomatoes
3 Pasta
4 Flour
5 Sugar
6 Tinned tuna
7 Biscuits
8 Soy sauce
9 Dried beans/ pulses
10 Tinned soup

HOW & WHERE TO KEEP VEG

1 Don't keep tomatoes in the fridge – it doesn't do their texture any good.

2 Keep salad vegetables in the bottom drawer of the fridge, which is designed to keep them slightly humid.

3 Store root veg in a cool, dark place. But put them in the fridge once you've cut them up.

4 Strong-smelling vegetables such as onions and leeks are best stored separately from other foods.

5 Take off all tightly wrapped packaging before storing vegetables.

6 Cut the tops off beets, carrots, parsnips and radishes before you store them.

7 Store the following veg in paper or perforated plastic bags: beans, broccoli, cabbage, carrots, cauliflower, cucumber, kohlrabi, lettuce, leafy greens, radishes, scallions and turnips.

8 Vegetables should be stored dry, so it's best not to wash them before you store them. Brush off any excess dirt, though.

9 String peppers together using heavy thread and hang them up to dry.

10 Glut of asparagus? Store in bundles, standing upright in just enough water to keep the stalks moist.

STORE FRUIT PROPERLY

1 Store only good-quality fruit. If it has blemishes or wounds not only will it rot, but it could encourage the rest of your store to go bad, too.

2 Store fruit at temperatures between 3–7°C (37–44°F), ideally in the dark.

3 If you have a lot of fruit to store, crates are ideal, as they allow air to circulate and they can be stacked.

4 Wrapped apples store better for longer. You can use newspaper, tissue paper or pierced polythene bags.

5 Fresh berries can be fragile. Don't pile them up too high.

6 To freeze soft fruit such as raspberries, blueberries, pitted cherries, redcurrants and blackcurrants, arrange on a baking sheet (not touching) and pop in the freezer until hard. Then transfer to freezer bags.

7 Soft fruit such as peaches and nectarines taste best at room temperature. Take out of the fridge a day or so before you plan to eat them.

8 Store all the following fruit at room temperature: bananas, pineapple, pomegranates and watermelon.

9 Pears won't ripen on a tree, but need to be stored cold after picking until they are almost ripe, then ripened at room temperature for three or four days.

10 Want to ripen your fruit faster? Pop it in a paper bag (top folded closed) at room temperature, with a banana or apple inside. Check regularly.

INGREDIENTS TO JAZZ UP A SALAD
1 Croutons
2 Blue cheese
3 Nuts
4 Herbs
5 Chillies
6 Pomegranates
7 Seeds
8 Spices
9 Lardons
10 Anchovies

ZINGY SALAD DRESSINGS

1 Choose olive oil with care. Extra virgin olive oil gives a delicious full flavour; a lighter olive oil or vegetable oil gives a lighter dressing.

2 Cheap balsamic vinegar can be a little bitter. Simply heat it with a little sugar, then cool it and add to your dressing.

3 For a standard vinaigrette, use about three parts of oil to one part of vinegar/lemon juice. Add salt and pepper to taste.

4 Add French or English mustard to a dressing for a bit of tang.

5 Flavoured oils and vinegars make an interesting difference. Try raspberry vinegar or walnut oil, for example.

6 An easy way to mix dressing is to pop it into a jar, screw on the lid and shake.

7 Make a yummy creamy dressing by adding cream, sour cream or mayonnaise and whisking in well. Keep refrigerated.

8 Add fresh herbs to a vinaigrette to impart a variety of flavours. Good ones include mint, coriander, parsley, chives, dill and tarragon.

9 **For extra pizazz** add crushed garlic with sea salt or anchovies (whole or mashed) to your dressing.

10 **Toss the salad** with the dressing lightly but thoroughly – so that all the surfaces are evenly coated.

YUMMY HOME-MADE BREAD

1 **Look for 'strong' flour** – it's the most suitable for home-made bread. It contains gluten that makes your dough elastic.

2 **Sticky dough?** Don't throw flour at it. Just leave it to rest for a bit. It takes time for flour to assimilate the water.

3 **Visit your local supermarket's bakery department** and ask for fresh yeast. Most supermarkets will let you have some at minimal cost.

4 **If you substitute dried or easy-blend yeast for fresh,** use half the quantity.

5 **Make your wholemeal bread delectably light** by adding a crushed tablet of vitamin C to your yeast.

6 **Water is the key to a good dough.** Use the right amount. A mere four tablespoons of water can make the difference between a farmhouse cob and a bap.

7 **When you are making pizza dough for a domestic oven,** add a couple of tablespoons of mashed potato to create a far more chewy, more authentic, texture.

8 **Don't let your head spin** with all the different advice out there. If you're a beginner, choose just one book to follow. If you like the results, stick with it.

9 **Letting a bread dough rise for longer before baking** makes for a lighter, better-quality loaf. If you halve the yeast asked for in a recipe, double the rising time.

10 **Freeze baked bread when it's cool** – it will keep for ages. Slice it beforehand and defrost what you need each day.

STORING & USING CHEESE

1 **Buy little and often.** Cheese goes downhill once you've cut it.

2 **To store cheese,** wrap loosely in waxed paper or foil – film may cause a damp surface to develop.

3 **Soft, fresh cheese should be kept** in the coldest part of the fridge; other cheeses are best in the least-cold part of the fridge, or in a nice cool larder.

4 **Unripe Brie or Camembert?** Leave them still in their packaging, at room temperature, until they are ripe and then refrigerate or else just microwave briefly.

5 **You can freeze** cream cheese, and bags of grated hard cheese.

6 **Chill your cheese** before you grate or slice it to make it easier.

7 **Making a cheese sauce?** Add the cheese at the end of the cooking time and just heat it gently enough to melt it in.

8 **Add your cheese to a sauce before you add the seasoning.** Cheese can be quite salty, so you may not need to season it as much as you think.

9 **Think ahead – if you're going to serve a cheese board,** bring all your cheeses up to room temperature in advance. They'll taste so much better.

10 **How to serve cheese politely.** Don't just cut the tip off the Brie, for example, but make sure each guest has an equal ratio of cheese to rind.

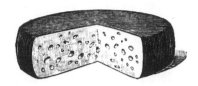

CULTIVATING YOUR OWN YOGURT

1 **However much milk you use** is the amount of yogurt you will make.

2 **For your first batch,** you'll have to buy plain yogurt with active cultures (choose one you like the taste of), or a freeze-dried yogurt starter culture. After that, you can use your own yogurt as a starter.

3 **For low-fat yogurt,** simply use low-fat milk. If you prefer a richer yogurt, mix cream with whole milk.

4 **If you are using non-fat milk,** adding a little non-fat dry milk will help it thicken.

5 **Temperature is crucial.** Heat your milk to 85°C (185°F), then cool to 32–49°C (90–120°F). Buy a good sugar thermometer for this.

6 **Bring your starter to room temperature** before you add it to the milk.

7 **Make yogurt last thing** before you go to bed, so the cultures can work undisturbed overnight. The yogurt needs to be kept still during incubation.

8 **If you haven't got an electric yogurt-maker,** find another way to keep the yogurt at a consistent, warm temperature while it incubates. Try using the pilot light in your gas oven, a rice cooker on a 'warm' setting, a warming tray, a slow cooker on its lowest setting, a large thermos or just wrapping your container in blankets.

9 **Don't make yogurt and bread on the same day.** Sounds crazy, but the yogurt cultures don't like competition from the yeast in the air.

10 **Keep going!** Make a new batch of yogurt every four or five days so the culture stays active. If your starter is too old, it won't work.

MUESLI EMBELLISHMENTS

1 Roasted nuts
2 Fresh/stewed fruit
3 Seeds
4 Maple syrup
5 Yogurt
6 Crème fraîche/ sour cream
7 Dried fruit
8 Chocolate chips
9 Coconut
10 Banana chips

ALL ABOUT CUTS OF MEAT

1 **The tenderest cuts** come from the parts of the animal that have had the least exercise (muscle and connective tissues are the toughest).

2 **Cuts with the bone in** (such as rib, shank and hock) tend to have more flavour. Cuts without the bone may be easier to carve and eat, but they can be dryer and less tasty.

3 **Talking turkey (and chickens)** – the white meat comes from the breast and wings. It has less fat than dark meat from the legs, backs and thighs, so be careful it doesn't dry out when cooking.

4 Beef should be aged from ten to 30 days. The longer it is aged the better (and the more expensive).

5 For the best mid-price steak, try a rib eye. The marbling of fat through the meat keeps it moist and flavourful.

6 To tenderize tough meat, marinate in something acidic – wine, lemon juice, vinegar, yogurt or tomatoes. Add oil for extra succulence.

7 Roast belly of pork and pork shoulder are cheaper than the leaner cuts. Slow-cooked, the fat helps moisturize the meat.

8 If you have opted for a cheaper cut the basic rule is to cook it for longer, in a moist heat. Braising or stewing are the best methods or use a slow cooker.

9 Another trick with a cheaper cut – score the surface of the meat in several directions with a sharp knife, or pound with a rolling pin before adding flavouring.

10 Lamb shoulder is underrated, but it's hard to beat for flavour and tenderness when you braise it gently in the oven for up to seven hours with some vegetables. herbs and stock.

ROAST A CHICKEN

1 Use the best quality, 'happy' chicken you can afford.

2 Take your chicken out of the fridge half an hour before cooking.

3 Placing the chicken breast-side down for the first 15–30 minutes of cooking, then turning it to finish, will make the breast moister.

4 Push herbs or stuffing under the skin (don't break it!) for extra flavour.

5 Baste your chook regularly during cooking with plenty of butter.

6 Pop in a lemon. Puncture a lemon all over with a fork. Microwave for 20 seconds full power, then insert it before roasting.

7 Use a roasting tin with a rack if you want to cook the chicken evenly all over. You can add wine to the bottom of the tin to add some moisture (and it will make a delicious gravy!).

8 Is your chicken fully cooked? Stick a meat thermometer into the thickest part of the thigh – it should read 76°C (170°F).

9 The French chicken known as 'poulet de Bresse' is considered the finest kind for roasting. Go on! Treat yourself.

10 Once the chicken has come out of the oven, cover it up with foil and let it rest for at least 15 minutes before you start carving.

ROAST BEEF, SIR?

1 Best cuts for roasting? Sirloin, rump, top rump and rib. Topside and silverside can also be roasted; they usually come with a layer of fat attached with string to make them even more succulent.

2 Roast with the bone still in: your joints will be sweeter, have more flavour and be more succulent.

3 Bigger is better: use a larger joint, cooked at a higher temperature, so that it browns on the outside but remains pink and juicy within.

4 Try seasoning your joint, rolling in a flour/mustard powder, before browning in a pan with a little oil.

5 You get what you pay for. Properly hung beef is more expensive, but it doesn't shrink. Cheap beef can shrink alarmingly.

6 Joints with a healthy layer of fat are self-basting.

7 It's far better to choose a cheaper cut from a good butcher than a more expensive cut from somewhere that sells lower-quality meat.

8 Leaner cuts, such as topside or silverside, take longer to cook and give you more time for preparing the roast potatoes and all the other tasty trimmings.

9 Lay your roast on a bed of vegetables to cook both at the same time. Add some stock and your beef will be moist and your veg melting and delicious.

10 Let your joint rest for 20 minutes or more before you start carving.

SAUCALICIOUS SAUCES & GRAVIES

1 Avoid lumps in a white sauce by taking your pan off the heat and adding small amounts of liquid – whisk in gradually.

2 To make cheese, mushroom, onion or parsley sauce, add to a basic white sauce.

3 Add spices of your choice for a bit of extra zip. Star anise is great in a beef gravy, for example.

4 Freeze leftover sauce. Re-use or add to another sauce later.

5 To stop a skin forming on your sauce, stir it regularly or cover the surface with buttered, greaseproof paper or tin foil.

6 Make sauce in advance: simply re-heat gently in a bain-marie or microwave.

7 Home-made stock makes for a great-tasting gravy.

8 If your gravy is thin or lacking colour, add yeast-extract paste or red wine.

9 If your gravy is bitter, add a dash of port, sweet sherry, sugar or syrup.

10 To make the best gravy, lift your roast carefully from its pan, add flour to the sediment, heat gently on the hob, add your home-made stock and stir it until it is smooth and delicious.

CHOOSING & STORING FRESH FISH

1 Your best option is to buy fish fresh from the quayside.

2 A really fresh fish is bright and shiny, with firm but springy flesh. Its eyes will be bulging, with black pupils.

3 Take a sniff – a good, fresh fish will smell agreeable. If it smells off, it is.

4 Ask where the fish has come from and how it has been treated.

5 Eat mackerel, herrings and sardines the same day you buy them. If you have to keep them till the next day, freeze them overnight. Other fish can be kept for a night, wrapped in layers of newspaper, in the coldest part of your fridge.

6 **It's hard to freeze fish at home –** domestic freezers can't work fast enough to prevent ice crystals forming, impairing texture and flavour. Better to buy commercially frozen fish.

7 **Sole and other flat fish are better for freezing** than fish with larger flakes of flesh, such as salmon. But don't ever keep fish in your freezer for too long – the less time it's in there, the better it will taste.

8 **Try freezing fish by 'glazing' –** clean and gut, then put it in your freezer on a 'fast freeze' setting. When it's pretty solid, dip it in cold water and put it back in. Leave until a layer of ice has formed all over. Repeat two or three times, so the fish is well coated in ice. Store in a freezer bag.

9 **Try to buy sustainable fish.** It may be labelled or you could ask your supplier.

10 **Defrost frozen fish thoroughly** before you cook it.

PREPARE FISH: A FEW HINTS

1 **No need to scale** if the fish are tiny or you're going to poach them.

2 **To scale a fish** lay it on newspaper, hold it by the tail and scrape towards the head with the blunt edge of a knife. Rinse under running water.

3 **For the juiciest results,** remove the scales but leave the skin on when cooking.

4 **If you're preparing flat fish,** the darker skin on the top side must be removed, but you can leave the white-side skin on.

5 **Never cook a fish with the guts in –** it can taste awful and could make you ill.

6 **When removing a fish head,** cut in a V-shape so as not to waste the thick piece of flesh behind the head.

7 **It's best to gut fish next to the sink.** Lay newspaper on your chopping board and bin it afterwards.

8 **After gutting,** rinse the fish inside and out with cold, running water and put back in the fridge until you need it.

9 **Filleting is easier** if you use a filleting knife, which has a flexible blade.

10 **If you're at all squeamish** ask your fishmonger to do the preparation.

FISH – HOW TO COOK IT

1 **Fish cooked on the bone** has more flavour, but if you can't be bothered with the bones, ask your fishmonger to fillet it.

2 **Marinate fish** in herbs, pepper and olive oil to enhance its natural flavour.

3 **Sprinkle fish with a little sea salt** on both sides and leave for ten to 15 minutes for brilliant flavour and texture.

4 If you plan to pan-grill your fish, dry with kitchen towel before cooking in a ridged pan coated with butter or oil.

5 Fish for kids – best to use cod, salmon or whiting because they have large bones which are easy to see and then remove.

6 Is the fish cooked? It will look opaque. Also, use a fork to prod the fish. If it flakes easily, it's ready to eat.

7 'Cook' very fresh, filleted fish in lime juice. Leave to marinate and eat.

8 The quickest way to cook fish is to microwave it. A salmon fillet could be ready in as little as three or four minutes.

9 Fatter fish (salmon, tuna, swordfish and shark) are ideal for grilling.

10 Steam fish on a bed of seaweed to create extra flavour. Cheap and unusual.

DRESS A COOKED LOBSTER

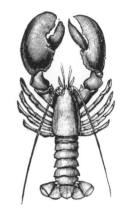

1 Twist off the claws and legs.

2 Use either a nutcracker, small hammer, lobster cracker or back of a heavy knife to carefully crack open the claws and legs.

3 Use a pick or the handle of a teaspoon to remove as much meat as you can.

4 Cutting the lobster in half is best done in two stages. Using a sharp knife, cut through the head from the base of the neck to the eyes. Then cut the tail, from the neck end to the tip of the tail.

5 When you've got two halves, take out any roe and save it for another recipe.

6 Throw away the pale stomach sac, the gills and the intestines.

7 You can either eat the coral and liver, or put them on one side for the fixings of a truly wonderful lobster sauce.

8 Remove the meat from the tail, and scrape out the soft flesh from the shell.

9 Serve with mayonnaise, melted butter or lemon juice.

10 You can use the shells to make some delicious fish stock.

ALL-TIME FAVOURITE: PASTA

1 Select the right pasta shape for the right sauce. Ribbed or folded shapes catch pieces of meat. Flat pasta is better to use with creamy or tomato sauces.

2 Always use plenty of water. Aim for 1 litre (2pt) per 100g (3oz) of pasta.

3 Add salt to your boiling water: it helps the pasta cook evenly and prevents it going slimy. One tablespoon per litre is about right. Most of it stays in the water.

4 Never add oil to your pasta while it's cooking in water. The sauce won't stick when you add it later.

5 The water should be at a rolling boil all the time the pasta's cooking. Best not to put a lid on – the water might boil over.

6 Choose a large pan. The pasta will double in size when cooking and if it's squashed it will be starchy.

7 If you're making a plain pasta dish, such as spaghetti with olive oil and garlic, use a high-quality and/or fresh pasta and

TYPES OF PASTA
1 Fusilli
2 Spaghetti
3 Linguini
4 Pappardelle
5 Lasagne
6 Orecchiette
7 Penne
8 Tagliatelle
9 Ravioli
10 Tortelloni

a really good extra virgin olive oil.

8 Is the pasta cooked? Break open a piece. If it has a white line or dot in the middle it's not ready.

9 If you're not going to add sauce to your pasta immediately, toss the pasta with either butter or oil so it doesn't become a sticky mass.

10 Serve pasta quickly – *presto pronto* – or it will become gluey.

CREATIVE WITH COUSCOUS

1 Couscous isn't particularly flavoursome in itself, but takes other flavours well. Add a teaspoon of ginger, cumin, coriander or chilli pepper for a classic dish.

2 Cook couscous in stock instead of water for extra flavour.

3 Couscous grains are delicate. Steam and fluff; don't boil and stir.

4 Leave the couscous to sit in its cooking liquid until it's completely absorbed. Don't be tempted to stir it.

5 When the couscous is ready, add some butter and fluff with a fork or use your fingers, coated with a little olive oil.

7 One cup of dry couscous will become two-and-a-half cups once cooked.

8 To cook traditional (rather than packet) couscous the authentic way, use a special pan called a couscoussière, or else a colander lined with cheesecloth, suspended over a saucepan containing simmering stock or water.

9 Use couscous as a breakfast or dessert – add sugar or maple syrup, dried fruit, chopped nuts and a pinch of cinnamon.

10 Add cheese: feta, halloumi, Gruyère or Cheddar to your couscous, before mixing with chopped tomatoes and baking.

WHAT TO ADD TO A RISOTTO

1 Peas & mint
2 Mushrooms
3 Asparagus
4 Balsamic vinegar
5 Parmesan
6 Blue cheese & squash
7 Truffle
8 Bolognaise
9 Wine
10 Tomato

WAYS WITH RICE

1 Most rice will need washing before cooking. It will be less sticky if you rinse off the starch on its surface.

2 Steam is the friend of rice. Slightly undercook rice in plenty of boiling water (no salt), then drain, put back in the pot and cover. Let it stand for ten minutes to steam. Finally, fluff gently with a fork.

3 Don't throw out old uncooked rice. It will keep for years. Like a good wine it will develop extra flavours as it ages.

4 Store rice in a cool place.

5 Be sure to soak basmati rice in water before cooking. It keeps its shape better.

6 Use chicken/vegetable stock instead of water to give your rice a lovely flavour.

7 Brown rice needs more water and more cooking time than white. Follow the instructions on the packet, but use a little less water than required. At the end of cooking, leave the rice to steam in its covered pot for 15 minutes.

8 If you slightly undercook basmati or long-grain rice, it will work well stir-fried in vegetable oil with onions, ginger, peppers, ham, prawns and omelette strips.

9 **There are scores of different types of rice.** Choose the right one for the cuisine you're cooking. And be adventurous!

10 **If you have any leftover rice,** make a nice salad by adding sweetcorn, peppers, chillies and olives, and a light dressing.

GO HERBAL

1 **To keep herbs fresh for longer,** snip the stems, rinse and leave in a glass or vase filled with cool water.

2 **Add a stalk of lemon grass** to your fish kettle when cooking whole fish. It gives the fish a wonderful, lemony hint.

3 **Leftover herbs can be chopped** and popped into the freezer in an airtight bag. Use them straight from the freezer to flavour any cooked dish.

4 **Want to freeze herbs?** Blend two cups of herbs with a third of a cup of oil. This will freeze beautifully in an ice-cube tray. Wrap in film to keep airtight.

5 **Preserve herbs** by microwaving between a couple of paper towels for two minutes, in 30-second bursts until the herbs are dry.

6 **Rub fresh/dried herbs into your meat before cooking.** Leave from one hour to overnight. The meat will become tender and gain loads of flavour.

7 **Parsley eats up odours fast.** If you have onion or garlic breath, chew on some. If your hands are oniony, then rub them with parsley.

8 **Dried herbs are stronger than fresh.** If a recipe calls for a tablespoon of fresh herbs, but you only have powdered, use just a quarter teaspoon. But if you have ground herbs, use one teaspoon.

9 **Tarragon, rosemary, basil, thyme and oregano are great** crushed in butter and spread on steaks, chicken, chops or pretty much any meat.

10 **Rosemary is sublime with lamb.** Make slits in the lamb with a knife and bury short lengths of cut rosemary in them, then roast.

HOT, HOT, HOT! COOK WITH CHILLIES

1 **If you want to cool down your recipe slightly,** remove the hottest part of the chilli (the white membrane that holds the seeds) along with the seeds themselves.

2 **If your mouth is on fire from chillies,** never drink water – it reacts with the chemicals in the chillies and makes it worse. Drink milk or eat plain rice instead.

3 **Put in too much chilli?** Add a little sugar and vinegar to tone your dish down.

4 **Try putting chillies and chocolate together – it's a dynamic combo.** Melt a couple of pieces of dark chocolate into chilli con carne for fab depth of flavour.

5 **Try the chilli lottery!** Fry padron peppers in olive oil with a little sea salt. Watch out – one in ten is hot!

6 **In general, red chillies are two or three times hotter** than green and dried chillies are up to ten times hotter than

fresh. Though there are exceptions (but do be careful...).

7 Chilli burn on your hands? Try dabbing with lemon juice, lime juice or vinegar. The acid counteracts the chilli's alkaline.

8 If you'd like an exotic, smoky chilli taste, add a few chipotles, which are fresh jalapeños that have been smoke-dried.

9 For a zappy addition to soups, stews or to splash on a pizza, slice some chillies down their lengths and add to a bottle of olive oil. Leave for a couple of months.

10 Got a cold? Eat a few chillies. They're an excellent source of vitamin C.

SUCCESS WITH SPICES

1 If you want maximum flavour, avoid store-bought, pre-ground spices, but grind your own whole ones just before using.

2 Grind spices with a pestle and mortar, or in an electric coffee mill (but be sure to use a separate one for your coffee!).

3 Store spices in a dry place, out of heat and light, and with their lids tightly on. This means that a rack by the cooker is not a great location.

4 Spices lose their ooomph after six to 12 months. If they've lost their smell, they won't have much flavour, either.

5 Don't be heavy-handed with spices, especially if you're not familiar with them. You can add more, but you can't take away.

6 If you are cooking a dish for a long time, only add the spices an hour or so before you serve up.

7 After measuring dried spices, crush them slightly to release more flavour.

8 Keep it simple. On the whole, use only three or four spices in one dish.

9 Just a tiny hint of star anise imparts amazing flavour to a bolognaise sauce.

10 Use freshly ground black pepper on almost anything. Try it crushed on strawberries and add a splash of balsamic vinegar.

OH LA LA! GARLIC

1 When buying garlic, look for round, fat, hard garlic bulbs with a purple tinge to the skin.

2 Careful how you go: one raw clove of garlic, pressed with the back of a knife, releases more flavour than ten whole cooked cloves.

3 The smaller you dice garlic, the stronger the flavour.

4 Garlic, braised in stock or wine, or baked whole, attains a sweet, mild, nutty flavour. Add to cakes or ice cream and surprise your taste buds.

5 When frying garlic, don't let it brown or burn. It will be bitter and inedible.

6 Remove any small green shoots before chopping, as they are bitter.

7 When sautéing onions and garlic, add the onions first. They take longer to cook and the garlic may quickly burn.

8 For extra zap, rub crushed garlic around your salad bowl, then add salad and toss lightly for a minute or two (with dressing).

9 **New season garlic** makes a nice change from the usual dried and is more subtle in taste. Slice finely into a salad.

10 **Want an amazing gravy?** In a small bowl, blend a tablespoon of roasted garlic with one of butter and mix into the pan juice of any roast.

YUMMY MARINATING

1 **Adding oil to a marinade** locks in the natural flavour of the food and stops it from drying out.

2 **Some good oils for marinating** are corn, canola or peanut oil. Be careful of strongly flavoured oils such as walnut or sesame.

3 **Rub the marinade into meat or poultry** with your hands – it will make the finished dish more tender and flavoursome. Don't do it with fish, though – it's too fragile.

4 **Use a shallow pan or dish,** so all your ingredients are covered evenly.

5 **The more acidic the marinade,** the less time needed.

6 **Never use a metal pan to marinate** for more than two hours. The acid in the marinade may react with the metal to produce unpleasant, or even toxic, flavours.

7 **Re-use leftover marinade?** Always boil it first to eliminate harmful bacteria from raw meat or fish.

8 **Watch your timings.** Don't leave fish for more than an hour, poultry for four hours and meat overnight in the fridge. Vegetables can marinate up to two hours.

9 **If you use a sticky marinade,** such as sweet chilli sauce, reserve some to add in the last few minutes of cooking, to keep that sticky, glossy coating on your food. Don't cook the food on too high a heat, or the sugar in the marinade will burn.

10 **An easy way to cook meat and veg in one go** is to marinate pieces of the same size on a stick, *à la* kebab, and then grill.

SENSATIONAL SOUFFLÉS

1 **Check your recipe and prepare your ingredients** and equipment in advance. It's really best not to be interrupted in the middle of making a soufflé.

2 **Your equipment must be absolutely grease-free** or your egg whites won't rise – meaning your soufflé will collapse.

3 **Separate the eggs when cold,** but let the whites reach room temperature before you start cooking – they'll incorporate more air that way.

4 **Mix a quarter teaspoon of cream of tartar** for every two egg whites to make the egg foam more sturdy.

5 **Use a balloon whisk** to get the most air into your egg whites.

6 **Stop whisking** when your whites just hold a peak when you lift out the whisk. Don't over-mix or your soufflé won't rise.

7 **Brush the inside of the soufflé dishes** with room-temperature butter, and use breadcrumbs, finely grated Parmesan cheese for dusting or (for a sweet soufflé) use cookie crumbs or sugar. This will give the soufflé something to hold on to as it rises.

8 Once your dish is full, run your thumb or a knife around the rim. It will give your risen soufflé that 'top hat' shape.

9 Whatever you do, don't open the oven door. A sudden change of temperature is what makes a soufflé sink.

10 Have your guests waiting at the table so that you can take the soufflé out of the oven and serve it immediately.

FLAKY OR NOT: MAKE THE BEST PASTRY

1 Keep your cool for best results – chill the ingredients and utensils first.

2 Work on a cool surface. Marble is ideal. It's also good if you have cold hands!

3 Work fast – it helps keep the pastry cool, but also stops the gluten developing and making the pastry too elastic or tough.

4 Incorporate as much air as you can. Hold the sieve high above the bowl when sifting flour, and when you rub the mix together lift it above the bowl and let it drop back in.

5 Minimize how much you handle your pastry. It can become greasy. A food processor may help (but don't overdo it).

6 Add water carefully. It's easier to add more than take it away!

7 Add an egg yolk to the water for a richer shortcrust pastry.

8 Once you've made the dough, wrap it in film and chill in the fridge for half an hour to relax the gluten and set the fat.

9 If you want to make pastry in advance, the film-wrapped balls of dough will keep in the fridge for two or three days before you need to roll and cook them.

10 Dust the rolling pin and surface with flour before rolling pastry out – but not too much, or you'll alter the proportions of the recipe.

MELT-IN-THE-MOUTH MERINGUES

1 Try to make meringues on a dry day. If it's humid, meringues can absorb moisture and become limp or sticky.

2 Eggs are easier to separate when cold, but whites should be beaten at room temperature. Separate straight from the fridge, then let your whites stand a while.

3 Don't let even a tiny bit of egg yolk get into your whites – they won't stiffen.

4 For the best volume of beaten egg white, use a metal or glass mixing bowl. It

must be clean, grease-free and dry. Plastic can retain a greasy film, so is best avoided.

5 An electric mixer is easiest, or use a balloon whisk. The beater should be clean and grease-free.

6 When you mix the sugar in, only add about a tablespoon at a time. Too much at once and you risk it not dissolving. Check it by rubbing some foam between your fingers – it should feel smooth.

7 Don't overbeat. Your final meringue mix

should be stiff and glossy, with peaks that have a lovely sheen.

8 **Test your meringue mix is ready** by holding a spoon of it upside down. None should drop off!

9 **Do you want the oven for anything else?** The best meringues are left in the oven once cooked until it has gone cold.

10 **To cut meringue without it crumbling,** use a knife dipped in cold water.

THE CAT GOT THE CREAM

1 **The more you whip cream,** the more air it contains so the more diluted the flavour is. If you want both flavour and light texture, use softly whipped cream.

2 **You can't whip single cream.** But you can whip both double cream and (stating the obvious) whipping cream.

3 **Cream won't whip properly** if it's not cold. Keep it in the fridge until just before you need it. If your room is warm, place your mixing bowl in a bowl of iced water.

4 **If you're whipping cream with an electric whisk,** be careful not to overdo it or you'll end up making butter!

5 **Don't leave whipped cream out** in a warm kitchen – it will become granular and may separate and be ruined.

6 **You can add double cream** to a stock or sauce, but if the base contains wine, reduce it first or the acid may make the cream curdle.

7 **Heat single cream** before adding it to another hot liquid. A difference in temperature can cause it to curdle.

8 **Use half-fat crème fraiche** as a lower-fat alternative to double cream.

9 **Mix ordinary whipping cream with plain yogurt** for a rich-tasting, lower-calorie alternative.

10 **To make your own sour cream,** blend a cup of creamed cottage cheese with a tablespoon of lemon juice and two table-spoons of milk until smooth.

ICE CREAM DREAM

1 **Use the best ingredients that you can afford.** Organic milk, fresh, free-range eggs and high-quality vanilla flavouring will make a tasty difference.

2 **After you've cooked the custard base** (eggs, sugar and milk/cream) leave it to cool before adding flavourings, or they won't be as pronounced.

3 **Chill the custard** until it's as cold as possible before pouring it into your ice-cream maker.

4 **Freeze your ice cream maker's bowl** for a day or so before you make your ice-cream, to ensure it's cold enough. In fact, why not always keep it in your freezer?

5 **Turn on the ice-cream maker's motor** before you actually start pouring in the custard, so that it won't freeze into a solid

GREATEST ICE CREAM FLAVOURS

1 Vanilla
2 Chocolate
3 Mint chocolate chip
4 Strawberry
5 Rum & raisin
6 Praline
7 Pistachio
8 Cherry
9 Lemon meringue
10 Coconut

block the moment it hits the bowl.

6 **Chill any extras** you plan to mix in before adding them, to avoid raising the temperature of the ice cream. Add them right at the last minute of churning – just to distribute them evenly.

7 **To stop your home-made ice cream going hard and icy,** store it in a shallow container rather than a deep dish, and cover the surface with a layer of film or greaseproof paper.

8 **Be sure to go easy on the alcohol –** it freezes at a lower temperature, so adding too much may prevent your ice cream from solidifying.

9 **Always use a container with an air-tight lid –** as ice cream can absorb other aromas in your freezer.

10 **Eat quickly!** Home-made ice creams are best kept for up to a week, but after that they may start to lose their flavour and texture.

BEST-EVER PANCAKES

1 **Don't overbeat your American pancake batter** or you'll have tough pancakes; it's OK to have small lumps in the mix.

2 **A traditional English pancake batter** should be left to stand for at least half an hour before frying. American-style pancakes should be cooked as soon as the batter has been mixed.

3 **How hot should your griddle/pan be?** A drop of water should 'dance' on it.

4 **Use just a small amount of butter** or flavourless oil (or a mix) to lightly grease your griddle or pan.

5 **Use a pan with a heavy bottom –** it will heat more evenly and is less likely to burn your pancake.

6 **Remember – once turned,** the second side cooks more quickly than the first.

7 **If you are making a batch of American-style, small-stack pancakes,** don't be overly generous. If they're fairly small, they are easier to turn.

8 **Want extra-light American pancakes?** Separate your eggs, mix the yolks into the batter and whip the egg whites till stiff. Fold them in just before you cook.

9 **Pancakes are best eaten straight from the pan,** though if you have no choice you can keep them for up to half an hour or so in a warm oven. They'll also freeze well.

10 **Try the following delicious toppings:** lemon and sugar, maple syrup, chopped fruit, whipped cream, chocolate spread, ice cream or anything else you fancy.

EASY FRUITY PUDDINGS

1 Fruit salad
2 Crumble
3 Fruit pie
4 Baked fruit
5 Sorbet
6 Coulis
7 Eton mess
8 Fruit tart
9 Pancakes
10 Fruity kebab

CAN'T-GO-WRONG CRUMBLES

1 **For a great basic crumble topping,** use butter, sugar and flour. Proportions should be roughly 1:1:2, but you can play around.

2 **Replace some of the flour** with chopped hazelnuts, pecans, almonds or walnuts for a pleasantly nutty taste.

3 **For other flavours and textures,** try adding crushed amaretti or ginger biscuits, desiccated coconut or crushed cornflakes.

4 **Make a savoury crumble topping** by substituting grated Parmesan, Cheddar or Stilton, and maybe Cayenne pepper, parsley or mixed herbs instead of sugar.

5 **Try popping the mixed topping** into the freezer for at least ten minutes. This should give it a delicious texture.

6 **If you use a food processor** instead of rubbing the crumble topping by hand, watch out that you don't overdo it and get a cake mix instead of a crumble.

7 **Try brown, demerara or golden caster sugar** for nice crunch and flavour.

8 **Scatter rolled oats or crushed almonds** on top of the crumble for a toasty texture.

9 **Use any type of fresh fruit for the base,** though if you choose apples, soften them first with a little sugar and water.

10 **Don't press the crumble down** when you sprinkle it over the fruit. You could rake it with a fork for great texture, though.

MORE, PLEASE! DELICIOUS COOKIES

1 **Don't be tempted to use up** old flour, baking soda or baking powder. Your cookies simply won't be as delicious.

2 **Don't overwork your dough –** mix it just until the flour disappears, then stop.

3 **Chill your dough** before you try and roll it out – you'll find that it will be much easier to work with.

4 **Use a special cookie scoop** (or an ice-cream scoop) to ensure you put the same amount of mix onto the baking sheet each time. Uniform cookies, ta da!

5 **Your baking sheet should be cold** or at room temperature when you put your cookie dough on it, otherwise the butter in them will melt, affecting both their texture and shape.

6 **Grease the baking sheet** with a little unsalted butter, or else use parchment paper or reusable silicone baking mats.

7 **For chocolate chip cookies,** flour the baking sheet as well as greasing it, so the chocolate doesn't stick and burn. Flouring also prevents any type of cookie from spreading out too thinly.

8 **Allow about 5cm (2in) between each cookie** to allow for spreading.

9 **Pay attention when baking** and check a few minutes before the minimum baking time is up. A minute too much and your sweet treats will be ruined.

10 **Once out of the oven,** use a fish slice or pancake turner to put your cookies on a wire rack. Do this immediately, otherwise they'll carry on cooking in the heat from the baking sheet.

MAKE CAKES LIKE A DOMESTIC GODDESS

1 **Before you start,** make sure your eggs and butter are at room temperature. Pre-heat your oven, too.

2 **Is your butter fresh out of the fridge?** You can speed up softening by slicing or grating it.

IDEAS FOR CAKE FILLINGS/TOPPINGS

1 Whipped cream
2 Butter cream
3 Jam
4 Cream cheese
5 Fresh fruit
6 Custard
7 Ganache
8 Fruit curd
9 Fruit compote
10 Icing

3 Sieve well – it will aerate your flour, giving you a much lighter cake.

4 Always use a metal spoon to fold the dry ingredients into the wet ones.

5 Work quickly once your wet and dry ingredients are mixed.

6 Chocolate cake? Use cocoa powder, not flour, to dust your greased cake tin.

7 A properly cooked cake should shrink from the edges of the tin and spring back slightly when pressed in the centre. Or pierce the cake middle with a fine skewer/toothpick – it should come out clean.

8 Place your cake tins in the centre of the oven. Make sure that they don't touch the sides of the oven or each other.

9 Once you've taken your cake out, leave it to cool for ten or 15 minutes before turning out onto a wire rack.

10 To make layered cakes sit evenly on top of each other, trim as necessary with a serrated knife.

TOTALLY AWESOME BROWNIES

1 Cake-like or fudge-like? The choice is yours. If you like gooey brownies, choose a recipe that calls for melted butter (instead of creamed with sugar) and very little flour.

2 For a fudgy flavour, use brown sugar.

3 Always use a good-quality chocolate. Cheap chocolate tastes – well – cheap.

4 Measure carefully and use the right-size pan. A pan that's too big will make dry bars, while a too-small one may give you undercooked brownies.

5 Use a well-greased, light-coloured, shiny pan. Glass or dark pans may bring about overdone or soggy brownies.

6 Bake in the centre of the oven, where the heat is most even.

7 Better to underbake than overbake. If the edges are slightly springy, whip them out. Gooey centres solidify while cooling.

8 Resist! Leave them in the pan and don't cut them until completely cool.

9 Serve with cream, ice cream, crème fraîche... or just gobble on their own.

10 If by a miracle you don't eat them all at once, you can keep brownies in an airtight container. They'll also freeze.

MAKING JAM & OTHER PRESERVES

1 Making your own jam is an ideal way to use up fruit gluts – though you shouldn't use over-ripe fruit, as it will have no pectin, which is what's needed for the jam to set. Choose strawberries, currants, blackberries, plums, raspberries, apricots and so on that are either just ripe or very slightly under-ripe.

2 Save time and effort by not bothering to stone your fruit first. Obviously, you should check it over (discard any damaged fruit) and wash thoroughly, but when you simmer it with water, the stones will rise to the surface for you to pick out easily.

3 Do you like to put whole strawberries or raspberries in your jam? After hulling and wiping with damp kitchen paper, layer them in your preserving pan with an equal amount of sugar and leave overnight. The sugar coating will draw out their juices and leave the fruit firm enough to stay in one piece when you boil them.

4 To stop the fruit and peel rising to the top of the jar, leave your pan to stand for about 15 minutes after removing it from the heat. It will begin to set, at which point stir the peel/fruit evenly throughout the mixture.

5 Make sure your sterilized jars don't crack when your pour the hot jam into them by warming them in the oven before-hand. About five minutes at 140°C (275°F) should be enough.

6 No sugar thermometer? Here's how to tell if your jam has reached setting point. Chill a saucer in the fridge. When ready to test, take your pan off the heat (you don't want the contents to overcook while you do this!) and spoon a little jam onto the saucer. Pop it back in the fridge. After a few minutes, push your finger across the jam. If the surface wrinkles, it's ready.

7 Not all fruit can set by itself. Some (in particular cherries, elderberries, rhubarb and strawberries) need extra pectin added. You can buy bottled pectin or use 'jam sugar', which is sugar pre-mixed with pectin. Some added lemon juice also helps.

8 While you're cooking the fruit, warm your sugar in the oven before adding it. This will reduce cooking time, so your jam will be a clear colour and fresher in taste.

9 Once your fruit has reached its setting point, skim any scum that has risen to the surface of your mix, using a metal spoon or ladle. Adding a small knob of butter at the same time as the sugar should reduce the amount of scum.

10 Don't be tempted to make too much jam in one batch. It will take forever to reach its setting point, meaning that the fruit will dissolve in the jam and you won't have that lovely, home-made texture. Store your jams in a cool, dry place away from heat and light – bet you'll be wanting to make more again soon!

COOK WITH CHOCOLATE

1 Choose the right chocolate for your recipe: unsweetened (or baking), semi/bittersweet, milk or white. Milk chocolate, though great to eat, is not often used.

2 Store chocolate in a cool, dark and dry place, away from strong aromas.

3 Don't worry if your chocolate develops a white bloom – it will be OK for baking.

4 Always chop chocolate up first, to help it melt more quickly. Chop dark choco-late into nut-sized lumps but chop milk or white chocolate more finely.

5 Never try to mix chocolate with water, as it will become stiff and grainy.

6 If you over-heat chocolate it will burn. Milk and white chocolate burn most easily, so beware.

7 Never try to cook chocolate in a pan

over direct heat. Instead, use a double boiler or cook it in a heatproof bowl suspended over a shallow pan filled with hot (not boiling) water.

8 **Stir regularly** so the chocolate melts evenly and parts of it don't start to burn.

9 **If you accidentally overheat** your chocolate and it starts to look lumpy, quickly add vegetable shortening – a level tablespoon per 170g (6oz) chocolate.

10 **You can actually melt chocolate** in the microwave – gently! Use medium power for a minute, then check. If necessary do a few seconds more, stirring when you check.

COOKING DISASTERS

1 **Burnt sauce or gravy?** Pour it into a clean pan (but without scraping the bottom) and add sugar, a little at a time, to take away the burnt flavour.

2 **Lumpy gravy?** Pass it through a sieve so that the lumps are removed.

3 **Add vodka to an over-peppered dish.**

4 **Added too much salt by mistake?** Peel a potato, cut into medium-sized pieces and add to your pan. When the potato is soft, lift it carefully out. It will have absorbed the saltiness.

5 **If you burn a pot of rice,** place a slice of white bread on top. Leave for five to ten minutes to soak up the flavour. Remove the rice without scraping the bottom.

6 **Put too much spice in?** Add a little honey, to counter-balance the heat.

7 **Add a little olive oil to a dish over-spiced with chillies.**

8 **If your home-made mayonnaise separates,** whisk in a little hot water and it should re-emulsify.

9 **Mushy veg in a casserole?** Stick it in the blender, turn into a soup, buy crusty bread and everyone will love it.

10 **Revive a stale loaf of bread** by wrapping it in a clean, damp cloth for 20 minutes. Remove and warm the loaf in the oven. You'll get that just-baked effect.

EATING FOR ONE

1 **No need to cook from scratch for every meal.** Make two servings and either re-heat leftovers the next day, or be creative and use them as the basis of a different meal.

2 **Buy your fresh fruit and veg in small amounts** to avoid them going off.

3 **Make big casseroles and stews, but freeze in single portions.** When you're ready to eat a helping, defrost and reheat.

4 **A well-stocked store cupboard will help –** cans keep for longer than fresh food if you're not using much at a time.

5 **Freeze sliced bread or rolls** in small portions to use one at a time.

6 **Cook a whole small chicken,** cut off the leftover meat and freeze. Make a stock from the rest, to make a soup or the basis of a risotto.

7 **Just because you are eating alone**

doesn't mean you can't eat healthily – in each meal, try to include ingredients from the main food groups: meats, wholegrains, legumes and veg.

9 **Pre-packaged foods don't always come in small quantities.** Instead use your butcher, fishmonger or deli counter to get a single fillet or a tiny container of olives.

9 **Plan meals in advance** so that if, for example, you need half an avocado for one recipe, you can use the other half the next day in a different dish.

10 **Use a food processor** to turn leftovers into soup.

CHOOSE A CHOOK

1 **Roasting a whole chicken?** Select one that has a rounded, plump breast.

2 **Skins may vary in colour** from cream to yellow, according to how the chicken has been reared, but it should not be grey, patchy or transparent.

3 **If you are buying chicken parts**, make sure they are plump and moist.

4 **Is the breast meat soft to the touch?** Then it should be tender to eat.

5 **Any visible bone ends should be pink**, not grey. The pinker the better.

6 **Never buy a chicken** that is wrapped in damaged packaging.

7 **Frozen chicken should be rock hard,** and have no frozen liquid or ice crystals contained in the package.

8 **Hair and feathers** should have been completely removed. The chicken should look clean and smell fresh.

9 **Read the label carefully:** you might want to opt for a bird that's been organically or humanely reared.

10 **If you are buying chicken on the bone, with its skin,** 0.5kg (1lb) will serve two to three people. The same amount, if it is already boned and skinned, will serve four people.

BUYING MEAT

1 **Meat should feel cold and look firm and silky** while not actually being wet. In a good butcher's, all the cuts should look appetizing.

2 **Rolled joints of meat** should be tied rather than skewered.

3 **Look for neatly chopped bones** and thorough, tidy trimming, with no excess fat left behind.

4 **Beef that looks very pink** won't have been aged and will have much less flavour.

Ideally, beef should be a deep, dark red.

5 **Pork should be firm** and have a greyish pink colour.

6 **Buy meat (especially pork) with some fat on,** as it will enhance flavour and juiciness. You can always discard it after you've cooked it. Fat should be white or creamy, rather than a yellowish hue.

7 **Buy meat with the bone in for fuller flavour.** But if you're buying by weight, remember to allow a little more.

8 **If you're buying lots of food at once,** pick up the meat last, to minimize time spent out of the fridge.

9 **Get to know your butcher –** he/she will be a source of valuable advice and will bone, cut, trim and even stuff, roll and tie joints for you.

10 **Store all meat in the fridge,** loosely wrapped in greaseproof paper, film or foil, at no higher than 5°C (41°F).

SUPERMARKET SHOPPING

1 **Plan your meals** and write a list before you leave home.

2 **Join the loyalty scheme** and get points, discounts, specials or whatever's on offer.

3 **To save money,** look for cheaper brands instead of the household name. They're often just as good.

4 **Giant packs** are often the cheapest, but not always. Take a calculator.

5 **Can't bear to queue?** Pick a quiet time to shop. Many supermarkets are open 24/7 – so avoid the after-work/Saturday crush.

6 **Take strong, reusable shopping bags** along with you. It's the green thing to do.

7 **Don't fill a huge trolley to the brim** if you've got to walk home.

8 **At the checkout,** put heavy things on the conveyor belt first. Then you can pack them in the bottom of your bags.

9 **Get to know one supermarket well.** It's so much faster if you can easily remember where to find everything.

10 **Best not to shop when you're hungry.** You'll only be tempted to buy too much.

SHOP AT A FARMERS' MARKET

1 **Take time to talk to sellers.** They'll be happy to give advice, tips and background information. Perhaps recipes, too.

2 **Remember that food sold at farmers' markets is seasonal.** Get to know what's in season and when in your area and you'll enjoy looking forward to the freshest produce all year round.

3 **Get there first thing in the morning.** The best stuff goes early.

4 **Or shop late.** You might get a good discount just as the market is closing.

5 **Ditch the list.** At a farmers' market not everything is available all the time, so you may need to be flexible.

6 **Experiment.** Now's the chance to try a range of interesting new foods.

7 **Bring cash –** in small denominations, not large notes.

8 **It's worth bringing your own bags.** They probably won't supply them.

9 **Expect a few imperfections.** A bit of mud, some roots, uneven shapes and so on. It's natural, after all.

10 **Don't rush.** Take it slowly and savour the experience.

SHOP FOR FOOD ONLINE

1 **Allow plenty of time** for your first online shop. You'll be setting it all up.

2 **Utilize the special offers page** so that you don't miss out.

3 **Use the opportunity** to get heavy and bulky items delivered without fuss.

4 **Find out what the delivery fees are** – they vary, so shop around.

5 **This is a great chance** to stick to your budget as there's no impulse buying.

6 **Buy healthy foods** – you can take your time to check out the nutritional content of every item.

7 **Research your quantities.** It can be hard to work out weights if you're used to seeing items for real.

8 **If possible, specify your requirements** – many online grocery stores allow you to say how you like fruit, for example.

9 **Make sure you have a reliable internet connection.** There's nothing more frustrating than spending hours on an order and losing it all.

10 **It's not just food.** You can also order flowers, wine, toys and clothes – anything your online supermarket also sells.

CHEAP/FREE FOOD

1 Discounts
2 Buy one, get one free
3 Vouchers
4 No-frills brands
5 Coupons
6 Bulk buys
7 Beyond 'best-befores'
8 Pick your own
9 Grow your own
10 Swap with gardener friends

VEGETABLE BOX SCHEMES

1 **Be prepared to experiment.** You may come across vegetables and fruit that you haven't cooked before.

2 **If you can't use all your vegetables,** make soups/stews and freeze them.

3 **It's best to use the greens and the ripest fruit first,** before they wilt.

4 **Use the internet** to search for ideas and recipes for preparing and cooking unfamiliar fruit and veg.

5 **Be flexible** – you'll need to be able to work around what's delivered.

6 **Store your veg properly.** Supermarket produce may have been treated, but your veg-box produce won't, so may wilt quickly.

7 **Resign yourself to gluts and shortages.** If you get the same veg for several weeks, you'll need to be a more creative cook.

8 **Opt out.** If you don't like something, then ask for it to be left out of your box.

9 **Decide where your box can be left if you'll be out.** Somewhere secure, but also cool and dry. Or you may be able to use a local collection point.

10 **Get what you need.** Play with the box sizes until you get the right one.

PICK-YOUR-OWN FRUIT

1 **Call the farm in advance** to check that the fruit you want are available to pick.

2 **Bring your own containers** for carrying the fruit home – some farms charge.

3 **Wear comfortable old clothes and shoes** that you don't mind getting muddy.

4 Read the farm's rules and regulations, and make sure children know what they can and can't do.

5 Walk carefully along the rows and avoid stepping or kneeling on any plants.

6 Only pick ripe strawberries – they won't ripen further once picked.

7 It's easy to get carried away when you're picking fruit – but there's no point in taking home more than you can realistically use.

8 Once you've filled a container, try not to leave it out in hot sunshine for long – the fruit will deteriorate.

9 Don't overfill containers or try to pack the fruit down – you'll only damage it.

10 Take the following with you: snacks, drinks, sunscreen and floppy hats.

SAVE ENERGY IN THE KITCHEN

1 Put lids on pans while cooking.

2 Choose the right size of pan to match the size of the ring on your hob.

3 Use residual heat to cook for free. Just before cooking is finished, turn the oven or hob off.

4 Pressure cookers and microwaves save on energy.

5 Use less liquid to cook faster and use less energy.

6 Try one-pot cooking instead of turning on lots of burners.

7 It's cheaper to heat things on the hob than in the oven.

8 Search for the highest-rating energy-efficient appliances.

9 Only boil the water you need in your kettle and boil it ahead of time.

10 Only preheat the oven in just enough time for it to be ready for your dish.

BUDGET EVENING MEALS

1 Baked beans on toast
2 Cheese/toast
3 Macaroni cheese
4 Jacket potato
5 Cauliflower cheese
6 Rice stir-fry
7 Noodle soup
8 Sausage & mash
9 Pasta & tomato sauce
10 Pasta & pesto

PLAN FAMILY MEALS

1 Keep a running list of foods that have been used up and that you'll need soon. Put it somewhere handy – a hook on the wall or hung from a fridge magnet.

2 Work around your shopping routine, so if you shop weekly, plan the week's meals around meat/vegetarian alternatives, adding foods from the other groups to create nutritious dishes.

3 Waste not, want not. Devise a menu that makes best use of all your ingredients, especially if they're not things you use regularly: if you need half an aubergine for one recipe, for example, make sure you include another recipe to use the other.

4 Plan for using up leftovers. It can save money and time if you make a little extra, store it in the fridge and reheat it the next day. Or make a lot extra and freeze whatever you don't use immediately.

5 If your family has likes and dislikes, make life easier with the occasional pick 'n' mix supper – a cheese and tomato pizza to which they add their own toppings, a home-made burger with extras, or a plain frittata with options on the side. It should get little ones interested in cooking, too.

6 **Check serving sizes in recipes** so that you buy correct amounts of ingredients and don't cook too much/too little.

7 **Stick to your shopping list and don't buy on impulse.** Little extras add up – especially if they're non-essentials. But if something's on offer, grab it.

8 **If you buy economy sizes,** split them at home into sizes that suit your family, then freeze. Defrost what you need.

9 **Cook a recipe that will make several meals** – a chicken, for example, can be the basis of a roast dinner one day, some slices for sandwiches the next, as well as some tasty morsels for a risotto. Additionally, you can boil the bones for stock to freeze and later make into delicious chicken soup.

10 **If you fancy a break from cooking every now and then,** work takeaways or restaurant meals into your budget, so that they don't come as an added extra.

KIDS IN THE KITCHEN

1 **Choose quick, simple recipes.**

2 **Check you've got all the ingredients before you start.** With young, impatient children, measure everything out and get all your ingredients and utensils ready on the worktop.

3 **Allow plenty of time** – rushing it won't be any fun for anyone.

4 **Expect mess.** It's inevitable and there's no point in getting upset about it.

5 **Tie long hair back,** wash their hands and get them to wear aprons.

6 **Cooking with more than one child?** Be rigorous about taking turns with stirring, measuring, sieving and so on. A kitchen timer may come to your assistance.

7 **Teach children how to use utensils properly** – cutting away from them with knives, for example (but under close supervision, obviously).

8 **Try not to interfere too much** – kids would much rather have messy dollops of dough than have you make perfect shapes on their behalf.

9 **Lavish praise is necessary,** whatever the final dish looks or tastes like!

10 **Encourage them to help clear up.** Good habits start young.

NO-BRAINER BABY FOOD

1 **Choose the freshest fruit and vegetables possible.** Try to use them within a couple of days of purchase.

2 **Good first fruits to try include:** peeled apples, apricots, bananas, pears, plums, blueberries, mangoes, peaches and prunes. First vegetables include: asparagus tips, peas, avocados, carrots, potatoes, sweet peppers, sweet potatoes and squash.

3 **You can use almost anything to mash the food:** a fork, a blender or processor, a grinder, a food mill or a specialist baby food-maker.

4 **Wash fruit and veg thoroughly** and, if

QUICK, EASY SUPPERS

1. Spaghetti, garlic, olive oil
2. Stir-fry
3. Omelette/frittata
4. Chicken nuggets
5. Tuna noodles
6. Grilled lamb chops
7. Pancakes, ham, cheese
8. Ham, egg, chips
9. Hot dogs, buns, mustard
10. Pasta & pesto

necessary, cook until soft, using a little water. Peel, pit and strain seeds.

5. **For meat and poultry,** remove skin and trim fat, cook, then purée with vegetables. Older babies will like meat chopped into small pieces.

6. **If the purée is rather solid,** add a little liquid – breast milk, formula or water.

7. **Add seasonings –** babies like different flavours. No need to sweeten, though. And whatever you do, don't add salt – ever!

8. **Serve baby food at body temperature.** If you heat it in the microwave, stir well to get rid of hot spots and let it sit for a couple of minutes before serving.

9. **Use ice cube trays or baby food trays** to freeze extra portions.

10. **Discard uneaten food.**

USE UP YOUR LEFTOVERS

1. **Store leftovers carefully,** in a clean, lidded container in the fridge or freezer, within two hours of cooking. Eat refrigerated leftovers within two days.

2. **Leftovers can become too dry.** Try adding water, stock, juice or cream.

3. **Reheat leftovers** until they reach 74°C (165°F). Don't use a slow cooker: it may not get them hot enough.

4. **Remember: you should only reheat leftovers once.**

5. **Bread that's not so fresh** is great for bread and butter pudding, or blitz it in the processor to make breadcrumbs.

6. **Use mashed potato** in soups, stews, bread, meatloaf or to make patties (add an egg, shape, then fry). Have a fry-up with leftover cooked veg to make bubble and squeak/colcannon.

7. **Odd fresh vegetables can be turned into a soup.** Sauté until soft in a mix of olive oil and garlic, then purée with stock.

8. **Use the internet –** there are sites into which you can type your leftovers to get a great recipe.

9. **Order too much takeaway?** Leftover Asian dishes can be turned into a noodle meal or omelette filling.

10. **Masses of milk or yogurt?** Whip up some milkshakes or smoothies.

VEGELICIOUS MEALS

1. **A balanced veggie diet includes** plenty of fruit, veg, legumes (beans, peas and lentils) and wholegrains (bread, rice, pasta, corn, millet, barley, bulgar wheat and tortillas).

2. **Tofu is a great meat substitute.** Cook it in a marinade for more flavour.

3. **Add fabulous flavour** with a variety of herbs and spices. Fresh basil, for example, is ideal for pepping up a tomato salad, while dried basil works well in a sauce.

4. **Beans are a brilliant veggie storecupboard essential.** Buy tinned or soak them overnight in a couple of inches of water to reduce cooking time.

5. **Want a quick, delicious veggie meal?**

Stir-fry chopped veg and add nuts, tofu or beans, soy sauce, garlic and ginger.

6 Don't include highly processed vegetarian ingredients/meals. This is because they tend to be high in sodium.

7 If a recipe calls for animal stock or flavouring, add a vegetarian alternative or white wine. Try making your own stock by simmering onions, carrots and celery, with garlic, bay leaves and other spices.

8 Meatless ingredients can stick to pans, so coat pans, dishes and baking sheets with a vegetable cooking spray or olive oil.

9 Mushrooms are a great meat substitute. Use them in omelettes, pizzas, shepherd's pie and burgers.

10 For a rich and satisfying base for a vegetarian meal, cook onions with oil until they are nicely brown, then add a splash of wine or lemon juice and scrape the pan. Then simply mix in all your other ingredients.

GOING VEGAN? NO PROBLEM

1 Base meals around beans, whole grains and fresh vegetables.

2 Craving cheese? Try slices of avocado.

3 Instead of butter, use vegetable oil in general cooking and non-hydrogenated margarine for baking and spreading.

4 Experiment with different brands of vegan milk – they have different flavours.

5 It's hard to replace eggs in baking. Experiment with flax meal, silken tofu, apple sauce or oil plus baking powder.

6 Miss fishy flavours? Add kelp powder.

7 Get your dairy. Calcium is essential. Include tofu, soya milk, leafy vegetables, sesame seeds or sea vegetables daily.

8 Instead of cottage cheese or ricotta, use crumbled tofu.

9 Ensure you are getting iodine (green leafy vegetables/seaweeds), vitamin B12 (fortified foods such as yeast extract, soya milk, breakfast cereal and margarine) and vitamin D (sun exposure/fortified foods such as margarine/soya milk).

10 Vegans also need to make sure they have enough good fats, in the form of omega 3: one heaped tablespoon of ground flaxseed or two of rapeseed oil each day will give you what you need.

SUPER-NUTRITIOUS FOODS/DRINKS

1 Blueberries
2 Salmon
3 Beans
4 Yogurt
5 Broccoli
6 Oats
7 Tomatoes
8 Turkey
9 Spinach
10 Green tea

EASY GLUTEN-FREE EATING

1 Get to know the grains that you can and can't eat. For example, buckwheat is OK, but semolina is not. Print out a list and stick it up in the kitchen.

2 Read product labels carefully; if you are in doubt, contact the manufacturer.

3 Buy another toaster. You can't toast ordinary bread for the kids in it one minute, and your gluten-free bread in it the next.

4 Keep gluten-free ingredients separate from others, in labelled, sealed containers.

5 Ready-made gluten-free products are expensive. Try making your own bread, cakes and other bakery items using gluten-free ingredients, or even get hold of a pre-packaged baking mix.

6 Don't be limited in what you cook. Beg, borrow or steal a good gluten-free cookbook. Go to the library and check out recipes on the internet, too.

7 Clean your worktops and utensils really well to protect yourself against cross-contamination from gluten.

8 Look at your baking containers. Gluten is what makes dough stretchy and helps it rise, so in gluten-free baking it helps to use a baking container with walls, so loafs and rolls can hold their shape. You can also try adding egg instead of water to recipes, and/or a gum such as guar or xantham.

9 Substituting gluten-free flours works best in recipes where there is a less-than-average amount of flour in the first place. Stay away from recipes that call for large quantities of flour – your substitution probably won't work well.

10 Always use a different sieve for gluten-free and standard flours.

LOW-GI FOODS
1 Porridge
2 Pumpernickel
3 Spaghetti
4 Cherries
5 Carrots
6 Yogurt
7 Lentils
8 Sausages
9 Peanuts
10 Milk

LOW-CALORIE BASICS

1 Cut down on fats. Use cooking sprays instead of a knob of butter when you are frying, for example. Liquid oils are better than solid fats.

2 Go for low-fat milk instead of full fat. The same goes for creams and yogurts.

3 Choose lean meats such as round, loin and sirloin.

4 Take the fat and skin off meat before you cook it.

5 If you really must have chips, pop them in a plastic bag with a little olive oil and shake. Bake in the oven.

6 Chuck out the deep-fat fryer and avoid all frying and sautéing completely. Instead, bake, braise, grill, poach, slow-cook, microwave or steam.

7 Step up the veg. They're lower in fat than other foods, so gradually increase them and decrease meats and carbs.

8 Choose strong cheeses – but use less of them. Or use reduced-fat cheese.

9 Love fried chicken and fish? A lower-fat alternative is to coat them in bread-crumbs and bake.

10 Can't resist a cake? Instead of some of the fat, try low-fat butter-milk, plain non-fat yogurt or apple sauce.

SUPERIOR SCHOOL PACKED LUNCHES

1 Packed lunch foods should be easy to open and eat with little fingers.

2 Smaller foods are not only easier to eat, but more interesting for little ones. Cut up sandwiches and fruit, and try out mini tortillas, waffles or buns, for example.

3 Use a cookie cutter to shape bread, sliced cheese, deli meats and so on.

4 Bread gets boring every day. Try bagels, wraps, pitta breads, rice cakes, crackers, croissants, muffins and tortilla.

5 Freeze a carton of juice and include it

in the lunch bag. It will thaw by lunchtime but keep everything else cool all morning.

6 Include some nuts or dried fruit for a delicious and nutritious snack.

7 Put in some finger-sized veg and a dip: sugar snap peas, baby carrots, cherry tomatoes, celery sticks, cucumber chunks and sliced red peppers are all ideal.

8 Tempt your child to eat fruit by making mini kebabs of fruit on a stick.

9 Always pack a drink – water or fresh fruit juice is best.

10 Why not include something fun to put a smile on your child's face? A home-made cookie tied with a ribbon, a note, joke, riddle, photo or a sticker.

PACKED LUNCHES FOR WORK

1 Buy sealable plastic containers that are the right size to transport your meal.

2 Avoid very runny food – it's all too likely to leak over your keyboard.

3 Don't offend your colleagues by eating anything too smelly at your desk.

4 Is there a microwave in your office? If so, why not bring your delicious home-made soups or leftovers from last night?

5 A good sturdy flask is invaluable for transporting home-made soups.

6 Are you taking a salad to work? Pack dressings separately in an old spice jar.

7 Pack bite-sized things that can be eaten with your hands.

8 A fridge at work will help by keeping lunch chilled until it's ready to eat. Otherwise, consider an insulated container.

9 Sandwiches are easy but can get boring. Alternatives? Wraps, flatbreads, crispbreads, rice cakes, flavoured oat cakes or savoury biscuits.

10 Wrap some leftovers in a tortilla for a quick, easy and inexpensive work lunch.

LUXURIOUS WEEKEND BREAKFASTS

1 Go for huevos rancheros – a spicy tomato sauce with peppers and chillies. Chuck the sauce into ramekins, crack an egg into it, then bake – hey presto!

2 The full English is to die for: sausage, bacon, eggs (any which way), mushrooms, fried bread, tomatoes and baked beans.

3 Breakfast burritos – do it your style: eggs, cheese, tomato, chorizo, veggies, rice, whatever – all wrapped in soft tortilla.

4 Home-made waffles are yummy and so much nicer than the shop-bought variety.

5 For a continental breakfast make a spread of fruit, cereals, toast, pastries, sliced meat and cheese.

6 To pep up your home-made granola. Add fresh fruit, natural yogurt and honey.

7 Champagne... with anything.

8 Smoked salmon and scrambled eggs. Need we say more?

9 French toast with roast apples. Add crème anglaise and caramel sauce.

10 Eggs Benedict. Muffin, ham, poached egg and hollandaise sauce. Yum.

SUPER-EASY BREAKFASTS
1 Cereal/muesli
2 Cinnamon toast
3 Bacon/egg
4 French toast
5 Fruit & yogurt
6 Blueberries & porridge
7 Pancakes
8 Ham baps
9 Mushrooms on toast
10 Last night's leftovers

LAY THE TABLE

1 **Lay cutlery so that utensils can be taken from the outside,** moving inwards.

2 **Glasses may either be arranged** in a triangle or a straight line.

3 **The bread plate** goes on the left, with a butter knife laid on top.

4 **At a more formal dinner,** place all the cutlery in a line either side of the plate. If it's less formal (three courses or less) place the dessert spoon and fork above the plate.

5 **Face knife blades** towards the plate.

6 **Forks –** prongs point upwards.

7 **If you need specialist cutlery** such as lobster crackers or escargot holders, bring them to the table with that course.

8 **Place condiments and serving cutlery** in strategic places – there's no set rule.

9 **Generally, bring the plates** (other than side plates) in with each separate course.

10 **A simply folded napkin** (in a rectangle or triangle) can go on the side plate or to the right of the glasses, but a more complex fold should go in the centre of the setting or on the side plate.

EATING ETIQUETTE

1 **Use cutlery, not fingers –** knife (or spoon) and fork, please.

2 **No chewing with your mouth open.** Or talking with your mouth full.

3 **Never put your knife in your mouth.**

4 **Break bread into small pieces** using your fingers, then butter a piece at a time.

5 **Always use your fork** with the tines pointing downwards. It's not a scoop.

6 **When you've finished a course,** leave your cutlery in the bowl/on the plate, together, the tail end(s) to six o'clock.

7 **Place your napkin on your lap** once your host or the guest of honour does. When you've finished, wait for the host to place their napkin on the table, then follow suit with yours, to the left of your plate, with no soiled areas showing.

8 **Don't grip your knife/fork** in a fist.

9 **As a guest,** wait until your host either starts eating, or invites you to do so.

10 **Absolutely no:** elbows on the table, reaching across other people, slurping, burping or picking teeth.

PLAN & SERVE A BUFFET

1 **Offer bite-sized finger or fork foods** that are easy to eat standing up/off a lap.

2 **Choose foods that are best served** at room temperature.

3 **Clear plenty of surfaces.** Where will guests put their glasses or empty plates?

4 **Make sure you can prepare** the whole buffet ahead of time.

5 **Think about where things go** on the table. Arrange a stack of plates at one end, then main dishes, then sides and salads, and utensils and napkins at the other end.

6 Put the buffet table in the middle of the room, if there is space, so guests can access it from both sides.

7 It's best to separate the bar area, so guests don't keep bumping into each other.

8 Don't let hot dishes sit out for more than two hours; an hour if the room is warm. Avoid food poisoning at all costs.

9 Adding height to your buffet table will create visual appeal. Simply hide a small box under the table cloth and pop your serving dish on top of it.

10 You'll need a lot of serving dishes! Have you got enough? Do they match?

STICK IT ON THE BARBIE

1 Remember that your coals must turn white before they are ready to use. Using gas takes away the guesswork.

2 Have snacks to hand while the food is cooking. It may take longer than you think.

3 Marinate your meat in advance – it will have much more flavour.

4 Make sure everything you cook is fully defrosted. Keep raw foods in the fridge until needed and don't leave anything in the sun before/after cooking.

5 Sardine and oily fish cook easily – you don't have to oil the barbecue first, just add a squeeze of lemon and black pepper.

6 Simmer sausages in advance for five minutes in water or stock on the hob. This will ensure they're cooked through before you brown them on the barbecue – no burnt outsides and undercooked insides!

7 Cook chicken gently in the oven in advance. Then brown it off on the barbie with an extra layer of marinade.

8 Soak wooden kebab sticks in cold water for 30 minutes before you need them. Otherwise they'll scorch.

9 Put foods near the hot coals to sear the outside, then move further away to cook thoroughly all the way through.

10 Be safe: wear an apron and gloves, use tools with long, heatproof handles, keep a bottle of water handy to douse flare-ups of flames; never leave a barbecue unattended.

THE PERFECT PICNIC

1 No chairs, no china, no glass. Minimal cutlery. Just a rug, a folding knife and a bottle opener.

2 Don't feel that you have to make everything yourself. Make life straightforward by buying crusty bread, yummy cheeses, pre-sliced ham, a selection of olives and a few gourmet crisps.

3 Make sandwiches once you get there, not in advance – less hassle in the kitchen.

4 Invest in a good (light and easy to carry) cool bag that's the right size for the number in your party. Remember that a full bag will stay colder than a half-empty one.

5 Condiments will be de rigueur. Don't forget to bring salt, pepper and sugar.

6 Don't dress salad in advance – it will go slimy. Instead, take the dressing along with you in a small, screw-top jar.

7 Think simple. Cherry tomatoes, hard-boiled eggs, quiches, pies, sandwiches or rolls. No need to make things stressful.

8 Avoid lugging around heavy crocks and glasses. Take lightweight melamine or disposable paper plates, plastic cutlery and cups instead.

9 Always clear up after yourselves – leaving rubbish lying about is totally unacceptable. Take along an empty plastic bag with you so you can bung it all in.

10 Take insect repellant, sun cream and some damp cloths or wipes.

MUNCHABLE CANAPÉS

DELICIOUS DIPS

1 Houmous
2 Taramasalata
3 Cream cheese & chives
4 Baba ganoush
5 Guacamole
6 Tomato salsa
7 Blue cheese
8 Satay
9 Spanakopita
10 Melted chocolate

1 No bigger than one bite.

2 Choose one main ingredient to be the focus, and make sure the others truly complement it.

3 Use the freshest ingredients.

4 What will be the base of your canapé? It could be toasted bread or a Parmesan crisp, slice of cucumber or a spinach fritter. Or rolled or served in a container.

5 Use utensils such as skewers or shot glasses to hold the canapés.

6 Make your canapés mini – a roast dinner could become a tiny slice of rare beef topped with horseradish; fish and chips could be a goujon of fish with a couple of chunky chips wrapped in a newspaper cone.

7 Don't forget dessert: your guests will love sweet canapés like mini scones with strawberries and cream, mini banoffee pies or tiny doughnuts.

8 Save time by using food that's already bite-sized, such as cherry tomatoes, king prawns, cocktail sausages or strawberries.

9 How many should you serve? Allow 9–12 per head over a two to three-hour drinks reception; 15–18 canapés each if they're replacing a meal.

10 How will you present them? Plates or trays are fine, or you may want to consider something like a slate tile (write the name of the canapés in chalk on the side) or a sheet of clear or coloured acrylic.

PARTY FOOD FOR KIDS

1 What time is the party? If it's between meals, limit the amount of food you offer.

2 For a main meal, allow three or four savoury choices and two or three sweets.

3 It's easier if they can eat with their fingers – sandwiches, cocktail sausages, mini pizzas and chopped-up raw carrots, cucumber and red peppers are perfect.

4 Ask your child what they would like, and take it into account. Healthy food can be off the menu – just for once.

5 Prepare in advance. You'll need your energy for other things on the day.

6 Kids love crisps. If you can't bear the idea, make your own veggie crisps by slicing root vegetables and deep-frying.

7 As a sweet course, how about some iced biscuits? You could make decorating them one of your party activities.

8 Make sure there's plenty to drink. No need for sweet, fizzy stuff (it will make them hyper). Water and squash is fine.

9 You can't beat a traditional jelly and ice cream combo. Add tinned fruit to jelly. Don't forget spoons!

10 Don't try to economize with cheap paper plates and cups. If they're flimsy they'll go soggy and mess will ensue.

DECORATING A CUPCAKE

1 Vanilla frosting
2 Other coloured/ flavoured frosting
3 Sugar flowers
4 Edible shapes
5 Small/chopped candies
6 Cream-cheese icing
7 Candied fruit
8 Edible glitter
9 Sprinkles
10 Chocolate curls

MAKE A CELEBRATION CAKE

1 Practise! Especially if it's an important occasion. Now's not the time to experiment with a new recipe. Try out icing skills first.

2 If it's a fruit cake, make it in advance. At least a month ahead of time is good.

3 Choose quality ingredients – no need to skimp.

4 To make a nice rich fruit cake, soak the dried fruit in brandy beforehand.

5 Want a really moist cake? Before you pop your cake in the oven, pour water into a baking tray and put it on the rack below.

6 Planning a novelty cake? If you want to carve it or add sugar paste, make it a Madeira, which won't crumble once baked.

7 If you freeze your cake first you will find it easier to carve it into shape.

8 If you go wrong when cutting the cake to shape, don't worry – you can slather on butter cream and cover up mistakes.

9 Using sugar paste? It's easier to work with it if you knead it first.

10 Use a rotating stand if you want to ice evenly all around the sides.

A TRADITIONAL CHRISTMAS

1 Plan like a pro. Set a time to eat and then, taking into account the turkey's cooking time, write a schedule of timings.

2 Add on how long it takes for the oven to heat. Allow about 45 minutes for the bird to rest after you've taken it out.

3 Set your phone, alarm clock or kitchen timer to remind you when to do everything.

4 Check you've got a roasting tin big enough for the bird and count up serving dishes and make sure you have enough.

5 Prepare some things the day before. Peel, trim, chop and parboil the vegetables and put in the fridge.

6 Take your turkey out of the refrigerator before you go to bed, so it's at room temperature by morning. Remove string, rubber bands and so on, cover with a clean tea towel and shut the cat away.

7 Lay the table the night before.

8 The secret to a yummy, moist turkey is to baste it regularly.

9 Is your turkey taking up all your oven space? Roast the vegetables for 40 minutes first and pop them back in to finish off while the meat is resting.

10 Accept all offers of assistance. Have a spare vegetable peeler ready to hand.

MARVELLOUS MEXICAN COOKING

1 **Buy avocados a week ahead** so they'll be fully ripe when you need them.

2 **Got some leftover chillies?** Make a slit down one side, remove seeds/membrane, stuff with grated cheddar, dip in egg batter and deep-fry till golden. Wow!

3 **Onions, tomatoes, chillies, coriander and lime are liberally used** to add crunch and a fresh, zesty vibrancy to your dish.

4 **Don't just use minced beef** for a chilli con carne. Try larger cuts, braised slowly.

5 **Use lime or lemon juice freely** to balance richness and spice.

6 **Try oven-roasting tomatoes, chillies, peppers and onions.** It will add a whole new layer of flavour to your recipes.

7 **Try making your own Mexican drinks.** Horchata mixes ground rice with a cinnamon stick, lime zest and sugar.

8 **Don't be scared of buying a big bag of chillies.** They freeze really well.

9 **Kidney beans can be a bit of a bore** – experiment with other types of bean.

10 **For a simple, healthy side dish** buy a tub of low-fat coleslaw. Dice some chillies, a little red pepper and fresh coriander. Mix.

CHINESE FOOD – NOTHING LIKE IT!

1 **Have all your ingredients chopped** and ready for action.

2 **A carbon steel wok** is a must-have.

3 **Prepare your wok before its first use.** Wash in hot water with soapy liquid, rinse, dry. Place on high heat until it smokes, turn the heat to low, add a little oil, cook for ten minutes, scrub with kitchen paper.

4 **For even cooking when stir-frying,** make the ingredients the same size.

5 **Use an oil that can cook at a high temperature without burning** – peanut or canola/rapeseed oils are ideal.

6 **Never overcrowd your wok with meat.** Cook in batches before you add vegetables, then add back when they're done.

7 **For an authentic Chinese taste,** add ginger and garlic to sizzling oil first.

8 **When stir-frying meat,** wait for ten to 20 seconds before moving it at all, so it can brown. But stir vegetables immediately.

9 **When adding sauce to meat or veg,** make a well in the centre. Allow the sauce to cook and thicken, then stir together.

10 **To get the best-cooked vegetables,** cut them on the diagonal.

BOW TO JAPANESE FOOD

1 **To eat a bowl of Japanese rice or soup,** lift the bowl with one hand and sip from it. Use chopsticks to eat the rice or noodles.

2 **Feeling a bit fluey?** Make shogayu to pick you up. Mix two teaspoons of freshly grated ginger and two teaspoons of sugar in a cup, add two-thirds of a cup of hot water, mix well and drink.

3 Add a smear of wasabi paste. Made of horseradish, it is eye-wateringly hot.

4 Try pickled ginger, another Japanese classic, with a bowl of boiled rice.

5 Add ingredients in this order: sugar/alcohol, salt, rice vinegar, soy, miso sauce.

6 Skim off the scum from vegetables or meat if cooking a Japanese broth. It's not good for you and removing it will improve the flavour.

7 Create some subtle Japanese flavours by soaking vegetables in water before use.

8 To cook the tenderest chicken Japanese-style, remove skin, chop it into bite-sized pieces, put in a plastic bag of salt for a few hours. When ready to cook, rinse in cold water, pat dry and fry.

9 Put beef in a plastic bag and hammer with a mallet to break down fibres/sinews. This will give you tender meat for teryaki.

10 Slurp soup and say 'gochisou-sama' when you've finished.

TERRIFIC THAI FOOD

1 Buy fresh. Dried/bottled lemon grass, is not a patch on lemony-fresh stalks.

2 Look in the freezer section of your local Asian store. This is where to find galangal, kaffir lime leaves or pandan.

3 Use palm sugar if a recipe asks for it. It has a deeper, more rounded character.

4 A pestle and mortar is better than a food processor for grinding your fresh spices or for pounding lemon grass or chillies to release their flavours.

5 If your dish isn't salty enough, try adding fish sauce. This way you get greater depth of flavour, plus saltiness.

6 Try using coconut or peanut oil for stir-frying.

7 Making noodles in a soup or stir-fry? But don't overcook them. Make sure they're slightly al dente, then set aside.

8 If you want really good stir-fried rice, cook it and then leave it in the fridge for a day or two until it is fairly dry. When you're ready to fry, stir in some oil and work it gently with your fingers. Ta da! Fluffy rice.

9 Try deep-frying your noodles for an attractive, crispy garnish. Cook in water, drain, dry with kitchen paper, then plunge into fairly hot oil till golden.

10 Give a bowl of rice to each person. They should mix a little of one dish in with their rice, then pass the main dish on, choose another dish, and so on.

SPICE UP YOUR INDIAN COOKING

1 Masala (spice mix) is the key to a great curry. One of the most popular is garam masala (cardamom, cumin seeds, black peppercorns, cloves, nutmeg and cinnamon). Add it at the end of cooking.

2 Make your own curry spice pastes to rub onto meat to form a delicious crust. Blend your choice of ground spices with puréed ginger, garlic or chillies, plus salt and pepper and a little oil.

3 To thicken a curry sauce, use yogurt, spice paste, tomatoes or coconut.

4 Add yogurt carefully when cooking a curry. Take the pan from the heat and add the yogurt one spoon at a time, stirring well, or it will separate.

5 Make your curry at least a few hours and up to three days in advance. Let it cool, place in the fridge and reheat.

6 Curry too hot? Add some potatoes, lentils, coconut milk, yogurt and/or cream.

7 If you come across 'tempering', it means heating spices in hot oil and adding to a dish. Mmmmm, maximum flavour

8 If you've made your own ginger, garlic or chilli paste, it will last longer in the fridge if you add a tablespoon of hot vegetable, canola/sunflower oil.

9 Curry and coriander leaves take centre stage in Indian cooking. Keep them fresh by popping them into an airtight plastic bag in the fridge.

10 Set up your own masala dabba. It's a useful Indian stainless-steel spice box containing separate tins and a spoon for your seven favourite spices.

GO ALL FRENCH

1 Chuck a brie in the oven at 180°C (350°F) for ten minutes. Drizzle with honey and serve with a crusty baguette.

2 If cooking with garlic, never let it brown. It will taste bitter and unpleasant.

3 For a classic French vinaigrette, mix two teaspoons of Dijon mustard, two tablespoons of red wine vinegar and finally six tablespoons of light olive oil.

4 Making a fondue? Use day-old bread, not fresh. It will retain body and crispness.

5 When adding cream, take the pan off the heat so the cream doesn't split.

6 Try roasting vegetables Provençal-style. Put a generous layer of onions, cooked for 20 minutes in a tablespoon of sugar and a little water, into a roasting pan. Lay on top rows of tomatoes, aubergines, courgettes and red peppers. Sprinkle with salt, pepper and rosemary, drizzle with olive oil. Bake.

7 Who can resist a steak frite? Let the pan smoke before adding the meat, flip every 15 seconds until done.

8 Make a superb sauce for lamb. Cover 50 to 60 peeled garlic cloves with sweet white wine. Roast the meat on top.

9 Let your crêpe mix rest for at least half an hour before using.

10 Coq au vin is enhanced by the addition of a side dish of fried bread.

BRILLIANT BRITISH NOSH

1 Don't even think about serving fish and chips without ketchup, salt, vinegar.

2 Why not add some British bitter to make your fish batter extra tasty and crispy?

3 Yorkshire pudding not rising? Sift the flour, make sure the batter mix isn't too thin and heat the oil in the oven until it's really hot before pouring in the mix.

4 After roasting a chicken, add a little flour, cooked apples, cider and cream, to make a delicious, British-style sauce.

5 To ring the changes with classic cauli-flower cheese, add diced, smoked ham to your sauce and chopped parsley, mixed with breadcrumbs on top.

6 Stale white bread in your bread-and-butter pudding makes it deliciously crispy on top and meltingly soft below.

7 For a shepherd's pie, try chunky cubes of leg of lamb instead of mince.

8 Stilton freezes beautifully. Cut it into whatever size you want, wrap it in film or foil and freeze for up to three months.

9 You can't beat fresh British asparagus. To get rid of the chewy stem base, hold it in your hands and snap – it will break at the division between edible and woody.

10 Porridge is a Scottish classic. Just be sure you add a pinch of salt to bring out the flavour.

ALL–AMERICAN DISHES

1 Dip chicken pieces into flour, then egg, and roll in Cajun spices mixed with bread-crumbs for Southern-fried cooking.

2 Buy a jar of American mustard for that authentic sweet kick with burgers.

3 Try American pancakes for a semi-healthy breakfast. Stack with grilled bacon and maple syrup and serve with fruit salad.

4 Try a hot dog without the bun. Mixed with American mustard dressing, red onion, shredded cabbage, romaine lettuce and tomatoes. It becomes a Chicago dog salad.

5 Have corn with sweet chilli glaze: maple syrup, chipotle chillies, garlic and salt.

6 Go for sweet potato chips instead of French fries.

7 Try apple pancakes by grating raw apple into your pancake mix.

8 Add an American twist by putting apples and pecan nuts in a rocket salad.

9 Want a genuine authentic American flavour? Add maple syrup to salad dressing.

10 Corn bread with a taste of the South? Add creamed corn, Cheddar and chillies.

IRRESISTIBLE ITALIAN COOKING

1 Use the freshest, best-quality ingre-dients – you'll notice the difference.

2 Reserve your expensive extra virgin olive oil to add authentic Italian flavour to salads or to drizzle on cooked dishes.

3 Basil is probably the most widely used herb in Italian cooking. Add it to any tomato dish or salad.

4 Antipasto dishes are intended to stimulate the appetite. Produce three or four, including cold meats, and you have the makings of a substantial, varied meal.

5 For the best, quick and easy tomato sauce, choose San Marzano tomatoes.

6 To cook up an amazing Italian stew add a little dark chocolate or a couple of chopped anchovies at the end of cooking.

7 **The secret to a great Italian soup** is to use a good stock instead of water.

8 **If you are adding wine to a dish,** make sure that it is an Italian wine.

9 **If you source just one ingredient** from the area your recipes comes from, you'll achieve a bit of that elusive local colour.

10 **An alternative to pizza is a calzone.** Fold your dough over the filling and bake.

MIX UP REFRESHING LEMONADE

GREAT FRUITS TO JUICE
1 Apples
2 Oranges
3 Carrots
4 Bananas
5 Kiwi
6 Strawberries
7 Mango
8 Beetroot
9 Tomato
10 Celery

1 **Be sure to select firm, ripe, glossy yellow lemons.** If they feel heavy for their size, they'll have the most juice.

2 **Eight to ten lemons** will make enough for a whole pitcher.

3 **Buy organic lemons,** or wash ordinary ones with soap/water to remove insecticide.

4 **Zest your lemons first,** then juice (the other way round is way too tricky).

5 **You'll get the most juice out of your lemons** if you warm them first.

6 **When mixing up your lemonade,** reserve a little lemon juice in case it's too sweet and you need to adjust the flavour.

7 **Freeze some lemonade in an ice cube tray,** so you can add it as ice to your drink without diluting it.

8 **Add a splash of cranberry juice** to make pink lemonade with a twist. Lime or orange juice also give an unexpected dash of delicious flavour.

9 **Choose tall glasses and add an extra zing** with a sugar frosting: rub their rims in lemon juice and dip in sugar.

10 **Chill your jug** and serve with plenty of ice and mint leaves.

MAGNIFICENT MILKSHAKES

1 **Add your milk a bit at a time.** Too much milk and your shake will be runny and not so tasty. Add a little and taste – you can always pour in some more.

2 **Use quality ice cream.** You'll be able to tell the difference.

3 **Flavoured syrup is quite OK, but fresh flavours are best,** whether it's fruit, espresso, chocolate or vanilla beans.

4 **How about blending up yummy leftovers** – cheesecake, cookies, brownies?

5 **Add flavouring after** you've put the ice cream and milk in your blender, so it doesn't just stay at the bottom of the mix.

6 **Don't even think about making a diet milkshake.** Use full-fat milk and ice cream for a delicious, creamy shake and start counting calories tomorrow.

7 **Indulge the kids** with a chocolate-bar milkshake. Just unwrap it and add it to the blender with the ice cream and full-fat milk. It's OK once in a while!

8 **Too thick?** Add more milk. Not strong enough? Add more flavourings.

9 **Fancy an adults-only shake?** Add rum, amaretto or whatever alcohol you feel like.

10 **A shake isn't complete** without some whipped cream, a cherry and a straw.

CHILL OUT WITH A COFFEE

1 Learn what's what: a lighter roast means more aroma and flavour, but if you like yours bitter, choose a darker roast.

2 The origin of the coffee is important: coffee beans from Indonesia are smoky and chocolaty, while Kenyan and Colombian beans are slightly fruity.

3 Use one to two tablespoons of coffee per 6fl oz (⅓pt) water.

4 Check the label and get the right grind size for your machine, There's no such thing as an 'all-purpose' grind.

5 For the ultimate in coffee freshness, you really must grind your own beans.

6 An open pack of coffee will deteriorate quickly. Store in an airtight container, away from heat, light, humidity and strong flavours. Use it fast or pop it in the freezer.

7 Water should be used at just less than boiling point.

8 Use a white porcelain cup to retain heat and show off coffee colour. Leave room for the aromas to flow above it.

9 You can't re-heat coffee, so don't microwave it. Chill it for an iced latte.

10 Use full-fat milk for best flavour.

AAAH, THE PERFECT CUP OF TEA

1 Always use freshly drawn water and descale your kettle regularly.

2 Consider using filtered water, if yours is a hard-water area.

3 Store tea in an airtight container, at room temperature.

4 A bag of English breakfast tea is best left to brew for about two minutes. Other teas may need longer to reach full flavour, or less to prevent them going bitter.

5 For black, fruit or herbal teas, use freshly boiled water. But green, oolong or white teas should be made with water at 82°C (180°F). Let the kettle cool for a couple of minutes after boiling before you pour out the water.

6 Using a teapot? Make sure it's clean, and warm it up with hot water.

7 Use one teaspoon of tea/one teabag per person. However, if you like it stronger, add 'one for the pot'.

8 Milk or tea first? Experts can't agree.

9 Your milk shouldn't be too creamy. But it should be chilled.

10 Wait six minutes before you drink your freshly made tea.

BECOME A BEER KNOW-IT-ALL

1 There are two basic types of beer: lager (light in colour and taste) and ales (darker, more robust, fruitier).

2 For quality and interesting flavours, try a micro-brewery. Go on a tour. You'll learn more and perhaps get free samples!

3 Experiment: think of beer appreciation just like wine appreciation and look for colour, body, smell and taste. A good beer deserves some time.

4 Beer should be clear and bright, with no sediment. The exception is cloudy beer, which should look appealing, not dull.

5 Not all beer is meant to have a 'head', but if it does, it should be thick/creamy.

6 Swirl the beer around your glass. If the head leaves a trail it usually means it's a better-quality beer.

7 Beer makes a better companion than wine with certain foods: egg dishes, anything very spicy, thick soups, and dishes with vinegary condiments.

8 Become a beer expert. Give a half-empty glass a swirl, place your hand over the top, then take a deep sniff.

9 Ditch the can. The taste of aluminium never improves the flavour of beer.

10 Beer purists prefer to serve theirs at room temperature. You'll find that real ale loses its complex flavours when chilled.

BREWING YOUR OWN BEER

1 The most important rule is that all your equipment must be properly sterile. Using brewing sterilizer is probably the simplest way to do this.

2 Sterilize just before you use your kit and then rinse it several times in clean tap water. If you don't sterilize it well your beer may end up being vinegary.

3 The easiest way to start is with a kit. All the ingredients will be measured out.

4 If you want more control over the final taste, buy ready-mashed syrup (or malt extract) and then add hops and the yeast separately.

5 Keep notes: what you've made and how it tasted, so you can refine your brewing.

6 Don't disturb your beer while it's fermenting. Keep it somewhere quiet while it does its stuff.

7 For bottling your beer, choose chunky bottles that can cope with the pressure. Cheap, flimsy ones might explode.

8 Is it time to bottle? The liquid (called 'wort') should be deep in colour and clearer than it was in its active phase. The bubbles in the airlock should have slowed to fewer than one a minute.

9 Practise siphoning with plain water before you try it on your precious brew.

10 Don't drink the sediment from your bottles – it's yeasty and will give you really bad wind!

MAKE YOUR OWN WINE – HIC!

1 The best time to get started on home-made wine is late summer or early autumn, when there's a glut of fruit. Or use a grape concentrate at any time of year.

2 Sterilize all your equipment really carefully, but take care to rinse it thoroughly. If you leave some sterilizing agent in your jar, it will kill the yeast.

3 Always use fresh yeast. Dead or damp yeast won't get fermentation going.

4 If fermentation doesn't start, try moving the jar to a warmer place or using a heating pad or belt.

5 Fermenting wine needs a constant, warm temperature. Putting it by a radiator that goes on and off just won't do.

6 If your wine is too sweet, simply blend it with a drier wine.

7 Don't try to save on cheap corks. The wine may seep through them.

8 Wine smells or tastes vinegary? It's infected with bacteria. Sorry – but you just have to be brave and throw it out.

9 Keep all your wines labelled at every stage, so you know what's what.

10 Go easy – home-made wine may be higher in alcohol content than you are used to drinking.

RED WINE, SIR?

1 To enjoy a red wine without food, a medium- or light-bodied one is best. With fewer tannins, it will slip down more easily.

2 If you buy an expensive red wine, research whether it's ready to drink or not. Younger wines may need time to mature.

3 Don't be tempted to go too cheap. On the most basic wine, you're paying mainly for the bottle and manufacturing costs as well as duties. If you spend more, it's going into the wine itself.

4 If you like a smooth, less dry, medium-bodied red wine, try the Merlot.

5 Don't serve red wine too warm. Some grapes, Pinot Noir and Gamay, especially, should even be served a little cool.

6 Shiraz, or Syrah, is one of the heavy-weights of the wine world. It's for you if you like something high in alcohol, big, bold, fruity and spicy.

7 For a smoother, lighter red wine, with less tannin but bags of flavour, opt for a Pinot Noir.

8 Try serving red wine in a bigger glass. You'll really get the aromas swirling around.

9 Look for the letters AOC on a bottle of French red. It's better quality.

10 Decanting any red wine will help improve the flavour. The older it is, the less time you should decant it for. Younger, cheaper wines could be poured from one jug to another for maximum effect.

I'LL HAVE WHITE

1 Almost all white wine tastes better chilled. But if it's too cold you just can't taste the wine.

2 For a crisp, clean flavour, white wine should be served in smaller glasses.

3 In the supermarket, read the back of the bottle to get an idea of the wine's character. But take it with a pinch of salt.

4 If you don't know what white wine to buy, try one recommended in the media.

5 The higher the alcohol content, the fuller and fruitier the flavour.

6 Make a change from the supermarkets, and try a specialist retailer, which will often have off-beat wines.

7 Don't expect sweet white wine to be as alcoholic as dry. It is bottled before all the grape's sugar is converted to alcohol.

8 Looking for a lighter, dry white wine? Choose one without oak, like Soave, Pinot Grigio, dry German Riesling or Muscadet.

9 For a fuller-bodied wine, without oak, try a New Zealand Sauvignon, a cheaper Côte du Rhône or a Chablis.

10 The bigger wines with oak include Australian and Californian Chardonnays, the more expensive Bordeaux, Rioja or white Burgundies.

STORING WINE

1 Keep wine in the dark. If you haven't got a cellar, wrap it in a cloth or in a box.

2 Bottles with corks must lie down. Stored upright, the corks may dry out; air would get into the wine and spoil it.

3 Keep a constant temperature. No more than 24°C (75°F) or it will start to oxidize.

4 Don't move wine. Even vibrations from heavy traffic may have an adverse effect.

5 Lots of bottles? Label your shelves.

6 Aim for a humidity of around 70 per cent, to keep the cork from drying out.

7 Wine 'breathes', so don't store it with anything strong-smelling.

8 Most inexpensive wines are not improved by storing. Drink most other white wines after two or three years, and red wines after two to ten years.

9 Opened, a bottle of white wine can be re-corked. Or use a stopper/pump and keep in the cellar/fridge for three to five days.

10 An open bottle of red wine is fine if you re-cork it and keep it in a dark place for a few days.

WHICH WINE WITH WHICH FOOD?

1 Try thinking of wine as a sauce, and match the flavours and weight of the dish with your wine.

2 Eating a herby salad? Try matching it with a herby wine: Sauvignon Blanc or Cabernet Sauvignon.

3 Cabernet Sauvignon is a grape with a thicker skin. This results in more tannins and a stronger, upfront wine, most suited to roast beef or other red meats.

4 Choose an oaky wine to go with salads or dishes with nutty, toasty ingredients.

5 Sometimes, opposites attract. Sweet Riesling/Gewurztraminer would go well with dishes including spicy red chilli.

6 Most people put white wine with fish, but to ring the changes, choose a light, low-tannin red – Beaujolais or Pinot Noir. But only if it's a meaty fish.

7 If you want wine with your barbecue, red is best – a fruity wine with sweetish hints is delicious. Try Beaujolais, Australian Shiraz or youthful Zinfandel.

8 Chocolate desserts are hard to match

with wine, but try Banyuls, a sweet red from the French Pyrenees.

9 **Good combos of desserts/cheese and wine:** stilton with port, crème brulée and Sauternes, Tarte Tatin and Monbazillac.

10 **Try pairing your dish with the wine you put into it.** For champagne chicken, break open the bubbly.

ALL ABOUT BUBBLY

1 **True 'Champagne' only comes from the Champagne region of France.** All other wine with bubbles in is sparkling wine. It can be just as delicious, however!

2 **Special occasion?** Find a specialist retailer and sample some of them.

3 **If your bottle says 'NV',** it's non-vintage. Vintage champagnes are more expensive because they come from a year when the grapes were at their best.

4 **If you want something really special,** look for a 'prestige cuvée'. These are even better than vintage (and more pricey).

5 **Learn about what you're buying –** read reviews in wine publications.

6 **Champagnes labelled 'sec' and 'doux' are sweet –** best served as dessert wines. Most people prefer 'brut' or 'extra dry'.

7 **Don't act like a racing driver** and fizz your champagne away. Place a towel over the top of the bottle before you open it.

8 **Serve champagne properly chilled.** To really get the benefit, chill your glasses.

9 **Drink the lower-priced champagnes straight away –** they're sold at their optimal age. Pricier champagnes improve with age – store for three to five years.

10 **Experts advise storing by standing bottles upright,** though still in a cool, dark, undisturbed place.

MAKE A BIG BOWL OF PUNCH

1 **If it fizzes, add it last –** this applies to champagne, colas and carbonated water.

2 **If the recipe calls for sugar,** use sugar syrup (dissolved in boiling water) to avoid undissolved granules in your drink.

3 **For a cold punch,** chill your ingredients before mixing and serving (just stand the bottles in the fridge). Chill the bowl, too.

4 **No need to use your best wines or spirits.** Drink them on their own.

5 **Save time by making hot punch in advance.** Prepare everything until the point of adding the spirits, then allow it to cool and store in the fridge. When you need it, simply bring to a simmer, add the spirits and you're done.

6 **Avoid diluting punch** with melting ice cubes. Instead, use a large block of ice (it melts more slowly) or else frozen juice or other non-alcoholic ingredients.

7 **If you want to make a fruit punch alcoholic,** add a slug of vodka/rum.

8 **Garnishes add the finishing touch –** but remember that they should complement the taste of the punch, not overwhelm it. Use mint leaves and lemon slices sparingly.

9 If you don't want to use a classic glass punch bowl, try making a hollowed-out pumpkin or watermelon, a clean plastic bucket or Hallowe'en trick-or-treat cauldron (for kids' parties) or a soup tureen.

10 Drink alcoholic punch with care – especially if you didn't make it yourself! You can't always tell how strong it is...

BARTENDER! I WANT A PERFECT COCKTAIL

FABULOUS COCKTAILS

1 Manhattan
2 Margarita
3 Whisky sour
4 Pina colada
5 Bloody Mary
6 Black Russian
7 Harvey Wallbanger
8 Martini
9 Mojito
10 Singapore Sling

1 Chill glasses in the freezer for half an hour before serving. Or, to chill a glass in a couple of minutes, fill with ice and water.

2 Chill alcohol to enhance the flavour.

3 Cocktails containing difficult-to-mix ingredients need to be shaken. A cocktail that only contains liquids can be stirred.

4 Add ingredients to the shaker in order of alcohol content – the highest first. Add three to six ice cubes – not crushed ice, which will over-dilute the drink.

5 When using a cocktail shaker, shake vigorously for about 10–15 seconds, or until condensation forms on the tin.

6 How to layer a cocktail: first, make sure your heaviest liquid goes at the bottom, then pour the second and subsequent liquids on slowly so they don't sink in. Pour over the back of a teaspoon.

7 When muddling to release the flavour of herbs/fruit, press and turn.

8 Measure your ingredients carefully. It's impossible to do it by eye.

9 What garnish? Fruit goes well with lighter spirits, while sweeter garnishes work with liqueurs/creamy cocktails. The higher the alcohol content or the darker the spirit, the more minimal the garnish.

10 Add extra-special ice cubes – use filtered/distilled water, boil it, then add to silicone trays while still hot. Your cubes will be sparklingly clear instead of cloudy.

CHEERS! DRINKING SPIRITS

1 When drinking whisky straight, add a dash of water to allow the aroma to emerge.

2 Adding ice cubes to spirits flattens their flavour, so let the ice melt a little first.

3 Add whisky to coffee and brown sugar and float whipped cream on top – a delicious alternative to a post-meal coffee.

4 Want to spice up your drinking life? Add chillies to vodka and leave for a week. Leave it longer to really feel the burn.

5 How you serve a spirit depends on the type/quality. High-quality whiskies, for example, could be served straight.

6 Vodka and gin will both give you less of a hangover because there are fewer chemical substances in them than in brandy, rum or whisky.

7 Before serving vodka, connoisseurs put the bottle in the freezer overnight, and a small, clear glass in the freezer for an hour. Pour, warm slightly in the hand and drink. No ice cubes.

8 Bored with gin in the usual way? Have a classic 'pink gin' – which is one part gin and a clever dash of angostura bitters.

9 **Impress your friends** by buying a bottle of 'rhum agricole' – it's the champagne of rums.

10 **Get into flambéing.** Only spirits with high alcohol will work. Flaming will add the flavour of the spirit to your dish, but lose the harshness of the alcohol. Looks good, too! Try brandy with beef stroganoff or roast lamb.

ALL ABOUT PORTS & SHERRIES

1 **Watch out!** Port is deceptively strong.

2 **Don't miss out on port** because you're worried it will give you a hangover. It won't – unless you've drunk too much!

3 **Serve white or tawny port,** chilled, before a meal. Serve red port after a meal.

4 **If you want to add port to a recipe,** ruby is the youngest, cheapest kind.

5 **Unless you want a mouthful of sludge** at the end of your bottle, decant vintage port through muslin into a jug or decanter.

6 **Use sherry instead of wine** for a different slant on a recipe. Just match the dryness of the sherry to the wine required.

7 **Don't bother to store sherry** in the hope that it will improve with age. It won't. Drink it straight away.

8 **Store sherry upright in the cool/dark.**

9 **For a healthy alternative cocktail,** try the elegant rebujito. It's fino sherry (the driest) mixed with lemonade or soda water and a dash or lemon of lime.

10 **If you ever visit a tapas bar,** try fino sherry with your little plates of food.

ENJOY A LIQUEUR

1 **Liqueurs don't have to be stored like wine** and many will last years. Keep cream-based liqueurs in the fridge once opened.

2 **Liqueurs are expensive and designed to be sipped slowly** in small quantities. So serve them in small glasses.

3 **Liqueurs may sometimes be called cordials, shots or schnapps –** they may, or may not, be the same thing.

4 **Avoid liqueurs if you're on a diet.** They're high in calories and low in nutritional value.

5 **When to serve a liqueur?** Usually after the main course, to go with dessert/coffee.

6 **If you like oranges, try curaçao –** it may be coloured orange, blue or green.

7 **Keep a good selection of liqueurs** in the house and you can either drink them straight or add them to your cocktails.

8 **It's a real cinch to make your own fruit liqueurs.** Combine fruit, sugar and a spirit and leave to steep for at least a fortnight. Add more sugar, if necessary, leave a bit longer, then sieve and bottle.

9 **If a recipe calls for orange juice,** try substituting a dash of orange-flavoured liqueur for added depth of flavour.

10 **Many liqueurs can be higher in alcohol than spirits.** The sugar rush, then crash, can cause a headache.

YOU & YOUR MONEY

Want to save money? Well, who doesn't? Here's how to get organized with personal finance, from reducing your outgoings to maximizing your income. We cover banking and borrowing, credit cards and debt, how to avoid fraud, all sorts of advice on property – probably your biggest asset – and even how to become a millionaire...

GET YOUR ENERGY BILLS DOWN

1 **Choose the most energy-efficient appliances –** look for a label. Running costs will be lower. Run full loads rather than half loads in dishwashers, washing machines and tumble dryers – two half loads use more energy than one full one.

2 **Your boiler is what makes the most difference –** it uses the highest proportion of energy in the home and the older it is the less efficient it will be. Replace an old model with an energy-efficient one. Have it serviced regularly to ensure it runs at peak efficiency.

3 **Fit thermostats and controls** so that your heating and hot-water system only comes on and off when you need them. Only heat the rooms you use and don't over-heat them. Putting on a sweater is cheaper than turning up the heating! Consider turning down the room thermostat by one degree – you will hardly notice the temperature drop, but you should notice the difference in your bank balance.

4 **Insulate your home as much as possible.** Do cavity walls, the loft, hot-water tank and pipework and under the floorboards, and draught-proof the doors and windows. Close curtains at dusk.

5 **Replace single-glazed windows** with double, triple or secondary glazing. Reducing heat loss through windows means your heating system won't need to work so hard, so over time you should make back the cost. You'll also have fewer draughts, experience fewer cold spots and enjoy better sound-proofing.

6 **A quick and easy way to save money** is to replace your traditional lightbulbs for low-energy ones. Choose from compact fluorescents (CFLs) or light-emitting diodes (LEDs). Switch lights off when you leave a room and don't over-light rooms – you may only need a small reading light rather than overhead lights. Have outside lights on a sensor, so that they only switch on when someone approaches or when it gets dark.

7 **Don't leave devices on standby –** buy energy-saving plugs and sockets with a single switch. Once you count up TVs, set-top boxes, DVD players, Xboxes, Wiis and digital radios, the bills to run them can mount up and many modern devices aren't really switched off until you turn them off at the plug.

8 **Keep computer equipment switched off unless you're actually using it** as it can use a surprising amount of energy. Laptops use less than desktop PCs, however, so consider changing. When buying peripheral devices such as printers, routers and scanners, make energy efficiency one of your main criteria.

9 **Reduce the costs of heating water.** Take showers instead of baths, replace your shower head with a water-efficient one, fill up your dishwasher and washing machine before you run them (using energy-efficient settings), don't run the hot tap while hand-washing and only fill your kettle to boil what you need.

10 **Make sure you're really getting the best value for money from your energy supplier(s).** If not, switch. Calculate how much you're currently paying or, for greater accuracy, how much gas and electricity you used in the last year. Go online and do comparisons between companies – there are plenty of reliable sites. Then choose the best new tariff to suit your needs – the cheapest ones available are usually dual-fuel (electricity and gas from the same supplier) with a monthly debit payment.

CUT YOUR PHONE BILLS

1 **Use comparison websites** to check you are getting the best deal with your phone provider. If not, switch.

2 **Make sure you're on the right package** for the times you call, and where you call.

3 **A cheaper option is a 'bundle' package** (combining phone with other products such as broadband or TV).

4 **Specialist phone providers can offer great rates** on international or mobile phone calls.

5 **Try online sites that give you a prefix to dial** before you call an international or mobile number – giving you a good deal.

6 **Set up an internet phone service.** It's free or, at least, reasonably priced.

7 **Avoid calling premium-rate numbers,** and if you have to do so, ask the business to ring you back – though this might be a bit cheeky.

8 **Make sure you use all your free phone minutes** every month. If you haven't done so, pick up your mobile phone instead of the landline to make your calls.

9 **Consider barring certain types of calls** from your phone if you have teenagers at home who run up huge bills.

10 **Make fewer calls,** make them shorter, send emails or even, perish the thought, write a letter!

SORT OUT YOUR BUDGETS

1 **Work out how much money you've got coming in** from every source. Don't just look at weekly or monthly earnings, but also benefits and savings interest.

2 **Calculate your regular outgoings** by gathering together several months' worth of bank and credit-card statements.

3 **To get a really good picture of your finances,** try to estimate annual outgoings – because otherwise things like Christmas or summer holidays could get left out.

4 **Pen and paper is fine, but a computer programme/spreadsheet will help you** work things out in detail quickly and easily.

5 **Evaluate your priorities.** Hopefully, once you've taken the outgoings off the incomings, you're left with a positive figure. Do you want to lock your money away in long-term savings, pay off your mortgage or put it towards a holiday?

6 **Hmmm – have you got a negative figure?** Having worked out your budget, at least you can now think about cutting back your expenditure.

7 **What about unexpected expenditure?** The car goes wrong or you need to replace your phone? Put some money aside each month so you can cope with such problems.

8 **If you have a job, aim to build up savings** worth at least three months of your outgoings in case you lose it; if you're self-employed, six months would be good.

9 **It can really help to set up telephone or online banking,** as it gives you instant access to check your balance or transfer funds in your bank account(s).

10 **Don't just go through your budget once and forget about it.** Track your income and expenditure regularly. Budgeting should be a part of your life.

WAYS TO CUT COSTS

1 Drive less; walk and cycle more
2 Eat less meat
3 Quit smoking
4 Stop drinking
5 Shop in sales
6 Shorten phone calls
7 Grow your own
8 Use coupons
9 Basics first, luxuries last
10 Swap/barter

MONEY PROBLEMS: WHAT TO DO?

1 Face up to your problems. The first step, however painful, is to calculate how much you owe and who to.

2 Prioritize your debts. Not in size order, but in terms of importance. Usually a mortgage, rent or any secured loans should be your highest priority.

3 Look at the bigger picture and work out your annual income and expenditure. Then you can look at all the possible ways of cutting your outgoings. The more you can save in regular expenditure, the more will be available to service your debts.

4 Check whether you are eligible for any sorts of benefits. If you are already on some, are you receiving the correct amount? This may well apply if you have found yourself in debt because of illness or redundancy.

5 Shift all your debts to the cheapest possible form of repayment. For starters, if possible, take out a credit card with a low or no interest rate for balance transfers, and put your credit card debts on it. But never, ever use it for purchases!

6 If you owe money to companies, get in contact with them and ask whether they can offer any help. You might be able to renegotiate your payment terms.

7 Cut the costs of your debts to as little as possible, then if you have any savings, use them to pay off debts. The interest paid on the savings is usually less than that charged on borrowing.

8 Look at remortgaging. A mortgage is most people's biggest debt. Shop around – it may be possible to remortgage and save substantial amounts of money.

9 Cut your expenditure by shopping around so that you pay less for your debts. If, at the end of the day, you really can't make a payment, tell your lender well in advance so that you can minimize repercussions. Try to work out a solution that is acceptable to both of you.

10 Talk to the professionals: there are charities and advice agencies whose job it is to help people with their debt problems and even mediate on their behalf. Get to know about them and then use them.

IF YOU HAVE MONEY PROBLEMS – DON'T:

1 Panic
2 Despair
3 Borrow more
4 Avoid making minimum payments
5 Ignore letters
6 Suffer in silence
7 Use a credit card for payments
8 Stop talking to your creditors
9 Pay the creditor who makes most fuss
10 Give up

GET MEAN & CUT BACK

1 Write shopping lists for everything you need. Only buy what's on the list.

2 Don't use cards or go online. Instead, put the week's cash into separate envelopes for each expense and stick to spending just that. If you underspend in one category you can move the money into another.

3 Keep a spending diary so that you can identify what's going where – and cut out anything unnecessary.

4 Look after your clothes and shoes so that they don't need replacing so often.

5 Join a car-share scheme or, if you live in a city where they have one, a car club where you simply pay to drive.

6 Swap named brands for own brands.

7 Make home-made presents for friends and family. Put some thought into them, wrap prettily and they'll be charmed.

8 Re-use, re-use, re-use. Last year's

Christmas cards can be trimmed down and turned into this year's gift tags. Pretty wrapping paper can be reclaimed. Plastic drinks bottles can be washed and refilled for gym outings. Get into the mindset and saving money will become automatic.

9 Entertain the family for free: country walks, board/card games, a treasure hunt in the garden, press flowers, make things out of old egg boxes…

10 Holiday for less by camping, hiring a static caravan or doing a home swap.

CUTTING CHRISTMAS COSTS

1 Set a budget
2 Make a list
3 Cheaper presents
4 Family presents only
5 Presents for kids only
6 Re-gift
7 Home-made gifts
8 Make your own cards
9 Buy through the year
10 Discounts with online vouchers

GET GOOD DEALS

1 Only buy what you need, not what seems like a bargain at the time.

2 Check out reviews and decide exactly what to buy in advance.

3 Do your research. Once you know what you're going to buy, work out exactly where the best bargains are to be had. Often this means going to an online retailer.

4 Remember: 'cheap' isn't the same as 'value for money'.

5 Buy from a good, reputable source and, where appropriate, check you're getting a good warranty and after-sales service.

6 Don't dismiss your local high street. Their prices may not often beat those on the net, but they will usually be far better than an online site for personal service.

They may even offer to price-match.

7 Once you've picked your product and retailer, check that you're getting exactly what you expect. Some goods are cheap because they are seconds or reconditioned, and it's not always easy to spot them. Read the small print.

8 Try getting discount coupons – there are actually websites that specialize in these. Simply type the name of your chosen store into your search engine.

9 If you can, wait for the sales. If you are shopping online, keep checking the site to watch for offers.

10 Look for possible reasons why it's so cheap – don't get ripped off. If it sounds too good to be true it probably is.

SAVVY SALES SHOPPING

1 Know your sales: sign up to newsletters so you'll hear when the sales are coming up in your favourite shops.

2 Work out what you want in advance. That way you'll avoid being side-tracked and can focus on the most necessary items.

3 Try clothing on before the sale starts. Then make a dash for exactly what you want without having to try on.

4 Get there early. The really huge bargains and the best stuff will go first. For the most amazing sales deals, some people camp outside for days. Just saying…

5 Would you have bought it if it had been full price? Don't go mad and buy stuff just because it's cheap.

6 What are your rights if you buy in the sale? If you don't like the item or it's the wrong size, for example, can you exchange it or get a refund?

7 Check that anything you're about to buy is in perfect condition. If it's labelled 'shop soiled', 'ex display' or whatever, do you know exactly what the damage is and are you happy to live with it?

8 Set yourself a budget – and stick to it.

It's all too easy to be tempted by a marked-down price tag.

9 Plan your day, wear comfortable shoes and take a drink and a snack. Sales shopping can be exhausting.

10 Don't forget online sales. Indeed, many websites now include permanent 'sale' sections.

USE A LOYALTY/STORE CARD

1 By all means sign up for a store card to get an initial discount, but then watch out: don't run up bills that you can't pay back in full each month – interest rates can be very high.

2 Look for special deals, promotional events and customer evenings intended for card holders, and use them in order to get further discounts.

3 Don't choose the place you shop just because you've got a loyalty card. Go where the bargains are, but once in store, always use your loyalty card.

4 Check the card's website regularly for updates on deals.

5 Save up your non-essential shopping

to do at times when your retailer is offering loyalty card holders extra points.

6 Look out for extra-points promotions on certain items – but, of course, only buy the product if you actually need it!

7 Know the actual value of rewards or points before you rack them up. Some are markedly more 'rewarding' than others.

8 Understand how your can redeem your points, and what methods are worth the most. Money-off in-store usually offers the least return.

9 Sign up to mailing lists and news-letters in order to keep up to date with special offers.

10 Remember to spend your points!

IT'S GOING CHEAP OR EVEN FREE!

1 Try out 'skip-dipping' or 'dumpster-diving'. The art of removing unwanted items from other people's skips. Take along some steps, heavy-duty gloves and perhaps a long pole with a hook on the end of it.

2 Ask the owner's permission if you're going to take something out of a skip or front garden, even if it appears to have

been thrown away. And never trespass.

3 Sign up to an internet-based network that connects people who want to dispose of things with people who will happily take them off their hands.

4 If you have a skill, offer it on online swap sites in return for something you need. Try this with family or friends, too.

5 Couch-surfing is the brand-new way of travelling around the world at minimal expense. Sign up to a website to connect with people willing to put you up.

6 Have a free makeover at department-store make-up counters. They will often give you sample products.

7 Lots of utility companies give away free gadgets such as lightbulbs or water-saving devices. Just ask.

8 Get free product samples of everything from nappies to fruit juice. The catch? You'll have to sign up and you may be bombarded by emails.

9 Opt for free or cheap haircuts, beauty treatments or even dental work. You have to be willing to be experimented on by a student. Ask at your local college.

10 Want to read books for free? Join a library. Some lend music and films, too.

WAYS TO MAKE EXTRA CASH

1 Evening/weekend job
2 Paid surveys
3 Enter competitions
4 Dog-walking
5 Home-tutoring
6 Artist's model
7 Mystery shopper
8 Cashback credit card/shopping
9 Home ironing service
10 Babysitting

SELL YOUR STUFF

1 Make sure everything you are planning to sell is in tip-top condition. Mend it and then clean it to within an inch of its life.

2 Get together with a friend and share the work. It's more fun and the more there is on offer, the more buyers you'll attract.

3 If you're planning to hold a garage or yard sale, tell people about it! Write out clear, attention-grabbing signs and pin them up where passers-by will notice them (but take them down afterwards). An ad in the local paper may be a good idea, too.

4 Check whether you need a permit to sell from your garage, drive or front lawn?

5 Be an early bird and get to car-boot sales as early as you can, and, if possible, choose a good pitch, not too close to other cars and with plenty of people passing by.

6 Set your goods out as attractively as possible. Hang the clothes on a rail and arrange other things at different heights, so they look their best.

7 Price reasonably, but not too low. A good starting point, for something in near-perfect condition, is half the new price.

8 Take plenty of small change. You don't want to lose a sale because you couldn't give your customer the right change.

9 Reduce your prices in the hour or so before you plan to shut up shop. The less there is to pack away, the better.

10 Give any leftover goods to charity. You may not have made money on it, but hopefully they will.

SELL AT AN INTERNET AUCTION

1 Take an excellent picture. Try for good natural light or, failing that, artificial light, rather than camera flash.

2 Choose the most appropriate category in which to list your item and give it a clear, accurate title – using words that people are likely to search for.

3 Write a description that sells your item without going over the top. Accuracy is important but emphasize the positive.

4 Think what a buyer would want to know. Be honest and go into detail without writing reams. Be grammatical and run the spell-check. You need to appear credible.

5 Set a reserve price – high enough for you to be happy if you only achieve that price, but low enough to attract interest.

6 To help you set a price, look for items similar to yours – see what they made.

7 People trust feedback ratings – you can build yours initially by buying some small items. Few people will buy something expensive from a zero-rated seller.

8 Pick a time to end your auction. You'll be aiming for a bidding frenzy in the last hour, so choose a time when people are likely to be online. Sunday evenings?

9 Set a fair postage cost.

10 Email customers at every stage of the process: to tell them they've won, to tell them payment has been received and to tell them that their item has been dispatched. You'll find that good customer service leads to good feedback.

MAKE MONEY FROM YOUR BLOG

1 Take a long-term approach. You'll need to build readers and experiment with different ways of making money.

2 Work hard. To bring in a full-time income, expect to put in full-time hours.

3 Choose an original subject that advertisers are likely to find appealing and that isn't already covered.

4 Come up with good content, regularly. This will need a combination of planning and inspiration. It helps if you're writing on a subject you're passionate about.

5 Make your blog stand out with brilliant writing, imagery and layout. You need to attract both readers and advertisers.

6 Drive traffic to your site. This means getting good at search engine optimization and article marketing.

7 Selling advertising is key. Design your site so that the ads are noticeable and appealing, and familiarize yourself with how blog advertizing works.

8 Sell products too – virtual and/or real. Ebooks are probably the most obvious, but what about webinars, courses, apps or reports? Or even T-shirts, DVDs, books or other merchandise?

9 Spin-off work may come from being a popular blogger – a newspaper column, consulting or after-dinner speaking.

10 Once your blog is a roaring success, syndicate it or sell it to the highest bidder.

SAFE SHOPPING ONLINE

1 Is the website secure? There should be a security icon (locked padlock or key) showing in the browser's window frame. The site name should begin 'https'.

2 Only access shopping sites by typing the address into your web browser yourself. Never go to a website from an email link and enter your personal details.

3 **Deal with reputable sellers only –** check that they have a physical address and landline phone number.

4 **Be more cautious** when the company is based overseas.

5 **Don't give out your card information** unless you feel completely happy about the website and seller.

6 **Check the seller's privacy** and returns policies carefully.

7 **Protect your PC better** by installing the latest operating system, browser and anti-virus system.

8 **Make sure you save the confirmation email.** This means that if there's a problem, you'll have a record of the transaction.

9 **Always log out after shopping online.**

10 **Contact your card issuer** immediately if you suspect your card details may have been misused.

OPEN A BANK ACCOUNT

1 **Make sure the bank is legitimate –** choose a well-known bank for safety.

2 **Does it have a branch near where you live or work?** Even in this internet age, sometimes it's nice to be able to sort things out face to face.

3 **How big and where?** Small banks are great – but perhaps not if you travel and need national or international facilities.

4 **Check out the fees!** Even small ones add up over time.

5 **Are you extremely rich?** Good for you! There are some banks that specialize in accounts for wealthy people.

6 **Will you struggle to maintain a certain balance in your account?** Look for one that is designed for a minimal balance.

7 **Check out the main features of the account –** is it run in branch, online or over the phone?

8 **What else is thrown in?** Some accounts offer you inclusive travel insurance, free overdrafts or interest payments – but you may have to pay for them in other ways.

9 **Shop around,** in person or online. Go into branches, make phone calls and look on comparison websites.

10 **Ignore the frills.** Don't get sucked in by a promotional deal that might only be short-lived. Once it has ended you may be stuck with an account that doesn't really suit you.

RUN A PERSONAL BANK ACCOUNT

1 **Keep an eye on your account** so you don't go into the red.

2 **Check statements regularly** so you will quickly spot any unauthorized activity.

3 **Set up automatic payments** if you're bad at remembering your bills, so that everything gets paid on time.

4 **Why not link your savings account to your current account** so that you can quickly and easily transfer money?

5 **Paying money in?** It won't be credited to your account immediately.

6 **Stick to the bank account's terms and conditions.** If you think you're going to go overdrawn, arrange it in advance.

7 **Maintain records** in an organized way.

8 **Keep a cash cushion** in your account so that you don't go accidentally overdrawn and incur a fee.

9 **Be cautious when using an ATM to withdraw cash.** Only use ones that are well-lit, check that the machine looks as it should, and tuck your cash safely away the moment it pops out of the machine.

10 **Review your bank account once a year** and ensure it's still the best for you.

SAFE ONLINE BANKING

1 **Beware copycat websites.** Check you have typed the correct web address before starting any transactions.

2 **Never ever send sensitive information** (passwords, PIN numbers) on an email.

3 **Think of a unique password** – avoiding the obvious ones like birth dates or your children's names. The longer they are the better, using upper and lower case letters, numbers and symbols.

4 **Change your password regularly.**

5 **Use different passwords** for different online accounts.

6 **Don't give your password out** to any-one else – especially someone who phones you out of the blue.

7 **Keep your virus protection up to date,** and install a firewall.

8 **Ignore emails supposedly from your bank** asking you to verify details – usually by clicking a link to a website. Your bank will never ask you to do that – it's a scam.

9 **Don't write down your log-in details,** password or PIN.

10 **Contact your bank** now if you think there's a problem with your card's security.

JOIN A CREDIT UNION

1 **Can you join a credit union?** You may be eligible because of where you live, work or worship, or because of an association to which you belong.

2 **Will you save on fees?** Check, and compare them to your bank's.

3 **Debit card and/or cheque book?** Check how the account will work.

4 **Does the credit union offer other financial products?** You may want to start a mortgage, credit card or a loan.

5 **Convenience counts.** Can you use an ATM easily? Where's the nearest branch?

6 **Ask whether your deposits will be fully insured.**

7 **Would you find electronic banking convenient?** Check whether it's on offer.

8 **Opening hours may be more limited** than with a large bank. Does that matter?

9 **Ask about the minimum balance.**

10 **If you decide to leave** be sure to let the old account remain open for at least 60 days to make sure all outstanding cheques have cleared.

CHILDREN'S BANK ACCOUNTS

1 **Choose a bank with a branch that's easy to get to –** children are less likely to use the account online.

2 **Check the minimum amount required** to open the account.

3 **What if the account is unused** for any length of time? It's more likely to happen with a child's account.

4 **What are the fees?** The account may have only a small amount deposited.

5 **Look for a high rate of interest –** it will encourage your child to save.

6 **How will your child withdraw money?** Is there a pass book or a card? Can he/she use an ATM?

7 **Read all the terms and conditions –** is it possible for the account to go overdrawn?

8 **Don't just go for the account with the fun freebies –** they're not always best.

9 **Be aware of security** and don't write down passwords.

10 **Check the tax situation.** It's unusual for a child's savings to earn enough interest for tax to be due, but you should ask.

MAKE YOUR KIDS MONEY–SAVVY

1 **Give kids pocket money,** when they realize what money is. This will teach them about budgeting, spending and saving.

2 **Encourage children to save.**

3 **Explain all about borrowing, earning, saving, credit –** the sooner they start to understand financial terms, the better.

4 **Teach young people about spending wisely,** and how to shop around.

5 **Help your kids understand** there's a difference between 'need' and 'want'.

6 **Allow children to make their own decisions** about spending their money. Let them learn from their mistakes.

7 **Set them to work!** Just helping around the house for small change at first, then bigger chores and maybe a part-time job for a teenager. Once they understand what it takes to earn money, they'll respect it.

8 **Involve kids in financial decisions.** Get them to look at options so they can learn how financial planning works.

9 **Get them to practise handling money** by setting up a mini-enterprise.

10 **Encourage your child to wait before spending.** They'll learn that sometimes the desire to have something goes and they can spend the money on something else.

SAVVY STUDENT BANK ACCOUNTS

1 **Are you eligible?** Check the criteria for being a student.

2 **What overdraft will the account give?**

Aim for the highest, that's guaranteed the longest at 0 per cent.

3 **Compare like with like.** Some overdrafts

are guaranteed, others are described as 'up to'. Know the difference.

8 **Don't just choose the bank that has an ATM or a branch on or near campus.** Banking online is easy and you can usually withdraw cash from other banks' ATMs.

4 **Your overdraft is really the bank's money,** and you will have to pay it back.

5 **Check the small print.** Make sure you're happy with every detail, including fees.

6 **Never go over your overdraft limit.**

The fees can be prohibitively steep.

7 **If you're struggling with money** and close to your overdraft limit, talk to your bank and try to agree to an extension to it.

9 **Never ever save your personal security details** on a shared or public computer.

10 **Don't stick with the same account for years** after you have graduated. Once you've grabbed all the benefits of a student account, move to the best account you can – it will probably be more suitable.

THE SECRETS OF SAVING

1 **Start young.** The earlier you start the more you'll save, and the easier it will come to you.

2 **Make it a habit,** not a choice.

3 **Do it automatically** – set up a standing order so you'll never miss a payment.

4 **Set a budget** – work out your income and expenditure and save as much as you can from the difference.

5 **Stick to it** – don't think of saving as a 'blue moon' activity, rather treat it as an essential part of life.

6 **Revise the amount you save regularly.** Can you try to save more?

7 **Are you tax-efficient?** Choose savings accounts that (legally) keep the money with you, not the tax man.

8 **If you want to maximize your savings, reinvest the interest.** Your account may do this automatically, but some move it to another account. Check.

9 **Get the timing right** – the money should leave your current account after you get paid. Less temptation to spend!

10 **Set goals.** What are you saving for? A car, a holiday, your pension, college fees? When you eventually hit your targets you'll feel a great sense of achievement.

CHOOSE A SAVINGS ACCOUNT

1 **How much money can you save to start off with?** Some accounts require little – others ask for a higher minimum.

2 **How easy will it be to get at your money?** Check how many withdrawals you're allowed to make per month/year.

3 **Is the account easy to use?** Do you get

a pass book, a card or the facility to bank by phone or online? How often will you get statements? Make sure it suits you.

4 **Find the highest interest rate.** Usually, the longer you are prepared to lock your money away for, the higher the rate.

5 **Check the small print.** Make sure an

account that offers attractive rates doesn't have lots of hidden fees or surcharges.

6 **Consider an account that pays higher rates** in return for locking your money away if you don't need it for a while.

7 **Putting money in regularly?** Consider an account that's set up to accommodate this and that pays good rates as a result.

8 **Choose an online account.** Convenient for some and they often offer good rates.

9 **What can your bank offer you?** Some have accounts paying higher interest for those holding other accounts with them.

10 **Is the account secure?** Check whether it has a insurance/compensation scheme. If so, what is the upper limit?

INVEST FOR YOUR FUTURE

1 **Get a good adviser** – unless you're prepared to spend time teaching yourself how financial markets work. You can still research potential investments yourself.

2 **Decide how much money you can set aside for investments.** Can you afford to invest regularly? This can help smooth bumps in the stock market.

3 **How long can you tie your money up?**

4 **When and how will you access your money?** What happens if you need it sooner than expected?

5 **Mind risking your money?** Usually, the safer the investment, the lower the potential profit will be.

6 **Make sure that any investments you make are tax-efficient.**

7 **Spread your money around** between all different types of investment. That way your exposure to risk will be limited.

8 **Track your investments** and make sure they're working hard for you.

9 **Read the small print.** Check for fees, penalties and conditions.

10 **If you're getting professional advice,** ask about fees or commission.

GREEN & ETHICAL INVESTING

1 **Find out which companies have ethical policies?** Many have disclosure policies, but you may have to do some digging.

2 **Choose whether you want to buy shares individually or via a fund,** where selection/management are done for you.

3 **How about a fund that invests in all sorts of sectors,** not necessarily ethical, but tries to influence company policy to encourage positive change?

4 **Get advice** from someone who is a specialist in this type of investment.

5 **Some ethical investment funds may be higher-risk** because they operate according to strict criteria.

6 **Shares go down as well as up** in ethical companies, just like any other shares.

7 **Check how 'ethical' is defined.** If a tobacco company looks after its workers well, is it ethical?

8 **Want to concentrate on certain areas,** (animals, fairtrade or the environment)?

9 **Want your money to go to companies that are actively 'ethical',** or simply ones that are not unethical?

10 **It's more than stocks and shares –** think about ethical banking, pensions, life assurance, savings and mortgages.

ALTERNATIVE INVESTMENTS

1 **Invest in something that you're really passionate about.**

2 **Don't bank on a regular income or short-term profit.** Your investment won't necessarily deliver.

3 **Understand the risks –** possibly greater than with other types of investment.

4 **Don't get caught by scams.** Cast-iron certainties don't exist; don't be conned.

5 **Art is a popular investment,** and at least you can look at your purchase while it (hopefully) increases in value. Choose either the safer route of an established artist or the riskier one of emerging talent. Keep the work for at least five years.

6 **If you choose to invest in wine,** you can have it stored for you, but you'll have to pay annual storage and insurance fees.

7 **Gold may seem like a dead cert,** but it can still fluctuate. You don't have to buy physical bars or coins, but could choose exposure to the price movements of gold instead.

8 **Investing in a racehorse is high-risk** – though if you have money to burn you may have a lot of fun. It's best done through a syndicate or fund.

9 **Whatever investment you choose, get good advice** and use a reputable dealer.

10 **Do you have other passions?** Stamps, jewellery, classic cars, glassware, silverware or pottery?

CHOOSE A CREDIT CARD

1 **What type of card is best for you?** Choose from the following: regular, premium, reward, student, prepaid or charity.

2 **Paying the balance off in full each month?** A charge card might be better.

3 **If you want to transfer a balance onto your credit card,** look for one with a low interest rate on balance transfers.

4 **Want to carry a balance over from month to month?** Choose a credit card with a low interest rate.

5 **Planning high-value shopping?** Get a card with an introductory deal, then pay off the balance before incurring interest.

6 **Know the finance charges –** they will probably vary for balance transfers, purchases and cash advances.

7 **Fees?** They may be applied if you're late paying or if you go over your limit.

8 **Know how much time you've got –** it's called the 'grace period'.

9 **If you're new to credit cards,** a small credit limit might be best.

10 **Check before applying** whether you are likely to qualify. If you're refused, it can damage your credit score.

USE YOUR CREDIT CARD WISELY

1 **Pay promptly.** Avoid late fees and maintain a good credit record.

2 **Don't go over your credit limit.** You might be charged and pushed onto a higher penalty rate of interest.

3 **You might be charged** for cash advances or transferring a balance.

4 **Pay more than the minimum –** as much as you can. Interest builds up.

5 **Watch for changes to terms.**

6 **Read your statement when it comes** and check for unexpected charges. If you have had an introductory deal, your bill should tell you when it's going to end.

7 **Getting a cash advance on your card is an expensive way** to get hold of money.

8 **Plan ahead.** What will you use the card for and how will you pay it off?

9 **Don't use a credit card to pay for loads of small things.** Before you know it, you'll have an enormous bill, with little to show for it. Set a limit on how often you use it, or the lowest amount you will pay on it.

10 **Leave credit cards at home!** Then you can't be tempted to use it. If you're worried about emergencies, take one card.

TAKE OUT A LOAN

1 **Never be tempted to borrow more** than you can afford to repay.

2 **The longer the life of the loan, the more interest you will pay.** Arrange the shortest term possible.

3 **Repayment fees?** A flexible, as opposed to a fixed-term, loan might suit you better, but watch for higher interest rates.

4 **Repay store and credit cards** (unless 0 per cent interest) in full each month, as their interest rates are usually higher.

5 **Don't choose a lender just because they offer you a few freebies.**

6 **Don't take a loan out under pressure.** Think about it in your own time.

7 **Study all the terms and conditions** with the greatest care.

8 **Do you really need loan insurance?** It can be expensive. You may find a better standalone policy elsewhere.

9 **Establish exactly how much you'll be paying back each month,** and what the total cost of the loan will be.

10 **Check how the interest rates will be described.** Monthly rates actually convert into much higher annual ones.

IMPROVE YOUR CREDIT RATING

1 **If you are rejected by one lender, you may not be by another.** Scoring systems vary from one lender to another.

2 **Get on the electoral register.** This is the most important way to make yourself more attractive to lenders.

3 Check your credit file regularly. There may be mistakes on it that will create problems for you later. If you find any errors, correct them immediately.

4 Don't apply for loads of credit in a short space of time.

5 If you're planning to move house, apply for credit beforehand, not after.

6 You'll do better if you have a job, so if you're about to be made redundant, go on maternity leave or otherwise take time off, apply for credit beforehand.

7 No credit history? Take out a small amount of credit, make each payment on time and don't go over the limit – you'll appear to be a good proposition.

8 Separate your partner's finances from yours, if he/she has a poor credit history.

9 Get a land line – just putting a mobile phone number on the application form doesn't look as good.

10 If you have lots of credit cards that you never use, cancel most of them. Too much available credit reflects badly on you. But keep long-held bank accounts – they'll work in your favour.

CHOOSE A MORTGAGE

1 How much can you afford to pay each month – not just now, but for years ahead?

2 Do you plan to move again fairly soon? Take this into account when you are choosing a mortgage.

3 Check your credit report. A higher score may mean a lower interest rate.

4 Understand the terminology and read financial pages online or in the press – you will be able to make better choices.

5 Shop around. Compare loan rates, fees, terms and conditions.

6 Think hard about a mortgage with a variable interest rate, you'll be well off if rates go down, but you must work out how you will cope if rates go up.

7 Think about whether you can afford to make the higher payments. Take out a mortgage over a shorter-than-average term and your total repayments will be less.

8 If you get specialist advice, check that the advisor is impartial and ask how their fees are structured.

9 Read the small print. What looks like a good deal may have hidden expenses.

10 Check what penalties you'd incur if you made overpayments or repaid your mortgage early.

HOW TO PAY OFF YOUR MORTGAGE EARLY

1 Pay off loans
2 Pay off credit cards
3 Monthly targets
4 Cut back
5 Get cheapest deals
6 Save straight after payday
7 Boost income
8 Small, regular overpayments
9 Watch for charges
10 Don't over-stretch yourself

PROBLEMS PAYING YOUR MORTGAGE?

1 Tell your lender as soon as you think you're going to have a problem. They will help you with a solution.

2 Pay what you can afford. It helps if you demonstrate that you are doing your best.

3 Increase the length of the loan? This will decrease monthly payments, though it's likely to increase the total amount.

4 You could change to an interest-only mortgage, but it's essential that you consider what you will do when the mortgage itself needs to be repaid.

5 Have you got a mortgage payment protection policy? This should cover the payments if you've been made redundant, have had an accident or become ill.

6 Perhaps add arrears to the outstanding mortgage amount and pay it off over the term of the loan, not all in one go.

7 Check what day you make payments on. Sometimes, just changing it to the day after payday will help.

8 Don't take out a loan to pay your mortgage that's at a higher interest rate than the mortgage.

9 Keep in touch with your lender; don't ignore letters or phone calls.

10 Get specialist advice.

GET ON THE PROPERTY LADDER

1 Build your deposit as fast as you can. Pay off any debts, consider taking on extra work and cut back on overheads.

2 Move back home. You'll save far faster.

3 Can the bank of mum and dad help with your deposit?

4 Keep a sharp eye out for bargain properties – repossessions, fixer-uppers and places that have been on the market for a while and might accept a low offer.

5 Is there a scheme to help you buy your first home? Some may offer the right to buy a share of the property at a discount

6 Buy a new-build and take advantage of developer's incentives. They may pay fees.

7 Club together with family or friends. But draw up a proper legal agreement first.

8 Make do with a smaller property. It's OK to change your mind if it's hard to find the money for what you'd really like.

9 Shop around for the best mortgage deal. Seek specialist advice.

10 Can you rent out a spare room to help pay the mortgage?

BUY A GREAT PROPERTY

1 First get an agreement from a lender before you start house-hunting. You will know how much you can borrow and sellers will take you more seriously.

2 Research the area. Look at local plans, check out transport and amenities.

3 Look for signs of the area smartening up. Attractive architecture is another plus.

4 Better buy the worst house in a good street than the best house in a bad street.

5 Search on the internet. A few clicks will show you hundreds of dream homes.

6 Look for a house in an area with good schools. Even if you don't have children, the property will be more attractive to more buyers when you come to sell.

7 Get to know a property by studying not just the written details and photographs, but also virtual tours, aerial maps and local websites.

8 Look at how much similar houses in the same area have sold for recently.

Base your offer on these prices.

9 Get a good home survey and inspection done, so you know all the details of the property's physical condition.

10 Don't bust your budget. Take into account all the expenses, from fees to tax and insurance, and make sure you really can afford the property.

ADD VALUE TO YOUR HOME

1 Convert the loft – it's usually cheaper than moving to a bigger house. Provided it has enough headroom, you can create a bedroom, perhaps with bathroom, a home office or a playroom.

2 Build an extension – but make sure it doesn't take up too much of the garden.

3 Build a room in the garden. Great for a home office, games room or chill-out zone. Ideally insulate it and run power to it.

4 Convert the basement into a family living space. No need to alter the exterior – though it may have low ceilings.

5 Add a conservatory on the back. It's not too dear and optimizes sunshine.

6 Convert your garage into a living space.

7 Redecorate. Buyers will likely pay more if your house is freshly painted.

8 Improve the kitchen. It's what every buyer will be interested in.

9 Add a parking space. If you live in an area where parking's at a premium, convert the front garden into off-street parking

10 Upgrade your outside space. A high-quality garden/hard landscaping will make your property more desirable.

MAKE MONEY FROM YOUR HOME

1 Take in a lodger but think it through carefully. You could make a new friend... or sharing your space could be a nightmare.

2 Rent out a room as a daytime office.

3 Be a friendly host for foreign students. This works best if you live in a big city or tourist destination. Some students want year-round accommodation, others are seasonal. You may be expected to provide meals, too.

4 Set up as a bed and breakfast. Best if you live in a desirable area and are really good with people – and at cooking!

5 Rent a room as a weekday let. Some people need a place to stay while they work Monday to Friday. You can still use your spare room at weekends.

6 Rent out your parking space. If you live in a town/city where parking is at a premium, you could rent to a commuter – or perhaps to the theatre or sports crowd.

7 Become a movie location. Make your home a star – though it helps if it has lots of parking. Though a bit unreliable and disruptive, the work pays well.

8 Rent out your home while you go on holiday. Why let it stand empty?

9 Make money from people who want to store their surplus stuff. Advertise your spare space: your garage, shed or attic.

10 **Sell your garden to developers.** It's a drastic move, but if you have a large garden and you can get permission to build on it, you could make a lot of money.

RENT OUT YOUR SPARE ROOM

1 **What space can you allocate to a lodger?** They'll need their own bedroom, but where will they do their cooking, wash their clothes and socialize with friends?

2 **Not prepared to share too much of your space?** Perhaps you could put a TV and sofa/chair in their bedroom. In a larger room, installing basic cooking facilities may even be a possibility.

3 **Tell your mortgage lender, landlord and insurer.**

4 **Work out how much you can charge.** Look online or in classified ads and see how much other landlords in your area are asking for a similar standard of room.

5 **Prepare the room carefully.** It should be spotlessly clean and fully functional.

6 **Write a clear, accurate, persuasive ad** for your local paper, online and local shops. Will the room be furnished or unfurnished?

7 **Always run a credit check and/or take up references** after you've interviewed prospective lodgers and made your choice.

8 **Both sign an agreement** that states the rights and obligations on both sides.

9 **Take a reasonable deposit.** This means you're covered if things do go wrong.

10 **Be around when your lodger moves in.** Be friendly and welcoming and answer questions. Go over ground rules, too.

HOW TO SELL A HOUSE

WHAT'S YOUR DREAM HOME?

1 Castle
2 Country cottage
3 Mansion
4 Penthouse
5 Beach hut
6 Lakeside hut
7 Log cabin
8 Glass house
9 Treetop
10 Igloo

1 **Do that value-adding alteration** before the house goes on the market.

2 **Invite several agents** round to value your property, then take an average.

3 **Research what people are asking for similar homes** near by and what prices have been achieved recently.

4 **Choose an agent who knows your area** and who sells your type of property. They should be proactive with phone calls, produce thorough details, listings and brochures and have a good internet presence.

5 **Check that your agent has all the information**, and that what they write about your property is accurate.

6 **Good photography helps.** Photograph the house on a sunny day. Ensure all interiors look bright and airy.

7 **Put most of your possessions away** and tidy up. If the house looks a little bare, that's probably about right.

8 **First impressions are extremely important** so ensure that your house looks immaculate from the outside.

9 **Sort out all the imperfections.** Chipped paintwork and dripping taps should be easy to sort out. Clean from top to bottom.

10 **'Stage' your home for viewings** with fresh flowers and plumped-up cushions. Open the windows, too.

PREPARE TO MOVE

1 **Give your landlord ample notice** if you are renting.

2 **Check your home insurance** and make sure cover will start on your new home on the day you move in.

3 **Choose a removal firm.** Check their references and insurance limits, too.

4 **Start to declutter.** The more you get rid of, the less you'll have to pack and unpack.

5 **Order furnishings and flooring** for the new house in good time, so that it will be delivered as soon as you move in.

6 **Pack as much as you can in advance.** Doing a little a day won't seem too painful.

7 **De-register from your doctor, dentist and optician** and sign up with new ones.

8 **Make arrangements for kids or pets** to be looked after elsewhere on moving day.

9 **List all those who need to know** that you've moved and write to them. Contact your bank and cancel/alter all the relevant payments such as your mortgage/house insurance.

10 **Finalize all the details** with your chosen removal company and arrange to collect the keys.

BUY A SECOND HOME

1 **Are you buying the property to rent it out?** Think carefully about how you will feel about being a landlord, dealing with tenants, collecting rent and so on.

2 **Purchase a property for rental** in an area where there is strong demand from students/workers/families. Ask advice from local rental agencies.

3 **If you are buying a property to use as a holiday home,** consider whether you could also rent it to others and cover some costs. Buy in an area popular with tourists.

4 **Check whether buying it will alter your tax situation.**

5 **Shop around for the best deal on insurance.** Some insurers won't cover you if the house is unoccupied for more than 30 days in a row, for example.

6 **Be aware of all the costs.** As well as the purchase itself, there'll be maintenance and repairs, insurance and new furniture.

7 **Analyse the cost of travelling to your second home.** Will it take too much time to get there and will this put you off going?

8 **Work out how best to maintain your second home.** One option is to use an agent or find someone local.

9 **Second homes that aren't used very often may attract burglars.** Be thorough about security and perhaps change door/window locks. Consider an alarm.

10 **For an infrequently used home, plug in lights on a timer** and find someone who can check it regularly. They should make it look lived-in by mowing the lawn, clearing leaves/snow and picking up post.

BUY IN ANOTHER COUNTRY

1 Want to earn a regular letting income? Buy in an area with proven strong demand.

2 Factor in the cost of travelling if you're buying abroad as a holiday home and will go there frequently.

3 Want to live permanently in your new home, either now or in the future? Choose a country where you feel comfortable and will settle in quickly and easily. Learning the language is top priority.

4 Research your area in depth – even more so than if you were buying at home. Visit and talk to locals.

5 Use a reputable agent who knows the local market inside out. Arrange to have all letters and documents translated.

6 Understand the inheritance tax laws in the country where you're planning to buy. They may be very different to what you're used to.

7 Get a grip on all the local laws and regulations relating to property – from planning to taxation.

8 Make friends with any expats already living there. They've already been through the whole process and will be an invaluable source of good advice.

9 Keep track of all the paperwork to do with the purchase and file them carefully – letters, emails, agreements, certificates, payments and so on.

10 Have your finances ready. In some countries you'll need to put down your deposit as soon as the sale is agreed.

LET A PROPERTY

1 Maintain the property in excellent condition. The higher quality the property to start with, the more likely it is that your tenants will respect it and look after it.

2 Make sure you are familiar with all the rules and regulations relating to letting a property in your area, from taking a deposit to electrical safety.

3 Do every safety check possible and repeat these as often as necessary. Use professional tradesmen – it's important not to cut corners.

4 Agent or DIY? You'll make more money if you look after the place yourself rather than paying a professional manager, but it will cost you in time, effort and, quite possibly, stress.

5 Always take up references and run credit checks on prospective tenants.

6 Why not join a landlord's association? These offer advice, information and contacts.

7 Take out the correct insurance.

8 Set aside finance to cover unexpected expenses, whether a period with no tenant or an uninsured accident.

9 Get a proper lease, tenancy agreement or contract drawn up. Do an inventory – use a video camera with a date stamp.

10 Good, long-term tenants are like gold dust. Hang on to them.

RUN A HOLIDAY LET

1 Make decisions about a few basics first. What market you are aiming for? Will you allow children or pets? What facilities?

2 Marketing is make or break. Be as pro-active as possible. The internet is most people's method of booking a holiday, so set up your own website and/or advertise on others that are suitable to your property.

3 On your website, be clear and simple, use great photography, and optimize it for search engines – it's what makes your site appear high on a list.

4 Consider signing up with a good lettings agency. They'll get you the right clientele and may offer other services such as cleaning, full management and even renovation. But it will cost you – usually around 15–20 per cent of the income.

5 Formulate your terms and conditions: deposits, payments, cancellations, damage and liabilities on both sides.

6 Decorate to the highest possible standard. Holiday guests expect better than at home. Install good-quality, durable, modern fixtures, fittings and appliances.

7 Expect to do regular maintenance, repair and replacement – to a higher standard than your own home. Chipped paint and broken wine glasses? Be prepared.

8 Ensure that your property complies with statutory regulations. Never, ever, skimp on safety.

9 Can you offer extras such as booking theatre tickets or a food hamper on arrival? This may dig into your profits, but they could secure extra bookings or allow you to increase your prices.

10 Be prepared to put the hours in.

BECOME A MILLIONAIRE!

1 Earn as much money as you can. You'll need a good income to have a chance.

2 Don't spend too much. Blow everything you've got on a fast car at this point and long-term goals will slip away.

3 Save as much as possible. Treat savings as if they were another bill you had to pay – not an afterthought that you can miss as often as you manage.

4 Invest your spare money. Get good financial advice and safeguard your money by putting it into a range of investments.

5 Get advice from other millionaires – take books from the library or check out reputable websites. Be wary of expensive courses where the ones making millions will be the teachers rather than you.

6 Step outside your comfort zone and use your entrepreneurial skills. You don't find all that many millionaire employees.

7 Provide something that people will really need and want. You won't make money from a business that everyone else is doing, too.

8 Work hard and don't expect things to be easy. Keep costs down. Educate yourself and find a mentor. Be nice to people.

9 Be prepared to take a risk when an opportunity comes, but never invest more than you're willing to lose.

10 When all else fails: inherit a fortune, marry a millionaire or win the lottery!

FUN & GAMES

Are you a crafty type or a go-getting sportsperson? Good with your hands or prefer reading or writing? From the cerebral delights of chess to the fun of crafting something at home, this chapter offers great tips for making the most of every second of your spare time.

HAVE FUN WITH YOUR FABRIC STASH

1 Doll's house furnishings only need little scraps so this is a great way to use up all your tiny bits and pieces. To make dolly-sized carpets, fray the ends of upholstery fabric so that they look realistic. Snip scraps of lace to make pretty curtains – just thread them onto elastic thread and staple them in place. Little squares of cotton can make pint-sized cushions.

2 Make a magic memory wall-hanging collage using all your bigger scraps. Use up old dressmaking pieces and cut up unwanted clothes to create a special trip down memory lane. Just place the scraps in a pleasing design – every time you see it you'll be reminded of happy times when you were wearing that special dress or top.

3 Patchwork is perfect for using up small pieces. You can place fabric scraps together and make decorative covers for a wide range of household items: curtains, bedspreads, cushions, runners, tablemats, pot holders and sachets.

4 Sew baby bricks using up leftover scraps. Cut colourful squares to make into soft bricks that are easy for the baby to pick up and stack. Choose all your brightest scraps of densely woven cotton. Position and pin rights sides together and stitch, leaving a small opening on one side, clip corners, press and turn. Stuff with washable synthetic wadding and stitch the opening.

5 Turn kids' art into fun cushions. To use up plain scraps of lining fabric or other light-coloured fabrics – get the children to draw dolls or animals in felt-tip pens – adding in all the features. Cut out a front and back – allowing a seam allowance all round the design. Sew front to back, right sides together, leaving a small opening. Turn right side out and stuff with washable wadding. Stitch up the opening.

6 Make something stylish for your home? Make cushion covers to match your curtains out of leftover fabrics. An envelope-style opening is the easiest to sew – no buttons or zips. For the cushion front cut around a cushion pad, allowing extra for turning. The back is the same width, but 10cm (4in) longer to make the overlapping opening.

7 What about an everlasting grocery bag from leftover fabric? You'll never have to accept a plastic bag again. Cut out two pieces of fabric 46 x 51cm (18 x 20in). Place them right sides together and stitch, leaving the top side open. Fold under and topstitch. Use webbing for handles.

8 If you've got lots of colourful old T-shirts, try making a rag rug. Cut the shirts into narrow strips. You need a two-metre length for the base 'cord' and lots of 12cm (5in) lengths to make the knots. First knot the base cord so that it's double and then loop the short ones around it to make tufts, arranging them close to each other. Coil the cord and stitch in place.

9 Cover notebooks with leftover scraps from dressmaking projects – they make great presents. Cut the fabric about 2.5cm (1in) larger than the book cover. Make notches the width of the spine and glue them under. Glue under the front flap, then the cover and back flap. Then glue top and bottom flaps and the first and last pages for endpapers.

10 Gift wrap and labels from fabric scraps? Forget about paper! Use beautiful cloth scraps instead. The technique is called Furoshiki and is Japanese. Wrap the item up and knot it neatly. For labels cut out fabric scraps and stick them on card. Add a coordinating ribbon to tie it on.

SEWING KIT ESSENTIALS

1 Needles
2 Pins
3 Threads
4 Scissors
5 Pinking shears
6 Seam-ripper
7 Thimble
8 Pin cushion
9 Sewing machine
10 Bobbins

SEW EASY HOME SEWING

1 Worn-out elbows? Cut patches out of sturdy fabric, matching or contrasting, and pin in place before stitching down firmly

2 A blind hem stitch is an effective hemming stitch that will prevent stitches from being visible on the right side of the fabric. Everything looks neater that way.

3 When you have finished sewing on a button, wind the leftover thread around the threads between button and coat to make a really sturdy 'stalk'. Your button will stay on for much longer.

4 Keep an ordinary magnet handy in your sewing basket – so that you can easily pick up any pins you have dropped.

5 To make it easier to find a needle in a pincushion – leave it threaded up with a short piece of thread.

6 When you sew, press as you go. For a really professional finish to any item you sew, press every seam open as you go along. It makes a real difference.

7 When making curtains, you need to allow enough fabric to cover twice the width of the window.

8 Get more wear out of your clothes by altering them. You can take in darts or let them out, and take hems up or down.

9 Repair your clothes whenever you see a small tear or a worn spot appear and mend them before the problem gets any worse. There's no need to discard favourite items just yet. Just look online for simple tutorials if you're not quite sure of the correct sewing methods.

10 Never sew when you're feeling tired and grumpy – you'll just rush and make mistakes, which may be hard to put right later. Sew when you're feeling fresh and upbeat – you'll have a great time!

SIMPLE KNITS

USING LEFTOVER YARN

1 Gift-wrap ribbon
2 Stripy scarf
3 Baby blanket
4 Blanket squares
5 Small bags
6 Lampshade fringe
7 Table runner
8 Baby mitts
9 Socks
10 Baby toys

1 Use large bamboo needles and light-coloured worsted-weight wool so that you can see what you are doing. Bamboo needles will glide more easily.

2 Wash your hands before you pick up the needles – sticky hands will stop the needles gliding over each other smoothly.

3 Learn how to cast on using the knit-stitch method.

4 If you've never knitted before, start by making a simple swatch of 20–25 stitches.

5 Practise the knit stitch until you are really good at it. Then you can move on to purling. Don't try to learn any other new stitches until you have mastered both of these basics as they're the most-used ones.

6 Now learn how to cast off – though it's best not to attempt this until you are a really confident knitter.

7 For your first project, choose something made from garter stitch – this way you don't have a pattern to remember.

8 Move on to alternating rows, knit/purl.

9 If you make a mistake, 'tink', or undo, your knitting until you get back to your mistake. Only do this if you haven't knitted on too far from your mistake.

10 Some simple first-knitting projects might be: a plain scarf, blanket squares, pot holders or an easy beenie hat.

SUPER-COOL CROCHET

1 Wind the skein of yarn into a ball before you start crocheting – this will make your progress easier, improve your tension and avoid tangling difficulties. Do it by hand or acquire a ball-winder.

2 Position the ball of yarn so that it can unwind easily as you go along. Keep it in your lap or have it on the floor at your feet. If you are in a vehicle/public place, put it into a bag to stop it rolling away.

3 If you tend to crochet too tightly – choose a larger crochet hook.

4 The hook size on your pattern is just a suggestion – it depends on your style of crochet. So experiment with hooks before you start making something important.

5 Don't change hook sizes in the middle of a project – your tension will change.

6 Try ergonomic crochet hooks – these are designed for those who have repetitive stress injuries and a range of other hand-related problems. However, they tend to be expensive compared to standard models and are prone to breaking.

7 If your work seems to be too loose, choose a smaller hook.

8 Make gauge swatches before you start a project. Don't skip this stage otherwise your project may turn out the wrong size.

9 Don't be afraid to unravel your crochet if you make a mistake. It's better to undo and go back rather than ploughing on. The mistake will be there forever.

10 Experiment and practise! Think about putting unusual colours together in a pattern or choosing unexpected yarns.

QUAINT PATCHWORK QUILTS

1 Create a design first of all. Think about where your quilt will be kept once finished and what style you would like. Is it intended for an adult or a child. You could make one to celebrate a special occasion.

2 Work out your design on graph paper and use coloured pencils. Research designs online or in books and magazines.

3 Cotton is a good quilt fabric – it's easy to work with and doesn't crease. It is not flammable and is generally allergy-free.

4 If you have plenty of time to spare and like hand-sewing, you can make the whole thing by hand. You will need to make templates from thin card and cut out your fabric pieces around them.

5 If you are using a sewing machine, cut out your patchwork pieces precisely, with special attention to turnings.

6 Rotary cutters can be a real time-saver when cutting out your pieces.

7 A few supplies you'll need: washable fabric markers, needles, hoops, thimbles, pins, threads and cottons.

8 Use cotton thread and if your quilt is brightly coloured select a grey colour. You may want to buy ready-waxed thread for extra strength and ease of untangling, or you can coat it in bees' wax yourself.

9 Choose batting or wadding with care. Both come in different thicknesses and can be natural or synthetic.

10 Machine-quilt if you want to get a quick result.

POPULAR QUILT PATTERNS

1 Amish
2 Hawaiian
3 Log Cabin
4 Cathedral Window
5 Wedding Ring
6 Crazy
7 Double Pinwheel
8 Grandmother's Flower Garden
9 Trip Around the World
10 Lone Star

STITCH YOUR OWN BUNTING

1 **Think about what the bunting will be decorating.** Will it be for a street party, to celebrate a new baby or for a birthday party? Instead of ordinary triangles, you could think about having letter shapes, hearts, cupcakes, flowers – you name it!

2 **Choose bias binding for the tape.**

3 **Get out your fabric scrap stash** and select the brightest and best for your bunting. Choose cottons. Think 'jolly'.

4 **Iron the pieces** before you start.

5 **Cut out the fabric into long-shaped triangles** – use a card template.

6 **You can hem the triangles,** if you like, along the long edges. Or you can trim them with pinking shears so that they don't fray.

7 **Position the triangles** at generously spaced intervals inside the bias binding folds. Think carefully about good colour juxtapositions.

8 **Allow a good length of bias binding at either end –** you may want to tie the bunting around a tree or lamp post.

9 **Machine-stitch twice along the bias binding,** catching in the tops of the flags. Add interesting trimmings, such as those bobbly ones used for lampshades, to the flag tops if you like.

10 **Hang up your bunting** in swagged loops and enjoy!

PRESSED FLOWERS – SO SWEET!

ESSENTIALS FOR ARRANGING FLOWERS

1 Freshly cut flowers
2 Suitable containers
3 Florist's knives
4 Wires & pins
5 Foliage stripper
6 Florist's scissors
7 Floral foam
8 Strings & tape
9 Ribbons & bows
10 Staples

1 **Pick flowers when they are at their freshest** and make sure that there's no moisture on them.

2 **If you don't press them straight away,** be sure to condition them in order to prolong their life.

3 **Think how the flowers will look when they are flattened.** If possible, prevent the petals from overlapping and lay the leaves out flat.

4 **Remove all the stamens from lilies,** otherwise the white petals will be stained yellow. The same applies to other delicately coloured blooms.

5 **Treat the plant with spray-on glycerine,** if you like, before you start the pressing process – especially with foliage and autumn leaves. You can buy it in a chemist or at a crafts store.

6 **You can curve straight stems** to make a more effective design – run it between your thumb and the blunt edge of a pair of scissors. Be sure to do this before pressing.

7 **Place the flower between two sheets of paper** and insert them between the pages of a heavy book.

8 **You could put the book into a micro-wave and zap it** in short bursts (30 seconds to a minute). Check and repeat until the flower is almost dry and flat.

9 **Buy a botanical flower press.** This is made especially to allow the air to circulate. Or try a special microwave flower press, which is purpose-made to use in microwave ovens.

10 **Use the pressed flowers for collages,** greetings cards or just put them into an album. You'll be able to create pretty designs and have memories of the day you picked them.

LIGHT YOUR WAY WITH CANDLES

1 **Use a double-boiler –** never melt wax over an open flame.

2 **Try making your own moulds** using a milk carton, yogurt pot or even an old-fashioned teacup.

3 **Choose a suitable container to use as a candle mould.** Make sure it won't catch fire, leak, crack or break. Glass jars are great because they're designed to withstand heat.

4 **Use a bit of masking tape to stick the wick** to the bottom of the mould and tie the other end to a pencil lying across the open end.

5 **If you want to be green** don't use paraffin wax – it's a versatile and common wax for candles, but it's a product of the oil-refinement process.

6 **Soy wax is a good alternative to paraffin wax** and it's much cheaper than bees' wax (the most ancient and traditional type – with loads of sweet fragrance, too).

7 **Collect up all the scraps of your old candles** by melting them down. Remove any debris and old wick ends and use them just as you would new wax. Take particular care if the wax is coloured and scented – mixing up different waxes will be a bit of an experiment, which may not always work. On the other hand you may end up a happy accident.

8 **Use the old candle scraps for testing out** new moulds or pouring techniques.

9 **Recycle wax drips and spills** when pouring your new candles.

10 **Refrigerate the candle** at least one hour before you light it to slow down the burning process.

LATHER UP YOUR OWN SOAP

1 **Safety first!** Always wear protective gloves and goggles.

2 **Never make soap with kids around.**

3 **If you are a first-timer –** start with the cold process or the melt-and-pour method.

4 **Use only suitable fragrance oils** that have been tested and then found to be OK for soap-making.

5 **Natural essential oils are the best choice.** They have health benefits and are the best green option.

6 **Have your moulds to hand –** before stirring the soap mixture, so that you're prepared when your mixture is ready.

7 **Use stainless steel, glass and plastic equipment –** other metals can react badly with the soap-making ingredients and cause them to become unstable.

8 **Take notes as you go along.** That way you remember the do's and don'ts and can recreate those accidental miracles the next time you have a soap-making session.

9 **It's best to line your moulds** with wax paper, lightly greased with vaseline, so that you can get the soaps out more easily.

10 **When cutting your soap** use a length of wire with two handles or a fishing line – and be careful.

CRAFTS FOR YOUR GARDEN

1 Glass-bottle terrarium
2 Woven fencing
3 Wirework sculpture
4 Salvaged timber bench
5 Pebble inlaid path
6 Painted plant pots
7 Painted pebbles
8 Willow tunnels
9 Mosaic table tops
10 Basket plant containers

SUPERIOR HOME–MADE GIFTS

FOODIE GIFTS
1 Chocolate-dipped pretzels
2 Preserves
3 Brownies
4 Fudge
5 Chutney
6 Flavoured popcorn
7 Biscuits
8 Bread
9 Sweets
10 Fruitcake

1 Make a memory calendar for an elderly relative. Get in touch with all your relatives and ask them if they have any photographs and/or memories of the person. Stick 365 onto a piece of stiff paper and put them into a box or jar. The person removes one a day for a year to remind themselves of times gone by.

2 Create candles in your teacups. Search for pretty cups and saucer sets in charity shops and car-boot sales. Make sure they are not cracked or damaged. Buy wicks and candle wax or use old candle stubs melted down. Melt the wax in a double boiler and add a fragrance if you like. Support the wick and pour the wax over it. Leave until it is set.

3 Compile a family recipe book. Ask all your rellies to contribute their favourite recipes and perhaps meet up for a day to stick them into a home-made album. Keep adding to it as your family grows.

4 Offer gifts of time if you're a bit cash-strapped. Consider babysitting, computer help, tuition, gardening chores, knitting a sweater – you name it. Just write your skills down on coupons and give them to someone as a gift.

5 Make a spice set for a keen cook – buy spices in bulk and decant them into pretty, small matching jars. Add nicely penned and decorated labels. You could also make customized spice blends and perhaps add a nice recipe for each spice.

6 Put together a hidden-treasure box. Find an interestingly bound old hardback – preferably worn – in your local charity shop. Hollow out the centre of the book with a craft knife and give it to someone for hiding valuables in. Fool those burglars!

7 Give a make-from-scratch shortbread/ biscuit or cake kit. Assemble the ingredients and measure them out carefully – put them into pretty bags and jars and label them attractively. Write out the recipe and decorate it. All the lucky recipient has to do then is get everything out and follow your recipe. Ta-da!

8 Give home-made truffles. Truffles are oh-so easy to make, but they do need to be put together and consumed quickly – they have a short shelf life. No problem! And a pretty box makes all the difference.

9 What about themed gift baskets? For example, if you gave a 'Little Italy' basket, you could use a colander as a container, add some garlic bulbs, a wooden spoon, a jar of your special pasta sauce and finish the whole thing off with gourmet pasta.

10 Make a personal gift box. Find an old shoe box and decorate it. Fill it with little things that mean a lot to the recipient such as charity-shop treasures, origami birds and hand-written jokes.

GORGEOUS GREETINGS CARDS

1 You can buy plain cards and envelopes all ready to decorate, but if you prefer to buy paper by the sheet – choose a sturdy card and separate envelopes to fit your size. Remember that the card doesn't have to be rectangular – necessarily.

2 Save up all your bits of scrap paper. Cut them up to use for collage designs or to punch out 'punchies'.

3 Use rubber stamps to embellish your cards – there's a vast range to choose from. Washable inkpads are a good idea – especially if you are card-making with kids.

4 Pressed wild flowers can be great for decorating cards. They make a striking centrepiece for your design – or put several together to make a bunch of flowers.

5 Make a mini patchwork out of fabric scraps and stick them onto your card.

6 Create personalized cards by including a photo of the person you are sending it to. Great for a special birthday.

7 Give a flamboyant Valentine's card – fashion a stuffed red satin heart and surround it with real lace.

8 Customize your cards according to the recipient and the occasion – think of their favourite colour, hobby or occupation. You can download templates for different events and occasions.

9 Go for exciting pop-up cards – using basic origami techniques.

10 Add embellishments: glitter, colourful braids, stars and stickers.

WRITE THAT NOVEL!

1 Devise a good plot. Write a brief outline or note down the different stages of the story on index cards.

2 Choose themes that really fascinate you – otherwise you will get bored and this will show up in your writing.

3 Your characters are important and they must seem 'real'. Let them come alive gradually by freeing up your imagination. They need to grow independently and have their own lives. You'll be surprised what you come up with.

4 Get the complete story down on paper while your ideas are still fresh.

5 Stick to a regular writing schedule. Writing needs to become a regular habit for you to achieve anything significant. Decide what timetable works best for you and make sure it combines well with all your other commitments.

6 Be prepared to revise your writing and then revise again – until it seems right.

7 Get feedback from those you trust – don't be dismayed if they don't mince words and you then need to go back and revise even more. It will be worth it.

8 Look at the big picture first – fix the large structural problems to begin with. Then go back and pep up the detail.

9 Let it rest! Put your work aside for a while and work on something else instead. Then come back to your writing and see it with fresh eyes – you'll be able to make some worthwhile corrections.

10 Be prepared to make drastic cuts – if something doesn't work, cut it. Don't leave it in just because you worked on it for hours. The end result might be a lot better.

FICTION GENRES

1 Thriller
2 Crime
3 Erotic
4 Adventure
5 Humour
6 Fantasy
7 Gothic
8 Romance
9 Medical
10 Literary

GET INTO PRINT

1 **Think about why you want to get published.** Is it because you have a really fantastic idea for a novel or you want to transmit your knowledge and expertise about a particular subject?

2 **Want to make money?** Publishing a book is probably not the way to do it. You have to be a best-selling author to see a good return on your efforts.

3 **Ask yourself whether what you write is any good.** What about your style? Does it suit the people you think will want to read your book? There are different styles for different purposes.

4 **Go on creative writing courses** and take any advice and feedback you can get on your work.

5 **Write and then rewrite.** Then be prepared to rewrite again. Writing is a craft and you need loads of practice in order to produce anything that might be any good.

6 **Ask other people to read your book** and get them to be honest in their reactions – each new reader will react individually. Take all their comments on board and incorporate them carefully.

7 **Find an author's agent.** They will make suggestions for improving your work and if they want to get behind it, they will find a publisher for it and negotiate a deal. In return for a percentage, of course.

8 **Research publishers** who might be interested and look at what is already on their list. Look at their catalogues and visit bookshops to see what they produce.

9 **Send a enquiry letter to the publisher** before sending in your manuscript. This is to find out whether they might be interested – that way you won't be wasting time asking the wrong company.

10 **Allow publishers about three months** to look at your manuscript. Some take longer, but if they aren't interested you want to know sooner rather than later.

READ UP AT A BOOK CLUB

1 **Book clubs can change lives.** They are great for reading titles you might not normally have thought of reading.

2 **You can hear a whole range of different, sometimes surprising, opinions.** Listening to other people's perspectives will help you get a lot more out of your personal reading.

3 **Being in a book group gives you the motivation to read.** No more excuses and sinking in front of the telly with a glass of wine of an evening – you are reading your book for a reason.

4 **Read the book carefully** and note two interesting things about it – so that you have something to contribute.

5 **No time to go to evening meetings?** Try an online reading group.

6 **Newspapers sometimes contain book reviews** aimed at reading groups.

7 **You may find notes in the backs of books** that are geared towards book club discussions.

8 **Choose your book club with care.** Some clubs are women-only and some deal only with certain literary genres.

9 Keep discussions focused on the book for at least an hour. Book groups are great social occasions, but there is a tendency for people to get a bit side-tracked.

10 A glass of wine and a few nibbles will help things go with a swing.

PENCIL POWER FOR SKETCHING

1 Use all of the different pencil grades to achieve your tonal range – from hard-grade pencils through to soft grade.

2 Use black to achieve depth in your drawing – if it helps, stick a black piece of paper on the corner of your drawing to remind you.

3 Which grade of paper? Use the correct texture drawing paper for the right effect.

4 Keep a sketch book and practise often – you need to train your eye and hand. Take it with you wherever you go and don't worry about people watching you sketch.

5 Draw light outlines to start with and fill in the shading – from light to dark.

6 Use a strong, single light source on your subject to give it dramatic shadows.

7 Sharpen your pencils using a scalpel not a pencil-sharpener – you can control the shape of the point more easily.

8 Try using blu-tac rather than a normal rubber – it doesn't damage the paper and is useful for creating highlights.

9 Don't rest your hand on the paper surface – it will be greasy. Put your hand on a second piece of paper.

10 Join a sketch group or club so that you can learn from others.

WATERCOLOUR WONDERS

1 Buy good equipment – the best you can afford. Your painting will benefit from good-quality paints, brushes and paper. Start with student-quality paints and don't be tempted to use children's sets.

2 Cakes or tubes? Tubes are more convenient and let you use uncontaminated colour at the start of a painting.

3 Buy paints separately– so that you can select the exact shades you want.

4 The best watercolour brushes to use are sable, but they can be expensive.

5 Choose a white, flat palette – slanted wells make it difficult to gauge the colour intensity. Or use a white dinner plate.

6 The water container should be clear and as large as possible – so that you can see how dirty the water is.

7 Try using two water containers – one for washing brushes and the other for mixing up the colours.

8 Experiment with papers from different manufacturers, with various surfaces, to find the one you prefer. Watercolour paper is best for many of the specific techniques.

9 Buy paper by the sheet, not pads or blocks – it's far cheaper.

BASIC WATER-COLOUR PAINT PALETTE

1 Cadmium Yellow Light
2 Cadmium Yellow Medium
3 Cadmium Red Medium
4 Alizarin Crimson
5 Ultramarine Blue
6 Pthalocyanime Blue
7 Pthalocyanime Green
8 Hooker's Green
9 Burnt Sienna
10 Burnt Umber

10 **Dab off colour and clean palettes** with facial tissue or kitchen roll – don't use toilet tissue as particles will dissolve and could transfer to your painting.

CLEVER CALLIGRAPHY

1 **Start with a cartridge chisel-point** (italic) pen with changeable nibs. Dipping pens are trickier to use.

2 **Use a 'stroke chart'** with a range of styles, samples and examples to study and copy. It will demonstrate how to make the strokes and how to combine them to form the letters.

3 **Practise strokes,** then try to combine them to form the letters.

4 **If you are left-handed,** try oblique nibs as they're cut on a slant to accommodate awkward angles.

5 **Don't let your fingers form the letters.** Learn the proper shoulder motion and wrist-and-forearm techniques.

6 **Don't use cheap copy paper** as your ink will bleed. Laser paper is good for practice.

7 **Use a baseline.** All your letters should sit on the same line and all the strokes should be at the same angle.

8 **Keep letters consistent.** The main body of the letters should be the same and you should be able to draw a line across the tops of the ascenders and descenders.

9 **Pressure and control are two of the key considerations.** In properly written script, the thins are consistent and clean, transitions to and from thick strokes are smooth and transitions occur at the same place for each letter.

10 **Don't worry if your italic looks different** from other calligraphers. Within any style there are many variations – you are an individual and you will develop your own style.

SCRAPBOOKING FOR FUN

1 **Choose a theme first of all.** Family archive? Baby or wedding album? Journal? Holiday record? Special birthday? Graduation? Silver or Golden Wedding?

2 **Use an acid-free, memory-safe pencil or pen** when you write on the backs of photographs. This is a good idea for recording dates and the ages of people.

3 **Each page should tell a different story.** Plan one focal point per page.

4 **Use special scrapbooking adhesive.** Normal white glue will make the pages buckle and crease and it will get brittle as the years go by.

5 **Paper must be acid- and lignin-free** to prevent degradation and discoloration as time goes by.

6 **Keep it simple!** Don't put too many embellishments on to your pages.

7 **To prevent newspaper cuttings from deteriorating** use a special achival spray to neutralize the acid. Scan the clippings and discard the original, or have them copied onto acid-free paper.

8 **Save all your wrapping paper scraps** and use them for borders, tiles or collages.

9 **Start up a scrapbooking group** – that way you can share ideas and supplies.

10 **Use page-protectors** in between your scrapbook pages to increase their life span.

BE A SHUTTERBUG

1 **Take the picture at the subject's eye level** – bend down to photograph pets and children at their level. The end result will be far more engaging.

2 **Shoot with a clean background.** Clutter behind the subject, such as a tree or pole sprouting from the top of someone's head, will spoil the picture.

3 **Don't forget flash for filling in shadow areas** – even when you are outdoors. This works especially well if the sun is overhead or behind the subject.

4 **Create more impact** by moving in close to your subject and filling up your frame as much as you can.

5 **Think about proportion** in the frame.

Your subject will probably look better if you frame it off-centre. Be sure to lock the focus on the main subject before you adjust the framing.

6 **Use the macro facility** when you are photographing very small objects and get right up close to get the detail.

7 **Turn your camera on its side** and take some vertical pictures. Many pics are vastly improved by this simple twist.

8 **Check that your subject is in focus.**

9 **Know what the range of your flash is.** It may only be short – check your manual.

10 **Watch the light – always.** Great light always makes great pictures – it's the difference that makes the difference.

GREAT FEATURES ON A PERSONAL CAMERA

1 Autofocus
2 Zoom lens
3 Face detection
4 Electronic viewfinder
5 Rechargeable batteries
6 Different-quality settings
7 Short shutter delay
8 Flash
9 Carrying case
10 Video feature

JUNIOR MOVIE-MAKERS

1 **Borrow a video camera,** but make sure the owners are in agreement first.

2 **Write your plot.** Brainstorm action ideas and think about the characters.

3 **Create a storyboard** by drawing what each shot is going to look like.

4 **Research locations.** Use your own home and garden as a set – if it's suitable.

5 **Find or make costumes** and raid the attic or charity shops for suitable props.

6 **Establish the cast** and decide who will be director and producer.

7 **Practise your acting skills.** Refine your art and learn to distinguish between 'good' and 'bad' acting.

8 **Rehearse each scene** thoroughly before you try to shoot it.

9 **Shoot the story according to your storyboard.** You will end up with several short movies that will then need to be put together to make a cohesive movie.

10 **Upload your movie** on to the computer and use a programme to cut and paste the scenes together. Piece the story together and use your editing skills, making sure the parts make a convincing whole.

SPACE-SAVING COLLECTIBLES

1. Thimbles
2. Matchbooks
3. Paperweights
4. Snow globes
5. Salt & pepper shakers
6. Autographs
7. Comics
8. Fabergé eggs
9. Netsuke
10. Hat pins

START A COLLECTION

1. **Decide how much you want to spend.** Collecting can require serious outlay, but you may end up with a great investment.

2. **What is your passion?** Collect things that you are interested in.

3. **How much room have you got** for your collection? Vintage cars or matchbox cars?

4. **Collect things that aren't difficult to obtain.** There's no point otherwise.

5. **Learn how to store your collection** so that it will be preserved – especially with delicate items such as stamps.

6. **Categorize and display your collection well.** Add little notes about some of the items which will make the collection interesting for others.

7. **Make friends with other collectors.** You might be able to swap or sell items to improve your collection.

8. **Join a local hobby club** and go to hobby fairs for networking and adding to your collection.

9. **Go for the unexpected.** It could be inexpensive and everyday, such as match boxes or beer mats.

10. **It's all about the thrill of the hunt.** Scour jumble sales, car boot sales and flea markets for cheap/free finds.

PICK OUT A TUNE ON A PIANO

1. **Start by playing pieces you like** and that you are familiar with.

2. **Try playing by ear.** Start with jingles, TV themes or popular tunes. This will help you with fluidity.

3. **Keep your fingers curved** and play on their tips.

4. **Touch the piano keys very lightly** and gently. A relaxed hand is much easier to get to the right place at the right time.

5. **Nearly always play with both hands,** don't try to separate them.

6. **Always keep the rhythm going** even if you make mistakes. Keep playing.

7. **Memorize the pieces you practise** and get them into your long-term memory. A good way to do this is by practising just before you go to bed.

8. **Learn music terminology** and how to read music.

9. **Practice makes perfect** and it's best to put aside time for it every day.

10. **Play in front of other people** whenever you get the chance.

STRUM A GUITAR

1. **Practise playing guitar scales slowly** at first, using the proper fingering, posture and technique.

2. **Set a metronome** at a slow speed, then go on to practise at faster speeds.

3. **Start your practice session** with the

bits that you find most difficult. When your mind is fresh you'll see more progress.

8 Break up your practice sessions into manageable chunks, if this makes things easier – and practise every day.

4 A chord book is a must-have for a beginner – and that's especially true if you are teaching yourself.

5 Learn to play one chord at a time. Or try practising three chords that can easily be played together.

6 Listen to the best guitarists and guitar-intensive music for inspiration.

7 Remember that your hands have to work together simultaneously. Don't stop strumming with your right hand when your left hand is changing position.

9 Play on the best guitar you can afford.

10 Take some guitar lessons. If you are frustrated with your lack of progress or find motivation tricky, consider finding a teacher – or a different teacher if you are not progressing fast enough with your current one.

BETTER SINGING – TRA LA!

1 Open your mouth! That's essential – but if you can put two fingers between your teeth, that's wide enough.

2 Relax your tongue so that the tip isn't resting on your bottom front teeth. You can't achieve maximum quality of tone if your tongue is tense.

3 Don't breathe in too much. It causes tension in your neck, hinders your ability to sing freely and can prevent you from singing high notes.

4 Rest your hand on your larynx while singing – make sure it stays steady.

5 Open and relax the back of your mouth. This is like the 'Aaah' sound.

6 Give it some oomph! You must feel energized about singing, otherwise you will lack passion and it will show.

7 Exercise before you start singing. Do some jumping jacks or jog on the spot – you'll improve your energy levels!

8 Believe what you're singing – connect with the song.

9 Don't force it. Singing should feel as natural as speaking.

10 Assume a good posture for singing. Keep your arms slightly away from your body, clasping your hands in front. Allow your ribcage to fully expand and your lungs to fill to capacity.

LEARN A NEW LINGO

1 Study the language every day – it's best to do this when you are fresh and when your brain is at its most receptive.

2 Revise regularly and go over your lessons several times to give your brain time to digest the material. Make sure gaps between sessions are not too long, otherwise you'll forget everything.

3 Get to grips with one lesson before you move on to the next.

4 **Learn the fundamentals** of the language properly first – before you move on to more advanced levels.

5 **Set yourself some targets.** But make sure they're reasonable – they can motivate you and you'll make progress.

6 **Focus on your interests.** Learn to talk, write and read about what you are most interested in – you are more likely to pick up the language that way.

7 **Don't worry** if you don't seem to be making much progress. This is quite normal.

8 **Don't be too concerned about making mistakes –** getting your message across is the most important thing.

9 **Ask your teacher to correct you** as you go along so that mistakes don't become ingrained habits that are harder to shift.

10 **Visit the country –** it's easier to pick up the language from the locals.

THE ART OF JUGGLING

1 **When you first start juggling,** just get confident throwing and catching one ball (or a beanbag will do, too).

2 **Now try with two balls.** Hold one in each hand. Throw one up and when it comes down, throw the second ball up and catch it again.

3 **Then take three balls.** Hold two in one hand and one in the other. Do the same as with two balls, but when Ball Two is coming down, throw up Ball Three.

4 **Pause between each throw** and try to throw each ball to the same height.

5 **Don't throw the balls too far in front.**

Throw them straight up in the air before your face.

6 **If you juggle by a wall** it helps with your angle discipline. Or else pretend that you're juggling in front of a glass window or while walking backwards.

7 **Focus on what you want to happen.** Visualize the end result.

8 **Work on consistent, steady throws.**

9 **Stay relaxed –** your brain learns the most when you are concentrating in a laid-back way.

10 **Find some other jugglers** and practise with them – more fun!

WE ARE SAILING!

1 **Search for calm and uncrowded waters** if you are a beginner.

2 **Choose a small boat to learn on –** it will be easier to handle, more manoeuvrable and more responsive.

3 **Start off with a boat that is rigged with one sail only.**

4 **Research** the tide, wind and weather

conditions so that you are fully prepared.

5 **Follow the basic safety basics:** tell someone where you are going, take a flotation device or wear a lifejacket. Importantly, be a confident swimmer.

6 **Always take food and drink** and waterproof clothing along with you.

7 **Learn how to adjust the sails** to take

advantage of wind and water conditions.

8 Practise capsizing – you can do this in shallow water or on a practice lake.

9 Watch out for the boom! Don't get a nasty bump on the head – or worse!

10 Learn all the basic sailing terms and perhaps go on a course to gen up on seamanship skills.

STARRY-EYED STAR-GAZING

1 Acquire a torch with a red light to find your way around and read in the dark. A white light will be too bright.

2 Cheap plastic planispheres are great for giving you the night sky from your location at any particular time of the year.

3 Join your local star-gazing society – you'll be able to ask others for advice and help and perhaps be able to try out different telescopes before you acquire your own. Find kindred spirits – it's always good to share knowledge.

4 Subscribe to an astronomy magazine. They come with monthly sky charts.

5 You'll need a powerful pair of binoculars or a telescope, but don't rush to buy – try out all the different types first. Binoculars are probably best to start off with as they take in a much wider field of view.

6 When you have decided to purchase a telescope, don't skimp on quality. It must be portable to get good use out of it, but the aperture needs to be wide.

7 Learn the names and patterns of the stars – familiarize yourself with what you're looking at.

8 Get some basic knowledge by raiding your local library and looking online. Books are probably the more reliable source to start off with.

9 Keep an astronomy diary – a log book of what you do and see will give you a focus and help concentrate your mind.

10 You need to be patient. Persistence will pay off as you may not necessarily see what you want to see for some time.

GIDDY UP! HORSE-RIDING

1 Find out all about your horse's personality. You need to connect with the horse, work as a team, spend time with them and really get to know them. This creates trust between the two of you.

2 Get professional tuition – there's a lot more to riding than may be apparent. It's important to get things right at the outset so that you do not learn the wrong methods and perhaps have accidents down the line.

3 Practise, practise, practise – as much as you can. At least once a week is a good idea if you want to make any progress. The more you ride, the more quickly you will feel comfortable in the saddle.

4 Talk to professional riders and glean as many tips as you can from the experts.

5 Read books on the subject, watch DVDs and pick up all the tips you can.

6 Use your hands and legs correctly.

Always keep your heels down in the stirrups. The right positions will help you interact with your horse far more effectively and your control will be better.

7 **Posture is important** – keep your head and shoulders up and sit straight.

8 **Learn what you can about tack.** You must get your horse ready to ride properly and know how to use all the equipment. For example, if the saddle is not put on properly it could be a safety hazard.

9 **Groom your horse after every ride** – so that you get to know them. And it needs doing anyway!

10 **Be patient with your horse at all times** – never shout at them or hit them.

WALKING FOR FUN

ENERGY-BOOSTING SNACKS

1 Bananas
2 Cereal bars
3 Popcorn
4 Nuts
5 Oatcakes
6 Dried fruit
7 Cheese
8 Chocolate
9 Soy crisps
10 Berry muffins

1 **Find a walking buddy.** It's great to walk and talk.

2 **Join a local walking club or ramblers' association.** They organize regular walks in groups, which makes motivation and planning much easier. Some groups arrange 'slow', 'medium' and 'fast' walks.

3 **Plan a sight-seeing day in detail** so that your walk can become interesting and educational, too.

4 **Listen to music/audio book while you are walking** to keep yourself amused over long distances. When you are wearing headphones remain aware of your surroundings at all times.

5 **Plan to take breaks on your walk** so that you don't wear yourself out. Aim for a café or pub along the route.

6 **Get the whole family walking** – the kids might walk to school and the dog probably needs regular trips out every day.

7 **Wear comfortable walking shoes or boots.** Make sure they are waterproofed to withstand bad weather.

8 **If kids get bored on walks, devise some walking games.** Supply them with bags to make a collection of objects found along the way. They can search for unusual pebbles, colourful leaves, wild flowers or feathers. If you're on a beach look out for driftwood and interesting shells.

9 **Dress to be seen.** You'll need reflectors and/or wear light-coloured clothing if you are walking near traffic in the early morning or at night.

10 **Wear a pedometer** to see how many steps you take. This could be useful if you want to get fit and lose weight.

LET'S GO FLY A KITE!

1 **You'll need a large open space** with plenty of room to lay out your kite and flying line plus the space to fly it in. It's important not to get in the way of other people or other kite-flyers.

2 **Steady, smooth winds are best** and ocean beaches have the best winds. Any turbulent air will negatively affect the way a kite flies. If you can't get your kite up in the air, there's probably not enough wind.

3 **Avoid buildings and trees.**

4 **Don't fly kites near power lines!** Never attempt to free your kite if it gets stuck.

5 **Don't fly kites in wet or stormy weather.** Static electricity can build up and be conducted down the line, so never use wire or anything metallic in the line.

6 **Always wear gloves –** they'll help you to grip on to strong-pulling kites.

7 **Consider taking lessons** if you have a dual-line sports/power kite. These kites can be dangerous if not flown properly.

8 **Tie ribbons to the tail of a diamond kite** to help stabilize it in gusty winds.

9 **If your kite starts diving and looping uncontrollably,** there's probably too much wind for that style of kite.

10 **Landing a kite is easier than takeoff.** Reel it in slowly or walk towards the kite as you reel it in. You can control the speed.

YOYO TRICKS

1 Gravity Pull
2 The Sleeper
3 The Forward Pass
4 Walk the Dog
5 Around the World
6 Skin the Cat
7 Rock the Baby
8 The Breakaway
9 Walk the Cat
10 Reverse Sleeper

LET'S GO ICE SKATING!

1 **Wear the right kit.** Get dressed in layers so that you can remove items once you've warmed up – you will definitely get hot.

2 **Skating boots should fit properly** and be comfortable. Your ankles need to be supported and your feet should be snug – so that they don't slide around too much.

3 **Tie the laces all the way to the top** to help support your ankles. Make sure the lace ends are secured – otherwise they might get caught under a skate and perhaps cause an accident.

4 **If you plan to skate regularly,** buy your own skates. You'll get a better fit, which will help your skating.

5 **Knee and elbow pads are a good idea.** Gel pads are available for figure skaters.

6 **Follow the rink's direction of traffic always –** crashes happen otherwise.

7 **Use skate guards** and only walk on rubberized surfaces – your skates will be ruined if you walk on other surfaces.

8 **Helmets are a must –** especially for children and beginner adults.

9 **Easy-glide equipment** could be a good idea. Beginners push them along in front of them. They're great for kids, too.

10 **It's a good idea to practise falling over** by anticipating the fall, bending your knees and squatting into a dipped position. If you put out your hands to save yourself, clench your fists.

RADICAL ROLLER SKATING

1 **Inline or roller skates?** It's up to you.

2 **Look for a good place to do it.** Many cities have rinks and special parks for roller enthusiasts to practise their skills. When you first start, you might want to go at times that are not too crowded – there'll be less crashing into others that way.

3 **Learn on your own as it's mostly about practice.** But you might want to enlist someone to get you started on the basics. There are certified instructors who can put you on the right track.

4 **Buy your own skates** if you are really serious, but you may be able to hire at rinks. And you'll need all the protective gear, too, such as arm and knee pads plus a helmet. There'll be plenty of thrills and spills – at least when you first start out.

5 **Try to keep your whole body relaxed** and avoid locking your knees. It's quite normal to find that your muscles tense up.

6 **Learn to stop safely** and concentrate on making turns in both directions.

7 **Don't get embarrassed** about your first attempts – everyone has to start somewhere. You'll soon build confidence.

8 **Avoid skating on uneven surfaces** to begin with – especially if you're outside. You'll lose control, and possibly your confidence, all too easily.

9 **Wait until you are highly experienced** before skating on the roads.

10 **Check your skates** constantly for signs of wear and tear.

SKATEBOARDING – HAVE A GO!

1 **Don't begin with jumping ramps!** Take your time, learn at your own speed and always operate within your ability.

2 **Falling over helps!** This sounds mad, but falling builds confidence and your body learns what to do. Practise when you can.

3 **You need to commit to seeing your tricks through** or you may hurt yourself. Don't stop once you've started a move.

4 **Learn skateboarding vocabulary.** Make sure you're referring to a trick by its rightful name – otherwise there may be confusion.

5 **Keep injury-free.** Wear a helmet and buckle it! Knee-pads, elbow pads and wrist guards are also necessary to keep your body all in one piece.

6 **Read reviews of skateboarding gear and skateboards** before you buy as there is a lot of kit to choose from and it is important to get the right board for you.

7 **Don't push on through tiredness and pain.** Injuries are more likely to happen.

8 **Always skate in safe places** and be aware of your surroundings. Notice who else is around and try not to get in other people's way.

9 **Don't worry if you find it a bit scary.** Skateboarding can be dangerous. But if you approach learning and safety correctly you can overcome your fears.

10 **Never stop right in the middle of the skate park!** You'll cause an accident.

STARTER FISHING KIT
1 Rod
2 Reel
3 Line
4 Floats
5 Plummet
6 Hooks
7 Bait
8 Rod rest
9 Landing net/pole
10 Disgorger

BE A TWITCHER

1 **When the bird is in view, fix your eye on it** and take in all its details.

2 **Listen out for distinctive calls and song.** This really helps you to identify the bird, but is all too easy to miss.

3 **Assess the size and shape of the bird** to pick up clues about its family origin.

4 **Notice any facial markings and bill characteristics.** Look at the head first for stripes and patches of colour.

5 **Look at wing bars, tail shape and colour patches.**

6 **Note the colour of the back and belly.** Watch for these details when the bird is still and when it's in flight.

7 **How long is its tail in relation to the body?** How does the bird hold its tail – is it forked, rounded or square-tipped?

8 **Look at the bird's legs –** are they long or short and what colour are they? Determine whether the feet are webbed or have talons. Some birds have toes.

9 **Study movement and flight patterns.** How does the bird walk and how does it jump from branch to branch?

10 **Look at the bird's feeding habits –** determine what it is eating and how. Does it cling to a tree trunk or forage for food?

KIDS! MAKE A DELIGHTFUL DEN

1 **Don't borrow** chairs, sheets, blankets or towels that someone may need to use before you want to dismantle your den.

2 **Build your den in an out-of-the-way place.** That way you may be able to keep it in place for longer. It won't annoy others.

3 **Sheets will let more light** and air into your den, but if you want a dark, spooky den, use blankets instead.

4 **Look for a structure** that will hold blankets up and create a space underneath: bunk beds, between two sofas, under a table or a few chairs in a circle should work perfectly well.

5 **Place heavy books along the edges** of the sheets and blankets so that they are held in place.

6 **Use safety pins, elastic bands, tape or pegs** to connect sheets/blankets together.

7 **Don't forget to make a doorway.** You can use a cushion or pillow for a door and you will be able to get in and out without having to take the den apart.

8 **Make 'walls' by hanging up sheets and blankets** inside the den, or try pinning smaller blankets to the 'roof'.

9 **Cover small gaps and spaces** with towels or pillow cases.

10 **Use extra chairs, sheets and blankets** to make a house with separate rooms.

KIDS' GARDEN PLAY STUFF
1 Hammock
2 Tire swing
3 Rope ladder
4 Treehouse
5 Wendy house
6 Den
7 Trapeze
8 High-jump rope
9 Tin-can stilts
10 Fort

TEACH KIDS TO RIDE A BIKE

1 **Lower the seat to the point** that the child can put their feet on the ground.

2 **Don't use a brand-new bike on the first day.** Use a bike that you are familiar with so that you and your child don't have to deal with a lot of new things at once.

3 **Keep the child's knees (and feet) close to the bicycle.** They will be able to balance better and won't swerve as much.

4 **Don't resort to the one-training-wheel method.** It doesn't teach balance.

5 **If you use the hold-the-back-of-the-seat or the run-beside-the-bike method,** don't trick your child by claiming you're holding on when you are not. If the child crashes, trust and confidence will vanish.

6 **Don't hold the handlebars** – the child cannot learn the feel of balancing if you are controlling the bike for them.

7 **When riding straight,** get your child to look ahead. If your child turns their head, arms/shoulders follow, causing swerving.

8 **From a standstill,** start with one pedal at two o'clock. This gives the rider a solid pedal stroke to power the bike and keep it steady until the other foot finds its pedal.

9 **Always wear a helmet;** tuck in shoelaces and long trousers. Gloves and knee pads may enhance confidence.

10 **Teach on a bike that has a coaster brake,** but add a hand brake to the front wheel, so that the child learns to brake.

FABULOUS FACE PAINTING

1 **Try different types of paint** to see which is best – it comes in tubs or sticks.

2 **Sponge, don't brush.** If you want to cover a large area or put on a base colour, it'll be quicker.

3 **Use a different sponge/brush for each colour.** This gets rid of the necessity to washing out the sponge every time.

4 **Apply the paint in thin layers** rather than putting on one thick layer of paint, which may crack. Let it dry before applying another layer. Let the first colour dry before adding a second. If you don't, the colours might mix and you could have to wipe everything off and start again.

5 **Decide what you're going to paint beforehand** – don't make it up as you go along. Kids aren't known for their patience and won't be able to sit still for long.

6 **The paint will also function as a glue.** To create bumpy noses or big eyebrows, soak a bit of cotton wool in the paint and position it on the face, cover with a piece of tissue and paint. Puffed rice or wheat make perfect warts. For an extra-ghostly effect, apply a light dusting of flour once you've finished painting the face.

7 **Use stencils.** These work well if you're not confident about painting freehand. Stars, hearts and flowers all stencil onto a cheek. Have a few sizes to hand, so that you can allow for small and larger faces.

8 **Beware of using temporary tattoos.** They are faster to apply than stencils, but some kid's skin reacts badly to them and they take longer to remove.

9 **Bring plenty of tissues.** You'll use more than you think for wiping hands and brushes. Baby wipes work fast and are easy for correcting little mistakes.

10 **Don't forget to bring a mirror** so the kids can see the result.

EASY-TO-MAKE FANCY-DRESS

1 **Raid the attic or charity shops** to track down old clothes to convert into fancy-dress items. Cut down and adapt any adult garments that are too large. Such fun!

2 **Look out for hats and cloaks** – these items are useful for a number of different

characters (pirates, nursery-rhyme, TV and story-book characters).

3 **Sew an all-in-one animal suit** made from fake-fur fabric – it's available from good fabric stores and craft shops.

4 **Old sheets and curtains** are exactly what you need! You can use them to make all kinds of characters: ghosts, desert sheiks and Roman centurians. Or cut them up and dye them different colours if you are sewing a special outfit.

5 **Old pillowcases are handy.** You can form the foundation garment for just about any fancy-dress idea. Just cut armholes and a hole for the head and you have a handy tabard-shaped garment to adapt for many costumes. For example, dye it grey and sew on metallic scales to make chain-mail armour.

6 **Save all your large pieces of card** such as cereal packets. You can make a simple sword by cutting it out and covering it with tin foil. Thin card can be used to fashion hats of all kinds, such as a poke bonnet for Little Bo Peep. Cover it with pretty flowery fabric and staple in place.

7 **The final touches can be added with simple accessories** and the child's own improvised clothes. Headscarves can form bandanas, earrings can be made from old curtain rings and shields made from dustbin lids covered in a layer of tin foil.

8 **Collect foil pie trays and milk bottle tops** – they can be used to make 'jewellery' – just cut up, make into balls and thread.

9 **You can do a lot with masks that just cover the eyes.** Cut them out of cardboard and cover with fabric, sequins, braid and ribbons. Go further and cover one with fake fur fabric if you're making an animal costume. Add elastic to hold it on

10 **Use face paints** to get a really convincing effect – paint on beards and moustaches, for example.

FANCY-DRESS IDEAS
1 Pirates
2 Cavemen/ cavewomen
3 Fortune-tellers
4 Spanish dancers
5 Cowboys & Indians
6 Circus clowns
7 Doctor/nurses
8 Gangsters/molls
9 Superheros/ heroines
10 Kings/queens

PUPPETS ARE GO!

1 **Finger puppets are great for entertaining little kids.** Cut the fingers off old gloves and stick felt scraps on for faces.

2 **Glove puppets are easy.** Lay a double thickness of sturdy cotton out and draw around the hand – allowing the thumb to stick out. Draw a face on one side. Stitch right sides together, turn and sew on wool/ string hair. Add buttons for eyes.

3 **Pipe-cleaner puppets are a cute idea.** Twist two pipe cleaners together to create a body. Twist a third around to make the arms and bend the ends to make hands and feet. Wind scraps of wool around the limbs and make clothes out of scraps. The head is a stuffed circle of stretchy fabric. Glue it onto the body and then add the features.

4 **Wooden spoons make great puppets** – the long handle is good for smallies to hold. Stick a paper face on and draw on features. Glue on wool hair.

5 **Collect old paper bags.** Smooth them out and draw faces on them. Colour the corners for animal ears. Gather the opening together around a piece of dowelling.

6 **Use a paper plate as a puppet face** and stick it to a broom handle. Cut paper tendrils for hair and stick on scraps to make the eyes, nose and mouth.

7 **Find a traditional mop** with a stringy head and wooden handle. You've already got the crazy hair (the mop), so just cut out a felt face and mark on features.

8 Use up old odd socks or the sleeves of a discarded sweater to make arm puppets. Stripy ones are great for making snakes. Add felt faces and ears and make horses' manes out of lengths of plaited wool.

9 Shadow puppets are fun. Draw your character onto stiff cardboard, colour it and cut it out – the more expressive the shape the better. Add clothes and then stick the arms on to chopsticks for easy manipulation. Rig up an old sheet and shine a light on it for the shadow effect.

10 Need a puppet theatre? Find two similar-sized boxes and cut an arch in the front of one. Cut slots in the sides and make scenery flats from the other box – suspended from dowelling rods. Make characters out of thin card and stick them to chopsticks for sliding on and off stage.

YOUR VERY OWN DOLL'S HOUSE

1 Why not use old cardboard shoe boxes to make an open-fronted dolls' house? Glue or tape the boxes together to form the rooms and pile them as high as you like to make a multi-storey building. Cut window shapes into the outside walls.

2 Paint the exterior with emulsion paint or go all French and paint *trompe-l'oeil* murals on the outside walls.

3 To create a period piece download vintage wallpapers.

4 Short of time? Paint the interior walls white and draw on fixtures and fittings such as shelves, kitchen cupboards, fireplaces and pictures using a black marker pen. Colour in the lines for extra authenticity. Then position your furniture.

5 Make curtains from lace fabric scraps, thread on to elastisized thread and staple into place. Add colourful ribbon tie-backs.

6 Create beds and chests of drawers out of old matchboxes. Add pillows and a bedspread made from scraps of fabric.

7 Fashion tables from thread spools and plastic lids, and chairs from halved corks, or cardboard tubes and egg cartons. Paint them with emulsion paint and add details such as minute cushions and tablecloths made from your smaller fabric pieces.

8 Personalize your house by using small photo-booth or postage stamps as pictures to hang on the walls.

9 Make living room and bedroom carpets out of carpet scraps or weave your own. Use a offcuts of lino for the kitchen.

10 Don't forget to people your house with small dolls and make it even more homely by adding a pet or two.

THINGS TO MAKE FROM TIN CANS

1 Vases
2 Plant/herb pots
3 Storage jars
4 Tea-light holders
5 Cookie cutters
6 Pin cushions
7 Table numbers
8 Party favours
9 Wine rack
10 Soap dispenser

HAPPY CRAFTING WITH KIDS

1 Decide what you want to make with the kids and assemble all the bits and pieces first. It's wise to do this in advance so that their patience isn't overly tested.

2 Expect a lot of mess and prepare for it. You might want to supply aprons and a plastic sheet to go beneath the work area.

3 Stay with the kids to make sure they know what they're doing and how. Don't assume you can just leave them to get on with it. They may be able to for a few minutes, but now's probably not the best time to go and get on with things elsewhere – it won't last.

4 Give help, but not too much – let the kids work out some things for themselves. They'll get far more satisfaction from what they're doing that way.

5 Don't expect perfection – it's the doing of it that counts to the child. So refrain from being too critical about techniques that are less than wonderful. If you're following instructions, be prepared to change them or just let the child do what they want. It's personal creativity that counts here.

6 Set up a craft shelf at home where you store all the bits and pieces that might be needed for projects.

7 Collect recyclables that might be useful for your child's junk modelling – yogurt pots, cardboard, cotton reels, bottle tops and plastic containers.

8 Find a place for displaying what your child makes – that way satisfaction lies. They can feel proud of what they make and show off achievements to all their friends and family.

9 See the project through to the end. If they don't finish what they're doing they won't learn that completing things is important – you can't just give up and walk away when you get a bit bored.

10 Offer lots of praise for the completed project and let them show it off to friends and family.

TEACH KIDS TO BE GOOD LOSERS

1 Be a good role model. Your child will model your behaviour, so always be a good sport. Admit your mistakes and explain how you learn from them.

2 Don't let your child win all the time. Losing is fact of life and it takes practice learning how to handle it.

3 Expose your kids to ordinary small disappointments. This will make them more resilient and teach them not to expect everything to go their way.

4 Avoid reprimanding a post-loss tantrum. Wait for a while and then ask how your child is feeling now. Suggest that throwing equipment around in anger wasn't the best way to deal with losing.

5 Wean kids off needing to win all the time. Explain that losing is just part of playing and the only person who really loses is the one who doesn't try.

6 If your child loses, discuss the other aspects of the game so that they realize fun can be had without winning.

7 Allow children to express feelings in words. Tell your child that it's OK to be angry, upset, frustrated or sad that they lost, but that no one can win all the time.

8 Encourage your children to handle defeat gracefully with a few after-the-game phrases such as 'Good race!', 'That was close' or 'Unlucky!'

9 Teach your child that good players and good losers support and encourage each other, especially in team games.

10 End on a good note. Suggest how your child could do better next time.

POPULAR PLAY-GROUND GAMES

1 King of the Castle
2 Tag
3 Blind Man's Buff
4 Simon Says
5 Giant Steps
6 Green Light, Red Light
7 Grandmother's Footsteps
8 Hop Scotch
9 Leapfrog
10 Skipping-rope games

GREAT SCRABBLE MOVES

1 Before beginning the game, decide which dictionary you are going to refer to. You will want to avoid disagreements.

2 Look to play a 'bingo', using all seven letters. You will get a 50-point bonus. The most common letters players save to create a bingo are A, E, I, N, R and S.

3 Don't be afraid to exchange letters, especially at the beginning when there are lots of spaces to play a bingo.

4 Plan ahead and aim to use the high-value letters on a double- or triple-letter or word square.

5 Memorize as many two-letter words as you can. They will be useful.

6 Place a new word alongside an existing word to dramatically increase your score.

7 Keep reshuffling your letters between turns to see what other possibilities you might have. Just don't forget the words that you have already found!

8 Play with good Scrabble players and pick up some of their tricks.

9 Don't be afraid to open things up on the board. Even if it seems that you are helping your opponents, you will be helping yourself, too.

10 Play defensively. Avoid giving other players easy access to bonus-point squares, especially the triple-word scores.

MONOPOLIZE MONOPOLY

1 Always buy railway stations and never buy utilities at their full price.

2 Get out of gaol quickly early in the game, even if you have to pay. Later on, when moving around the board is more dangerous, stay in gaol as long as you can.

3 Focus on acquiring a complete colour group at the beginning of the game.

4 When you build, get to three houses quickly – the rent goes up significantly between two and three houses.

5 Remember that the fourth square (red group) after 'free parking' is the most often landed on (besides 'gaol').

5 If you're stuck with some low-income properties, build to four houses quickly in order to create a building shortage, hurting other players' chances to build.

6 Pick up available properties if: no other player owns one of the same group;

the purchase would give you two or three of the same group; it blocks someone else from completing a set.

7 Don't forget that you can buy houses and do swaps during your turn or between the turns of any other players.

8 The orange set is an excellent one to own because of its relationship to gaol. A dice roll of six or eight (two of the most common rolls) from gaol lands you on an orange site.

9 Try to avoid mortgaging where you own two or more of the properties. If one property in a set is mortgaged, you cannot build on any of the properties in that particular group.

10 Show no mercy! If a player is going through a downturn, try to eliminate them. Luck plays too big a role in Monopoly to risk a player making a comeback.

CONQUER AT DRAUGHTS

1 Leave your pieces in your home row for as long as possible. If your opponent cannot king their piece, they will be at a disadvantage.

2 Don't play defensively. No defence that you build can stand up over time.

3 Be willing to sacrifice a draught piece if necessary. Move where you sacrifice one of your pieces, knowing that you have set your opponent up to take two or three of their pieces in return.

4 Your goal should be getting a draught piece to the end of the board. A kinged piece is powerful.

5 Dominate the centre. Pieces in the middle of the board have greater options than those along the edges.

6 Examine every possible move in your mind first before you actually make it.

7 Centralize your kings towards the end of the game.

8 Side moves can be beneficial as you cannot be jumped when your pieces are along the sides. Don't do this too early.

9 If you do not have many pieces left or do not have a king, move your piece into the corner and move back and forth from that point. It will be more difficult for the other player to take your piece and you may even capture a few of your opponent's pieces in the meantime.

10 Remember the blocking option. If you cannot move a piece on your turn, this means you lose. If you can block in your opponent's draughts such that none of them can move, you will win.

GET BETTER AT CHESS

1 Pawns are strong when they are in a chain. Try to avoid splitting them into isolated groups.

2 Bishops, if not developed early, may get blocked by your own pawns blocking the diagonals. Be aware of this.

3 Knights play well in the centre of the board. Avoid keeping them at the sides.

4 Rooks positioned in the seventh or eighth row becomes a headache for the opponent. Two rooks on that row can often provide mating attack.

5 Even though the queen is always the strongest piece, it needs a rook or another minor pieces for its most effective use.

6 Avoid taking the queen too far out during the openings as it is likely to get 'harassed' by the opponent's minor pieces, causing you to lose tempo.

7 If the king is at its original position, aim to rook it at the earliest opportunity.

8 You gain tempo when you can achieve two objects in one move. For example, a pawn move may attack a piece while opening a line for your own pieces. Look for such opportunities.

9 Don't try to launch a premature attack. Develop your pieces so that they coordinate well with one another and then plan your attack. Otherwise, you may find your attack losing steam, to put you at a disadvantage.

10 When you hit trouble, remember that attack is often the best form of defence. Look for such possibility.

FOUR WHEELS & TWO

Are you a petrolhead or a freewheeling cyclist? Either way, this chapter will get you going, on four wheels or two. Look no further for the low-down on choosing a new car or bike, getting about safely, and how to deal with roadside problems. And if you love your caravan, camper van or motorhome, here's the inside track on everything from towing to decorating it.

BUY A NEW CAR

1 **Look for a car that's high up in the fuel efficiency tables.** Generally, the smaller the engine size, the more economical it will be to run, but check for the exact make and model, as fuel consumption can vary enormously, even between different versions of the same car.

2 **When setting a budget for a new car,** it's not just about the purchase cost. Don't forget all the extras: insurance, tax, fuel, general running costs and repairs. These will all vary, depending on the type of car you choose although, in general, they do relate to the size of the engine and the car's overall value.

3 **Safety first.** There are league tables: check them out. One of the best car safety features to look for is electronic stability control, which stops you losing control in a sudden manoeuvre or a skid.

4 **Choose between diesel and petrol.** Diesel emits less CO_2, but gives off more nitrogen oxide, which leads to poor air quality. A diesel engine is more economical if you make a lot of long trips (motorways or coast-to-coast), and diesel cars tend to hold their value better.

5 **Go green – get an electric, hybrid or super-efficient car.** Electric cars have to be plugged in to charge their battery and they won't take you long distances between charges. However, they are ideal if you have a private driveway where you can plug it in and mainly make short journeys around town. Hybrids use energy recovered from the brakes to charge an electric motor – which either helps the engine or can propel the car at low speeds. These super-efficient cars use new technology to produce fuel economy that can be better than that of hybrids.

6 **Make sure your car will fulfil your needs.** Although smaller is better for economy, your car should also be comfortable for you and any other drivers, and for passengers both big and small. This is particularly important if you make long trips as a family. Check that all necessary child seats and boosters can be fitted safely, too.

7 **Do you have a horse box, a caravan or a boat?** In that case your new car would need to have a tow bar and be capable of pulling the extra weight. Diesel engines are better at towing than petrol ones.

8 **Think family-sized car,** especially for holidays, but also shopping trips, days out and so on. How much boot space do you need for the luggage, the dog and the kitchen sink? Maybe a seven-seater would be the right choice for you. The most convenient types have seats that fold down flat, so you can easily swap between extra seats or luggage space.

9 **Comfort counts.** Do you like to feel that you are high up in the car? How about the back-seat passengers? Is there enough leg room? Are the seats supportive and fully adjustable? Try out all the permutations before you buy.

10 **A test drive on a new car is essential.** And not just for the driver – anyone else who is likely to use the car regularly (probably the kids) should sit in it, too. Drive far enough to get a good idea of how the car handles, as well as overall size, space and comfort. A quick checklist would include steering, brakes, gears, acceleration, ride comfort and visibility.

GOOD THINGS TO KEEP IN YOUR CAR

1 Owner's manual
2 Bottle of water
3 First-aid kit
4 Sat nav or map book
5 Compact multi-tool
6 Blanket
7 Pen and paper
8 Wipes/hand sanitizer
9 Multi-use car charger
10 Spare sunglasses

HOW ABOUT A PRE-LOVED CAR?

SECOND-HAND CAR CHECKS

1 Service history
2 Seat belts
3 Tyres
4 ID number
5 Lights
6 Oil
7 Bodywork
8 Gaps between panels
9 Paintwork/rust
10 Door function

1 **Would you prefer to buy privately, or from a dealer?** Dealers are usually more expensive, but the car may come with warranties or a free service.

2 **How much will your insurance, road tax and fuel costs be?** Assess as for a new car, before signing on the dotted line.

3 **Always look at the car in daylight.** You'll spot any faults more easily.

4 **Get the car history-checked** to see if it has any financial issues or has been stolen or written off.

5 **Check all the lights on the display (air bags, engine and brakes) come on** when the key is in 'start' position. They should all go out when the engine is switched off.

6 **Check for water in the exhaust system.** With the car switched off and cold, stick a finger up the exhaust pipe. If you find moisture it could indicate serious problems.

7 **Has the car been 'clocked'?** That is, is it a high-mileage car passed off as a low-mileage one, because the seller has wound back the milometer. The reading should tally with its documentation.

8 **Why not pay for a mechanic** to check the car over?

9 **Make sure you're given all the car's official documents.** Read them carefully.

10 **Always test-drive the car** to assess performance. How does it feel? Does its equipment function properly?

SHOP FOR A CAR ONLINE

1 **Research used car prices** and compare.

2 **It is usually safer to buy from a seller who gives a detailed description** of the car and multiple photos

3 **Email the seller with any questions.** Making personal contact helps both buyer and seller assess each other.

4 **If you're bidding online,** set yourself a strict limit and stick to it.

5 **Try to buy locally;** then you can view the car properly before you bid.

6 **Ensure you're happy with the seller's terms/conditions** before you bid.

7 **Always check the seller's feedback ratings.** If they are dodgy, don't bid.

8 **Beware of brilliant-sounding deals.** They probably are too good to be true.

9 **Be suspicious of requests for cash.**

10 **Never send money abroad** unless you know the seller personally.

THE BEST PRICE FOR YOUR WHEELS

1 **Clean the interior yourself, or take it to be valeted.** Vacuum and wipe down all surfaces and remove personal belongings.

2 **Go to a car wash** or use pro cleaning products to give the car a clean and a wax.

3 **Make sure you clean the car thoroughly**

enough to remove pet hairs and the smell of cigarettes or stale food.

4 Change the oil so it's clean.

5 Don't respray unless you can cover the cost through its better appearance.

6 Clean smudges from windows/mirrors.

7 If the car is due for a service soon, do it before you put it up for sale.

8 Show all receipts for work done, and all documentation, to reassure the buyer.

9 Place ads in the paper/online. Include pictures, model, registration date, mileage, colour and previous owners.

10 If you are meeting a buyer, take a friend who knows about cars. Don't let a potential buyer test-drive unaccompanied.

WHERE TO SELL YOUR VEHICLE

1 Online ad
2 Local dealer
3 Specialist dealer
4 Classified ad
5 Supermarket ad
6 Local club or society
7 Friends
8 Car auction
9 Internet auction
10 Poster in window

BUYING CAR TYRES

1 Don't ever buy cheap tyres! They may require a longer stopping distance and you would have less control in an emergency.

2 Don't spend too much on your tyres! Most well-known manufacturers produce excellent tyres, but there are lesser-known brands that cost less and are just as good.

3 Ask advice about which tyre to buy from a tyre dealer you trust, or try online on a specialist site.

4 Don't necessarily replace your tyres with the same kind that came with your car. They may be good all-rounders, but your own requirements may be more specific.

5 Performance tyres may wear out more quickly, but are better for cornering.

6 Tyres providing a comfortable ride may last longer, but do worse on corners.

7 If you can, buy four tyres at the same time. Or buy and fit in pairs for a more even grip. Never replace a single tyre.

8 When buying a tyre online, make sure delivery and fitting in a reputable local garage are included in the price.

9 Make sure the new tyre is suitable for your car. Check your owner's manual or inspect the old tyre wall: it will have markings that will tell you all you need.

10 After fitting new tyres, don't forget that you may need to realign your wheels.

LOOK AFTER YOUR TYRES

1 Check the tread depth regularly, and replace tyres as soon as they appear worn.

2 Check your tyres' pressure about once a month and before a long journey, but wait until the tyres are cold.

3 What should the tyre pressure be? Look in your user manual, at a label on the door frame or inside the fuel flap – NOT on the tyre wall (that's maximum pressure).

4 When you replace a tyre, have your wheels balanced.

5 Fit new tyres or the least worn tyres, on the rear wheels, to ensure better road holding and control.

6 Make sure your valves and valve caps are in good condition.

7 Got a problem? Call in a tyre specialist. Repairing or replacing a tyre is complicated.

8 **Check your tyre manufacturer's replacement recommendations** and follow them. If you've had tyres for ten years, even if not worn, replace them.

9 **Changes in the weather affect the tyre pressure.** The higher the atmospheric temperature the higher the pressure.

10 **Check tyres** for bulges, cuts, cracks, irregular wear and visible signs of damage. If they keep losing pressure or you feel vibration or pulling, get them checked by a specialist. Damaged tyres may fail suddenly.

LEARN TO DRIVE

1 **Start your lessons by learning in the passenger seat.** Ask the driver questions, and practise road rules, assessing hazards and judging distances and speeds.

2 **Don't be content to settle for the cheapest lessons.** If you employ a good instructor you'll need fewer lessons, thereby saving money in the long run. Ask about discounts for block booking.

3 **Aim to have at least one or two hour-long lessons per week.** You'll find that the more time you spend behind the wheel, the more comfortable you will become with driving. Once you have reached a competent level, perhaps also practise with family or friends.

4 **Get personal recommendations** for an instructor. Find someone who makes you feel confident as it will make an enormous difference. Change instructors if you're not completely happy.

5 **Learning on a manual car?** Here's how to tell when you've found the bite point.

Press on the accelerator lightly and steadily, so the engine hums gently. Slowly bring the clutch up towards halfway, until you hear the engine note get deeper and the bonnet lifts very slightly.

6 **Fine-tune your clutch control** by raising and dipping the clutch around the bite point to control forward movement. It's important to get this right.

7 **On a hill start,** release the hand brake gently and slowly. If you haven't got the bite point exactly right, this will give you time to react.

8 **Try to practise in varying weather conditions,** at different times of day and night, and in all types of traffic.

9 **Develop good habits** – do everything correctly and repeat it. If you make a mistake, work out what went wrong and correct it.

10 **Don't take your test too soon.** If you're not ready and fail it will cost you in both extra lessons and lost confidence.

BASIC CAR CHECKS

1 Oil
2 Coolant
3 Screen wash
4 Brake fluid
5 Lights
6 Tyre pressure
7 Tyre treads
8 Wiper blades
9 Battery
10 Exhaust

SAFE EVERYDAY DRIVING

1 **If you've stopped in a queue of traffic,** leave a gap between you and the car in front. If someone drives into the back of you, it's less likely to cause a pile-up.

2 **If visibility is very poor,** use your hazard warning lights. It's also a good idea to put them on if you have to come to a sudden stop – to warn cars approaching from behind.

3 **In rain or poor conditions,** increase your distance from the car in front.

4 **Go slower.** Speed is the biggest cause of road deaths. Keep to speed limits, give yourself time to cope with the unexpected, and if you spot a hazard, slow down.

5 **Have your vehicle serviced regularly** and maintain it in good condition. Keep windows, mirrors and lights clean; check lights, tyre pressures and treads regularly, and never ignore any warning lights.

6 **Expect other people to make mistakes.** Drive cautiously and be aware of other road users.

7 **Keep calm and don't rush.** If you get stressed, angry or upset, pull over safely and take a few deep breaths.

8 **Be secure.** Always wear a seat belt and make sure that all child passengers use properly fitted car seats. The centre of your head rest should be at eye level. Secure all luggage tightly.

9 **Be alert.** If you find it hard to chat with passengers while driving, don't. Never use a mobile phone while at the wheel – it's illegal as well as unsafe. The moment you feel tired, pull over and take a break.

10 **Consider taking some more lessons.** Whether you've just passed your test or have been driving for years, it will help you drive more safely.

CAR SAFETY FEATURES

1 Smart seat belt reminder
2 Air bags
3 Dynamic head restraints
4 Speed limiter
5 Antilock/ automatic/ intelligent brake system
6 Traction control
7 Electronic stability control
8 Lane/attention assist
9 Blind spot monitors
10 Active headlights/night vision

ADVANCED DRIVING

1 **Never stamp hard on the brake pedal.** It's all about progressive application of the brakes. Release them smoothly, too.

2 **Don't accelerate too early or too aggressively.** Accelerating should be a progressive action, otherwise the wheels will start spinning.

3 **When steering, both hands should do the work.** You'll have more control.

4 **Smooth gear changes** are the mark of a great driver. Passengers should not be aware that you've changed gear. Practise changing, matching revs to speed.

5 **Before you take a corner, brake first,** then change down into the correct gear.

6 **Practise anticipation** and leaving space in front to cope with likely/unlikely events. Adapt driving to the environment.

7 **Be careful when there are horses on the road.** Drive slowly past them, leaving plenty of room. Don't rev the engine or sound your horn. A horse turning right may not move to the centre of the road first – look for rider's signals.

8 **When you are overtaking,** choose a safe location – can you see far enough ahead, are there junctions or obstacles that are obscuring your view? Hang back before you overtake so that you can get a good view of the road. And then don't cut in too quickly afterwards.

9 **If you are going on a long or unfamiliar journey,** plan your route carefully; get plenty of sleep the night before and allow enough time so that you can avoid rushing or feeling stressed.

10 **Expect the unexpected** and have a plan to deal with it. Look out for ways to avoid problems – for example, a child running into the road or a load falling off a lorry. Steer for safety – if necessary, this may have to be off the road.

PERFECT PARKING EVERY TIME

1 **Get to grips with the basic principles of parallel parking** by watching a competent friend or videos on the internet.

2 **Find a quiet stretch of road** or an empty car park and lay out cones or markers to stand in for cars. Now practise parking in between them. If you go wrong it's much better than hitting the real thing!

3 **If you find you keep getting it wrong, go slower.** Better to make other drivers wait a few seconds than rush and have an accident. Also, if you scrape a nearby car it just might not cause so much damage.

4 **Use your mirrors – rear and both wings.** They'll give you more awareness of where you are than just craning your neck.

5 **For parallel parking, can you actually fit into the space?** It must be one-and-a-half times longer than your vehicle.

6 **If you park on a level street, keep your wheels straight.** If you park facing uphill, leave the car in a forward gear and turn your wheels away from the kerb. If facing downhill, select reverse and turn the wheels towards the kerb. If your brakes fail, your car will come to a rest against the kerb instead of rolling straight back.

7 **If you get it wrong first time,** pull out and try again.

8 **Parking sensors may make life easier,** though some drivers do find them overly cautious, and they are no substitute for good spatial awareness. And never reverse without looking, even with sensors.

9 **Be considerate to other drivers.** Don't park so close that they can't open their doors or move their car out of the space.

10 **Practice makes perfect.**

DRIVING ON A MOTORWAY

1 **If you feel nervous about motorway driving,** take some specialist training.

2 **Leave at least two seconds between you and the car in front;** four seconds in poor weather.

3 **Know what junctions you're going to be taking in advance.**

4 **Take breaks:** 15 minutes every couple of hours is about right. If you feel drowsy, open windows or sing out loud. Pull off at the next service station and have a coffee or take a power nap.

5 **When entering from a slip road** make your speed match that of the cars in the slow lane.

6 **Use the correct lanes.** If you sit in the fast lane you may cause congestion – not to mention road rage.

7 **Keep clear of drivers who drift across lanes** or suddenly slow down or speed up.

8 **Allow plenty of time for every manoeuvre.** Use your mirrors and make sure there is time for your signals to be seen before starting to manoeuvre.

9 **When moving into the middle lane,** look across to the lane beyond to check that another driver isn't also moving into the same space from the other side.

10 **Coming off the motorway:** check your speed as soon as you enter the slip road and slow down if necessary. You may be going faster than you think.

DRIVE SO YOU USE LESS FUEL

1 **Avoid aggressive driving.** Fast starts and hard braking can increase fuel consumption by as much as 40 per cent.

2 **Develop the habit of turning off all your accessories** before you turn off the ignition. Watch out for extra items that plug into your car's cigarette lighter.

3 **If you're stationary for more than 30 seconds,** turn off the engine.

4 **Pump your tyres up to the correct pressure.** Under-inflated tyres can increase fuel consumption by six per cent.

5 **Change up through the gears as quickly as you can,** to reach top gear without accelerating more than necessary. Driving in a lower gear than you should increases fuel usage.

6 **Do you really need air conditioning?** It increases fuel consumption by up to ten per cent on short, stop-and-start journeys.

7 **Don't use too high a gear in hilly areas;** it makes the engine work harder.

8 **On long stretches,** use fifth gear and cruise control to save fuel.

9 **Choose the best fuel.** Premium fuels aren't always the right choice. Many cars are designed to take lower-octane fuels.

10 **Have regular services.** A poorly tuned engine can use up to 50 per cent more fuel and produce the same emissions.

ECO CARS ARE IN!

1 **Electric cars go further when it's warm,** which is worth bearing in mind.

2 **Wrap up warmly** when driving your electric car – if you turn on your heater it will decrease the car's range. The same may be the case for using the radio.

3 **It is possible to do a long journey in an electric car.** But you must make sure you know where the public charging points are and factor in charging time.

4 **In an electric car, you go further if you reduce your speed,** reduce weight to a minimum and keep your tyres inflated.

5 **If you are a speed fiend** an electric car probably isn't for you.

6 **To be really green,** charge your car using electricity supplied by a producer using 100 per cent renewable sources.

7 **Be aware that driving an electric car is a little different from a petrol car.** The engine is silent and there are no gears. When you remove your foot from the accelerator there's a more rapid speed loss.

8 **Driving a hybrid car is similar to a normal car,** except when the car stops for more than a few seconds, the petrol engine shuts down – the car goes silent.

9 **Are electric cars too expensive?** Then consider an electric motorbike or scooter.

10 **Hybrid cars operate most efficiently** in urban, stop-start driving situations. If you do regular long-distance driving, a clean diesel car would probably be the better choice for you.

ALTERNATIVE FUELS

1 Waste vegetable oil
2 Bio-alcohol/ ethanol
3 Electricity (plug-in)
4 Hydrogen
5 Non-fossil methane
6 Compressed natural gas
7 Waste animal fats
8 LPG or autogas
9 Solar
10 Compressed air

FIND YOUR WAY WITH A SAT NAV

1 Check what area(s) the sat nav covers. If you are planning to travel abroad, make sure it covers the places you want to go, or can be updated to do so.

2 Look for a sat nav that provides up-to-the-minute traffic updates.

3 Get a sat nav with a voice instruction, so that you can keep your eye on the road.

4 Sat navs that provide warning signals about speed cameras are very useful. However, radar detection is illegal in some countries so, if you're planning to travel, check out the law first.

5 Consider some extra features, such as parking locations, cash points, restaurants, petrol stations and cinemas to help you get the best from your sat nav.

6 Think about the size of the sat nav you want to buy. Would you benefit from a larger screen or would it be too bulky?

7 Spend more to get voice recognition technology. You simply tell your sat nav where to go without taking your hands off the wheel.

8 Consider a higher priced machine that provides an advance lane-warning feature showing you the lane you need to be in at difficult or confusing junctions.

9 Is the keyboard easy to use, with big buttons, and is the screen visible in bright sunlight? By the way, if you buy one that requires you to use a stylus to type with – make sure you don't lose it!

10 If you don't want to invest in a car-mounted sat nav, you can download a sat nav app to many mobile phones. Some are even free. You'll need to buy a car charger and a holder for your phone.

GET THE BEST OUT OF YOUR SAT NAV

1 Load the journey details before you set off, and check the route in advance.

2 Update your sat nav regularly. Otherwise it won't be able to tell you about any new features of your route.

3 Some destinations share names. Check you're going to the right place.

4 Don't programme your sat nav to your home address and label it. If you're out and your car is stolen, all a thief has to do is follow the sat nav to your home and burgle it.

5 Make sure voice instructions can be heard over the radio or conversations.

6 Novelty sat nav voices are funny but infuriating. Use a neutral voice.

7 Use the device's extra features – it may let you take a photo of a recently discovered place and geo-tag it so you can find it another time.

8 If you're using your smartphone as a sat nav, remember that you can often locate a point of interest, then display its phone number and call it – perhaps to check opening times.

9 Don't leave your sat nav in the car. Thieves will notice tell-tale signs like an empty mount, and will easily find your sat nav in a glove compartment/under a seat.

10 Looking for a device that doesn't need a charger or batteries and doesn't mind being dropped? Get a road map.

CAR WON'T START?

1 **The most common problem is a weak or dead battery,** or poor battery connections. Check by turning on an interior light – if it doesn't come on, or goes dim when you turn the key in the ignition, it's the battery. If it's bright, and stays that way when you turn the key, something else is at fault.

2 **If you think the problem isn't the battery, check your fuses** and look under the bonnet for loose connections. Only do the latter if you know how to do it safely.

3 **Pump the clutch,** or move the shift selector in and out of P or N a couple of times, then try starting again.

4 **Er – have you got fuel in the tank?**

5 **If the key doesn't turn,** check that you're using the correct key. Or maybe it's damaged or worn. Try a spare.

6 **Key still won't turn?** There may be too much pressure on the steering lock, due to the wheels being fully turned to one side. Wiggle the steering wheel to turn the key.

7 **If your car has problems starting in cold weather,** the battery may be on its way out. Replace it – you should be fine.

8 **Don't wear your battery down.** If the key turns and the engine starts, but then stops again when you release the key, your battery and starter motor are fine, but your engine is not firing. You must stop cranking the engine.

9 **Automatic transmission?** Check you are in park or neutral. Otherwise, you may have a problem with the neutral safety switch – time to call in the pros.

10 **Swearing at your car** or beating it with a stick won't help.

JUMP-START YOUR CAR

1 **Don't even think about jump-starting a car** unless you can do it safely.

2 **Check jump leads** for wear or damage.

3 **Some cars should never be jump-started.** Others can only be jump-started after certain steps have been taken. Check manuals or you may cause damage.

4 **Park the two cars** so that the distance between both batteries is small, but the cars don't touch. In both cars, turn off the engine, radio, lights, air conditioning and anything else electrical. Put gears in neutral or P, and apply the handbrakes.

5 **Keep metal clear of the batteries** – take off all jewellery/watches, and take care that tools, clips and wires don't dangle and that nothing can fall into the engine. Tie back hair and remove scarves, ties or any other loose clothing. Don't smoke.

6 **Never try to jump-start a battery** that is leaking, cracked or looks damaged.

7 **Wear goggles and gloves** for safety.

8 **Remove the dead battery's cables** or terminals and clean them with a stiff wire brush. They may be dirty or corroded.

6 **Make sure that the red and black ends of your leads** never touch each other once they are connected to the batteries – serious shocks or damage could occur.

7 **Once both leads are connected,** don't start either engine just yet. Wait three minutes for the voltages to equalize.

8 If the jump leads get hot, switch off both engines and allow them to cool.

9 Let both of the engines run for about ten minutes. Then switch off both and disconnect the leads. Don't touch the clips against each other or the cars' bodywork.

10 If your battery doesn't now have enough power to restart the engine, it's a more serious problem – get it checked out by a professional.

CHANGING MOTOR OIL

1 Use the right oil and change it (and the oil filter) when necessary to help your engine last longer and perform better. Check manufacturer's recommendations.

2 Do an oil change when the vehicle is still a little warm. Run it for 20 minutes, then leave to rest for another 20. Check the temperature of the dipstick beforehand.

3 Do you have to jack the car up? It may be possible to remove the drain plug and oil filter without it. It's easier and safer, though you must still turn off the engine, chock the wheels, put the car in neutral and engage the handbrake.

4 Put up the bonnet and take off the oil filler cap. This will help the oil to drain out faster.

5 Don't wrench off the oil plug all in one go – the oil will start to pour out straight away. Loosen it with the wrench, then place the drip pan underneath and remove the cap with your fingers, holding on tight so it doesn't drop into the pan.

6 Be as patient as possible. When the oil is draining, leave it for 20 to 30 minutes. The last drips will contain the most dirt and debris, which is what you really want to get rid of.

7 When you unscrew the oil filter, make sure that the rubber gasket comes off with it. If it remains on the car, the new oil filter may not act as a proper seal.

8 Wearing gloves, coat the rubber gasket on the new filter with a smear of oil and thread the filter back into the hole.

9 Once you've drained the oil, replaced the filter and put the oil plug back in, fill your car with new oil to the correct level and replace the oil cap. Then close the bonnet and run the engine for a few minutes to regain proper oil pressure and check for any leaks.

10 Take the old oil and filter it into a proper disposal location.

CHANGE A WHEEL SAFELY

1 No spare tyre? Many cars just have a puncture repair kit – sealant and compressor – instead. Familiarize yourself with your car's kit, so you'll be prepared.

2 If your car has a spare tyre, practise changing a wheel while at home.

3 **Never try to change a wheel on the hard shoulder of a motorway** or at the side of a road – it's too dangerous. Turn off the main road and find a safe spot. If this really isn't possible, pull over away from the traffic and call for help.

4 **Have the spare and all necessary tools close by.** Lay the spare on the ground next to the damaged wheel.

5 **Keep the car stable while on the jack.** Chock the road wheel diagonally opposite the one to be replaced.

6 **Expect the wheel nuts to be very tight.** When you are loosening them, be sure to keep your back straight and your body weight as evenly distributed as possible.

7 **When removing the slackened wheel nuts,** leave the top one until last, so it holds the wheel on the hub.

8 **Once the spare is on,** secure the wheel with the top bolt/nut first. Then tighten the nuts in a diagonal sequence.

9 **Don't oil the bolts/nuts before you refit them,** as this will make them more likely to work loose.

10 **Drive to the nearest garage,** and have the wheel nuts loosened and re-tightened to the correct torque, and the pressure checked in the 'new' tyre. Repair or replace the damaged tyre as soon as possible.

SAFE JACKING UP

1 **Never work under a car** when there's only a jack supporting it. Hydraulic jacks are intended to lift cars, not actually support them. You must use jack stands to ensure safety.

2 **If you have a ground-hugging car** a low-profile jack will fit underneath.

3 **Don't try to jack up a car with people still inside.** If you're in an emergency situation, move everyone to a place of safety, well clear of the road.

4 **Only use a jack when the car is on firm, even ground.** Concrete is the ideal surface. Even asphalt or tarmac may be too soft. If in any doubt, use thick plywood boards to support the jack/stands so that they don't sink into the ground.

5 **Hydraulic floor jacks are rated according to the weight they can lift.** Check your vehicle's weight (look in the owner's manual or on the driver's door jam) and never try to lift a car that's too heavy for the jack.

6 **Only use the jack at the specified jacking points** – look them up in your manual. If you attach the jack in the wrong place you could damage your car and/or it could collapse when lifted.

7 **Always check that the jack head** has properly engaged with your car before you start lifting it.

8 **As you raise the jack, watch it closely.** If it slips or jumps, lower the car again immediately and check that the jack is in the correct position and properly engaged before raising it again.

9 **Release the jack very gently** and slowly when lowering your car. Always check that there are no hazards beneath the car. You might want to practise raising and lowering the jack on its own first, to get a feel for how it works.

10 **With your vehicle on the jack,** check that it's really solidly supported by giving the bumper a good shake before getting to work underneath.

CLEANING A CAR BRILLIANTLY

1 **Don't use washing-up liquid.** It can remove wax and leave marks.

2 **Start at the top of the car and work down.** Use a hose first, then a bucket with hot, soapy water and a sponge.

3 **Have a second bucket full of clean water –** you can wash your sponge in this, keeping your washing bucket clean.

4 **Don't forget** about the windows, wheel arches, bumpers, skirts and inner door panels. Lift the wipers right out of the way to do the windscreen. It's best to do the wheels last.

5 **Rinse with clean water,** and dry with a chamois leather.

6 **If you want to be thorough,** take off the wheels and clean separately, as well as the wheel arches and the mud flaps.

7 **Tyre shine may look smart,** but don't get it on the treads – it can reduce grip.

8 **For superb bodywork,** wipe with a softened clay bar, then use polish, glaze, sealant and wax.

9 **Clean windows** using specialist glass cleaner and a microfibre cloth.

10 **Take out all the things that are removable** and wash them separately. Vacuum, then spray and wipe using a special dashboard cleaner, upholstery cleaner and/or a damp cloth.

FIND A GOOD MECHANIC

1 **You can't do better than a personal recommendation** from someone who has used the mechanic for years.

2 **Use your common sense –** if the place looks well organized and maintained, there's a good chance that the mechanics will care about their work, too.

3 **What qualifications or affiliations do they have?** Don't be afraid to ask. Perhaps they have certificates on display.

4 **Trust your instincts.** Does the place feel right? If you feel uncomfortable or poorly treated there, just walk away.

5 **Independent mechanics work hard** to compete with the big chains and will be keen to build up a long-term relationship with you. They're often the best bet.

6 **Ask members of a local car club** who they would recommend.

7 **Online reviews may be informative –** though, as with anything online, treat everything said with a pinch of salt.

8 **Do they have a warranty policy?** Is it just on parts, or labour, too? The longer the better – it shows they have confidence in their work.

9 **Will they let you sit in a safe place near by and watch?** A good mechanic will be quite happy for other people to oversee his or her work.

10 **Make sure that the mechanic is completely upfront** about pricing and why the work needs to be done. You don't want to get stung with an unexpected bill.

YOU & YOUR MECHANIC

1 Stick to what you came in for. If you just need a new tyre, don't be pressurized into other services. Ask the mechanic to list recommendations to consider later.

2 If the garage says your car needs work, ask what needs doing. Does it comply with manufacturer's recommendations?

3 Be confident. You may not know much about cars, but you're still the one in charge. Ask for things to be explained in language you can understand.

4 Ask if there are alternative options – the dramatic, expensive, replace-everything one may not be the only solution.

5 Build up a good relationship with your mechanic. They'll get to know your car.

6 If your car has a problem, work together to find the best solution.

7 Be honest. Tell them everything you can about the car, what's been done to it, past problems, current problems and so on. They more knowledge they have, the better they will be able to help you.

8 Friday afternoons are often a garage's busiest times. Take the car in early on Monday instead.

9 Even good mechanics make mistakes. Give them the chance to put it right. If they really are good, they won't mind.

10 If you find a good mechanic – stick with them! They're like gold dust. They may also offer loyal customers discounts.

HAVING YOUR CAR SERVICED

1 You don't have to take your car to be serviced at the same place you bought it. Shop around to get the best deal.

2 Make sure the garage is accredited.

3 Check your owner's manual for the service schedule. Every vehicle has a specific tune-up schedule, recommended by the manufacturer.

4 Understand what type of service you need and when. It can get a bit complicated, with interim, full, major and annual services.

5 Keep your car records in order and take them with you to the service. They can help the mechanic diagnose a problem. Always get them stamped – a good service history will be helpful if you sell.

6 Make sure the mechanic is trained to carry out work on your specific make of vehicle. Not all car mechanics can work on all cars – sometimes they need specific tools or to have had special training.

7 Don't let them actually start work without quoting you a price.

8 Understand that the quoted price for just the service will go up if faults are found and repairs required. Ask the garage to call you, so you can decide what to do. They shouldn't just go ahead.

9 Make sure that parts and fluids used are genuine manufacturer's products, or manufacturer-approved and not generic. They may cost more, but can make a big difference to performance and longevity. Ask for receipts and/or part serial numbers.

10 Ask for an itemized copy of the service checklist, so you know what was done, and keep it in your files.

AFTER A MINOR ACCIDENT

1 **Stop, turn the engine off,** and switch your hazard lights on. Try to keep calm.

2 **Check that no one is injured.** If possible, pull over so you are not obstructing the road or, if you have to leave the vehicles there, move everyone involved to a safe waiting place.

3 **Don't apologize or discuss who was to blame.** This could cause problems with your insurance claim later.

4 **Both drivers should exchange** names, addresses, phone numbers and insurance details. If the other driver was driving for work, make a note of their employer's details, too. Take the names, addresses and phone numbers of any passengers and/or witnesses.

5 **Note the time and date,** the location, the make, model, colour and registration number of each vehicle, and what damage was sustained.

6 **Write down how the accident happened,** including the type of road, any markings, signs or obstructions, approximate vehicle speeds, and the weather, visibility and lighting conditions. Were you and/or the other driver using lights or indicators?

7 **If possible, take photographs of the vehicles.** Also, try to sketch a diagram for your insurers including the positions of the vehicles and any relevant road markings.

8 **Inform the police,** even if there's no need for them to attend.

9 **Contact your car insurers** as soon as possible.

10 **Is your car still roadworthy?** If you are in any doubt, have it checked over by a trusted mechanic.

DEALING WITH A BREAKDOWN

1 **If you are forced to pull over** onto a motorway hard shoulder, park as far to the left as possible, turn your wheels to the left, and switch on your side and hazard lights. Get all your passengers out of the car and retreat up the bank. However, it's best to leave pets in the car as it may prove too hard to control them once they are out of the car.

2 **Never attempt any sort of repair** on the hard shoulder of a motorway.

3 **If your car suffers a problem on a minor road,** try to get it to a safe place where it won't be an obstruction.

4 **Turn on your hazard warning lights** to let other vehicles know that you have a problem. If the general visibility is poor, switch your side lights on, too.

5 **Unless you are stopped safely off the road,** ask passengers to leave the car and wait, well clear of the traffic.

6 **Put a warning triangle on the road** about 45m (50yd) behind your car. Be very careful when doing this: wear a reflective jacket if you have one.

7 **Can you repair the car safely?** If you can't, telephone for help and stay with your vehicle.

8 **Be very careful if you decide to open up the bonnet.** The engine may be very hot and steam may escape forcefully and dangerously.

9 **When reporting the breakdown,** give as many details as you can about your location, as well as your car's make, registration and colour.

10 **If you are stuck for a long time in an isolated area,** be sure to remain inside the car in order to keep warm. It's OK to switch on the vehicle engine occasionally, but make sure that the exhaust pipe is clear of obstruction and keep the downwind window open.

AVOID CAR CRIME

1 **Treat your car keys as if they were cash –** to the value of your car. Keep them in a secure place in your home (not in the hall where they could be 'fished' through the letter box) and never leave your car unattended with the keys in it.

2 **If your car number plates are stolen,** contact the police immediately. They are likely to be used to change the identity of another vehicle – which could be involved in criminal activities, or serious offences such as speeding.

3 **Don't leave your sat nav in the car,** and remove its mount or suction pad. Clean off any suction marks as these are tell-tale signs that you use a sat nav.

4 **Park in the safest place possible –** your garage, a driveway, a well-lit, busy street, or a well-lit car park, preferably one with barrier entry and exits.

5 **Set the alarm or immobilizer** every time you leave the car unattended.

6 **If your car is considered high in value** or an obvious target for thieves, consider buying a tracking device.

7 **Close the windows and sunroof,** and lock the doors every time you leave the car unattended.

8 **Don't leave tempting items around in the car,** such as a mobile phone or tablet, laptop, handbag, portable DVD player, cash or CDs. It would only take seconds for a thief to smash a window and grab them.

9 **If you're buying a new car,** ask whether security glazing is installed.

10 **Be suspicious if you're stopped by a stranger,** especially if they want you to get out of your car. If you're crashed into at low speed from behind, be wary of getting out to check for damage – it's the latest method of car-jacking. If in doubt, stay in the car and call the police.

BAD-WEATHER DRIVING

1 **Make sure your vehicle is in the best possible condition.** Check brakes, battery, hoses, belts, fluid levels, wipers, heater and defroster, lights and tyres.

2 **A working radio is important –** you'll be able to pick up the latest weather and traffic reports.

3 **Pack a winter emergency kit** and keep

it in your car. The following could all be useful: phone and charger, torch and batteries, battery-operated or wind-up radio, jump leads, snow shovel, first-aid kit, warm clothing, a blanket, ice scraper, snow shovel, bottled water and non-perishable food.

4 If you're travelling as a family, think about what else might be needed if you get delayed or stuck – medication, nappies, wipes, changes of clothes or pet food.

5 Listen to all warnings. If the weather forecast is bad, don't travel unless you absolutely have to.

6 Top up your tank regularly so that you always have at least half a tank of fuel.

7 Drive defensively. In poor weather, leave loads of space between you and the car in front.

8 Avoid sudden stops and starts, where you're more likely to skid. Go slowly.

9 Tell someone else where you are going and when you expect to arrive. They can start a search for you if you don't turn up.

10 In poor conditions, put your lights, wiper and de-misters on, and make sure you'd be able to stop within the distance that you can see ahead of you. Remember to switch lights off again once conditions start improving.

COPE WITH SKIDDING

1 If you have the chance, choose a front-wheel-drive car for dealing with wintry conditions. It gives you more grip.

2 In snowy conditions, accelerate, steer and brake as smoothly as possible. Think ahead, so you don't have to brake abruptly. Bear in mind that skids are more likely on curves and turns.

3 Remember: most skids can be avoided by having good tyres and adjusting your driving to the conditions.

4 On slippery roads, drive so that you don't have to rely on your brakes to stop. Leave a much longer clearance between you and the car in front, and be constantly on the lookout for escape routes in case there's a problem.

5 Gone into a skid? Don't slam on the brakes. You could lock the wheels and make it worse.

6 Don't suddenly wrench the wheel. You will over-compensate and possibly go into a spin.

7 The main objective is to steer out of trouble. Keep your eyes on where you want the car to be and steer towards it.

8 In a front-wheel-drive car, once you have corrected the steering, controlled acceleration will pull the car out of the skid. In a rear-wheel-drive car, though, you should ease off the accelerator.

9 During a skid, forget what your driving instructor told you about feeding the wheel through your hands when steering. Keep your hands in the same position on the steering wheel, so that you can tell which way the wheels are facing.

10 Don't think that your ABS brakes will help you stop in a shorter distance. They won't. But they will stop the wheels from locking, which helps prevent you going into an uncontrollable skid.

DRIVING IN SNOW & ICE

1 **Before and during your journey, completely remove all snow and ice f**rom mirrors, windows, lights, roof and bonnet.

2 **Frozen locks?** Use a cigarette lighter to warm your key.

3 **Plan your route** so that you use main roads that are more likely to have been cleared or grilled.

4 **Pack warm clothing** if you are going out in snow: hat, gloves, boots, blankets, food and drink. Put a shovel in the boot in case you have to dig yourslf out of a drift.

5 **If the sound of your tyres suddenly goes quiet,** you may be driving on ice. Slow down and don't carry out any abrupt manoeuvres. Be extremely careful.

6 **Tyres should be inflated properly**.

7 **Fit snow tyres or chains** if you live in an isolated area hit with heavy snow. But take them off before driving on a normal road that isn't covered with snow.

8 **Don't drive in big, snow-covered boots** – you'll find it hard or impossible to manipulate the pedals.

9 **Remember that stopping distances are ten times longer on icy, snowy roads.** Keep well clear of the car in front!

10 **To get up a slippery hill,** avoid having to stop halfway up by waiting at the bottom until the road is clear. Choose a low gear so you don't have to change down on the hill. Going downhill, reduce speed in advance, choose a low gear and try not to brake. If you do, apply the brakes gently.

HELP! I'M STUCK IN SNOW

1 **If you can, put the transmission into four-wheel-drive.** Use the lowest gear and, if you can't go forward, try backing. Rock backwards and forwards, gently, and you may free the car.

2 **Try turning the wheel slightly** to get some traction in a different direction.

3 **Scrape away as much snow as possible from around the wheels.** You did remember your snow shovel, didn't you?

4 **Let's hope you have cat litter with you.** Why? You can sprinkle it in front of the wheels to give you traction. Sand or an old sack or rug will do the same trick.

5 **In severe weather, don't try to walk for help** unless you can see it within 100 metres or so. It's easy to get disorientated.

6 **Hope for a good Samaritan to pass by.**

Some extra muscles behind the car could push you out of the problem.

7 **In very cold weather, don't try to dig your way out of snow.** You could succumb to hypothermia very quickly.

8 **If you're trapped in your car,** stay warm by running the engine. But no more than ten or 15 minutes per hour, and check that the exhaust pipe is not blocked by snow: you could risk dangerous fumes in the car. Open a window just a little.

9 **Hang something brightly coloured** to your aerial or outside the car, so rescuers will find you more easily.

10 **If snow is falling and you are in your car,** only clear the settled snow off the windscreen. The rest of the cover will provide insulation for you.

SAFETY FOR WOMEN DRIVING ALONE

1 **Take all the steps you can to avoid breaking down in the first place.** Make sure that your car is in good condition. With enough fuel for the whole journey and good tyres.

2 **If a warning light comes on,** it doesn't always mean you have to stop and call for help. Check your owner's manual. In some cases, it will still be safe to drive home or to a garage.

3 **Avoid getting lost on unfamiliar roads** by planning your journey thoroughly before leaving. Use a sat nav, but take a map book to use as a backup – machines have been known to malfunction.

4 **Stick to the main roads** as far as you possibly can.

5 **Have a fully charged mobile phone** with you. Invest in a car charger or take a spare battery with you, too.

6 **While driving, keep all your valuables well out of sight.**

7 **Lock the doors and don't open windows fully,** especially if you're stopping and starting in towns and cities.

8 **Don't open a window or get out of the car for strangers.** If you have broken down, a car mechanic or police officer will be happy to show their ID to you through a closed window.

9 **Never give lifts** to anyone you don't know well. And hitch hikers are definitely a no-no.

10 **Park in either a well-lit car park** or on a bright, busy street. Have your keys in your hand as you return to the car.

CHOOSE & FIT A CHILD'S CAR SEAT

1 **Plan ahead.** Buy a car seat before you have your baby. You'll need one from the day you take them home from hospital.

2 **Always choose a baby's car seat that faces the rear of the car.**

3 **Buy a new child car seat.** Second-hand seats, if they weren't installed or adjusted correctly, may have developed a fault.

4 **Buy the most suitable seat** for the height and weight of your child. Their age isn't relevant.

5 **You can buy a car seat as part of a travel system,** which means the seat can also fit into a buggy. But remember: they are often large/heavy, and you'll need the space to store the bits you're not using.

6 **Always follow the instructions** when fitting your seat. If you have lost them, contact the manufacturer.

7 **Make sure the seat you purchase will actually fit in your car.** If you have three children who need them, is there room for three seats in a row on the back seat?

8 **Take care when locking the seat belt.** Make sure that you push all your weight onto the child's seat as you tighten the belt, so there is no slack.

9 **Never fit a rear-facing child's seat in the front passenger seat** if the car has an active air bag.

10 **Fit the seat belt around a booster seat** to make sure it rests on the child's shoulder and not their neck, and from hip bone to hip bone.

KEEP KIDS SAFE ON THE ROAD

1 **Whenever you're on the road,** make sure your child – whatever their age – is safely buckled into the appropriate seat.

2 **The back seat is safer for children** than the front. The centre rear is the safest place of all.

3 **If you're the only adult in the car,** it can sometimes be less distracting to put your child in the front next to you. If you do, use the correct safety seat and move the passenger seat as far back from the dashboard as possible.

4 **A baby in a rear-facing seat should never ride in the front seat** of a vehicle that has an airbag, unless deactivated.

5 **Don't let your children play with car keys.** If they hop in the car and activate the central locking – they're locked in, and you're locked out.

6 **Most children try to undo their seat buckle at some point.** Stop the car as soon as you can do so safely and do the buckle up again. Keep doing this until the child learns that undoing the buckle means they don't go anywhere. Also, try giving them a distraction such as a toy

7 **Make sure child locks are on** whenever children are in the car.

8 **Never be tempted to sit a child on an adult's or another child's lap,** even for a short trip.

9 **Children who are demanding attention or fighting** can be a dangerous distraction to the driver. Give them plenty to do and reward them for being good. If all else fails, ignore them. Keep your attention on the road until you can pull over safely and sort them out.

10 **Portable games consoles** or DVD players are a marvellous way to keep kids amused in the car for hours. But give them headphones to wear, as the noise of the soundtrack can be just as distracting for the driver as children arguing!

BUY A RECREATIONAL VEHICLE

1 **Don't even think about buying a recreational vehicle (RV)** unless you've rented one first, so you know what to look out for and what to avoid.

2 **Think about size –** if you can afford it, an extra berth space would probably come in very handy. So if you need three berths, go for four, for example.

3 **How often will you use your RV?** If it will only be every now and then, it makes sense to save as much as possible and buy second-hand.

4 **Test-drive your motorized RV** before you actually commit to a purchase. You need to get an idea of how it handles.

5 **If you want a towable vehicle,** make sure your car is powerful enough.

6 **Find a manufacturer and a dealer who will give you post-sale support** and who knows your vehicle.

7 **Look at getting an extended service deal.** It should work out cheaper in the long run.

MOTORHOME ESSENTIALS

1 Fresh water
2 Gas bottle and spare
3 Torch
4 Campsite/park guide
5 Tin opener
6 Plastic bags
7 Clothes pegs
8 Toilet chemicals/ paper
9 Plastic tubs
10 First-aid kit

MOTORHOME LUXURIES

1 Home entertainment system
2 HD TV
3 Microwave
4 Fridge-freezer
5 Ice-maker
6 Reclining chair
7 Washer/dryer
8 Security cameras
9 Induction hob
10 Gaming console

8 **Make sure you know where you can use your RV.** There's no point in buying one if it's not feasible to use it in your favourite holiday spots.

9 **Research all the possible accessories,** for example, a refrigerator, cooker, shower, lavatory and washing machine and decide what will be useful and what's not worth the money.

10 **Join an owner's club –** you'll get information on absolutely everything to do with buying and using an RV.

CARE FOR YOUR MOTORHOME

1 **Have your motorhome serviced** as recommended by the manufacturer. Use a garage that knows your make of vehicle.

2 **You'll also need an annual 'habitation' service,** done by a specialist, to check and maintain water, gas, electrical and heating systems, as well as for general damp/leaks.

3 **Check for signs of water penetration,** which can be caused when the mastic on the bodywork seams and around windows, doors and other joins dries out.

4 **Window rubbers can lose elasticity and become damaged.** You may be able to prevent this by applying chalk dust or talcum powder; or replace the rubbers.

5 **Wash all outside surfaces** with a good-quality car shampoo. Avoid using pressure washers, though – they're too strong and could cause damage.

6 **Use a liquid car polish on the outside** to help prevent dirt from sticking.

7 **Take good care when you are washing plastic windows –** they can scratch easily. Use a soft cloth. You may be able to treat minor scratches with a cream metal polish – try it out on an inconspicuous area first.

8 **Do you get condensation in between double-glazed acrylic windows?** Look for plugs near the top of the window. Take them out until the window is dry again.

9 **Not planning to use your motorhome for a while?** Take the weight off the tyres using axle stands. Or rotate the wheels by a quarter turn at least once a month.

10 **Vacuum upholstery regularly** and use upholstery cleaner. When the caravan is not in use, either store the upholstery in a warm, dry place, or stand it on end to air.

VAMP UP YOUR CAMPERVAN

1 **A crochet blanket/throw** adds colour and softness, as well as warmth at night.

2 **Put out colourful bunting –** it will always cheer you up.

3 **Why have boring bedding** when you could add a beautiful patchwork quilt?

4 **Protect your table** in the nicest way possible with a cheery oilcloth cover.

5 **No self-respecting camper should be without** solar-powered fairy lights.

6 **Cushions add comfort** and are an inexpensive way to introduce colour. Try ones with embroidery, appliqué or fun trims such as bobbles or ric rac.

7 **Peel-off, stick-on wall transfers** are a great way to transform a bare inside wall. Or there's nothing stopping you from putting up some flowery wallpaper.

8 **Fit some chintzy, gathered curtains** for privacy and prettiness.

9 **There's really no need to settle for naff accessories.** Go vintage, flea market or hand-made instead.

10 **Unbreakable kitchenware needn't be boring –** choose classic enamelware for a practical-but-cool vibe.

MANOEUVRING YOUR CARAVAN

1 **Invest in a good map and/or a sat nav.** With a larger vehicle the last thing you want to do is end up on the wrong route.

2 **Plan where you are going to park each night in advance.** For popular campsites you may need to book several months ahead.

3 **Allow plenty of distance between you and the vehicle in front,** and slow down in plenty of time for corners.

4 **Keep the weight down inside your vehicle –** this will improve handling and stopping distances. Don't over-pack it, don't overfill the water tank and, before you leave the site, empty the waste tank.

5 **When parking, or manoeuvring into tight spaces,** ask a passenger to get out and guide you. It's all too easy to misjudge where you are.

6 **Watch out for low trees that overhang the road!** Scratches and bumps on the bodywork can be expensive.

7 **You'll need a hard-standing pitch,** as a motorhome may sink into softer ground.

8 **Avoid parking under trees –** branches may break off in high winds.

9 **Park where you can access power,** but not too close to other vehicles.

10 **In a park, check the location of all the amenities** such as the toilet block, children's play area, café and decide whether you want to be near to them or as far from them as possible.

TOW A TRAILER/CARAVAN

1 **Do you need a special driving licence?** Know the regulations and check.

2 **What is your car's maximum recommended towing weight?** You'll find it in the owner's manual.

3 **Find out legal maximums** for towing width and length and stick to them.

4 **You may need to fit towing mirrors** and/or trailer brakes. Even if not legally required, would they be useful?

5 **What about breakdown cover?** You may need to go to a specialist.

6 **It's important to check that caravans and trailers are serviced** and fit for use. Check lights, tyres and coupling.

7 **Fit a breakaway cable** to apply the brakes of a braked trailer if it becomes separated. Or, on an unbraked trailer, a short, strong cable or chain to stop the nose of the trailer touching the ground.

8 Towing is different. You'll be slow pulling away and when you slow down and stop. Bends and reversing could be tricky.

9 Watch out for side winds, which can affect towed vehicles. Do take care when crossing a bridge/emerging from a cutting.

10 Don't overload a trailer or caravan. Pack the heaviest items lower down, close to the axles, with weight evenly distributed and everything securely restrained.

A ROOF BOX IS THE ANSWER

1 If you don't already have roof bars you will have to fit them. Make sure you choose a box that's compatible with them.

2 Consider the distance between the roof bars. Larger roof boxes often need the bars further apart, to ensure stable fitting.

3 Check measurements and dimensions before you buy – make visual comparisons. Claims about storage space may suggest that the roof box has more capacity than it really does.

4 What are you going to transport most regularly? The different shapes of roof boxes suit different contents.

5 Be aware that almost all roof boxes are fairly easy to steal from. Choose one that's more secure if this could be an issue.

6 If you are using your roof box for skiing or snowboarding, be careful: cheaper roof boxes can crack in cold weather.

7 A sturdy roof box is essential. In a crash, the contents could break through the casing of a cheap version.

8 If you're not sure about buying a roof box, hire one for a week to see if it suits you and your needs.

9 Get your roof box fitted by someone who knows what they're doing. It may appear to be an easy job, but it's really important to get it right.

10 Manufacturers' websites are worth looking at. Some tell you whether their box will fit on your car, and some will even show you a picture of what it will look like.

HURRAH FOR A HORSE BOX!

1 Pull away slowly, so that your horse can get its balance.

2 Allow double the braking distance than you would in a car. The trailer and load create extra weight and sudden braking may upset your horse.

3 Avoid any sudden braking by carefully reading the road ahead of you.

4 Give yourself plenty of time and space to manoeuvre at junctions.

5 Check the horsebox in your mirrors.

6 Get your horse accustomed to the box before going on a long journey – make some short trial trips.

7 Plan your journeys and check traffic information to avoid long delays.

8 Be careful on fast-moving roads, using mirrors and leaving room before pulling out. Slipstream may pull the horsebox, so hold it steady and don't over-correct.

9 **Take plenty of hay or feed and water,** and a warm coat for the horse, in case you are delayed. Take your vet's phone number.

10 **If you break down,** keep your horse in the vehicle, making sure there is plenty of ventilation. Stay with it if possible.

CHOOSE A BIKE

1 **Choose a style of bike according to where you plan to cycle:** a road bike for paved roads and a mountain bike for trails.

2 **Prefer racer or relaxed?** Road bikes are generally classified as being either racing (lightweight and low handlebars) or touring (more durable, upright, with racks). Hybrid bikes are a good compromise.

3 **Buy the best bike you can afford.** You are investing in better quality and more durable components and features. It will be well worth it.

4 **Think about where you will store the bike.** If it has to be kept outside, the bike needs to be properly secured and protected from the weather.

5 **Are you intending to carry a basket, panniers or a child seat?** If so, you need to ensure that the frame of your chosen bike is compatible.

6 **It's worth visiting a good bike shop** for knowledgeable advice and to make sure that the bike you buy is checked and set up for you.

7 **Test-ride a bicycle** for at least 20 minutes, to make sure the size, weight, riding position and gears to suit you. The bike should perform, brake and shift gears comfortably.

8 **If you opt for a cheaper bike,** make a small investment in your personal safety by immediately replacing the brake pads with better-quality ones.

9 **Look for a good helmet** that's durable, smooth and round on the outside, visible, comfortable to wear and with a strong strap that can be tightened or loosened.

10 **Unless you can always keep your bike in a secure place,** buy a good lock. In fact, two tight-fitting D-locks are ideal: one for the front wheel and frame and another for the back wheel and frame.

CUT BACK ON CAR USE

1 Car share
2 Bus
3 Walk
4 Cycle
5 Work from home
6 Jog/run to work
7 Car club
8 Work car-pool
9 Park & ride
10 Local holiday

LOOK AFTER YOUR BIKE

1 **Expect to spend a couple of hours a month checking your bicycle over,** and cleaning and lubricating it.

2 **Always keep your tyres pumped up** to the right pressure.

3 **Use a specially formulated bike lubricant** on moving parts, where metal moves against metal. Wipe away excess lube, however, as too much can attract dirt and abrasive particles.

4 **Keep your chain clean –** it's the most important moving part. With the chain in the biggest gear, scrub with a bristle brush and hot water mixed with washing-up liquid. Apply degreaser, wipe clean, lightly apply lubricant and allow to soak in for a

ESSENTIAL CYCLING KIT

1 Spare inner tube
2 Patch kit
3 Tyre lever
4 Pump
5 Multi-tool
6 Bright clothes
7 First-aid kit
8 Helmet
9 Drink
10 Sun glasses

couple of hours before you climb into the saddle again.

5 **Nuts, bolts and screws can loosen or wear.** Listen for rattles and squeaks when you are riding and look out for wobbles. Tighten when necessary, but don't over-tighten as this can cause damage.

6 **Have your bike checked professionally** and adjusted and serviced regularly – once or twice a year, depending on how often you cycle.

7 **Inspect the brake pads for wear.** To improve braking, sand them a little. Replace brake pads when there's only about 0.5cm (¼in) left.

8 **Check wheels and tyres –** you want upright valves that don't leak, straight and true wheels and unbroken spokes (tighten up loose ones).

9 **Inspect the brake cables –** if they are worn or frayed, replace them.

10 **Make sure that the handlebars and pedals aren't loose,** and that the pedals spin freely.

CHANGE A FLAT BIKE TYRE

1 **Be prepared –** an occasional flat tyre is inevitable. Carry a patch kit, spare inner tube, tyre levers and pump with you at all times. They'll fit in a bag under the saddle.

2 **Practise changing a flat tyre at home,** when you're not under any pressure.

3 **If the flat tyre is on the rear wheel,** put the chain on the smallest cog – it will be much easier to remove the wheel.

4 **You may need to loosen your brakes** before you can get the wheel off.

5 **Check the inside of the tyre** before fitting a new tube – it may have a shard of glass or piece of metal lodged in it.

6 **If you inflate the tube by a tiny amount** before working it into the tyre, it will hold its shape, making your job easier.

7 **When you install the new tube,** inflate it about halfway and then check that it's not pinched between the rim and the tyre before you fully inflate it.

8 **The new tube should inflate evenly all round.** Any bulges mean it's twisted or pinched inside. You'll have to let the air out and refit it.

9 **When reinserting the new tube's valve stem,** check that it comes out straight and not at an angle. If it's angled, it means it's not centred over the hole, and you'll need to slide the tube and tyre around the rim a little to correct it.

10 **Once you've put the wheel back on,** check that it is properly aligned, secure and spins cleanly before riding off.

CYCLING SAFELY

1 **Before you ride off, check that your tyres** are properly inflated and undamaged, and that your wheels are securely fastened.

2 **Set the handle bar and seat at the right height,** and ensure that they are both fixed on securely.

3 **Squeeze your brakes** and check that they're working properly. Make sure that the brake pads are hitting the wheel rims and not the tyres.

4 **Wear a well-fitting helmet –** it could save your life. The front of the helmet should sit just above your eyebrows – too high and it won't protect your forehead if you have an accident.

5 **Keep your chain clean and lubricated,** and check that it turns cleanly, without rubbing against the derailleur gears. As you pedal off, run through the gears to check for any problems.

6 **Be aware of your own ability,** and don't attempt anything you can't handle.

7 **Take all essential tools with you,** and understand how to use them.

8 **Wear clothing that won't get caught** in the chain or wheels. Light or fluorescent for daytime/poor light; reflective clothing/accessories for cycling in the dark.

9 **Always carry a working set of lights.** Even if you set off in daylight you might end up cycling home in the dark.

10 **Anticipate what a driver might do;** make eye contact where possible. Look and signal before manoeuvring, stay clear of the kerb and keep a car-door's distance from parked cars.

BIKES ON THE MOVE

1 **Don't fit a roof-mounted bike carrier** if you're short or not particularly strong. It's hard work lifting a bike onto the roof of a car.

2 **Family of five?** The only way to carry more than four bikes on a tow-bar rack is if you buy a four-by-four with a towball nose weight of 100kg (220lb) or more. Otherwise, at least one bike will have to go on the roof or inside the car.

3 **Even if you already have a roof box,** you can often still carry a couple of bikes on a roof carrier next to it.

4 **Some car roofs aren't suitable.** You can't carry bikes if you have a soft top, a moon roof, on some curved roofs, or a car with very close-together roof bars.

5 **Strap-on cycle carriers are less expensive,** but less secure and more likely to damage your vehicle. And if the straps fit below the bumper, you won't be able to open the tailgate during your journey. This could be very inconvenient.

6 **Choose a roof-mounting system** with a quick-release handle at shoulder height. You'll be very grateful for it when you are heaving bikes up and down.

7 **There is no such thing as a universal rack –** so check carefully that it is suitable for your car and bike weight/style.

8 **Some boot or towbar-mounted carriers** obscure your vehicle's lights and number plate – budget for buying an auxiliary lighting board.

9 **For security when using a towball -mounted rack,** fit a cable lock around all the bikes, the carrier and the towing loop.

10 **Carrying your bikes on the roof?** Be aware of your overall height. Perhaps best to avoid going into multi-storey car parks, beneath overhead barriers, under low bridges and below overhanging branches – just to be on the safe side.

INDEX

A

accessories: fashion 120–1
accidents: driving 396
addiction: preventing 177–8
adventure holidays 240
ageing:
  foods to prevent 138
  looking good 117
air travel:
  with babies/toddlers 249
  carry-on luggage 248
  cheap flights 246
  flight delays 247–8
  flight upgrades 246–7
  jet lag 247
  long-haul 248
alcohol: safe drinking 182
allergies: environmental 182
American cooking 325
Amsterdam: sights 252
anger management 152–3
anniversaries: holidays for 259
anti-addiction tips 177–8
antiques: buying 33
appearance:
  getting older 117
  in photos 123–4
aromatherapy:
  oils 151
  uses 155
astronomy 371
Australia: holidays in 256

B

babies:
  bathing 193
  bonding with 191
  bottle-feeding 192–3
  breastfeeding 192
  colic 195–6
  first days with 90–1
  flying with 249
  food for 313–14
  layette 190
  name: choosing 90
nappy changing 191–2
  safety gear 194
  sleeping 193–4
  teething 195
  using highchair 196–7
  weaning 196
baby monitor 194
baby shower 87
babysitters: finding 218–19
backache: minor 171
backpacking:
  choosing backpack 271
  packing for 272
bad breath 183
banking:
  for kids 344
  online: safety 343
  opening account 342
  running account 342–3
  student accounts 344–5
bar/bat mitzvah
  celebrations 82
Barbados: holidays in 255
barbecues:
  cleaning 44
  cooking on 319
Barcelona: sights 251
basins: unblocking 18
bathroom:
  cleaning 42–3
  designing 15
  renovating 34
beach holidays: basic
  wardrobe 234
beans: cooking 290
beauty treatments: quick 135
bed linen: buying 32
bed-wetting 92
beds:
  headboard 27–8
  selecting 31–2
beef: roasting 294–5
beekeeping: starting 62
beer 327–8
  brewing 328
bereavement: coping with 107–8
best man's speech 77
bikes:
  carrying on car 407
changing tyre 406
  choosing 405
  looking after 405–6
  teaching kids to ride 375–6
bird-watching 374–5
birds:
  garden: feeding 62
  as pets 113
bites and stings 176
biting (by child): response to 99
blender: choosing 282
blog:
  making money from 341
  writing 47
blood pressure: reducing 179
blues: beating 172
body language 215
body odour: banishing 139
book clubs 364–5
boots: care 122
bottle-feeding 192–3
bow ties: tying 125
brain exercises 154–5
brainstorming 212
bras: fitting 118–19
bread: making 292
breakfasts:
  luxurious weekend 317
  super-easy 317
breastfeeding 192
breasts: examining 170
breathing: improving 180
British cooking 324–5
brownies: making 306
budgets: sorting out 336
buffet: planning and
  serving 318–19
buggies 197
bulbs 57
bullying: at school 223
bunting: sewing 360
burns: minor: treating 175
buses: surviving long
  journey on 245–6
business:
  meetings: handling 214
  networking for 213
  starting up 206

C

cakes:
  celebration: making 321
  cupcakes: decorating 321
  fillings and toppings 306
  making 305–6
  wedding 72–3
calligraphy 366
calmness: sense of 150–1
cameras: features 367
camper van: vamping up 402–3
camping:
  in bad weather 268–9
  choosing site 268
  crises: averting 269
  cuisine 267
  essentials 265
  at festivals: essentials 269
  games and activities 266–7
  glamorous 267–8
  health hazards 269–70
  with kids 266
  kitchen essentials 267
  low-impact 268
canapés 320
candles: making 361
caravan:
  manoeuvring 403
  towing 403–4
carbon footprint: reducing 24
career:
  changing 207
  choosing 199
  return to after break 208–9
cars:
  accident in 396
  alternative fuels 389
  avoiding car crime 397
  basic checks 386
  bike-carriers on 407
  breakdown 396–7
  buying online 384
  changing oil in 392
  changing wheel 392–3
  child's seat 400
  cleaning 394
  driving abroad 244
    essential kit 244
  eco 389

hiring 244
jacking up 393
jump-starting 391–2
mechanic for 394–5
new: buying 383
parking 388
refusing to start 391
roof box for 404
safety features 387
second-hand:
    buying 384
    checks on 384
selling:
    preparing car 384–5
    where to sell 385
servicing 395
skidding 398
stuck in snow 399
things to keep in 383
tyres:
    buying 385
    looking after 385–6
carving meat 285
caterers: for wedding 73
cats:
    giving medicine to 115
    as pets 111
cellulite 139
chairs: restoring 26
Champagne 331
cheese: storing and using
    292–3
chess 381
chicken:
    choosing 309
    roasting 294
chickens: keeping 62–3
childbirth:
    adjusting after 190–1
    birth plan 189
    bringing on labour 189
    packing for hospital 188
childcare:
    choosing 217–18
    choosing nursery 217
children:
    ailments 98
    bank accounts for 344
    bed-wetting 92
    biting 99
    boosting confidence 93

camping with 266
car safety 401
car seats 400
coping with parents'
    divorce 105
crafts to make with 378–9
dyslexic: helping 224
    extra tutoring for 225
garden play stuff 375
gifted 223–4
hair-washing 96
headlice 97
home-schooling 224–5
homework 221
on internet 99
juggling work and 101–2
learning musical
    instrument 96–7
learning numbers 220–1
learning to read 220
learning to spell 220
left-handed 92
making den 375
making friends 95
money-savvy 344
party food for 320–1
pocket money 98
safety in pools 263–4
sex education 100
sibling rivalry 93
stranger danger 97
teaching to cook 313
teaching to lose at games
    379
teaching to ride bike
    375–6
teaching to swim 95–6
travel activities 246
travel with 233
tweenagers 99–100
writing 220
see also babies; toddlers
chillies: cooking with 299–
    300
Chinese cooking 322
chips: making 290
chocolate: using in cooking
    307–8
chopping: vegetables 285–6
christening parties 88
Christmas:

cutting costs 338
decorations 84–5
planning meal 321
stocking fillers 84
wreath 84
Christmas tree 84
cinema, home: setting up 49
city breaks 249
cleaning:
    household: regular 40
    kit:
        alternative 42
        essentials 41
    spring 40
clothes:
    bargain: shopping for 129
    for beach holidays 234
    bras 118–19
    capsule wardrobe 117
    care 122–3
    classics 118
    cleaning: energy-
        conscious 25
    clearing out 128
    for cold weather 235
    colours 124
    customizing 129–30
    detoxing wardrobe 128
    ethical 127
    for hot weather 234–5
    little black dress 126
    maternity 187
    for night out 119–20
    panties 118
    sewing 130
    for skiing 164–5
    slimming 118
    storage 39–40
    swimsuits 119
    things to bin 128
    vintage 127
    women's shirts 121
    working girls' 202
clothes-swapping parties
    128–9
cocktails 332
coffee: making 327
cold relief 169
colic 195–6
collecting 368
colours: for room 8

composts: making 52
computer: choosing 45–6
concentration: improving
    153–4
condolence letters 108
confidence: boosting in
    children 93
conflict resolution 213
conjunctivitis 174
constipation 173
contact lenses 146–7
cooker:
    choosing 280–1
    cleaning 42
cookies: making 305
cooking:
    on barbecue 319
    basic rules 275
    with children 313
    disasters 308
    essential kit 275
    gadgets 277
    for one 308–9
    safety 276
    saving energy 312
cookware 277–8
    care 278
couscous: using 298
crafts:
    for garden 361
    to make with children
        378–9
cravings: food: foiling 153
cream: using 303
credit cards:
    choosing 347
    using wisely 348
credit rating: improving
    348–9
credit union: joining 343
crochet 359
crowds: safety in 157
cruises 259
crumbles: making 304–5
cupcakes: decorating 321
currency: exchanging 242
curtains: ideas for 27
cushions: from old fabrics 27
cuttings (plant) 58
CVs: writing 201
cycling: safety 406–7

D

dads: successful 102
damp: dealing with 23
dandruff 144
dating:
    first date:
        safety 66
        venues 66
    first impressions 66
    internet profile 65
    long-distance 67–8
    making oneself irresistible
        66–7
de-stressing 150
deadheading 58
decluttering 11
decorations:
    Christmas 84–5
    Thanksgiving 83
den: for kids 375
dentures 145
desk:
    ergonomics 204
    posture at 171
detox 181
diarrhoea: causes 173
dinner parties 80
dips: delicious 320
discipline: of toddlers 94
dishwashers: choosing 280
displays: designing 12
division of plants 58
divorce:
    dealing with 104
    helping kids get over 105
DIY: safety 17
dogs:
    care 110
    choosing 109
    giving medicine to 115
    puppy-training 110
doll's house: making 378
doors: sticking: easing 30
draughtproofing 22
draughts (game) 381
dress codes 81
dress-making 130
dresses:
    little black dress 126
    wedding 71
drilling 18

drinks: nutritious 315
driving:
    abroad 244–5
    advanced 387
    in bad weather 397–8
    learning 386
    on motorway 388
    safe 386–7
    saving fuel 389
    in snow and ice 399
    women alone: safety 400
drug-taking: tell-tale signs
    101
duvets: choosing 32
dyslexia 224

E

Easter eggs: colouring 82–3
eating: etiquette 318
eco (green):
    cars 389
    clothes cleaning 25
    decorating 26
    travel 240–1
    weddings 75
eczema 183–4
eggs:
    cooking 287
    Easter: colouring 82–3
    omelettes 287–8
    storing and using 286–7
    testing freshness 287
Egypt: holidays in 258
elderly:
    caring for 106–7
    choosing care for 107
    travel with 237
energy:
    alternative 24–5
    beefing up 156
    reducing bills 335
engagement parties 81–2
environmental allergies 182
ergonomics: desk 204
essays: writing 229
etiquette:
    of eating 318
    office 204
examinations:
    college 230–1
    poor results 223

school 222
exercise:
    getting six-pack 166–7
    plan 159
eyebrows: plucking 132–3

F

fabrics: scraps: using up 357
face: cleansing 133–4
face lifts: scalpel-free 137
face masks 133
face-painting 376
facial cleansers: making 133
facial scrubs: making 133
fainting 176–7
fake tan 137
family get-togethers 87
family tree: tracing 89–90
fancy-dress: easy-to-make
    376–7
farmers' market: shopping
    at 310
feet: care 147–8
fence: erecting 20–1
fiction: genres 363
fireworks: safety 85
first-aid kit 175
fish:
    choosing and storing
        295–6
    cooking 296–7
    preparing 296
    tropical 113
fishing: starter kit 374
fitness: at work 204
flags: for Fourth of July 86
floorboards:
    laying 21
    sanding 23
flooring: types 29
floors: squeaky 29
Florida 254–5
flowers:
    arranging 360
    pressing 360
    for wedding 75–6
flying: fear of 151–2
food cravings: foiling 153
food poisoning: avoiding
    177
food processor:

choosing 282
    uses 282
food(s):
    age-defying 138
    American 325
    to avoid for wind 172
    for babies 313–14
    British 324–5
    budget evening meals 312
    cheap 231, 311
    Chinese 322
    free 311
    French 324
    as gifts 362
    gluten-free 315–16
    Indian 323–4
    Italian 325–6
    leftovers: using up 314
    low-calorie basics 316
    low-GI 316
    Mexican 322
    nutritious 315
    for school packed lunches
        316–17
    shopping online for 311
    snacks: energy-boosting
        372
    storage 277
    Thai 323
    for vegans 315
    for vegetarians 314–15
    wines to go with 330–1
    for work packed lunches
        317
Fourth of July: flags for 86
France: holidays in 250–1
freezers:
    choosing 281–2
freezing 276–7
French cooking 324
fridge:
    buying 281
    cleaning 41–2
    using 276
friendships:
    children making friends
        95
    good 69
    platonic 67
frost: protecting plants
    from 59

fruit(s):
  growing 57
  to juice 326
  pick-your-own 311–12
  storage 291
funeral: arranging 108–9
furnishings: buying 32
furniture:
  damaged: resuscitating 31
  free 36
  garden 61
  second-hand 36
  upcycling 26
  wooden: care 43

G

gadgets: for experimental
  cook 277
games:
  indoor 380–1
  learning to lose at 379
  playground 379
gardening:
  basics 50
  organic 53
  tools 50
  wildlife 53–4
garden(s):
  birds in: feeding 62
  crafts for 361
  erecting fence 20–1
  furniture for 61
  hard landscaping 60
  kids' play stuff 375
  lighting for 61
  for outdoor living 60
  water features 60–1
garlic: cooking with 300–1
gifted children 223–4
gifts:
  food as 362
  home-made 362
  wedding list 74
gluten-free food 315–16
goals: achieving 216
golf:
  buying clubs 161–2
  improving swing 162
grandparenthood 103
gravies: making 295
greenhouse: using 63

greetings cards: making
  362–3
guest room 13
guests: welcoming 88–9
guinea pigs: care 112
guitar: playing 368–9
gym:
  choosing 160
  value from 160

H

haggling 243
hair:
  curly: care 142
  dandruff 144
  dyeing 143
  long: care 141–2
  loss 144
  straightening 143
  washing 142–3
hair removal 132
hair-washing: for children
  96
hairbrushes 139–40
haircuts: DIY 140–1
hairdryers 140
hairstyles 141
Hallowe'en:
  pumpkin carving 83
  trick-or-treat 83
handbags 121–2
hanging basket: planting 54
hangover: curing 182
happiness 150
hats: for wedding 72
hay fever 182–3
headlice 97
hearing aids: choosing 149
heart: healthy 179
heartburn 172
heat: surviving 262–3
hedges: growing 54–5
herbs:
  to grow on window sill 63
  using 299
hiccups 184
highchairs 196–7
hobs: choosing 282–3
holiday lets 355
holidays:
  accommodation: saving

on 238
  activity 239
  adventure 240
  all-inclusive 239–40
  beach wardrobe 234
  car hire 244
  cheap travel 245
  city breaks 249
  currency exchange 242
  eating out 243
  family trips 259–60
  green travel 240–1
  hotel hints 238
  house-swapping 238–9
  jobs before leaving for
    236
  last-minute trips 240–1
  mini-breaks 241
  most popular spots 259
  package 239
  packing for 234–6
  romantic 258
  saving on 238
  self-catering 237
  shopping during 242
  ski wardrobe 235
  skiing 261–2
  in sun 262–3
    survival 262–3
  tour groups 240
  traveller's tummy 243–4
  UK breaks 249–50
  volunteering breaks 270
  weekend breaks 260
  winter-sun 255
home:
  adding value to 351
  dream 352
  making money from 351–2
  renting out spare room
    352
  second: buying 353
home cinema:
  setting up 49
home spa 135
home-schooling 224–5
homework 221
honeymoon: organizing 78
horse boxes 404–5
horse-riding 371–2
hotels 238

house-swapping 238–9
houseplants: cultivation 63
houses see property

I

IBS 173–4
ice: driving in 399
ice cream:
  flavours 303
  making 303–4
ice-skating 373
identity theft: preventing
  49–50
illnesses: childhood 98
inbox: dealing with 210
incontinence: averting 149
India: holidays in 257
Indian cooking 323–4
indigestion 172–3
insomnia: fighting 185–6
insulation: places for 22
internet:
  blog: making money from
    341
  children using 99
  dating profile 65
  selling goods on 340–1
  shopping for car 384
  shopping for food 311
  shopping safely 341–2
  studying online 229
interviews: job 201–2
introducing people 81
investments:
  alternative 347
  for future 346
  green and ethical 346–7
ironing 39
irons: choosing 35–6
Italian cooking 325–6
Italy: holidays in 251–3

J

jam: making 306–7
Japan: holidays in 256–7
Japanese cooking 322–3
jet lag 247
job see work
job-sharing 208
juggling 370
juicers 279–80

K

kids' room: designing 15
kitchen:
  cleaning kit 41
  designing 14
  renovating 34
kite-flying 372–3
knitting 358
knives:
  carving with 285
  kitchen 278–9
  using 279

L

labour (childbirth): bringing
  on 189
ladder: using 17
lamps: revamping 28
landscaping 60
languages: learning 369–70
Lapland 253
laundry:
  aids 37–8
  removing stains 37
  using vinegar 38
  in washing machine 38
  whitening 38
lawns:
  laying 51
  mowing 51
layette 190
left-handedness 92
lemonade: making 326
lentils: cooking 290
letters:
  condolence 108
  thank-you 81
letting property 354
  holiday lets 355
library: for study 229
lifting: safe method 170–1
lighting 10–11
  garden 61
lipstick 132
liqueurs 333
loans: taking out 348
lobster: dressing 297
London: sights 250
loyalty cards 339
luggage:
  for beach holiday 234

carry-on 248
  for cold weather 235
  essentials 234–5
    extras 235–6
  packing 234
  for ski holiday 235

M

make-up:
  applying 131
  buying 130–1
  essentials 131
  lipstick 132
  removal 131–2
manicure 136
map-reading 245
marinating 301
marriage:
  keeping alive 103–4
  proposal 68–9
  second: success with 105
maternity clothes 187
meals:
  etiquette 318
  evening: budget 312
  family: planning 312–13
  suppers: quick and easy
    314
  vegetarian 314–15
meat:
  buying 309–10
  carving 285
  cuts 293–4
mechanics:
  dealing with 395
  finding 394
medicine: giving to pets 115
meditation 150
meetings: business 214
memory: improving 154
menopause 185
meringues: making 302–3
Mexican cooking 322
microwaves:
  choosing 283
  using 283–4
migraine 181
milkshakes: making 326
millionaire: becoming 355
mini-breaks 241
mobiles:

choosing 47
  texting: faux pas 47
money:
  cutting costs 337–8
    at Christmas 338
  making extra 340
  problems 337
  saving: free goods and
    services 339–40
monopoly 380
mood board: for room 8
morning sickness 187
mortgage:
  choosing 349
  paying off early 349
  problems paying 349–50
Mother's Day: treats for 85
motion sickness 180
motor oil: changing 392
motorhome:
  care 402
  essentials 401
  luxuries 402
motorway driving 388
movie-making: for juniors
  367
moving house:
  moving day essentials 353
  preparations 353
moving in together 68
muesli: embellishments 293
mulches: making and using
  53
mums:
  juggling work and
    children 101–2
  miracle-working 103
music systems: choosing
  48–9
musical instruments:
  learning 96–7

N

naming parties 88
nappy changing 191–2
nappy rash 194–5
neighbours: good 70
networking: in business 213
New York: sights 253–4
newborn:
  bonding with 191

first days with 90–1
night out: dressing for 119–
  20
nosebleed 176
novels:
  genres 363
  getting into print 364
  writing 363
numbers: teaching child
  220–1
nursery: equipping 190
nursery school:
  choosing 217
  settling child into 219

O

office etiquette 204
omelettes: cooking 287–8
onions: cutting 286
open-plan designs 12–13
organic gardening 53
outdoor living: garden for
  60

P, Q

package holidays 239
packed lunches:
  for school 316–17
  for work 317
packing 234
  backpack 272
paints (for decorating):
  choosing 9–10
paintwork: perfect 18–19
pancakes: making 304
pans: choosing 277–8
panties: buying 118
parents: single 102
Paris: must-see sights 250
parking 388
parties:
  adult: themes 79
  christening 88
  clothes-swapping 128–9
  dinner 80
  engagement 81–2
  entertainment at 79–80
  essentials 80
  guests: behaviour 79
  hosting 79
  kids':

food for 320–1
games for 86–7
themes 86
naming 88
tea 80
partners: finding 65
pasta:
cooking 297–8
types 297
pastry: making 302
patchwork quilts 359
patterns (for decorating):
choosing 9
pay rise: negotiating 203
peas: cooking 290
people management 213–14
perfumes:
buying 136
making 135
period pains 184
personal trainer: finding 160–1
Peru: holidays in 255–6
pests: household: dealing with 44–5
pet-sitter: choosing 114
pets:
choosing 109
eliminating smells 114
lost: finding 115
protecting from loss 115
safety in home 114–15
travel with 236–7
phobias: overcoming 151–2
phones:
cutting bills 336
mobile: choosing 47
provider: choosing 47–8
photography 367
photos: appearance in 123–4
piano: picking out tune on 368
picnics 319–20
pictures: hanging 19
pilgrimages: reasons for 261
pillows: choosing 32
pizzas: making 288
plants:
cuttings 58
deadheading 58

dividing 58
frost protection 59
growing from seed 57
houseplants 63
pruning 58–9
scented 60
plastering 21–2
pocket money 98
port (drink) 333
posture 147
at desk 171
potatoes:
chips 290
cooking methods 289–90
roasting 288–9
pots and pans: choosing 277–8
Prague: sights 253
pre-teens 99–100
pregnancy:
becoming pregnant 186–7
concerns 188
exercise in 189
foods to avoid in 187
presentation: preparing 229–30
presents: wrapping 88
preserves: making 306–7
primary school: starting 219
printer: choosing 46
problem-solving 211
project managing 211
property:
adding value to 351
buying 350–1
abroad 354
extending 16
exterior 16
getting on ladder 350
holiday lets 355
letting 354
maintenance 16–17
making money from 351–2
renting out spare room 352
second home 353
selling 352
pruning 58–9
public speaking 210
pumpkins: carving 83
punch: making 331–2

puppets: making 377–8
puppy-training 110
quilts: patchwork 359

R
rabbits: care 112
reading: helping child with 220
recreational vehicle (RV):
buying 401–2
see also caravans; motorhomes
recycling 24
redundancy: coping with 205–6
references: writing 216–17
relationships:
breakup: coping with 104
ending 69
long-distance 67–8
moving in together 68
relatives:
choosing care for 107
elderly: caring for 106–7
relaxation 155
renovating: cutting costs 37
report: writing 215–16
restaurants: saving money 243
retreats 260–1
rice: using 298–9
risotto: ingredients 298
road safety 157
roller-skating 373–4
Rome: sights in 252
room planning 7
awkward spaces 14
bathroom 15
colours 8
decluttering 11–12
decorating style 9
displays 12
guest room 13
kids' room 15
kitchen 14
lighting 10–11
mood board 8
open space 12–13
paints 9–10
pattern 9
storage space 11–12

tiny spaces 13
window treatments 10
roses 56
running 163–4

S
safaris 258
safety:
banking online 343
camping 269–70
children in cars 401
children on internet 99
cooking 276
in crowds 157
cycling 406–7
DIY 17
driving 386–7
fireworks 85
on first dates 66
gap-year travel 271
gear for baby 194
lifting 170–1
out on foot 156–7
of pets in home 114–15
on roads 157
at seaside 264
on ski slopes 262
stranger danger 97
teenagers 101
women driving alone 400
sailing 370–1
salad dressings 291–2
salads: jazzing up 291
sales shopping 338–9
sales skills 212
San Francisco: sights 254
sat nav:
finding way with 390
getting best out of 390
sauces: making 295
savings:
accounts: choosing 345–6
green and ethical 346–7
secrets of 345
school:
bullying in 223
choosing 221
coursework 222
exams 222
poor results 223
extra tutoring 225

homework 221
packed lunches for 316–17
play-ground games 379
primary: starting 219
secondary: starting 221
school holidays: surviving 218
school uniform 219
schooling: at home 224–5
scrabble 380
scrapbooking 366–7
seaside: safety 264
secondhand goods:
   selling 340
      on internet auction 340–1
seeds: growing plants from 57
self-esteem: raising 152
sewing:
   easy 358
   kit: essential 357
sex education 100
shaving: for men 134
shelves: putting up 19
sherries 333
shirts:
   man's 125
   women's 121
shoes:
   care 122
   fitting 148
   high heels 120
shopping:
   at farmers' market 310
   good deals 338
   haggling 243
   on holiday 242
   loyalty/store cards 339
   online:
      for food 311
      safety 341–2
   in sales 338–9
   in supermarkets 310
   vegetable box schemes 311
shorthand 209
shower: cleaning 43
shyness: overcoming 156
sibling rivalry 93
silver: cleaning 44

singing 369
single parents 102
six-pack: achieving 166–7
skateboarding 374
sketching 365
skidding 398
skiing 164–5
   basic wardrobe 235
   holidays 261–2
skin: dry: soothing 134–5
sleep:
   good 186
   insomnia 185–6
slimming 168
slow cooker: using 284–5
slugs 52
smells:
   eliminating 45
   animal 114
smoking: giving up 178
snacks: energy-boosting 372
snoring: stopping 185
snow:
   car stuck in 399
   driving in 399
snowboarding 165
soap: making 361
sofas:
   choosing 33
   reviving 28
sore throat: treatment for 169
soufflés: making 301–2
soundproofing: installing 22–3
spa: home 135
Spain: holidays in 251
spectacles: choosing 146
speeches: best man's 77
spelling: helping child with 220
spices: cooking with 300
spirits: drinking 332–3
sports:
   avoiding injuries 161
   indoor 160
   outdoor 159
sports kit 167
   trainers 167
   wetsuits 167

spots: zapping 134
sprains: treating 174–5
spring cleaning 40
stains: laundry: removing 37
star-gazing 371
stationery: wedding: saving money on 74
steaming: methods 284
stepchildren 105–6
stings 176
storage:
   cheese 292
   of clothes 39–40
   of eggs 286–7
   of fish 295–6
   of food 277
   of fruit 291
   of garden tools 59
   of vegetables 290–1
   of wine 330
storage space 11–12
store cards 339
store-cupboard essentials 290
stress: reducing 178
student accommodation:
   choosing 226–7
   sharing 227
students:
   bank accounts for 344–5
   budget ideas 231
   cheap eats 231
   essay writing 229
   mature 227–8
   online study 229
   part-time jobs 230
   presentations:
      giving 230
      preparing 229–30
   social life 231
   study methods 228
   using library 229
suits:
   man's: choosing 125–6
   wedding 71–2
sun:
   protection from 138
   surviving 262–3
sunburn: mild: treating 175
sunglasses 263

supermarket shopping 310
suppers: quick and easy 314
supplements: to boost wellbeing 154
surfing 165–6
swimming 166
   teaching child 95–6
swimming pools: kids' safety in 263–4
swimsuits 119

T
table: laying 318
tan: fake 137
tantrums:
   mealtime 93–4
   toddler 91
taps: dripping 29–30
tea: making 327
tea parties 80
team work 215
teenagers:
   co-existing with 100–1
   drug problems 101
   mistakes to avoid with 100
   safety 101
teeth: care 144–5
teething 195
temperature: taking 170
tennis: playing 163
tennis racquets: choosing 162–3
tents:
   buying 264
   care 265
   pitching 265
   types 264
text messages: faux pas 47
Thai cooking 323
thank-you letters 81
Thanksgiving: decorations 83
theme parks 260
ties:
   bow 125
   ideal 125
tiling 20
time management 155
   at work 214–15
tin cans: making things

from 378
toddlers:
  bedtime 95
  discipline 94
  tantrums 91
    mealtime 93–4
  teaching to talk 94
  toilet training 91–2
  trips out 93
toilet training 91–2
Tokyo: sights 256–7
tomatoes: growing 56
tools:
  gardening: storage 59
  kit: essentials 8
toothbrushes 145–6
touch-typing 209
tour groups 240
trailer: towing 403–4
trainers: buying 167
travel:
  activities for kids 246
  alone 236
  cheap 245
  with children 233
  with elderly 237
  gap year 270–3
    earning during 273
  interrail 273
  with pets 236–7
traveller's tummy 243–4
trick-or-treat 83
tumble drying 39
TVs: choosing 48
tweenagers 99–100
twitchers 374–5
tyres:
  bike: changing 406
  buying 385
  looking after 385–6

U
uniform: school 219
university:
  choosing 227
  choosing degree 225–6
  exams 230–1
  finding digs 226
  as mature student 227–8
  preparing for 226
  social life 231

student essentials 228
surviving first term 228
USA: holidays in 253–5

V
vacuum cleaner: choosing
  34–5
Valentine's Day 86
varicose veins: avoiding 148
vegans: foods for 315
vegetable box schemes 311
vegetables:
  chopping 285–6
  growing 55
  storing 290–1
vegetarians: meals for
  314–15
Venice: sights 252–3
vinegar: use in laundry 38
voluntary work 208
volunteering breaks 270

W
walking: for fun 372
wallpapering 20
wallpapers: unusual 20
wardrobe:
  beach holiday 234
  capsule 117
  classics 118
  detox 128
  ski holiday 235
  working: girl's 202
washing machine:
  buying 35
  use 38
water: economizing with 25
water features 60–1
watercolours:
  colours 365
  equipment 365–6
WCs: unblocking 18
weaning 196
website: creating 46
weddings:
  best man's speech 77
  bride's day 75
  cake for 72–3
  caterers for 73
  departure plans 78
  dress for 71

entertainment at 75
flowers 75–6
gift list 74
green 75
hats for 72
invites 73
planning 70
pre-wedding breaks 261
reception:
  table plans 76–7
  tables 76
saving money on 72
stationery: saving money
  on 74
suit for 71–2
venues 70–1
vows: personalized 77
weekend breaks: ideas for
  260
weight gain 169
weight loss 168
wellbeing:
  boosting with
  supplements 154
  sense of 152
wetsuits 167
wildlife: gardening for 53–4
wills: making 106
wind (flatulence): foods to
  avoid 172
windows:
  broken: repairing 30–1
  cleaning 41
  curtain ideas 27
  treatments 10
wine:
  to complement foods
  330–1
  making 328–9
  red 329
  storing 330
  white 329–30
work:
  achieving goals 216
  business meetings 214
  changing 207
  choosing 199, 200
  difficult boss 217
  during gap-year travel
  273
  fitness at 204

from home 206–7
gap year 270
girl's working wardrobe
  202
interviews 201–2
job-sharing 208
office etiquette 204
packed lunches for 317
part-time 207–8
  for students 230
pay rise: negotiating 203
people management 213–
  14
promotion 202–3
redundancy: coping with
  205–6
report writing 215–16
skills related to 200
team work 215
time management 214–15
under threat 205
voluntary 208
watercooler don'ts 205
wreath: Christmas 84
wrinkles: keeping at bay
  138
writing: helping child with
  220

Y
yarns: leftover: using 358
yoga 164
yogurt: cultivating 293

Quercus Editions Ltd
55 Baker Street
7th floor, south block
London
W1U 8EW

First published in 2012

Produced by Bookworx
Editorial and additional writing: Jo Godfrey Wood
Design and additional research: Peggy Sadler
Proofreading: Brittany Bauschka
Indexing: Dorothy Frame

A catalogue record of this book is available from
the British Library

UK and associated territories:
Paperback ISBN 978 1 78087 310 7
Hardback ISBN 978 1 78087 923 9

Printed and bound in China
10 9 8 7 6 5 4 3 2 1

AUTHOR ACKNOWLEDGEMENTS
Huge thanks to my husband Martin, not just for his
patient help and support when the going got tough,
but also for putting his prodigious talent for
cooking to invaluable use in writing the Food &
Drink chapter.

NOTE TO READERS
The information in this book provides general
guidance on a range of family and household
issues. The book is not a do-it-yourself guide to
every issue but gives general advice and hints
and tips. It is not a substitute for professional
care, but advice based on information available
to the author. Where there is any question
regarding a problem, the author and publisher
urge the reader to consult a qualified
professional. The author and publisher expressly
disclaim any responsibility for any adverse effects
arising from the use or application of the
information contained herein.